AF663580

A SOCIO-POLITICAL STUDY
OF THE
VĀLMĪKI RĀMĀYAṆA

RAMASHRAYA SHARMA,
M. A. (Skt. & Hindi), Ph.D.
Delhi College, Delhi University, Delhi

MOTILAL BANARSIDASS
DELHI : VARANASI : PATNA

©MOTILAL BANARSIDASS
Head Office : BUNGALOW ROAD, JAWAHARNAGAR, DELHI-7
Branches : 1. CHOWK, VARANASI-1 (U.P.)
2. ASHOK RAJPATH, PATNA-4 (BIHAR)

First edition
1971

Printed in India
BY SHANTI LAL JAIN, AT SHRI JAINENDRA PRESS, BUNGALOW ROAD, JAWAHAR NAGAR, DELHI-7, AND PUBLISHED BY SUNDARLAL JAIN, FOR MOTILAL BANARSIDASS, BUNGALOW ROAD, JAWAHARNAGAR, DELHI-7.

TO

My late father Pt. Shiva Dutta Sharma
From whom I received the letter of Sanskrit

AND

My revered guru Dr. S.N. Shastri
M.A.D. Phil., L.L.B. F.R.A.S. (LONDON)
Who revealed its meaning to me.

FOREWORD

Dr. Ramashraya Sharma's "A Socio-political Study of the Vālmīki Rāmāyaṇa" stands in a class by itself. He has studied the entire text thoroughly, taught it to post-graduate classes, and pondered long over the problems it raises. And the study has been fruitful, because it was carried on, not so much to gain the degree of Doctor of philosophy as for the sheer love of the subject. He has found in the Rāmāyaṇa not only the best source of information about post-Vedic social and political institutions, actual as well as ideal, but also the "standard on the basis of which one can evaluate all cultures, Indian as well as foreign". I am glad to find also that he does not fail to notice instances when the admirable standard could not be put into practice even by Rāmāyaṇic heroes.

There is a certain freshness about Dr. Ramashraya's treatment of the subject. Tired of *obiter dicta*, he takes the reader to the original text, giving him a chance to decide for himself; and when no definite conclusion can be reached on the basis of available evidence, he is frank enough to say so. I have liked also his study of institutions, not as static entities, never changing whatever be the period of time, but as human creations evolving and changing according to the needs of the individual and the society of which he is a part and parcel. The questions of the age and text of the Rāmāyaṇa have also been considered, because no authoritative study of the poem would be possible without answering these questions satisfactorily.

I am glad to write these few words to introduce this thorough-going monograph to the world. It has entailed a vast amount of research. No relevant source has been neglected, and no well-known view on the subject left undiscussed and unrecorded. May it be read long by scholars and enquirers after truth.

Dasharatha Sharma

Director,
Rajasthan History Project,
Jodhpur University,
JODHPUR.

PREFACE

I was first introduced to the complete text of Vālmīki's Rāmāyaṇa in 1952 when the Sanskrit Department of Delhi University included the Sundara-Kāṇḍa in the syllabus for the M.A. (Sanskrit) Examination and invited me to teach it under the co-operative teaching scheme. Very soon the *Ādi-kāvya* became my favourite subject of study, for I discovered that besides possessing superb literary excellence it also presents a very authentic and at the same time a very comprehensive picture of ancient Indian culture and civilization. Noticing my deep interest in the Rāmāyaṇa, my revered teacher and Head of the University Department of Sanskrit, Dr. N. N. Chaudhury, suggested that I should take up 'Social and Political Conditions as Reflected in Vālmīki's Rāmāyaṇa' as a subject for research for the Ph.D. degree. I was, accordingly, enrolled as a Ph.D. student in the University of Delhi in 1956 and completed my research after eight years of devoted study, in 1964. It is a matter of great pleasure now to present the same in the form of this published volume. I have tried to do justice to the subject to the best of my capacity and competence. But its real worth can be judged only by the experts, for, as says Kālidāsa,

hemnaḥ saṃllakshyate hyagnau viśuddhiḥ śyāmikāpi vā[1].

I know that there are already a number of valuable works touching upon one or several aspects of the present study. Recently Dr. S. N. Vyas has even brought out a parallel work entitled 'India in the Rāmāyaṇa Age.' However, it is my firm conviction that inexhaustible and deep like the sea, with layers of information unexplored and sometimes even unsuspected, our epics would, inspite of the studies made so far, reward even now the efforts of a diligent investigator. My humble submission, therefore is that I have tried to build on the foundation laid by my predecessors in the field of Rāmāyaṇic studies

1. (......it is in the fire alone that the purity or the impurity of gold is tested) Raghuvaṃśam, I 10.

and tried to pay the *guru-ṛiṇa* thus incurred by carrying the work a little further. I sincerely hope that a better equipped scholar would some day carry the torch of knowledge still further and reveal many a hidden corner of Rāmāyaṇic studies.

The Rāmāyaṇa of Vālmīki is available in three recensions —the *dākshiṇātya*, the *baṅgīya* and the *paścimottarīya*. Of these the *dākshiṇātya* recension published by the Nirṇaya Sāgara with the Tilaka commentary in 1930 has long been the most popular recension. But the fact that it contains the largest number of verses, many of which are not found in the other two and also that its readings generally give an impression of later grammatical refinement perhaps indicates that it was the latest to assume a settled form. The *baṅgīya* recension was published by Dr. Gorressio in Italian characters in 1847 and by Paṇḍita Pancanana Tarkaratna in Bengali characters in 1908. The present study is primarily based on the *paścimottarīya* recension published by Paṇḍita Bhagavad Datta, Ramlabhaya and others from Lahore in 1931. My study of the Rāmāyaṇa has convinced me that this recension too has its own shortcomings and that the *dākshiṇātya* and the *baṅgīya* recensions have at places preserved better readings and a better order of narration. I have therefore not refrained from consulting them and adapting their readings in some cases. In recent years the Oriental Institute of Baroda has undertaken to bring forth a critical edition of the Vālmīkīya Rāmāyaṇa. The critical edition is as yet incomplete and doubts have also been expressed about its being a more authentic version of the Rāmāyaṇa than the editions already before the public. I have therefore used it only sparingly. For the translation of the Rāmāyaṇa I have freely utilised Shri Manmatha Nath Dutt's English translation, though it has not always been possible to indicate this in the foot-notes.

In the original thesis, almost invariably, the relevant text of the Rāmāyaṇa was quoted in the foot-notes. Apart from affording immense help in ready reference, that practice served for me as an effective check against writing anything which would not be supported by the original source. Due to limitations of space in the present volume I had to drop the original text at several places. I can still without breach of modesty,

claim to share Mallinātha's *pratijñā—*
nāmūlaṃ likhyate kiñcit.[1]

It is my proud privilege and solemn duty to express my deepest sense of gratitude to Dr. N. N. Chaudhury and Dr. Dasharatha Sharma under whose able guidance I carried on this work. In fact, it is not possible for me to express in words my indebtedness to Dr. Dasharatha Sharma who helped me at every step during the course of writing the thesis and its publication. I should also like to take this opportunity of thanking Shri R. R. Gupta, Dr. Bhisham Sahni and Shri S. N. Nigam who were unsparing in making available to me their very useful suggestions. My thanks are also due to my sincerest friends, Shri Charu Candra Shastri, Dr. Nikhilesh Shastri and Shri Sudarshan Shastri who took great pains in preparing the manuscript for the press.

I am conscious of the fact that despite the able guidance of my learned teachers and the generous assistance of a large number of friends and colleagues the present work suffers from a number of errors and shortcomings. I offer my sincere apologies to my readers in this behalf and crave their indulgence, for : *haṃso hi kshīramādatte tanmiśrā varjayatyapaḥ.*[2]

Dhanatrayodaśī Ramashraya Sharma
Saṃvat 2028.

1. (Nothing is written without a (sound) basis.) Mallinātha's Sañjīvinī on Raghuvaṃśam, Ii.

2. (The swan sips the milk, and leaves aside the water mingled wlth it.) Abhijñāna Śākuntalam, VI 28.

SCHEME OF TRANSLITERATION

Whereas all extracts from the original Sanskrit works and also various technical terms and phrases are given in the Roman characters in this monograph, the mode of Transliteration adopted while doing so, is noted below for reay reference :

अ	a	ट्	ṭ
आ	ā	ठ्	ṭh
इ	i	ड्	ḍ
ई	ī	ढ्	ḍh
उ	u	ण्	ṇ
ऊ	ū	त्	t
ऋ	ṛi	थ्	th
ॠ	ṛī	द्	d
लृ	lṛi		
ए	e	ध्	dh
ऐ	ai	न्	n
ओ	o	प्	p
औ	au	फ्	ph
·	ṃ	ब्	b
:	ḥ	भ्	bh
क्	k	म्	m
ख्	kh	य्	y
ग्	g	र्	r
घ्	gh	ल्	l
ङ	ṅ	व्	v
च्	c	श्	ś
छ्	ch	ष्	sh
ज्	j	स्	s
झ्	jh	ह्	h
ञ्	ñ		

MODE OF CITATIONS

In case of the Rāmāyaṇa citations are given by reference to *Kāṇḍas* (Books), *Sargas* (cantos) and *Ślokas* (verses). References to the cantos and the verses have been separated by an oblique stroke—the first figure referring to the canto and the second to the verse. To take an example in V 5/17 the first figure refers to the *Kāṇḍa* (i.e. *Sundara-Kāṇḍa*), the second to the canto (i.e. fifth canto) and the last to the verse (i.e. seventeenth verse). References from the Nirṇaya Sagara Edition of the Rāmāyaṇa have been marked by the letters N. S. at the end, whereas the letter B has been used for referring to the Critical Edition of the Rāmāyaṇa from Baroda. In all cases where there is no special indication the references are from the Lahore edition of the Rāmāyaṇa.

Run on references are signified by means of quoting the initial page, canto or verse as the case may be. Comparative references are indicated by the abbreviation 'Cf.' and references to the preceding page (or pages) as Vide p. (or pp.)—Supra, whereas to the following page (or pages) as Vide p. (or pp.) —Infra. For this purpose even Appendices are folioed in continuation of the text.

ABBREVIATIONS

B.	Critical Edition of the Rāmāyaṇa, Oriental Institute, Baroda.
B.I.	Bibliotheca Indica.
B.O.R.I.	Bhandarkar Oriental Research Institute (Poona).
Cf.	Compare.
Chand.Up.	Chāndogya Upanishad.
C.I.I.	(Volumes of) Corpus Inscriptionum Indicarum.
Ed.	Edited.
E.I.	Epigraphia Indica.
ff.	Following.
I.H.Q.	Indian Historical Quarterly.
J.A.O.S.	Journal of the American Oriental Society.
Manu	Manu Smṛiti.
M.Bh.	Mahā-bhārata.
N.B.	Nota bene.
No.	Number.
N.S.	Nirṇaya Sagara edition of the Rāmāyaṇa, Bombay. 1930.
p.	Page.
pp.	Pages.
R.	Rāmāyaṇa.
Yājñavalkya	Yājñavalkya Smṛiti.

CONTENTS

Chapter I

INTRODUCTION

The Rāmāyaṇa is regarded as the *Ādi-kāvya* (the first poetical composition) of Classical Sanskrit; and rightly too, as in this particular field, its great writer, Vālmīki, was the first to have arrived intuitively at the true concept of poetry and to have created in the Rāmāyaṇa a literature with the object of providing aesthetic joy to its listeners and readers. It was he who discovered the great truth that true poetry is a spontaneous outflow of the poet's heart in response to the pain and anguished cry of the universe.[1]

Sanskrit literature, nay the entire Indian literature, is highly indebted to Vālmīki, for in the Rāmāyaṇa he created a *kāvya* which, besides providing perennial joy to all lovers of poetry has served as an immortal and inexhaustible source of inspiration to poets through the ages. It has, as rightly remarked by Winternitz, "become the property of the whole Indian people, and scarcely any other poem in the entire literature of the world, has influenced the thought and poetry of a great nation for centuries."[2] There is no form of Sanskrit poetry in which the *Rāma-Kathā* has not been retold and there is no Indian language—living or dead—which does not possess its own Rāmāyaṇa.

No doubt, we have the earliest picture of Indian culture and civilisation in Vedic literature. But since that literature is primarily religious and metaphysical and the information supplied by it on secular subjects meagre and casual, the cultural picture that emerges from it is rather dim and hazy. The credit of presenting the first clear picture of Aryan culture, complete almost in every detail, belongs to the Rāmāyaṇa, which gives us a vivid portrait of a living human society and furnishes ample details with regard to its food and drink habits,

1. Cf. *Śokaḥ ślokatvamāgamat* R. I 2/44.
Vide also Sankaran, A.—Some Aspects of Literary Criticism in Sanskrit, pp. 6-7.

2. Winternitz, M., A History of Indian Literature, Vol. I, p. 476.

dress and ornaments, sports and amusements, superstitions and customs as also its religion and philosophy. The epic also supplies valuable information relating to its various social, economical and political institutions. In fact, for a student of the history of post-Vedic Aryan institutions the Rāmāyaṇa is simply indispensable.

Among its characters there are, indeed, some who, on account of their prodigious physical strength and uncouth behaviour, have been represented as demons; and others who seem to correspond to gods on account of their benign disposition and illustrious conduct. But the fact remains that all the characters of the epic are essentially human. They cherish in their hearts aspirations and ambitions like ordinary men and women; their life passes through vicissitudes of hope and despair, pleasure and pain, success and failure; they endure disease, old age and death; and they are also subject to human weaknesses like greed, jealousy and the like.

The Rāmāyaṇa appeals to the human mind also on account of its lofty idealism. It represents a struggle between good and evil, between truth and falsehood, between selfishness and self-sacrifice, between the highest ideals that an *Ārya* entertained and their reverse cherished by the Rākshasas. In this struggle and in the robust idealism of the poet, which makes good in the end triumph over evil, lies the universal appeal of the Rāmāyaṇa.

To a devout Hindu, the Rāmāyaṇa culture supplies the standard on the basis of which he can evaluate all cultures, Indian as well as foreign. Down to the present day the ideals of filial devotion, brotherly and parental love, wifely fidelity and friendliness are judged with reference to the characters of the Rāmāyaṇa—Rāma, Lakshmaṇa, Daśaratha, Sītā and Sugrīva. Likewise, the *Rāma-rājya* is still the cherished embodiment of the golden age, of all-round peace and prosperity and the highest regard for the people—their will and welfare.

Traditionally the Rāmāyaṇa is regarded as an ideal representative of *kāvya* (artificial epic) as opposed to the Mahābhārata which is an *Itihāsa.*[1] Probably it is on this account

1. Cf. "Sanskrit epic poetry falls into two main classes. That which comprises old stories goes by the name of *Itihāsa*, "legend", *Ākhyāna*,

that modern scholars have mostly turned to the Mahābhārata for collecting information on various subjects of historical and cultural interest about ancient India. The encyclopaedic character of the Mahābhārata encourages such efforts by easily rewarding even a casual enquirer. More often than not even the scholars who claim to present an account of the entire epic period rely principally upon the Mahābhārata, referring to the Rāmāyaṇa only casually—either to strengthen the evidence of the Mahābhārata or sometimes to draw the attention of the readers to certain very well-known facts of this epic. Serious, independent studies of the material contained in the Rāmāyaṇa have been made only within the last few decades. Dr. (Miss) P. C. Dharma presented in 1941 an account of Rāmāyaṇa Polity and Dr. S. N. Vyas published in 1958, his two studies in Hindi, viz. 'Rāmāyaṇa-kālīna Samāja' and 'Rāmāyaṇa-kālīna Saṃskṛiti'. But we believe that inexhaustible and deep like the sea, with layers of information unexplored and sometimes even unsuspected, our epics would, inspite of the studies made so far, reward even now the efforts of an adventurous investigator. It was in this spirit that we ventured to undertake the present study.

Apart from presenting additional data the present work differs from its predecessors in three important respects. Firstly, in forming an estimate of the social and political consciousness of the Rāmāyaṇic people we have not been guided by the *obiter dicta*, interspersed throughout the poem but by the actual behaviour of the various characters of the epic. We have taken due care to appreciate the subjective as well as the objective side of a question, i.e. the circumstances of a particular behaviour as also the motives—covert or overt—which prompted that behaviour. This has, in a number of cases, led us to conclusions different from those of earlier writers. Secondly, we have tried to present the data in a systematic manner; and we hope that the reader would, with the minimum of effort, find before himself a clear picture of a particular institution of the Rāmāyaṇic times. Lastly, in our treatment of every social and

"narrative", or *Purāṇa*, "ancient tale", while the other is called *kāvya* or artificial epic. The Mahābhārata is the chief and oldest respresentative of the former group, the Rāmāyaṇa of the latter."

Macdonell, A. A., A History of Sanskrit Literature, p. 281.

political institution we have tried to give in the beginning a brief resume of its evolution from the Vedic times to the epic period. This way of treating the institutions, not as static but dynamic parts of an evolutionary process, has helped us in understanding, and we hope, in also presenting a clearer picture of the progress or decline of the Aryan society.

A few words about the period to which the social and political conditions reflected in the Rāmāyaṇa may be said to belong would be relevant here. According to tradition, Vishṇu descended on earth as Rāma in the *Tretā Yuga* (approximately 867,102 B.C.) and Vālmīki, who was Rāma's contemporary composed the Rāmāyaṇa in the life-time of his hero. As against this we have the view of some Western scholars who put the date of the composition of the epic as late as the 3rd or the 4th century A.D. Such differences of opinion with regard to the date of a Sanskrit poet or his work are not uncommon, for in many cases, we have no conclusive internal evidence to decide such questions. Therefore, one has generally to depend upon indirect evidence, which can at best help arrive at the relative age of a composition as anterior or posterior to certain other well-known works or poets.

If we proceed on these lines to determine the age of the Rāmāyaṇa—and there is none else on which we can—one thing becomes absolutely clear, viz. the period of the Rāmāyaṇa falls posterior to the entire Vedic literature. Not only does the comparison of the form, the matter and the spirit of the Vedic literature with that of the Rāmāyaṇa confirm the above conclusion, but the epic expressly recognises the existence of the Vedas and the Vedāṅgas as prior to itself.[1] In fact, the Rāmāyaṇa was intended to be an exposition of the *śruti* and the *smṛiti*[2] And as the Vedic period is generally believed to have ended by the 6th century B.C., this can be termed the upper limit for the composition of the Rāmāyaṇa. The lower limit of the Rāmāyaṇa can also be fixed with some certainty by the fact that the Rāmāyaṇa displays no familiarity with the Buddha or with Buddhism.[3] Equally significant is the fact that in the

1. R. I 4/49; R.II 2/8; R. IV 29/14; R. VI 4/24.

2. Cf. *Dharmakāmārtha saṃyuktam Śrutismṛityupabṛiṃhitam*. R. I 5/4.

3. Cf. "The only mention of Buddha in the Rāmāyaṇa occurs in a passage which is evidently interpolated. Hence the balance of the evidence

entire Rāmāyaṇa there is no reference to the Māhābhārata or its characters, while the Māhābhārata, besides giving a summary of the *Rāma-kathā* (in the Rāmopākhyāna) and referring to Vālmīki and his characters, actually contains a verse from the Rāmāyaṇa.[1] Moreover, a large number of non-Pāṇinian grammatical forms in the Rāmāyaṇa also indicate that the composition of the epic took place prior to the age of Pāṇini (i.e. 5th century B.C.) In view of all this it is quite safe to assign the Rāmāyaṇa to the 6th century B.C. and to state that the epic principally draws before us a picture of ancient Indian culture and civilisation of the period of its composition. This fact is also confirmed by the resemblance of its data to that of early 'Sūtras' which are generally assigned to the 6th century B.C. or so. Of course, everything that Vālmīki says, does not reflect his times. Some allowance has to be made for a mixture of the factual with the imaginary, in the work of a poet writing on a more or less historical theme, belonging to his period or prior to his own.

It is necessary for a serious student of the Rāmāyaṇa to discuss also the question of its text. That some part of it is interpolated is recognised not only by the western scholars but also by our old commentators. But exactly what portions of the Rāmāyaṇa can really be regarded as *prakshipta* (spurious) is a question that needs some serious thinking.

The extant Rāmāyaṇa opens with a conversation between Vālmīki and Nārada. In the first canto of the Bāla-Kāṇḍa the sage, Nārada, recounts, in reply to Vālmīki's query, the virtues of Rāma and relates in bare outline those incidents connected with Rāma's life which go to prove that Rāma was the ideal man—or rather an ideal king—of Vālmīki's conception. It was this outline which Vālmīki later on developed into a *Rāma-*

in relation to Buddhism seems to favour the pre-Buddhistic origin of the genuine Rāmāyaṇa."

Macdonell, A. A., A History of Sanskrit Literature, p. 307.

1. *Na hantavyāḥ striyaśceti yad bravīshi plavaṅgama,*
Sarvakālam manushyeṇa vyavasāyavatā sadā,
Pīḍākaram amitrāṇāṃ yat syāt kartavyameva tat.

R. VI 60/29.

Cf. *Api cāyam purā gītaḥ śloko Vālmīkinā bhuvi,*
Na hantavyāḥ striya iti yad bravīshi plavaṅgama,
Sarvakālam manushyeṇa vyavasāyavatā sadā
Pīḍākaramamitrāṇām yat syāt kartavyameva tat.

M. Bh. VII 143/67-68.

carita at the behest of Brahmā. But in giving it the shape of a full-fledged *kāvya*, he added to it a good deal of religious and didactic matter, so that his poem, besides affording supreme artistic pleasure should also serve as a means of attaining the *trivarga*, viz. *dharma*, *artha* and *kāma*.[1]

The account in the opening canto of the Rāmāyaṇa is not the *anukramaṇī* (table of contents); it is merely the *kāvya-bīja*, i.e. the seed out of which grew the *Rāmāyaṇa kāvya*.[2] The *anukramaṇī* (table of contents) comes only in the third canto of the Bāla-Kāṇḍa and it takes full cognisance of the events related throughout, including the Bāla-Kāṇḍa and the Uttara-Kāṇḍa. We, therefore, find it difficult to agree with the view which would exclude the Bāla-Kāṇḍa and the Uttara-Kāṇḍa, merely on the ground that the incidents related therein have not been referred to in the first canto of the Bāla-Kāṇḍa.[3]

Nor can we agree with the argument that Books II-VI of the Rāmāyaṇa show no familiarity with the incidents of the Bāla-Kāṇḍa,[4] for such a view militates against the evidence of the Rāmāyaṇa. Actually, all the three recensions of Books II-VI allude in fair detail to the following incidents from the Bāla-Kāṇḍa :

(i) Viśvāmitra's approaching king Daśaratha with the request that he should lend him the services of Rāma for guarding his *yajña* (sacrifice) against the raids of the notorious Rākshasas (Mārīca, Subāhu and their followers);[5]

(ii) Rāma's staying with Viśvāmitra in the latter's *āśrama* (hermitage) and driving away the Rākshasa, Mārīca;[6]

1. R. I 2/46.
2. R. I 4/1.
3. Cf. "It further contains two tables of contents (in cantos i. and iii.) which were clearly made at different times; for one of them takes no notice of the first and last books, and must, therefore, have been made before these were added."

Macdonell, A. A., A History of Sanskrit Literature, p. 304.

4. Cf. "Moreover in the genuine parts of the poem there is never any reference to the events in Book I..........."

Winternitz, M., A History of Indian Literature, Vol. I, p. 496.

5. R. III 41/3-5.
6. R. III 41/10, 17.

(iii) Rāma's visit to Mithilā;[1]

(iv) Rāma's marriage with *ayonijā* Sītā in consequence of his fulfilling the condition of stringing the Śiva's bow.[2]

Likewise, there are several passages in the Sundara-Kāṇḍa of the Rāmāyaṇa[3] which refer to incidents that are given in detail only in the Uttara-Kāṇḍa. Moreover, many facts like the circumstance in which Nandī cursed the Rākshasas (particularly Rāvaṇa), the past history of Laṅkā and Rāvaṇa's victory over Kubera and the other gods, can be understood clearly only with the help of the details contained in the Uttara-Kāṇḍa. Thus, the poem has an organic unity which would be seriously impaired if some of its parts were arbitrarily declared as interpolations.

The Bāla-Kāṇḍa is treated as spurious by some scholars, for they believe that it contains details which are contradicted by Books II-VI. The contradictions cited are :

(a) Rāma in the Araṇya-Kāṇḍa calls Lakshmaṇa as *akrita-dāra* (a bachelor) even though his marriage with Urmilā has been described in the Bāla-Kāṇḍa.

1. R. III 3/7, 9.
2. R. III 2/24; R. III 3/14, 20.
3. Note the following :

(i) *Nirmitām Viśvakarmaṇā (Laṅkām)* R. V 1/21.

(ii) *Kuberādhyushitām purā.* R. V 1/25.

(iii) *Brahmārtham hi kritam divyam divi yad Viśvakarmaṇā,*
Vimānam Pushpakam nāma sarvakāmagamam śubham.
Pareṇa tapasā lebhe yat Kuberaḥ Pitāmahāt,
Kuberādojasā lebhe Ravaṇastadgrihottamam.
R. V 5/23-24.

(iv) *Airāvaṇa vishāṇāgrāirāpīḍitakritavraṇau,*
Vajrollikhitapīnāṃsau nānāyudhaparikshatau.
R. V 9/109.

(v) *Nirjitā hi mayā devāḥ saṃyutā saṃyuge purā,*
Tairavaśyam vidhātavyam vyalīkam kiñcideva naḥ.
R. V 42/10.

(vi) *Avadhyatā tapovīryād bhavatā yadi manyate,*
Ātmanaścāsurairdevair hetustatrāpyayam mahān.
Sa hi Rāmaḥ sa Sugrīvo naiva Devo na Pannagaḥ,
Nāsuro naiva Gandharvo na Yaksho naiva Kinnaraḥ.
Mānusho Rāghavo rājan Sugrīvaśca Harīśvaraḥ,
Tābhyām prāṇaparitrāṇam katham rājan karishyasi.
R. V 47/26-28.

(vii) *Kim esha bhagavān Nandi bhavet sākshād ihāgataḥ.*
Yen saptosmi Kailāse mayā prahasite purā.
R.V 50/2-3 N.S.

(b) Bharata, who was, according to the Bāla-Kāṇḍa, carried by his maternal uncle to Kekaya after his marriage is referred to as a *bāla* (child) by Mantharā in the Ayodhyā-Kāṇḍa.[1]

The former objection, it may be pointed out, does not hold good because the words of Rāma to Śūrpaṇakhā were not meant to be taken seriously. We have to be guided in this respect by the poet's express remark that Rāma was only jesting with Śūrpaṇakhā.[2] Similarly, the words of the elderly maid-servant, Mantharā, are only expressive of her almost motherly affection for Bharata and cannot be interpreted as indicative of Bharata's age. Such a usage of the words *bāla, jāta* etc. in such a manner is common enough even now.

As regards the apparently supplementary nature of the Uttara-Kāṇḍa indicated by the *kāvya-praśasti* at the end of the Yuddha-Kāṇḍa we fully agree with the following remarks of C. V. Vaidya : "The history and greatness of Rāvaṇa required to be detailed somewhere, for without them the poem would have been incomplete and the greatness of Rāma without a strong relief."[3] Some of the great poets even of the West, we know, have added, subsequent to the composition of the main body of their poems, fresh portions to their original works[4] or written sequels.[5] Thus, it is not unnatural or preposterous if Vālmīki appended a supplement to his poem. Judged from this point of view the two *kāvya-praśastis* at the end of the Yuddha-Kāṇḍa and the Uttara-Kāṇḍa will not indicate two distinct authorships, but the composition of the Uttara-Kāṇḍa by the same author at a time subsequent to that of the Kāṇḍas I-VI.[6]

Nor do we feel convinced by the argument that the authorship of Books I and VII must be different from that of the other

1. Cf. Bulcke, C., Rāma-Kathā, p.123.
2. *Krūrair anāryaiḥ Saumitre saṃprahāsaḥ kathañcana, na kāryaḥ...* R. III 23/19.
Cf. *Parihāsa vijalpitam sakhe paramārthena na gṛhyatām vacaḥ.* AbhijñānaŚākuntalam, II 18.
3. Vaidya, C. V., Riddle of the Rāmāyaṇa, p. 48.
4. Vide for example, Shelly's Act. IV of Prometheus Unbound.
5. Vide, for example, Milton's Paradise Regained.
6. Vide also Sastri Ramaswami, K.S., Studies in Rāmāyaṇa, Part I, p. 30.

Books, as in Books I and VII Rāma is deified and identified with Vishṇu whereas in Books II-VI he is a mortal, though of heroic stature.[1] Western scholars, we know, perceive three successive layers in the development of Rāma's character. From an ordinary human being originally, perhaps the leader of a small clan, he is said to have been fast converted into an ethical and national hero and then raised to the plane of a divine being and identified with Vishṇu.[2] But, such an idealisation of the 'real' is a natural and well-known feature of Indian poetry. Even recent rulers like Pṛithvīrāja II[3] and Pṛithvīrāja III[4] were regarded as incarnations of Rāma. About Samudragupta it was said that only in routine functioning was he a mortal; else, he was a god incarnate.[5] In ancient India this tendency to idealise and deify great heroes might have been even more marked, with the result that these heroes, though of the same flesh

1. Cf. "Only in Books I and VII is Rāma throughout conceived as a divine being, an incarnation of Viṣṇu. In Books II-VI apart from a few passages which are doubtless interpolated he is always only a mortal hero and in all indisputably genuine parts of the epic there is no indication whatever of his beng conceived as an incarnation of Viṣṇu."

Winternitz M., A History of Indian Literature, Vol. I, p. 496.

2. Cf. "Through this very work the hero of the Rāmāyaṇa became converted to the ethical hero of the people and from the hero of a clan to a national hero. The honour apportioned to him, raised him forthwith from the human to the divine sphere and brought about his identification with Viṣṇu..."

Jacobi, H., Das Rāmāyaṇa, Eng. Tr. Ghoshal, S. N. p. 50 (See also pp. 95-96.).

N.B. Dr. Jacobi draws a distinction between the Books II-VI on the one hand and I and VII on the other, primarily because, according to his version, Rāma is a human being in the former whereas he is represented as an incarnation of Vishṇu in the latter. But he seems to have remained unsatisfied with this conclusion also, for he suggests furtheron a division between Book II on the one hand and Books III-VI on the other. According to him, "everything is human and natural" in Book II. But in Books III-VI, "evertyhing is supernatural and phantastic." Dr. Jacobi, would like us to believe that Rāma in Book II is a human being; in Books III-VI he is Indra, who with the help of Hanūmat, the genius of the monsoon recovers his wife Sītā, the Furrow, from the captivity of Vṛitra, the king of the Rākshasas, viz. Rāvaṇa; and in Books I and VII he is an incarnation of Vishṇu.

3. See the Hānsī inscription of Pṛithvīrāja II's reign, E. I. Vol. I.

4. Vide Jayānaka's Pṛithvīrāja-vijaya Māhākāvya canto XI (p. 262 ff.)

5. Vide Samudragupta's Allahabad Pillar inscription (Line 28). C.I.I. Vol. 3.

and blood as the rest of humanity, excel even the gods in respect of their virtues and character. Vālmīki's portrayal of Rāma creates a difficulty for the westerners and for those others who view things wholly Indian with western eyes. Vālmīki has indeed portrayed Rāma as a human being but he is at the same time so conscious of the divine element in him that he conveys through numerous passages scattered all through the several Kāṇḍas of the Rāmāyaṇa the fact of his being essentially divine and incarnation of Vishṇu.[1]

As to the remark that in Books II-VI, "it is not Vishṇu but the god Indra who as in the Veda is regarded as the highest god,"[2] we do not find any substantiation of this assertion in the Rāmāyaṇa. Indra, it may be pointed out, had been pushed into the background already in the later Vedic period. As will be shown in a subsequent chapter, the Indra of the Rāmāyaṇa is only a poor copy of the Indra of the Rigveda. In the Rāmāyaṇic mythology the supereminent position is enjoyed by two gods, Brahmā and Vishṇu,—Brahmā here being the thinker and Vishṇu the executor of plans for the welfare of all gods, (especially Indra) who, without them, would have been, nowhere in their conflict with the Rākshasas.[3]

Nor can we establish on the basis of their metre, language and spirit that the Books I and VII are a later composition, for even the findings of the western scholars themselves show that in these respects these Books are in no way distinguishable from Books II-VI. Hermann Jacobi writes : "In fact these (two) Books do not at all differ from the remaining (Books) so far as the metrical peculiarities are concerned. The (metre) *śloka,* which shows the same regular features, has been utilised in them and been handled with the same dexterity."[4] About the grammatical peculiarities he says; "they are pretty uniform all over the poem" and "as a result there is no means of making this feature as a test of distinguishing the spurious element from the genuine."[5] Lastly, with regard to the spirit

1. R. VI, 98/20. Vide also chapter on "Mythology."
2. Winternitz, M., A History of Indian Literature, Vol. I,p. 496.
3. For details on this point vide chapter on "Mythology".
4. Jacobi, H., Das Rāmāyaṇa, Eng. Tr. Ghoshal, S. N. p. 21.
5. Ibid, p. 25.

of these two Books he observes: "We can speak of biased revision, only when the existent material is remodelled in order to incorporate into it views and dispositions, which differ from those of the old work or are perhaps in glaring contrast to them. Nothing of this sort can be traced in the Rāmāyaṇa because the annexed matters breathe the same spirit as the original poem."[1] And as in the presentation of the social and political conditions of the Rāmāyaṇa, it is the general spirit that is most important, we should hardly be justified in excluding the Bāla-Kāṇḍa and the Uttara-Kāṇḍa from our purview.

Further, we may be permitted to add that even if there were within any *kāvya* variations of language and style these would not in themselves serve to establish multiplicity of authorships, for in a literary composition language and style do have a rhythm of their own which fluctuates with the subject, character, circumstance and context. As an illustration from the Rāmāyaṇa itself, we may note that in the Sundara-Kāṇḍa the language of dialogues, of nature descriptions, of the accounts of the affluence and splendour of the Rākshasas and of the battle-scenes is not the same throughout.

We may also add that while discussing the position of the Bāla-Kāṇḍa and the Uttara-Kāṇḍa one should not forget the fact that the Rāmāyaṇa is an account of the struggle for political domination between the Aryans and the non-Aryans—principally the Rākshasas. The beginning of this struggle is found in the Bāla-Kāṇḍa where Rāma kills Tāṭakā and uproots Mārīca, Subāhu aud their followers; and it finally ends in the Uttara-Kāṇḍa with the killing of Lavaṇa by Śatrughna. In other words, the Bāla-Kāṇḍa and the Uttara-Kāṇḍa occupy a definite place in the plan. of the entire epic which will be materially disturbed if these two Books were rejected as spurious.

As to the interpolations in the other cantos various criteria have been proposed. Mr. C. V. Vaidya for instance suggests that all verses in metres other than the *Anushṭup* should be treated as later interpolations, particularly when they occur at

1. Jacobi, H., Das Rāmāyaṇa, Eng. Tr. Ghoshal, S. N. p. 47.
Compare also : "They are, however, pervaded by the same spirit as the older part. There is, therefore, no reason for the supposition that they are due to a Brahman revision intended to transform a poem originally meant for the warrior caste."
Macdonell, A. A., A History of Sanskrit Literarure, p. 304.

the end of a canto. He is of the opinion that such verses were added later with the object of making the original poem conform to the definition of a *Mahā-Kāvya*.[1] But, as 'theory' initially presents in a systematic form the actual practice of the great masters of the day and is derived from it, would it not be more reasonable to presume that the definition of a *Mahā-Kāvya* itself is based on the *Ādi-Kāvya* of Vālmīki—that it supplied the norms which determined whether a certain composition could or could not be called a *Mahā-Kāvya*. Moreover, in view of the fact that longer metres are freely found employed even in the earlier Vedic literature there is absolutely no ground for holding that the *Ādi-Kavi* was incapable of composing verses in *Upajāti*, *Vaṃśastha*, *Pushpitāgrā* or *Mālinī*.

Equally unacceptable is Mr. Vaidya's suggestion that all those episodes, which contain the element of marvel ,should be discarded as spurious[2], for 'marvel' has been an essential ingredient of early heroic poetry all over the world.[3] In such poems, the poet has sustained the interest of his audience principally by introducing the 'marvellous' in his accounts. If episodes like the flight of Hanūmān, his encounters with Surasā and Siṃhikā and certain battle-scenes in the Yuddha-Kāṇḍa were to be dropped from the poem it will, we fear, no longer be the Rāmāyaṇa which Indians have learnt to love and admire. Besides, if its various legends of didactic and religious character as well were to be summarily discarded, it will cease to be "an incarnation of the Hindu spirit and a supreme shrine of the Hindu ideals."[4] It will, then, be reduced to an insipid chronicle, presenting only the account of the life and adventures of a *kshatriya* prince; and this, as pointed out earlier, has never been the ambition of a Sanskrit poet.

In the light of the discussion above, regarding the text of the Rāmāyaṇa we may briefly present our position thus :

There is a distinct tradition that Rāmāyaṇa is an archaic

1. The Riddle of the Rāmāyaṇa, pp. 37-38.
2. Ibid, pp. 43-44.
3. Cf. "Heroic poetry seems to be a development of narrative from a magical to a more anthropocentric outlook."
Bowra, C. M., Heroic Poetry, p. 8.
4. Sastri, Ramaswami, K. S., Studies in Rāmāyaṇa, Part I, p. 1.

work of 24,000 verses divided into seven 'Kāṇḍas'.[1] Moreover, Kālidāsa and all subsequent writers display their familiarity with the *Rāma-Kathā* as contained in the seven 'Kāṇḍas' of the extant Rāmāyaṇa. Since there is so far no sound reason to disturb this time-honoured tradition we feel that it should be respected. Further, though we admit that from time to time interpolations have been introduced into the original poem we cannot subscribe to the view that there has been a wholesale revision (or revisions) of the *kāvya* in any subsequent period (or periods). And as regards the additions which might have been made to it later by the author himself, or made within a period not far removed from that of the poet, since they breathe the spirit of the original they do not disturb its integrity; they rather present a social and political picture identical with that of the core of the Rāmāyaṇa and can, therefore, be utilised in the account that we are presenting in the following chapters.

---

1. It is believed that by putting together the opening letter of the first verse and of every thousandth verse thereafter in the Rāmāyaṇa the *gāyatrī mantra* becomes complete. (*Gāyatryāśca svarūpam tad Rāmāyaṇam anuttamam*).

For details vide Sastri, Ramaswami, K. S., Studies in Rāmāyaṇa, Part II, p. 18.

Chapter II

THE VARṆA AND THE ĀŚRAMA

I

The concept of *varṇa*, as suggested by its literal meaning, originated in the early Ṛigvedic period as a racial distinction between the fair *Āryas* and the dark-skinned *Anāryas*, the *Dāsas*, and the *Dasyus*. Shortly afterwards, the complexity of life necessitated a further division among the *Āryas* themselves, so that among them, men devoted to learning and priesthood came to be known as the *brāhmaṇas*; kings, noblemen and warriors as the *rājanyas* (*kshatriyas*); and the rest, i.e. artisans, agriculturists, traders and others as the *vaiśyas*. The *Anāryas* who were by this time almost completely subjugated were also included in this scheme as the *śūdras*, though they were placed at the lowest rung of the social ladder as subservient to the *Āryas*.[1] A verse in the Purusha-sūkta, wherein, in the Ṛigveda the four *varṇas* are collectively mentioned for the first and the only time clearly illustrates this.[2] "The whole social organisation is here conceived symbolically as one human being—"the Body Social", we may say, with its limbs representing the social classes based on the principle of division of labour."[3] This four-fold division of the society into the *brāhmaṇas*, the *kshatriyas*, the *vaiśyas* and the *śūdras* had become fully established by the time of the Rāmāyaṇa[4] and a passage in the Araṇya-Kāṇḍa[5] very distinctly reproduces the idea of the afore-said verse of the Purusha-sūkta.

From the story of Viśvāmitra as given in the Bāla-Kāṇḍa (where it is primarily intended for the glorification of the *brahmarshi* ideal) it may appear that the society of Vālmīki

1. Kane, P. V., History of Dharma-śāstra, Vol. II, part I, pp. 25-36.
2. Ṛigveda, X 90/12.
3. Prabhu, Pandhari Nath, Hindu Social Organization, p. 292.
4. Note the use of the word *cāturvarṇya* in R. I 1/94.
The four *varṇas* are collectively mentioned in R. I 6/21; R. I 9/77; R. II 118/13; R. III 19/53; R. VI 106/37.
5. R. III 19/54.

recognised the principle that *varṇa* was to be determined by *karma* (action) and not by *janma* (birth).[1] However, the evidence of the rest of the epic shows that heredity was actually the main principle in determining the *varṇa* of an individual. The rights and privileges of the different *varṇas* in the society had by that time been distinctly laid down and members belonging to a particular *varṇa* were expected to follow the course applicable to their own *varṇa*. In the description of Ayodhyā the poet repeatedly emphasises the fact that all the *varṇas* living there were intent upon performing the duties prescribed for their own *varṇa*[2] and that among the people there was no *ācāra saṅkara* (confusion of conduct).[3] The concept of *sva-dharma* as one's duty as a member of a particular *varṇa* was being gradually evolved[4] and even the principle that by the faithful discharge of one's duty as a member of a particular *varṇa* one could achieve the highest glory here and hereafter is also found in the Rāmāyaṇa, though in an elementary form.[5]

One remarkable fact about the *Ārya varṇas* in the Rāmāyaṇa needs noting. In the Dharma-śāstras the first three *varṇas*, viz., the *brāhmaṇa*, the *kshatriya* and the *vaiśya* are termed *dvijas* or *dvijātis*—twice-born ones, for the *upanayana-saṃskāra* which introduces a young boy to the Vedic studies and which was, therefore, regarded as his second birth, as it were, was a privilege only of these three *varṇas*; the *śūdra* was denied this right. In the Rāmāyaṇa, however, where the words *dvija* and *dvijāti*[6] are of very frequent occurrence, there is not a single passage in which these have been employed in relation to any non-*brāhmaṇa*.[7] It is rather strange that the Rāmāyaṇa

1. By gradually modifying his conduct Viśvāmitra, who was a *kshatriya* by birth succeeded in becoming a *brahmarshi*.

R. I cantos 51-61.

2. R. I 7/14.

3. R. I 6/22.

4. R. I 1/94; R. I 6/14; R. I 19/9; R. IV 4/6 N.S.; R. IV 18/11 N.S. R. VI 110/9.

5. R. III 7/15-16.

6. R. I 10/15; R. II 32/8; R. II 46/15; R. II 47/14; R. II 73/12; R. II 77/18; R. III 5/29, 31; R. V 22/5; R. VII 6/6.

7. In the Bombay recension of the Rāmāyaṇa there is, however, one passage in the Sundara-Kāṇḍa in which the word *dvija* seems to have been

does not directly mention even the *upanayana-saṃskāra* in relation to any *varṇa* (or individual), even though its first three *varṇas* (viz. the *brāhmaṇa*, the *kshatriya* and the *vaiśya*) constituted one group[1] as distinguished from the last viz. the *śūdra*. The study of the Vedas, offering sacrifices and giving gifts were held to be the duties of the *brāhmaṇas*, the *kshatriyas* and the *vaiśyas* alone. It may also be added here that though in the Rāmāyaṇa the gradation of the *brāhmaṇas*, the *kshatriyas* and the *vaiśyas* as each preceding one, being considered higher than the one following, was fixed,[2] there is not the slightest evidence to show that the differences among them had reached such extents as to require different qualities and measurements in their dress and equipment.[3] The Rāmāyaṇa, on the other hand, depicts most cordial relations subsisting among the different *varṇas*. In the description of Ayodhyā it is said that all the *varṇas* lived there in perfect amity. The *kshatriyas* were obedient to the *brāhmaṇas*; the *vaiśyas* respected the *kshatriyas* and the *śūdras* lived there doing ungrudging service to the three higher *varṇas*.[4] In the Rāmāyaṇa there are many accounts of friendliness and co-operation between the *brāhmaṇas* and the *kshatriyas*;[5] even though, as revealed by the stories of Paraśurāma[6] and Viśvāmitra[7] there might have been a period of rivalry between these two highest *varṇas* in the society.

At the head of the *varṇa* scheme, in the Rāmāyaṇa, stood the *brāhmaṇas*—men dedicated to learning,[8] veracity,[9] tran-

employed to distinguish the regenerate *varṇas* from the non-regenerate one. The verse reads as follows—

"*Bhāvam na cāsyāhamanupradātum alaṃ dvijo mantramivādvijāya*." R. V 28/15

It may be noted in this connection that the reading of this passage in the North-Western recension is different and in consistence with the rest of the Rāmāyaṇa it retains the sense of a *brāhmaṇa* for the word *dvija*. The verse in N. W. reads :

"*Bhāvam na cāsyāham anupradātum alaṃ dvijo brahma yathāntyajāya*" R.V 22/5.

1. R. II 114/51.
2. R. I 6/21.
3. Cf. Manu-smṛiti II 41-47.
4. R. I 6/21.
5. R. I 16/23-25; R. I 43/22; R. II 104/6-8; R. III 4/19-20.
6. R. I 71/25 ff.
7. R. I cantos 49 and 51.
8. R. I 10/38; R. II 1/22.
9. R. VII 76/7.

quillity[1] and austerity,[2]—in fact, to everything that was good and righteous.[3] The study of the Veda was their primary concern and they considered the Vedas to be their highest treasure.[4] While introducing a *brāhmaṇa*, the Rāmāyaṇa generally speaks of him as "proficient in the Veda and its auxiliaries."[5] *Śruti-dṛishṭārtha* (one who has understood the meaning of the Veda), *bahu-śruta*, (very learned), *śrutānvita* (possessed of learning) and *sarva-vidyāntaga*[6] (conversant with all lores) are the usual epithets employed for the *brāhmaṇa* by Vālmīki. But besides the Vedas and other scriptures, the *brāhmaṇas* studied other subjects of practical utility also, for example, politics, logic and grammar.[7] They were further considered experts in *loka-vṛittānta* (custom and usage?)[8] and were regarded supreme authorities on all matters of religion.[9]

Another activity to which the *brāhmaṇas* devotedly applied themselves was the performance of sacrifices. The daily *agnihotra* and the various periodical sacrifices were zealously performed by them. In Ayodhyā, the poet says, there was not a single *brāhmaṇa* who did not maintain the sacrificial fire and perform *yajña*.[10] Thus *yajña* and *adhyayana* were the two main duties of a *brāhmaṇa*.[11] *Tapas* is also intimately associated with the *brāhmaṇas*[12] as a severe course of bodily and mental training leading towards complete self-restraint. Alms-giving has not been specifically mentioned in the Rāmāyaṇa as a duty of the *brāhmaṇas*. But from the emphasis on 'hospitality' and the general high tone of morality among the *brāhmaṇas* it can easily be inferred that 'benevolence' was also obligatory upon them.

In addition to *adhyayana*, *yajana* and *dāna*, the Rāmāyaṇa, like the Dharma-śāstras, seems to recommend three more

1. R. I 71/6.
2. R. I 1/1.
3. R. II 47/14.
4. R. II 47/25
5. R. I 5/19; R. I 7/1; R. I 10/16; R. II 29/15; R. II 77/18; R. VI 108/3.
6. R. I 8/14; R. II 4/19; R. II 47/14; R. II 1/22 respectively.
7. R. II 114/9; R. VII 93/20.
8. R. I 8/14.
9. R. II 32/19.
10. R. I 6/13.
11. R. I 6/14; R. VI 11/20.
12. R. V 90/47.

duties for the *brāhmaṇas*, viz. teaching the Vedas, officiating at sacrifices, and receiving gifts. In fact, these latter were the peculiar privileges of the *brāhmaṇas* to serve them as their principal means of livelihood.[1]

Teaching was generally done by the *brāhmaṇas* in the third stage of their life, when, having completely renounced the pleasures of the world they lived in the hermitages as *vānaprasthas* (anchorites). Large numbers of students lived with Vālmīki, Vasishṭha, Viśvāmitra, Bharadvāja and the sages of Daṇḍakāraṇya.[2] Teaching must also have been imparted by those *brāhmaṇas* who were living as householders in the towns (and villages). This seems all the more likely in view of the fact that for various reasons it might not have been feasible for quite many young scholars to leave their homes and live for studies with a teacher in the forest. We actually see that the sons of Daśaratha did not leave their home and stay with a *guru* in an *āśrama* for their education; on the other hand, their education was arranged in Ayodhyā itself. In case of Bharata and Śatrughna we hear that they received their lessons in various *śāstras* from the *brāhmaṇas* in the royal palace of Kekaya itself.[3] From these references it is also clear that the *brāhmaṇa* teachers provided instructions not only in religion and philosophy, but also, in such practical subjects as archery and politics.

Priesthood was another office exclusively reserved for the *brāhmaṇas*. Any attempt of encroachment on this privilege of a *brāhmaṇa* by a person belonging to any other *varṇa* was vehemently resisted by the *brāhmaṇa* community and condemned by the society. Thus the *brāhmaṇas* refused to co-operate with Viśvāmitra who, though being a *kshatriya*, was acting as a priest in the sacrifice of Triśaṅku.[4] Not only that, as the story goes, the *Devas* themselves declined to accept the offerings made by a *kshatriya* priest. In fact, the zealous devotion with which the *brāhmaṇas* applied themselves to the study of the Veda qualified them alone to undertake and discharge with efficiency such a responsibility.

1. Kane, P. V., History of Dharma-śāstra, Vol II, part I, p 105.
2. R. I 2/43; R. I 48/5; R. II 103/1, 7; R. III 16/1.
3. R. II cantos 1-2.
4. R. I 55/14.

Note that the *brāhmaṇas* who participated in the performance did so for fear of Viśvāmitra's curse and not willingly. R. I 56/6.

The *brāhmaṇas* were considered the worthiest recipients of gifts[1] and 'acceptance of gifts' remained their principal means of livelihood. Rich and profuse gifts were given to them by the kings on various occasions such as sacrifices, coronations and other ceremonies like the birth or marriage of a prince (or princess).[2] Vālmīki alludes to large numbers of *brāhmaṇas* honoured with gifts by Daśaratha, Kauśalyā and Rāma.[3] In certain cases, it must be added here, the *brāhmaṇas* accepted state service also. A number of *brāhmaṇas* constituted the *mantri-parishad* of the king in Ayodhyā.[4] Perhaps in every kingdom there was a *brāhmaṇa purohita*, who very often was also the king's Chief Counsellor.[5] Vasishṭha in Ayodhyā enjoyed very wide powers and high position.[6] Likewise, Sudhanvā who was a past-master in archery and the use of missiles and well-versed in the science of polity was another *brāhmaṇa* attached to the royal household of Ayodhyā as a military teacher of the princes.[7]

It is necessary to add here that in return for their services the *brāhmaṇas* did not expect much. Many of them subsisted on mere alms, regarding poverty as their ornament and contentment as their chief characteristic. In the Ayodhyā-Kāṇḍa, Vālmīki refers to a class of *brāhmaṇas* named by him as *bhikshā-bhujaḥ*,[8] i.e. subsisting on alms. Contrary to the suggestion of the term *bhikshā-bhujaḥ* these *brāhamaṇas* were most probably not mere beggars. On the other hand, it is very much likely that this class comprised of those who were completely given over to such pursuits as study and performance of sacrifices, but whose living depended solely on the charity of the people. Kaikeyī in her childhood invited a curse from such a *brāhmaṇa* when, in the pride of her beauty, she scoffed at him, judging him by his looks to be a simpleton.[9]

1. R. II 56/20.
2. R. I 10/39-40; R. I 68/27-28; R. VI 109/87-88.
3. R. II 20/4; R. II 35/2 ff.
4. R. I 7/1; R. II 73/2-3.
5. Vide Chapter XVIII.
6. Daśaratha is described as *Vasishṭhavaśavartī* in R. I 17/2.
7. R. II 114/9.
8. R. II 35/26.
9. R. II 11/38-39 (Note,—*brāhmaṇam mūrkharūpiṇam*)

Inspite of physical hardships a *brāhmaṇa* on an average displayed in his conduct very high moral and spiritual standards. The *brāhmaṇa* in the Uttara-Kāṇḍa, whose son had prematurely passed away, accused Rāma of being responsible for the death saying, that he himself could not be blamed for it, as in all his life he had never uttered a lie nor in any way caused injury or affliction to a living being.[1] That the covetable position of a *brahmarshi* which required as a pre-requisite fortitude, forbearence, austerity, tranquillity, graciousness and complete control over one's anger and lust, and which was attained by Viśvāmitra only after a protracted herculean effort[2] was again no mere ideal, but that it was actually embodied in the lives of a number of *brāhmaṇas* can be seen from the examples of Vasishṭha, Bharadvāja, Atri, Agastya and others. Naturally, such *brāhmaṇas* commanded very high respect in the society. They were universally regarded as *varṇa-śreshṭhas*[3] (best among the *varṇas*) and even glorified as *bhūmi-devas*[4] (divinities on the earth) and as the prime cause of a man's well-being.[5] They are seen invariably present in all social and religious functions as harbingers of auspiciousness.[6] The *kshatriya* kings and princes cherished their friendship and took pride in doing them service.[7] The estimation in which kings held the *brāhmaṇas* is amply illustrated in the outpourings of Daśaratha's heart at the visit of the sage Viśvāmitra to his court. Welcoming the sage he said that the arrival of the sage in the court was like the obtaining of ambrosia; like a shower in a land suffering from drought; like the birth of sons by worthy wives to one without issue; like the recovery of a lost thing; yea, like the dawning of a mighty joy.[8] In times of a national emergency or any other crisis a king sought the guidance of renowned *brāhmaṇas*. When his country was facing a grave famine due to drought, king Lomapāda referred the matter to the *brāhmaṇas* and on their advice took steps to fetch Ṛishya-Śṛiṅga from his

1. R. VII 76/7 ff.
2. R. I 59/26-27; R. I 61/13-15.
3. R. I 6/20.
4. R. II 1/23.
5. R. II 1/21.
6. R. II 1/22; R. VI 109/41.
7. R. I 48/18; R. II 59/10.
8. R. I 16/23-24.

father's hermitage.[1] Similarly, Rāma invited the *brāhmaṇas* Mārkaṇḍeya and others and requested them to guide him to a course whereby the deceased son of the *brāhmaṇa* could be revived.[2]

In consideration of their austere life and the selfless services rendered to itself the society granted the *brāhmaṇas* a few privileges. The person and property of a *brāhmaṇa* were considered inviolable. The *brahma-sva* (*brāhmaṇa's* property) was free of state taxation[3] and any person (be he a prince) who unlawfully seized it or caused damage to it was severely punished by the king.[4] Similarly no corporal punishment could be given to a *brāhmaṇa* and under no circumstance he could be killed.[5] *Brahma-hatyā* was one of the most grievous sins which degraded not only men[6] but also gods like Indra.[7]

The second *varṇa* was the *kshatriya varṇa* which was constituted of the martial section of the community. As rulers, the *kshatriyas* were sometimes glorified even more than the *brāhmaṇas*, for the belief was that a king was created from the elements of the four *Lokapālas*, viz., Indra, Yama, Kubera and Varuṇa[8]. The status of a *kshatriya* in the society, however, was next to that of a *brāhmaṇa*. Rāma, though a king, warmly received the deputation of *brāhmaṇas* living on the bank of the Yamunā and asked them to command him.[9] He submitted to them that his kingdom and his very life were at the service of the *brāhmaṇas*.[10]

Granting protection to the weak and the oppressed was the primary duty of the *kshatriyas*. They were believed to bear bows (weapons) only to see that the word 'distressed' did not exist on the earth.[11] As Daśaratha was hesitating to send Rāma with Viśvāmitra, Vasishṭha reminded him that there was no

1. R. I 8/14 ff.
2. R. VII 77/4 ff.
3. Cf. "*brahmasvasyāvihiṃsakāḥ*" R I 7/10.
4. R. II 78/45-46.
5. R. VII 62/30.
6. R. II 45/11.
7. R. VII 86/3 ff.
8. R. III 43/12-13.
9. R. VII 64/11 (Note : *ājñāpyo(a)ham*).
10. R. VII 64/12.
11. R. III 11/3.

duty of the *kshatriyas* more cherished than protection.[1] Thus only *kshatriyas* were considered competent to become rulers[2] and in that capacity they had to ensure a free and due observance of *dharma* by everyone in the society.[3] The cow and the *brāhmaṇa* were symbolic of Aryan culture and their protection was the special charge of a *kshatriya* prince.[4]

Bodily strength was one of the chief attributes of a *kshatriya*[5] and as such he was expected to make exertions for the fulfilment of all his needs and desires; accepting anything in charity from others was ignominious for a *kshatriya*. Unlike a *brāhmaṇa* the *kshatriya* was expected to give rather than accept from others.[6] Similarly to exercise pressure upon others for the acceptance of his demand by fasting (or any similar method) was unworthy of a *kshatriya*.[7] Performance of sacrifices was strongly recommended to a *kshatriya*,[8] for it served a dual purpose. On the one hand, it brought merit to the performer and, on the other, it offered subsistence to the *brāhmaṇas* who, as we have seen, depended mainly on the charities given to them by the other *varṇas*.

In the Rāmāyaṇa, which is primarily a *kāvya* of the *brāhmaṇas* and the *kshatriyas*, references to the *vaiśyas* are comparatively very few. The *vaiśyas* are often mentioned just to complete the list of the *varṇas*. However, by gleaning information scattered loosely in the Rāmāyaṇa it appears that they were a community engaged in trade, agriculture and cattle-rearing.[9] While describing a town the poet often refers to the markets and shops of the *vaṇig-jana* laden with merchandise.[10] Sometimes, he refers to their organisations (*nigamas* and *śreṇis*) also.[11] It is noteworthy that not a single individual belonging to this *varṇa* has been mentioned by name in the whole of the Rāmāyaṇa.

1. R. I 19/9.
2. Cf. R. I 1/101.
3. R. I 19/8.
4. R. I 23/13.
5. R. VII 32/29.
6. R II 99/18-19.
7. R. II 124/16.
8. R. II 53/30.
9. R. II 114/24.
10. R. II 8/12; R. II 18/7.
11. Vide chapter XXI.

The last *varṇa* comprised of the *śūdras*—the servant class. In various capacities (such as washermen, barbers, masseurers, attendants etc.) they served the higher three *varṇas*.[1] It is not unlikely that the families of the *śūdras* were attached as servants to various families of the higher *varṇas* whose concern it was to see that they (the *śūdras*) were provided with food and raiment. While preparing to proceed to the forest, Rāma gave specific instructions to Lakshmaṇa for making provisions for the maintenance of his servants during his absence.[2] As the *śūdras* originally belonged to a different racial stock, the *Āryas* had withheld from them the privilege of Vedic study. From the evidence of the Rāmāyaṇa also it is clear that the *sāvitrī* which symbolises the *upanayana-saṃskāra* and the commencement of Vedic studies was under no circumstance to be imparted to them.[3] However, in the Rāmāyaṇa there is not the slightest indication of hatred or contempt being cherished by the higher three *varṇas* towards the *śūdra*. On the other hand, as we have already noted in the poet's reference to Ayodhyā, the *śūdras* were living in perfect goodwill with the rest of the people.[4] It is worth mentioning that Daśaratha asked Sumantra to invite to his sacrifice the *śūdras* also, along with the other three *varṇas*.[5]

The *caṇḍālas, antyajas* and *pukkasas*[6] were the most degraded ones among the *śūdras*. The *caṇḍālas* were perhaps employed for such menial service as cleaning the faeces and carrying the corpses. Naturally, their presence at the sacrificial altar was considered contaminating.[7] They dressed themselves in black lower garments with red upper garments and put on ornaments of iron.[8] Perhaps they lived away from the

1. R. I 6/21; R. II 35/21 ff.
2. R. II 35/21-25.
3. R. II 92/18.
4. R. I 6/21.
5. R. I 9/77.
6. N. B. "The *pukkasas*", observes P. V. Kane, "are included by the Mahābhāsya under *Śūdras* that are *nirvasita* (i.e. those who are so low in the caste system that if a vessel is used by them for eating their food it cannot be used by any one of the other castes even after the vessel is purified by fire etc."

History of Dharma-śāstra, Vol. II, Part I, p. 92.

7. R. III 62/19.
8. R. I 54/11-12.

habitation of the other *varṇas* and unlike the common *śūdra* these *caṇḍālas* were untouchables.[1] The food of a *caṇḍāla* was considered to be polluting and no *brāhmaṇa* (perhaps no member of the higher three *varṇas*) was expected to eat it.[2] It is not very clear whether the *caṇḍālas* (also the *vṛishalas*) were such by birth or were a class formed of those members of the higher *varṇas* who were degraded to this position for having committed some heinous act. The word *patita* (fallen) occurs in a number of passages of the Rāmāyaṇa which makes it amply clear that a member of the higher *varṇa* being made to lose his privileges, could be relegated to a lower position and even reckoned as one among the *śūdras*.[3]

In addition to the four *varṇas* discussed above the Rāmāyaṇa mentions on the one hand *Nishādas*, *Mlecchas*, *Ābhīras* (*Śabaras* ?), *Kirātas*, *Yavanas*, *Cīnas*, *Pahlavas* and *Śakas*,[4] and, on the other, *sūtas*, *māgadhas*, *bandins*[5] *dantakāras*, *sudhākāras* etc.[6] In the Dharma-śāstras these are described as ramifications of the primary four *varṇas* caused chiefly by inter-caste marriages and also in some cases by following a particular occupation.[7] We may point out in this connection that even though there appear to be no rigid restrictions in the Rāmāyaṇa with regard to inter-caste marriages, there is no attempt to explain the existence of *Cīnas*, *Yavanas* etc. as offshoots of the four *varṇas* based on cross-marriages among themselves. The Rāmāyaṇa at the same time does not offer unambiguous evidence to show that members of the society following a particular occupation had formed themselves into independent castes.[8]

1. R. I 54/13.
2. R. I 55/15.
3. Vide the Triśaṅku account in R. I 54/9 ff.
Compare also : '*Kaccit tvām nāvajānanti yājakā patitam yathā.*' R. II 114/39.
4. For references vide R. II 50/27; R. II 3/55 (and R. II 5/11); R. IV 35/6 (and R. V 96/34); R. III 80/10; R. I 50/2-3; R. II 5/10-11; R. IV 32/19-22; R. IV 33/14; R. IV 35/21; R. IV 36/15-16, 22).
Note : Leaving the references to *Nishādas, Mlecchas,* and also perhaps *Ābhīras* and *Kirātas* the passages in which *Śakas, Yavanas, Cīnas* and *Pahlavas* are mentioned seem to be later interpolations.
5. R. II 16/56.
6. R. II 94/12 ff.
7. Kane, P. V., History of Dharma-śāstra, Vol. II, Part I, pp. 69-100.
8. Like the word *varṇa* the word *jāti* is also employed sometimes

A few words about the *dāsas* will not be out of place here. It may be stated at the very outset that besides employing the words *dāsa* and *dāsī*[1] the epic provides little information about the institution of 'slavery'. One passage of the Ayodhyā-Kāṇḍa simultaneously mentions *preshyas* and *dāsas*. The former are explained by the commentators as *bhṛityas* (i. e. servants).[2] This may indicate that the status of the *dāsas* differed from that of the ordinary servants; presumably the *dāsas* were slaves. One may draw a similar hint about the *dāsas* from another passage in the Sundara-Kāṇḍa where, complaining to his mother Kaikasī about the rough treatment meted out to himself by his brother Rāvaṇa in the Assembly of the Rākshasas, Vibhīshaṇa said that he was insulted like a *dāsa*.[3] Moreover, the palaces of the kings, queens and the princes were usually crowded with *dāsīs* and the practice of giving *dāsīs* as presents seems to have been a fairly popular one in the times of Vālmīki. Janaka gave *dāsīs* wearing gold necklaces (*nishka*) as part of the marriage dowry[4] and the term *jñāti-dāsī* for Mantharā[5] indicates that she was also given by Kekaya-rāja as dowry in the marriage of Kaikeyī. Besides marriage, on other occasions also, one could confer upon another *dāsīs* as a mark of his pleasure. Kaikeyī promised to Mantharā that if the plans of Rāma's banishment and Bharata's installation as *yuvarāja* succeeded she would appoint duly-bedecked *dāsīs* to wait upon Mantharā.[6] Similarly when Hanūmān brought the news about Rāma, Bharata conferred upon him sixteen *bhāryās* who were waited upon by hundreds of *dāsīs*.[7] Again,

to convey the sense of 'castes'. It may be noted that the term *varṇa* emphasises the element of race and culture in determining the castes whereas in the term *jāti* it is birth and heredity which predominate. In the Rāmāyaṇa the word *jāti* occurs in III 5/25; V 91/45 and VI 65/12, but nowhere it seems to connote the idea of 'caste'.

1. The word *dāśa* employed for the boatmen among the *Nishādas* is a different word and need not be confounded with the *dāsas*. (Vide R. II 96/15 and R. II 101/13, 22, 27).

2. R. II 28/3
The word *preshyāḥ* is explained as *bhṛityāḥ* by Govindaraja and Rāmāyaṇa-śiromaṇi-ṭīkā.

3. R. V 91/98 (Note : *dāsavaccāvamānitaḥ*).

4. R. I 70/6.

5. R. II 9/1.

6. R. II 12/15.

7. R. VI 106/53.

dāsīs were received by Rāma as presents from kings after his coronation in Ayodhyā.[1]

Dr. Dev Raj Chanana is of the opinion that the institution of slavery existed only among the Aryans (the people of Ayodhyā particularly); the Vānaras and the Rākshasas did not employ slaves. Further, he explains this contrast between the Aryans and the non-Aryans of Vālmīki's times by pointing out that the Vānaras and the Rākshasas "had not, at that time arrived at the stage of the domestication of cattle and of agriculture and, as a consequence, did not enjoy a complete mastery over a regular production of their food stuffs."[2] We do not find the reasoning very convincing. As already noted above in the words of Vibhīshaṇa the concept of *dāsa* is known to the Rākshasas. Moreover, silence of the poet in referring to agricultural fields in Laṅkā, in our opinion, does not necessarily indicate that agriculture was unknown to the Rākshasas; specially in view of the fact that food-grains have been specifically mentioned as forming part of their meals.[3] It is also to be noted that the number of concubines and female attendants in the palace of Rāvaṇa, far exceeds that of the number of concubines and female attendants at Ayodhyā.[4] If food could be procured for them, we wonder, how the paucity of food could stand in the way of the *dāsas* or *dāsīs* alone. One should have more of evidence to accept unreservedly Dr. Chanana's view.

II

As complementary to the *varṇa*-scheme the ancient Indians evolved another social institution, viz., the *āśrama*, and the two together sought to establish harmony between the seemingly opposite aims of the society and of the individual. The *varṇa*-scheme viewed man as a member of the Aryan society and from that angle laid down his rights, privileges, duties and responsibilities. The *āśrama* scheme, on the other hand, considered him as an individual and tried to so shape his life that preparing himself variously at the different stages

1. R. VII 41/9.
2. Slavery in Ancient India, pp. 28-29.
3. R. VI 38/32 (Note : *Rāśim annasya cādbhutam*).
4. R. V canto 5.

he finally achieved his spiritual goal, viz., of liberation from the travails of mundane existence. The word *āśrama*, derived as it is from the root *śram* 'to exert oneself', etymologically stands for (i) a place where exertions are performed, as also (ii) the action of perfor ming such exertions.[1] Technically it refers to the four stages of *brahmacarya*, *gṛihastha*, *vānaprastha* and *sannyāsa* through which every Aryan was normally expected to pass during his life. These four *āśramas* have been mentioned in the Rāmāyaṇa both collectively[2] as well as severally[3] and there is sufficient evidence to show that the Aryans of Vālmīki's times resorted to these stages, broadly in consonance with the directions contained in the Dharma-śāstras.

The *brahmacarya-āśrama* (or the stage of an unmarried student of the Veda) was, the first stage in an Aryan's life. It commenced with the *upanayana saṃskāra* which marked the beginning of the Vedic study in an individual's life and concluded with the *samāvartana* with which a *brahmacārī* being now termed a *snātaka* became qualified to enter the next stage viz. the *gṛihastha-āśrama*. In the Rāmāyaṇa the word *brahmacarya* occurs a number of times,[4] but there is no specific refe rence to the *upanayana* or the *samāvartana saṃskāra*. However, the fact that the *upanayana* was in vogue in Vālmīki's society is indicated by the references to the *yajñopavīta* and the *sāvitrī* in the passages of the Kishkindhā-Kāṇḍa[5] and the Ayodhyā-Kāṇḍa respectively.[6] The *samāvartana* can be easily inferred from such words as *vidyāsnāta*, *vrata-snāta*, *veda-vidyā-vrata-snāta* and *vidyā-veda-vrata-snāta*.[7] Moreover, in view of the popularity of the Vedas among the higher three *varṇas* and the rigid exclusion of the *śūdra* from the Vedic studies we should be justified in assuming that in the period of the Rāmāyaṇa

1. Prabhu, Pandhari Nath, Hindu Social Organization, p. 83.
2. R. II 104/64; R. II 118/14.
3. R. I 71/10; R. II 27/16;R. II 92/10; R. III 7/18.
4. R. I 8/9; R. I 30/36; R. II 53/14; R. II 14/10; R II 37/23; R. II 92/10; R. IV 42/10.
5. R. IV 21/15.
6. R. II 92/18
7. R. II 92/10; R. I 59/1 and R. V 16/17; R. I 9/42 and R. VI 71/59 respectively. For the meanings of these terms vide Kane, P. V., History of Dharma-śāstra, Vol. II part I, pp. 370-374 and 407.

also the *brahmacarya-āśrama* was compulsory for every child of the first three *varṇas* and that the *upanayana* and the *samāvartana* marked its range.

The evidence in the Rāmāyaṇa about the duration of the *brahmacarya-āśrama* is extremely meagre. Writing in the Bāla-Kāṇḍa about the princes (Rāma and his brothers) the poet suggests that when their studies were complete the king Daśaratha thought of their marriage.[1] Shortly afterwards while speaking to Viśvāmitra the king stated that Rāma had not till then completed his sixteen years.[2] This will indicate that roughly the sixteenth year, the time when one attained to adulthood, was the limit of this *āśrama*. It is also very likely that those *brāhmaṇas* who wished to master the Vedas along with their auxiliaries had a longer period of *brahmacarya*.[3]

Ordinarily a student was expected to leave his home and stay with his teacher during the period of *brahmacarya*, but in certain special circumstances he could even prosecute his studies while living with his parents. The fondness of Daśaratha for his sons (specially Rāma) kept them at home during their *brahmacarya*; otherwise there are copious references to students living with their teachers in the hermitages.

The life of a *brahmacārī* was an austere one. A verse in the Araṇya-Kāṇḍa indicates that he was an *eka vastradhara*[4] i. e. wearing only the lower garment; (the *ajina* was perhaps used by him, as the upper garment). Moreover, he was required to acquire learning in various subjects and at the same time to observe certain strict disciplines. When Kaikeyī put forth her demands before Daśaratha he apprehended that Rāma who had lately become emaciated by observing severe vows of *brahmacarya* would now again be called upon to suffer the hardships of forest life.[5] In addition to this a *brahmacārī* was also required to render certain services to his teacher. Some

1. R. I 16/5-6.
2. R. I 18/2.
3. About the duration of the *brahmacarya-āśrama* the Dharma-śāstras prescribe fairly flexible rules which try to accommodate the needs and ambitions of different *varṇas* and individuals.

For details vide Kane, P. V., History of Dharma-śāstra, Vol. II, Part I, pp. 351-352.

4. R. III 38/14 N. S.
5. R. II 14/10.

idea of these can be had from the account of Indra when he was attending upon Diti in her penance. With great diligence he administered to all her needs by providing her with fruits, roots, holy grass, faggots for (the sacrificial) fire and water.[1] Bharadvāja, a pupil of Vālmīki is also seen fetching for his *guru* his bark garments[2] and a bucket of water.[3] Besides, the *upanayana* also introduced the *brahmacārī* to religious performances and, now, he was required to offer *sandhyā* both in the early mornings (*pūrvā-sandhyā*) and the evenings (*paścimā-sandhyā*). The *japa*, i. e. muttering of *gāyatrī* and other sacred mantras and the *udaka* or *arghya*, i. e. offering water out of respect to the sun formed important items of this *sandhyā*. It may incidentally be added here that an individual continued to perform this *sandhyā* throughout his life.

A word about the position of girls with regard to *brahmacarya* may be deemed necessary here. As we have discussed this question in some detail in another chapter[4] it would be sufficient to say here that by introducing Svayamprabhā in the Kishkindhā-Kāṇḍa as a *tāpasī brahmacāriṇī*[5] Vālmīki has left unambiguous evidence regarding the presence of *brahmacāriṇīs* in his society.

On completion of the *brahmacarya* period, an individual usually took to himself a wife (or wives) and entered the next stage, viz. the *gṛihastha-āśrama* (or the house-holder's stage). No doubt, each *āśrama* being an important stage for the development of an individual has to be regarded as the best in its own place;but the *gṛihastha āśrama* holds a unique position in the *āśrama*-scheme. It was indispensable for the individual because it afforded him an opportunity to discharge his obligation to the gods, manes and sages.[6] Moreover, this was the only stage where he could ardently apply himself to the pursuit of *artha* and *kāma* (though only so far as they did not stand opposed to *dharma*).[7] From the social point of view this stage was essential because all the other three *āśramas* subsisted on what

1. R. I 42/10.
2. R. I 2/9.
3. R. I 2/23.
4. Vide chapter V.
5. R. IV 42/10.
6. Cf. R. II 6/13; R. II 118/20.
7. R. II 114/64.

they received from the *gṛihastha*. Vālmīki has recognised the importance of this *āśrama* by calling it most distinguished and praiseworthy.[1]

With the advance of age, when the senses grew weak and the mind became surfeited with the material pleasures of the world a man naturally developed a disregard for the hustle and bustle of town life and longed to repair to the calm and quiet corner of the forest for spiritual advancement. The *āśrama*-scheme provided scope for the fulfilment of this need of the individual by including within it the *vānaprastha* and the *sannyāsa*. These stages were to be resorted to by him in the last years of his life after he had lived an active life as a *gṛihastha* and entrusted the responsibilities of the household to the care of his competent son (or sons). The *vānaprastha āśrama* which means, "a stage of life in which one stays in a forest in a pre-eminent way" (by observing a strict code of life)[2] provided a start for this new life.

The term *vānaprastha* occurs a number of times in the Rāmāyaṇa[3] and that it connoted the idea found in the Smṛitis is borne out by various references and statements. Thus king Aṃśumān installed Dilīpa, his son, over the kingdom and himself practised penance on the Himavat mountain.[4] King Daśaratha wanted to be relieved of the responsibility of looking after the subjects by the appointment of Rāma as *Yuvarāja*.[5] According to Lakshmaṇa, dwelling in the forest was permitted for the kings only after they made over their subjects to their sons.[6]

1. R. II 118/14.
N.B. From a simile employed in a passage of the Araṇya-Kāṇḍa (*Tathā sandarśanenaiva copākarshata Rāghvam. Kuṭumba bharaṇāsaktaṃ naram mokshapathādiva*. R. III 49/6) a certain censure seems to be expressed against the *gṛihastha-āśrama*. We may point out in this connection that for the reasons noted below we consider this passage to be spurious :
(i) The verse is not found in the *Baṅgīya* and the *Dākshiṇātya* recensions of the Rāmāyaṇa;
(ii) The spirit of the simile goes against the general attitude of Vālmīki towards the *gṛihastha-āśrama*;
(iii) The idea of *moksha*, as will be shown in a subsequent chapter, is, on the whole, missing in the Rāmāyaṇa.
2. Kane, P. V., History of Dharma-śāstra, Vol. II, Part, II, p. 918.
3. R. II 70/20; R. III 7/18; R. III 16/25; R. V 8/47.
4. R. I 39/3.
5. R. II 4/8 ff.
6. R. II 23/29.
For details about the living of the *vānaprasthas* vide chapter VII.

One interesting fact related about the *vānaprasthas* in the Rāmāyaṇa is their organised living. Almost everywhere in the Rāmāyaṇa they are seen living in large groups in the *āśramas* (hermitages). In the Bāla-Kāṇḍa we are told that various types of hermits were residing in the hermitage of Vasishṭha[1] and the Araṇya-Kāṇḍa expressly mentions a big *Vānaprastha-gaṇa* in the Daṇḍakāraṇya.[2] The *āśrama* (hermitage) of a forest hermit, as shown elsewhere, was usually an academy in which resided large numbers of teachers and students. Besides, the presence of the notorious Rākshasas in the neighbourhood might also have necessitated group-living.

The stage that followed the *vānaprastha-āśrama* in what may be termed the right and natural sequence was that of the *yati* or the *sannyāsa-āśrama* (or the stage of an ascetic who had abandoned all worldly concerns).[3] In this *āśrama* a person broke off all worldly ties and becoming indifferent to pleasure and pain he quietly waited for the last hour to come. His only pursuit was the control of the senses and the mind, and meditation. The word *yati* is fairly popular in the Rāmāyaṇa.[4] The word *parivrājaka* which is a synonym of *yati* has been employed with reference to Rāvaṇa when he approached Sītā in Pañcavaṭī.[5] The word *sannyāsī* does not occur but *sannyāsa* has been employed in connection with Paraśurāma[6] and seems to convey the idea of renunciation. Taking all the evidence into consideration we can not agree with Dr. S. N. Vyas in holding that the Rāmāyaṇa does not shed any special light on this *āśrama*.[7]

1. R. I 47/24-26.
2. R. III 7/18.
3. In order to avoid any confusion that might arise it may be made clear that the terms *sannyāsī*, *yati* and *parivrājaka* are employed synonymously in the Dharma-śāstras. Thus Manu employs all these terms with reference to the treatment of the fourth order (vide Manusmṛiti VI 33-87.
4. R. II 19/83; R. II 57/2; R. VII 80/15.
5. R. III 51/2.
6. R. I 71/9-10.

The word *sannyāsa* also appears in R.III 10/14. But comparison of this passage with that of the Bombay recension (III 9/18 N. S.) reveals that in the Lahore edition it is a case of scribal error—*sannyāsa vidhinā* being wrongly put for *sa nyāsa vidhinā* (=by way of a deposit).

7. Vyas, S. N., Rāmāyaṇa-Kālīna Samāja, p. 96.

From the description of Rāvaṇa in Pañcavaṭī we learn about the outward marks of a *parivrājaka* as follows : "He wore a soft madder-coloured garment; had a lock of hair on his head and a pair of sandals on his feet; and he carried a staff, a *kamaṇḍalu* and an umbrella on his left shoulder."[1] Among the other salient features of the fourth order the Dhramaśāstras mention three things :

(1) The first requirement of this order was that the *yati* was to renounce all worldly possessions (except the elementary articles of daily use). Thus even for his food he was to depend on begging.[2]

(2) He was to break off all family ties. As against the *vānaprastha* who had the option to live in the forest in company with his wife, a *sannyāsī* was required to pass his time in strict loneliness;[3] he was not allowed even to keep company of fellow ascetics. For the strict observance of this rule he was advised not to stay at one place, but to keep ever moving. He was to pass the night wherever evening betook him. The only exception to this rule was during the rainy season for which period he was allowed to stay at one place.[4]

(3) The last and the most important requirement was the abandonment of all actions that spring from the desire to secure one object or the other (*kāmya-karmas*). Thus even *agnihotra* was no longer necessary for him. He was concerned principally with restraint or quiescence of the senses and the mind and contemplation of the highest Reality.[5]

It may be pointed out that practically each one of the above points is found mentioned in the Rāmāyaṇa. In the Śveta account in the Uttara-Kāṇḍa there is a direct reference

1. R. III 46/3 N.S.

2. Cf. The *Sarvavedas* sacrifice in the Kaṭhopanishad (I 1/1). In the later period it was known as the *Prājāpatyeshṭi* which a person was required to perform in order to qualify himself for his entry into the *sannyāsa-āśrama* : (Vide Manusmṛiti, VI 38).

3. Cf. Manu., VI 42.

4. Cf. Vasishṭha Dharma Sūtra (X 12-13, 15) quoted by Kane, P. V., History of Dharma-śāstra—Vol. II, part II, p. 932 (f. n, 2150).

5. Cf. Manu., VI 43.

For details vide Kane, P. V., History of Dharma-śāstra, Vol. II, Part II, pp. 931-938.

to the practice of begging of food by a *yati*.[1] The same Kāṇḍa introduces Durvāsā, (an ascetic presumably of the *yati* order) approaching Rāma for food.[2] That a *yati* was indifferent to pleasure and pain is testified by a figurative reference in the Ayodhyā-Kāṇḍa where Rāma has been compared to a *yati* because his face bore no sign of perturbance even when he was called upon to relinquish the *Rājya-Lakshmī*.[3] Sītā has also paid a homage in the Sundara-Kāṇḍa to those high-souled sages who had their senses in control and who had no objects of love or displeasure.[4] That a *yati* lived in solitude having completely renounced his family is shown by such references to him as *vimuktaḥ*[5] and *ekacaraḥ*.[6] Vālmīki even alludes to the practice of a *yati* keeping ever moving and making his quarters wherever evening overtook him.[7] The *cāturmāsya* idea is also noted in the case of Durvāsā who passed this period in the hermitage of Vasishṭha.[8] About the pursuits of the *yati* the Rāmāyaṇa clearly states that he was ever engaged in meditating on the self.[9]

With regard to these *āśramas* the Dharma-śāstras express three views, viz. of orderly co-ordination (*samuccaya*), option (*vikalpa*) and annulment (*bādha*). According to those who hold the first view a person is required to resort to the four *āśramas* one after the other in order; he is not expected to skip over any one or more and pass on to the next. The second view allows one to drop the middle two *āśramas*, viz. the *gṛihastha* and the *vānaprastha* and to adopt straight away the *saṁnyāsa-āśrama* on the completion of the *brahmacarya-āśrama*. The third view regards the householder's stage as the only stage fit to be adopted ; the *brahmacarya* being treated as only pre-

1. R. VII 80/15.
2. R. VII 107/13.
3. R. II 19/82-83.
4. R. V 20/67.
5. R. II 57/2.
6. R. II 73/21.
7. R. II 73/21.
8. R. VII 53/2.

Note. *Ṭilaka-Ṭīkā*: *Vārshikyaṃ varshāsu bhavaṃ cāturmāsyaniyamamuddiśyovāsa. Yatīnāṃ varshākāle bhramaṇa nishedhād vārshikamāsa catushṭayaṃ ekatraiva sthitavānityarthaḥ.*

9. R. II 73/21; R. V 11/31.

paratory to it.[1] There is no direct discussion on this point in the Rāmāyaṇa, nevertheless, the epic displays full familiarity with all the three views stated above. The first view, viz. *samuccaya* is clearly expressed in a passage of the Ayodhyā-Kāṇḍa which states that one should repair to the forest only in one's ripe age after entrusting the household to the care of the son (or sons)[2]. *Vikalpa,* the second view, seems to be indicated in the account of Ṛishya Śṛiṅga whose life was perhaps being modelled for perpetual celibacy (*naishṭhika brahmacarya*) by his father, the sage Vibhāṇḍaka.[3] But by showing that the youthful sage, Ṛishyaśṛiṅga fell an easy prey to the enticement of the courtezans employed by king Lomapāda the poet perhaps indicates his disapproval of the adoption of such an irregular course. The third view, viz. *bādha* is apparently recognised in those passages of the Rāmāyaṇa which glorify the *gṛihastha-āśrama* as the best of the *āśramas* and celebrate it as a division of the *brahmacarya-āśrama.*[4] On consideration of all this evidence together with the actual lives of the characters described in the Rāmāyaṇa we shall not be wrong to conclude that Vālmīki did not favour the dropping of the *gṛihastha-āśrama*; on the other hand, he recommended a natural course of reaching the *sannyāsa* stage by gradually passing through the earlier three stages.

1. Vide Kane, P. V., History of Dharma-śāstra Vol. II, part 1, pp. 424-425.
2. R. II 23/29.
3. R. I 8/41 ff.
4. R. I 9/5 N. S.
   Note Tilaka-Ṭikā : Mekhalājinādi dhāraṇarūpam mukhyam (brahmacaryam); dāreshu ṛitu gamana rūpaṃ gauṇam (brahmacaryam).

CHAPTER III

FAMILY LIFE

Man is a "civic animal"[1] and it is "in the family life alone that the social instincts can find any basis for growth."[2] Family is the foundation of society. "Of all the organisations, large or small, which the society unfolds," observe MacIver and Page, "none transcends the family in the intensity of its sociological significance. It influences the whole society in innumerable ways, and its changes.........reverberate through the whole social structure."[3] The individual imbibes the basic traits of his personality while living in the family and it is through the family again that the society transmits the cultural heritage to him. The importance of the family for providing proper conditions for the more stable satisfaction of the sex-need of the man and the woman, and for procreation, care and nurture of the offspring cannot be gainsaid. In short, it is in the family that the 'biological , psychological and sociological forces meet in giving the individual his start in life."[4]

The study of this important institution in the Rāmāyaṇa is of particular interest, for at the root of the whole drama of the epic are the intrigues of several persons of a family who were striving to secure power and prominence by pushing to the throne his or her nominee. In his creation of the family of Daśaratha which was constituted of men and women of diverse aptitudes and interests, the poet has fully brought to light the strength and weakness of the Hindu family structure.

The two principal characteristics of the Aryan family, namely, its joint structure and patriarchal organisation are

1. Aristotle.

2. Compte, Positive Philosophy, Vol. II, chapter V (quoted by Prabhu, Pandhari Nath, Hindu Social Organization, p. 209).

3. MacIver, M. R., and Page, C.—Society, p. 240 (quoted by Prabhu, Pandhari Nath, Hindu Social Organization, p. 203).

4. Young, Social Psychology, p. 237 (quoted by Prabhu, Pandhari Nath, Hindu Social Organization, p. 208).

found in tact in the times of the Rāmāyaṇa. With the father at the head, the family was made up of brothers, their sons and son's sons, together with their wives and unmarried daughters. Though its extent was flexible, normally, it included three generations, for the life span of three generations is around a hundred years and it is extremely rare for an individual to outlive a century. The Aryan family reckoned its descent from father to son;[1] daughters were invariably given in marriage to suitable husbands, outside the family.

These members of the joint-family generally lived under one roof, partook of food that was cooked at one hearth, held property in common, participated in common family worship and were related to each other as some particular type of kindred.[2] In royal families, however, the condition of living under one roof and that of partaking of food cooked at one hearth could not have been fulfilled, for the general practice obtaining among them was of separate palaces for wives and grown up princes. In Ayodhyā, Kauśalyā, Kaikeyī, Rāma and Lakshmaṇa are seen living in separate palaces. In such cases the family retained its joint character in the sense that all its members continued to recognise the authority of the one patriarch from whose common fund each received the material requirements of his life, and that they all participated in common family worship.[3]

The mainspring of the strength of the family is the affectional bond which holds its members together. This bond is, in fact, the very genesis of the family institution.[4] In the Rāmāyaṇa particularly, this aspect of the family life is very important in as much as herein are preserved some of the unique instances of ideal relationships subsisting between the parents

1. Vide the genealogies of Daśaratha related by Vasishṭha in R. I 66/17-31 and of Janaka related by himself in R. I 67/2-13.

2. Cf. Karve, Irawati, Kinship organisation in India, p. 10.

Note : For kinship terms in the Rāmāyaṇa see appendix to this chapter.

3. Vide, for example, the princes, participating along with their brides in the various religious ceremonies on returning to Ayodhyā from Mithilā (R. I 77/12-13 N.S.).

4. Cf. "Through the affectional bond in the family man, woman and child learn the technique and expression of affectional virtues which stand them in service in dealing with the outside world."

Prabhu, Pandhari Nath, Hindu Social Organization, p. 211.

and the children, wife and the husband, and the brothers themselves. It will be worthwhile, therefore, to give a review of the Rāmāyaṇa-family in respect of the relations of the members among themselves.

At the head of the family was the father. The Sanskrit term *pitā* for the father, derived as it is, from the root *pā* to protect (or to preserve) points at the primary responsibility of the father to protect his children and also to look after the needs of their life. Rāma recalled with gratitude the extreme affectionate care with which his father had brought him up, providing him with food and raiment.[1] Bharata also had very sweet memories of the fondling care with which his father treated him in his early years. He recalled, when, as a child, he approached his father, he greeted him, by smelling his head, and placed him on his lap.[2] In fact, Daśaratha's love for his sons, particularly for Rāma, has become proverbial among the Hindus. Just as arms issuing from the same body are equally dear to a person so were the four princes dear to Daśaratha.[3] Rāma, however, was the favourite of his father. In his separation from Rāma Daśaratha felt his very existence impossible. He earnestly implored Kaikeyī not to press her demand for Rāma's banishment too much, for that would mean death for him.[4] His apprehensions proved true, for on the seventh day after Rāma's departure he breathed his last and during the interval elapsing between Rāma's departure and his death he remained mostly unconscious.

The importance of a son in the family was many-sided. From the religious point of view, he was believed to be the deliverer of his father from hell. The word *putra* is explained in its derivative sense by Vālmīki as the protector (*trātā*) of his father from the hell named *put*.[5] A son was also indispensable, for the continuity of the family line depended upon him.[6] Moreover, in times of distress, a father looked upon his son as his deliverer and hoped that he would be his refuge in old age.[7]

1. R. II 124/9-10.
2. R. II 85/12.
3. R. II 3/6-7.
4. R. II 13/52-53.
5. R. II 120/12.
6. *vaṃśakaraḥ sutaḥ*—R. I 8/1. Also R. I 9/11.
7. R. I 58/8.

Naturally, the craving of an Aryan for a son knew no bounds. He did not feel secure or satisfied unless a son was born to him from his befitting wife.[1] In a number of cases, we find in the Rāmāyaṇa that the people invoked divine help through fasts, penances and sacrifices for the birth of a son. Daśaratha, it is well known, performed the *putreshṭi* for the fulfilment of his longing for a son.[2] It may be added, that the emphasis in all such cases was, not on the birth of a mere son, but on that of a virtuous one[3], for in him alone the father's heart could find its real solace. Moreover, a virtuous son was a living image of his father even after his death, while a wicked son brought ignominy upon the father and the family. It seems that a father often renounced his wicked son.[4]

A father, who was responsible for bringing the child into being in this world was the first claimant of his devotion. The father (along with the mother and the teacher) was a child's *guru* and was to be looked upon with the highest veneration.[5] According to Rāma, a father was a living embodiment of divinity more real than any other god and hence the most adorable.[6] He believed that it was not easy for a son to repay what the father (and the mother) always did in behalf of their son by providing food, sleep, clothing, constant pleasant speech and sport.[7] Therefore, in order to fulfil the wish of his father Rāma was readily prepared to burn or drown himself.[8] Obedience to the father was at once a duty and a virtue in a son;[9] it was indicative of his divine disposition, discernment and future prosperity.[10] By obedience to his parents the son could acquire wealth, learning, progeny, happiness and even heaven.[11] Natu-

1. *vinātmajenātmavatāṅ kuto ratiḥ*—R. II 12/111 N.S.
2. R. I 8/1-2.
3. R. II 120/13.
4. R. I 58/16-17; R. II 39/20-25; R. II 78/45-47.
5. R. II 124/2, 10.
6. R. II 19/18-19.
7. R. II 124/8-10.

Cf. *Yam mātā-pitarau kleśaṃ sahete sambhave nṛiṇām,*
Na tasya nishkṛitiḥ śakyā kartuṃ varshaśatairapi.
Manusmṛiti, II 227.

8. R. II 19/31.
9. R. II 30/32, 38 N.S.
10. R. II 68/3.
11. R. II 30/36 N.S.; R. II 70/47.

rally, disobedience was condemned and was considered one of the symptoms of anarchy.[1]

Vālmīki depicts most cordial relations among brothers. The four sons of Daśaratha bore the warmest affection towards one another. Rāma, being the eldest of them all, looked upon the rest almost with fatherly affection and they also accorded him almost filial regard. Lakshmaṇa had great attachment for Rāma. Disregarding his personal comforts, he remained ever intent on fulfilling the wishes of Rāma. He did not partake of any sweets offered to him unless Rāma also partook of them. When Rāma went ahunting he followed him with bow in his hand in order to protect him. Without Rāma's company he found himself unable to enjoy even on most joyous occasions.[2] The sacrifice that Lakshmaṇa made in voluntarily following Rāma in the forest for fourteen years is a singular illustration of fraternal relationship. Likewise, it is difficult to find a parallel in the whole Sanskrit literature to the sentiments expressed by Rāma about his brother (Lakshmaṇa) when he found him lying on the ground mortally wounded by the enemy.[3] Equally unique was Bharata's love and devotion for Rāma. He considered Rāma as his father, mother, friend and lord.[4] And to the surprise of everyone, he displayed utter contempt towards the 'Royal Splendour' secured for him by his mother.[5] Just as Lakshmaṇa was devoted to Rāma so was Śatrughna attached to Bharata whom he regarded more than his own life.[6]

Even when Vālmīki paints most glorious pictures of fraternal affection among his characters he does not completely rule out the possibilities of rifts and clashes among brothers. Among princes, the most powerful and common ground for transforming this fraternal affection into rivalry was the kingdom. At one place Vālmīki remarks that the 'Royal Splendour' washes away

1. R. II. 73/9
2. R. I 14/25-28.
3. R. VI 25/7, 16.
4. R. II 78/31.
5. Kālidāsa has paid a very deserving tribute to Bharata on this account—

Pitrā visṛishṭām madapekshayā yaḥ, śriyaṃ yuvāpyaṅkagatāmabhoktā.
Iyanti varshāṇi tayā sahogram, abhyasyatīva vratamāsidhāram.

Raghuvaṃśa XIII 67.

6. R. I 14/29.

affection from the hearts of brothers.[1] Elsewhere he says that the 'Royal Splendour' was competent enough to cause to break in a moment's time even powerful ties of fraternal affection.[2] Even in the times of Vālmīki, a cousin, it seems, had become well-known in his capacity of a rival, for in order to express the utter inappropriateness of his accepting the kingdom Bharata said that such an (unworthy) act would be worthy only of a cousin.[3] This very character of the cousin appears to have been echoed in the words of Mantharā also when she called Rāma a *sahaja-ripu* of Bharata.[4]

Women (i.e. wives) were considered another equally important factor in creating factions among the brothers. The very structure of a patrilineal Hindu joint-family is such that its strength lies in the unity of its men, but it is always threatened by an eruption emanating from the quarters of its women who are brought into the family from different houses. As a poet with insight, Vālmīki was conscious of this inherent weakness of the Hindu family-structure and has remarked that women tend to create dissensions among brothers.[5] In certain rare cases, brothers could also be expected to behave inimically to each other if one got enamoured of the charms of another's wife.[6]

Sometimes, this cordial relationship was also impaired by the impact of polygamy. Vālmīki's society made it possible, at least for a *kshatriya* to marry youthful maidens at different periods of his life, even when his previous wife (or wives) was (were) living. And a polygamous husband, naturally, had the greatest attachment to his youngest and fairest wife, who on that account was also the most charming one. Ups and downs in the lives of women married to a polygamous husband were very frequent, and the one, who was the seniormost and the dearest of her husband at one time could lose her position the other moment when her husband got enamoured of another woman. Rāvaṇa, after he had set his heart upon Sītā, offered

1. R. II 11/56.
2. R. II 95/6.
3. R. II 118/4.
4. R. II 10/29.
Mantharā perhaps looked upon Rāma as a cousin of Bharata, for he was born of a different mother.
5. *bhrātṛibhedakarāḥ striyaḥ*—R. III 50/29.
6. R. III 50/23-24.

her a position of pre-eminence among his wives[1], nay, he even promised that if she consented to accept him as her lord his previous wives would serve her as maids.[2] Almost a similar change of fortune can be witnessed in the harem of Daśaratha after his marriage with Kaikeyī. This lovely princess from Kekaya was married by Daśaratha at a late period of his life and the 'old man' loved his 'youthful wife' more than his own life.[3] Introduction of Kaikeyī into the harem of Daśaratha resulted in a serious loss of status for Kauśalyā who had to live on that account a life of neglect and disregard.[4]

Rivalry of a co-wife has become proverbial in Hindu life and literature, and everyone knows that inspite of the most sincere admonitions of the sages, poets and elders, serious rifts occasionally cropped in family life and vitiated the whole family atmosphere. Polygamy must also be regarded as responsible for the Indian's uncharitable view of feminine character. Women have been regarded as fickle-minded, jealous, indifferent to merit and virtue, callous and cruel. Rarely has one tried to analyse the circumstances which are the breeding ground of such vices in women and state honestly that such vices whereever they existed, were mostly due to the unnatural demands of men, who subjected their women to the most detestable and unjust conditions.

Introduction of a co-wife in the life of a Hindu lady, who so helplessly and entirely depended upon her husband not only for her happiness and well-being, but even for her physical existence was, naturally, an unfortunate and dreaded event. There is nothing strange, then, to find that a lady poisons or otherwise murders her co-wife. An unfortunate wife, a victim of polygamy, when feeling frustrated, may even be expected in her despair to plot against the son of her co-wife,[5] nay, her

1. R. V 15/16.
2. R. V 15/32.
3. R. II 13/3.
4. R. II 12/70 N.S.; R. II 25/6.
5. Vide the legendary case of Diti whose sons were killed by the sons of her co-wife. She complained to her husband and said—*Hataputrāsmi bhagavan putraiḥ śakrādibhistava, Śakra-hantāramicchāmi putram*...... (R. I 42/2.)

It is to be noted that the husband conceded—*Evam bhavatu*........ *Janayishyasi putraṃ tvaṃ Śakrahantāram*..... (Ibid 5).

The role played by Kaikeyī in dispossessing Rāma of his right is too own husband, who had been mainly responsible for her misfortune.[1] Vālmīki supplies ample references to testify to the genuineness of such possibilities. The mother of Sagara was poisoned during her pregnancy by her co-wife[2]; Hanūmān on not finding Sītā in Rāvaṇa's palace suspected that she might have been devoured by the wives of Rāvaṇa in order to do away with the possibilities of the emergence of a strong rival;[3] and Rāma on a number of occasions expressed his apprehensions about Kaikeyī administering poison to Kauśalyā, Sumitrā and Daśaratha.[4]

Not very rarely the ambition of a lady—the mother, but not of the eldest, would be to lay her hold upon the kingdom and the throne through her own son. In such an event it would become absolutely necessary to override the claims of the eldest son. One is surprised to notice that in the context of Rāma's coronation, in the Ayodhyā-Kāṇḍa, the poet alludes to the presence of rival camps of Kauśalyā and Kaikeyī, each wishing its own nominee to be appointed the heir-apparent.[5] Of these, one interested in Bharata, exploited the weakness of Daśaratha for Kaikeyī. Kaikeyī's *jñāti-dāsī*, Mantharā, succeeded in impressing upon her mistress that :

(i) if, for once Bharata, her son, failed to occupy the throne, he along with all his descendants would for ever be thrown out of the royal line;

(ii) personally she would be deprived of the status of a *rājamātā* (ruling prince's mother);

(iii) Kauśalyā, becoming powerful with the coronation of her son, could, naturally, be expected to return to her all the insults and injustices that she had hitherto suffered at the hands of her co-wife, the favourite of their husband.[6]

well known. It is to be noted that by sending Rāma to the Daṇḍakas, she actually wished him to perish.

1. R. II 21/2.

Moreover, when Lakshmaṇa suggested to Rāma—*Yāvadeva na jānāti kaścidarthamimaṃ naras tāvadeva mayā sārdham ātmasthaṅ kuru śāsanam.*

—Kauśalyā pleaded in favour of Lakshmaṇa's proposal. (R. II 21/8 ff)

2. R. II 110/19 N.S.
3. R. V 8/19.
4. R. II 53/18 N.S.; R. II 57/8-9.
5. R. II 6/37-38; R. II 10/28.
6. R. II 10/5-31.

We would like to point out in this connection that Kaikeyī did not feel satisfied by merely securing the throne for her son, Bharata, but in her anxiety to make her son's position free even from a danger likely to arise in future from the quarter of Rāma, she insisted on Rāma being sent to the Daṇḍakas and hoped that he would meet his end there before the expiry of the period of fourteen years.

The evils of polygamy did not remain restricted to the co-wives, but very often extended to the coming generation also. In such cases cordial fraternity was transformed into deep-rooted hostility. Vālmīki has alluded to the perpetual enmity subsisting between the legendary sons of Diti and Aditi.[1] He also records the popular case of Yadu who was neglected by his father because his mother (Devayānī) was not her husband's favourite; Yadu, on that account, bore a strong hatred not only for his brother, Puru, but also for his father.[2] Among Vālmīki's own characters the attitude of Lakshmaṇa towards his brother, Bharata, is worthy of notice. On learning that Rāma's rights were being forfeited in favour of Bharata, he got furious and started regarding Bharata as his enemy. In defence of Rāma's title to the throne he was prepared to indiscriminately fight against his brother, Bharata, father or any one else.[3]

1. R. I 41/14 ff.
2. R. VII 60/5.
3. R. II 21/11; R. II 110/14-28.

Appendix to Chapter III

Kinship Terms

The following is a table noting the various kinship terms occurring in the Rāmayāṇa in relation to the Aryans, the Rākshasās and the Vānaras :

		Aryans	*Rākshasas*	*Vānaras*
1.	Father	Pitā II 73/9	Pitā V 44/14	Pitā IV 17/27
2.	Father's father	Pitāmaha I 38/22		Āryaka IV57/5 N.S.
3.	Father's father's father (ancestors)	Prapitāmaha II 107/18 Pūrva-pitāmaha I 40/36		
4.	Mother's father	Āryaka II 1/19 Mātāmaha II 1/3	Mātāmaha VII 31/25	
5.	Mother's father's brother		Āryaka VII 31/26	
6.	**Father's brother :** younger elder	Pitā I 38/2, 7	Pitṛivya VI52/2 Jyeshṭha Pitā (Also Āryaka) VII 25/23 N.S.	Pitṛivya V 15/46.
7.	Mother's brother	Mātula II 1/2		Mātula V58/15
8.	Mother	Jananī V 36/2 Mātā II 20/3	Jananī V 91/15 Mātā VII 8/37	Mātā IV 47/4
9.	Mother's sister		Mātṛishvasā VII 30/37	
10.	Brother	Bhrātā I 66/2 (a) Jyeshṭha II 116/2 (b) Anuja I 66/2	Bhrātā V 34/9 (a) Jyeshṭha V 76/13 (b) Anuja VII 10/1	Bhrātā IV 47/4 (a) Jyeshṭha IV 47/4 (b) yavīyān IV 10/22
11.	Father's brother's son	Bhrātṛivya II 118/4		
12.	Mother's sister's son		Mātṛishvaseya VII 30/37	
13.	Sister	Bhaginī I 31/9	Bhaginī VII 11/1 Svasā VII 30/23	
14.	Mother's sister's daughter		Mātṛishvaseyā VII 31/27 Svasā VII 31/27	
15.	Son[1]	Putra I 43/18 Suta I 8/1	Putra V 44/9 Suta VII 4/7	Putra IV 17/39

1. The words *aurasa* and *kshetraja* standing respectively for a legitimate son and an illegitimate one (who is the offspring of the wife by some one else) are also found in the Rāmāyaṇa. (II 54/22 and IV 57/17).

		Aryans	Rākshasas	Vānaras
16.	Sister's son	Svasrīya I 69/5		
17.	Son's son	Naptā I 38/1 (Also for son's son's son VI39/25)	Naptā VI 46/106	Naptā VI 6/24
		Pautra I 48/10	Pautra VI 37/23	
		Suta I 8/1		
18.	Daughter's son	Dauhitra VII 28/20 N.S.	Putra VII 10/4	
19.	Daughter	Sutā I 12/8	Putrī VII 8/7	Duhitā IV 16/100
20.	Daughter's daughter		Dauhitrī VII11/23	
21.	Husband's father	Śvasura I 12/15		
22.	Wife's father	Śvasura I 13/6		Śvasura IV 35/2
23.	Wife's mother	Śvaśrū I 11/33		
24.	Husband	Bhartā I 72/12	Bhartā VII 11/11	Bhartā IV 15/4
		Pati III 2/22		Pati IV 15/36
25.	Husband's brother	Devara II 42/26	Devara VI 92/22	
26.	Sister's husband		Jāmātā VII30/28	
27.	Son's wife's father	Sambhandhī I 13/8	Sambandhī (a general term for the wife's relations VII 31/50)	
28.	Daughter's husband's father	Sambandhī I 68/3		
29.	Wife	Dārā I 6/10		
		Patnī I 35/3	Patnī V 5/122	Patnī IV 17/32
		Bhāryā II 30/4	Bhāryā V 5/122	Bhāryā IV 15/42
30.	Daughter's husband	Jāmātā II 33/3		
31.	Son's wife	Vadhū I 72/8		
		Snushā I 13/24	Snushā VI 36/15	
32.	Father's wife (other than ego's mother)	Mātā I 43/11		
33.	Father's son (from a wife other than ego's mother)	Vaimātra III 52/17	Dvaimātra III 53/3	
34.	Co-wife	Sapatnī II 20/30	Sapatnī V 5/81	

CHAPTER IV

MARRIAGE

Sex[1] and the offspring[2] are the two primary factors responsible for the evolution of marriage as a social institution. The Hindus carry the idea of marriage a step further by recognising it as a sacrament. More than a biological or social necessity, marriage for a Hindu is a religious requirement,[3] for without a wife he cannot discharge his debt to the *Devas* and the *Pitṛis*, and cannot secure heaven for himself after death. Thus, for a Hindu, happiness in this life and in the life to come primarily depends on marriage. A study of this institution in the Rāmāyaṇa is all the more interesting because herein are preserved, on the one hand, accounts of almost promiscuous sex relations and also references on the other, which point to the recognition of a permanent, rather eternal bond of unity through marriage between man and woman, in all phases of their life. These accounts are of particular interest as they incidentally help in understanding the evolution of 'marriage' in different forms, described in the Hindu Dharma-Śāstras.

Let us first take the Vānaras of Vālmīki. They are a very primitive race. Sex relations among them appear to be very loose. But very often the poet's description of these people is coloured with his own ideas. Thus at the death of Bālī, Tārā gives vent to her bereavement in a manner that would make one think that a Vānara lady had the same ideal of conjugal relations

1. Cf. "Marriage in the biological sense, and even to some extent in the social sense, is a sexual relationship entered into with the intention of making it permanent, even apart from whether or not it has received the sanction of the law or the church."

Ellis, Havelock, Psychology of Sex, p. 256.

2. Cf. "The source of marriage is to be sought for elsewhere. We can look for it in the utter helplessness of the new born offspring and the need of both the mother and the young for protection and food during a varying period of time."

Pandeya, Rajbali, Hindu Saṃskāras, p. 268.

3. *Ayajño va esha yo(a) patnīkaḥ.*
Taittirīya Brāhmaṇa ii, 2, 2, 6.

and fidelity as her Aryan sister.[1] The word *vidhavā*, with the train of all that entailed for an Aryan woman, has been mentioned by Vālmīki in this context. Likewise, the words, "who wants to violate my *eka-patnī varta*",[2] spoken by Añjanā to Vāyu, as he tried to embrace her, also give the same impression. But, in view of other facts mentioned in course of the story it is very difficult to recognise these sentiments as expressive of Vānara character. We know, for instance that Tārā and Rumā, who are normally described as the wives of Bālī and Sugrīva respectively, were both at one time living with Sugrīva as his wives,[3] and at the other with Bālī and then again with Sugrīva. It is worth remembering that as they pass from one brother to another the poet neither mentions any course of penance or purificatory ordeal, nor does he refer to a formal marriage. The reader only finds that those who had until yesterday been the wives of one, are now the wives of the other.[4] This was a common practice among the Vānaras, is also shown by a statement of the Vānaras loyal to Bālī in which they expressed their apprehensions that they would be dispossessed of their women by the victorious Vānaras coming into Kishkindhā with Sugrīva.[5] Moreover, the accounts of Hanūmān's birth[6] and that of Bālī and Sugrīva,[7] (in fact, of the entire contemporary Vānara population)[8] clearly indicate that the Vānara standard of sex morality was very much different from that of the Aryans.[9] The pride with which Jāmbavān declared before

1. R. IV 17/2 ff.
2. *Ekapatnīvratamidaṁ ko nāśayitum ichati*. R. IV 57/15.
3. R. IV 37/22.
4. N.B. In cantos 17 and 18 of the Kishkindhā-Kāṇḍa, Tārā laments over her widowhood. In the 19th canto upto the verse 43 the poet describes the coronation of Sugrīva and installation of Aṅgada as *Yuvarāja*. The reader is taken aback to find that in the next verse, which is also the last verse of the canto (viz., 19th) Tārā is found with Sugrīva as his wife—

   "*Nivedya Rāmāya mahātmane tadā, Mahābhishekaṅkapivāhinīpatiḥ,*
   Uvāsa bhāryām pratilabhya Tārām, Śaśāsa rājyan tridaśādhipo yathā."
5. R. IV 15/15.
6. R. IV 57/7-18.
7. R. VI 4/31-44.
8. R. I 15/7-12.
9. It seems, to allow a stranger to share her bed even during the life time of her husband (?) was neither resented by a Vānara lady nor disapproved by her society.

his Vānara colleagues that Hanūmān was the *aurasa* son of Vāyu begotten on Añjanā, the *kshetra* of the Vānara Kesarī, also proves this very fact.[1] On the evidence of the above facts and in the absence of even a single instance of sacramental union, we are probably justified in concluding that in the Vānara community a person took to himself a wife by the assertion of his physical power and not through marriage.[2]

Sometimes, it is argued that polyandry obtained among the Vānaras. Such a proposition is asserted on the evidence of Tārā and Rumā who lived in different periods as wives of Bālī and Sugrīva. What is noteworthy in this connection is that at no time, either of them has been described by Vālmīki to be simultaneously living as wife of Bālī and Sugrīva; and in the absence of such a reference polyandry cannot be recognised in their society.

One more point may be touched upon in this very context. From the account of Hanūmān's birth and also that of Bālī and Sugrīva one may feel inclined to believe that the custom of *niyoga* was popular among the Vānaras. This again would be found to be a fallacy, for according to the Dharma-Śāstras there are three necessary requirements of *niyoga*, viz.,

(i) the lady should either be a sonless widow or the wife of a husband who is incapable of procreation;

(ii) the intercourse should take place only with a near relation of the husband or with an appointed *brāhmaṇa*, and lastly

(iii) intercourse should be for procreation and not for the satisfaction of lust.[3]

The above noted cases of the Vānaras do not satisfy any of these conditions. On the other hand Vāyu, Indra and Sūrya are specifically said to have approached the Vānara ladies being enamoured of their beauty. They blessed them with sons, brave and strong, by way of compensation, so to say, for the privilege of sharing their beds.

The Rākshasas represent a transitional stage between the promiscuity of the Vānaras and the *vivāha-saṃskāra* of the Aryans.

1. R. IV 57/18.
2. Cf. *Rājyam prāptaṃ yaśaḥsphītam balāt Tārātmasātkṛitā*. R. IV 22/8.
3. Vide Kane, P.V., History of Dharma-Śāstra, Vol. II, part I, p. 601.

The poet has described Rāvaṇa's marriage with Mandodarī in a characteristic Aryan style. Maya, the father of Mandodarī, having related the birth of his daughter and also having tacitly pointed out that she had two brothers as well, performed the *kanyādāna* in the presence of fire with the words—"She is my daughter, O king, borne by the Apsarā, Hemā; she is a maiden, Mandodarī by name. Do thou accept her to become your *patnī*."[1] Earlier, in this very canto, Rāvaṇa is shown to have discharged his duty of giving his sister, Śūrpaṇakhā, in marriage to a befitting husband.[2] These references point at the fact that the Rākshasas had come to recognise the necessity of marriage both for men and women. Still, the sex ideals practised by their men and women varied. The sex freedom of women in their community was considerably curtailed. They were not polyandrous and sex relations outside the wedlock were completely banned for them. They were even denied the privilege of remarriage after the death of their husbands.[3] Thus, in their ideals and practices relating to conjugal life they approximated very closely to the women of the Aryan community of their times.

In contrast to their women, the Rākshasa men were extremely lascivious. They viewed women only as instruments of satisfying man's lust. Seizing other's women, raping and abducting them was a custom of theirs from times immemorial.[4] The Rākshasas sincerely believed in this rule, is shown also by the words of Vibhīshaṇa, who, while reporting to Rāvaṇa the forcible seizure of their cousin Kumbhīnasī by Madhu, approved of the act by characterising it as lawful.[5] Rāvaṇa himself, returning from his conquest of the *Lokas*, brought from various quarters, a large number of women as prizes of war.[6] These women included not only maidens, but also numerous ladies whose husbands and children were living.[7] To this host of Rāvaṇa's wives and concubines, we have to add another section

1. R. VII 11/13-19.
2. R. VII 11/1-2.
3. Vide the section on 'Widows' in Chapter V.
4. R. V 15/5.
5. *Śrutvā cedam mayā sarvam, kshāntan tasya hato na saḥ,*
   Yasmādavaśyan dātavyā, seyan dharmena vai hṛitā. R. VII 31/30.
6. R. VII 30/2-12.
7. R. VII 30/11-12.

of maidens (including Rākshasa girls) who voluntarily offered themselves to him.[1] Not satisfied with this, Rāvaṇa very often, criminally assaulted women, violently pulling them by the hair and forcibly locking them into his arms when the latter did not yield to his lewdness.[2] Other methods were also tried by the Rākshasas to secure a lady. They would also, for instance, try to induce the father (or guardian) to willingly surrender his daughter (or ward) in consideration of large and valuable presents, they could offer to him and his daughter. An indication of such a practice is given by Rāvaṇa when he tells Sītā that he would confer upon Janaka rich and vast dominion for her sake and also satisfy her relations.[3]

The above account of the Rākshasas shows that in their community the following five modes of securing a woman were current :

1. By regular marriage—here the father (or the guardian) of the maiden gave her to a deserving person in order that she may become his partner in life.
2. By voluntary offer —here a maiden herself approached a person and when accepted by him lived in his house as his wife. Such a voluntary offer could be possible from the side of a male Rākshasa also.
3. By purchase —here a maiden was obtained from her kinsmen on payment of bride-price.
4. By capture —here a woman (whether a maiden or a married lady) was seized as a prize of war.

1. R. V 5/91.

N.B. In addition to the indication found in the verse referred to above of Rākshasa maidens themselves selecting their life-partner, there is the instance of Kaikasī, who herself approached the sage Viśravā and married him (R. VII 8/9 ff). It is, no doubt, true that she was directed by her father to act in that manner, but in effecting the marriage he played no active role. Heti's is an example of a Rākshasa male, who perhaps directly approached Bhayā and married her (R. VII 3/16).

2. Vide the accounts of Vedavatī and Rambhā in R. VII 16/22 and R. VII 32/34 respectively.

3. R. V 15/18, 24.

5. By force —here a lady was criminally assaulted on the spot against her will and generally carried away.[1]

The Aryan society of Vālmīki's times recognised the authority of a father to arrange marriages of his children;[2] especially in case of a daughter this authority of a father was absolute. Wherever in the Rāmāyaṇa, a suitor is seen wooing a maiden, we find that his request has been turned down by the maiden, on the ground that she was incompetent to exercise her discretion in the matter, for the authority in this respect rested with her father.[3]

1. These forms correspond to the *Prājāpatya*, *Gāndharva*, *Āsura*, *Rākshasa* and *Paiśāca* forms of marriage respectively. They are defined in the Manusmṛiti as follows :

(i) The gift of a daughter (by her father) after he has addressed (the couple) with the text, 'May both of you perform together your duties', and has shown honour (to the bride-groom), is called in the Smṛitis the *Prājāpatya* rite.

(ii) The voluntary union of a maiden and her lover one must know (to be) the *Gāndharva* rite, which springs from desire and has sexual intercourse for its purpose.

(iii) When (the bride-groom) receives a maiden after having given as much wealth as he can afford, to the kinsmen and to the bride herself, according to his own will, that is called the *Āsura* rite.

(iv) The forcible abduction of a maiden from her home, while she cries out and weeps, after (her kinsmen) have been slain or wounded and their houses broken open, is called the *Rākshasa* rite.

(v) When (a man) by stealth seduces a girl who is sleeping, intoxicated, or disordered in intellect, that is the eighth, the most base and sinful rite of *Piśācas*.

The Laws of Manu, Eng. tr. Buhler, G., III 30, 32, 31, 33, 34.

2. It is interesting to observe that Rāma who had won Sītā in consequence of fulfilling the condition laid down by her father, Janaka, for the purpose, did not immediately assent to his marriage with her. He waited for the approval of his father in the matter. Elsewhere also it is said that Sītā was dear to Rāma because she was *dārā pitṛikṛitāiti* (R. I 77/26 N.S.)

As a solitary departure to the above rule there is the case of Ṛishya-Śṛiṅga who married Śāntā without making any reference of the matter to his father, Vibhāṇḍaka. Presumably he feared that his father would not readily give his consent and so perhaps, he wanted to confront him with a *fait accompli*.

3. For further details see the section on 'Maidens' in Chapter V.

A society, which insisted on a bride being given to the bride-groom in marriage by the father (or her guardian), naturally, could not be expected to look with favour upon a marriage which was the outcome of mutual negotiation between a maiden and her lover.[1] Not only that Vālmīki has not described any form of courtship preceding a marriage, but he has condemned such an attempt as a transgression of the limitations of *dharma*.[2] In case of Sītā's marriage which is believed to have been brought about by a *svayaṃvara*,[3] it must be made clear that contrary to the suggestion of the term Sītā had no free choice in the selection of her life-partner. The condition of the selection had already been laid down by her father. He had decided to select that person as his son-in-law who would prove his worthiness by successfully undergoing a certain test in archery. Sītā, the prospective bride, it is to be noted, had no right to express her approval or otherwise with regard to a suitor, who participated in the competition or came out successful in it.[4]

Incidentally, we may draw the attention of scholars to another term, which has been employed by the poet in connection with Sītā's marriage. Janaka is said to have declared before the participants in Sīta's *svayaṃvara* that his daughter was a *vīrya-śulkā*, i.e., intended for one who could pay for her the price in the form of prowess.[5] This idea of price (*śulka*) was present even in the marriage of Daśaratha with Kaikeyī. She was *rājya-śulkā* in the sense that Daśaratha had to promise to appoint as his successor a son begotten on Kaikeyī.[6] These cases

1. Cf. "It seems that from the time of the Sūtras this form of marriage (viz. *Gāndharva*) was falling into disuse. The Gṛihyasūtras speak of *dattā* or *prattā*, "the given one" bride, whose hand was to be grasped by the husband." Pandey, Rajbali, Hindu Saṃskāras, p. 280.

It may be added that in the Rāmāyaṇa (VII 91/4 ff) there is a solitary instance of Budha's marriage with Iḍā which comes under the *Gāndharva* form. Here Iḍā submitted herself to the wooing of Budha. But this case belongs to a period much earlier than Vālmīki's times and hence does not point at the prevalence of the *Gāndharva* form of marriage in his society.

2. (*Utkramya dharma-maryādām*) R. I 30/25.

3. R. III 2/26.

4. R. III 2/29-30.

5. *Vīryaśulkā ca me kanyā divyarūpaguṇānvitā*. R. I 62/14.

6. ....*Mātāmahe samāśraushīdrājyaśulkamanuttamam*. R. II 107/3 N.S.

of *śulka* marriage in the Rāmāyaṇa only speak of the anxiety of a father for the future security and well-being of his daughter and are to be distinguished from the practice of securing a bride by purchase[1] which, as we have seen, obtained among the Rākshasas. This latter form of marriage (viz. by purchase), too, might have existed among the Aryans, but we have no definite evidence for it in the Rāmāyaṇa.

But the only form of marriage,[2] popular and held praise-

1. Dr. S. N. Vyas has termed the marriage of Daśaratha with Kaikeyī as *Āsura* marriage, i.e. a marriage by purchase. (Rāmāyaṇa-Kālīna Samāja, p. 120) Obviously he has been guided in his observation by the word *rājya-śulka*. It may be pointed out that in the *Āsura* form of marriage the bride price is paid to the father or the guardian of the girl for his own use. But the promise which was elicited by Kaikeyī's father from Daśaratha was not in his own interest. It is to be remembered that at the time of his marriage with Kaikeyī Daśaratha was much advanced in age and that there was great disparity between his age and that of Kaikeyī (Cf. *Sa vṛiddhastaruṇīṁ bhāryām*.. R. II 13/3). The object of the Kekaya-Rāja in making that condition was only to make Kaikeyī's future secure rather than benefit himself from his daughter's marriage.

Dr. Vyas has further observed that the *Āsura* marriage was a dignified one so far as the girl was concerned, for it shows that the society attached some importance to women ; it recognised that for securing a woman a man has to pay her value. (Rāmāyaṇa-Kālīna Samāja, p. 121) We beg to differ from the learned scholar in this respect. In our opinion such a marriage did not enhance the prestige of a woman; on the other hand it was most derogatory to her status. It reduced a maiden to the wretched position of a marketable commodity, a personal possession of a father who could at his will dispose her of in consideration of money or other personal benefit.

2. The Hindu Dharma-śāstra-kāras also recognise marriages by capture and seduction, which they term as *Rākshasa* and *Paiśāca* marriages respectively. The object in doing so was not to encourage such practices, but to sympathise with the unfortunate girl. The society in this way compelled the abductor and the seducer to grant the status of a wife to the lady who had been the victim of his passion. Vālmīki's society, as we have elsewhere shown, was very particular with regard to the sex purity of its members and was not prepared to be moved even by the helplessness of such a victim. His society considered such cases to be cases of licentiousness on the part of both man and woman and as far as possible punished both of them. Arajā was abandoned by her father when she was ravished (though against her will) by Daṇḍa. (R. VII cantos 82 and 83). Under similar circumstances Vedavatī committed suicide, for she felt that on being criminally assaulted by Rāvaṇa it was not possible for her to live any longer. (R. VII 16/24). Similar sentiments were expressed by most of the ladies who were forcibly snatched away by Rāvaṇa from the home of their fathers or husbands. (R. VII 30/12).

worthy among the Aryans, was the one in which the daughter's father selected as his son-in-law a worthy man of noble parentage, who possessed all the desirable qualities of learning and character. He invited him to his house and having received him respectfully along with his friends and relations, offered according to the rites, in the presence of fire, his daughter, who was duly bedecked with dress and ornaments.[1] Marriages of Śāntā, the daughters of Kuśanābha, Sītā, her sister and cousins, and Tṛiṇabindu's daughter were performed according to this form.[2] In order to enable the reader to have a full idea of this important *saṃskāra* we summarise below the necessary details from Rāma's marriage with Sītā.

1. This form of marriage corresponds to the *Brāhma* marriage of the Sūtras.

2. Dr. S. N. Vyas distinguishes between the marriage of Sītā and that of the rest enumerated above. In his opinion Sītā's marriage was performed according to the *Prājāpatya* form and that of the rest according to the *Brāhma* one. He has not clearly shown the basis of this distinction. In connection with the *Prājāpatya* he says that in this form the bride's father duly honours the bride-groom and directs the bride and the bride-groom to become partners in the practice of *dharma*. (Rāmāyaṇa Kālīna Samāja, pp. 119-120). In this connection we may draw the attention of the reader to the observations of Dr. Altekar in his book, 'The Position of Women in Hindu Civilization (p. 46). "The distinction between the two (viz. *Prājāpatya* and *Brāhma*) is not clearly explained by Smṛitis. We are told that in the *Brāhma* marriage, the bride, properly bedecked and ornamented, is offered to a bride-groom who is specially invited for the purposes, while in *Prājāpatya*, the bride is offered according to due rites, but with an injunction to the couple that they should be always inseparable companions in the discharge of their religious duties. These definitions do not really state the difference between the two forms. It is sometimes argued that the injunction to the couple in the *Prājāpatya* marriage to remain inseparable companions in the performance of religious duties renders polygamy impossible and prohibits the husband from entering into the *vānaprastha* or *sannyāsa* stage without the consent and company of his wife. This view, however, is not correct, for the same corollaries can be drawn from the usual exhortation in the *Brāhma* marriage, enjoining the husband and the wife to be inseparable companions of each other in all their activities in the sphere of religion, love and wealth. *Brāhma* and *Prājāpatya* are synonymous words......" Vālmīki, it may be further added, has not employed any of these terms. He has either simply stated that the two were married or in certain cases given some description of the ceremony. We have not been able to notice any distinctive particulars in the marriage of Sītā on the basis of which it could be differently treated from the rest of the cases cited above.

On finding Rāma to be a suitable match for his daughter, Sītā, Janaka with the approval of the sage Viśvāmitra and the *purohita* Śatānanda sent his messengers to Ayodhyā to inform Daśaratha that his eldest son, Rāma, had fulfilled the conditions of Janaka's vow and thus qualified himself to receive Sītā's hand in marriage. On reaching Ayodhyā, the *dūtas* requested the king to proceed to Mithilā along with his *upādhyāya* and relatives, provided the alliance was agreeable to him. Daśaratha consulted Vasishṭha and his *brāhmaṇa* counsellors and on their suggestion resolved to leave for Mithilā the next day.[1] Meanwhile, he ordered the officers in charge of the treasury to go in advance with plenty of money and precious gems. He himself reached Mithilā with Vasishṭha and others after four days of journey.[2]

The ceremonies of marriage performed at Mithilā lasted for four days. On the first day of his arrival in Mithilā the king Daśaratha was accorded a very warm reception by Janaka accompanied by his *purohita*, Śatānanda.[3] The party was comfortably lodged in 'quarters' which were collectively known as *upakāryā*.[4] The next day the bride-groom's party was respectfully invited to his own place by the bride's father. Since 'noble parentage' was an important consideration in marriage-alliances, both for the bride's and the bride-groom's party, a ceremony of 'Relating the lineage' was held as a preliminary of marriage. Daśaratha had appointed Vasishṭha as his spokesman and he narrated the genealogy of Daśaratha.[5] He also formally solicited from Janaka the hands of his worthy daughters, Sītā and Urmilā, for Rāma and Lakshmaṇa respectively. From the bride's side, Janaka himself related his pedigree, for he considered it necessary that in the matter of giving one's daughter one should relate one's line himself.[6] At the end, he also on his part, formally announced his resolve to

1. R. I 64/8-18.
2. R. I 65/2-7.
3. R. I 65/9-13.
4. R. I 66/10.

The word *upakāryā* in the sense of a 'king's quarters' occurs in Raghuvaṃśa also (V 63). Mallinātha quotes the Viśva on it :

Upakāryā rājasadmanyupacāracite (a) nyavat.

5. R. I 66/14-15.
6. R. I 66/35.

offer his daughters as daughters-in-law to Daśaratha.[1] After this ceremony, the bride-groom's party returned to its 'Head quarters' where other ceremonies like the (*Nāndī*)*śrāddha* and the *Godāna* were performed.[2]

The principal rites of the marriage ceremony took place on the following day. It was an auspicious day, for the *Phālguna* was to commence on that day.[3] The bride-groom arrived in a gorgeous procession at Janaka's house for the principal ceremonies and was taken immediately to the *vedī*. In the presence of the nuptial fire, three important rites, viz., the *Pāṇi-grahaṇa*, the *Agni-pariṇayana* and the *Svastyayana* were performed. Under the first, the bride's father, viz., Janaka, did the *kanyā-dāna* by placing his daughter's hand into that of the bride-groom namely, Rāma, with these words—"Good betide you, O Rāma, please hold her hand in yours and accept her as your partner in the fulfilment of all duties."[4] After the *Pāṇi-grahaṇa* the next rite was *Agni-pariṇayana*, in which the bride and the bride-groom were led round the nuptial fire, which was lodged in the sacred altar. The marriage being complete with this rite, the *brāhmaṇas*, parents and other relations who were present on the occasion showered blessings on the weds (*Svastyayana*).[5] It is interesting to note that dowry (*kanyā-dhana*) was given by the father at the time of his daughter's departure to her husband's home,[6] though it was never stipulated or held indispensable.

A few ceremonies were performed at the bride-groom's place also when the party returned there after the wedding. The brides were received by the mother-in-law (or mothers-in-law) and other ladies and were ceremoniously taken into the new home. Perhaps it was also customary to take the brides to the temples for paying homage to the family deities.[7] Perhaps *Caturthī-karma* formed the final rite of the marriage ceremony

1. R. I 67/19
2. R. I 68/23-28.
3. R. I 67/23.
4. R. I 69/19-20.

That it was also customary for the bride's father to impart a few lessons of practical importance to his daughter at the time of the principal rites of the marriage is indicated by R. III 1/68.

5. R. I 69/25-26.
6. R. I 70/3-7.
7. R. I 72/8-11.

in the times of Vālmīki also and there is a faint reference to it in a passage of the Bāla-Kāṇḍa.[1]

From the consideration of the above account and also of other references, the following points emerge about marriage in the times of Vālmīki :

1. In Vālmīki's times, the marriage ceremonies had attained a complex form. Marriage comprised of various ceremonies, some of which were symbolic in character (e.g. the *Pāṇi-grahaṇa*), while some were purely religious (e.g. invocation of gods and sacrifices), some others had a social significance (e.g. the assemblage of friends and relatives of the bride and the bride-groom), and lastly some were expressive of the aesthetic sense of the society (e.g. decoration of the house and adornment of the bride and the bride-groom).

2. The object of marriage was a two fold one. Firstly, to bring together a man and a woman (maiden) for life-long partnership in the discharge of all their duties. It was clear from the words of Janaka that he gave his daughter, Sītā, to Rāma specifically with the understanding that he would accept her as his companion in the observance of *dharma*. Various other passages, it may be added, also indicate that marriage was believed to create an eternal bond between a wife and a husband which could not be terminated even by death.[2] Secondly, the birth of a son was the very fruition of marriage, for he was the perpetuator of the family line and the deliverer of his father from the hell named *Put*.[3] There was no greater occasion of happiness for a married person than the birth of a son and conversely, no greater misfortune than not to be blessed with a son even after marriage.[4]

1. *Remire muditāstatra bhartṛipriyahite ratāḥ* R. I 72/12.

N.B. The account of the marriage of Rāma with Sītā in the Bombay recension of the Rāmāyaṇa is very elaborate in respect of its details and appears to belong to a later period. (For details of the ceremony vide Vyas, S.N., Rāmāyaṇa-Kālīna Samāja, pp. 122-126).

2. R. II 29/18 N.S.

3. R. II 120/12.

Cf. *Punnāmno narakād yasmāt trāyate pitaraṃ sutaḥ.*
Tasmāt putra iti proktaḥ svayameva Svayambhuvā.

Manusmṛiti, IX 138

4. Viśvāmitra's visit to his court was hailed by Daśaratha 'like the birth of sons of worthy wives to one without issue' (R. I 16/23). And

3. It seems there were no child marriages in Vālmīki's society and at least in the cases of the marriages of the *kshatriyas* described in the Rāmāyaṇa, we do not find a single instance of child-marriage. Janaka thought of marrying his daughter, Sītā, only when he found that she was 'fit for the company of a husband'.[1] Her marriage with Rāma actually took place even later than this; a considerable time elapsed between the failure of the *svayaṃvara* arranged by Janaka for selecting his daughter's life-partner and Rāma's incidental arrival in Mithilā with Viśvāmitra.[2] In view of these references, it is not surprising to find that 'consummation' formed the last item in the ceremonies of marriage. The girls were married only after attaining puberty is also shown from the cases of Kuśanābha's daughters, Vedavatī and Arajā who were all mature ladies.[3]

A passage in the Araṇya-Kāṇḍa suggests that Sītā was married to Rāma when she was only six years old. She told Rāvaṇa (who had approached her in Pañcavaṭī, disguised as a *parivrājaka*) that having lived in Ayodhyā (after marriage) for twelve years, she repaired with Rāma, her husband, to the woods at the age of eighteen.[4] This statement of Sītā not only goes against her own statements made earlier before Anasūyā,[5] but at the same time, is not in accordance with the spirit and practice of her age.

4. One of the primary considerations in the marriage alliances was 'nobility of birth'. Neither in Rāma's marriage with Sītā nor in any other case there is any reference to the consideration of restrictions of exogamy or endogamy in marriage. There is no reference in the Rāmāyaṇa to the idea of *pravara* or *sapiṇḍa* relationship. In the absence of any specific reference, it is not possible to state, whether these matters were taken into consideration or not at the time of fixing marriage. Vālmīki

in order to convince Kauśalyā of his innocence in Rāma's banishment, Bharata said that one, who had connived to that act might die without a son. (R. II 75/35 N.S.)

1. R. III 2/22.
2. R. III 3/1 ff. (note 7—*atha dīrghasya kālasya Rāghavaḥ......*)
3. R. I 30/14 ff.; R. VII 16/4 ff; R. VII 82/6 ff. respectively.
4. R. III 52/4-9.
5. R. III 2/22.

requires that a wife should be a befitting one (*sadṛiśa*),[1] but what he exactly means by the term, it is difficult to bring out. From general remarks of Hanūmān in the Sundara-Kāṇḍa, one may guess that the main things that valued in Vālmīki's consideration, were age, beauty, family and character.[2] Perhaps the personal features of the bride and the bride-groom were also considered.[3] It was presupposed that the bride was a virgin[4] and that the couple (the bride and the bride-groom) was fit for procreation.

5. Caste was not a serious barrier in marriage. There are frequent references to marriages of a man of higher *varṇa* with a maiden of lower *varṇa* i.e. *anuloma* marriage. Thus Ṛishya Śṛiṅga and Pulastya, both *brāhmaṇas*, married *kshatriya* girls, Śāntā and Tṛiṇabindu's daughter respectively.[5] The boy Yajñadatta, who was killed in ignorance by Daśaratha, was the son of a *brahmaṇa* and was born of a *śūdra* wife.[6] There is, however, only a solitary instance of *pratiloma* marriage in the Rāmāyaṇa. The Uttara-Kāṇḍa records Yayāti's (a *kshatriya*) marriage with Devayānī (a *brāhmaṇa* girl).[7] It is obvious that the case does not belong to Vālmīki's society.

It may be added here that in Vālmīki's times the Aryans strongly disapproved of the idea of giving their daughters in marriage to the non-Aryans. Sītā declared her marriage with Rāvaṇa an utter impossibility, for as she said, a *mānushī* could never be the wife of a Rākshasa.[8] However, the Aryans were not disinclined to accept girls of the non-Aryans in marriage. Śūlī married Somapā, a Gandharvī[9] and Viśravā married Kaikasī, a Rākshasī.[10]

6. Dowry was, no doubt, given by the bride's father; but it was a voluntary gift and did not weigh as a consi-

1. R. I 30/51.
2. R. V 10/56.
3. Vide R. VI 24/8-13 for bride's marks and R. V 29/15 ff. for bride-groom's marks.
4. *aparigrahām......ananyapūrvām......*R. I 30/42.
5. R. I 8/73 and R. VII 1/51-53 respectively.
6. R. II 69/44.
7. R. VII 59/9.
8. R. V 19/9.
9. R. I 30/37-42.
10. R. VII 8/16-18.

deration for either party in fixation of marriage. Sometines immovable property was also given as a gift to the bride by her father. This formed the bride's *strīdhana*—her personal property, throughout her life. Kauśalyā had a thousand of such villages, with the income of which she maintained a number of destitutes.[1]

7. The practice of consulting horoscopes had not yet come into being. However, the auspiciousness of the hour for the performance of the wedding was kept in view.[2]

8. The ceremonies were held in an atmosphere of extreme cordiality. The words of Daśaratha and Janaka are worth noting in this connection. The day Daśaratha and party arrived in Mithilā, Janaka received them with due honour and requested Daśaratha to wait for the marriage ceremonies till he became free from his *yajña*.[3] Daśaratha readily replied, "Verily, O king, the recipients are dependent upon the giver. We shall do as and when you will bid us to do."[4] Later on the day of the principal ceremonies, when the bride-groom and party arrived at the *vivāha-maṇḍapa*, and when Daśaratha announced to Janaka that the party was waiting to be ushered in by him, he shouted, "What warder (*pratihāra*) stands there (to stop you from coming in)? Whose orders are you awaiting? This kingdom is (as much) yours (as mine), then, what fix prevents you from entering your own house? You may freely come in."[5]

Polygamy was the order of the day. Great *brāhmaṇa* ascetics like Kaśyapa and Viśravā[6] are also known to have had more than one wives, and everywhere the kings are seen with large harems. Daśaratha had three hundred and fifty wives besides the well known three.[7] The term *jyeshṭhā*[8]—senior, frequently occurring with reference to a particular wife of a king points to the existence of some system to determine the relative status of a polygamist's wives.

1. R. II 31/22 N.S.
2. R. I 68/13.
3. R. I 65/14-15.
4. R. I 65/16-17.
5. R. I 69/14-15.
6. R. III 19/11 and R. VII 8/16-18 respectively.
7. R. II 38/10.
8. R. I 35/3; R. III 2/21.

Inspite of this popularity of polygyny Rāma was a strict monogamist.[1] Even for the performance of a great sacrifice like *Aśvamedha* in which, normally several wives were required, Rāma had only the golden image of Sītā as his partner[2]—Sītā having been earlier forsaken by him.

A modern reader might feel curious to enquire whether Vālmīki visualised a circumstance in which the marriage tie between a husband and wife could be recognised as broken, during their life time. As to this we may state that generally speaking 'divorce' is against the spirit of Hindu view of marriage. The same was the view of Vālmīki according to whom, as we have noted above, marriage created an indissoluble tie between a husband and his wife, not only for this life but also for subsequent ones.

In the words of Rāma, spoken to Sītā, at the conclusion of the Laṅkā war[3] one may attempt to seek a recognition for 'divorce'. But an appreciative reader will not fail to observe that these words were uttered by Rāma at a time when the sudden consciousness of his society's rigidness in respect to the chastity of women had completely unnerved him; when under the pressure of two conflicting emotions—of love for his beloved wife and fear of the society, simultaneously arising within his heart, he had lost all his mental balance.[4] Naturally, we can not give much credence to his words as they do not represent his well-considered opinion. Moreover, we know for certain that even when he finally abandoned Sītā in the Uttara-Kāṇḍa, he continued to recognise her as his wife, for in every *Aśvamedha* that he performed he kept the golden image of Sītā, as his partner.

The position, in fact, was like this. Vālmīki's society insisted very rigidly on the chastity of its women and treated

1. This is, however, to be noted that Rāma was an exception rather than the rule. This is made amply clear by the statement of Sītā in the Sundara-Kāṇḍa where she apprehends that Rāma might not take pains to recover her from her abductor, Rāvaṇa, for on returning to Ayodhyā at the expiry of the period of exile he would easily take to other wives. (R. V 22/14).

2. R. VII 101/8.
3. R. VI 96/19-25.
4. R. VI 96/11.

with severity cases of lapse. A lady accused of adultery was immediately deserted by her husband and in consequence of that she forfeited her conjugal and religious rights. But this desertion did not mean a dissolution of marriage. She continued to be the wife of her husband and after a certain course of expiation which made her husband (and society) feel assured that she had returned to moral life, she was to be re-instated on her former position. Ahalyā, who was previously deserted by her husband, Gautama, for deliberately committing adultery with Indra, regained her right after she had undergone a severe and protracted course of penance and shown hospitality to Rāma.[1]

Desertion of a wife could also be possible when her behaviour was felt to be a threat to the life and security of her husband. Kaikeyī's mother is said to have been deserted by her husband because she insisted on knowing the cause of his laughter even when it was made plain to her that such a disclosure would mean death to him.[2]

Some scholars feel inclined to believe that Kaikeyī was also deserted by her husband, Daśaratha, on the ground that her thoughts were sinful and that in her avariciousness she had renounced *dharma*.[3] When Kaikeyī remained adamant in her demand of the kingdom for Bharata and banishment of Rāma Daśaratha felt extremely desperate and said that he renounced her hand that he had clasped at the time of marriage in the presence of fire with the recitation of *mantras*, and also his son, Bharata, born of her.[4] He re-iterated his resolve when Rāma and party actually left Ayodhyā.[5] Further, to show that these words were spoken by Daśaratha in all seriousness, it is pointed out that in the Yuddha-Kāṇḍa Rāma requested Daśaratha (the spirit of Daśaratha) to withdraw his curse from Kaikeyī and Bharata.[6]

1. R. I 44/29-32.
(note—*dhutapāpā bhavishyasi* and *matsamīpam mudopetā samupaishyasyasaṃśayam*. 31, 32).
2. R. II 35/21-26 N.S.
N.B. This account does not appear in the N.W. and has been discarded as spurious in the critical edition from Baroda.
3. Vyas, S.N., Rāmāyaṇa-Kālīna Samāja, pp. 159-160.
Also Jayal, S., The Status of Women in the Epics, p. 67.
4. R. II 15/12-13.
5. R. II 45/8-9.
6. R. VI 100/35-36.

We may specially state here the comments of Shri Tryambaka Raya Makhi who is a staunch advocate of the above view.[1] He quotes a verse from the Purāṇas according to which a wife could be deserted by her husband under the following four conditions :

(i) If she impeded the pursuit of *dharma*;
(ii) If she was unchaste;
(iii) If she was excessively wrathful;
(iv) If she always spoke unkindly.[2]

Mr. Makhi was conscious of the fact that Kaikeyī's case did not fall under any of the four conditions laid above, for he himself states, in asking the fulfilment of a promise previously made to her by her husband she was in no way transgressing the course of *dharma*; she was not unchaste (*asatī*)—Daśaratha had not the slightest of suspicion with regard to her chastity; she was not *atikopanā*....moreover, if that could be recognised as a fit ground for desertion, Draupadī also, who spoke angry words to Yushishṭhira should have been deserted by him; and lastly she could not be deserted on the ground of speaking unpleasant words, for in that case Kauśalyā and Sītā also should have been deserted.

Inspite of this, Mr. Makhi, starting with the presumption that Kaikeyī was legally deserted by her husband has laboured hard to show the justifiableness of Daśaratha's act. He argues :

(i) Kaikeyī's demand was impeding the course of *dharma*, for it was in contravention of the general *dharma*—the rule of primo-geniture in the Ikshvāku family, and compliance with Kaikeyī's request would have involved Daśaratha in another *adharma*, viz., of abandoning a dutiful son.
(ii) She was an *asatī*, not in the restricted sense, but in the sense that she was acting in complete disregard to the will of her husband.

1. Dharmākūtam Vol. II, part I, pp. 183-196.
2. *Dharmavighnakarīm bhāryām asatīñcātikopanām,*
Tyajed dharmasya rakshārthaṃ sadaivāpriyavādinīm.

Makhi, Tryambaka Raya, Dharmākūtam Vol. II, part I, p. 183.

(iii) She was an *atikopanā* because Bharata called her so. He further adds that Kaikeyī can not be equated in this respect with Draupadī whose *kopa* was expressed in the interest of her husband.

(iv) She was an *apriya-vādinī*, for she uttered very harsh words to her husband. Kauśalyā and Sītā are to be distinguished from her in this respect because Kauśalyā later repented over what she had said and Sītā's words helped Rāma to discharge his duty of *bharaṇa-poshaṇa* towards her.

Thus Mr. Makhi concludes that when a husband could desert his wife on any one of the four grounds enumerated above, king Daśaratha was perfectly justified in deserting Kaikeyī who was in default in all the four respects.

Mr. Makhi and others holding the same view, we feel, would have arrived at a different conclusion had they considered a few important points in this respect. It is true that Kaikeyī was acting against the wishes of Daśaratha, but merely on that ground it can not be said that she was sinful or that her behaviour was unrighteous. Moreover, we know from the statement of Rāma noted earlier that the kingdom was already pledged by Daśaratha at the time of his marriage with Kaikeyī for the son to be born of her, and presently she was asking something only in consideration of the two promises already made by Daśaratha. In a polygamous family, as we have elsewhere shown, it was but natural that each wife tried to make secure her interests as also of her son, and so Kaikeyī could not be held guilty if she was also trying to safeguard the interests of her son. It is pertinent to note in this connection that there is not the slightest change in the status of Kaikeyī after this incident. Unlike Ahalyā and Sītā, who, when deserted by their respective husbands, were forced to live a wretched life, Kaikeyī continued to live as a queen (though widowed) in the palace. Her religious rights were also not affected. She joined the funeral of Daśaratha as did the other queens;[1] she accompanied Bharata and party to Citrakūṭa;[2] and was again present to welcome Rāma returning from the forest.[3] In the absence of any change

1. R. II 87/27-28.
2. R. II 105/27-28.
3. R. VI 108/43.

whatsoever in her status, we feel, that we shall not be justified in asserting that she was actually deserted by Daśaratha. We are more inclined to treat the words of Daśaratha as an expression of his fury, when he found that his plans with regard to Rāma's installation as *Yuvarāja* were being frustrated.

Chapter V

POSITION OF WOMEN

Man and woman are the two basic supports on whom rest the family and the social structures. In fact, they are like two wheels of a cart without either of whom no progress is possible, the one is incomplete without the other. It is, no doubt, true that in a patriarchal pattern of family life, man is in a more privileged position than woman. However, from the early literary records of the Indians it is clear that the woman in the family was in no way made to live a life of subjugation. About a wife in the times of the Ṛigveda, writes A. A. Macdonell, "………she participated with her husband in the offering of sacrifice. She was mistress of the house (*gṛihapatnī*), sharing the control not only of servants and slaves, but also of the unmarried brothers and sisters of her husband."[1] Early Sanskrit literature has preserved the names of Apālā, Lopāmudrā, Viśpalā, Gārgī, Damayantī, Sāvitrī, and many others who were paragons of beauty, wisdom, learning and even chivalry.[2]

The Rāmāyaṇa, too, contains names of Arundhatī, Anasūyā and Sītā who have commanded reverential appreciation from all oriental scholars in India and outside.[3] Of these, too, the position of Vālmīki's Sītā is a unique one. She has been declared a "divinity clad in flesh"[4] and has remained throughout the ages "the grand exemplar to Hindu women as the embodiment of purity, chastity and wifely fidelity."[5] It may be pointed out at this very stage that the Rāmā-

1. A history of Sanskrit Literature, p. 162.

2. For details see Upadhyaya, Bhagwat Saran, Women in the Ṛigveda, (note p. 216).

3. Note that the 'Ācāra-ratna' (p. 10a) (quoted by Kane, P. V., History of Dharma-śāstra, Vol. II, part I, p. 648) states that the names of Sītā, Ahalyā, Tārā, Mandodarī (and Draupadī) should be repeated by a person every day in the morning.

4. Dutt, M. N., The Rāmāyaṇa, Eng. Tr., Introduction, p. iii.

5. Ibid, p. iv.

yaṇa often presents conflicting opinions and picture regarding women. In the capacity of daughters, wives and mothers they are loved, admired and adored but when independent comments are made about them as women, most disparaging remarks are passed. Not only that, in actual practice, when they are seen placed in a situation where the interest of man clashes with that of the woman, the bulk of the evidence contained in the Rāmāyaṇa shows that the interest of the man was upheld and that of the woman abandoned. It is interesting that on such occasions all sorts of moral and religious pressures were brought to bear upon the woman in order that she resigned to her lot without resistance and without murmur. The present subject calls forth a very careful study specially when it is remembered that the position in which a particular society places its women serves as a touchstone for evaluating its worth.

We shall proceed with a consideration of women in their different capacities of a maiden, a wife, a mother and a widow and in the end note the various general remarks made with regard to their character, capacities and status. For arriving at a true estimate of their position in family and society we shall not limit ourselves only to the stray opinions of the poet or his characters expressed in a moment of leisure, but shall place greater reliance on the incidents of the story where, we feel, they can be seen in their true perspective.

(a) As maidens :

In the Rāmāyaṇa parents are seen performing sacrifices or practising penance for the sake of a son,[1] but there is no prayer for the birth of a daughter.[2] This is not at all surprising,

1. Vide the *Putreshṭi yajña* of Daśaratha. R. I 10/46-49 Also R. I 23/4-6.

2. Dr. Vyas, S.N. writes : "*guṇavatī kanyā kī prāpti dīrgha tapasyā se hī sambhava hai.*" (Rāmāyaṇa-Kālīna Samāja p. 151).

This might suggest that parents undertook to perform penances for the birth of such a daughter. In support of his view Dr. Vyas has cited the case of Tāṭakā who was born to her father Suketu in consequence of great austerities. But it is to be remembered that Suketu practised austerities for the sake of a son and not for a daughter, and since perhaps, his designs were suspected by Brahmā, the Lord granted him only a daughter and not a son.

(Contd. on next page)

for the son as a perpetuator of the family line and as deliverer of his father from hell has ever remained a source of greater delight to the heart of a Hindu fáther. In his conception of an ideal state Vālmīki also expected the mothers to bring forth sons.[1] The sight of the first male issue was an occasion of immense joy for the mother;[2] in fact, nothing was more dear to a mother than a son born of her limbs and coming out from her heart as it were.[3] There are no such sentiments expressed with regard to the daughter and we shall not be far wrong in surmising that the birth of a daughter in Vālmīki's society was not so welcome an event.

The references, however, in the Rāmāyaṇa, in which a daughter is brought up with fond care by a father are numerous and very explicit. About Sītā it is said that she was fondly brought up, amidst all comforts in the house of her father.[4] Unique is the case of king Kuśanābha who had as many as hundred daughters. They enjoyed themselves, dancing, singing and playing.[5] This and the evidence of Tṛiṇabindu's daughter, who freely visited lovely spots for sports in company with her girl friends,[6] show that there was no restriction in the family on the movement of a daughter. In fact, in a well-administered state maidens of noble birth, bedecked with ornaments, sporting and frolicking freely in the streets was a common sight.[7] Moreover, the maidens were considered as harbingers of good luck and prosperity and their presence was held propitious on all occasions of social and religious importance. The poet seldom misses to describe them on the occasion of a prince's coronation[8] or the reception of a dignitary.[9]

The Rāmāyaṇa is very explicit on the point. Moreover, the daughter born as a result of that penance was also not illustrious. About her conduct, suffice it to say that inspite of the immunity granted to women from death, Viśvāmitra required Rāma to finish her, for she was a menace to the security and well-being of the society at large.

1. R. VII 43/18.
2. R. II 49/6.
3. R. II 80/16.
4. R. II 66/8.
5. R. I 30/12.
6. R. VII 1/38.
7. R. II 73/16.
8. R. II 16/11; R. IV 19/27; R. VI 109/79.
9. R. II 46/15.

With regard to the maidens Vālmīki alludes to a unique practice of 'girls being given and taken in adoption'. King Daśaratha gave his daughter Śāntā to another king, Lomapāda, his friend, when the latter requested him saying, "O knower of *dharma*, I am without a child. So, with a peaceful heart you give this daughter, Śāntā, to me, for I am desirous of a *putra* (son)."[1] That it was not casually said is evidenced from the frequent use of such terms as *dīyatām*, *dāsyate* and *pratigrihya*[2] which emphasise the act of giving (*dāna-vidhi*). This is further corroborated by the fact that Śāntā is referred to by Daśaratha himself as the daughter of Lomapāda, her adopting father.[3] The only association that she is known to have retained with Daśaratha and his family was that she once paid a visit to her former parental home along with her husband when the latter was brought to Ayodhyā by Daśaratha to preside over his *Aśva-medha* cum *Putreshṭi* sacrifice. It is to be noted that Ṛishya-Śṛiṅga was approached by Daśaratha through Lomapāda, who requested the sage to look upon Daśaratha with the same regard of a father-in-law as he had for him.[4] The passage makes it

1. R. I 9/5.
2. R. I 9/5-7.
3. R. I 9/20.
4. R. I 9/24

The Smṛiti works visualise only the possibility of a boy (and not of a girl) being taken in adoption. The object of adoption as they could see it was a twofold one—religious and secular. The adopted son was to absolve his adopting father of the ancestral debt, i.e., to save from extinction his family line. He was also to become his legal successor. A daughter, according to the Smṛitis was by herself neither competent to offer *śrāddha* etc. nor could she retain (after her marriage) the *gotra* of her genitive or adopting father. She could at the same time not be a legal successor of her father. In IX 127 (*Aputro(a)nena vidhinā sutāṅ kurvīta putrikām.*
Yadapatyam bhavedasyāṃ tanmama syāt svadhākaram.)

Manu allows a provision under which a daughter's son could offer *piṇḍa* etc. for his maternal grand-father provided, as says Kullūka, such a condition was specifically made with the daughter's husband at the time of marriage. (*Jāmātrā saha kanyādānakāle sampratipattirūpeṇa vidhānena*)

The Smṛitis call such a son as *putrikā suta*. The case of Śāntā only partially corresponds to the *putrikā* of Manu. In his statement Lomapāda says, *an-apatyo(a)smi* and *putrārthī* (or *putrārthe*—another reading) which might speak of his future plans, viz., of giving Śāntā in marriage with the specific condition of receiving her son in adoption. For the present the point under consideralion is 'the first adoption', viz., of Śāntā herself for which the

perfectly clear that Daśaratha is called a father-in-law of Ṛishya-Śṛiṅga not in his own right, but gratuitously—out of regard for a friend. What is more significant is the fact that later Śāntā (or her husband) is not mentioned or remembered by the people at Ayodhyā even on such important occasions as Rāma's coronation or Daśaratha's death.

That the adoption of a girl was a possibility in Vālmīki's society is further evidenced from the case of Sītā herself. It is too well known a fact that Janaka was not her genitive father; he had only adopted her. The only difference between her case and that of Śāntā is that in the latter the *dātā* (giver) and the *grahītā* (receiver), both are mentioed and so is the act mutually consented to by both the parties. In the case of Sītā, however, only the *grahītā* is there, but not the *dātā*. Still the fact remains that to all intents and purposes she was the child of her adopting father, Janaka.

Considering the circumstances in which Sītā is described to have been found by Janaka,[1] and a simile employed by the poet in the Sundara-Kāṇḍa, Dr. S. N. Vyas opines that the exposure of female children was not unknown in the times of Vālmīki.[2] However, in view of what has been noted above in this section with regard to the position of a 'daughter' in the family and the society, such an extreme opinion seems difficult to be maintained. Moreover, the passage of the Sundara-Kāṇḍa on which primarily rests Dr. Vyas' theory does not unambiguously support him. It can safely be asserted that the

Smṛitis do not offer any term. Bhavabhūti, it may be noted, calls her—*apatya-kṛitikā* in the Uttara-Rāmacarita :

Kanyāṃ Daśaratho rājā Śāntāṃ nāma vyajījanat.
Apatyakṛitikāṃ rājñe Lomapādāya yāṃ dadau. (I 4).

1. It may incidentally be noted that perhaps to wash away the calumny that might cling to the heroine of the Rāmāyaṇa in view of the circumstances of her birth the N. W. recension of the Rāmāyaṇa concocts a story which purposes to establish that Sītā was in fact, Janaka's own daughter. It is related that once on seeing the beauteous Menakā passing through the aerial path Janaka was stricken with passion for her and longed for a child from her. He was then informed by the divine announcer that his wish had been granted—(R. III 2/12-13).

2. Rāmāyaṇa-Kālīna Samāja, pp. 150-151.

poet is only referring in the simile to the piteous state of a helpless girl fortuitously left behind in a wood.[1]

Marriage of a daughter was a vexatious problem even in the times of Vālmīki. It is true that 'dowry' was not the source of this anxiety, but to find a suitable match for one's daughter was not an easy task even in those days.[2] Love-marriages (*Gāndharva-vivāhas*) were not the order of the day—not even among the *kshatriyas*, and this added to the responsibility of the father. In the Rāmāyaṇa the authority of the father to select a partner for his daughter is unequivocally recognised by the maidens themselves,[3] and the Rāmāyaṇa-fathers have admirably exercised this authority in the interest of their daughters. Janaka, in order to secure the greatest hero of the times as his daughter's life-partner, not only suffered a long period of anxious waiting but also courted the displeasure of several princes whom he had declined to offer his daughter's hand, for they did not qualify themselves in the test fixed for the purpose.[4] Often a father fought shy of proposing to a person to accept his daughter's hand for fear of refusal.[5] The plight of the father of a maiden of marriageable age was, indeed, pitiable, for even if he were like Śakra himself on earth, he was sure to reap odium at the hands of his son-in-law equal or even inferior in status to himself.[6] The self-respecting persons finding such a situation to be an unpalatable one considered this state (viz., of being a maiden's father) an accursed one.[7] Moreover, it was an added source of misery, if after marriage the union did not prove to be a happy one. Thus it was felt that the birth of a daughter placed the three families (of father, mother and husband) in uncertainty (about future).[8]

1. R. V 22/2.
2. R. III 2/23-24.

Do the verses sugg st that Janaka faced some difficulty in fixing Sītā's marriage, also on account of the circumstances of her birth ?

3. R. I 30/19-20.

(Note also Vedavatī's case who respected in this respect the wish of her deceased father. (R. VII 16/11-15).

Also Arajā, R. VII 82/10.

4. R. I 62/15-19.
5. R. VII 8/5.
6. R. III 2/23
7. R. VII 8/7.
8. R. VII 8/8.

Vālmīki has left no appreciable information regarding the education of girls. In the early Vedic times *upanayana* marked the beginning of the period of studentship both for boys and girls.[1] In the later Smṛiti period, *upanayana* was denied to maidens and along with that the sacred scriptures were made inaccessible to them.[2] This resulted in the curtailment of the religious rights of women. Now, a wife became only a silent partner in the sacrifices of her husband; she was neither having the ability nor the right of uttering the Vedic verses. Smṛitikāras like Manu argued that the marriage ritual in the case of girls really served the entire purpose of *upanayana* ; that service of the husband corresponded to the service of the preceptor ; and that household duties were a fit substitute for the service of the sacrificial fire.[3]

The commentators of the Rāmāyaṇa who invariably belong to a period posterior to the latest of Smṛitis, and following them the modern scholars too, advocate a similar state even in the times of Vālmīki. Commenting on the words *saṃskāram āpannām* occurring in a verse of the Sundara-Kāṇḍa,[4] Nāgojī-Bhaṭṭa opines that by *saṃskāra* in the verse under reference is meant the *pāṇi-grahaṇa-saṃskāra* (and not the *upanayana saṃskāra*), for the former (viz. *pāṇi-grahaṇa*) in case of women (of the upper three *varṇas*) caused regeneration (*dvitīya-janma*).[5] A dispassionate consideration of the context in which the verse under reference occurs will reveal that on seeing Sītā in that miserable state Hanūmān felt that the misfortunates suffered by Sītā were incompatible with her birth and accomplishments. The last quarter of the verse (viz. *jātām iva ca dushkule*) expressly states that the sufferings of Sītā were like those of one who had been born and bred in a low (or degraded) family which was

1. Note : *Purākalpe kumārīṇām mauñjībandhanam ishyate.*
Adhyāpanañca Vedānāṃ Sāvitrī-vācanan tathā.
(Yama quoted by Kane, P. V., History of Dharma-Śāstra, Vol. II, part I, p 295, f. n. 697).
2. Kane, P. V., History of Dharma Śāstra, Vol. II, part I, p. 295.
3. *Vaivāhiko vidhiḥ strīṇāṃ saṃskāro vaidikaḥ smṛitaḥ.*
Patisevā gurau vāso grihārtho (a)gniparikriyā. Manusmṛiti, II 67.
4. R. V 14/10.
5. ....*punaḥ saṃskāram pāṇigrahaṇa saṃskāramāpannām........ strīṇāṃ vivāhasyaivopanayanavad dvitīyajanmasthānatvāditi bhāvaḥ.*—Tilaka-Ṭīkā on R. V 14/10.

devoid of education and culture—in other words, of a *śūdra* who was denied the right of *upanayana* and Vedic studies. In the light of this the meaning *upanayana* will be found to be more appropriate.

Moreover, it is very clear in the Rāmāyaṇa that women of that age had not lost even a bit of their religious rights. As in the times of the Ṛigvedic period so in the days of Vālmīki a wife was held indispensable for the performance of sacrifices. She could by herself perform the daily *sandhyā* and worship the gods and manes,[1] offer *śrāddha* to her deceased son,[2] receive a guest according to the Vedic rites,[3] and with the recitation of the Vedic verses perform the *svastyayana* for her husband or son proceeding on a journey or to the battle-field.[4] All this presupposes *upanayana*, for without it she could neither acquire the ability nor the eligibility to pronounce the Vedic *mantras*. The presence of female ascetics like Svayamprabhā, Vedavatī and Anasūyā also points to the same fact. These ladies were leading a similar religious life as men of their age were doing. They observed similar vows, practised similar austerities and acquired similar merit. To argue that all this was possible for them without *upanayana* would be taking away of the *upanayana* all its importance and significance.

The roles played by Tārā, Mandodarī, Kauśalyā and Sītā make it amply clear that at least the daughters of the nobility received such education as went a long way in the full growth of their personality. Worthy of mention in this connection are the words of the dying Bālī spoken to Sugrīva about Tārā. He said, 'This Susheṇa's daughter is wonderfully expert in ascertaining subtle things and giving counsels in the hour of danger. Do thou, without the least of doubt perform what shall the chaste lady instruct thee to do; for Tārā's advice never goes without effect."[5] Similarly Sītā's readiness and determination to share her husband's misfortunes[6] and her discourse with Hanūmān[7] instantsneously impress upon the reader the stamp

1. R. V 9/58; R.II 20/9.
2. R. VI 71/54.
3. R. III 51/29-32.
4. II 28/16 ff. ; R. IV 12/10.
5. R. IV 16/100-101.
6. R. II Cantos 30 and 32-33.
7. R. V. Cantos 32-37.

of her lofty character. We can not help referring here to a passage in the Sundara-Kāṇḍa. While in his fondness Hanūmān was dilating before Sītā upon Rāma's deep attachment for her saying that Rāma was so much overtaken with grief that he was even forgetting himself; so much so that he did not even drive away from his body flies, insects and snakes, Sītā exclaimed, "Your account, O Vānara, that Rāma is still attached to me but is worn with grief is like nectar mixed with poison."[1] Her words at once reveal that she was not subject to self-indulgence and also that she had a penetrating vision to see that her redemption could not be effected if Rāma allowed that stupour to continue. Like the message of Kuntī to her sons in the Mahābhārata, her message and the token sent through Hanūmān were extremely timely and potential in raising the spirits of Rāma. She conveyed to Rāma through Hanūmān, "For my sake, against a mere crow, you employed the *brahmāstra*; how do you then, suffer the enemy who has carried me away from you ?"[3] Her token was a head-dress which she had received from Daśaratha at the time of marriage. It was an emblem of her personal honour and at the same time of the family of Rāma.[4] Now, such a character could only

1. R. V 34/2.
2. M. Bh. V 133/3 ff.
3. R. V 35/35.
4. It is necessary to point out here that the token selected by Sītā to be sent to Rāma was at once a symbol of her personal respect and the honour of Rāma and his family, for it was an article of her head-dress and a family ornament which was given to her (as the wife of the eldest son) by her father-in-law.

Cf. *Maṇiṃ drishṭvā tu Rāmo vai trayāṇāṃ saṃsmarishyati.*
Vīro jananyā mama ca rājño Daśarathasya ca. R. V 36/2.

It may be added here that Nāgojī Bhaṭṭa is wrong when commenting on this verse he writes :

Ayam maṇirvivāha kāle majjananyā hastānmatpitrādāya Daśarathahaste mama śirobhūshaṇatayā datta iti mama jananyāśca matpitur Daśarathasya ceti trayāṇāṃ smāraka iti bhāvaḥ.

This *maṇi*, it may be noted, has been mentioned elsewhere also in the Rāmāyaṇa. Verse 59 of Canto 96 in the Sundara-Kāṇḍa says that this *cūḍāmaṇi* was presented to Daśaratha by the *Devas* in consideration of his destroying the Dānavas.

Vastrāṇi caiva divyāni rathaṃ yuktañca suprabham.
Cūḍāmaṇintathā śubhraṃ divyañcāmṛitasambhavam.

And verse 4 of canto 65 in the same book states that this was presented to Sītā by her father-in-law at the time of marriage :

be the product of an efficient system of education which she must have found available to herself in her father's house.

The royal princesses, it seems, were given special training and education to equip them for their coming life. Kaikeyī had some sort of first-aid training in her childhood which enabled her to render service to her husband on the field of battle.[1] Kauśalyā was fully familiar with the various religious rites which her son and daughter-in-law were required to perform in connection with the coronation.[2] Sītā was conversant with the *rāja-dharmas* (royal rites or duties)[3] and Tārā[4] and Mandodarī[5] are actually seen participating in political deliberations along with their husbands. In Laṅkā one can see ladies being employed as military guards[6] and even acting as spies (—unofficially though).[7] Further, women, it seems, had a fairly wide knowledge of ancient legends and folk literature;[8] and they must have also been receiving education and training in fine arts like dance and music.[9]

It was perhaps customary to give a few lessons of practical wisdom to the daughter at the time of her marriage either in the presence of the nuptial fire or when she was leaving as a bride for her husband's home. With pride and confidence Sītā told Anasūyā that all the instructions of her father given to her on

Maṇiratnam idan dattaṃ Vaidehyā śvaśureṇa vai.
Vadhūkāle purā baddham adhikam mūrdhnyaśobhata.

This shows, as we have stated above, that ever since the ornament was received by Daśaratha from the *Devas* it became a family ornament. This might have remained in the beginning with Kauśalyā (the senior queen) and later passed on to Sītā, the wife of the eldest son. Thus the three persons referred to in the verse above are 'myself' (i. e. Sītā), the 'mother' (i.e. Kauśalyā) and the 'king' (i.e. Daśaratha).

1. R. II 11/14-15.
2. R. II 6/35-36.
3. (Abhijñā rājadharmāṇām) R. II 29/4.
4. R. IV 28/6 .
5. R. VI 35/10 ff
6. R. V. 4/32; V 12/15 ff.
7. R. VI 10/3 ff.
8. R. II 154-5; R. II 33/6; R. III 1/70-71; R. III 10/11 ff; R. V 24/10-13 N. S. ; R. VI 94/40-43.
9. In the harem of Rāvaṇa, a galaxy of fairies was seen by Hanūmān reclining against various musical instruments. R. V 5/127-140.

the occasion of marriage lay inscribed over her heart.[1] Some idea of these lessons can be had from the words of the mothers spoken to Śāntā when she was leaving with her husband at the conclusion of Daśaratha's *Putreshṭi*. They advised her to serve regardfully her father-in-law and especially to attend upon her husband affectionately and courteously.[2]

(b) As wives .

The next and the most important stage in the life of a woman is wifehood. It may be pointed out here that the affection and care enjoyed by a daughter or the reverence shown to the mother is not the real guide in determining a woman's status in society. The true outlook of a people towards women can be gauged, primarily from the status enjoyed by them as wives. Even a cursory notice of the relative rights and duties of a wife and husband makes it amply clear whether the society treats its women as equal partners of men or accords them a higher or lower position.

Among the Hindus, the bond of marriage which unites a man and woman as husband and wife has been considered from the earliest times not as a contract but as a sacrament; it seeks to unite two souls together, establishing between them a perfect identity of interests;[3] and it makes a woman a man's *ardhāṅginī*—an equal partner in all his undertakings, religious as well as secular.[4] According to Vālmīki a wife's association with her husband was so intimate that it continued even in the subsequent lives.[5] A father, mother, brother, son or other relations reaped after death the fruits of their own respective actions while a wife was believed to partake of the lot of her husband.[6] A loving and dutiful wife was her husband's unfailing companion in his misfortunes.[7] No other relation—neither a father, nor a mother, nor any one else surpassed or even equalled a wife in love.[8] She looked after the household of her

1. R. III 1/68-72.
2. R. I 12/15-16.
3. *Jāyāpatyorna vibhāgo vidyate. Pāṇigrahaṇāddhi sahatvaṃ karmasu.* Āpastamba Dharma-Sūtra II 6. 14. 16-17.
4. *Ardho vā esha ātmano yatpatnī,* Taittirīya Saṃhitā VI. 1.8.5.
5. R. II 32/20-21 (Cf. II 29/18 N. S.)
6. R. II 30/2-4.
7. R. III 65/3.
8. R. V 32/32.

husband like a maid; enjoyed his confidence like a friend; counselled him on his welfare like a sister; supplied him food and other requirements of life like a mother, and acted as a partner in his religious undertakings. Likewise, the husband was his wife's friend (*bandhu*) and refuge (*gati*).[1] He brought her all happiness and enjoyment.[2] In fact, all that belonged to him belonged to his wife as well.[3]

The sweet and courteous manner of a wife's counsel has become proverbial in Sanskrit literature.[4] Sītā, who preceded her speech with a smile,[5] freely and emphatically expressed her disapproval of Rāma's action in killing without provocation the Rākshasas. But she removed all sting in her speech by adding in the end that it was only out of affection that she reminded him of that matter; she did not mean to instruct him[6]. Such counsels were naturally welcomed by the husbands and received in good spirit by them.[7] It is interesting to note that Tārā preferred a husband to a son, for, on hearing wholesome but disagreeable words of a mother, a son felt offended, but on hearing the same the husband felt extremely gratified.[8]

Unfortunately, the above described bright side of the relations between a husband and a wife is not the only side. The popular terms *bhāryā* and *bhartā* for wife and husband respectively, emphasise the dependence of a wife on her husband (specially for food and shelter). This dependence was more often than not overdone. It was being dinned into the ears of a lady that her entire world was centred in her husband;[9] that he was her highest stage of life (*āśrama*) and the holy place of pilgrimage (*tīrtha*)[10]; and that she ought to consider him as a veritable deity, her lord and God.[11] The popularity of this

1. (Bhartā bandhurgatiścaiva) R. II 72/42.
2. (Sukhabhogārthadātāram) R. II 72/15.
3. R. II 42/11; R. IV 16/34.
4. Note the conception of *kāntā sammita-upadeśa* referred to in Mammaṭa's Kāvya prakāśa, I 2.
5. (*Smitapūrvābhibhāshiṇī*) R. III 48/9.
6. R. III 10/19.
7. R. III 11/2.
8. R. IV 16/8.
9. R. II 42/10.
10. R. II 72/42.
11. R. II 26/4.

ideal reduced a wife to the position of a simple maid, rather the slave of her husband. Unswerving devotion, perfect obedience and unmurmuring resignment to the will of her husband were now considered to be the highest virtues in a woman.[1] It was being advocated that a husband was the only spring of religion for a woman.[2] The lure of a seat in heaven was offered to her if she rendered ungrudging service to her husband.[3] Good name in this life and a position of eminence in heaven in the life to come, a lady could win only by being devoted to her husand.[4] Service to her husband was the only penance for a lady[5]; without service to her husband she, even if engaged in excellent religious rites and fasts was bound to meet a wretched end. As against this, even she who did not worship and bow to the celestials was sure to attain welfare, only if she served her husband devotedly.[6]

There is no wonder that this school of thought preached to a lady that she should love her husband even if he was ill-disposed towards her.[7] Nay, she was advised to regard him as her supreme deity even if he was not virtuous, but wicked and libidinous.[8] To cite as an example Kauśalyā, in whose heart these ideals were deeply ingrained, even after being ill-treated and neglected by her husband all her life, considered it a great sin for herself when her 'veritable deity' (Daśaratha) propitiated her with folded hands.[9] Women were so educated and trained that they could never think of uttering even a harsh word to their husbands.[10] In short, a wife lost all her individuality and was reduced to a state of nothingness; she was a mere shadow of her husband, following him as he walked, staying as he stopped and com pletely devoted to him and longing only for his association.[11] Naturally, such women did not deserve to enjoy their husband's

1. R. II 27/13-14; R. VI 95/20.
2. R. II 72/42 (Also R. II 24/27-28 N. S.).
3. R. II 27/14-16 ; R. III 1/69; R. VI 8/33.
4. R. II 27/14-15.
5. R. III 1/69.
6. R. II 24/25-27 N. S.
7. R. II 27/8; R. VII 49/19.
8. R. III 1/55
9. R. II 67/10 (Cf. R. II 62/13 N. S.)
10. R. II 65/32.
11. R. II 32/20-21.

confidence.[1] They helplessly depended upon the vagaries of their husbands and could be easily owned and disowned by them.[2]

It is painful to remark that the actual treatment received by the Rāmāyaṇa-wives from their husbands corresponds more to the above-drawn picture than to the 'ideal' presented earlier. As an example, we may cite the cases of Sītā and the queens of Daśaratha. Sītā, the lovely daughter of Janaka, bred with most affectionate care by her loving father, was an ideally dutiful wife. She had learnt to love and regard her husband more than her own life and her fidelity towards her husband even in most trying circumstances, was simply exemplary. But even she at the conclusion of the Laṅkā war, was very unjustly and cruelly treated by her husband. Apart from the refusal by Rāma to accept her back as his wife, the entire treatment meted out to her on this occasion was extremely rough and humiliating.

In Laṅkā she was confined by her abductor in the *Aśokavana* and as behoved a lady separated from her husband she was observing the *viraha-vrata* (vow of separation) which, according to the conventions of that age required her not to wear her toilette before she was united with her husband. Rāma, disregarding her vow, insisted that she should present herself before him duly bathed and ornamented. Sītā was betaken with surprise to hear such unreasonable command of her husband. However, she submitted to the will of her lord.[3] Again, as she was proceeding in a palanquin towards Rāma and as Vibhīshaṇa was driving away the crowd to clear her passage Rāma angrily shouted and ordered Vibhīshaṇa not to prevent the crowd from having a look at her. He passed a surreptitious remark at this juncture that neither the houses, nor clothes, nor stately honour was

1. R. II 114/26.

2. Vide the discussion in the following pages about Kaikeyī and Sītā. In the light of what has been noted above the remark of E. W. Hopkins, viz., "In the Epics woman is only a chattel, her good points or her defects have their meaning and being only with reference to the man—to his sexual pleasure, his feelling of power and his vanity", appears to be no exaggeration. (Position of Ruling Caste in Ancient India, J.A.O.S., 1897)

3. R. VI 95/16-20.

N. B. Even the Vānaras wondered :

Alaṅkṛitāyāḥ Sītāyāḥ bhūshitāyāśca darśane,
Ko hetuḥ kimabhipretamiti caiva viśaṅkitāḥ. (R. VI 95/32.)

the veil for a woman; her character (alone) was her true shield.[1] He even bade Sītā to leave the palanquin and approach him on foot. It was only with difficulty that Sītā, thus insulted, could hold her rage.[2] It is to be noted that this behaviour of Rāma struck as a discordant note to all present—Lakshmaṇa, Sugrīva and Hanūmān, who were pained at it.[3] The climax was reached when Rāma declared that his unparalleled exertions in the battle-field were not for her sake but to uphold the dignity of his own family.[4] What is most derogatory in Rāma's address is his suggestion to Sītā that (being renounced by him) if she wished, she could live with Lakshmaṇa, Bharata or Śatrughna, or with Sugrīva or the Rākshasa Vibhīshaṇa.[5] Her abandonment by Rāma in the Uttara-Kāṇḍa is still more objectionable.[6] As soon as the news was brought by his spy that the people were suspecting the character of the queen, Rāma resolved to abandon her. He summoned his brothers for consultation, but exhorted them to accept his decision and not utter a single word regarding Sītā's banishment.[7] It is to be remembered that this abandonment took place after the *agniparīkshā* at Laṅkā gone through by Sītā in the presence of Rāma. Yet, when it came to choose between "honour (public popularity to say it correctly) and wife" the latter was ruth-

1. R. VI 95/56.
2. R. VI 95/52.
3. R. VI 95/65.
4. R. VI 96/16 (reading adopted from f. n. 13).
5. R. VI 96/24-25.
6. Remarks of Shri V. S. Srinivas Shastri are worth considering in this respect :—

"........a woman whom you otherwise honour and love and adore and hang all your jewels upon and allow to dominate your whole life—well, a woman whom you treat with all this consideration, when however she is weighed in the balance of real values in a crisis like this, sinks into the position of *Indriyārtha*, a means of gratifying our senses, no more. Now Rāma decrees that Sītā should be banished. This time Rāma sinks lower and lower. Not only does he, against the testimony of his conscience, agree to banish Sītā but he does it secretly."

(Lectures on the Rāmāyaṇa, p. 179).

Dr. Pinkham Mildrethworth also writes :

"The unsupported suspicions concerning the character of womanhood which were expressed by the revered Rāma have not helped forward th ethical progress of womanhood in India."

(Woman in the sacred scriptures of Hinduism, p. 184).

7. R. VII 47/20.

lessly cast away. Rāma expressly told his brothers : "Even the celestials speak ill of bad name—whereas fame is adored in all the regions. Therefore the high souled ones exert their best to acquire reputation."[1] The callousness with which the husbands could treat their wives is further shown by the mean suggestion of Rāma (made later) that Sītā should again submit herself in public to some purificatory ordeal to convince the people of her purity.[2] We call it mean because earlier when it was the proper time for such a test he cast her off even without acquainting her of her misfortune, and now when he was perhaps tempted to own her sons Kuśa and Lava, he threw that suggestion. It was worthy of the self-respecting Sītā that she proved the purity of her character but did not suffer a situation in which she would have been compelled to live once again, as the wife of such a husband.

Daśaratha's treatment of his wives also relates the same story. The Rāmāyaṇa does not provide any detail about the way in which Sumitrā was treated by her husband. This is, however, clear that she was the juniormost and enjoyed only a low status. Of the other two queens, Kauśalyā, though she was the chief queen, was not the favourite of her husband. She was extremely dutiful and submissive yet her married life was an extremely unhappy one. She complained to Rāma that she had not experienced in her life that blessing and pleasure which women generally felt when their husbands were devoted to them.[3] Since her husband did not regard her with respect, not only Kaikeyī but even other co-wives of much lower status insulted her and tormented her with unpleasant heart-rending words.[4] Wily Kaikeyī perhaps bore special malice towards her and did not tolerate even a maid serving Kauśalyā devotedly.[5] That this is not merely the exaggerated account of an injured mother to evoke the sympathy of her son and to dissuade him from going to the forest leaving her behind, is shown by the words of Daśaratha himself. He is seen repenting that on account of Kaikeyī he had not regarded with honour his dutiful wife Kauśalyā who was ever studious of his welfare

1. R. VII 47/12-14.
2. R. VII 97/5.
3. R. II 20/27.
4. R. II 20/29-30.
5. R. II 20/32.

and who deserved homage at his hands.[1] One is simply stupefied to observe that even such husbands had the audacity to preach to their wives that being women cognizant of virtue, they should look upon their husbands as veritable deities, irrespective of their merits or demerits.[2]

Daśaratha's treatment of Kaikeyī also can not be considered as entirely fair. He was aware that he had at the time of his marriage, vowed before Kaikeyī's father that a son born of her alone would succeed him on the throne of Kosala.[3] But to hoodwink Kaikeyī, he prepared a plan of installing Rāma as *Yuvarāja* when Bharata was away[4] and when he could conveniently keep Kaikeyī's father and brother, ignorant of the event. Later when at the instance of her *jñāti-dāsī*, Mantharā, Kaikeyī demanded in consideration of her two boons (promises), previously voluntarily made by the king, the installation of Bharata in the place of Rāma and Rāma's banishment he became furious. He not only condemned her as a wretch and an imp but also threatened to desert her along with her son.[5]

1. R. II 12/70 N. S.
2. R. II 67/4.
3. *Purā bhrātā pitā naḥ sa mātaraṃ te samudvahan,*
'*Mātāmahe samāśraushīd rājyaśulkam anuttamam.* R. II 107/3 N. S.

Note : This is the solitary reference in the Rāmāyaṇa to show that the kingdom of Ayodhyā was already pledged by Daśaratha to the son, to be born of Kaikeyī. The N. W. recension of the Rāmāyaṇa does not contain this verse. Instead it reads—

Purā tāta mahārājo mātaram te samudvahan,
Devāsure ca saṅgrāme jananyāstava pārthivaḥ,
Prahṛishṭaḥ pradadau rājā varau dvau yācitaḥ prabhuḥ.
Tataḥ sā tau pratiśmṛitya tava mātā yaśasvinī,
Ayācata nṛipaṃ gatvā dvau varau varavarṇinī,
Tava rājyaṃ naravyāghra mama pravrājanan tathā.

R. II 120/3-6.

A careful reader will not fail to notice that the compiler was recalling two grounds in justification of Kaikeyī's demand, but the first either by slip or deliberately got dropped. Moreover, the way Daśaratha planned Rāma's coronation makes a strong suggestion upon the mind of the reader that he was trying to square up a tangle which earlier in his unguarded moment he had created for himself. That parents of a maiden elicited such promises from a bridegroom specially when the match was an incompatible one from the side of the bridegroom—is corroborated from Satyavatī's marriage with Śāntanu in the Mahābhārata.

4. Note the word *nishkāsitaḥ* in R. II 6/23.
5. R. II 15/12-13.

It is necessary to add here that among the non-Aryans the wives, in actual practice also received a better treatment. Unlike Sītā, Tārā and Rumā, were not abandoned by their respective masters, Bālī and Sugrīva, even when they had actually lived as wives of the other brother. Apart from this, Tārā enjoyed a unique position of honour and love from Bālī.[1] Rāvaṇa's treatment of Mandodarī is also full of regard for her.[2]

An account of the mutual rights and duties of a wife and a husband will further help us to assess the position of women in the society and the same we now proceed to present.

The scriptures of the Hindus lay down that man by himself is only half; the second half being his wife.[3] The theory of 'Three Debts' requires every man to take to himself a wife, for without her he cannot discharge two of his (three) debts. By associating with her husband in sacrifices a wife helps him to discharge the debt to the gods and by giving birth to a son (or sons) she absolves him of the debt to the *Pitṛis*.[4] Partnership in the religious and the sexual life of the husband was, therefore, the primary right and duty of a wife. The word *patnī*, as Pāṇini explains, becomes applicable to a wife only when she shares in the sacrifices of her husband.[5] Vālmīki also seems to recognise the word *patnī* in this very sense, for he employs specifically this term when he refers to the golden image of Sītā which was got prepared by Rāma every time to be installed as his partner in sacrifices.[6] This idea is made more explicit in the compound word *dharmapatnī* which is dissolved as *dharmāya patnī*, i.e., a wife who was given to her husband to be his companion in the performance of all religious acts.[7]

1. R. IV 16/100-101.
2. R. VI 35/17 ff.
3. *Ardho ha vā esha ātmano yajjāyā, tasmādyāvajjyāyāṃ naiva vindate naiva tāvat prajāyate (a) sarvo hi tāvadbhavati. Atha yadaiva jāyāṃ vindate (a) tha prajāyate tarhi hi sarvo bhavati.* Śatapatha-Brāhmaṇa V 2. 1. 10.

Also : *Tasmāt purusho jāyāṃ vitvā kṛitsnataramivātmānam manyate.*

Aitareya Āraṇyaka I 2.5.

4. Cf. *Apatyaṃ dharmakāryāṇi śuśrūshā ratiruttamā, Dārādhīnastathā Svargaḥ pitṛiṇāmātmanaśca ha.* Manusmṛiti, IX 28.
5. *Patyurno yajña saṃyoge*—Ashṭādhyāyī, IV 1/33.
6. R. VII 101/8.
7. R. III 3/20.

The marriage vow of the Hindus too emphasises this point. Janaka offered the hand of his daughter Sītā to Rāma that he may accept her as his *sahadharma carī.*[1] It is worth remembering that Kauśalyā though not the favourite of her husband had her position secure in this respect. As the seniormost queen of Daśaratha (*mahishī*) it was, her privilege to slay the horse with three strokes in the *Aśvamedha* sacrifice.[2] In the distribution of the *pāyasa* also hers was the lion's share. She received half whereas the rest was distributed between Kaikeyī and Sumitrā.[3] Tārā in a figurative statement complained that Bālī deprived her of her right in taking without her the *avabhṛitha-snāna* in the water of Rāma's shafts at the end of the sacrifice in the form of the battle.[4] Participation of the wife in the religious acts was considered so necessary that husbands even when they repaired to the forest for practising penance, did not forget to take their wives along with them. The sages Viśvāmitra, Gautama and Atri are all described as accompanied by their wives. To fulfil this very requirement Rāma installed the golden image of Sītā, she being not available in person.

Partnership of the wife in the sex life of her husband was as intimate as in the religious sphere. Vālmīki expects both husband and wife to be mutually faithful in the preservation of conjugal fidelity. In a polygamous society it will not be unnatural to expect that a man is not required to observe a very high standard of sexual morality. In the Rāmāyaṇa, however, one is gratified to note that almost equal standards were expected in this respect both of man and woman. In Ayodhyā, we are told, men were devoted to their own wives and wives were faithful to their husbands.[5] Adultery was a heinous crime and Vālmīki's society dealt with severity the parties to such a crime. An adulterous wife was abandoned forthwith by her husband.[6] Likewise, an adulterous man was liable to be banished to the forests.[7]

1. R. I 69/19-20.
2. R. I 10/24-25.
3. R. I 11/27-28.
4. R. IV 17/32.
5. R. I 6/10
6. See the cases of Ahalyā and Sītā in R. I 44/28 ff. and R. VI 96/19 ff. respectively.
7. R. II 78/47.

"Marriage", writes Havelock Ellis, "in the biological sense, and even to some extent in the social sense is a sexual relationship."[1] To demand and provide sexual satisfaction was, therefore, the mutual right and obligation of a wife and husband. It was the sacred duty of a husband to visit his wife (for coitus) every month after her menstrual bath and it was his privilege not to be refused intercourse by her when he wished to cohabit with her.[2] A barren wife (*vandhyā*) was condemned as wretched[3] and so was an impotent (*klīva*) husband.[4] In the wider sense a wife was her husband's *krīḍāsahāya*—companion in sport.[5] There are copious references in the Rāmāyaṇa of wives enjoying sports in the company of their husbands in gardens, in the waters of a river or on a hill.[6]

Though the marriage ideal declares husband and wife as equal partners in all spheres of life, in actual practice, absolutely equal rights and privileges in case of either of them are an impossibility. In India, from very early times, the physical limitations of a wife aided by the conditions of a patriarchal society helped the Hindu husband to acquire ultimate supreme authority over his wife. He was the *bhartā* (the protector and the maintainer) and she was the *bhāryā* (the protected and the maintained). A wife could thus insist on living with her husband and being maintained by him. Under no circumstance the husband was allowed to refuse this privilege to his wife. When Rāma was unwilling to take Sītā along with him to the forest and was advising her to receive calmly food and raiment from Bharata, she asserted her right and rebuked him for hesitating in the discharge of his duty towards her. She said that she could in no case be persuaded to look to any one else as her refuge and could never accept maintenance at the hands of Bharata.[7] Of course, a wife was to regard as 'much' whatever her husband could provide for her. Sītā assured Rāma that whatever fruits or roots he will give her in the forest she shall relish as *amṛita*.[8]

1. Psychology of Sex., p. 256.
2. R. I 44/18.
3. R. II 20/26-27.
4. R. IV 13/19.
5. R. VI 111/63 N. S.
6. R. II 73/17, R. II 108/13, R. VII 20/23, R. VII 44/14.
7. R. II 33/7.
8. R. II 33/17.

The Rāmāyaṇa calls a husband, besides *bhartā*, a 'giver of pleasures and enjoyments.[1] He was the fountain from which flowed unbounded earthly pleasures for his wife.[2] During the period of her confinement a wife deserved to be looked after with still greater care not only because, now she was all the more helpless but also because if her needs were not fulfilled or if she kept melancholy during this period it was likely to react adversely on the prospective child. As soon as Rāma came to know that Sītā was in confinement he requested her to express her desires so that they might be fulfilled by him.[3]

Protection of the wife was the principal duty of a husband[4] not only because she belonged to the weaker sex[5] but also because she was the symbol of his personal and family honour. Mārīca pointed out to Rāvaṇa that Rāma could perhaps overlook any other offence; but in no case the molestation of his wife. He called that move of Rāvaṇa (viz. of abducting Sītā) as extremely dangerous, for, he pointed out that in defending their wives or in order to redress the wrong when the wife had been abducted people brought all their strength to bear upon the enemy, showing utter disregard even to their lives.[6] Rāma had employed the *brahmāstra* (the atom-bomb of those days) against a mere crow when the latter attempted to offend Sītā;[7] and he killed Rāvaṇa to wipe away the stain that had stuck to the fair name of his family, for his wife had been taken away by the enemy.[8] On seeing Sītā, Hanūmān also observed in the Sundara-Kāṇḍa that it was she on whose account Rāma was filled with compassion because he could not protect one who was his protege (*āśritā*).[9]

Generally speaking, a husband was expected to be kind and loving to his wife but it will be seen that this cannot strictly be specified as his duty, for much depends upon the personal

1. (*sukhabhogārthadātāram*) R. II 72/15.
2. (*amitasya hi dātāram*) R. II 42/11. Also R. VI 92/21.
3. R. VII 44/24.
4. R. IV 56/75.
5. R. VII 32/43.
6. R. III 45/8-9.
7. R. V 35/35.
8. R. VI 96/17 (reading adopted from f. n. 17).
9. R. V 15/49-50 N. S.

accomplishments of the wife and the disposition of the husband. The same Daśaratha who was completely indifferent to Kauśalyā was extremely courteous and fondling to Kaikeyī.

Corresponding to her rights and privileges a wife had a number of duties also to discharge. If maintenance and protection were her prerogatives, obedience, reverence and diligent service to the husband, were her obligations. Women of Ayodhyā, we are told, were engaged in diligently serving their husbands[1]. Doing service to her husband was the highest penance for a wife and through that she could secure heaven.[2] Even Sītā is shown by Vālmīki as waiting upon Rāma in the palace with a tiny fan in her hand (*bāla-vyajana*).[3] In the forest also she could be seen ready with the bow, quiver and sword for her husband as he prepared to go out.[4]

Equally important was 'obedience to her husband'. Rāma advised his mother not to go against the command of her husband.[5] Sītā also considered it her duty to submit to the command of her husband irrespective of the consideration whether it was good or bad.[6] Iḍā offering herself (as a wife) to Budha, the son of Soma, said that she was surrendering herself to him of her own accord and was prepared to carry out his command.[7]

A wife was to be devoted to her husband in word, mind and deed.[8] The *pativratā* was to be solely devoted to her husband, and to think in her heart of none other than her husband.[9] Eternal regions (of Bliss) were promised to those

1. R. I 1/91.
2. R. III 1/68-70.
3. R. II 17/8.
4. R. III 9/18.
5. R. II 26/4.
6. R. VI 95/20.
7. R. VII 91/6.

It is to be added that the Vedic marriage ritual does not enjoin the duty of implicit obedience upon a wife; but by the time of Vālmīki, it seems, it had found a place there. Sītā recalled the words of her father spoken to her at the time of her marriage, viz., there was no other penance for a lady than rendering service and obedience to her husband. (R. III 1/68-69).

8. R. II 33/9.
9. R. VII 49/19.

ladies who loved their husbands dearly.[1] On the earth also only that lady was considered as praiseworthy by the good, who was devoted to her husband and who diligently followed him.[2] It is said about Sītā that she was very dear to Rāma; but he was doubly dear to her.[3] Hanūmān was so much impressed by her that he felt that in separation from Rāma she could hold her life only because she bore within her heart the image of her lord.[4]

A wife was not to disregard her husband even in the worst circumstances.[5] Those ladies who renounced their husbands in adversity were condemned as low in the society.[6] About her devotion to Rāma Sītā said to Kauśalyā, "I should not, O noble lady, say with my own mouth that I am *pativratā*. The manner in which I shall behave with my lord (in the forest) you will only hear from the good later on."[7] Rāma ever recognised her (Sītā) as his "companion in adversity."[8] She was so much devoted to him at heart that without him she felt her very existence impossible.[9] In his company in the forest she enjoyed as in heaven and in separation from him even the palace in Ayodhyā was like hell to her.[10]

Devotion to the husband does not, however, mean blind following. If her husband appeared to her to be swerving from the path of duty or was likely to transgress the limits of righteousness, it was the wife's duty to bring him round by her sweet and persuasive words. Sītā tried to stop Rāma from killing without provocation the Rākshasas, for she felt that in doing so he was going against *dharma*.[11] Her counsel was greeted by Rāma though on certain grounds he declined to accept it. The wife of king Saudāsa successfully prevailed upon her husband and prevented him from cursing (in return)

1. R. III 1/54.
2. R. V 57/15; R. II 27/13-14.
3. R. I 14/23-24.
4. R. V 10/53.
5. R. I 12/16; R. II 42/5.
6. R. II 27/13-14.
7. R. II 42/18.
8. (duḥkha-sahāyā me) R. III 65/3.
9. R. II 33/21-22.
10. R. II 33/20.
11. R. III 10/2 ff.

the family preceptor, Vasishṭha.[1] Tārā was so much regarded by her husband for her wholesome counsels that she even took liberty in commanding him.[2]

A wife was the mistress of the household. Her home was her domain. Vālmīki has not left much information about the house-wife managing her household. There are only a few casual references about Sītā performing the routine of a house-wife during her stay in the forest. Thus to manage the kitchen was her primary business in the house.[3] She also used to smear the floor with earth,[4] cook the meals and serve them to her husband and his brother after making due offerings to the creatures.[5] It is to be noted that a wife perhaps did not take her meals with her husband. While in the forest Sītā ate her food after the brothers had eaten and then, too, in a lonely corner (*ekānte*).[6]

To serve the elders, especially the parents of her husband was also the duty of a wife. The queen-mothers advised Śāntā to revere her father-in-law and to serve him by helping him in the performance of his daily sacrifices.[7] Rāma also advised Sītā to stay behind him in Ayodhyā and to diligently serve his father and mother and to treat his brothers affectionately.[8] In the Uttara-Kāṇḍa she is actually seen regularly attending upon her mothers-in-law.[9]

During the period of separation from her husband a wife led a life of continence.[10] She not only refrained from all sexual enjoyment but also avoided all sorts of amusements and merry-

1. R. VII 68/33-34.
2. R. IV 16/7.
3. R. II 109/39.
4. R. II 60/22.
5. R. II 109/37-38.
6. R. II 60/31; R. III 63/25.

N. B. According to Shakuntala Rao Shastri "This practice of the wife taking her food after her husband had finished his, is noticed for the first time (in Sanskrit literature) in the Śatapatha Brāhmaṇa."—Women in the Vedic Age, p. 79.

7. R. I 12/15.
8. R. II 29/25.
9. R. VII 44/21.
10. R. II 29/29.

makings. She forsook (till the return of her husband) the wearing of toilette, ornaments and also rich and tidy dress.[1] She kept her hair undressed (only carelessly tying them together in one braid) and perhaps, she even avoided regular baths.[2] She did not eat sumptuous food. In fact, she took the minimum that was needed for keeping herself alive and that too she took only after mentally offering it to her husband in sojourn.[3] Moreover, like an ascetic living in a forest she passed the days in performing various types of penance. She not only endeavoured to acquire control over her appetites by the observance of manifold disciplines and fasts, but like an ascetic she also exercised complete control over her anger (and other passions).[4] Her thoughts were all directed towards the welfare of her husband and she stayed longing for the happy day of his return.[5] Since in a joint family, in the absence of her husband, she depended for her maintenance upon her father-in-law (or brother-in-law) she was expected to be gentle in her behaviour to all and to be particular in showing regard to her seniors and affection to the juniors.[6]

Vālmīki has liberally showered his encomium on the wife who served her lord with single-minded devotion and who strictly adhered to the rules of conduct prescribed for her. Wonderful powers are accredited to such a *pativratā* by the poet. Sītā has been described in the Rāmāyaṇa as competent to reduce to ashes her abductor.[7] On learning that Hanūmān was being led around Laṅkā by the Rākshasas with fire set to his tail she prayed to the Fire-God that if she had served her lord, if she were of pure character, if she had ascetic merit, and if she had been the wife of one alone, He should prove cool to Hanūmān.[8] And her prayer is said to have been granted.[9] Hanūmān was of the opinion that by dint of the power got

1. Vide Sītā viewed by Hanūmān in the Aśoka garden, R. V 10/20.
2. Sītā was seen by Hanūmān wearing the same garment in which she was clad in Pañcavaṭī when Rāvaṇa abducted her. (R. V 10/48).
3. R. III 63/25.
4. R. V 17/25.
5. R. V 11/14.
6. R. II 29/25 ff.
7. R. V 17/25.
8. R. V 49/27.
9. R. V 49/32-33.

through the purity of her character Sītā could maintain the entire animal creation or burn it with her ire.[1] The fire of a *pativratā's* character is considered superior to that of the Fire-God Himself,[2] so much so that when she approached Him with the intention that He should testify to the purity of her character He was to bear her within His flames in the presence of all and return her to her lord unscathed.[3] In fact, she could command the elements and they had no option but to obey.

(c) As mothers :

The highest glory of a woman's life lies in motherhood. One of the principal purposes of marriage according to the Hindus is the preservation and progress of society through the procreation of progeny. A wife is known as *jāyā* because the husband is born in her as a son.[4] Motherhood is, therefore, the cherished ideal of a Hindu woman and childlessness her worst misfortune. A legend in the Rāmāyaṇa powerfully presents the fury of a wife who was prevented from attaining to motherhood.[5] Wives unable to bring forth an issue in the normal course resorted to the observance of several vows and fasts to enable them to become mothers.[6] The sight of the first-born son was a great joy to the lady.[7] In fact, there was no object dearer to the heart of the mother than a son born of her own

1. R. V 57/3.
2. R. V 57/5.
3. Vide Sītā's *agni-parīkshā*. R. VI 99/2 ff.
4. Cf. *Patir bhāryāṃ sampraviśya garbho bhūtveha jāyate,*
Jāyāyāstaddhi jāyātvaṃ yadasyāṃ jāyate punaḥ. Manusmṛiti, IX. 8.
5. It is said that in days of yore, lord Śiva, having entered into matrimony with Umā engaged himself in sport with her. A divine hundred years thus passed away; and yet no child was born of her. At this the Gods became anxious and wondered who would be able to bear the offspring of that union. In the interest of the welfare of the *Lokas*, therefore, they requested Mahādeva to rein within himself his energy and practise austerities with Umā. The lord granted them their prayer. Enraged at this Umā cursed the gods. (R. I 33/24-25.)
6. R. II 25/3.
The Rāmāyaṇa also refers to several cases of women who approached a distinguished sage to be able to bring forth from his union an illustrious son. Thus Somapā Gandharvī attended upon the sage Śūlī (R. I 30/38) and Kaikasī approached Viśravā (R. VII 8/12 ff)—each with the object of having a highly distinguished issue.
7. R. II 49/6.

limbs and springing from her heart, as it were.[1] Rāma is often described as the promoter of his mother's joy,[2] and Vālmīki often observes the practice of addressing a son after his mother.[3]

For describing the mother's affection for her son Vālmīki often employs the 'cow and her calf'[4] as a symbol. He also refers to a legend according to which Surabhi, the divine cow, was stricken with grief and had her eyes overflown with tears when she saw her sons (—a pair of oxen) toiling hard on earth in the scorching heat of the midday sun. This made Indra understand that none was an object of affection (for a mother) more than her son.[5] Mothers were naturally very eager to see that their sons were well established in life. In the times of Vālmīki also mothers felt very much gratified on seeing their sons married to a befitting wife.[6] In fact, all their thoughts were directed towards the welfare of their sons.[7]

Vālmīki has portrayed in Kauśalyā a very true picture of the Hindu mother which continues to be the same down to this day. Kauśalyā is said to have begotten Rāma by dint of severe penances.[8] Ever since Rāma was born she fixed her hopes and expectations on him.[9] She earnestly prayed for his welfare. In the Ayodhyā-Kaṇḍa, specially, she is frequently seen engaged in various types of *pūjā* and *arcanā* for his prosperity.[10] The news of Rāma's prospective coronation filled her with extreme joy and she liberally distributed wealth among the poor.[11] But when suddenly the tables were turned and she learnt that instead of being installed as the *Yuvarāja* Rāma was

1. R. II 80/16.
2. R. I 1/20; R. II 20/10.
3. R. I 21/2; R. II 34/13.

Note : "This tendency of addressing a son after his mother is not generally indicative of matriarchy, although it may be a custom surviving or borrowed from some matriarchal clan, for in the Epics patriarchal clans freely addressed sons after mothers." Jayal S., The Status of Women in the Epics, p. 147.

4. R. II 28/8; R V 65/3; R. VI 8/11.
5. R. II 80/17 ff.
6. R. I 30/51.
7. R. III 74/11-13.
8. R. II 20/37; R. II 25/3.
9. R. II 20/28.
10. R. II 6/29, 32; R. II 20/6.
11. R. II 9/5.

required to repair to the forest for a long period of fourteen years she instantaneously fell on the ground like a stem of a plantain tree cut asunder (by an axe).[1] Unable to bear separation from her loving son she resolved to follow him to the forest,[2] but Rāma refusing her entreaties and insisting on going alone she somehow restrained her tears lest his departure should be rendered inauspicious. She got ready to perform the benedictory ceremonies in connection with his departure[3] and did not forget to tie on his arm the twigs of auspicious plants as amulet.[4] Her parting words to Sītā also are saturated with the love and care for Rāma, her son. She advised Sītā not to disregard Rāma though he was now banished to the woods ; reminding her that a husband, whether he was wealthy or poor was like a god for a chaste woman.[5]

A mother who held the son in her womb and nurtured him with extreme loving care, naturally, had the greatest claim on her son's devotion.[6] The apotheosis of a mother in Vālmīki can be seen in a verse of Ayodhyā-Kāṇḍa which declares that a mother exceeded ten times in greatness a father : she surpassed (in glory) the entire earth. Who was equal in veneration to the mother ?[7] Vasishṭha advised Rāma to regard the words of his mother (Kauśalyā) and declared that by doing so he would be following the path of the good.[8] Matricide is declared by Vālmīki as a most heinous crime.[9] The poet, as a matter of fact, prescribes that a son must never renounce his mother even if she were an outcast (*patitā*) (though other elders were to be renounced under such circumstances).[10]

Here again, we are sorry to remark that the practice was not very much in conformity with the ideal. Bharata was positively disrespectful to his mother. Even before the happenings at Ayodhyā became known to him he enquired of the messengers

1. R. II 20/22.
2. R. II 28/8.
3. R. II 28/15 ff.
4. R. II 28/19.
5. R. II 42/5.
6. R. II 25/15.
7. R. II 25/13-14. Cf. Vasishṭha Dharma Sūtra XIII. 48.
8. R. II 124/5.
9. R. II 21/28.
10. R. II 25/15.

coming from Ayodhyā,.........."And that wrathful and conceited one, ever intent on her own interest, my mother Kaikeyī—all well ?"[1] And on returning to Ayodhyā as he learnt the whole happening his rage knew no bounds. He addressed her as 'Stainer of the line', (*kulapāṃsini*) 'Deserving censure' (*garhite*), 'Ignoble' (*akalyāṇi*) 'Of evil designs' (*pāpasaṅkalpe*), 'Shameless' (*nirapatrape*) 'Cruel' and 'Wicked' (*nṛiśaṃse, pāpaniścaye*).[2] In fact, he wished to kill her, but desisted from doing so for fear of inviting Rāma's displeasure.[3] His manner of introducing Kaikeyī, his mother, to the sage Bharadvāja was also reproachable. Pointing to Kaikeyī he said : "And her in consequence of whose act those foremost of men have been despatched to the forest, and the king Daśaratha has gone to heaven, ignoble and slayer of her own husband, setting her heart on wealth, do thou know this wicked one, as Kaikeyī, my mother."[4] Rāma himself, who professed to regard even his step mother Kaikeyī with the same veneration in which he held his father, Daśaratha[5], declined to respect the wish and command of his real mother, Kauśalyā. He plainly said that though he was fully aware of the fact that separation from their sons was extremely painful to the mothers, yet, he was not prepared to go against the orders of his father.[6] In fact, he expected his mother to make him obey the orders of the father, in case due to childishness or weakness he appeared disinclined to obey.[7] In support of his stand he cited the cases of Paraśurāma—who even committed matricide at the behest of his father—and of the sage Kaṇḍu who, in deference to his father's command committed an equally heinous act in killing a cow.[8]

In the midst of this dark picture occurs also the case of Śatānanda, the son of Ahalyā, in whose words deep affection for the mother is expressed. On meeting Viśvāmitra who had come to Mithilā accompanied by Rāma and Lakshmaṇa he made anxious enquiries about his unfortunate mother. He was

1. R. II 76/10.
2. R. II 79/2 ff. ; R. II 80/2 ff.
3. R. II 81/27.
4. R. II 103/26-28.
5. R. II 115/18.
6. R. II 21/31-32.
7. R. II 26/11.
8. R. II 21/35-36.

eager to learn from the sage whether in consequence of showing hospitality to Rāma his mother was purified and united with her husband or not ?[1] But here also one cannot fail to note that Vālmīki has made no suggestion that Śatānanda in any way regarded his mother more than his father or that he disapproved of his father's action in abandoning Ahalyā. The truth is, as we have indicated in the previous section, a husband or a father whether right or wrong in his behaviour had always an upper hand, and it was his will that prevailed. Vālmīki's sons, generally speaking, were highly respectful to their mothers, but vis a vis a father they held the mother only second in importance.

The above discussion incidentally makes also clear the relative position of a son and a husband for a lady. When placed in a situation where she found that the interests of her son and of her husband were clashing against each other she was expected to take sides with the husband. Kaikeyī who made a departure from the general expectation in trying to guard the interests of her son against the wish of her husband was severely and unreservedly condemned not only by her husband but also by the *Mahāmātya* Siddhārtha,[2] Kauśalyā[3] and the whole population of Ayodhyā.[4] Kauśalyā also was (mildly) reproved by her own son when she appeared to be acquiescing in the tempting offer of the outraged Lakshmaṇa to secure the crown for Rāma by the use of arms against senile Daśaratha.[5] The position in this respect is made expressly clear in the words of Sumantra, viz., "the wish of a husband (to a wife) outweighs a *koṭi* (crores) of sons."[6]

(d) As widows :

There is no greater calamity for a woman than widowhood, specially so in a society in which the dependence of a woman on her husband is to its extreme. Vālmīki remarks that the life of a lady who had lost her husband was, indeed, wretched (*kṛipaṇa*).[7] A husband was the centre and symbol of

1. R. I 47/4-7.
2. R. II 39/18 ff.
3. R. II 72/19-26.
4. R. II 44/18; R. II 49/23; R. II 50/7.
5. R. II canto 26.
6. R. II 35/8 N. S.
7. R. IV 16/18

all joy and happiness of his wife. Naturally, along with his death all mirth and merriment departed from her life.[1] Bewailing the death of her husband, Rāvaṇa, Mandodarī exclaimed, "Formerly (when you were living) I toured in a befitting car according as it pleased me. But alas ! henceforth I shall only be longing (in vain) for pleasures to return in my life."[2] Tārā also remarked, "A lady may be prolific in wealth, food and sons, yet, after the demise of her husband she cannot escape being called a widow"[3] A lady, therefore, considered it extremely meritorious to die while her husband was still alive.[4]

There is no wonder that the news of her husband's death completely unnerved a lady; and unable to bear the shock her first thoughts were of putting an end to her own life. Kauśalyā, Tārā and Sītā[5] thought of following their husbands when they saw them dead. Particularly the words of Kauśalyā in this connection seem to refer to the immolation of widows. She said, how fortunate, indeed, would she be if her body was also to be consumed by fire along with that of her husband.[6] The Uttara-Kāṇḍa actually records the case of Kuśadhvaja's wife who immolated herself in fire along with the dead body of her husband.[7] These references, however, do not conclusively establish the prevalence of the *satī-prathā* in the times of Vālmīki.

The origin of the *satī-prathā*, it may be pointed out, lies in the belief of the primitive man that the needs of the dead in the next world were more or less similar to those in this life and hence just as the usual paraphernalia of a noble man was sent for him through 'Fire' so was sent his wife.[8] In the times of Vālmīki, however, the society had become sceptical about this belief. Tārā was prepared to follow Bālī provided she could be convinced of her union with him there. She, on the other hand, knew that the departed ones followed each his (or

1. R. II 42/10.
2. R. VI 92/21.
3. R. IV 17/17.
4. R. VI 8/9.
5. R. II 72/34; R. IV 16/2; R. VI 8/30, 32 respectively.
6. R. II 72/34-35.
7. R. VII 16/13.
8. Altekar, A. S., The position of women in Hindu civilization, pp. 115-116. Compare also the attempt of the Kīcakas to burn Draupadī along with Kīcaka, M.Bh. IV 23/6.

her) own separate course determined by his (or her) own actions.[1] This knowledge cuts at the very root of the belief which was at the back of burning of widows with their husbands and we do not find Tārā, Mandodarī or the queens of Daśaratha following their deceased husbands. In fact, the Rāmāyaṇa expects a widow to survive her husband. The counsellors of Tārā advised her to look after her son after the death of Bālī.[2] There are frequent references to Kauśalyā eagerly awaiting the arrival of her son at the expiry of the period of exile and seeing once again the returning of the days of prosperity and power.[3]

It may be added that a new incentive in the form of the concept of *pātivratya* was steadily emerging in the society of Vālmīki for the rejuvenation of the *satī-prathā*. It was being held that a woman belonged to one person only, viz., her husband. Sītā echoes the faith of her society when she says that a woman who was duly given as a wife by her father to one, was his, even in her after life.[4] In order to adjust this new concept to the earlier religious notions a modification, as it were, was made in the *karma* theory. It was, now propagated that a father, mother, brother, son or other relations, each enjoyed in the next world the fruits of his (or her) own respective actions; only a wife, devoted solely to her husband, partook of the lot of her husband.[5] It is true, as noted above, that in the Rāmāyaṇa there is just one case of actual *satī*. However, the Rāmāyaṇa is important in as much as it set the stage for the appearance, with full vigour of this custom in subsequent times.

In the times of Vālmīki also a widow was required to lead an austere life. She was neither to wear ornaments[6] nor dress her hair.[7] The idea underlying was that she was not to appear attractive. Hers was a melancholy sight and naturally she strikes the poet as a standard of comparison (*upamāna*) for

1. R. IV 17/36-37.
2. R. IV 15/11-13.
3. R. III 74/11-12.
4. R. II 29/18 N. S.
5. R. II 30/2-4.
6. R. IV 16/12.
7. The widows of Daśaratha joined the funeral with *prakīrṇasitamūrdhajāḥ* (R. II 87/27).

everything that had lost its charm.[1] It is, however, relieving to note that in the period of the Rāmāyaṇa a widow was not required to disfigure herself by undergoing a tonsure. We frequently read about the dishevelled and soiled hair of the widow.[2] There is no indication in the Rāmāyaṇa, at the same time, that widows were held inauspicious or that they were not allowed to be present on such religious and ceremonial occasions as, funeral, marriage or coronation. The widows of Daśaratha are found among the assembly that had collected to welcome Rāma and party returning from the forest.[3] They are also seen participating in the rejoicings held in connection with Rāma's coronation.[4] Moreover, from the regard shown by Rāma and his brothers, and Sugrīva and other Vānaras to Kauśalyā and the other queen-mothers it is clear that the widows received a humane and considerate treatment from the family and the society.

A widow could not perhaps, even in the times of Vālmīki inherit in her own name her husband's property. After the death of her husband she was dependent for maintenance on her son. Tārā found the situation unpalatable in which a widowed mother was required to live on the subsistence provided by her son.[5] Kauśalyā recognised Bharata as her guardian (*nātha*), the king Daśaratha being dead and Rāma being away in the forest.[6] Rāma found it improper to look after his mother so long as his father was living.[7] This must, however, be noted that even in those days a widow was allowed to retain her *strī-dhana* (woman's property) which could include besides gold, silver and other valuables, immovable property. Kauśalyā, it is said, owned one thousand villages which were exclusively for her personal use.[8] Widows (who had none to look after them and whose sons were not yet come of age and hence not in a position to support their mothers, and who being

1. R. III 21/8; R. V 20/48, 49.
2. R. II 87/27; R. VII 91/2.
3. R. VI 108/42-43.
4. R. VI 109/22.
5. R. IV 16/9.
6. R. II 99/9.
7. R. II 27/8.
8. R. II 34/16.

poor and old had no other source of income) were maintained by the charities of the king liberally distributed on the occasion of sacrifices.[1]

The question of widow remarriage in the Rāmāyaṇa is a controversial one. Scholars like J. J. Meyer[2] and Dr. Dhairyabala[3] admit the provision for a widow in ancient India, of remarrying her deceased husband's younger brother. In support of her contention three items of evidence are cited from the Rāmāyaṇa by Dr. Dhairyabala.

1. It is stated in the Rāmāyaṇa that Rāma killed Bālī because he had appropriated to himself Rumā, the wife of his younger brother, Sugrīva, during the very life time of her husband. Commenting upon this Dr. Dhairyabala writes : "This shows an advance in the idea of the relation between different family members. As compared to the older tradition according to which all brothers had a right to the wife of a dead brother, the right of the elder brother over younger brother's wife is curtailed"[4] She further adds, "While a person's approach to his younger sister-in-law was completely prohibited, relation of the elder brother's widow with the younger brothers of the dead husband was still in vogue as illustrated by Tārā's remarriage with Sugrīva as recorded in the Rāmāyaṇa."[5] Rāma's acquiescing in this union of Sugrīva with Tārā is also sometimes interpreted as a tacit recognition of the custom of a widow's remarriage with her younger brother-in-law in the Aryan Society.

2. In her haughty address to Lakshmaṇa in Pañcavaṭī Sītā accused him of harbouring a base design within his bosom eversince he resolved to follow them to the woods, viz., of appropriating to himself the wife of his elder brother when he perished in some calamity in the forest.[6]

3. At the end of the Laṅkā war Rāma made an offer to Sītā that being renounced by him she could, if she wished, fix her mind on any of his younger brothers—Bharata, Lakshmaṇa or Śatrughna.[7]

1. R. I 10/42.
2. Sexual Life in Ancient India, part II, p. 436 f.n. 1.
3. Evolution of Morals in the Epics, pp. 71-74.
4. Ibid, p. 72.
5. Ibid, pp. 72-73.
6. R. III 50/24.
7. R. VI 96/24-25.

The above data, it will be seen, is of a very flimsy nature and does not succeed in establishing convincingly the proposition advocated by the scholar referred to above. Rāma, it is to be remembered, when interrogated by Bālī as to why he had killed him without any ground of enmity subsisting between the two, was at great pains to justify to him his act. Unwilling to confess the political motive with which he had entered into alliance with Sugrīva he adduced all sorts of lame excuses in support of his act. One of them was that Bālī as an elder brother of Sugrīva was in relation to Rumā like her father-in-law, and that his sex relation with her was in the nature of an incest and hence punishable.[1] It is to be clearly understood that Rāma has not at all discussed in the present context the possibility or otherwise of a brother marrying the widow of another brother. As to the point why Rāma did not object to Sugrīva's marriage with Tārā, there are two explanations. The first is that it was

1. *Jyeshṭho bhrātā pitā vāpi yaśca vidyām prayachati,*
Trayaste pitaro jñeyā dharme ca pathi vartinaḥ.
Yavīyān ātmanaḥ putraḥ śishyaścāpi guṇoditaḥ,
Putravatte trayaścintyā dharmaścaivātra kāraṇam.
Asya tvaṃ dharamāṇasya Sugrīvasya mahātmanaḥ,
Rumāyāṃ vartase kāmāt snushāyāṃ pāpakarmakṛit,
Aurasīm bhaginīṃ vāpi bhāryāṃ vāpyanujasya yaḥ,
Pracareta naraḥ kāmāttasya daṇḍo vadhaḥ smṛitaḥ.

R. IV 18/13-23 N. S. (For parrallel verses in the N. W. vide R. IV 16/70-75. It is to be noted that the verse 'Aurasīm bhaginīm etc. is missing in the N. W.)

Catching suggestion from the word *dharamāṇasya* in number 19, Nāgoji-Bhaṭṭa tries to argue a defence for Sugrīva. Referring to the custom of a younger brother marrying his elder brother's widow, a distinction is drawn between the behaviour of Sugrīva and Bālī. But the statement of Aṅgada viz., *Bhrāturjyeshṭhasya yo bhāryāṃ jīvato mahishīm priyāṃ, Dharmeṇa mātaraṃ yastu svīkaroti jugupsitaḥ* (R. IV 47/4) creates a difficulty, for it does away with the distinction of an elder brother or a younger brother so far as the approachability of the other brother's wife is concerned. If the wife of one is a daughter-in-law (*snushā*) in one case, she is mother in the other case. Thus a sexual relation of a brother, younger or elder, with the other brother's wife would, in either case, come under incest. Whatever suggestion one may try to catch from the word *dharamaṇasya,* it will fail to alter this basic position. Hence Rāma did not raise the point of possibility, of the younger brother marrying the widow of his elder brother, but took his stand on 'incest'. (Note R. IV 16/73-75).

none of Rāma's concern. His only motive in killing Bālī and installing Sugrīva in the former's position was to divide the allies (the Rākshasas and the Vānaras) and later to make the strong Vānara power stand in opposition to the Rākshasas themselves. So long as this object of his was secure, he was not interested in worrying his head over the way Sugrīva or Tārā went. Secondly, he might have known that the sex relations between men and women of the Vānara community were of an extremely loose character and presented no difficulty if one brother, elder or younger appropriated the wife of another —whether living or dead.[1]

In the speech of Sītā also it is to be noted that besides the fact that it was made when she was out of temper she not only declared in most unequivocal terms the utter impossibility of accepting in Rāma's position Bharata, Lakshmaṇa or any one else[2] but also condemned as base and evil (and not lawful) the very (suspected) desire of Lakshmaṇa.[3] Sītā 's vehemence and sharpness would appear meaningless if it were to be presumed that the marriage of a widow with her younger brother-in-law was the norm in her society and that she was herself aware of it.

Lastly, with regard to Rāma's proposal to Sītā in the Yuddha-Kāṇḍa, we fail to understand on what internal or external testimony, Dr. Dhairyabala concludes, "Here it is clear that Sītā selecting any of her brothers-in-law as her husband was not against *dharma*."[4] Rāma did never mention that Sītā was to select any of his brothers as her husband. He simply stated at the end of his rejection that if it gave her pleasure Sītā could live with Lakshmaṇa, Bharata or Śatrughna; or if she so wished she could even fix her heart upon Sugrīva, Hanūmān or Vibhīshaṇa.[5] The fact that he included in this list the names of Sugrīva, Hanūmān and Vibhīshaṇa makes it amply clear that his words were spoken not with the sincerity of suggesting an alternative marriage to Sītā, but sarcastically. In plain language, he only meant that if once he renounced

1. Vide pp. 46-48 supra.
2. R. III 50/25.
3. R. III 50/23-24.
4. Evolution of Morals in the Epics, p. 74.
5. R. VI 96/25.

her after doubting the purity of her character it did not concern him whether she lived for the rest of her life as a virtuous lady or passed her time as a debauchee. Failing to recognise that Rāma in the present context was in the grip of a similar emotion as had seized Sītā in Pañcavaṭī Dr. Dhairyabala finds herself in a very uncomfortable position. She observes, "It is very curious that Rāma who refuses to accept Sītā, points out his brothers as an alternative because all belonged to the same family and it is for the noble family tradition that he refuses Sītā."[1] We further wonder why she fails to recognise another important point in the present context. The proposal of Rāma was made to Sītā while her husband was living. His words in the present context, obviously, can not be utilised to prove the custom of widow-remarriage. If on the strength of this statement of Rāma one would advocate the case of remarriage, then, first he (or she) shall have to acknowledge legal 'divorce' in the Rāmāyaṇa,—and such an absurd proposition we believe, no one will be prepared to uphold.

The prevalence of the custom of widow remarriage in the Aryan society of Vālmīki is further rendered impossible in view of the ideal of *pātivratya* according to which as we have shown earlier, a lady was required to be faithful to her husband not only during his life time but also after his death.

Widow remarriage was perhaps not obtaining even among the Rākshasas. There is, indeed, a singular instance of Śūrpaṇakhā, the widowed sister of Rāvaṇa, attempting to remarry Rāma (or Lakshmaṇa),[2] but it is more likely that it was a clandestine move on her part, unwarranted by her own society;

1. Evolution of Morals in the Epics, pp. 73-74, f.n. 13.

It is interesting to observe that the problem of interpolations in the epics has reduced their texts to a peculiar mockery. Scholars readily accept a passage as genuine if they find it agreeing with the line of their thinking, but easily discard it as spurious if it offers the least of resistance to their preconceived theories. To wit, Dr. Dhairyabala, in order to get rid of her present difficulty writes : "This shows the incongruency of the passage which can be regarded as a later interpolation." But earlier, disagreeing with Dr. A. S. Altekar (who treats the whole passage as an interpolation) she argued, "Instead of considering the episode in the Yuddha-Kāṇḍa as an interpolation it would be better to consider it as an indication of the evolution towards a stricter code of sex ethics for which the Epics stand." (Ibid, p. 46)

2. R. III 22/21.

for when she went first to Khara[1] and then to Rāvaṇa[2] to lodge her report against Rāma's misbehaviour, she studiously avoided any reference to her own role in inviting upon herself the calamity. Moreover, had widow-remarriage been a regular feature among the Rākshasas, Rāvaṇa would have certainly placed such a proposition before her when she accused him of rendering her a widow. He, no doubt, tried to redress her loss by the promise of gifts, honour and favour during all her life, but did not visualise a remarriage for her.[3] Again, the anxiety with which Kumbhīnasī tried to save her husband's life from the outrage of Rāvaṇa also seems to point at this very fact.[4] Moreover, the sentiments expressed about widowhood by the Rākshasa women also show that this state was as much an object of dread for them as for their Aryan sisters.[5] They would not have been so much horrified at the prospects of widowhood, had there been a provision of remarriage to take away its poignancy.[6]

(e) Sex relationship :

That sex relations in the early Vedic society were fairly loose is evidenced among other facts, by the frequent occurrence of such words as *kumārī-putra* (son of a maidem),[7] *mahānagna* (paramour) and *jāra* (paramour of a married woman)[8] in Vedic literature. Immediately after the period of conquest when social intercourse of the Aryans with the non-Aryan population of India became more and more free and intimate, the Aryan social thinkers became apprehensive of the pollution of the blue-blood and in order to prevent contamination they evolved stricter codes of sex morality, especially for their women. By the time of Vālmīki, as we have seen above, the ideal of *pātivratya* which demanded of a woman fidelity to her husband

1. R. III 24/11-16.
2. R. III cantos 37-28.
3. R. VII 30/30.
4. R. VII 31/42-48.
5. R. VI 92/30 ff.
6. 'Forcible seizure of another's women' (married or otherwise) was, however, very common among the Rākshasas, but that does not necessarily prove that remarriage of widows was recognised by their society.
7. Vājasaneyi Saṃhitā, XXX, 6. (quoted in the Vedic Index, Vol. I, p. 396).
8. Vedic Index Vol. I, p. 140. Vide also Upadhyaya, B. S., Women in the Ṛigveda, p. 195.

not only physically but even mentally was almost grounded in society. Thus the principal merit in a lady which could entitle her to be called virtuous (*sādhvī*) was her single-minded devotion to her husband.[1] She was to consider her husband as a veritable deity and was not to offend him in word, deed and mind.[2]

Incest and adultery could naturally be considered as unpardonable offences in such a society. Distinguishing such sex pleasure from *dharma-rati*, Vālmīki declares it as punishable.[3] We find preserved in the Rāmāyaṇa the popular story of Ahalyā who out of curiosity, engaged in coition with Indra. No sooner than Gautama, the husband of Ahalyā, detected the crime committed by his wife he discarded her till she became purified by the performance of severe austerities and by paying homage to Rāma.[4] So sensitive was Vālmīki's society with regard to conjugal fidelity that not only a wife who willingly defiled her husband's bed was severely punished but even that lady who was abducted against her will in most helpless circumstances was shown no sympathy.[5] Rāma declined to receive Sītā back as his wife because he feared that his society would be unwilling to regard a lady as chaste who was kept in confinement by her abductor for a long time.[6] His apprehensions were, indeed, genuine, for his society was even more conservative than what he had suspected. Laying no credence on the testimony of the god Vibhāvasu his people unreservedly condemned him for deriving pleasure out of Sītā's company whom they considered polluted by the touch of Rāvaṇa.[7]

It is somewhat gratifying to note that in Vālmīki's times

1. R. V 57/15.
2. R. II 33/9.
3. R. II 75/55 N. S.
4. R. I, 44/28 ff.

This episode has been explained as an allegory by Ravindranath Tagore. He writes : "………Next, at his skilled touch, the desert soil which had lain for long years bound in the hardness of stone, becoming *a-halyā*, not fit for ploughing, resumed the bloom of life. It was the self same soil which Rishi Gautama, the foremost of the early Aryan pioneers who had striven to drive the plough southwards had found treacherous and had abandoned in despair. (A Vision of India's History, p. 19).

5. Vide the cases of Sītā abandoned by Rāma (R. VI 96/19 ff.) and Arajā by her father Bhārgava (R. VII 83/13 ff.)
6. R. VI 99/17-21. (Note no. 18).
7. R. VII 45/17-18.

conjugal fidelity was the mutual obligation of husband and wife, and according to Vālmīki either defaulting party was severely dealt with. In the Ahalyā legend, it was not only Ahalyā who was punished; but Indra, the male partner in the committing of the crime, was also cursed by Gautama to become impotent.[1] Rāma also before rejecting Sītā punished with death the wrongdoer, Rāvaṇa. Bharata, it is to be noted, on being told by Kaikeyī that Rāma had repaired to the forest in consequence of Daśaratha's orders wondered if such a punishment was inflicted on him for criminally assaulting another's wife.[2] Further, in order to convince Kauśalyā of his innocence in Rāma's banishment he sweared saying that let the person who had approved the exile of the noble Rāma take a fancy for the wife of his friend and of his preceptor.[3]

The moral sense of Vālmīki's society in this respect was so acute that it felt touched even when a person cast an evil glance at another's wife.[4] Hanūmān felt extremely uneasy when he suddenly realised that in conducting his nocturnal search for Sītā in the inner apartments of Rāvaṇa he had become guilty of beholding another's wives while they were asleep. He feared that this would surely cause loss of righteousness (*dharma lopa*).[5] He felt relieved only on reflecting that he was not revelling in glancing at another's wives and that his mind was completely unperturbed.[6] It is surprising to note that Vālmīki who was aware of the general principle of human behaviour (viz., in respect of the enlistment of the senses on behalf of any course of action, good or evil, it was verily, the mind which was the cause)[7] could not sympathise with his unfortunate heroine, Sītā. She pleaded before Rāma that her person was, no doubt, touched by another, but it was not within her power to prevent it, nor was that a wilful act of hers. Her heart was under her control and that was fixed in him.[8]

1. R. I 44/25-26.
2. R. II 78/47. (Also R. III 10/3; R. III 55/5).
3. R. II 83/6.
4. Kubera was punished even for gratuitously casting his look upon Umā (Śiva's wife) R. VII 12/22-24.
5. R. V 6/40.
6. R. V 6/43.
7. R. V 6/44.
8. R. VI 97/8-9.

In view of this Dr. Dhairyabala is right in observing that the Rāmāyaṇa shows a stricter code of sex ethics.[1]

A society which laid so great an emphasis on conjugal fidelity could naturally be not expected to tolerate pre-marital or post wedlock sex relations. At the time of marriage a bride was strictly required to be a virgin. The Somapā Gandharvī approaching the sage Śūlī to have from him an illustrious son, first proposed a marriage with him and declared that she was a 'virgin'.[2] This makes it clear that sex relations outside the wedlock were not approved of by Vālmīki's society and there too they were to exist, as we have seen above, strictly between a wife and her husband. There is only a legendary case of Tṛiṇabindu's daughter who conceived while she was yet a maiden. The hurry with which her father married her to the sage Pulastya (who was indirectly responsible for her conception) further shows that under no circumstance a child's birth could be tolerated by the society without a wedlock.[3] To what an extent pre-marital sex relations of a maiden were abhorred by the society is evidenced from Arajā's case who was criminally assaulted against her will by the king Daṇḍa. Her father, the sage Bhārgava, brought disaster on Daṇḍa and his kingdom and ruthlessly discarded his daughter although he knew fully well that she was only an unwilling, helpless partner in the committing of the crime.[4]

Presence of prostitutes and concubines in the Rāmāyaṇa strikes as a jarring note in this strong emphasis on sex fidelity. One is betaken with surprise to notice that Vālmīki is almost incapable of conceiving a town without prostitutes. He even accords them state recognition and state employment. Prostitutes were employed by king Romapāda to entice Ṛishya-Śṛiṅga whose visit alone to the Aṅgadeśa, it was declared, could avert famine in the kingdom.[5] Prostitutes were also invited by kings to join the reception of a royal visitor,[6] and to be present on ceremonial occasions.[7] They were usually

1. Evolution of Morals in the Epics, p. 45.
2. R. I 30/42.
3. R. VII 1/38 ff.
4. R. VII 83/4 ff.
5. R. I 8/38 ff.
6. R. II 1/40; R. VI 108/3.
7. R. VI 109/85.

invited to the palace to entertain by their performance the kings and princes.[1] These prostitutes employed by the state were of the superior *gaṇikā* class, most accomplished and proficient in various arts.[2] They were youthful and possessed very sweet and courteous speech. Besides, they had mastered various technicalities of dance and music.[3]

In addition to the high class *gaṇikās* who probably made their living only by the display of their arts there were the *rūpājīvas*. These latter seem generally to have accompanied the royal army obviously to provide entertainment to the soldiers.[4] This class, it seems, was constituted of prostitutes who probably made their living by selling their person. Sometimes their customers even manhandled them. Describing the Aśoka garden of Rāvaṇa ruthlessly trampled down by Hanūmān Vālmīki presents by way of comparison the picture of a prostitute with sparkling teeth and lovely upper lip, who (in course of an intercourse with her paramour) had her hair dishevelled, her paste worn off and her person torn with nails and teeth.[5]

Vālmīki is silent about the origin of prostitution. He has given a legendary account of the birth of *Apsarasas*, the divine prostitutes. It is said that they sprang from the cream (*sāra*) of the waters (*āpaḥ*) of the ocean being churned by the Devas and the Dānavas. But neither the Devas nor the Dānavas accepted them. In consequence of this non-acceptance they were known as *sādharaṇīs*, i.e., common to all.[6] This legend only brings out the character of a prostitute, viz., that she was a woman belonging to all; and unfit to be married by any one. Through a casual reference to *śailūsha* Vālmīki also seems to testify to the existence of clandestine prostitution in his society.[7]

Mention must also be made here of a separate class of

1. R. VII 44/16.
2. R. I 8/35.
3. A *gaṇikā* is defined by the Kāmasūtra as a *veśyā* who is most accomplished and proficient in the sixty-four *kalas*—

   Ābhirabhyucchritā veśyā śīlarūpaguṇānvitā,
   Labhate gaṇikā śabdaṃ sthānañca janasaṃsadi. I 3/20.
4. R. II 39/3.
5. R. V 9/23.
6. R. I 41/25.
7. R. II 33/8.

women held in concubinage by a king or a prince. The kings in the epics are generally described with unusually large harems. To wit, in the Rāmāyaṇa, Daśaratha is said to have possessed three hundred and fifty women in addition to his three principal wives, viz., Kauśalyā, Kaikeyī and Sumitrā.[1] No doubt, these ladies are loosely termed wives of Daśaratha and especially Rāma is represented to have been highly respectful to them. Nevertheless, we feel disposed to believe that their actual status was that of concubines, and not of regular wives. This position is very distinctly brought out by the fact that none of them was made a sharer in the divine *pāyasa* offered by the Prājāpatya-nara for the *anurūpa* wives.[2]

Now it remains for us to consider the attitude of the Rāmāyaṇa society towards its women and also to make a general estimate of their position in society.

The first thing that strikes the reader of the Rāmāyaṇa is the regard and the kindness which the poet requires his men to show towards the fair and the weaker sex. In the presence of women he required men to behave suavely and not to put on a stern demeanour. An extension of this very principle was the privilege granted by the society to women, viz., they should not be killed. To Śatrughna manhandling Mantharā Bharata said that ladies were granted immunity from capital punishment and hence he should spare her life.[3] The same was the rule even among the Vānaras and the Rākshasas. Bālī said that the magnanimous did not strike at a woman;[4] and Rāvaṇa was also dissuaded by his councillor Supārśva from killing Sītā, for the killing of a woman did not behove him who was born of a noble family, had performed sacrifices, and, above all, was magnanimous.[5] The highest punishment accorded to a woman guilty of a severe offence was 'deformity'—her ears and nose were chopped off.[6] However, it is to be noted that Vālmīki was not in favour of allowing the above privilege to become a licence for women for committing atrocities. He required his prince (or king) to show no clemency towards a woman who

1. R. II 38/10.
2. R. I 11/20.

Note : For the sex relations among the non-Aryan societies of the Rāmāyaṇa vide pp. 46-51 supra.

3. R. II 81/26.
4. R. IV 16/28.
5. R. VI 71/60.
6. R. III 23/21.

was a menace to the security and well-being of the society at large.[1] In support of this view the poet has recorded the legendary evidence of Indra who killed the Rākshasī Dīrghajihvā who threatened to swallow the whole earth, and of Vishṇu who killed the Kāvya-mātā, for she was plotting to appropriate to herself the dominion of Indra.[2]

It is to be observed that the above noted concession shown by Vālmīki's society to its women appears very inequitable when we look at the limitations imposed upon them. Vālmīki advocates absolute dependence of women upon men in society. We have noted that as a maiden, a woman was under the control of her father. In the times of Vālmīki there was a curtailment in her right of selecting her husband. She was not, as in the earlier period, free to choose the partner of her life. The *svayaṃvara* of earlier times was reduced to a mockery, for instead of affording an opportunity to the maiden for selecting her husband from among the assembly, now it was transformed into an arena for competitive princes where they made a display of their knightly powers and won a wager in the maiden.[3] Marriage did not improve her lot either, for it only meant the transference of guardianship from the hands of the father to those of the husband. As a wife, she was in complete subordination to her husband and any one trying to go against his will, stood the risk of being deserted by him. In old age (if she happened to be a widow) she was under the control of her son and in his absence, of the near relations. Vālmīki declares that the first refuge of a woman was her husband, the second her son, the third her relatives, and fourth she had none.[4]

The reason for disallowing any independence to women is not hard to seek. Vālmīki's society did not accredit its women with any sense of sound and independent judgment. Vālmīki says that it was the very nature of women that they readily accepted, without themselves reflecting (over the soundness or otherwise of the advice given) what their own people, though fools, preached to them.[5] Moreover, generally when there is

1. R. I 23/15, 21. 2. R. I 23/18-20.

3. Cf. "Thus epic *svayaṃvara* was only a method of selection which more or less served the same purpose as matrimonial advertisements of to day." Jayal, S., The Status of Women in the Epics, p. 54.

4. R. II 61/24 N. S. 5. R. II 11/34.

a reference to a woman's nature in the epic it is in a spirit of contempt; a sense of frivolity often remains inherent in such a reference.[1] It is the considered opinion of an august personality like Agastya that a woman combines in herself the fickleness of lightning, sharpness of weapons and the rashness of fire and wind.[2] Covetousness which sometimes prompts them to disregard their husband's will, and at others to create dissensions among the brothers (—husband and his brother) was believed to be another important trait of their character.[3] Actuated by their greediness they were said to regard their husbands only so long as they remained installed in high positions. Ingratitude was so ingrained in their nature that the moment they found them in the grip of misfortunes due to the sudden adverse turns of fate, they deserted them.[4] Sometimes such disparaging remarks about feminine character are put in the mouth of the women characters themselves. Thus, Kauśalyā while briefing Sītā on the manner she was to conduct herself in the service of her husband in the forest declared that verily, this was the nature of women that even though fondled and honoured by their husbands, due to pride of youth and beauty they did not recognise past associations or affections.[5] Even Sītā is made in the following words to defend Rāma, suspecting her own character, —"You are right in suspecting me, for women are untrustworthy."[6]

1. (i) *So(a)marshastacca me jñānaṃ, tat tapaḥ sa ca niścayaḥ. Nashṭānyekapadeneha sarvathā kimapi striyā.* R. I 59/15-16.
   (ii) *Strīcāpalāttu tacchrutvā Kaikeyī punarabravīt,* R. II 78/48
   (iii) *Yoshit svabhāve Kaikeyi nṛiśaṃse nirapatrape.* R. II 80/2.
   (iv) *Striyā nāma kathaṃ Rāmo vanam pravrājito (a) vaśaḥ* . R. II 81/3.
   (v) *Viklavaṃ dharmasaktañca yanmāmevaṃ viśaṅkase. Strī-svabhāvena dushṭena.........* R. III 50/31.
   (vi) *Yaḥ striyo vacanād rājyaṃ vihāya sasuhṛijjanam...* R. III 54/13.
   (vii) *Vidyate strīshu cāpalyam.........* R. V 90/47.
   (viii) *Upakāro na kartavyastvadvidhānām mahātmabhiḥ, Mūrkhāṇām akritajñānāṃ strīvaśāṇāṅkadācana.* R. IV 27/19.
   (ix) *Athavā strī-svabhāvena cāpalyavaśamohitā......*R. VI 23/7.
   (x) *Rañjanīyaṃ hi bhartāraṃ vinashṭam avagamya sā, Vairāgyāt strī laghutvācca tvadvaśam pratipatsyate.* R. VI 43/33.
2. R. III 17/6.
3. R. II 37/10; R. III 50/29.
4. R. III 17/5.
5. R. II 42/3-4.
6. R. VI 97/7.

Had the analysis of the women characters of the Rāmāyaṇa approached even in a small measure the above estimate of their nature made primarily by the male characters of the epic we would have readily joined them in advocating that a woman from her cradle to the grave should live under perpetual guardianship of man. Their study, however, relates a different story and forces one to arrive at an opposite judgment.

In fidelity to their spouse, in rendering ungrudging service, in enduring untold hardships, in showering serene love and affection, in displaying courage and fortitude in the hour of distress, in being ever vigilant about the welfare of their husband, in making sacrifice for the interest of their lord, in ready obedience and in their promptness to stand by the side of their husbands in the hour of need the women characters of the Rāmāyaṇa are simply exemplary. If one could pause a while to see the true picture of their own character presented by the men of the Rāmāyaṇa one would not fail to realise that their glitter immediately fades away in the presence of the inherent lustre of the illustrious women characters. The clamour against the avariciousness of Kaikeyī fails to attract the attention of the reader when it is disclosed to him that in consideration of securing Kaikeyī's hand in marriage the kingdom was already pledged by Daśaratha in favour of the son to be born of her.[1] Moreover, in the light of this disclosure when one is able to see through the scheming of Daśaratha, to see as to how he was trying to hoodwink Kaikeyī, her father and Bharata the cloak of ignominy instantaneously falls on his shoulders.[2] Daśaratha's guiltiness is also felt in his neglect of his simple and dutiful wife, Kauśalyā, which was caused on account of his marrying in advanced years the youthful Kaikeyī. Rāma himself, the ideal of Vālmīki's manliness, is much inferior to Sītā, his better half (—in the literal sense of the term). Passion for fame was his greatest weakness[3] and in rushing after it he became blind not only to finer human sentiments, but even to duty, for which he claimed to stad.

The treatment meted out by the society to women overtaken by the misfortune of falling into the hands of ruffians or

1. R. II 107/3 N. S.
2. Cf. R. II 6/23-24.
3. R. VII 47/12-14. Also R. VI 96/15.

enemies has been held by Dr. A. S. Altekar as the real touchstone to test the genuineness of a society's sympathy towards the weaker sex. According to him, "...it enables us to find out how far man is prepared to rise above the prejudices of his sex and judge the woman by equitable standard."[1] Looking from this point of view we find that the society of Vālmīki was most apathetic to its women. It cruelly shut its doors upon the unfortunate woman who was raped against her will by a libidinous monster,[2]—nay even upon one who even at the risk of her life kicked the wealth and glory of the three worlds being offered to her by her abductor and returned faithful to her own lord. How stern was the attitude of the society in this respect can easily be gauged from the fact that Rāma, who was through out the period of his separation from Sītā craving to clasp her within his arms dared not accept her when she stood before him at the conclusion of the Laṅkā war. The thought of the severe criticism of Sītā's character by the conservative in Ayodhyā made frozen within his heart all the love and sympathy that he bore to his dear spouse and instead of warmly pressing her to his bosom he himself put on a stiff demeanour and uttered those harsh words of repudiation to her.[3] Already by the time of

1. The position of women in Hindu civilization, p. 305.

2. Vide the case of Arajā raped by Daṇḍa—R. VII 82/13-17 and R. VII 83/13-16.

3. Sītā's repudiation by Rāma in the Yuddha-Kāṇḍa has created difficulty to many a scholar. Moreover, the inequity of Rāma's behaviour towards Sītā deeply hurts the sentiments of a devout Hindu who holds Rāma not only as an ideal of manliness but also as a veritable god. Scholars have been at great pains to defend Rāma by showing the incongruity of the episode under reference with Rāma's previous attitude towards Sītā. Thus they assert that the episode in question is a later interpolation in the epic. Dr. Altekar (in his work, the Position of women in Hindu civilization, pp. 306-307), for example, "finds it difficult to believe that the sentiments above expressed really represented the views of Rāma." In support he cites the following passages from the Rāmāyaṇa which speak of his deep love for Sītā :

Śyāmā padmapalāśākshī priyā virahitā mayā,
Katham dhārayati prāṇān vivaśā Janakātmajā.
Gatvā Lakshmaṇa paśya tvam Bharatam bhrātṛivatsalam,
Na hyahañ jīvitūṃ śaktastāmṛite Janakātmajām.

(R. IV 1/105, 113 N. S.)

Vālmīki a wave of asceticism had swept over the minds of the Indians and with growing enthusiasm the leaders of the society were painting women in very black colours to dissuade men

Kadā nu cāru bimboshṭhaṃ tasyāḥ padmamivānanam,
Īshadunnāmya pasyāmi rasāyanamivāturaḥ.
Kadā nu khalu me sādhvī Sītā surasutopamā,
Sotkaṇṭhā kaṇṭhamālambya mokshatyānandajam payaḥ.

(R. VI 5/13, 20 N.S.)

In fact, it is possible to add to the list many more such verses; but the point is not that. A reader has to appreciate that Vālmīki has supplied a very graphic and at the same time subtle analysis cf the simultaneous emergence of two opposite seniments in the heart of Rāma. There was on the one hand a strong urge to clasp to the bosom the dear spouse whom he was seeing after a long period of separation and on the other there was the fear of public condemnation. Rāma's heart, as Vālmīki has expressly put it, was being torn into pieces under the pressure of the inner conflict of his own conscience.

Paśyatastāntu Rāmasya samīpe hṛidayapriyām,
Janavādabhayād rājño babhūva hṛidayaṃ dvidhā.
Paśyatastāntu Rāmasya bhūyaḥ krodho (a) bhyavardhata,
Prabhūtājyāvasiktasya pāvakasyeva dīpyataḥ.
Sa baddhvā bhrukuṭīm vaktre tiryak samprekshya Rāghavaḥ,
Abravīt parushaṃ Sītām madhye Vānara Rākshasām.

R. VI 96/11-14.

It is to be noted that in the beginning he was waivering, being unable to decide in what manner he was going to receive Sītā. In the first part of his speech there was nothing to suggest that he was going to disown Sītā. He had only recounted the untold hardships that he, along with his allies had undergone for recovering Sītā. The result was—

Ityevam bruvataḥ Sītā śrutvā Rāmasya tadvacaḥ,
Kshaṇañ cotphullanayanā babhūvāśru pariplutā.

R. VI 96/10.

Sītā was moved to tears on learning of the unhuman exertions that Rāma had to put in in order to recover her from the hands of her abductor. Her heart was, perhaps, at the same time, filled with a sense of joy and pride feeling that her husband did all that for her sake. It was only later when the fear of public criticism had preyed upon the heart of Rāma who had a weakness for public popularity, that he spoke those harsh words.

We fully agree with Dr. Dhairyabala in holding that the present episode be considered a genuine portion of the Rāmāyaṇa not only because "it is an indication of the evolution towards a stricter code of sex ethics for which the Epics stand", (Evolution of Morals in the Epics, p. 46) but also because the attitude displayed towards women in the present lines is, we find, in perfect agreement with the sentiments of the society variously expressed throughout the Rāmāyaṇa.

from marriage and family life.[1] The remarks of Agastya that a woman was a conglomeration of sharpness, fickleness and rashness,[2] and the contempt shown towards them by Viśvāmitra in his soliloquy, viz., for the sake of a mere woman he had lost simultaneously his energy, his wisdom and his determination[3] clearly reveal that the society though still sticking in theory to the old ideal of partnership between husband and wife in all the phases of their life, was, in actual practice losing its concern in women. This is also corroborated from the fact that already in the times of the Rāmāyaṇa the process of confining women to the four walls of the house had commenced It is true that in the Rāmāyaṇa wives are seen freely moving in the company of their husbands, sporting with them in the public gardens, in rivers and over hills, visiting the holy places and personages, yet, this can also be clearly seen that the elites did not approve of their absolutely free movement in public. The women of the princes and the nobles were permitted to come out only well-escorted,[4] and they were required to wear a veil when they met strangers or appeared in public. About Sītā going with Rāma to the woods the poet remarks. "The same Sītā who previously could not be beheld even by the heavenly beings was today being seen by the common man on the street."[5] The statement of Rāma in the Yuddha-Kāṇḍa that the public appearance of a woman in times of misery, in war, in extraordinary circumstances, in *svayaṃvara* , and in marriage was not held objectionable,[6] is also a record of concessions granted to women on certain special occasions and testifies to the fact that seclusion was the norm. Sītā is actually described to have covered her face with her cloth to hide her shame when she appeared before the assemblage of people after the Laṅkā war.[7]

1. Cf. *Ye (a) pyaṅganānam pravadanti doshān, Vairāgya mārgeṇa guṇān vihāya.*
Te durjanā me manaso vitarkaḥ, Sadbhāva vākyāni na tāni teshām.
Bṛihat Saṃhitā, 74/5.
Also see Altekar, A. S., Position of women in Hindu Civilization., pp. 323-324.
2. R. III 17/6.
3. R. I 59/15-16.
4. Vibhīshaṇa when asked by Rāma to present Sītā before him, brought her duly escorted, and when Rāma compelled her to leave the palanquin and move on foot, she resented it—R. VI 95/52.
5. R. II 36/9.
6. R. VI 95/57.
7. R. VI 95/68.

The above account might appear to go against the description of Sītā in Pañcavaṭī where she is shown to have freely conversed with Rāvaṇa and entertained him. It is to be remembered in this connection that in Pañcavaṭī Rāvaṇa appeared disguised as a *parivrājaka* (hermit).[1] It seems, even in the times of Vālmīki there was no restriction on women on approaching the ecclesiastic people.[2] The distinction is clearly brought out by the fact that later when Rāvaṇa appeared before Sītā (without any disguise) she invariably placed a blade of straw between herself and Rāvaṇa to symbolically represent a veil or a curtain.[3]

That woman were even treated as chattels is evidenced by the fact that they usually constituted an article of gift on such occasions as coronation or marriage of a prince.[4] Royal palaces, it seems, were crowded with *dāsīs* and most probably the chowry-bearer, the jug-bearer, the lamp-bearer the parasol-carrier and the seat-lifter mentioned in the Sundara--Kāṇḍa belonged to this very class.[5]

1. R. III 51/2.
2. Nowhere during her stay in the forest Sītā is said to have put on a veil.
3. R. III 62/1; R. V 16/3.
4. R. I 70/6; R. II 9/1; R. VI 106/53-54; R. VII 41/9.
5. R. V. 13/10, 13-15.

Chapter VI

EDUCATION

Lives of men and women in any society serve as the surest index of the achievements or failures of its educational system. Judged from this standard the educational system of Vālmīki's times comes out very triumphant as it produced illustrious characters like Rāma, Sītā, Bharata, Atri, Anasūyā, Vasishṭha and Vālmīki[1]. Among these, Rāma, the hero of this epic, stands above every one else, for in him is embodied, "a harmonious development and combination of the excellencies of body,mind and character."[2] The presence of an efficient educational system in this period is further revealed by the wide range of literature with which the Rāmāyaṇa displays its familiarity and by the devoted pursuit of various fine arts by the people of these times. Thus Vālmīki furnishes ample evidence to show that the Veda and the Vedāṅgas,[3] the Arthaśāstra, the Daṇḍanīti or Rājanīti, Vārtā, Itihāsa, Purāṇa, Kalpasūtras,[4] the practical sciences like medicine, anatomy, astrology and astronomy formed interesting subjects of study for the people in that period.[5] Further, the popularity of such epithets as *vidvān*, *paṇḍita*, *vedavit*, *śruti-pāraga*, *bahu-śruta*, *saṃskāra-sampanna* etc. also point at the same fact. Moreover, there is evidence to show that the people zealously cultivated useful arts like carpentry, spinning, weaving, tailoring etc.[6] and also fine arts like music, dance, drama, paint-

1. (a) For the sketches of these characters vide Shastri, Srinivasa, Lectures on the Rāmāyaṇa.
   (b) For the education of Rāma and his brothers vide Sarkar, S. C., Edu. Ideas and Insti.

Note : That we do not agree with some of Dr. Sarkar's views will be seen from the following pages.

2. Sarkar, S. C., Edu. Ideas and Insti., p. 44.
3. The Uttara-Kāṇḍa of the Bombay recension mentions by name *Chanda*, *Jyotish*, *Kalpa*, *Vyākaraṇa* and *Svara-Lakshaṇa* (*Śikshā*?) (VII 94/5-8 N. S.).
4. In addition to the above the Yoga, Sāṅkhya, Nyāya and Mīmāṃsā systems of Indian philosophy are also mentioned in a few passages. The passages, however, appear to be palpable interpolations. (R. V 91/66; R. VII 93/20).
5. For references to these subjects vide R. I 3/6; R. I 10/30; R. II 2/8, 28, 29; R. II 3/12; R. V 22/6.
6. R. II 94/12 ff.

ing, architecture and poetry.[1] In spite of all this it is rather strange to observe that the purely educational evidence in the epic is so very meagre that one is left guessing about such interesting and important aspects of Rāmāyaṇic education as the curriculum, examinations, vocational education and the like. Hence the information culled from the epic, which we present in the following pages has naturally to be rather sketchy.[2]

It may be observed at the very outset that the idea of education is generally conveyed by Vālmīki by the following four terms, viz., *śikshā*, *adhyayana*, *vinaya* and *upadeśa*. An examination of the meanings of these words[3] indicates that Vālmīki's conception of education was either (i) an action in which one leads oneself in a particular manner or (ii) an action in which inborn faculties are led out (i.e. trained) in a particular

1. R. V 15/10.

It may be noted that Vālmīki calls fine arts by the name, *Vaihārika Śilpa* R. II 3/17.

(*Vaihārikāṇāṃ krīḍāprayojanānāṃ śilpānāṃ gītavādyacitrakarmādīnāṃ vijñātā* —Tilaka-Ṭīkā).

2. It may be noted that the meagreness of information on the point does not appear to have deterred some of our earlier predecessors in the field (like Doctors S. C. Sarkar and S. N. Vyas) from presenting an elaborate account of the Rāmāyaṇic education. But they have mostly dilated upon the personal attainments of Rāma, Sītā and a few other characters of the Rāmāyaṇa. No doubt, as already indicated earlier, an individual embodies in himself (or herself) the educational system of his (or her) own times. However, he (or she) only indirectly reflects the system. In our opinion it is difficult to draw concrete points on the basis of such data.

Note : (i) For the education of a prince vide chapter XVII infra.
(ii) For female education vide pp. 72-76 supra.

3. The word *śikshā* is derived from the first conjugational *ātmanepadī* root *śiksha* 'to learn' or 'to acquire knowledge'. (For its use in the Rāmāyaṇa see —*śikshāmastreshu darśayan* III 33/5).

The word *adhyayana* is a noun from the second conjugational *parasmaipadī* root *i* 'to go', preceded by the preposition *adhi*. It expresses the idea of a pupil (or pupils) going to some teacher for education. (For its use in the Rāmāyaṇa vide—*yadā tu śāstram adhyetum*......VII 39/14).

The word *vinaya* is a derivative from the first conjugational *parasmaipadī* root *ni* 'to carry' preceded by the preposition *vi*. It literally means 'to lead out in a particular way' (For its use in the Rāmāyaṇa in this sense vide—*rājavidyāvinītānām* and *Yajurvedavinītaśca* in V 29/13, 14).

The last word *upadeśa*, a noun from the first conjugational *ubhayapadī* root *diś* preceded by the preposition *upa* literally means 'to explain', 'to

cular way.[1] It will be seen that of these two the former conveys a comprehensive sense being synonymous with self-culture, while the latter refers to the instruction and training imparted to a youth by the society through the various agencies devised by it for the purpose. The object of all such training and instruction in the times of Vālmīki may be summed up as "making the student know the *dharma* and help him practise the same."[2]

Very much against this view is the opinion of Dr. S. N. Vyas. On the basis of an interpolated passage of the Rāmāyaṇa[3] and the illustration of Rāvaṇa and his brother, Kumbhakarṇa, who though sons of a renowned sage conducted themselves in their lives in a very unrighteous manner, Dr. Vyas has concluded that good behaviour according to the Rāmāyaṇa primarily depended upon one's inborn tendencies and not so much upon one's education and nurture.[4] Actually, the question of determining the role of 'Heredity' and 'Environment' (or 'Nature' and 'Nurture') in shaping a child's individuality is a very vexed one, and since the earliest times it has engaged the attention of all educationalists in our country and elsewhere. We feel that the question, whether a person or people attach higher or lower importance to 'Nature' or 'Nurture' is basically linked with their general outlook on life. Therefore, to pass a judgment in favour of either of them merely on the basis of a few stray references or individual illustrations would be misleading. We have shown in the chapter on 'Philosophy' that Vālmīki had unflinching faith in human action and that his outlook on life was predominantly one of optimism.[5] In view of this it would be difficult to hold that in comparison to 'Nature' Vālmīki assigned a subsidiary position to 'Nurture'.

instruct' or 'to teach'. (For its use in the Rāmāyaṇa vide —*upadishṭaṃ susūkshmārthaṃ śāstram tattvena dhīmatā* II 83/12).

1. Das, S. K., Educational system of the ancient Hindus, p. 18.

2. The word *dharma* is to be understood here in a comprehensive sense as connoting everything that was good and right for an individual and as including all his duties and obligations as a member of a particular *varṇa* and an *āśrama*.

3. *Vinītavinayasyāpi prakṛitirna vidhīyate.*
Prakṛitiṅgūhamānasya niścayena kṛtirdhruvā. R. VII 59 'Prakshipta 2/26' N.S.

4. Vyas, S. N. Rāmāyaṇa-Kālīna Saṃskṛiti, p. 115.

5. Vide Chapter X infra.

It may further be recalled in this connection that the conception of the *saṃskāras* and particularly the importance of the *upanayana-saṃskāra* clearly shows that a higher place for training and educational refinement is inherent in Hindu culture. The Hindus have recognised since the earliest times that by (physical) birth a man is like a *śūdra*; it is only by the *saṃskāras* that he is regenerated. The importance of educational refinement is, again, responsible for the high estimation of a teacher in Hindu society. The parents, it is said, produce only the body (of the child), but the teacher causes him to be born from *vidyā* (i.e. by imparting vedic study); and that such a birth was superior to physical birth from the mother's womb.[1] We would like to assert confidently that this position was basically unaltered in Vālmīki's times.

According to the *āśrama* scheme every Aryan was necessarily required to undergo the *upanayana saṃskāra* and after that to pass the first period of his life as a *brahmacārī*. During this period he normally stayed with his preceptor in the latter's *āśrama* receiving such education from him as, on the one hand, initiated him into the nation's cultural heritage and, on the other, prepared him for the calling that he was expected to pursue in his future life as a member of a particular *varṇa*. Obviously this arrangement had a distinct merit—it ensured compulsory education for every one and at the same time harnessed the energies of the entire nation for the preservation of the Veda, the national treasure of learning.

The Rāmāyaṇa speaks of a network of *āśramas* (hermitages) which were spread all over the country, most of them situated in the forest along the banks of rivers like Sarayū, Gaṅgā, Yamunā and Godāvarī. Many of these *āśramas*, apart from carrying on various activities of religious and cultural importance, served as important centres of learning.[2] One notes

1. Kane, P. V., History of Dharma-śāstra, Vol. II, part I, pp. 188-189.

2. With reference to the Mahābhārata Dr. R. K. Mookerji writes in his 'Ancient Indian Education' (p. 333) :

"A full fledged *Āśrama* is described as consisting of several Departments which are enumerated as follows:

(1) *Agnisthāna*, the place for fire-worship and prayers; (2) *Brahmasthāna*, the Department of Veda; (3) *Vishṇusthāna*, the Department for teach-

in them the presence of *śishyas* (pupils) gathered around a celebrated sage.[1] One occasionally reads also of a *śishya* fetching water for his teacher,[2] following him with his garments to a river bank[3] or helping him in according reception to his guests,[4] but unfortunately the epic does not introduce a single scene depicting a student (or students) receiving his (their) lessons from the teacher.

Not every *āśrama*, however, was a seat of learning. We cannot agree with Prof. S. C. Sarkar when he represents even the *āśramas* of the Andha muni (whose son was by mistake killed by prince Daśaratha) and of Rāma at Citrakūṭa and Pañcavaṭī as educatonial centres.[5] About Rāma living at Citrakūṭa he writes : "While at Citrakūṭa, Rāma seems to have joined other *ṛshis* in the *āśramas* there in the work of teaching; for when ....the *kulapati* of Citrakūṭa abandoned his *kula*.........the

ing Rājanīti, Arthaniti, and Vārttā; (4) *Mahendrasthāna*, Military section; (5) *Vivasvatsthāna*, Department of Astronomy; (6) *Somasthāna*, Department of Botany; (7) *Garuḍasthāna*, section dealing with Transport and conveyances; (8) *Kārtikeya sthāna*, section teaching military organization, how to form patrols, batallions, and army." But unfortunately Dr. Mookerji does not refer to the verses, chapter or book where this description is given in the Mahābhārata.

In connection with the description of Agastya's *āśrama* the Rāmāyaṇa also refers to *Brahma-sthāna*, *Śiva-sthāna*, *Agni-sthāna*, *Indra-sthāna*, *Vivasvata-sthāna*, *Soma-sthāna*, *Bhaga-sthāna*, *Kubera-sthāna*, *Dhātṛi-sthāna*, *Vidhātṛi-sthāna* and *Vāyu-sthāna*. (III 16/17-18). The commentators explain them as sanctuaries of different deities. If, however, Dr. Mookerji's interpretation be correct we can interpret these words in the Rāmāyaṇa also in the same manner.

1. R. I 2/43; R. I 48/5; R. II 103/7; R. III 16/1; R. VII 51/6 ff.
2. R. I 2/23.
3. R. I 2/9.
4. R. VII 51/6; R. II 103/7;
5. "Finally, at Pañcavaṭī he (Rāma) joined and organised a fairly large *āśrama-padam* or educational settlement."

Sarkar, S. C., Edu. Ideas and Insti., p. 56.

It may be incidentally added that Dr. Sarkar takes *andha* (in *andha-muni*) not in the sense of blindness but as referring to his family name. He writes : "So this *Andhaka* family must have belonged to the ruling or *kshatriya* classes; there are several instances of Purāṇic tradition of princes being described as *vaiśyas* (perhaps for owning farms and pastures.)" (Ibid. f. n. 4 on page 123).

Obviously, Dr. Sarkar's suggestion is a very fanciful one. The āmāyaṇa clearly alludes to the blindness of the *muni*—

Jānannapi hi kiṇkuryādandhatvādaparākramaḥ. R. II 69/39;
Agaterme gatiryastvaṃ tvamme cakshuracakshushaḥ. R. II 70/8.

remaining *tāpasas* (students) clung to the side of Rāma........"[1] Obviously such an assertion can not be upheld, for not only is there not the slightest indication in the Rāmāyaṇa to show that Rāma at any stage of his long sojourn in the forest acted as a teacher imparting education to bands of students, but also because it goes against the *varṇāśrama vyavasthā* of which Rāma is believed to have been such a rigid adherent that he evenbe-headed Śambūka who tried to violate it. Equally fallacious would be the suggestion that some of these *āśramas* were such extensive or powerful institutions as to accord a luxurious reception to the full-fledged army of a prince[2] or to repel its onslaught by employing mercenery barbarians like the Śakas, Yavanas, Pahlavas and others.[3] In our opinion such descriptions in the extant Rāmāyaṇa either represent the flights of the poet's imagination or point to later interpolations.

Besides the *āśramas* situated in the forests there must have been various educational institutions in the towns as well. Vālmīki has expressly mentioned teachers of different Vedic traditions[4] living in Ayodhyā and being honoured with gifts by Rāma at the time of his departure to the forest. Moreover, Rāma and his brothers appear to have received their formal education in Ayodhyā itself.[5] Perhaps Vasishṭha supervised

1. Edu. Ideas and Insti., p. 55.

2. Cf. "Lastly we may mention one of the biggest *āśramas* of the times, that of *Ṛishi* Bharadwāja at Prayāga, which accommodated Bharata and his royal retinue, including the ladies of the Palace. The *āśrama* was equipped with white *chatuḥ-śālās*, stalls which accommodated the royal elephants and horses; *harmyas* or mansions; *prāsādas* or palaces, and their *toraṇas* or gateways, a separate *rāja-veśma* or royal guest house fitted with several *toraṇas* and furnished with beds, seats, and vehicles, coverlets and carpets, stores of food. The *āśrama* also entertained its royal guests with the performances of musicians and dancing girls. All this lavish hospitality was extemporized for the occasion, showing the resources which *Ṛishi* Bharadwāja could command in the locality by his personality."

Mookerji, R. K., Ancient Indian Education, pp. 343-344.

3. Sarkar, S. C., Edu. Ideas and Insti., p. 176 (also foot-note 5 on p. 176).

4. R. II 35/15 ff.

5. According to Prof. S. C. Sarkar, the education of Rāma and his brothers took place at several places—in Ayodhyā and outside. He writes : "........and as we have already seen, Daśaratha sent his sons to be educated not only to the various Vedic schools and *ṛṣi-āśramas* in the city

their religious education[1] while another *brāhmaṇa* teacher, Sudhanvā, gave them lessons in *Daṇḍa-nīti* and also trained them in the use of various missiles and weapons.[2] The excellent *brāhmaṇas*, Agastya and Kauśika who were also invited to receive gifts from Rāma seem to have been teachers residing in Ayodhyā,[3] if they be different from the well-known sages of this name. Like the *āśramas* of the forest these institutions in the towns also seem to have enrolled large numbers of resident students and provided for them free boarding and lodging. For their maintenance, they seem to have depended largely upon royal patronage which was received by them in various forms .A large number of *brāhmaṇas* is thus mentioned in the Ayodhyā-Kāṇḍa as depending upon Kauśalyā and Sumitrā for help and receiving liberal donations from Rāma at the time of his departure to the forest.[4]

On the basis of a stray passage appearing in the Kishkindhā-Kāṇḍa Prof. S. K. Das suggests that the session (or annual term) in the educational institutions began in the rainy or the winter season when the heat was less intense. He is further of opinion that the commencement of Vedic study took place on the full moon day either of the month of *Āshāḍha*, *Śrāvaṇa* or *Bhādra*[5]. Another passage in the Sundara-Kāṇḍa of the

of Ayodhyā, but also to the *Vāmanāśrama*, south of the Ganges, run by a Kauśika *ṛṣi*, to the Bhāradwāja (Āṅgirasa) *āśrama* at Prayāga, and to several *āśramas* further south, within the Daṇḍaka monasteric zones, amongst which was apparently the major 'Agastyan *āśrama*' of the time."

Edu. Ideas and Insti., p. 112.

We may point out that in the Rāmāyaṇa there is not the slightest direct or indirect evidence to support Dr. Sarkar's view.

1. Commenting on the word *janmakriyādīni* (occurring in R. I 18/24 N. S.) Nāgojī-Bhaṭṭa writes : *janmakriyādīni tadādyupanayanāntānītyarthaḥ*. This expressly supports the contention that Vasishṭha supervised the religious education of the princes. But the verse referred to above is missing in the N. W.

2. R. II 114/9. (Perhaps the *ācārya* referred to in R. II 34/26 from whose house Lakshmaṇa was directed by Rāma to fetch the bow was this very *ācārya*, Sudhanvā.)

3. R. II 35/16.

4. R. II 35/26-27.

N. B. The N. S. mentions instead a big host of *brahmacāris* approaching Kauśalyā for help and receiving liberal donations on her behalf from Rāma. (R. II 32/21 N. S.)

5. Educational system of the Ancient Hindus, p. 106.

(contd. next page)

Dākshiṇātya recension indicates that the first day of the fortnight was considered the most objectionable one for studies.[1]

About the methods of teaching and learning employed in the times of Vālmīki we know but little. Though writing was known in that period[2] and the use of the verb *paṭh* and its derivatives is copious in the epic, still teaching and learning, at least of the sacred texts, must have been largely oral.[3] In fact, personal attention of the teacher towards every individual student has been a special feature of ancient Indian education and this eliminated to a great measure the intervention of a written book between the teacher and the taught. Thus the popular modes of learning seem to have been recitation, conversation, discussion and debate. In the bewailing of the *Andhamuni* in the Rāmāyaṇa, we get a glimpse of a student preparing his lessons at early dawn. The bereaved sage said that he would no longer be able to hear the scriptures being studied in sweet speech by his son.[4] The Rāmāyaṇa was also perhaps taught orally by Vālmīki to Kuśa and Lava and there is no mention of the written text of the Rāmāyaṇa being utilised by them at the time of reciting it before the distinguished assembly in Rāma's *Aśvaemdha.* Conversational method is evidenced in the account of Rāma's and Lakshmaṇa's temporary stay with Viśvāmitra. In course of the journey with the sage from Ayodhyā to Siddhāśrama and later from Siddhāśrama to Mithilā Rāma's inquisitiveness was aroused by the sight of holy rivers and places that he passed by, and he made a number of enquiries about them of the sage. Viśvāmitra not only gladly answered every one of them, but incidently he also supplied interesting details of past history and theogony, which proved extremely educative for the princes.[5] Narration of moral and religious stories in

(The verse under reference is :
Proshṭhapādo vineyānām māso brahmavivakshatām.
Ayamadhyāyasamayaḥ sāmagānām upasthitaḥ. R. IV 21/10.

1. R. V 59/31 N. S.

2. The name of Rāma was inscribed on the ring which Hanūmān presented to Sītā in the Aśoka-vana. (R. V. 31/17) Likewise, the name of a knight was generally written on his arrows (R. V. 16/22). Moreover, 'writing' and 'written books' are also expressly mentioned in the Rāmāyaṇa (II 2/2 and VII 39/43).

3. Note the use of the root *vac* 'to speak' in R. IV 21/10.

4. R. II 70/33.

5. R. I, cantos 21-27 and cantos 29-45.

the evenings appears to have been a daily routine in the *āśramas.*[1] Debates and discussions are seen being specially held on the occasion of sacrificial sessions when scholars of distant lands assembled at one place and exchanged their views.[2] This method must have been found particularly useful for senior students who carried on their studies in specialised branches of learning

It may be added here, that in an age in which libraries were practically non-existent and even written books were mostly inaccessible, a student always stood the danger of soon forgetting what he had learnt during the period of his formal study. Vālmīki actually refers to this danger in a simile employed in the Sundara-Kāṇḍa where the *virahiṇī* Sītā is compared to the learning of a person, reduced for want of regular revision.[3] As a safeguard against such a contingency not only great pains were taken to develop memory highly, but at the same time it was enjoined upon every Aryan to continue the *svādhyāya* throughout his life; this required daily recapitulation of a portion of what had been learnt earlier.[4]

The Dharma-Śāstras speak of different grades of teachers such as *guru, upādhyāya, ācārya* and *kulapati.*[5] Each of these is mentioned by Vālmīki in the Rāmāyaṇa,[6] though he does not provide any clue to specifically determine their relative position. Perhaps an *ūpādhyāya*, as in the Smṛitis, imparted instructions in consideration of regular fees and the *kulapati* used to be the head of a big *āśrāma* in which large numbers of students resided with him and received under him education in various subjects. The Araṇya-Kāṇḍa alludes to a *kulapati*, who lived at Citrakūṭa, but on sensing danger for the academy he moved away with all his followers to a place of safety.[7]

1. R. I 31/14.
2. R. I 10/14.
3. R. V. 74/18.
4. Kane, P. V., History of Dharma-śāstra, Vol. II, part I, p. 356.
5. For definitions vide Manusmṛiti II 140-142.
6. (i) *Prajñāṃ dadāti cācāryas tasmād gururucyate.* R. II 124/3
   (ii) *Sa kaccid brāhmaṇo vidvān dharmanityastapodhanaḥ*
   Ikshvākūṇām upādhyāyo yathāvat tāta pūjyate. R. II 114/5
   (iii) *Kṛitāñjaliruvācedamrishiṅ kulapatintadā.* R. III 1/4.
7. R. III 1/12-33.
Prof. S. C. Sarkar introduces a new class of 'itinerant teachers' who,

Since very ancient times a teacher has been regarded by his students in India with the highest respect. The Rāmāyaṇa also says that the father and the mother were responsible only for the physical being of a child but the *ācārya* granted him wisdom (*prajñā*) and was, therefore, higher than them.[1] In another passage a teacher is likened to a father and a mother, i.e. relations deserving highest respect.[2] That modest deportment towards his teacher was specially characteristic of a student is indicated in a passage of the Sundara-Kāṇḍa in which Hanūmān, when he was gently approaching Sītā, has been described as a modest pupil approaching his *ācārya*.[3] A statement of Rāvaṇa further

according to him, were "sent forth from the monasteries at regular intervals on semi-religious educational missions." The basis of Prof. Sarkar's view is the following verse of the Rāmāyaṇa :

Sarvam mamaitad viditan tapasā dharmavatsala.
Sampatanti ca me śishyāḥ pravṛittyākhyāḥ purīmitaḥ. R. VI 124/16 N. S.

Strangely enough Prof. Sarkar reads *pravṛitta- ākhyāḥ* for *pravṛittyākhyāḥ* and renders it as pupils designated *pravṛittas*. He further comments, "......*pravṛtta* is clearly a school word of the same class as *samāvṛtta*—students who have returned to home life after finishing their school course; apparently the *pravṛtta* stage just preceded the *samāvṛtta* status."

(Edu. Ideas and Insti. p. 128 — (note, f.n. 2)

Dr. Sarkar, it is obvious, tries to build a little too much on slender foundation. No doubt, there is a similarity in the sound between the words *pravṛitta* and *samāvṛitta*, but merely on that basis *pravṛitta* can not become technical term designating a certain stage of studentship. It is to be remembered that no where in the Dharma-śāstras there is any reference to the *pravṛitta* class of students. Moreover, as already indicated, in order to force his interpretation on the text Prof. Sarkar alters the reading of the text into *pravṛittākhyāḥ* for *pravṛittyākhyāḥ* of the original.

The verse under reference simply means, "I have known all this by virtue of my asceticism, O thou, fond of virtue. My disciples used to go hence to that city to bring tidings." It is well known that *bhikshāṭana* was the routine business of the *brahmacāris* and sometimes when the disciples of the sage Bharadvāja used to go to Ayodhyā they also incidentally brought news (*pravṛitti*) about Bharata and the people of Ayodhyā. It is further interesting to observe that in the text there is expressly a reference to the disciples. One wonders how Prof. Sarkar catches a hint from it to introduce a new class of teachers. The meaning is simple and perfectly suited to the context. Prof. Sarkar unnecessarily tries to twist the text and attribute to it a novel interpretation.

1. R. II 124/3.
2. R. II 124/2.
3. R. V 35/63.

indicates that even a person of advanced age and experience when approaching another person for learning was expected to shake off all vanity and to consider himself a junior and to put on a modest demeanour.[1] A more vivid idea of a student's behaviour towards his teacher may be had from the account of Rāma and Lakshmaṇa when they were living with Viśvāmitra. Throughout their stay with the sage they displayed the highest deference for him. Every morning, after attending their daily duties they used to approach the sage to pay him their respects,[2] and even though they were princes they used to announce themselves to him as his *kiṅkaras* (servants) waiting to receive his orders.[3]

As a corollary to the above position a teacher was also expected to regard his pupils with affection and kindliness; in fact, he was to look upon them as his very children.[4] Such an attitude on the part of the teacher was all the more necessary, for in majority of cases a student left his natural home at a tender age and came to live with the teacher as a member of the latter's family. Under such an arrangement the entire personality of a child was principally of the teacher's making and any harsh or indifferent treatment on his part could prove fatal to the interests of his ward. We find that the sage Viśvāmitra always accosted Rāma in such sweet terms as 'Rāma', '*tāta*' and 'Kauśalyā māta'[5], and whenever he had to direct him to perform his duties he would do so in very pleasing speech.[6] Moreover, he appreciated inquisitiveness in Rāma and encouraged it by his replies. He was so much pleased with him that he voluntarily imparted to him advanced training in several secret missiles[7] of which, perhaps, he was the only repository in his times.

---

1. R. V 88/9.
2. R. I 21/4; R. I 27/23.
3. R. I 29/4.
4. R. IV 18/14 N. S.
5. R. I 21/2; R. I 32/2; R. I 36/3.
6. R. I 21/2.
7. R. I 25/2.

Chapter VII

ASCETICS AND THEIR LIFE

Ascetic practices were very widely prevalent in India in Vālmīki's times. In the Rāmāyaṇa we come across two classes of ascetics which we may term as 'regulars' and 'occasionals'. The first class comprised those *vānaprasthas* who, having led an active worldly life as *griha-medhins* had retired to the forest, mostly in company with their wives. In the forest, they habituated their bodies to all sorts of privations and mortifications[1] by living a life of severe discipline. As this mode of life devolved upon these persons in their ripe age and in consequence of a more or less natural scheme their effort was mainly directed not towards the attainment of any worldly objective but towards the cultivation of moral virtues like humility, compassion, truthfulness, continence, abstinence from anger and the like. They aimed at mental peace and for that endeavoured to acquire complete control over passions and to rid their hearts of all sorts of desires,[2] except perhaps that of a permanent place in Heaven after death.[3] To this class belong the inmates of Bharadvāja's *āśrama*, the sages living at Citrakūṭa, Atri and Anasūyā, the big host of sages living in the *tāpasāśrama-maṇḍala* of Daṇḍakāraṇya (which included Śarabhaṅga and Sutīkshṇa), Agastya and his brother, Mātaṅga and Vālmīki. In case of some of these, Vālmīki has himself employed the word *vānaprastha*[4] and that others also belonged to this category is clear from the fact that they had an organised living, and had not given up the maintenance of fire.[5]

The second class consisted of those who viewed *tapas* as a method of exercising pressure upon the gods for conferring upon them the highest rewards of place and power. To this

1. R. II 31/17-23.
2. R. III 80/10-12; R. V 81/16.
3. R. III 6/23; R. III 9/10.
4. (i) *So(a)yam brāhmaṇa bhūyishṭho vānaprasthagaṇo mahān.* R.III 7/18
   (ii) *Vānaprasthena vidhinā sa tebhyo bhojanaṃ dadau.* R. III 16/25.
5. Vide pp. 30-31 supra.

class belonged people of different ages and stations;[1] and naturally, their austerities were more protracted and severe. One interesting thing about this class is that the gods are represented as being always suspicious of their motives; and they try by various means to make them give up the *tapas*.[2] Equally interesting is the bargaining, which sometimes takes place between the god and the ascetic. Thus the Yaksha Suketu who was aspiring for a son was granted only a daughter.[3] Viśvāmitra, who in his rivalry with Vasishṭha, wanted to become his equal (i. e. a *brahmarshi*), achieved his end only after he had undergone several tests.[4] The Pitāmaha appeared a number of times before him—once to reveal to him the *Dhanurveda* with all its secrets, and then to declare him, in order, a *rājarshi*, a *maharshi* and a *brahmarshi*.[5] That ascetics of this class almost compelled the gods to fulfil their ambition is clear from such statements of the gods as :

(a) Let this son of Kuśika attain the title *maharshi* and let him no longer torment us by his severe penance.[6]

(b) Before this great treasure of penances decides to acquire the celestial dominion, grant him his heart's desire.[7]

1. Mālī, Sumālī and Mālyavān (R. VII 4/8-14), and Rāvaṇa, Kumbhakarṇa and Vibhīshaṇa (R. VII 9/2 ff), are cases of ascetics who practised *tapas* before their marriages. Umā (R. I 32/25) and Vedavatī (R. VII 16/2 ff.) are cases of female ascetics of this very category, each of whom resorted to *tapas* for winning her cherished husband.

The Yaksha Suketu and Viśvāmitra are cases of *gṛihasthas* who took to asceticism for the attainment of their goals . Of these Viśvāmitra was living with his wife and during the long period of his penance he got sons as well (R. I 52/5).

2. For example Indra tried to seduce Viśvāmitra through Rambhā and Menakā. (R. I cantos 59 and 60).

3. R. I 23/6.

4. The story of Viśvāmitra suggests that a definite quantum and character of *tapas* were fixed for a particular wish to be granted (cf. the words of Brahmā—*Jito rājarshilokate sumahān Kuśikātmaja, Anena tapasā yuktaṃ rājarshi tvāṃ samarthaye*. R. I 53/2.)

5. R. I 50/17-20; R. I 53/2; R. I 59/23-24; R. I 61/10

6. R. I 59/21.

7. R. I 61/8.

The gods are said to have tried many ingenious methods to detract such ascetics from their objective. Deputing the celestial damsels for the purpose was a well known practice[1] (and in times of need even men on earth had recourse to it).[2] But the way the Devarāja excited Gautama's anger and thus impeded the course of his penance is really interesting. In the interest of the gods he appeared before Gautama's youthful wife, impersonating Gautama himself and seduced her and thereby invited upon himself (and also Ahalyā) a curse of the sage.[3] Equally interesting is the case of Kumbhakarṇa who was, by the machination of the gods, made to ask for sleep for six months and one day of wakefulness (whereas he had really wished to ask just the reverse of it.)[4]

The attitude of the gods is entirely different towards ascetics of the former group. They are friendly towards them. They pay them occasional visits[5], offer to take them in their celestial cars to Heaven[6], and participate in the final services of their sacrifices.[7] And these ascetics did well deserve it, for the attainment of the position of *brahmarshi* after which they strove, involved no infringement of the interests of others. For attaining this coveted position (viz. *brahmarshitva*) it was not so necessary to pass through the severe ordeal of physical disciplines and tortures as the cultivation of high moral culture. After an unusually protracted and severe course of austerities when Viśvāmitra expressed his desire before Brahmā to be named *brahmarshi* the latter rebuked him saying, "You have not yet mastered your senses. How do you aspire for *brahmatva* without subduing *kāma* and *krodha*?"[8] The title was conferred on him only when he had observed the vow of 'complete silence' for a thousand years and allowed no quarter in his heart to lust and anger.[9]

1. R. I cantos 59 and 60.
2. King Lomapāda employed prostitutes to entice Ṛishya-śṛiṅga. (R. I 8/35-70).
3. R. I 45/2-3.
4. R. VII 9/36-40.
5. R. III 16/31.
6. R. III 6/23; R. III 8/10.
7. R. VII 78/33-35.
8. R. I 59/26-27.
9. R. I 61/1-10.

Various views have been held about the origin of these ascetic practices. Dr. A. S. Geden, for instance, holds that practice of *tapas* was, in great part at least, adopted by the Aryans from the aboriginal or other tribes among whom the new-comers settled.[1] He points out that "in the earliest Sanskrit literature, the hymns of the Ṛigveda, neither the word *tapas* nor the conception and thought that underlies it is of frequent occurrence."[2] He further argues that "to the bright joyous spirit of the Aryans—the spirit that finds expression in the hymns—the sad and despairing outlook which is the motive power and inspiration of ascetic practice was repugnant. To them the gods were open-handed, and did not need to be forced or cajoled by human suffering; and life was not yet clouded by the pessimistic tendencies of a later age."[3] The basis of this approach, it is obvious, is the conviction that asceticism is only a manifestation of the escapist tendency which makes one endure self-imposed hardship and suffering in the hope of future deliverance.

Such a view is, however, one-sided and displays total lack of appreciation of the Aryan concept of the *āśramas*. The word *āśrama* derived from a root meaning 'to toil', shows, as Dr. Radhakrishnan points out, that "the Indians realised that suffering was incidental to all progress."[4] One had to 'toil' to reach the highest stage. The complete control over one's body and intellect by means of regulated prayers and fastings, was not an unimportant part of this 'toil'. Actually this remained a part of the Hindu culture almost throughout its evolution; and we can trace best its course in Yogic *sādhanā*, where *ṛitambharā prajñā* is preceded by culture—physical, mental as well as intellectual.[5]

In the Rāmāyaṇa the struggle between Vasishṭha and Viśvāmitra very impressively emphasises the supremacy of mental culture over physical torture. We have already indicated that the ideal of a *brahmarshi*, which was attained only

1. Asceticism (Hindu), Encyclopaedia of Religion and Ethics, Vol. II p. 88.
2. Ibid.
3. Ibid.
4. Indian Philosophy, Vol. I, p. 132 (f.n. 2).
5. The Yoga System of Patañjali, H.O.S., Vol. XVII p. 94.

after complete victory over the human frailties like *kāma* and *krodha*, was held as supreme by all in the Rāmāyaṇa. Moreover, it was resorted to by people wishing to make their worldly life 'full' according to their own ideals and ambitions.

There is also in the Rāmāyaṇa, no doubt, another type of asceticism which includes much that is degenerate in character, and out of tune with the Aryan spirit. The spirit of coercing gods by excessive self-mortification and physical torture does not, indeed, represent the healthy side of asceticism. Moreover, the fact that the followers of this selfish asceticism, in the Rāmāyaṇa, are predominantly Rākshasas and Yakshas might indicate that this trend in its origin belonged primarily to the non-Aryan tribes of India. It is, however, to be added that even people belonging to this class of ascetics did not take to asceticism as an escape from the struggle of worldly life.

The life of an ascetic was a voluntary choice for hardships. His main object was to accustom his body to the severest disciplines and vows and for that purpose he had evolved for himself a strenuous routine. Very early in the morning, he walked to the nearby river (or lake) for a dip and by sunrise returned to his hut with water still dripping from his wet bark-garments.[1] He was required to take three baths in a day[2]—one, just before sunrise, the other at noon, and the last just before sunset. On his way back from the river he brought sometimes a jar full of water and sometimes the sacrificial fuel and the bundle of *kuśa* blades.[3] On the river bank, perhaps standing in water, he offered libations of water to the *Pitṛis*[4] (manes) and muttered in his heart the sacred verses, the *Gāyatrī* and the like.[5] In a lonely corner of the river-bank he also offered sweet-smelling flowers to the gods[6] and at the time of the evening bath, he also worshipped the sun.[7]

1. R. I 44/24; R. III 3/27.
2. R. II 108/18; Also R. II 28/15 N.S.
3. R. I 44/24; R. III 3/27.
4. R. I 2/11.
5. R. I 2/10.
6 R III 14/9
7. R. VII 83/21.
N. B. Usually Sūrya is worshipped in the morning.

Maintenance of fire was the most important obligation of an Aryan's life of which he became free only at the end of the *vānaprastha āśrama.*[1] After his bath, therefore, the ascetic, both in the morning and in the evening performed the *agnihotra*[2] in which the *haviḥ* offered to the gods and the manes generally consisted of clarified butter and *muni-anna*, viz. *śyāmāka* and *nīvāra.*[3] Besides the daily *homa* the ascetic performed the periodical sacrifices, which were known as the *parva-kāla-homa.*[4] These were performed usually on the occasion of the sun or the moon passing through the node. The *Darśa* and the *Paurṇamāsa ishṭis*, performed respectively on the *amāvasyā* and the *purṇimā* were the most important of this group.[5] The performance of the daily *agnihotra* and the periodical sacrifices was in the discharge of the debt which every Aryan was believed to owe to the gods and the manes, and as already remarked, it was obligatory on him.

Besides these, the ascetic of the second type invariably and those of the first sometimes, undertook to perform certain special *yajñas* with the object of achieving some definite results. The *yajñas* of Rāvaṇa which he performed in the course of his extremely protracted penance and in which he offered his nine heads—one each time, belong to this class.[6] It appears that similar was the character of the *yajña* of Viśvāmitra which lasted for six days and in which he sought the assistance of Rāma.[7]

An equally important obligation, enjoined upon the ascetic, was the 'receiving of a guest'. The doors of an ascetic's hut were ever open for a guest and whatever viands were available with him he was always eager to offer them to the *atithi.* The ascetic strongly believed that one who, without sharing his food with

1. Vide p. 32 supra.
2. R. III 3/28.
3. R. I 48/39-40.

Note : The *svāhā* and *vashaṭkāra* occurring in these verses refer to the sacrifices in which accompanied with the uttering of these words offerings were made to the gods and the manes respectively. (vide Ṭilaka-Ṭīkā).

4. R. III 11/13.
5. R. I 48/48.
6. R. VII 9/7-9.
7. R. I 28/4.

the *atithi* (who had announced himself at his doors) swallowed one's morsels lived on one's own flesh in the next world.[1]

Regulation of one's habits of 'food' was one of the most important disciplines of ascetic life and sometimes this ideal has been exaggerated to fabulous lengths in the Rāmāyaṇa.[2] By training his body the ascetic aimed at reducing his requirements to the barest minimum. In the forest, he subsisted on fruits, roots and other green vegetables that were procurable without any special effort.[3] Gradually, he accustomed himself to live on leaves of trees, grass, water, rays of the sun or the moon and lastly wind.[4] The ascetic used only those fruits and leaves which had fallen from the trees of their own accord.[5] Sometimes he also used corn procured by gleaning.[6] Mostly the corn that he used was of a coarse quality.[7] Some of the ascetics used corn but without cooking. They have been named as *aśmakuṭṭas* (i. e. breaking it on stone) and *dantolūkhalins* (i. e. those who employed their teeth as the pestle).[8] The practice of living on a single handful or mouthful also seems to have been popular in the times of Vālmīki.[9] The ascetic was normally required to abstain from the eating of meat.[10]

In fact, the entire life of the ascetic was subjected to extreme rigours. He acclimatised himself to the roughness of weather by sitting in summer surrounded by four blazing fires and the scorching sun over his head,[11] by passing the winter

1. R. III 16/26.
For further details on this point vide chapter VIII infra.
2. R. I 50/13.
3. R. II 31/18; R. III 11/5; R. VII 84/3.
4. R. I 47/25; R. III 7/2, 8.
5. R. I 47/25 (note *śīrṇaparṇāśanaiḥ*).
6. Vide Tilaka-Ṭīkā on R. II 28/16 N. S.—*ārshovidhiruñchādivṛittiḥ*.
7. R. II 31/18.
8. R. III 7/3.
9. R. V 8/47.
10. This was not a rigid practice is shown by the account of Rāma, who mostly subsisted in the forest on the meat of deer. (Vide chapter XI infra) Moreover, the occasion of *śrāddha* was definitely an exception to the prohibition of meat-eating by the ascetic is shown by the account of Agastya, who is described to have made a meal of the notorious Vātāpi in a *śrāddha* feast (R. III 14/12-17).
11. This was technically known as *pañcāgni-tapa* (R. II 31/23).

sitting or standing in water[1] and by exposing himself in the *vīrāsana* posture to the showers and thunders of the rains.[2] The nights he generally passed in the open on beds prepared on the bare ground by himself of grass or leaves.[3] In the *āśrama* of Vasishṭha and among the big host of ascetics in Daṇḍakāraṇya, Vālmīki has mentioned several ascetics, who had wonderfully adapted themselves to one or the other type of rigour. Thus there were *ab-bhakshas* (living on water), *vāyu-bhakshas* (living on wind), *śirṇa-parṇāśanas* (living on leaves fallen from the trees of their own accord), *phala-mūlāśins* (living on fruits or roots), *samprakshālas* (literally meaning those who washed their utensils after meals i.e. those who did not store for the second meal), *aśma-kuṭṭas* (eating uncooked corn after breaking it on stone), *dantolūkhalins* (employing teeth as their pestle), *marīcipās* (living on the rays of the sun or the moon), *ākāśa-nilayas* (living in the open air and not in a hut or cave), *sthaṇḍila śāyins* (passing the night on bare ground), *udavasanas* (always standing in water), *avastra-dhārins* (nudes), *pañca-tapās* (concentrating on the sun in summer being surrounded by four burning fires), *caturmāsa-kṛitāhāras* (taking food only once in four months), *nirāhāras* (taking no food), *vṛikshāsaktāgrapādas* (suspended on tress with heads turned down wards), *ekāṅgushṭhāgrasthitas* (standing on the thumb of one foot), *śashpa-bhakshas* (living on grass), *aśayyas* (ever awake), and *ārdra-paṭavāsas* (always wearing wet garments).[4] In these very enumerations occur the *Pṛiśṇis*, the *Bālakhilyas* and *Vaikhānasas*.[5]

The most important engagement of the ascetic was *svādhyāya*.[6]

1. R. I 39/14; R. II 31/23; R. VII 9/4.
2. R. I 39/14; R. II 31/23; R. VII 9/4. The *vīrāsana* is described as,
Ekam pādamathaikasmin vinyasyorau tu saṃsthitaḥ,
Itarasmiṃstathaivoruṃ Vīrāsanamudāhṛitam.
(Vide Mallinātha on Raghuvaṃśa XIII 52).
3. R. II 31/17.
4. R. I 47/25-26; R. III 7/2-8.
5. The *Pṛiśṇis* is the name of an ancient family of *ṛishis*, one of the seers in Ṛigveda, IX 86. The *Bālakhilyas* seem to be urchins initiated in the ascetic practices at a very early age. The *Vaikhānasa* class appears to be a remnant of ascetics of the earliest period who lived upto the ideals laid down in the Vaikhānasa Śāstra.

For details vide Kane, P. V., History of Dharma-śāstra, Vol. II, part II, p. 917.

6. R. I 1/1; R. I 8/33; R. VII 1/57.

Vālmīki has not thrown much light on this aspect of ascetic's life, but it is clear from various terms like *dharma-kovidaḥ*, *dṛishṭa-parāvaraḥ* and *brahmavādinaḥ*[1] that reading and recitation of the sacred texts along with reflecting and profoundly meditating over their sense was a part of his daily programme. This is corroborated also by the fact that the task of imparting education to the new generation was also in the main, the business of the ascetic.[2]

By subjecting himself to such privations and mortifications did the ascetic achieve anything apart from the mythical gains of heaven and the like ? For the modern enquirer's benefit, especially, we shall attempt to draw below a sketch of the ascetic's personality leaving it to him to judge whether such a life was worth its while or not.

The life of the ascetic was simple and his needs elementary. He wore matted hair on the head,[3] long and thick beard and moustaches on the face,[4] a *yajñopavīta* (*brahmasūtra*) across his left shoulder,[5] a pair of bark garments (or skin of an antelope and even leaves) over his body[6] and a pair of sandals on his feet.[7] Usually he also carried in his hand a staff and a *kamaṇḍalu.*[8] The more advanced in age had wrinkles on their face and their hair were silvery.[9] The observance of severe vows and disciplines, which his order entailed, emaciated the body of the ascetic but at the same time it added loveliness and lustre to his personality. Thus, on the one hand, his appearance inspired confidence even in the hearts of birds and beasts of the forest,[10] and on the other, became overbearing to the evil minded like burning fire of the summer sun.[11]

1. R. III 4/15; R. III 12/14 and R. I 21/16 respectively.
2. Vide pp. 31 and 119 supra.
3. R. III 8/5.
4. R. II 31/20.
5. The *yajñopavīta* is not specifically mentioned in the Rāmāyaṇa with reference to an ascetic. However, *upanayana* was in vogue in that society is proved by various indirect references in the epic. (Vide p. 27 supra).
6. R. II 31/20.
7. R. II 126/1.
8. R. III 46/3 N. S.
9. R. III 1/50.
10. R. II 58/13; R. IV 52/15.
11. R. I 44/25; R. III 7/4.

Restraint was the password of the ascetic order. All efforts of the ascetic were directed towards the complete subduing of passions and rising above the appetites, specially of sex. *Akrodhana* (i. e. without anger), *niyatendriya*, *jitendriya* or *dānta* (i. e. with senses under control) and *jitamaithuna* or *ūrdhva-retas*[1] (i.e. one who has conquered the appetite of sex and lives in perpetual celibacy) are epithets which are commonly applicable to all ascetics. Though himself living a life of poverty the ascetic was of liberal disposition. He received his guest warmly and generously. In fact, he endeavoured to treat everyone (including the birds, beasts and plants of the forest) with love and kindness. *Bhūtāvihiṃsaka* (i.e. causing no injury to creatures) and its positive form *sarva-bhūtahite rataḥ* (i.e. devoted to the good of all creatures) are of invariable association with the ascetic.[2] By penance the ascetic shook off all his sins[3] and with his soul thus rendered pure, he realised within himself the identity of his individual self with the universal self.[4]

1. R. III 1/45; R.I 47/25; R. III 1/8; R. III 4/20; R. III 9/7; R. I 39/14; R. I 30/36 respectively.

It may be noted that *kāma* and *krodha* were the worst infirmities of the noble ascetic mind. The gods quite often created conditions for the ascetics under which they fell a prey to these weaknesses. Thus there are outstanding cases of Viśvāmitra (R. I cantos 59-60) and Madakarṇi (R. III 12/13) who were way-laid by the gods by rousing in them *kāma*. The cases in which, being moved by the onrush of anger a sage pronounced curse are numerous. Thus Gautama (R. I 44/25-29), Viśvāmitra (R. I 60/14), the father of Yajñadatta (R. II 70/54), Sthūlaśirā (R. III 78/4), Vedavatī (R. VII 16/25), Nalakūbara (R. VII 32/46-51), Vasishṭha (R. VII 56/18) and Śukra (R. VII 83/7-10) are seen indulging in this practice. However, the true spirit of the ascetic is evinced in the appeal of the sages of Daṇḍakāraṇya in which they said, "We have been immensely harassed in the forest by the Rākshasas.......Do thou deliver us.......... We can by virtue of the energy of our asceticism easily destroy the Rākshasas, but we are loath to lose our asceticism earned in a long time" (R. III 11/12-15).

It may also be noted that the ideal of *jita-maithuna* was not strictly observed by the ascetics, for there are a number of cases of ascetics who departed from this rule when they were approached by young maidens (R. I 30/36ff.; R. VII 1/54; R. VII 8/18). In their defence, however, it can be said that they were not prompted by the desire of satisfying their lust.

2. R. III 4/14; R. III 7/7; R. III 15/17; R. V 81/16.

3. R. I 21/16.

4. R. III 7/19.

No doubt, the ascetic, when he repaired to the forest, renounced the world with its pleasures and pursuits. But it will be wrong to say that he was completely cut off from the town and its people or that he became totally indifferent to the affairs of the society. His *āśrama*, as already indicated before, was a centre of great literary activity and it was he, who prepared the coming generation for its undertakings in future life. Moreover, the rules of conduct and the ideals of morality which inspired the king and the clown alike in their behaviour emerged from the hermitages of these *ṛishis*.

Since the *āśramas* were generally situated not very far from the towns, communication between the towns and the *āśramas* was neither difficult nor very rare. The sages used to be invariably present at the big sacrifices performed by kings.[1] They also approached him in the hour of their need.[2] It is noteworthy, that the king always considered the visit of a sage to the royal court a matter of great pleasure and honour for himself. The king Daśaratha hailed the visit of Viśvāmitra to his court saying, "Like unto the obtaining of ambrosia, like unto a shower in a land suffering from drought, like unto the birth of sons of worthy wives to one without issue, like unto the acquisition of a desired object and the return of a dear one, like unto the recovery of a lost thing, yea—like unto the dawning of a mighty joy, I consider this thy arrival."[3] When a great repository of penance (*tapodhana*) announced himself at the royal gate, the king rushed with the *mantrins* and *upādhyāya* (or *purohita*) to receive him with due honours.[4] Not only that, the king also made arrangements for the reception of a sage when the latter passed through his territory.[5] As far as possible the

1. R. I 9/42; R. I 10/8; R. I 29/6-7; R. VII 93/19-21; R. VII 95/1.
2. Viśvāmitra approached Daśaratha—R. I 17/3.
   Pulastya went to Māhishmatī to effect his grand-son's release—R. VII 21/16.
   Cyavana and others approached Rāma to request him to do away with the notorious Lavaṇa—R. VII 64/1 ff.
   Durvāsā approached Rāma for food—R. VII 107/13-15.
3. R. I 16/23-25.
4. R. I 16/14-16; R. I 46/6; R. VII 21/6-9.
5. R. I 13/11-14.

king himself came out to offer *pādya* and *arghya* to the sage.[1] The king also visited the *āśramas* in the course of his routine tours or expeditions.[2] On such occasions he took every care not to cause obstruction to the activities of the *āśrama*.[3] The king considered it to be his extreme good fortune, if he succeeded in winning the sympathy of a renowned sage.[4]

The relationship between the kings and the sages was intimate. Since the king was the political head of the state, the ultimate responsibility of providing proper and adequate conditions for the carrying out of the righteous pursuits of the sages lay upon him.[5] Thus on meeting the sages he enquired about the welfare of their person, the *agnihotra*, the *tapas* and the disciples, about birds and beasts, and trees and creepers.[6] The sages on their part were the guardians and promoters of culture and as such they were deeply interested in the peace and progress of the state. Since this depended primarily on the soundness of the government machinery they made anxious enquiries with regard to the welfare of the king's person (body) and family, the treasury and the allies, and the capital and the country with all their people. The sages also enquired whether the officials were paid well and whether they abided by the discipline determined by the king in this regard, whether the king had suppressed his enemies, or whether he did not falter in the discharge of his duty viz., of governing his people according to law.[7] Moreover, if we accept Shri Satavalekar's interpretation of the Rāmāyaṇa it will appear that in the Rāmāyaṇic age the interest of the sages in the affairs of the country was not casual but continuous.[8] The period of the Rāmāyaṇa respresents the heyday of the *āśramas*, which were spread in a continuous chain along the banks of rivers (or lakes) from North to South. The *āśramas* of Vālmīki, Vasishṭha, Viśvāmitra, Gautama, Bharadvāja, Atri, Śarabhaṅga, Sutīkshṇa,

1. R. I 43/22.
2. R. I 47/22; R. II 102/24; R. VII 74/13.
3. R. II 104/6-8.
4. R. I 48/18; R. II 59/10.
5. R. III 4/19-20.
6. R. I 48/5; R. II 103/11; R. III 80/10-12.
7. R. I 48/7-10; R. II 103/10.
8. For Shri Satavalekar's view on the story of the Rāmāyaṇa see appendix to this chapter.

Agastya and Mataṅga were important centres of religious activities. Hundreds of ascetics who had become indifferent to mundane pleasure and wealth, led here a life of purity and self- restraint. These *āśramas* were generally situated at some distance from the towns. A *ṛishi* usually selected a pleasant site in the interior of a forest for building his *āśrama*. He took special care to see that the site was fit for healthy living, being free from gnats and gadflies[1] and that it was rich in the supply of his daily requirements.[2] Thus Rāma on reaching Pañcavaṭī, directed Lakshmaṇa to raise a cottage for their living on a spot where the forest presented a charming spectacle, where water was healthy and fuel, flowers and *kuśa* were easily available.[3]

The heart of an ascetic was an ever-flowing fountain of love for the entire creation and the stamp of his kindliness could, naturally, be perceived on the trees, birds and beasts of the *āśrama*. Rāma could easily recognise the vicinity of Agastya's *āśrama* from the fact that the leaves of the trees were glossy and the deer were lovely.[4] The appearance of a rising cloud of (sacrificial) smoke, a long line of trees laden with fruits and flowers, heaps of fire-sticks, grounds from which *darbhas* were plucked, the offerings of flowers lying in the solitary corners of the river-banks[5] and the barks suspended on the branches of the trees to serve as way marks[6], were the sure signs of the presence of an *āśrama* nearby. In the description of the *āśramas* in the Rāmāyaṇa the cow is conspicuous by its absence.[7] She fares only in the *āśrama* of Vasishṭha, but there she appears in all her glory.[8]

The presence of the meritorious sage infused the whole atmosphere with such serenity and holiness that even the beasts of prey, renouncing their malignant nature behaved like pets. Thus the bears, *sṛimaras*, tigers, lions, elephants and reptiles

1. R. III 8/18.
2. R. III 18/3.
3. R. III 20/4-5.
4. R. III 15/8.
5. R. III 14/5-9.
6. R. II 113/9.
7. May be, this indicates the paucity of cows in the South even in the days of Vālmīki.
8. R. I 48/39-41.

followed the sage Niśākara as babies do their mother.[1] And such was the influence of Agastya that a liar, or a sinner, or a crafty person, or a wicked wight, or one who was licentious could not live in his *āśrama*.[2] Sometimes, with the association of a great repository of penance the place itself acquired such merit that it remained ever green, was delightful with fragrant breezes[3] and became competent to bless people with the fulfilment of their desires.[4]

The fear of the Rākshasas, perhaps, compelled the ascetics to live in large groups. The words *muni-saṅgha*, *ṛishi-saṅgha* and *gaṇa*[5] are of frequent occurrence in relation to the ascetics. The place of their dwelling was known as *āśrama-maṇḍala*.[6] It was a big locality consisting of several *tāpasālayas* or *āśramas*.[7] The outer portion of the *āśrama* was known as *uṭaja*[8] while the chambers meant for dwelling in it were known as *parṇaśālās*.[9] Attached to every *āśrama* was an *agni-śālā* or *agni-śaraṇa*[10] in which were established a *vedī* (an altar), and perhaps sanctuaries for different deities.[11] It was in the *agni-śālā* that the sage performed his daily *agnihotra* and delivered religious discourses.[12] The whole structure of the *āśrama* was raised on walls of wood and clay, and pillars of bamboos with coverings of branches of trees, reeds, leaves and grass tightly fastened with strong cords.[13] Before entering the newly erected hut a ceremony, *vāstu-śamana*, was performed.[14]

The paraphernalia of the *parṇa-śālā* was simple. It consisted mostly of those articles that were of use for the ascetic in his daily life. Thus there were cushions (*bṛisī*), seats of

1. R. IV 52/15.
2. R. III 15/20.
3. R. IV 52/12.
4. R. III 15/23.
5. R. III 7/1; R. III 8/17; R. III 1/27 respectively.
6. R. III 4/1.
7. R. III 13/1-6.
8. R. II 113/24.
9. R. II 60/21.
10. R. II 104/10; R. III 16/5.
11. R. III 16/17-18.
12. R. II 58/12-13.
13. R. III 15/21-22 N. S.
14. For *vāstu-śamana* vide chapter VIII infra.

kuśa grass, spade (*khanitra*), basket (piṭaka), ladle (*sruk*), jars (*kalaśa*) and other necessary utensils for the performance of a sacrifice (*yajña-bhāṇḍa*), bark garments, deer-skin, the holy thread (*yajña-sūtra*), *kamaṇḍalu*, a *mauñja* girdle, *kaupīna*, axe, thread for tying the matted locks, a twine for binding faggots with, an umbrella, a pair of sandals and a staff.[1] Sometimes *ṛishis* (or their wives) are said to possess ornaments, costly apparels and cosmetics. These, it seems were received by them as presents and were preserved only for giving as presents to the people of the town, who occasionally visited them.[2]

The head of an *āśrama*, more correctly of an *āśrama-maṇḍala*, was a *kulapati* or a *kulapa*.[3] He was a man advanced both in age and penance.[4] It was under his guidance that other ascetics of the *āśrama-maṇḍala* made efforts for their spiritual uplift. It was his primary concern to see that the whole atmosphere of the *maṇḍala* remained congenial for the pursuit of ascetic practices and that the inmates of the *āśrama-maṇḍala* maintained inward and outward purity. It was his responsibility also to protect the inmates of the *āśrama* and at times when living became perilous at a particular place, he moved with his followers to a new place.[5]

Mention may be made, at this place, of a practice prevailing among the ascetics of the Rāmāyaṇic period, viz., of ending their lives by wilfully entering into the flames.[6] Generally speaking, suicide was condemned. The *śrutis* despatch the slayers of the self to regions that were enshrouded in blind darkness.[7] But suicide was looked upon with contempt only when people resorted to it on suffering a shipwreck in their life. The cases of Śarabhaṅga and Śabarī are to be distinguished from general cases of suicide, because they consigned their bodies to the flames only when no desire was left in them for the pleasures of any of the senses.[8]

The inmates of the *āśrama* were principally the *Vānaprasthas*

1. For references see—R I 4/20-25 N.S.; R. II 20/28 N. S.; R. II 40/5; R. III 1/22, 24; R. III 46/3 N. S.
2. R. III 1/78; R. VII 79/12.
3. R. III 1/4, 31.
4. R. III 1/8.
5. R. III 1/25, 31.
6. R. III 6/31; R. III 80/33.
7. Vājasaneyī Saṃhitā 40/3.
8. Vide *Mahā-prasthāna* in Kane, P. V., History of Dharmaśāstra, Vol. II, part II, pp. 924-927.

and their *brahma-cārī* disciples. In some cases, the wives of the ascetics also lived with them. These women had also renounced the world with its wealth and pleasures and along with their husbands they were also engaged in ascetic practices.[1] One interesting thing mentioned in the Rāmāyaṇa is the presence of a separate and independent *āśrama* of female ascetics which was situated close to the *āśrama* of Vālmīki.[2] The fact that like men women too were free to adopt the ascetic's life is proved beyond doubt, by the instances of Anasūyā, Śabarī, Svayamprabhā and Vedavatī. Of these, the cases of Śabarī and Svayamprabhā are of special interest because they correspond to the *brahmavādinīs* of later times.

1. Vide Anasūyā with Atri (R. III cantos 1-3.)
2. For details about the *brahmavādinīs* vide Kane, P. V., History of Dharma-śāstra, Vol. II, part I, pp. 293-296.

APPENDIX TO CHAPTER VII

(A brief summary of Shripada Damodar Satavalekar's comments on the role of the *Devas* and the *Ṛishis* in the Rāmāyaṇa)

According to Shripada Damodar Satavalekar these sages were not engaged in meditation only; their life was imbued with politics guided by philosophy.[1] The truth of this statement cannot be fully grasped without being acquainted with the background of the Rāma story as understood by Shri Satavalekar after his profound study of the Rāmāyaṇa. According to him, the Rāmāyaṇa is a poetic record of a vehement struggle for supremacy which was going on between the *Devas* and the Aryans on the one side and the Rākshasas on the other. In the beginning, we find that the Rākshasas, after suffering a great reversal in the past, were emerging once again as a strong power under the leadership of Rāvaṇa and his brothers.[2] With their seat in the strong-hold of Laṅkā they were proclaiming their supremacy in various directions. Rāvaṇa had consolidated his position by entering into an *ahiṃsaka* alliance with Bālī, the leader of another big power of those times, viz., the Vānaras. The Rākshasas were from the beginning inimical to Aryan life and ideals and they particularly spurned the sages and their practices. The same was their attitude towards the *Devas*; rather it was more hostile in their case because the *Devas* always favoured the Aryans in general and the sages in particular.[3] Rāvaṇa had established a strong outpost at Janasthāna under the command of Khara through whom he carried out the malicious design of harassing the sages.[4] The story of Rāma's personal life is principally the success of a campaign directed against the malignant Rākshasas by the *Devas* in conjunction with the *Ṛishis*.[5]

1. Rāmāyaṇa Mahākāvya, Araṇya-Kāṇḍa, p. 356.
For details vide his introductions to the Ayodhyā--Kāṇḍa and the Araṇya-Kāṇḍa.
2. R. VII 10/1 ff.
3. R. I 10/61-63.
4. R. III 39/44-46.
5. Note the message of Kubera sent through his messenger to Rāvaṇa. : (next page)

The first step towards carrying out this plan was to take out Rāma from a life of ease and comfort that he was passing in the palace of Ayodhyā.[1] The words of Viśvāmitra spoken to Daśaratha on this occasion were extremely significant. He said, "I will confer upon him (Rāma) manifold blessings, by means of which he will secure the good of the three worlds. ....I know full well the lotus-eyed Rāma,—as also the highly energetic Vasishṭha and all others that are stationed in asceticism."[2] By making Rāma wander through the woods and by making him chastise the wicked Tāṭakā, Mārīca, Subāhu and others Viśvāmitra made his muscles hard and his spirit dauntless. By transferring to him the secret of all the wonderful missiles that he possessed, the sage helped the young prince to develop into the most formidable hero of his time.[3] The sages (and the *Devas*) did not disclose their plan to any-

Tadadharmishṭhasaṃyogād vinivartasva kilvishāt.
Cintyate hi vadhopāyaḥ sarshisaṅghaiḥ suraistava. (R. VII 12/32)

1. R. I 20/4.
2. *Śreyaścāsmai vidhāsyāmi bahurūpamamatsaraḥ.*
Trayāṇāmapi lokānāṃ yena kāmo bhavishyati.
Ahaṃ vedmi mahātmānaṃ Rāmaṃ rājīvalocanam.
Vasishṭhaśca mahātejā ye cānye tapasi sthitāḥ. R. I 17/11-12, 15-16.

To illustrate the soundness of the statement *ye cānye tapasi sthitāḥ* in the verse above, we note below the statements of various characters of the Rāmāyaṇa which smack of a fore-knowledge of the plan being pursued.

Bharadvāja : *Rāmapravrājanaṃ hyetat sukhodarkambhavishyati.* R. II 105/32.
Devas : *Bho bho Bharata siddhārtha nivartasva svato laghu.*
Devakāryamaśesheṇa kartavyaṃ Rāghaveṇa vai. R. II 125/4.
Tumburu : *Adhyardha yojane tāta maharshiḥ sūryasannibhaḥ.*
Ito vasati dharmātmā Śarabhaṅgaḥ pratāpavān.
Taṃ śīghram abhigaccha tvaṃ sa te śreyo (a) bhidhāsyati. R.III 5/46-47
Śabarī : *Citrakūṭaṃ tvayi prāpte vimānairatulaprabhaiḥ.*
Munayo divamārūḍhāḥ ye mayābhyarcitā purā.
Taiścāhamuktā dharmajñairmahābhāgair mahātmabhiḥ.
Āgamishyati Kākutsthaḥ supuṇyam imam āśramam. R. III 80/15-16
Sampāti : *Eshyantyanveshakāstasya mahādūtāḥ plavaṅgamāḥ.*
Ākhyeyā Rāmamahishī tebhyaste Janakātmajā.
Sarvathā ceha tishṭha tvamīdṛiśaḥ kva gamishyasi.
Etaṅkālam pratīkshasva lapsyase tvaṃ tanūruhau. R. IV 54/12-13.

3. Cf. *Mune Kauśika bhadrante sendrāḥ suragaṇāstvayā.*
Toshitā karmaṇānena Rāmasyāmitatejasaḥ.
Asmanniyogāt bhadrante snehandarśaya Rāghave.
Tapoyogabalenainamāpyāyitumarhasi.
Pātrabhūto hi te śishyo Rāmo Daśarathātmajaḥ.
Kartavyañca mahatkāryamasmākaṃ rājasūnunā. R. I 24/18, 19, 21.

one lest it should prove abortive.[1] So much so, that even Rāma was made acquainted with it only when the hostility between Rāma and Rāvaṇa had become almost an insoluble fact with the deformation of Śūrpaṇakhā and the mass massacre of the 14,000 Rākshasas in Pañcavaṭī along with their leader, Khara. The *Rājarshis* and the *Parmarshis* (including Agastya)[2] confessed that it was in compliance with a strategy that he (Rāma) was brought by the great sages (*Maharshis*) to that place, specifically for the destruction of those foes—the wicked Rākshasas.

1. Cf. *Yāmaḥ śīghrataraṃ Rāmo yāvanmāṃ nābhibhāshate.*
   Kṛitārthamenaṃ dhvastāriṃ drakshyāmi nacirādiva. R. III 6/17.
2. *Tato Rājarshayaḥ sarve saṅgatāḥ Paramarshayaḥ.*
   Sabhājya muditā Rāmaṃ sāgastyā idamabruvan.
   Etadartham mahātejā Mahendraḥ Pākaśāsanaḥ.
   Śarabhaṅgāśramam puṇyam ājagāma Purandaraḥ.
   Ānītastvamimaṃ deśam upāyena maharshibhiḥ.
   Eshām vadhārthaṃ śatrūṇāṃ Rakshasām pāpakarmaṇām.
   R. III 35/42-43.

It is to be noted that in the verse above the word *upāyena* shall convey no meaning if what Shri Satavalekar says in this connection is not accepted. A similar difficulty will be envisaged in understanding the meanings of the words *kṛitaṁ kāryam* in the verse :

Drishṭvā Sītām parāmṛishṭāṃ devo divyena cakshushā.
Kṛitaṅ kāryamiti śrīmān vyājahāra Pitāmahaḥ. R. III 58/10-11.

CHAPTER VIII

MORALITY AND RELIGION

Chronologically speaking the rise of the epics comes in Sanskrit literature at the close of the Vedic period. Between the Saṃhitās and the Sūtras elapsed a long period which witnessed effective changes in the various departments of life of the people. Summing up the religious changes in the first three stages of this period Dr. E. W. Hopkins writes : "In the Vedic hymns man fears the gods, and imagines God. In the Brāhmaṇas man subdues the gods, and fears God. In the Upanishads man ignores the gods, and becomes God."[1] The Sūtras present a harmonised form of the various currents of religious activity of the preceding stages. Here one finds that the division of *varṇas* and the scheme of *āśramas* is fully established and that the rules of conduct laid down for a person belonging to a particular *varṇa* or *āśrama* have been accorded a religious sanctity; some of the rituals of the Brāhmaṇa period have been made a part of man's daily life and many others are recommended to be performed on certain special occasions, for example on the *amāvasyā* and the *paurṇamāsī*, royal inauguration and the like; the *ātmā* philosophy and religion are held in esteem but a person is advised to devote himself to the pursuit of the knowledge of *ātmā* on becoming an ascetic.[2] This religion of the Sūtras was the direct bequest that the epic age received from the Vedic period. Around this nucleus, however, is found gathered an abundant mass of heterogeneous character; for in the cultural march of ancient India this was a period when Brahmanism, in the interest of self preservation, was unconsciously assimilating the beliefs and religious practices of alien communities that had newly entered the Aryan fold.[3] The Brāhmaṇa, while he continued to take pride in the ancient religious beliefs and practices, also tried to allegorise the myth and symbol, the fable and legend, in which the new tribes

1. History of Religions, p. 216.
2. Ibid., p. 265.
3. Radhakrishnan, S., The Hindu View of Life, pp. 39-40.

delighted.[1] These facts coupled with the problem of interpolations which are the largest in this field in the Rāmāyaṇa render the present study a very difficult task.

The difficulty is further aggravated by the fact that the word *dharma* which is popularly held as a synonym of religion answers to no definite connotation. "Unlike the word religion it can be used in various senses according to the context. Thus it may mean law, justice, morality, custom, duty, established order, virtue, and so on."[2] In the Rāmāyaṇa also the use of this word in various meanings is very common. In passages like the *nānyo dharmaḥ kshatriyāṇāṃ rakshaṇāt tāta ishyate*[3] and *imāṃ dharmadhuraṃ gurvīm ahaṃ vakshyāmi Lakshmaṇa*[4] it stands for the duties of a particular *varṇa* and a particular *āśrama* respectively; in *dvau eva kathitau sadbhiḥ panthanau vadatāṃ vara, ahiṃsā caiva satyañ ca yatra dharmaḥ pratishṭhitaḥ*[5] it is a synonym of righteousness and moral excellences; in *upadishṭaṃ susūkshmārthaṃ śāstraṃ tattvena dhīmatā, sa nāśayatu tad dharmaṃ yasyāryo (a) numate gataḥ*[6] it connotes all rites and ceremonies that are ordained by the scriptures; and in *yat kṛitvā na bhaved dharmo na kīrtiḥ na yaśo bhuvi, śarīrato bhavet karma katham prājñas tad ācaret*[7] it signifies the merit acquired by the performance of religious rites.

From a careful consideration of these passages, however, it can be concluded that Vālmīki's conception of *dharma* comprises two elements, namely, the general (*sādhāraṇa*) and

1. Radhakrishnan, S., Indian Philosophy, Vol. I, p. 477.
2. Deshmukh, P. S., The Origin and Development of Religion in Vedic Literature, pp. 20-21.
3. R. I 19/9.
4. R. II 24/12.
5. R. II 65/18.
6. R. II 83/12.
7. R. III 55/19.

Note : In passages like *Vyavahāreshu te dharmaḥ kartavyo hṛidi nityaśaḥ* (R. I 12/21) and *Śāśvato (a)yaṃ sadā dharmaḥ sthito (a)smākaṃ nararshabha, jyeshṭhe tvayi sthite rājan na kanīyān bhaven nṛipaḥ* (R. II 116/2) the word *dharma* stands in the Rāmāyaṇa also in the sense of law, both statutory and customary. We have not mentioned this use of the word *dharma* separately, above, for, broadly speaking in the Hindu Dharma-śāstra, this sense is covered under the comprehensive term 'duty'.

the particular (*viśesha*). His conception of general *dharma* embodies the entire set of ethical virtues, such as truth, benevolence, compassion and the like, which are manifestations of a refined spirit and without which no spiritual development is conceivable.[1] In Dharma-śāstras these are known as *sāmānya* (or *sādhāraṇa*)—*dharmas* being applicable to entire humanity, irrespective of distinctions of caste, colour and creed.[2] The second element of *dharma* is concerned with the various rules of outward conduct which have been framed primarily keeping in view the *varṇa* and *āśrama* schemes.[3] As distinguished from the *sādhāraṇa-dharma*, *dharma* in the latter sense varies from man to man (*adhikārī-bheda*)[4], place to place (*deśa-bheda*)[5] and from time to time (*kāla-bheda*).[6] A broad idea of these variations has already been given in the chapter on "the *varṇas* and the *āśramas*". In the present chapter we shall first present an account of the Rāmāyaṇa ethics (*sādhāraṇa-dharma*) and then pass on to the consideration of the various religious ceremonies and observances that were in vogue in the Rāmāyaṇic society. These latter will be treated under two separate heads—the first comprising those rites and rituals which bear a direct link to the Vedic tradition as found in the early Kalpa-sūtras, and

1. Cf. *Nāvirato duścaritān nāśānto nāsamāhitaḥ,*
Nāśāntamānaso vāpi prajñānenainamāpnuyāt.
Kaṭhopanishad, I 2/24.

2. Kane, P. V., History of Dharma-śāstra, Vol. II, part I, pp. 3 ff.

3. Cf. : "It will be noticed from the above that all matters (except *sādhāraṇa* or *sāmānya dharma*) have *varṇa* and *āśrama* as the pivots round which the whole of Dharmaśāstra revolves." Ibid. p. 3.

4. Vide, for instance the the case of Śambūka in the Uttara-Kāṇḍa, who on account of being a *śūdra* was not an *adhikārī* for *tapas*. When he tried to transgress the limitations of his own *varṇa* it resulted in a chaos in the society (in the form of untimely death) and the king had to chastise him. (R. VII cantos 77-78)

5. *Kva ca śastraṅ kva ca vanaṅ kva ca kshatraṃ tapaḥ kva ca,*
Vyāviddhamidamasmābhir deśadharmastu pūjyatām.
R. III 9/27 N. S.

N. B. The verse occurs in the N. W. also (III 10/22). But there the reading in the last quarter is *esha dharmastu pūjyatām*. Looking to the context the reading in the N. S. appears to be more appropriate.

6. *Pūrvarājarshivṛittena vanavāso vidhīyate,*
Putreshvante vinikshipya rājyaṃ vayasi paścime. R. II 23/29.

the second consisting of such practices as were originally non-Aryan in character but, as indicated above, had been adopted with certain modifications by the Aryan society as well.

Ethics is the very essence of religion and the study of this subject in the Rāmāyaṇa is of special interest, for a moral ideal is at the very root of the composition of this *kāvya*.[1] Along with Rāma who "typifies the spirit of good"[2] several other characters of the Rāmāyaṇa are cherished by the Hindus as the embodiments of distinct moral virtues. Thus Daśaratha stands as an ideal of paternal affection, Lakshmaṇa and Bharata of fraternal love, Sītā of "purity, chastity and wifely fidelity",[3] Sugrīva of friendship and Hanūmān of devotion and service to the master. The sage Aurobindo is so much impressed by the morality that breathes in the Rāmāyaṇa that according to him, "The Rāmāyaṇa gives us the picture of an entirely moralised civilisation, containing indeed vast material development and immense intellectual power, but both moralised and subordinated to the needs of purity of temperament and delicate ideality of action."[4]

It may not be out of place to point out here that of the three objects of human pursuit,[5] namely *dharma* (righteous conduct), *artha* (acquirement of wealth) and *kāma* (gratification of desire) Vālmīki attaches highest importance to *dharma*. The Rāmāyaṇa refers also to people whose vision is limited to what they can see only through their senses and who are, therefore, impatient to derive immediate satisfaction. They are votaries of *kāma* and *artha* and deny any place to *dharma*, arguing that it was unreal, for it was not perceptible.[6] Vālmīki is unsparing in his condemnation of these people. He criticises through Lakshmaṇa, Kauśalyā and Bharata the behaviour of

1. Cf. "The Rāmāyaṇa is the bedrock of Hindu morality". Khan, B., The Concept of Dharma in Vālmīki Rāmāyaṇa, p. 6.
2. Dutt, M. N., The Rāmāyaṇa, Eng. tr., Introduction, p. i.
3. Dutt, M. N., The Rāmāyaṇa, Eng. tr., Introduction, p. iv.
4. Kālidāsa, pp., 6-7.
5. The Rāmāyaṇa speaks only of the *trivarga*; the word *caturvarga* is conspicuous by its absence in the Rāmāyaṇa. The word *moksha* no doubt, appears in the Rāmāyaṇa, but as will be shown in a subsequent chapter its conception is more or less alien to the Rāmāyaṇa.
6. R. VI 61/16.

Daśaratha who fell a prey to the unreasonable demands of his beloved wife, Kaikeyī.[1] Even Rāma is made to remark that one who like Daśaratha followed *kāma* to the sacrifice of *dharma* and *artha* was confronted with great difficulties.[2] Equally disparaging are the poet's remarks for Kaikeyī who, for the sake of *artha* (kingdom) became indifferent to *dharma*[3] (for she disregarded the lawful claim of Rāma to the throne and also her duty to her husband).

Though aware of the fact that the course of *dharma* entails severe hardships, the poet very strongly recommends its pursuit on the ground that even if *artha* and *kāma* brought immediate gratification of the senses, it was through *dharma* that men derived mental peace and a sort of spiritual joy.[4] *Dharma*, according to Vālmīki, was the quint-essence of life; it was the spring of wealth and happiness; and it was through *dharma*, again, that one attained heaven.[5] *Dharma* in this sense included moral excellences like truth, charity, benevolence, mercy, modesty, continence, abstinence from anger and injury to life—sterling qualities to be cherished by all humanity irrespective of the distinctions of class, colour or creed—and was to be distinguished from that *dharma* which became applicable to certain persons in well defined circumstances.

Of all the virtues counted under *sāmānya-dharma* again, *satya* was held to be of paramount importance in the period of the Rāmāyaṇa. In fact, glorification of *satya* knows no bounds in Vālmīki's epic. His hero, the most rigid adherent of *satya* declares that the divine *Dharma* was grounded in its entirety in *satya*.[6] He even extols *satya* as the very source of creation.[7] Elsewhere it is remarked that *satya* was the supreme *dharma*[8] and that in the three worlds there was nothing superior to *satya*.[9] It is significant also to note that in an age in which various sacrifices and penances were so popular Vālmīki has recognised that *satya* excelled (in merit) ten thousand *Aśvamedhas*;[10] that

1. R. II 81/5; R. II 25/9; R. II 23/15, 18; R. II 65/3 ff.
2. R. II 57/14-15.
3. R. II 45/7.
4. R. V 89/13-14.
5. R. III 10/25.
6. R. II 65/15.
7. R. II 65/12-15.
8. R. II 15/3.
9. R. II 65/11.
10. R. II 65/10.

the (celestial) regions that the veracious could attain through the pursuit of *satya* could not be attained by the untruthful even by performing hundred sacrifices[1]; and that *satya* was the essence of penance.[2]

It is, however, painful to observe that inspite of all the praise showered upon *satya* by the poet a reader of the Rāmāyaṇa does not become convinced that Vālmīki's age had a right conception of truth; and this is borne out both by the express statements of the characters in the Rāmāyaṇa and their behaviour. Vasishṭha, for instance, said to Daśaratha when he was unwilling to send Rāma with Viśvāmitra : "Having promised that you would, O king, if you did not act upto your word you would lose all the merit you have earned by *ishṭāpūrta* (i.e. by acts of personal piety and those done for the benefit of others)."[3] The considered opinion of the *brāhmaṇa* counsellors of Rāma's court similarly was that *dharma* would be destroyed if a promise was not fulfilled.[4] Rāma himself considered that person most wretched who did not fulfil whatever he uttered, whether it was good or bad.[5] He was gladly prepared to renounce his life or Sītā along with Lakshmaṇa but not the promise made to the *brāhmaṇas.*[6] *Hīna-pratijña* (fallen from the promise) was such a serious term of reproach in the Aryan sections of the Rāmāyaṇa society[7] that one could sacrifice all that was dear to him in life,—nay life itself, but could not be willing to court that unworthy term. Daśaratha having failed to dissuade Kaikeyī from her demand, in his great fury and despair threatened to disown Kaikeyī and her son, and even went to the extent of suggesting to Rāma that he should put him in prison and take over the administration by force, but not once did he think of breaking his promise to Kaikeyī. Rāma himself remained indifferent to the entreaties of his mother, the convincing arguments of Lakshmaṇa, the commands of his preceptor, and the strongest appeals of Bharata and did not budge an inch from the words he had given to his father (and Kaikeyī) that relinquishing the kingdom in favour of Bharata he would live in the forest

1. R. II 65/16.
2. R. VII 78/17.
3. R. I 19/10.
4. R. VII 108/10.
5. R. IV 23/29.
6. R. III 11/20.
7. Cf. *Hīnapratijñaḥ Kākutstha...sukhī bhava*...R. I 19/3.

for a period of fourteen years.[1] Rāma's fondness for the fulfilment of his promise was so great that he could even be prompted to commit an unrighteous act like the killing of a non-hostile person (or persons) provided he had earlier promised to do so.[2]

The legendary evidence in the Rāmāyaṇa also confirms the above view. To the request of the gods, who were entreating Viśvāmitra in the name of eternally established order not to press Triśaṅku's entry into heaven with his human body and not to create separate *Lokas* with new sets of gods for him the sage only partly agreed; and on the express condition that what he had till then created would be allowed to stay. He was not prepared to allow his promise (to Triśaṅku) to become false.[3] The fear of the promise made (in bygone ages) to Kaśyapa becoming false transformed the erstwhile haughty and conceited Paraśurāma into a meek suppliant[4] and likewise, the great god Pitāmaha, was made to rush to Yama to request him not to employ his *daṇḍa* (club) against Rāvaṇa for, if the *daṇḍa* became futile his (i.e. of Pitāmaha) words to Yama would be broken and if, on the other hand, Rāvaṇa were to be dead in consequence of its blow he would still be a liar.[5]

Another constituent of *sāmānya-dharma*, hospitality, was a pious duty which found a place among the five 'Great sacrifices' which a householder was enjoined upon to perform everyday. In fact, not only a householder, but every person in whatever station of life, was obliged to perform (according to his means) the rites of hospitality to a guest, however ordinary the latter might be.[6] It was the sincere belief of the people that if

1. It is interesting to recall that the shrewd Mantharā advised Kaikeyī to exploit this weakness of her age. She advised her mistress to disclose her demands (boons) to Daśaratha only after binding him in the *satya-pāśa*. (*Satyena parigṛhyainaṃ yācethāḥ*. R. II 11/24. Cf. also Daśaratha's words to Sumantra—*satyapāśanibaddho* (*a*)*smi*—R. II 16/42). It is further to be remembered that the cause of Daśaratha's anguish was revealed to Rāma by Kaikeyī only after she had elicited from him the promise that he would surely do anything and everything that he would be called upon to do in the matter—R. II 19/33.

2. Note the talk between Rāma and Sitā in cantos 10-11 of the Araṇya-Kāṇḍa.

3. R. I 56/26-28.

4. R. I 71/47.

5. R. VII 25/40.

6. R. IV 61/125.

a guest returned unattended from one's house he carried with him the merits (of the negligent householder) and left behind, his own evils;[1] and that one, who, without receiving his guests ate his food by himself was fed in the next life on his own flesh[2]. It is significant to remember in this connection that the sage Śarabhaṅga declined to accompany Indra to the *Brahmaloka*, for he was waiting to receive a distinguished and a dear guest in Rāma.[3] Similarly the sages of the hermitage at the Pampā lake, before leaving for heaven deputed Śabarī to offer the rites of hospitality to Rāma when he came there; and immediately after discharging her task the lady followed their course.[4]

Elaborate rules are given in the various Gṛihya-sūtras with regard to the reception of a guest. The evidence contained in the Rāmāyaṇa shows that the rules observed in Vālmīki's society in this behalf were essentially the same as in the Gṛihya-sūtras. Immediately learning of the arrival of a guest the host was required to offer *pādya* (water for washing feet),[5] *arghya* (water for sipping and a few other articles) and a seat along with salutations and greetings.[6] Next, he was to offer him *madhuparka* or some light refreshment such as fruits.[7] Receiving Rāvaṇa, who came disguised as a *parivrājaka* Sītā said, "O Brāhmaṇa, here is this *bṛisī* (a cany seat); do thou sit on it. Here is *pādya* (to wash thy feet); accept it. Here is the good cooked food for you; please partake of it."[8] In the times of Vālmīki also, it seems, the *madhuparka* of a distinguished *brāhmaṇa* or prince included the offering of a cow. The king Daśaratha, in accordance with the rules (*vidhi*), included the cow in his reception for Viśvāmitra; the sage Bharadvāja did so for Rāma; and the sage Pulastya was received by Kārtavīrya being followed by his *purohita*, who had the cow ready in the

1. R. III 16/27.
2. R. III 16/26.
Vide also the Śveta account in R. VII canto 80.
3. R. III 6/24.
4. R. III 80/17, 31-33.
5. R. II 103/7.
6. R. I 16/15-21.
Note : *Gandhamālyādi saṃyuktam udakamarghyamityucyate.*
(Nārāyaṇa, quoted by Kane, P. V., History of Dharma-śāstra, Vol. II, part I, f. n. 1259 on p. 543).
7. R. VII 21/7.
Note : *Madhuparka* was a mixture of curd, honey and clarified butter. (Pāraskara Gṛihya-sūtra, I 3/5).
8. R. III 51/32.

madhuparka.[1] Aryan kings invariably had a *purohita* in their courts whose duty among other things was to receive the guests (or to advise the king on matters of reception for the guests). A king receiving a sage has invariably been described in the Rāmāyaṇa as being accompanied by the *purohita*.[2] It is understandable, therefore, that the various rites of reception accorded by the kings were performed with the recitation of the Vedic *mantras*.[3] It may also be added that just as it was the duty of the host to perform rites of hospitality to the guest, so it was obligatory for the guest to inquire into the welfare of the host (and being satisfied confer blessings upon him—provided the guest was a *brāhmaṇa* and the host a *kshatriya*).[4]

Benevolence, as expressed in acts of charity and kindness is another virtue which is highly extolled and stressed by Vālmīki. The Rāmāyaṇa contains a beautiful account of Rāma distributing his entire possessions as gifts to the *brāhmaṇas* and scholars, as alms to the poor, the destitutes and the orphans, and as subsidies to the servants and dependents.[5] Even during the course of his journey he is said to have given ample charities at all holy places.[6] Liberal charities also formed an important part of the performance of an *Aśvamedha*. Large quantities of food, cloth and gold were distributed from the exchequers of Daśaratha and Rāma when they performed the *Aśvamedha*.[7] Besides, the full moon days of the months of *Āshaḍha*, *Kārtika*, *Māgha* and *Vaiśākha* were held in Vālmīki's society as days of compulsory alms-giving. One, who, for any reason, failed to give charities on these days considered himself as extremely unfortunate.[8] Givers of land, cows and gold were promised special (blessed) *Lokas* after death;[9] whereas one who frustrated the expectations of the suppliants was considered a very wretched person.[10] It is important to note that the true acts of charity were required to be absolutely free of any feeling of contempt (on the part of the

1. R. I 16/21; R. II 54/17 N. S. and R. VII 21/7 respectively.
2. (*Sopādhyāyaḥ*) R. I 16/14; R. I 43/23; R. I 46/6; R. VII 21/7.
3. R. I 46/7.
4. R. III 80/10-13; R. VII 21/13.
5. R. II 35/4 ff.
6. (*dadaddānāni tīrtheshu*) R. II 39/8.
7. R. I 10/7-13, 39-45; R. I 9/72-74; R. VII 94/10-16.
8. R. II 83/17.
9. R. III 75/34.
10. R. IV 23/28.

giver towards the receiver), for through a charity given contemptuously a giver incurred demerit.[1]

Compassion has been declared by Vālmīki as the supreme *dharma*[2] and granting refuge to one who came seeking it, as the solemn duty (especially of the *kshatriyas*).[3] It is said that granting asylum to the affrighted was more meritorious than even the performance of a costly *Aśvamedha*.[4] It was in recognition of this principle that Rāma forgave the offender in Jayanta and owned Vibhīshaṇa as a friend even when the latter came from the enemy camp. Men are required by Vālmīki to be kind not only to their fellow-beings but also to other creatures. Too well known in this connection is th story of Śibi who is said to have offered his own flesh in order to save a pigeon from a hawk.[5] In another legendary story farmers are advised to employ in their work only strong and sturdy bulls and not those that were weak, exhausted and sickly.[6]

In addition to the above Vālmīki refers to various other moral excellences. He observes at one place that service to the elders, restraint of the senses, compassion and tolerance alone constituted the (real) ornamentation of a person.[7] Rāma regarded obedience to elders and carrying out their orders as his supreme *dharma*.[8] Fortitude in times of difficulty was the virtue of a wise man[9] and modesty was indicative ef one's fitness to shoulder heavy responsibilities.[10] Perfect self-control was an indispensable qualification in a *brahmarshi* and under no circumstance was he to allow quarter to *kāma* (passion or lust) and *krodha* (anger).[11] *Krodha* rendered futile all penance, recitation of the sacred *mantras* and acts of charity and hence one was advised to completely renounce *krodha*.[12] The ascetics of the Rāmāyaṇa have displayed extreme self-control in this respect, for even when oppressed by the Rākshasas they did not allow

1. R. I 9/90.
2. R. V 35/43.
3. R. I 19/9; R. II 109/52.
4. R. V 93/12-13.
5. R. II 15/4.
6. R. II 80/30-31.
7. R. II 103/34.
8. R. II 21/47.
9. R. II 84/15.
10. R. II 125/15.
11. R. I 59/27-28.
12. R. VII 62/19.

krodha to take possession of themselves.[1] Honesty in all public dealings was another quality on which Vālmīki has laid great emphasis. Thus partisanship in (legal) disputes,[2] and non-payment of wages to the servants[3] or of fees to the officiating priests in a sacrifice[4] were regarded as grievous sins.

The religious practices observed in the strictly Vedic tradition by the people of the Rāmāyaṇic age can be classified under two different categories as :

(i) The Compulsory—comprising those religious rites and ceremonies the performance of which was obligatory upon every member, belonging to the three higher *varṇas*.

These again may be further distributed as :

(a) the routine rites to be performed everyday and

(b) the special rites and ceremonies to be observed only on special occasions.

(ii) The Optional—consisting of certain distinct rituals which were the privilege of a few in the society and were performed even by them only for the fulfilment of certain definite desires or ambitions.

An account of the various rites and ceremonies occurring in the Rāmāyaṇa under these heads is given below.[5]

Daily rites :

The daily rites began with the morning *snāna* (bath) which was performed usually before sunrise.[6] From the earliest times Indians have recognised the importance of *snāna* not merely from the point of personal hygiene, but also as a primary act conducive to inner purity. Therefore,

1. R. III 11/15.
2. R. II 83/13.
3. R. II 83/9.
4. R. II 83/10.
5. Sometimes a sixfold classification of *karmas* as *nitya-karmas, naimittika-karmas, kāmya-karmas, nishiddha-karmas, prāyaścittas* and *upāsanas* is given. (Vedānta Sāra I 7-12) With the exception of *prāyaścittas* these terms are not to be found in the Rāmāyaṇa. The epic at the same time does not display its familiarity with such a classification. We have, therefore refrained from employing these terms in our treatment.
6. R. I 21/13. Also : Rāma, Lakshmaṇa and Sītā after they had finished their bath and other morning duties saw the sun rising —R. III, 9/1-5.

snāna as the preliminary of prayers both in the morning and the evening[1] was considered very necessary. The ascetic usually performed certain religious rites in the noon also for which an additional third bath was recommended in his case.[2]

Immediately after the *snāna* one was required to perform *sandhyā*, i. e. the rite performed at the twilight. The morning *sandhyā* which was performed facing the sun in the East was known as the *pūrvā-sandhyā*[3], whereas the evening *sandhyā* known as the *paścimā-sandhyā*[4] was performed facing the sun, in the West. *Udaka* (or *arghya*), offering water out of respect to sun,[5] *japa*[6], muttering of the sacred *Gāyatrī mantras*, and *tarpaṇa*[7], offering water to gods, sages and manes, formed the principal items of *sandhyā*.

Agnihotra (or *homa*) was the next item in the daily rites and like the *sandhyā* it was also performed twice, in the morning and in the evening.[8] In every home the householder maintained the holy fire in which along with his wife he offered oblations of clarified butter and cooked food to various *Devas* and *Pitṛis* to the accompaniment of Vedic *mantras*.[9] The chamber in which the sacred fire was lodged and maintained was known as *agnyāgāra*[10] or *vedīgṛiha*[11] and the person, who maintained this fire (or fires) was known as *āhitāgni*. About the people of Ayodhyā, the poet says, that there was no one who did not maintain the sacred fire, (*nānāhitāgni*) or did not perform sacrifices (*nāyajvā*).[12] He also speaks of the special *Lokas* attained by the *āhitāgni* and the *yajvā*.[13]

1. (Evening snāna) R. I 29/19.
2. (*upaspṛiśaṃstrishavaṇam*) R. II 108/18.
3. (*pūrvāṃ sandhyām upāsva ha*) R. I 21/2; R. II 8/6; R. II 50/2.
4. (*sandhyāmanvāsya paścimām*) R. II 51/26; R. II 57/1; R. VII 83/20-21; R. VII 84/2.
5. (*snātvā kṛitodakau*) R. I 21/3.
(Nāgojī-Bhaṭṭa explains *udaka* as *arghya*—vide Tīlaka-Ṭīkā).
6. (*jepaturjapyamāhnikam*) R. I 21/3.
(note Tīlaka-Ṭīkā—*paramañjapaṃ Sāvitrīm*)
7. (*santarpya Pitṛidevatāḥ*) R. I 32/14.
Also R. I 2/10-11.
8. Morning : R. III 9/4.
Evening : R. I 29/19.
9. R. II 8/1-2.
10. (*agnyāgāramabhyetya*) R. II 35/2.
11. (*vedigṛihañjagāma*) R. VII 40/11
12. R. I 6/13.
13. (*āhitāgneśca yā gatiḥ*) R. III 75/34, (*yajvanāñca lokāḥ*) R. II 70/41.

Another religious institution, round which centred all the daily religious rites, was the conception of the five *mahā-yajñas*, namely :

(i) The *Deva-yajña* —which consisted in the daily *homa*;

(ii) The *Pitṛi-yajña* —which consisted in the daily *tarpaṇa*;

(iii) The *Brahma-yajña* —which consisted in the daily *svādhyāya* and *japa*;

(iv) The *Nṛi-yajña* —which consisted in honouring a guest by offering him *pādya*, *arghya* and *madhuparka*; and

(v) The *Bhūta-yajña* —which consisted in making offerings of food on the ground, in various directions for the guardians of the directions, spirits and other living creatures.[1]

The word *pañca-mahāyajña* does not occur in the Rāmāyaṇa but there are numerous direct and indirect references to its components. We have, already noted, references to *homa*, *tarpaṇa*, *japa*, *svādhyāya* and *atithi-pūjana*. References to the offerings (*bali*) for the *bhūtas* (creatures) are to be met with twice in the Ayodhyā-Kāṇḍa. In the first reference it is said that Rāma took his bath, duly performed his *japa*, kindled fire with the sacred *mantras* and then offered oblations into it for gods and manes. He also offered water to the *Pitṛis* and then offered in the prescribed manner *bali* to the *bhūtas*.[2] In the second reference, directed by Rāma, Sītā cooked the meat brought by Lakshmaṇa and offered a portion from it to the *bhūtas*.[3] The above references, in very unambiguous terms, testify to the prevalence of *Bhūta-yajña* in the society of Vālmīki, and at the same time, indicate, as to how the ancient Indians tried to inculcate in every person, the spirit of universal kindliness.

1. It may be observed that the conception of the five *mahāyajñas* in the Vedic religion is a very ennobling one. Unlike the *śrauta* sacrifices where the main spring of action is the desire to secure for oneself one or the other object of pleasure, in the five *mahā-yajñas* the householder is actuated by the feelings of gratitude, reverence, devotion, loving memory and kindliness.

2. R. II 60/27-29.

3. R. II 109/36-37.

Special rites and ceremonies :

In addition to this daily routine, one was required to perform certain other rites and ceremonies under certain well-defined conditions. Their number must have been considerable but in the Rāmāyaṇa only two of them have been mentioned, viz., the *Āgryāyaṇa* and the *Vāstu-śamana*. Of these, the former was performed towards the end of *Śarad* when the new crops were ready. The principal rite of this ceremony was the offering of the new produce to the gods and the manes, presumably as a mark of gratitude towards them.[1] The second ceremony, viz., *Vāstu-śamana* was performed before entering a newly built house. The main rite in *Vāstu-śamana* consisted in performing a *homa*, in honour of the presiding deity of the *śālā* (viz. Vāstoshpati) in which offerings of *aiṇeya-māṃsa* (cooked meat of the deer) were made. The chief object of this rite, as its very name suggests was the averting of evil. Moreover, it was believed that it brought longevity to the inmates.[2]

Under this very head mention must also be made of the various *saṃskāras* which a householder was required to perform on certain stated occasions.[3] Vālmīki displays his familiarity with the *jātakarma* (birth ceremonies), the *nāma-karaṇa* (name giving), the *upanayana* (initiation), the *samāvartana* (end of studentship), the *vivāha* (marriage) and the *antyeshṭi* (funeral ceremonies).[4] In connection with the birth of the twins of Sītā, the Uttara-Kāṇḍa refers to certain rites performed by the sage Vālmīki with the object of guarding the offspring

1. R. III 21/6.
   N. B. Perhaps the correct spelling is *Āgrayaṇa*.
2. R. II 56/22-32 N. S.; Also R. III 20/21-22.
3. The word *saṃskāra* which literally means refinement stands in the technical sense for those rites and actions which impart fitness by the generation of fresh qualities. (Vide Tantravārtika quoted by Kane, P. V., History of Dharma-śāstra Vol. II, part I, f.n. 448 on page 190).
4. It may be pointed out that the names *jātakarma*, *upanayana*, *samāvartana*, and *antyeshṭi* do not occur in the epic. We have, however, included them in the list above, for ceremonies described under these *saṃskāras* in the Dharma-śāstras are to be found mentioned in the Rāmāyaṇa. It may also be added that in course of the marriage rites of the princes of Daśaratha the Rāmāyaṇa refers to *godāna* and it is said that on this occasion king Daśaratha gave four hundred thousand cows, each having her calf. (I 68/26-28) It is not clear whether this is a reference to the *godāna saṃskāra* (the shaving of the beard) or just to the giving of cows.

against evil spirits.[1] It seems that these rites formed part of the *jātakarma*. The *nāmakaraṇa* is mentioned in connection with the sons of Daśaratha. This *saṃskāra* was performed on the twelfth day after the birth of the child and in this connection the *brāhmaṇas* were fed and liberal gifts were distributed among them.[2] The *upanayana* and the *samāvartana* are nowhere directly mentioned in the epic. But as has been shown in our treatment of the *brahmacarya-āśrama*, the prevalence of these two *saṃskāras* in the society of Vālmīki is to be inferred from indirect references.[3] With regard to the *vivāha* and the *antyeshṭi* the epic provides ample material. Of these the *vivāha* has already been treated in an earlier chapter[4] and we shall presently be taking up the *antyeshṭi*.

From the earliest times down to the present day, various modes of disposal of the dead have obtained among the different peoples of the world. The ancient Indians adopted cremation at a very early period[5] and in the Rāmāyaṇa, too, this was the only popular mode of disposing of the dead body.[6] Luckily, we find in the Rāmāyaṇa, not only a fairly detailed account of the funerl ceremonies of the three important kings, Daśaratha, Bālī and Rāvaṇa,[7] but also of Yajñadatta and Jaṭāyu.[8] A consideration of the entire material available on the point, in the epic, reveals that the principal rites of this *saṃskāra* were the same as laid down in the Sūtras and the Smṛitis.

1. R. VII 69/4 ff.
2. R. I 18/21-23 N. S.
3. Vide pp. 27-28 supra.
4. Vide Chapter IV supra.
5. Ṛigveda X 14.
6. A solitary passage put into the mouth of Virādha (R. III 5/48) alludes to burial as the popular mode of disposing of the dead among the Rākshasas. However, this passage itself refers to this mode as the *sanātana dharma* indicating thereby that it was an ancient practice. The contemporary Rākshasas had changed over to cremation, presumably under Aryan influence. A stage of transition is perhaps represented in the account of Kabandha where a burial cum cremation was adopted. (R. III 78/19, 30).
7. R. II Cantos 87-90. (Daśaratha)
   R. IV Cantos 18-19 (Bālī)
   R. VI 92/58-59 (Rāvaṇa)
8. R. II 70/45 (Yajñadatta)
   R. III 75/32-40 (Jaṭāyu)

The rites connected with the cremation of the deceased were collectively known as *aurdhvadehika*,[1] *preta-kārya*[2] or merely *saṃskāra*.[3] The performance of the last rites of the deceased by his son was considered meritorious[4] and a son, who was for any reason deprived of discharging this duty to his father considered himself extremely unfortunate.[5] Moreover, there seems to have been a belief that until the corpse was duly consigned to the flames, the spirit of the deceased kept lingering about, in this very world and that it was only with the performance of this *saṃskāra* that it attained to heaven.[6]

The principal ceremony of the *antyeshṭi* was cremation. In order to carry the corpse to the cremation ground, first a bier (*śibikā*) befitting the status of the deceased was prepared.[7] Next, the corpse duly dressed and decked with ornaments was placed on the bier.[8] The son (or sons), near relatives, friends and old servants then lifted the bier on their shoulders and marched to the cremation ground in a procession.[9] The widow (or widows) of the deceased also formed a part of that procession in those days.[10] At the head of the procession some people distributed wealth among the poor and the destitutes.[11]

On the cremation ground, which was usually situated away from the town and near the river side (—in case of towns on river banks) a spot was selected for raising a pyre.[12] This, in case of a king (or a wealthy person) was prepared with

1. (*rājñastasyaurdhvadehikam*) R. II 90/3.

Cf. "The Hindus call the cremation ceremony *Aurdhvadaihika-kriyā* or the eremonies that release the soul from the body for its upward journey to heaven. Unless the ceremony is performed, the departed soul is believed to linger about its late habitation and hover about without consolation, and in great distress as a *Preta*."

Pandey, Rajbali, Hindu *Saṃskāras*, p. 424.

2. (*kriyatāmeva Sugrīva pretakāryamanantaram*) R. IV 18/2.
3. R. II 87/3.
4. R. VI 71/13.
5. R. II 78/28.
6. R. II 87/40.
7. R. II 87/7 and R. IV 18/10.
8. R. II 87/15.
9. R. II 87/17.
10. R. II 87/27-28.
11. R. II 87/21.
12. R. II 87/29.

fragrant wood (e.g. sandal), incense and other fragrant material.[1] It was then, sprinkled over with clarified butter and oil,[2] and the corpse was laid over it. A *medhya-paśu* was slaughtered and its fat was cast over the dead body.[3] Next, the son (or a near relation of the deceased) set fire to the pyre[4] and the *brāhmaṇa* priests recited *mantras* from the Veda.[5]

It is to be noted here that the cremation of an *āhitāgni* was performed with the help of the three sacred fires, which were carried by the priests to the cremation ground.[6] These fires as also the utensils (*sruvā* etc.) used by the deceased in the performances of sacrifices, were laid on the pyre and were cremated along with him.[7]

When fire was set to the pyre, the son (or the near relative performing the *saṃskāra*) accompanied by other relatives circumambulated it (keeping the right side towards the pyre).[8] Next, he repaired to the adjoining river (or tank etc.) where standing in water he offered handfuls of water (perhaps mixed with sesamum seeds and *darbhas*) to the departed soul;[9] and this marked the conclusion of the principal rites of cremation. However, the formal mourning continued for ten days, for that was the period of *aśauca* (impurity).[10] During this period the son or the near relative who had performed the *saṃskāra* slept on the ground in the chamber where the deceased had breathed his last.[11]

On the twelfth day the *śrāddha* was performed in which food, dress, cows and other valuables were conferred on the

1. R. II 87/29-30.
2. R. II 87/ 6-7.
3. R. II 87/36.
This animal was intended to serve as a guide for the soul (of the departed) in his upward journey to heaven.
Vide, Pandey, Rajbali, Hindu Saṃskāras, p. 421.
4. R. II 87/38.
5. R. II 87/40.
6. R. II 87/4.
7. R. II 87/33-35.
8. R. II 88/1.
Also R. IV 18/29.
9. R. II 89/2-3.
Also R. IV 18/30-31.
10. R. IV 19/1.
11. R. II 89/26.

brāhmaṇas[1] for the welfare of the departed soul. Perhaps a ceremony of collecting the bones was also performed after the thirteenth day.[2]

A few words about *śrāddha* will not be out of place here. According to the belief of the people of the Rāmāyaṇic age, death did not completely sever the relationship of the deceased with that of the survivors. The latter cherished the memory of the deceased for a long time and in various ways tried to secure for him a life of happiness in the other world. No doubt, a few heretics expressed their scepticism about the efficacy of such practices as offering of food etc. (in *śrāddha*) for the departed one;[3] but the devout Aryan sincerely believed that he owed a debt to his ancestors. For the discharge of this debt daily *tarpaṇa* and periodical *śrāddhas* were considered to be absolutely necessary. Moreover, on such festive occasions as the marriage of one's son a distinct *śrāddha*, known as *nāndī-mukha śrāddha* was performed for securing the blessings of the ancestors and other gods. According to the Gṛihya-sūtras, it was dedicated principally to the *Devas* and not *Pitṛis*.[4] In the Rāmāyaṇa such a *śrāddha* was performed by Daśaratha, at the time of the marriage of his sons.[5]

Vālmīki has not supplied any details about the procedure of the *śrāddha* performance. All that we can gather from the stray references appearing here and there in the epic is :

(i) that feeding the *brāhmaṇas* with meat preparations,

1. R. II 90/1-3.

The Gṛihya-sūtras recommend in this connection a *śrāddha* known as *ekoddishṭa-śrāddha*. As is suggested by its name the *ekoddishṭa-śrāddha* is intended for a single dead person who has recently passed away. This *śrāddha* is performed every month for one year after the death. After that the *sapiṇḍīkaraṇa* takes place.

For details vide Ram Gopal, India of Vedic Kalpasūtras, p. 370.

2. (*trayodaśāhe (a) tīte tu kṛite cānantare vidhau*) R. II 90/4.

(The N. S. reads in this connection : *tataḥ prabhātasamaye divase ca trayodaśe......śabdāpihitakaṇṭhaśca śobhaānrtham upāgataḥ*. R. II 77/4-5 N.S. The commentators explain it as *asthisañcayanārtham*. Vide Tilaka and Bhūshaṇa commentaries.

3. R. II 121/14.
4. Ram Gopal, India of Vedic Kalpasūtras, p. 370.
5. R. I 68/26.

especially of castrated rams was an important part of the ceremony;[1]

(ii) that an offering made by one, who had been dear to the deceased during his life time, became a source of extreme happiness for him in the other world;[2]

(iii) that the person performing the *śrāddha* ordinarily offered the same food as he ate himself;[3] and

(iv) that the performance of the *śrāddha* rites in Gayā was considered specially meritorious.[4]

Optional rituals :

For the proper appreciation of the rites of this section, it is desirable to make, by way of preamble, a few general remarks on the position of Agni, in Vedic religion. It is a well-known fact that ever since the times of the Ṛigveda and perhaps even earlier fire (Agni) had been the principal medium of worship with the Aryans. The Ṛigvedic Aryans worshipped various gods like Indra, Varuṇa, Sūrya, Ushas etc. by offering oblations to Agni (fire) who was housed by them as the cherished *atithi* in the altar. Subsequently this fire cult gained more and more importance and at the same time, became extremely complex. By the time of the Sūtras, we find that besides the ordinary fire (the *laukika-agni* or the fire meant for cooking) people recognised four sacred fires known as *āvasathya*, *gārhapatya*, *āhavanīya* and *dakshiṇa*.[5] Of these the first (viz. *āvasathya*) was also known as the *gṛihyāgni* (or the *smārtāgni*) and all the domestic rites prescribed in the Gṛihya-sūtras were performed in it. The last three fires (viz. *gārhapatya*, *āhavanīya* and *dakshiṇa* were known as *śrautāgni* or the *tretāgni* and their presence was absolutely necessary for the performance of the *śrauta* rites, prescribed in the Śrauta-sūtras. The *gṛihyāgni* was established by every householder (in his home) usually at the time of his marriage when he entered the *gṛihastha-āśrama*[6], and in every rite, to be performed in it, he had the option to act as his

1. R. I 45/9.
Also the Ilvala-Vātāpi account in R. III 14/12 ff.
2. R. II 116/7.
3. R. II 116/36.
4. R. II 107/13 N. S.
5. By adding *Sabhya* to the above list the sacred fires are sometimes referred to as five.
6. *Āvasathyādhānaṃ dārakāle*, Pāraskara Gṛihya-sūtra, I 2/1.

own priest. The śrauta fires, on the other hand, were maintained only by few and for their administration, the services of four priests (*ṛitviks*) were absolutely necessary.

In the Rāmāyaṇa, the three fires have been mentioned in several passages[1] and there are clear indications that the ascetics living in the hermitages regularly performed such *śrauta* rites as *darśa* and *paurṇamāsa*.[2] As regards the people living in the town, we have already noted, that Vālmīki declares all the people of Ayodhyā as *āhitāgnis*.[3] Even if this reference may be taken as loose or exaggerated there is not the least doubt that at least, a section of *brāhmaṇas* living in Ayodhyā had performed *Vājapeya* sacrifice and maintained the sacred fires.[4] Likewise, there are frequent references to various *śrauta* sacrifices being performed by *kshatriya* princes. In various contexts, the Rāmāyaṇa mentions *Vājimedha*, *Vājapeya*, *Agnishṭoma*, *Atirātra*, *Gosava*, *Sautrāmaṇi*, *Rājasūya*, *Jāruthya*, and *Puṇḍarīka* sacrifices to have been performed by one or the other *kshatriya* prince.[5] As against the daily and periodical rites described earlier, whose performance was obligatory upon every Aryan, these rites (viz. the *śrauta-rites*) were optional. The belief was that the due performance of each of these rites yielded specific results in favour of the *yajamāna*. Therefore, he normally undertook to perform these rites only when he had a particular object in view like heaven or a son. However, so far as the Rāmāyaṇa is concerned, we find that every individual who had the resources, took pride in performing these rites.[6] In fact, he considered the fulfilment of his life's purpose only in such performances.[7]

The most important of these *śrauta* sacrifices was the *Aśvamedha*, which a *kshatriya* hero generally performed towards the fag end of his career. Its performance was a matter of glory and pride for the prince[8] and a carnival for the people

1. R. II 87/33; R. II 117/35; R. VII 4/6;
2. R. I 48/48.
3. R. I 6/13.
4. R. II 47/21-23.
5. For references note : R. I 8/2; R. II 114/4; R. VI 8/25; R. VI 110/12; R. VII 101/9-10.
6. (Cf. *dravyavāniva nishkṛiyaḥ*) R. II 53/30.
7. R. I 54/23; R. II 6/11
8. *Tataḥ prītamanā rājā prāpya yajñamanuttamam,*
Svargyam pāpmāpahañcaiva dushprāpaṃ sarvapārthivaiḥ R. I 10/45-46.

(contd. next page)

at large. Lakshmaṇa called it a *mahāyajña*, a *kratūttama* and a 'purifier from sins'.[1] Sagara is believed to have performed it for the sake of *svarga* (heaven);[2] Triśaṅku for the attainment of heaven in human body;[3] and through it Indra and Kārdama Iḍa are said to have become free of *brahma-hatyā* and Śiva's curse respectively.[4] Among the characters of the Rāmāyaṇa Daśaratha and Rāma are said to have performed several *Aśvamedhas* in their life time and the Bāla-Kāṇḍa and the Uttara-Kāṇḍa contain fairly detailed descriptions of the *Aśvamedhas* performed by them.

The *Aśvamedha* was a big affair usually extending over several years.[5] Naturally, it required preparations on a massive scale.[6] First of all, in consultation with his family priest (or priests) the *yajamāna* resolved to perform the *Aśvamedha*[7] and immediately after that he selected the chief priest[8] and his associates[9] to preside over the sacrifice. The principal priests in an *Aśvamedha* were four, viz., *adhvaryu*, *hotā*, *udgātā* and *brahmā*.[10] All the priests were invariably *brāhmaṇas* by *varṇa*. They were renowned for their Vedic learning and were proficient in all branches of sacrifices.[11] On a site,[12] selected by these priests for the performance of the sacrifice a vast *yajñavāṭa* (enclosure for sacrifice) was constructed to accommodate the large number of invitees consisting of sages and ascetics, *brāhmaṇas*

Cf. "The performance of the *Aśva-medha* involved an assertion of power and a display of political authority such as only a monarch of undisputed supremacy could have ventured upon without humiliation."

(Eggeling quoted by Law, N. N., Aspects of Ancient Indian Polity, p. 19).

1. R. VII 86/2.
2. R. I 38/28.
3. R. I cantos 55-56.
4. R. VII 86/3 and R. VII 92/25 respectively.
5. R. I 9/61.
6. R. I 9/40; Also R. VII 93/24-27.
7. R. I 9/44, 45.
8. R. I 9/64.
9. (*sahāyāśca dvijātayaḥ*) R. I 9/40.

The total number of priests administering an *Aśvamedha* was sixteen.

N. B. The N. S. specifically mentions this number in I 14/38 (*shoḍashartvijaḥ*). However, the verse is missing in the Lahore edition.

10. R. I 10/33-34.
11. R. I 9/42.
12. The site was generally the bank of a river.

distinguished in various branches of learning, kings, princes, dancers and singers.[1] In fact, the *yajñavāṭa* was a miniature township which contained, besides the *yajñavālā*, markets (sacrificial hall), granaries and other store houses.[2] On an auspicious day which was selected by the priests for the purpose, the *yajamāna* moved from his residence to the *yajñavāṭa*[3] and perhaps, immediately after that, he took the *dīkshā* (initiation) for the sacrifice.[4] After taking the *dīkshā*, till the completion of the sacrifice, the *yajamāna* was expected to conduct himself in a very suave manner, allowing no quarter in his mind to cruelty.[5] He was also expected not to leave the *yajñavāṭa*.[6]

The *Aśvamedha* was a solemn performance and it was supposed to bring merit and power to its performer. So, while, on the one hand, one could be assured of the co-operation from the good,[7] on the other, one could apprehend various types of obstructions and impediments being caused in the way by several forces—human, divine and demoniac.[8] Not only, meticulous care was therefore taken with regard to every rite and ceremony[9] but certain expiatory and propitiatory rites were also performed in the beginning to avert evil and calamity.[10]

In the beginning the secular object of the *Aśvamedha* was to proclaim the supremacy of the *yajamāna* over the rest of the princes.[11] So, a horse possessing auspicious marks was selected by the priests to go round the earth being followed by the *upādhyāya* and escorted by a renowned hero (from the family of the *yajamāna*) and his army.[12] With the return of the horse

1. R. I 9/69-71; R. VII 93/17-27.
2. Ibid.
3. R. I 9/95.
4. For the word *dīkshā* vide R. I 10/72; R. I 28/4; R. I 36/17; R. VII 17/15.
5. R. VII 17/15.
6. R. I 36/17.
7. R. III 71/14.
8. Note the obstruction caused by Indra in the sacrifice of Sagara. R. I 57/6-8.
Also : *Chidraṃ hi mṛigayante tu vidvāṃso brahma-rākshasāḥ.* R. I 9/55.
9. R. I 9/56-57.
10. R. I 9/54.
11. Vide Kane, P. V., History of Dharma-śāstra, Vol. II, part II, pp. 1228-1229.
12. R. I 9/53; R. I 36/6.

from its journey the regular performances started and everything proceeded according to the injunctions of the *śāstras*.[1] In an open space (usually the bank of a river) close to the *yajñaśālā*, twenty-one smooth-faced sacrificial posts, each having eight angles, were erected.[2] They were duly decked with cloths and to them were tied various animals of offering.[3]

In the beginning the *pravargya* and *upasada* ceremonies took place in which to the accompaniment of the *mantras* (sacred verses) various offerings of *soma* were made to the gods by the priests.[4] The principal rite in the *Aśvamedha* was the offering of the *aśva* (horse). After the performance of the preliminary rites the animal was, therefore, cut into three pieces by the three strokes of the *mahishī*[5] and she passed the night with that dead horse.[6] The priests then started duly making oblations into the fire with the fat of the horse.[7]

The duration of the (main rites of the) *Aśvamedha*, according to the Kalpa-sūtras is said to be of three days[8] and on these three days the *catushṭoma*, the *uktha* and the *atirātra* were performed respectively.[9] Subsequently, the various great sacrifices (the *Jyotishṭoma*, the *Āyushṭoma*, the *Atirātra*, the *Abhijit*, the *Viśvajit* and the *Āptoryāma*) were celebrated with due rites.[10] The last important ceremony of the *Aśvamedha* was the *avabhṛitha* with which the sacrifice concluded. This was a purificatory bath which the *yajamāna* took along with the *mahishī*[11] and after this bath he returned from the *yajñavāṭa* to his capital and resumed his normal work.[12]

1. R. I 10/1-3.
2. R. I 10/17-19.

These *yūpas* were—six each of *Bilva*, *Khadira* and *Palāśa* and two and one of *Devadāru* and *Śleshmātaka* respectively.

3. R. I 10/20-23.
4. R. I 10/4-5.
5. R. I 10/25.
6. R. I 10/26.
7. R. I 10/28-29.
8. R. I 10/30.
9. R. I 10/31 (variant I Bha)

The reading in the first quarter seems to be wrong. We have adopted the N. S. reading—(viz. *catushṭomamahastasya*, R. I 14/40 N. S.).

10. R. I 10/32-33.
11. Cf. R. IV 17/32.
12. R. I 38/25-26.

These sacrifices were important not only as religious rites but at the same time they also possessed great economic[1] and cultural significance. The *kshatriyas* were a prosperous community and in order to prevent accumulation of wealth at one place, the performance of periodical sacrifices was enjoined upon them as a religious obligation. Vālmīki refers to these sacrifices as *bahusuvarṇakaiḥ*[2] *annavadbhiḥ*,[3] *bhūridakshiṇaiḥ*[4] and *āpta-dakshiṇaiḥ*[5] and according to his descriptions liberal distribution of wealth among the poor and the needy was an important part of such performances. In course of his *Aśvamedha*, Daśaratha is said to have generously distributed food and clothes among beggars, orphans, women and poor *brāhmaṇas*. He made gifts of wealth (gold) to destitutes, imbeciles, cripples and widows.[6] Liberal eharities were also made to young graduates who wanted to pay fees to their spiritual preceptors and to poor house-holders who wanted to perform sacrifices.[7] Besides, these sacrifices provided work for a large number of manual labourers, artisans, dancers, actors and musicians.[8]

These sacrificial sessions went a long way in preserving the cultural unity of this vast land by providing an opportunity to the scholars of the country to assemble at one spot and exchange views on points of literary and cultural interests.[9] Thus in response to the invitations of Daśaratha and Rāma great Vedic scholars arrived to attend their *Aśvamedhas*. Among these were scholars who had mastered the *saṃhitās* along with their (six) auxiliary sciences; *snātakas* who had studied the Vedas and observed the *vratas*; *ṛitviks* who were proficient in the *yajñakarma*; knowers of the Vedic texts along with their

1. For the economic importance of the *Aśvamedhas* vide Shama Sastry, R, (article). "Śrī Rāmacandra Jī Kā Aśvamedha Yajña Aur Usakā Mahattva"—Kalyāṇa, Rāmāyaṇāṅka, pp. 129-131.
2. R. 1/93.
3. R. II 6/11.
4. Ibid.
5. R. VI 8/25.
6. R. I 10/7-13.
7. R. I 10/43.
8. R. I 9/66-67.
9. R. I 10/14.

expositions; and logicians and grammarians.[1] The kings provided encouragement and patronage to these people by bestowing liberal gifts upon them.

Popular Practices :

Parallel to the Vedic religion described above, various other religious practices were also current in the society of Vālmīki, which perhaps represent the popular religion of those times. To avoid any misunderstanding, which, the use of the word 'popular' is likely to inspire, it may be stated at the very outset that the practices to which we are now going to refer, were not popular in the sense that they obtained only among the lower sections of the society. The fact, on the other hand, is that most of the information that we are able to gather about these practices, comes from the accounts of the elites, who resorted to these practices also, as and when necessary. Students of Indology know that in the Vedic period, a stream of popular religious practices, represented in the Atharvaveda, was trying to gain recognition along with the Vedic religion, represented by the cult of sacrifice. This process continued in subsequent ages, mainly due to the influx into the Aryan fold of new communities professing alien beliefs and traditions. What is remarkable is that, by the time of the epics, not only the spirit of contempt towards this strange mass had disappeared but much of it had been embraced even by the higher sections of the Aryan society, though not without modifications and refinements. Nevertheless, it is necessary to bear in mind that the two streams were not so mixed together as to render their identity indistinguishable. A careful reader can easily discover a distinct tradition behind the practices of each set and it is on that ground that we have ventured to call these latter, as popular religious practices (as distinguished from the Vedic rites and ceremonies.)

One of the most striking illustrations representing the popular phase of Rāmāyaṇa religion, is the 'image worship.'[2]

1. R. I 9/42; R. VII 93/18-21.

2. It may be noted that according to C. V. Vaidya "there was yet no idol worship" in the epic period. He writes in his Epic India (pp. 303-304), "Idol worship was the outcome of Buddhism and Jainism and the orthodox Indo-Aryans were influenced by the catching example of Jains and

Vālmīki has repeatedly referred to the presence of *devatāyatanas*[1] and *caityas*[2] in Ayodhyā. In the Bāla-Kāṇḍa it is said that the town Ayodhyā looked splendid with the presence of *devatāyatanas*.[3] In connection with Rāma's coronation in the Ayodhyā-Kāṇḍa, the *devatāyatanas* of the town are said to have been decorated with lofty banners bearing the emblems of the deities and ordinary flags of various colours.[4] In connection with Rāma's reception in the Yuddha-Kāṇḍa, Bharata had also issued specific instructions with regard to the worship of *Devatās* (in the temples) and the *caityas* of the town.[5] Kauśalyā was seen by Rāma in the *devāgāra* devotedly invoking the blessing of various *Devas*.[6] The Uttara-Kāṇḍa seems to refer to the *brāhmaṇa pujārī* (brahmin priest) of the temples in the reference to the *deveshvadhikṛitaḥ*.[7]

In addition to the *devatāyatanas* and *caityas* in the town, mentioned above, which were perhaps public places,

Bauddhas worshipping idols of Buddha and of Jina and imitating their example had temples raised to Vishṇu and Shiva and other Vedic deities." Such a view, it may be pointed out, has been refuted by Dr. P. V. Kane. In his History of Dharma-śāstra (Vol. II part II, p. 711) he writes, "If modern chronology about Buddha's ministry is to be followed (he was born about 563 B. C. and died about 483 B. C.), it is almost impossible to hold that images of gods originally came to be made in imitation of images or statues of Buddha, since, as we saw above, temples and images of gods had already become widespread throughout India in the 4th or 5th century B. C.". It may be added that on a consideration of the various views on image worship in India Dr. Kane arrives at the conclusion that "this practise was a natural and spontaneous growth."

(For details vide History of Dharma-śāstra, Vol. II, part II, pp. 706-712)

1. R. I 5/10.

2. In fact, the word *caitya* occurs at various places in the Rāmāyaṇa and according to the context the commentators explain it variously. Thus in R. I 10/20 (and II 100/43 N. S.) it stands for the spot where the *yūpas* were raised in an *Aśvamedha*; in R. III 42/4 and R. V 7/17 it is a tree, presumably on the cross road; in R. II 8/11 and R. V 7/13 it is a *maṇḍapa* (temple ?) on the cross road; in R. V 10/17 and R. V 39/1, it is a circular palace (in the shape of a *stūpa*); and in R.V 22/29 N. S. it is explained as a Bauddha monastery by the Tilaka-Ṭīkā and as a 'tree on the cremation ground' by Govindarāja.

3. R. I 5/10.
4. R. II 8/11, 13.
5. R VI 108/2.
6. R. II 20/8.
7. R. VII 62/42.

there were also separate chambers (or corners) in the houses in which images of gods were installed and regularly worshipped. There is not the least doubt that the royal family of Ayodhyā had its separate temples, which perhaps housed the family deity (or deities) and as a family custom the new bride was taken to them for special services.[1] Moreover, there are very clear references to independent shrines in the houses of Kauśalyā and Rāma.[3] That independent shrines were probably maintained in every house is further corroborated by the reference in which the people of Ayodhyā, on hearing the happy news of Rāma's coronation are said to have repaired to their houses and worshipped the *Devas*.[4] In the description of Agastya's *āśrama* there is reference to separate places for Brahmā, Śiva, Agni, Indra Vivasvān, Soma, Bhaga, Kubera, Dhātā, Vidhātā, and Vāyu, which may indicate that the ascetics were also maintaining a sort of separate temple in their *āśramas*.[5]

The word *pratimā* or *mūrti* (standing for idol) does not occur in the Rāmāyaṇa, nor is there any direct reference to idols, except in the Uttara-Kāṇḍa where Rāvaṇa is said to have raised and worshipped a Śiva-liṅga.[6] However, the existence of images of gods can be easily inferred from various other references available in the earlier Kāṇḍas. About the figures and attributes of various gods we propose to write in a separate chapter on mythology. That information need not, therefore, be repeated here. Suffice it to indicate in the present context that the form of worship of an idol is distinctly different from that of fire worship. Already in the Rāmāyaṇa, there are indications of it in the references to *gandha* (perfume),[7] *mālya* (garland),[8] *modaka*[9] *naivedya* (or an offering of eatables presented to a deity) and *dakshiṇā* (a gift or fee to the *Brāhmaṇa*).[10]

1. R. I 72/11.
2. R. II 6/29.
3. R. II 8/3-7.
4. R. II 5/36.
5. R. III 16/17-18.
6. R. VII 19/39-43.
7. R. VI 108/2.
8. Ibid. Also R. II 67/27 N. S.
9. R. II 67/27 N. S.
10. Ibid.

Mention must also be made in this connection of tree, river and mountain worship.[1] Sītā, on being advised by the sage Bharadvāja,[2] worshipped the *Śyāma-vaṭa* (fig tree) on her way to Citrakūṭa and prayed to it for the long life of her husband and other members of the family.[3] That mountains were objects of worship is shown by the reference to Citrakūṭa which was circumambulated by Bharata as a mark of his respect to the hill.[4] Rivers as a general rule and the confluence of rivers particularly were held to be sacred and were usually worshipped.[5] While crossing the waters near Prayāga, Sītā prayed to Bhāgīrathī to help Rāma, her husband, to successfully carry out the orders of his father. She promised an elaborate *pūjā* (worship) in honour of the river on her return from the forest.[6] It seems that this practice of promising a *pūjā* to a deity in consideration of a wish sought to be fulfilled by the grace of the deity was fairly popular in the Rāmāyaṇic society.[7] Besides rivers, various places situated on the banks of the rivers and sacred lakes had also become holy and a visit to these was also considered to be an act of religious importance. The names of Pushkara,[8] Gayā,[9] Prayāga and[10] Prabhāsa[11] may be cited by way of illustrations.

Occasional fasts and such other disciplines (which were normally resorted to only by the ascetic living in the forest)[12] were popular even among the townsmen, particularly women.[13] The *praśasti* (panegyric) of the Rāmāyaṇa (in the early cantos of the Bāla-Kāṇḍa and at the end of the Yuddha-Kāṇḍa and the Uttara-Kāṇḍa)[14] and also a remark in the Bāla-Kāṇḍa about the long narrative, giving the account of the descent of the

1. Cf. Atharvaveda XI, 3/6.
2. R. II 59/5-6.
3. R. II 59/16-18.
4. R. II 126/3.
5. R. I 22/9; R. II 102/20.
6. R. II 56/15-20.
7. R. II 46/17.
8. R. I 57/3.
9. R. II 107/13 N. S.
10. R. II 102/20.
11. R. IV 58/14.
12. Vide pp. 133-134 supra.
13. R. II 29/29.
14. R. I 3/144-145; R. VI. 110/19-33 and R VII 112/29 respectively.

Gaṅgā on earth from *svarga*,[1] show that to recite a religious work and also to listen to such a recitation, were both considered meritorious and various rewards were promised for such acts.

---

1. R. I 40/57.

Appendix to Chapter VIII

Customs and superstitious belief in good and bad omens

We have noted earlier in this chapter that the word *dharma* covers also the sense of 'custom' in the Rāmāyaṇa.[1] But the more popular terms standing for custom in Sanskrit are *samaya, ācāra* and *vṛitta* which are usually preceded in this sense by the word *loka*.[2] Custom is very near to habit, being distinguished from it in the sense that unlike habit which is an individual rule of conduct, 'custom' is the habitual action of the community. Naturally, in the observance of a custom it is not so much the religious merit which counts but the fear of public censure. It is therefore true to say that custom "is a picture of the moral consciousness of the community."[3]

The study of the evolution of customs is both interesting and important, for generally the 'ritual' in religion is largely influenced by custom and again custom is the chief factor in the evolution of law.[4] Such a study, however, is beyond the purview of the present work. We shall only refer to a few striking customs alluded to in the Rāmāyaṇa.

Vālmīki has referred to a number of customs that obtained in the Ikshvāku family. Thus it was the privilege of the wife of the eldest son to receive at the time of her marriage the family ornaments.[5] The Bāla-Kāṇḍa refers to a custom according to which the brides, immediately after the wedding, were taken to the *devatāyatanas* for paying respects perhaps to the *kuladevatās* (family deities).[6] The most important customary rule of the Ikshvākus, however, was the rule of primo-

1. Vide foot note 7 on page 147 supra.
2. Cf. (i) *Dharmamarthañca kāmañca samayaṃ vāpi laukikam, Avijñāya katham bālyānmāṃ vigarhitumarhasi.* (R. IV 14/4)
   (ii) *Laukike samayācāre kṛitakalpoviśāradaḥ.* (R. II 3/12 f.n.30)
   (iii) (a) *Rājavṛittaviruddhañca lokavṛitte ca garhitam.* (R.V 48/4)
   (b) *Na hi lokaviruddhasya lokavṛittā dupeyushaḥ...* (R. IV18/21 N. S.)
3. Wundt, Encyclopaedia of Religion and Ethics, Vol. IV, p. 374.
4. Cf. Ibid, p. 375.
5. Vide foot note 4 on page 74 supra.
6. R. I 72/11.

geniture to which Bharata referred as their *śāśvata dharma* (eternal rule).[1] The violation of it in the case of Rāma tremendously distressed Daśaratha, infuriated Lakshmaṇa and made Bharata despise his mother.

In addition to the above practices which are in the nature of *kula-dharmas* (family customs) the epic also refers to a few general customs in the society. Thus *prāyopaveśana* was a practice of 'abstaining from food and awaiting in a sitting posture the approach of death.' Originally it seems to have been evolved for ascetics and persons completely worn out and exhausted by old age or disease. But in the Rāmāyaṇa it seems to have also become popular as an instrument of enforcing one's will upon another. Bharata resorted to it at Citrakūṭa when Rāma refused to return to Ayodhyā.[2] Rāma also seems to have taken recourse to it to persuade Samudra to grant a passage to him and his army.[3] Another popular custom was the *agni-parīkshā* or the fire ordeal in which in cases of suspicions Agni was called upon to declare the purity or otherwise of a woman's character.[4] Allied in character to the *agni-parīkshā* was the *śapatha* in which a lady invoked any divine agency to testify to her purity.[5] Mention may also be made of the practice of *triṇāṇtarābhāshaṇa* (or speaking with the intervention of a straw) resorted to by ladies when they were forced to speak to an unworthy person. Sītā did so a number of times while speaking to Rāvaṇa.[6]

There were also a few political conventions such as the non-killing of a *dūta*[7], the taking round through the principal crossroads of the town of a foreign spy when detected[8] and the expelling from the country in one garment of a person accused of treason.[9]

1. R. II 116/2.
2. R. II 124/12-13.
3. R. V 94/18-20.
4. Cf. R. VI 97/25-26.

N. B. The earlier Vedic literature also refers to trials by ordeal of fire. Compare for example Chāndogya Upanishad, VI 16/1-2.

5. R. VII 99/11 ff.
6. R. III 62/1; R. V. 16/3.
7. R. V 48/5.
8. R. V 49/5 (f.n. 11).
9. Cf. R. IV 7/66.

Belief in good and bad Omens :

The Rāmāyaṇic society also cherished a very large number of superstitious beliefs in good and bad omens which were based on the appearance and movements of heavenly bodies, the behaviour of plants, birds and animals, the spontaneous expressions of one's own limbs, and dreams. We present below an account of these omens broadly under the different categories just now indicated.

The Rāmāyaṇic people had strong faith in astrology and before commencing an act they took into account the position of the stars. Daśaratha arrived at the wedding ground in Mithilā to perform his son's marriage at an auspicious moment called *Vijaya.*[1] The marriage actually took place when the *Phālgunī* was in the North.[2] The camp for Bharata was laid near Prayāga at an auspicious hour and Bharata crossed the Gaṅgā and proceeded to Prayāga-vana in the *Maitra-muhūrta.*[3] Rāma's victorious march against Rāvaṇa was also undertaken in the *Vijaya-muhūrta* and the *Uttarā Phālgunī* was in the ascendant then.[4] In course of the war Rāma suffered a momentary repulse because, portending evil for the world, the *Budha* stood overpowering the *Prājāpatya* and the *Rohiṇī-nakshatras.*[5] On learning from the astrologers (*daivajñas*) that the star of his life had been invaded by *Sūrya*, *Aṅgāraka* and *Rāhu* Daśaratha concluded that his death was then imminent.[6] Jaṭāyu assured Rāma that he would surely be able to recover Sītā, for her abduction was caused by Rāvaṇa in a *muhūrta* in which the *svāmī* (master) regained his lost thing.[7]

The different aspects of nature and the movements of birds and animals were also believed to be indicative of good or bad happenings. Thus the dreadful fall of fire-brands from the sky, the cracking of the lightning, a shower of blood and bones from the firmanent, the sudden appearance of a dark circle in the vicinity of the sun, the abrupt darkening of the

1. R. I 69/9 (f.n. 11).
2. R. I 67/23.
3. R. II 91/18; R. II 101/27.
4. R. V 71/3.
5. R. VI 83/27, 30.
6. R. II 6/16-18.
7. R. III 75/14.

quarters by the emergence of dusky clouds, the untimely occurrence of eclipse, the roughness of wind, the pale and unpleasant appearances of the sun and the moon, the quaking of the earth and the mountains, the strong and unnatural agitation in the waters of the sea, the whirling winds and the burning of fire without flames but with a column of smoke were all considered ominous.[1] As against this the only striking propitious phase of nature referred to in the epic is that of fire burning with steady and gracious flames a little bent towards the right side of a person.[2]

The evil omens indicated by the behaviour of the birds and beasts also number very large in the epic. Thus the flight of birds from one's right to the left, the howling of the jackal, the sudden slipping of the horses even on level ground, the appearance of a vulture on the banner, the hoarse cries of carnivorous birds and beasts, the cry of *Śakuni* (a bird), the encricling of cranes very close over the head, the shrieking of the flocks of cranes and crows, the sudden emergence of ants and *sarīsṛipas* (reptiles) in sacrificial chambers, the trickling down of milk from the udders of the cow, the stopping of the flow of rut from the temples of the elephants, the piteous neighing of the horses and their aversion to fodder, the cross breeding of asses and cows, rats and mongooses, cats and tigers and pigs and dogs, the appearance of an army of rats in the streets and the appearance of tears in the eyes, and fire in the hooves of the horses portended a calamity.[3] But the movement of animals from left to right and the note of the *Vañjulaka* (bird) were indicative of good luck.[4] The crow was a very trustworthy harbinger of good news.[5]

The throbbing of the left eye, the left thigh, the left breast and the left arm of a lady[6] were auspicious while it was

1. For references see R. II 6/16 (R. III 28/15; R. VI 16/6); R. VI 74/38; R. III 28/1; R. VII 5/48; R. III 28/4 (R. VI 16/8); R. III 28/8 (R. V 44/46); R. III 28/10; R. VI 16/7; R. VI 74/33; R.III 28/16; R.VI 82/63; R. V 76/15; R. VI 16/4; R. VII 5/48; R. III 28/14; R. VI 29/31.
2. R. V 49/31.
3. R. I 70/10 (R. VI 44/47), R. III 64/4 (R. VI 11/31), R. III 28/2 (R.VI 31/5 and R.VI 33/39), R. III 28/3 (R.VI 29/29), R. III 28/5, R. III 28/6, R. III 28/7, R. III 28/15 (R.VI 11/33), R. V 76/16, 19, R. V 76/17, R. VI 11/34, R. VI 11/36; R. VI 33/35 and R. VI 87/32.
4. R. I 70/11; R. III 76/13.
5. R. V 21/38.
6. R. V 21/35, 37; R. V 23/2-5.

inauspicious in case of a male.[1] Turning pale of the face, the clouding of vision, the hoarseness of voice, pain in the head and a depression in spirits were also evil omens.[2] It was also believed that when death was impending a person lost his sight and memory and perceived certain peculiar sights.[3]

There are references to two dreams in the Rāmāyaṇa—one of Bharata in the Ayodhyā-Kāṇḍa[4] and the other of Trijaṭā in the Sundara-Kāṇḍa.[5] Perhaps it was believed that the dream of the early morning came out to be true. The sight of a person in a dream as being driven to the South while riding an ass or a camel was indicative of his impending death. Likewise the sight of a monkey,[6] the drinking of oil and falling into a tank of cowdung in a dream were considered ominous.[7] But a ride on a white bull, elephant or an aerial car were very propitious.[8] To touch the orb of the sun and the moon with one's hand in a dream was believed to be a very good augury and promised great prosperity in very near future.[9]

---

1. R. III 66/2, R. VI 31/6; R. VI 74/35.
2. R. VI 74/35, R. III 28/17, 18; R. VII 48/12-13.
3. R. II 45/30; R. II 70/57; R. II 118/7; R. III 75/13.
4. R. II 75/8 ff.
5. R. V 21/4 ff.
6. R. V 26/4.
7. R. II 75/13.
8. R. V 21/19 ff.
9. R. V 21/17.

Chapter IX

MYTHOLOGY

A study of the conception of the divine and supernatural powers in the Rāmāyaṇa is of absorbing interest, for in this epic the relationship between the human and the divine worlds is of a very intimate character. The gods of the Rāmāyaṇa are not just benevolent spirits coming down to earth to bless a pious sacrificer or an austere hermit but their fellowship with men extends over various other fields as well. Thus they show their concern (by their presence) in any marvel occurring on earth[1] or in any momentous event happening in the life of a great hero.[2] Their interest in the proceedings of a combat between contending heroes is unceasing. On such occasions when the hero of their choice comes out triumphant they even greet him and express their joy by showering flowers and playing upon their instruments.[3] They contract marital relations with mortal beauties[4] and not infrequently seek partnership of renowned kings in their efforts to repel the forces of evil.[5] In fact the gods of the Rāmāyaṇa are seen making special efforts to manoeuvre the activities of human heroes in a specific direction, for they feel that their own security and well-being depend in a large measure upon them. Thus the whole course of Rāma's journey to the Daṇḍakas was planned and even directed by the gods in their own interest.[6]

The conception of a divinity in the Rāmāyaṇa comprises all spiritual characters. The divine family is thus constituted of heterogeneous units which include, broadly speaking (1) gods,

1. (a) Witnessing *Gaṅgāvataraṇa*—R. I 40/13-15.
   (b) Witnessing the construction of the bridge on the sea—R. V 97/1-2.
2. E.g. present in Rāma's coronation—R. VI 109/29-30, 83-85.
3. R. III 35/46-48; R. VI 69/40; R. VI 89/25.
4. E. g. Vāyu addressing the daughters of Kuśanābha—
   Ahaṃ vaḥ kāmaye sarvā bhāryā bhavata me(a)balāḥ,
   Tyaktvā mānushyakam bhāvamamaratvam avāpyatām. R. I 30/14-15.
5. R. II 11/11 ; R. V 96/43-62.
6. For details vide Appendix to chapter VII supra.

(ii) mythical saints, (iii) divine races, (iv) evil spirits and (v) divine rivers, mountains, trees, birds etc. An exhaustive account of the material available under each of the above heads will be too elaborate a study for us to attempt within the scope of the present work. We will, therefore, content ourselves for the present with important details of the first head (viz. the gods) and with few general remarks about the rest.

(i) Gods

Among the gods themselves four distinct groups may be traced, namely (i) Vedic gods like Soma, Āditya, Vāyu, Indra, Agni etc. who, though originally representative of the various phenomena of nature had this character obscured due to the tendency of anthropomorphism; (ii) deified abstractions like Dhṛiti, Smṛiti, Medhā, Śrī, Hrī, Kānti etc.; (iii) comparatively modern gods like Diśaḥ, Vidiśaḥ, Māsāḥ, Saṃvatsarāḥ, Vedāḥ, Mantrāḥ etc. who like the earlier Vedic gods were products of animism and naturism; and (iv) gods like the Gṛiha-devatā, Āśrama-devatā and Vana-devatā who enjoy the term *devatā* but "do not share the characteristics of the supernal *Devas*."[1]

Traditionally the number of the gods is cited as thirty-three (—eleven Rudras, twelve Ādityas, eight Vasus and two Aśvins)[2] but actually they are innumerable. Indra retains the title *devarāja* but in prominence he has already yielded to Brahmā and Vishṇu (and also to Śiva sometimes). The *Lokapālas* viz. Indra, Varuṇa, Kubera and Yama, the guardians of the East, West, North and South respectively, command slightly greater respect than the rest but in his own sphere a particular god is supereminent. Thus Soma is noted for his gentleness and the quality of being pleasing to all;[3] Kandarpa for his beauty;[4] Aśvins for their grace and ideal fraternity;[5] Vāyu for his strength and velocity;[6] Kubera for his wealth and

1. Hopkins, E. W., Epic Mythology, p. 57.
2. R. III 19/16.
3. *Lokapriyatve candrasya*, R. II 3/22 and *Lokakānto yathā śaśī*, R. V 28/26
4. *Rūpavān subhagaḥ śrīmān Kandarpa iva mūrtimān*, R. V 28/28.
5. *Aśvināviva rūpeṇa*, R. I 44/4 and *Aśvinoriva saubhrātram*, R. II 10/25.
6. *Balavān mātariśveva*, R. V 28/26 and *Vegaste vāyunā tulyaḥ*, R. VII 40/5.

benevolence;[1] Mṛityu for his wrath;[2] Āditya for his lustre;[3] Vishṇu for his valour;[4] Indra for his prowess and invincibility;[5] Vasudhā for her forbearance;[6] Brahmā for his endurance and equanimity[7] and Bṛihaspati for his wisdom and eloquence.[8]

Human imagination did not remain satisfied only with providing forms to the gods but gradually other accessories of life were also supplied to them. Thus gods were provided with wives and children, palaces and gardens, horses and elephants, dress and ornaments and besides, certain special characteristics which differentiated them from men. As a general rule, the gods are benign spirits devoted to the pursuit and promotion of righteousness.[9] *Tridaśa* is a term of general application for them,[10] for with the drinking of ambrosia obtained by churning the ocean they are said to have overcome old age and death.[11] Likewise, it is believed that they do not touch the earth with their feet nor wink with their eyes; their apparel does not bear dust and their flowers do not fade.[12] As a mark of their divinity the gods possess a car (*vimāna*) which moves in the air.[13] In this car they travel to partake in a sacrifice or to attend any other business of their interest. As a rule, the gods remain

1. *Dhanadena samaścārthe*, R. I 1/22 and *Dānaṃ dhanapatestulyam*, R. VII 40/6.
2. *Yasya mṛityoriva krodhaḥ*, R. VI 4/22.
3. *Āditya iva tejasvī*, R. V 28/26.
4. *Vikrameṇopapannaśca yathā Vishṇurmahāyaśāḥ*, R. V 28/27.
5. *Purandarasamo vīrye*, R. II 4/9, *Mahendramiva durdharsham Mahendramiva duḥsaham*, R. IV 13/1 and *Mahendra iva durjayaḥ*, R. V 28/26.
6. *Kshamayā pṛithivīsamaḥ*, R. V 29/9.
7. *Kshamayā Brahmaṇā samam*, R. V 28/30.
8. *Buddhyā Bṛihaspatertulyaḥ*, R. II 3/21-22 and *Mitavāgapi kāryeshu vaktā Vācaspateḥ samaḥ*, R. II 3/21.
9. *Dharmo hi śrūyate pakshaḥ surāṇāṃ hi mahātmanām.*, R. VI 11/15.
10. R. I 33/23; R. III 4/22.
11. R. I 41/19.
12. R. III 63/20.
In Śarabhaṅgā's hermitage, it may be noted, Rāma could easily recognise a god in Indra because he was possessed of a resplendent body resembling in effulgence the sun and fire; was mounted on a superb car to which were yoked green steeds; was stationed in the sky—not touching the earth; was putting on a bright attire which was without dust; and moreover, he looked to be a young man of twenty-five years—for that was the ever enduring age of the celestials. (R. III 6/3-13).
13. *Etattu Pushpakaṃ nāma vimānaṃ sūryasannibham,*
Pratigṛihṇīshva yānārthaṃ tridaśaiḥ samatāṃ vraja. R. VII 2/18.

invisible to the human eye but when they so will it, they reveal their forms to men.

There are only fragmentary accounts in the Rāmāyaṇa relating to the early history of the gods. From a canto of the Bāla-Kāṇḍa we learn that the gods were the sons of Kaśyapa born of his wife Aditi. In order to overcome disease and death through *Amṛita* (ambrosia) to be obtained from the waters they churned the ocean in collaboration with their step brothers, the sons of Diti. For churning the ocean they employed Vāsukī (a serpent chief) and Mandara (mountain) as the churning cord and pole respectively, and as a result obtained the Apsarasas, the Ucchaiḥśravā, the Kaustubha, the *Amṛita* and the physician Dhanvantarī. In the process there also arose from the ocean Vāruṇī (alias Surā), the daughter of Varuṇa, seeking a suitor for herself. Since the sons of Aditi (viz. the gods) accepted her they are known by the name *Surāḥ* (whereas the sons of Diti who declined to accept her are known as *A-surāh*). There ensued a bloody struggle between the *Suras* and the *Asuras* for the *Amṛita* in which the *Suras* ruthlessly destroyed the *Asuras* and captured the *Amṛita* for themselves.[1] Thus the gods alone are the drinkers of *Amṛita* and as such they alone enjoy immortality in the universe.[2]

From the account of Kubera in the Uttara-Kāṇḍa it appears that his divinity was the reward of severe *tapas* (penance).[3] That others too attained divine status in the same way is proved by the fact that those already enjoying the divine status were terribly afraid of an ascetic, for they suspected that the ascetic if allowed to carry on his enterprise uninterruptedly, would in the end usurp their position.[4] It may be added that Vālmīki distinctly states that there were vicissitudes in the life of the gods and that they fell from their

1. R. I 41/14-33.

2. Cf. Brahmā's statement :

Nāsti putrāmaratvaṃ hi kasyacit prāṇino bhuvi. R. VII 36/10.

N.B. Mainda and Dvivida are, however, said to have tasted of the *Amṛita* with the permission of Brahmā. (R. VI 4/7).

3. R. VII 2/10 ff. (Note the words *tridaśaiḥ samatāṃ vraja* in 18) Compare also the ambition of Śambūka—*devatvam prārthaye,* R. VII 78/19.

4. R. I 61/8; R. III 12/13.

positions; the reason of such a fall probably being an end of the merit that they had accumulated to reach heaven.[1]

The habitation of the gods is in the sky, and is variously known as *Trivishṭapa*, *Svarga*, *Tridiva*, *Surālaya*, *Devaloka*, *Nāka*, *Amarāvatī*, *Purandarapurī*, *Viṭapāvatī* and *Vasvokasārā*.[2] Here Vālmīki mentions separate courts of Brahmā, Vishṇu and Indra.[3] Possibly only the highest gods were regarded as possessing a separate court; the smaller gods living mostly at the court of the chief, Indra.[4] These residences of the gods are called *puras* (cities), *lokas* (worlds) and *vimānas* (cloudlike vehicles).[5] Occasionally the gods repair to the mountains for sports. The Kailāsa is the favourite rendezvous of Siva[6] and Meru of the gods in general.[7]

Brahmā :

Brahmā of the Rāmāyaṇa stands midway between the neuter *brahman*, the universal world-power of the earlier Vedic period and Brahmā representing the force of creation in the later trinity. The Rāmāyaṇa, in fact, presents that stage of transition in which Vishṇu was emerging as the pre-eminent leader of the gods but had not yet completely overshadowed Brahmā.[8] In the extant Rāmāyaṇa, Brahmā and Vishṇu both are the leaders of the gods—the former plans for them[9] and the latter executes the plans.

Though there are passages in the Rāmāyaṇa according to which Brahmā seems to be associated with the preservation and destruction of the worlds,[10] yet his principal function is

1. R. II 85/24; R. II 117/18; R. VI 105/7.
2. For references vide R. II 121/9 ; R. II 85/24; R. I 56/15; R. IV 60/22 ; R. IV 13/3 ; R. II 119/28 ; R. IV 62/83 ; R. V 1/46; R. V 2/5 ; R. IV 46/16. respectively.
3. *Brahmalokaṃ sanātanam*, R. I 31/4 ; *Tad Vishṇoḥ paramam padam*, R. VI 42/24 ; *Gaccha lokān Mahendrasya*, R. IV 16/113.
4. Cf. *Vasvokasāram Indrasya puraṃ suragaṇairvṛitam*, R. IV 46/16.
5. R. IV 46/16; R. IV 13/3 ; R. V 50/16.
6. R. VII 15/8.
7. R. VI 41/39.
8. Compare his epithets :
sarvadevanamaskṛitaḥ (R. I 40/3), *sarvalokanamaskṛitaḥ* (R. I 34/5), *sarvalokaprabhuḥ* (R. II 28/35) and *lokaguruḥ* (R. V 44/43).
9. Compare his epithet, *mahābuddhe* (R. V 91/58). Also note R. I 10/64.
10. R. I 36/26-28 ; R. V 50/35.

creation[1] and as such his most popular epithets are *viśvakṛit* and *lokakṛit*.[2] His several other epithets such as *pitāmaha, lokapitāmaha, lokaguru* and *prajāpati*,[3] also point to the same relationship. It is, however, to be added that in the Rāmāyaṇa, Brahmā's relationship with the creation does not cease with the mere act of creation; on the other hand one finds that as the divine patriarch it is primarily his responsibility to ensure well-being of the universe and he is actually seen anxiously engaged in preserving the worlds from the atrocities of the wicked.[4]

Brahmā is the loving and impartial father of the *Suras* and the *Asuras* alike. Still, being the upholder of righteousness he is more intimately in association with the *Suras*, the Spirits of justice and welfare. When in distress they look upon him as their highest refuge and rush to him for advice[5] and Brahmā never disappoints them. Brahmā is a great believer in penance and anyone and everyone can obtain from him his desired object by performing penance.[6] Exploiting this weakness of Brahmā, several Rākshasas obtained special powers from him and in consequence became a menance for the entire creation. In fact, the whole drama of the Rāmāyaṇa could be possible only because Brahmā granted invulnerability to Rāvaṇa. It is, however, to be observed that the indifference with which Brahmā grants boons to the Rākshasas whereby they became a threat to the security and well-being of the worlds is not indicative of his rashness or ignorance; on the other hand, it shows that he is equable to all. He rewards goodness irrespective of the consideration that it is found in the gods or demons and he knew too well that by any misuse of his kindness the wrongdoer was only inviting his ruin in the end. Thus un-

1. R. I 10/59 ; R. I 11/4 ; R. V 15/13 ; R. VI 4/29-33 ; R. VI 11/14 ; R. VI 98/13; R. VII 36/21-22.

2. R. V 15/13 and R. I 2/25 respectively.

3. For references see R. V 15/14; R. I 2/29; R. V 44/43 and R. IV 57/29 respectively.

4. R. I 15/1 ff. ; R. VII 38/56 ff.

5. R. I 10/64 ; R. I 34/4 ; R. I 36/27-28 ; R. VII 38/57 ff.

6. R. I 23/5-6 ; R. I 39/15 ; R. I 50/15-20 ; R. I 53/1 ; R. III 78/7 ; R. IV 42/13; R. IV 57/28-29 ; R. V 44/2 ; R. V 57/30 ; R. VI 63/13; R. VII 2/15.

hesitatingly he granted to Rāvaṇa his heart's desire and later felt relieved at seeing him molesting Sītā, for thus Rāvaṇa was only signing his own death warrant.[1]

In order to convey the idea of infalliability Vālmīki usually employs the name of Brahmā because his decrees are known to be unfailing.[2] Kabandha, who had propitiated Brahmā by severe penance and obtained from him a boon of long life could not persuade Indra to take his life because the words of the Pitāmaha were to prove true.[3] Thus it will be seen that in this respect Brahmā incorporates within himself the conception of 'Fate'.[4] Sometimes Brahmā is faced with difficult situations when two of his own decrees stand opposed to each other. In the fight between Yama and Rāvaṇa Brahmā found himself placed in a very great difficulty on seeing that Yama was preparing to hurl his *Kāla-daṇḍa* against Rāvaṇa, for if by that deadly weapon Rāvaṇa died or did not die—either way the consequence was falsehood for Brahmā. For upholding the veracity of his words in this case, therefore, he had to appeal to Yama to desist from employing the *Kāla-daṇḍa* against Rāvaṇa.[5] A similar situation was likely to develop in the fight between Hanūmān and Indrajit in the Sundara-Kāṇḍa. But it was averted by the prudence of Hanūmān who voluntarily consigned himself to the operation of the *Brahmāstra* (employed by Indrajit), for he thought that he should pay due regard to (the decree) of the Ātma-yoni.[6]

Brahmā is self-existent as his epithets *svayambhu*, *ātmayoni* and *avyakta-janmā* indicate.[7] But when he is subjected to figurative anthropomorphism he is described as *caturmukha* (or *caturānana* or *caturvaktra*)[8] and is identified with Dhātṛi, one of the sons of Aditi.[9] Some passages (particularly of the Uttara-Kāṇḍa) also refer to his birth from the lotus in the

1. R. III 58/10.
2. R. V 3/48 N.S.
3. R. III 78/10.
4. Note the terms *Dhātṛi* and *Dhātṛiśāsanam* in R. II 80/33 (Also vide pp. 226-228 infra).
5. R. VII 25/36-41.
6. R. V 44/43.
7. R. I 2/25; R. V 44/43 and R. VII 11/5 respectively.
8. R. VII 38/68 (R. V 51/44 N. S. and R. VII 4/11).
9. R. II 105/23.

navel of Vishṇu[1] (or from the mundane egg).[2] The same tendency assigns to him the *Brahmaloka* which is described as *anāmaya* (free from disease) and as situated above heaven.[3] Here Brahmā who is lover of *brāhmaṇas*[4] and sages receives[5] in company with his followers the noble souls arriving from the earth after a brilliant pious (or heroic) record.[6] Here again he is said to be awakened every morning by the personified four Vedas and the host of *Ṛishis*.[7]

Vishṇu :

In contradistinction to Brahmā's paternal affection and care there stands Vishṇu in the Rāmāyaṇa with his grandeur and martial haughtiness. Though known as Upendra,[8] junior Indra or Indra's younger brother, he snatches from Indra many of his titles and even behind Indra's past heroic deeds the presence of Vishṇu's might (as success-giver) is asserted.[9] Indra is himself made to attribute to Vishṇu his own status as lord of the gods and of the worlds.[10] Indra's glory as the martial hero completely fades in the presence of Vishṇu who now becomes the god's typical fighter and saviour.[11] It is declared about Vishṇu that ever since the gods came in contact with him they found in him their protector (*nātha*).[12] "I never return from the battle-field without killing my adversary",[13] is now the proud boast of Vishṇu and not that of Indra who has to run about manoeuvring (behind the curtain) against the Rākshasas;[14] they not only defeat him but even carry him as a war prisoner.[15]

1. R. VII 9/33; R. VII 63/42; R. VII 106/7.
2. R. VII 56/7 N. S.
3. R. I 40/54.
4. *Brahmā brāhmaṇavatsalaḥ*, R. VII 4/14.
5. Cf. *Pitāmahamivarshayaḥ*, R. IV 19/3.
6. R. III 6/34.
7. R. II 16/23-24.
8. R. IV 2/4.
9. Cf. R. VII 87/6-7.
10. R. VII 33/11.
11. R. VII 5/16.
12. R. VII 86/15.
13. R. VII 33/17.
14. Cf. R. III 6/17; R. III 35/43.
15. R. VII 35/38.

But about Vishṇu even the Rākshasas confess that it was difficult to conquer him.[1] Vishṇu is known to have killed or vanquished a number of enemies of the gods. Notable among them are Hiraṇya-kaśipu, Madhu, Namuci, Kālanemi, Prahlāda, Bali, Naraka and the Kāvyamātā.[2]

Vishṇu is not only the chief of the gods but in a number of passages he is glorified as God—the creation, preservation and annihilation of the universe being attributed to him.[3] He is identified with Dhātṛi and Kāla[4] and is described as the great *yogī*, the lover of his devotees[5] and the goal of man's religious acts such as charity and sacrifice.[6] Not only men but even gods are seen worshipping him. Thus in order to be cleansed of the sin of *brahma-hatyā* and for being re-instated on his former position, Indra celebrated a sacrifice in honour of Vishṇu.[7] On the lines of the Gītā, one passage of the Uttara-Kāṇḍa describes him as the re-establisher of the lost principles of *dharma*, the creator of beings, ever ready to destroy the enemies of the gods and ever cherishing those seeking his refuge.[8] The epithets *suranātha*, *surottama*, *maheśvara*, *trilokanātha*, *bhūta-bhāvana*, *akshaya* and *avyaya* are freely employed for him.[9] In several passages the whole universe with its oceans, mountains and quarters, and the various gods like the Maruts, the Vasus, the Viśvedevas etc. are conceived as forming the various parts of Vishṇu's body.[10]

Of all the gods in the Rāmāyaṇa the personification of Vishṇu is the most complete one. He bears a bright brown-

1. *Duḥkhaṃ Nārāyaṇam jetum*, R. VII 5/31.
2. For references vide R. VII 5/31; R. VII 5/15; R. VII 5/32; R. II 15/8; R. VI 48/7 and R. I 23/20 respectively.
3. R. VI 27/36; R. VI 98/43-45.
4. R. VII 27/35-38, 53.
5. *Yogī bhaktajanapriyaḥ*, R. VII 27/52.
6. R. VII 27/37.
7. R. VII 87/21.
8. *Nashṭadharma vyavasthātā kāle kāle prajākaraḥ,*
Nityodito dasyuvadhe śaraṇāgatavatsalaḥ. R. VII 7/27.
Cf. *Paritrāṇāya sādhūnāṃ vināśāya ca dushkṛitām,*
Dharmasaṃsthāpanārthāya sambhavāmi yuge yuge. Gītā IV 8.
9. For references vide R. VII 27/51, 36; R. II 28/36; R. VII 6/33 and R. I 37/26 respectively.
10. R. VI 27/29 ff.; R. VI 98/33 ff; R. VII 37/16 ff.

blue-hue.[1] The loveliness of his figure is enhanced by the yellow robe, the garland of flowers and the *Kaustubha* gem that he wears. His eyes are broad and gay like fully bloomed lotuses and on the chest he wears the *śrīvatsa* mark. His arms are four in which he holds the conch *Pāñcajanya,* the thousand-edged disc *Sudarśana,* the mace (and a lotus).[2] His bow is *Śārṅga,* also known as merely *Vaishṇava-dhanuḥ*[3], and on several occasions it becomes the property of heroes.[4] Vishṇu's favourite conveyance is Garuḍa, the lord of birds.[5] Sometimes a lotus (which forms the seat of Brahmā) is said to grow from his navel and on this account Vishṇu is known as *Padma-nābha.*[6] Śrī or Lakshmī with whom lotus is intimately associated[7] is his wife and this gives Vishṇu his popular name Mādhava—the husband (*dhava*) of Lakshmī (*Mā*).[8] Vishṇu's residence is in the sea of milk[9] (Kshīra sāgara—that is why he is known as Nārāyaṇa)[10] where at the end of an aeon, he rests on his serpent cot having drawn the universe into himself.[11] A separate habitation of Vishṇu in the heavens known after his name as the *Vishṇu Loka* or Vishṇu's *Parama-pada* is also mentioned[12] and some passages refer to the sky as the *Madhyama pada* of Vishṇu.[13]

At times when sin and evil overwhelm the creation in consequence of some wicked soul acquiring irresistible strength and when the creation cries for a redeemer it becomes incumbent upon Vishṇu as divine saviour to descend upon earth. It was

1. *Śyāmāvadātaḥ,* R. VII 6/2.
2. R. V 91/63-65.

N.B. According to R. IV 35/34-36 the thousand-edged disc and the conch *Pāñcajanya* were seized by Vishṇu from the Dānava Pañca-jana and Haya-grīva respectively.

3. R. VII 6/16; R. III 33/19.
4. R. I 71/23-25 ; R. III 16/33.
5. R. VI 28/19. Also note R. VII 5/58 where Vishṇu is shown riding over Garuḍa.
6. R VI 41/49; R. VII 7/1.
7. Cf. *sapadmayā sevyamānaṃ Śriyeva Madhusūdanam,* R. II 17/8.
8. R. VII 5/59.
9. R. V 91/69 ; R. VI 27/26.
10. Cf. Manusmṛiti, I 10.
11. R. VI 98/39; R. VII 6/4; R. VI 27/33.
12. R. VI 42/24.
13. R. VI 15/22.

in response to such a call of Brahmā and the other gods that Vishṇu is said to have been born as sons of Daśaratha.[1] The Rāmāyaṇa thus recognises the principle of incarnation and it mentions besides Rāma, Varāha, Nṛisiṃha (or Narasiṃha), Vāmana, Paraśurāma and Kṛishṇa as forms of Vishṇu. Of these, the references to Vāmana as incarnation of Vishṇu are frequent and spread over almost all the Kāṇḍas of the Rāmāyaṇa.[2] The reference to Varāha in the Sundara-Kāṇḍa indi-

1. R. I 10/70-73

It may incidentally be pointed out that there are three principal views with regard to Rāma in the Rāmāyaṇa :

According to those who consider the Rāmāyaṇa to be a representation of "a celestial myth of the Veda transformed into a narrative of earthly adventure" Rāma is only a new edition of the Indra of the Ṛigveda, battling with the demons of drought. (Jacobi, H., Das Rāmāyaṇa, Eng. tr. Ghoshal, S. N. p. 98 ff.). This view is untenable because the historicity of the epic story is proved among other things by the fact that the Ṛigveda mentions Ikshvāku, Daśaratha and Rāma as historical personages. (Bulche, C., Rāmakathā, pp. 27-29).

Some scholars lay greater reliance on the Nārada-Vālmīki episode appearing in the opening canto of the epic and opine that Rāma was a national hero. Accordingly they consider as spurious all those passages of the epic which refer to the divine character of Rāma.

Lastly, there are scholars who recognise the divinity of Rāma. In their opinion the attitude of the poet towards Rāma is best expressed in the following verse of the Yuddha-Kāṇḍa:

Ātmānam mānusham manye Rāmaṃ Daśarathātmajam,
Yo(a)haṃ jāto yathā cāhaṃ Bhagavāṃstad bravītu me. R. VI 98/20.

This clearly shows that the poet was conscious of Rāma's divinity but he represented him as a human being because Rāma's behaviour on earth corresponded to that of a normal human being.

Since the passages referring to the divinity of Rāma are frequent in all the Kāṇḍas of the Rāmāyaṇa and since there is not very convincing evidence to prove that all these passages are later additions we would like to submit that the tradition in respect of Rāma's divinity should be respected.

N. B. For Rāma's divine character following passages may be noted: R. I 10/73; R. I 17/15-16; R. I 20/4-5; R. I 71/48-49; R. II 49/10; R. II 55/17-18 ; R. II 125/3-4; R. III 6/17; R. III 16/35-36; R. III 35/44; R. V 96/24; R. VI 4/45; R. VI 11/28; R. VI 37/101; R. VI 41/49 ff.; R. VI 42/2 ff.; R. VI 72/38-39; R. VI 98/17 ff.; R. VI 110/29; R. VII 36/40-41; R. VII 100/15 ff; R. VII 106/1 ff. ; R. VII 112/8 ff.

2. R. II 15/8; R. III 69/12; R. IV 56/52; R. IV 59/12; R. V 16/25; R. VI 98/38.

cates that it belongs to the genuine portions of the Rāmāyaṇa.[1] Paraśurāma fares as a character in the Bāla-Kāṇḍa and there is not the slightest indication of his being an incarnation of Vishṇu there. In a spurious passage of the Yuddha-Kāṇḍa, however, he is mentioned as one of the incarnations of Vishṇu.[2] References to Kṛishṇa and Narasiṃha also are to be found only in the interpolated passages of the Rāmāyaṇa.[3] It may incidentally be added that there is no reference, direct or indirect, in the Rāmāyaṇa, to the exact number of Vishṇu's incarnations.

Śiva :

In Indian mythology Śiva's career is a very chequered one. It is interesting to find that the extant Rāmāyaṇa has preserved ample evidence to illustrate this fact. The Daksha story is a clear evidence to show that there was a period when Śiva was not admitted to the fold of the gods and that no share was accorded to him in sacrifices. Śiva had to resort to arms to secure for himself equal status with the rest of the gods.[4] The Bāla-Kāṇḍa expressly mentions a struggle for supremacy between Śiva and Vishṇu in which Śiva was paralysed by Vishṇu.[5] That under sectarian influence efforts continued to be made even after that to raise Śiva to the level of Brahmā and Vishṇu and even to push him over them is evidenced among other things from the fact that epithets like *maheśvara, sarvalokamaheśvara, devadeva, viśveśa, akshaya, avyaya* and *sarvadevanamaskṛitaḥ*[6] became common for him.

Again, a study of his features and traits also reveals almost a double personality. On the one hand on account of his

1. *Trātumarhasi majjantīṃ Varāha iva medinīm*, R. V 35/58 (Note also R. VI 27/22).

2. R. VI 27/25.

3. Kṛishṇa : R. VI 27/27; R. VII 55/20.
Narasiṃha : R. VI 27/23; R. VI 98/40; R. VII 27/50.

4. *Yasmād bhāgārthino bhāgaṃ na kalpayatha me surāḥ,*
Tasmādaṅgāni sarvāṇi dhanushā śātayāmi vaḥ. R. I 62/10.

5. R. I 71/17-22

6. For references see—R. I 33/29; R. I 33/15 f.n. 10; R. I 62/20; R. VI 98/13; R. VII 3/29; R. I 40/3

terrific disposition he is identified with Rudra;[1] and on the other he is known as Śiva or Śaṅkara,[2] the benign and propitious. From a man of arms, the commander of divine forces[3] he is transformed into a *yogī* of severe penances.[4] Vālmīki simultaneously describes him as a *kāmāriḥ*[5]—the enemy of Cupid—and excessive indulger in amorous sports with Umā.[6] His one epithet is *prajādhyaksha*[7] but his principal function is the annihilation of the worlds.[8]

Among the feats of Śiva the most noteworthy are (i) his bearing the Ganges on his head in compliance with the request of Bhagīratha,[9] (ii) the killing of Tripura and razing his castles to the ground,[10] and (iii) the drinking of *hālāhala* (venom) at the request of Vishṇu and the other gods.[11] Among the characters of the Rāmāyaṇa Janaka is a staunch devotee of Śiva, for the Lord is said to have rescued him from the besiegers by granting him assistance in a critical period.[12] Another devotee of Śiva is Rāvaṇa who is mentioned in the Uttara-Kāṇḍa as offering *pūjā* to *Śiva-liṅga*.[13]

The wife of Śiva is Umā, the daughter of Himavān, with whom, as already stated, he is often described sporting in the woods and on the peaks of the Himālaya. His son is Skanda who succeeded his father as the *senānī* of the gods.[14] Śiva's suite

1. R. I 32/26 ; R. III 21/36; R. VI 36/18; R. VI 52/83
2. R. III 46/11
3. R. I 34/3.
4. *yogasiddho mahāvīryaḥ*, R. IV 59/4.
5. R. I 21/10 ff.

It is interesting to note that Śiva's epithets *trinetra*, *trilocana* and *tryambaka* (R. VII 4/5; R. III 19/61; R. VI 72/38) are common in the epic still Kāma (Cupid) is said to have been consumed by the fire of Śiva's curse (R. I 21/12) and not from the flame issuing out of his eye in the forehead.

6. R. II 109/30; R. III 46/11; R. VII 15/8.
7. R. VII 5/3.
8. R. VI 72/36.
9. R. I 40/4 ff.
10. Note his epithet *tripuraha*, R. VI 73/35.

Note also R. IV 59/5; R. VI 52/83.

11. R. I 45/25-26 N. S.
12. R. I 62/20-22.
13. R. VII 19/39-45.
14. R. II 28/27.

is said at one place to be comprised of *Bhūtas*[1] (who are most probably of terrific forms and whom he also employs sometimes as his conveyance). He is very intimate with Kubera[2] who dwells in the North which is also the residence of Śiva. His fondness for animals can be gathered from his popular epithet *paśupati*[3] and also from the fact that his favourite conveyance is the bull, Nandī.[4] The bull also serves as Śiva's insignia on which account he is known as *Vṛisha-dhvaja*, *Vṛishabha-dhvaja* or *Vṛishabhāṅka*.[5] Śiva's favourite weapons are a bow and a trident. He is thus often referred to as *Pinākī*[6] and *Śūlahastaḥ* or *Triśūlapāṇiḥ*.[7]

Indra :

Indra of the Rāmāyaṇa presents an interesting instance of a god who was subjected to opposite influences with the result that in his career, one can observe a simultaneous rise and a fall. Indra of the Rāmāyaṇa retains almost all the prominent characteristics of his predecessor of the Vedic period. Thus he is chief of the gods,[8] their leader in battles,[9] the slayer of Vṛitra, Śambara and Namuci,[10] the chopper of the wings of the mountains[11] and the benefactor of mankind by bringing rains.[12] Anthropomorphism has further exalted his appearance and reflection by weaving around him a complete paraphernalia of an earthly emperor. Still, in the presence of the pressing prominence of the three principal gods, Brahmā, Vishṇu and

1. R. VI 37/3.
2. R. VII 12/29.
3. R. I 40/3

N. B. Primarily on account of this characteristic of Śiva Sir John Marshall connects him with a Harappan deity whom he calls Proto-Śiva. For details see J. Marshall, Mohenjo Daro and the Indus Civilization, Vol. I p. 52.

4. R. VII 3/27.
5. R. II 28/35; R. VI 98/13.
6. R. II 109/30.
7. *Śaṅkaraḥ śūlahastaśca*, R. V 8/74; R. VI 98/13.
8. Note his epithets *suragaṇeśa* (R. I 10/62), *tridaśeśvara* (R. I 10/76), *devarāja* (R. I 30/44) *surādhipa* (R. I 60/2) *surapati* (R. I 60/4) and *tridaśapati* (R. III 4/22).
9. R. VII 34/24-28.
10. R. III 35/41; R. V 10/60 and R. IV 8/17 respectively.
11. R. IV 61/133.
12. R. IV 23/8.

Śiva Indra of the Rāmāyaṇa is only a poor replica of the original overlord prominently extolled in the Ṛigveda. We now find that in supremacy he has lost to Brahmā whose advice he has always to seek in times of distress[1] and even as a martial leader he is junior to Vishṇu who is now the sheet-anchor of the gods against all formidable enemies.[2]

A few facts about the personal life of Indra are related in the Rāmāyaṇa. He is described as the favourite son of Aditi and Kaśyapa.[3] His wife is Paulomī[4] (also named Śacī,[5] the daughter of the Daitya Pulomā) from whom he has a son Jayanta.[6] Besides, he is said to be the father of Bālī[7] and the grand father of Aṅgada. It is said that he killed in battle his step-brothers, the sons of Diti, and consecrated himself as king of the gods in heaven.[8] Though particularly guardian of the eastern quarter[9] Indra is referred to as ruling over the three worlds[10] from his capital, Amarāvatī.[11] This town contains, besides the residence of Indra, his council hall, Sudharmā[12] and the famous garden, Nandana.[13] On account of the presence of the wish-yielding tree (Kalpavṛiksha) and the divine cow Surabhi,[14] the town is conceived as an ideal place of enjoyment so much so that it is the goal which even an ascetic would like to attain after all his severe penance.[15] Here Indra lives in the midst of luxury enjoying the choicest pleasures of divine life.

Indra is chiefly a war god. He is often described as invincible and indomitable[16] and there are frequent references to his power and prowess. The epic likens to Indra one who

1. Cf. R. V 91/58.
2. R. VII 5/16.
3. R. I 41/15; R. II 20/12.
4. R. V 57/9.
5. Note his epithet *śacīpati* (R. III 6/16; R. VI 58/4).
6. R. V 35/26, R. VII 34/8.
7. R. IV 13/1.
8. R. I 41/33.
9. The eastern quarter is referred to as *Mahendra-kāntā*, R. IV 32/60.
10. Compare his epithets *trailokyādhipati* (R. III 69/21) and *trilokarājaḥ* (R. V 86/5).
11. R. I 5/13; R. VI 15/5.
12. R. II 86/9.
13. R. V 10/13.
14. R. II 80/19 ff.
15. Cf. R. VII 80/10.
16. R. IV 13/1.

possesses power and glory[1] and conveys fondness of Indra for valour by adding, that a great hero who dies on earth after performing a valourous deed goes to *Indra-loka* where he is accorded a grand reception.[2]

For battles against his enemies Indra dresses himself in a warrior's suit[3] and sits in a car which moves in the air and is driven by green horses. His charioteer (as well as war time councillor) is Mātali who baffles the enemies by his skill in driving and thus makes the task of the knight easier.[4] Sometimes Indra fights his enemies sitting on Airāvata[5] (more often Airāvaṇa), the mighty elephant, who along with Añjana, Vāmana and Mahāpadma guards the cardinal points[6]. Uccaiḥśravā, the horse sprung from the sea[7] is also believed to belong to Indra though Indra is never described in the Rāmāyaṇa as riding it. There are frequent references to Indra's bow and other weapons,[8] but his favourite weapon is *vajra* with which he smites the enemies as well as mighty mountains. *Vajra-bhṛit* is thus his most popular epithet.[9] His other prominent epithets are *sahasra-cakshu, śata-kratu, pāka-śāsana, purandara* and *puruhūta*.[10] Popularly he is also known as Tridaśeśvara, Surādhipa, Śakra, Vāsava, Kauśika and Maghavat.[11]

The Rāmāyaṇa mentions the names of Vṛitra, Namuci, Bali, Naraka, Virocana, Śambara, Hiraṇya-Kaśipu, Maya and Dīrghajihvā whom Indra defeated or killed in the past.[12] It is, however, to be remembered that in the epic Indra is not the invincible hero of the Ṛigvedic period. The Rākshasas present themselves as formidable enemies of Indra. They corner him almost at every front. Hence he is found resorting to clandes-

1. R. II 66/7; R. II 83/40; R. IV 16/113; R. IV 25/23.
2. R. IV 16/113.
3. Note his suite in R. VI 83/10.
4. R. VI 87/11; R. VI 89/3.
5. R. III 46/8.
6. R. I 6/24 N. S.
7. R. I 41/28.
8. R. VI 83/10.
9. R. III 6/19; R. VI 1/23.
10. R. I 24/17; R. III 6/28; R. III 35/43; R. II 4/9 and R. V 8/73 respectively.
11. R. I 10/76; R. I 60/2; R. VI 39/14; R. II 43/16; R. V 91/59 and R. II 115/8 respectively.
12. For references vide : R. V 16/29; R. III 35/41; R. VII 33/9; R. III 73/13; R. V 10/60; R. V 15/28; R. IV 42/15.

tine means to defeat them instead of facing them in an open fight.[1]

Mention may also be made here of certain undertakings of Indra which fail to be consistent to his dignity and position and moral law. For these the great god had also to suffer. Thus for killing Vṛitra, the sin of *brahma hatyā* clung to him and in consequence he had to abdicate his office. He was, however, reinstated as king of gods when he performed a horse-sacrifice in honour of Vishṇu and when his sin was taken by water, trees women and earth.[2] A similar sin is attached to him for betraying his friend Namuci. He was cured of this impurity when the gods administered a specific course of purificatory bath for him.[3] Indra's seduction of Ahalyā, the beautiful wife of the sage Gotama is frequently mentioned in the Rāmāyaṇa. For this misconduct he was unmanned by Gotama by a curse[4]—(the Pitṛis later fitted him with ram's testicles) and was also made to suffer the humiliation of being captured in war by Indrajit.[5] Of such of his practices another one is the enticement of ascetics through celestial damsels lest they should dethrone him by accumulating merit.[6] Indra defends these lapses on the plea that such an act was necessitated in the interest of universal welfare. Thus in the Ahalyā episode it is said that Indra deliberately offended Gotama to excite his anger (and invite a curse) and thus cause a loss of penance to the sage.[7] The same plea is given in the enticement of Viśvāmitra through Rambhā.[8]

Varuṇa :

Another great Rāmāyaṇic god, is Varuṇa. The only

1. Cf. "This is due not so much to a new cult of special Rākṣasas as to the lowered position of Indra, which permits the poet to play with the idea of fiends capable of defeating the king of the gods but defeated by Rāma, an indication of later age or of a place where Indra's cult was much reduced."

Hopkins, E.W., Epic Mythology, p. 140.

2. R. VII 87/22, R. VII 88/2 ff.
3. R. I 22/17-19.
4. R. I 44/26; R. I 45/8.
5. R. VII 36/19 ff.
6. R. I 59/17 ff.; R. I 60/1.
7. R. I 45/2-3.
8. Note the words—*surakāryamidaṃ Rambhe*......R. I 60/1.

connection that he has with his counterpart of the Vedic period is in respect of retaining the epithet *pāśa-hasta* and the association with waters.[1] The passages in which he is bracketed with Indra[2] might be a reminiscence of the Ṛigvedic period where he fares as an associate of Indra in wars. In the Rāmāyaṇa, Varuṇa (like Indra, Yama and Kubera) is a *Lokapāla* guarding the western cardinal point.[3] Though in the account of the western quarter by Sugrīva in the Kishkindhā-Kāṇḍa Varuṇa's home is placed on the peaks of the western mountains,[4] he is more commonly said to be dwelling in the depth of the *Rasātala* in the waters.[5] The ocean is in a very large number of passages alluded to as the home of Varuṇa[6] and he himself is more popularly known as *Ambupa*, *Ambupati* and *Jaleśvara*.[7] The palace of Varuṇa is described in the Uttara-Kāṇḍa as a splendid and imposing mansion, white and huge like the pale clouds and standing like another Kailāsa.[8] There in the home of Varuṇa is the divine cow Surabhi (or the Kāmagau) whose flow of milk forms the *kshīroda* which is the source of the moon.[9]

The spiritual liquor produced from the ocean as a result of churning by the *Devas* and the *Asuras* is conceived as the daughter of Varuṇa.[10] His sons and grandsons are also mentioned and they are believed to be great heroes fighting on chariots moving at will.[11] Varuṇa's minister is Prabhāsa[12] and the Yādogaṇas (aquatic creatures) are his attendants.[13]

1. *Varuṇaḥ pāśahastaḥ*, R. V 8/74.
Note his epithet, *salileśa*, R. VII 26/26.
2. *Mahendra-varuṇopamaḥ*, R. III 40/3.
Cf. the Indra-Varuṇa Sūkta, Ṛigveda, VII 83.
3. *Varuṇaḥ paścimām āśām*, R. II 17/22.
4. R. IV 35/56-57 and 66-67.
5. R. VII 26/16.
Note that before reaching Varuṇa's home Rāvaṇa had to cross in Rasātala the Bhogavatī, the town of the Nāgas, and Maṇimatī and Aśmanagara, the towns of the Daityas., R. VII 26/3-16.
6. *Sāgaraṃ Varuṇālayam*, R. IV 8/4.
7. R. VII 2/17, R. VII 26/42 and R. VII 26/46 respectively.
8. R. VII 26/16.
9. R. VII 26/17-18.
10. *Varuṇasya tataḥ kanyā Vāruṇī*......R. I 41/25.
11. R. VII 26/24-25. (Also R. V 78/11.)
12. R. VII 26/45.
13. *Ramyaṃ yādogaṇairvṛitam*, R. VII 26/20.

Yama :

Yama of the Rāmāyaṇa also is the son of Vivasvān (and hence he is more popularly known as Vaivasvat)[1] but, unlike his proto-type in the Ṛigveda he is not a mortal who died first and became the chief of the souls of the departed.[2] Yama of the Rāmāyaṇa is a *Lokapāla* guarding the southern cardinal point.[3] Among his earlier epithets like *antaka*, *kāla* and *mṛityu*[4] which are primarily based on the idea of death there is now an important addition; the doctrine of *karma* transforms him from a reckless and ruthless Death-god into a *Dharma-rāja*,[5] the king of right and justice. The Rāmāyaṇa pictures him as seated on the *dharmāsana* and ordaining happiness and misery to the lives of people according to their acts.[6]

Yama's realm is variously known as the *Yama-loka*, *Yamālaya*, *Yamakshaya*, *Yamavishaya*, *Yamasadana* and also *Pretarājapura*.[7] On account of being the common resort of the blessed as well as the accursed it consists of two parts—one for the meritorious and the other for the sinners. The latter is characterised by darkness and absence of happiness (*nir-aya*). Here is a *Śālmalī* tree which though outwardly very attractive with its foliage of bright lapises and shining golden blossoms actually causes the greatest torture on account of its sharp iron briers.[8] More dreadful still is the *Vaitaraṇī*, the stream of blood with sand comprised of hair, marrow and such other filth,[9] and is surrounded by an awful wood of trees having swords as their leaves.[10] In this part of the *Yamaloka* are even seen creatures undergoing torments and pains and emitting loud cries and sharp shrieks.[11] The poet does not dwell upon the details of the life of the good in the *Yamaloka*. All that he

1. *Tatra Vaivasvato rājā*, R. IV 33/65.
2. Cf. Ṛigveda, X 14/2.
3. *Dakshiṇām pātu te Yamaḥ*, R. II 17/21; Also R. VII 2/16.
4. R. IV 15/11; R. VII 23/23; R. VII 25/7.
5. *Dharmarājavaśaṅgatam*, R. II 70/25.
6. R. IV 33/65; R. VII 24/2.
7. R. VII 23/26 ; R. III 41/30; R. III 53/23; R. III 14/20 and R. VII 23/16 respectively.
8. R. III 59/24.
9. R. IV 36/69.
10. R. III 59/23.
11. R. VII 21/12 N. S.

says about them is that being honoured by the attendants of Yama they enjoy life on account of their good deeds.[1]

Diseases which are represented as the 'envoys of Death'[2] are employed by Yama as his agents to fetch creatures from all over the worlds and present them before him in the *Preta nagara*. The two dogs, the sons of Saramā, are also supposed to discharge the same function.[3] Yama is believed to possess a terrible club known as the *Kāla-daṇḍa*, which was presented to him by Brahmā for the discharge of his functions and was for the same reason made unfailing in its work.[4] It is said that in times of war Yama proceeds to the battle-field seated on a chariot equipped with various weapons and is accompanied by Mṛityu and Kāla—personifications of his own aspects of 'death' and 'time' respectively.[5] Of these Mṛityu claims to have brought under his sway the most powerful ones—Hiraṇya Kaśipu, Namuci, Śambara etc.—, the great royal sages, the knowers of the *śāstras*, the Gandharvas, the Apsarasas and the Yakshas. But this he accomplished not because of his own might, but because such is the established law of nature (*maryādā*).[6]

Kubera :

Kubera, more popularly known by his patronymic name Vaiśravaṇa, is son of Viśravā by Devavarṇinī, the daughter of the sage Bharadvāja.[7] As a worthy son of his illustrious parents, Vaiśravaṇa propitiated Brahmā by his austerities and obtained from him the position of *Lokapāla* and the guardianship of 'Riches'.[8] Brahmā not only raised him to the class of Indra, Varuṇa and Yama, but as behoved his status, bestowed upon him the aerial car, Pushpaka.[9] The story may be pointer

1. R. VII 24/10-11.
2. *Mṛityudūtāśca vyādhayaḥ*, R. III 17/23.
3. *Saramīyāḥ sutau śvānau Yamasyānucarau smṛitau*, R. III 19/33.
   Compae Ṛigveda X14/11 where these dogs are believed to guard the path along which the dead man hastens to join the Fathers.
4. R. VII 25/38.
5. R. VII 25/3-5, 18.
6. R. VII 25/22-25 (note the words —*maryādā me nisargataḥ*.)
7. R. VII 2/3-7.
8. R. VII 2/10-14.
9. R. VII 2/18.

This account of Kubera (particularly the phrase, *Tridaśaiḥ samatām*

(Contd. next page.)

to the late inclusion of Yaksha worship in the Hindu pantheon and to the late recognition accorded to it by the *Āryas*. Earlier, the worship was perhaps popular only in the South, among the non-Aryan people of that area. His adoption by the North perhaps signifies the worship of a similar god in the northern regions and the assimilation of Kubera cult with that of the northern deity.

It is interesting to note here that in the boon asked by Kubera and granted to him by Brahmā there is no mention of the North. Moreover, the place where Kubera first settled as a *Lokapāla* was Laṅkā, in the South.[1] It was only later when he was driven out by Rāvaṇa from Laṅkā that he settled with his family and following on Kailāsa in the North.[2] However, Kubera's guardianship of the North seems to be a settled fact in the Rāmāyaṇa, for Sītā invoking the gods to protect Rāma said, "May Vajradhara (Indra) protect you in the East, Yama in the South, Varuṇa in the West and Dhaneśa (Kubera) in the North."[3] In view of all this Hopkins appears to be correct in holding that originally the three world-protectors protected not the cardinal points of the directions but the three worlds, viz. the earth and the worlds below and above it. But when Kubera was pushed to the rank of the *Lokapālas* a new assignment was made and the four *Lokapālas* now became the guardians of the four cardinal points.[4]

Strictly speaking, Kubera is the lord of the Yakshas.[5] But the Rāmāyaṇa lists under him, besides the Yakshas, the Gandharvas, the Kinnaras, the Rākshasas, the Nairitas, the Bhūtas and the Guhyakas. *Nairita-rāja* and *Nairitarshabha*, *Gandharva-rāja* and *Bhūteśa*[6] are among his popular epithets and one

vraja, occurring in this context) is extremely useful to illustrate how ordinary men with brilliant pious record could not only be promoted to the divine class but could also be assigned a position of eminence in divine hierarchy.

1. R. VII 2/28.
2. R. VII 10/32.
3. R. II 17/21-22.
4. Epic Mythology, p. 150.
5. *Yakshādhyakshaḥ*, R. VI 109/84.
6. R. VII 13/7; R. VII 2/30; R. II 3/57; R. V 71/17.

passage calls him *Yaksha-Rākshasa-Gandharva-Kinnareśa.*[1] *Ekapiṅgekshaṇa* is another usual epithet of Kubera and it alludes to the loss of his one (left) eye by inviting a curse of Uma through his unintended misbehaviour in looking upon her as she was sporting with her lord, Rudra. Later, however, Kubera so much pleased Śiva with his penance that the Lord offered him his friendship and also declared that he (Kubera) will be renowned by the name *Ekapiṅgekshaṇa.*[2] A large number of the epithets of Kubera refer to his guardianship of wealth. Thus he is *Dhaneśvara*, *Dhaneśa*, *Dhanādhyaksha*, *Draviṇādhipati*, *Vitteśa* and *Vittada.*[3] Śaṅkha and Padma, the personifications of treasure are his chief assistants.[4] They transported him to a place of safety after he fell unconscious as a result of Rāvaṇa's attack.[5] *Rāja-rāja*,[6] King of kings, is another usual epithet of Kubera, but its correct import is hard to explain.

The estate of the Dhanapati is naturally unique in respect of its richness and luxury. His dwelling place is a splendid white mansion built by Viśvakarmā, the divine architect on the snow-covered Kailāsa. Its gateway is garnished with gold and decked with lapises. The whole structure is embellished with the settings of gold and resembles in beauty the white clouds.[7] Attached to the palace is a grove, *Caitraratha* which is another *Nandana* in beauty.[8] It is provided with a delightful lake (*Nalinī*) which looks lively with its flocking *haṃsas* and *kāraṇḍavas*, and ever bristles with its wealth of blooming lilies.[9] The most striking among the possessions of Kubera, however, is his aerial car, Pushpaka which, as noted above, was fashioned by Viśvakarmā and presented to Kubera by Brahmā.[10] It is endowed with the celerity of thought and is most richly and agreeably furnished. It is borne by thousands

1. R. IV 36/4.
2. R. VII 12/22-30.
3. R. VII 10/32; R. II 17/22; R. VII 13/19; R. V. 71/17; R. VII 10/10 and R. VII 8/3 respectively.
4. R. VII 14/13.
5. R. VII 14/31.
6. R. II 108/4.
7. R. IV 36/31.
8. R. V 10/13.
9. R. IV 36/32.
10. R. VII 2/18.

of *Bhūtas* (Spirits ?) possessing the velocity of thought.[1] It is perhaps on this account that Kubera is known as *Nara-vāhana*.[2]

Agni :

It is but natural to expect that an age which insisted on daily *agnihotra* and commended special sacrificial sessions should regard Agni in great estimation. Agni in the Rāmāyaṇa retains several of his earlier epithets like *pāvaka* (purifier), *citrabhānu* and *vibhāvasu* (shining with light), *havya-vāha* (oblation carrier) and *araṇi-suta* (son of *araṇis*).[3] Still, that intimacy with Agni which existed in the Ṛigvedic times, when he was the lord of the house (*gṛihapati*), the favourite guest (*atithi*) and the esteemed priest (*ṛitvik*) is missing in the Rāmāyaṇa. Presumably the intervening Brāhmaṇa period which held the ritual to be all important was responsible for this. Agni as a god in the Rāmāyaṇa is more prominent in his role of a witness of the world (*loka-sākshī*);[4] he observes everything done overtly or covertly.[5] Thus he is invited to be a witness in marriage;[6] alliances are contracted in his presence;[7] and a wife whose fidelity to her husband is questioned invokes Agni to her aid to declare her purity.[8]

Popularly speaking the fires are three (*trayognayaḥ*),[9] though sometimes five fires are also alluded to.[10] The Rāmāyaṇa also mentions the *Ananta* fire which consumes the worlds.[11] Agni's seat is the *vedī* (altar) in the *agnyāgāra*, *agniśālā* or *agniśaraṇa* (the fire chamber)[12] where he dwells feeding himself on the *havya* (offerings to the gods) and the *kavya* (offerings to the

1. R. V 5/40.
2. R. III 36/15.
3. R. IV 4/14; R. IV 62/43; R. VI 97/23; R. VI 97/19; R. V 8/49.
4. R. VI 41/40; R. VI 97/26.
5. R. VI 99/11.
6. R. VII 11/19.
7. R. IV 4/15.
8. R. VI 97/28.
9. Cf.—*jvaltitāstrayo* (*a*)*gnayaḥ*, R. II 117/35. The names of these three fires are *gārhapatya*, *dakshiṇa* and *āhavanīya*. But they are not mentioned in the Rāmāyaṇa.
10. These five fires are the four fires blazing in four altars and the sun as the fifth fire over the head.
11. R. VI 107/98.
12. R. II 35/2; R. V 76/16 and R. III 4/4 respectively.

manes).[1] In the homes of the *āhitāgnis* he was perpetually maintained and people like Indrajit and Rāvaṇa before going to the battle-field drew omens from the flaems of the *yajñāgni* to ascertain their victory in the fight.[2] Similarly, on Sītā's prayer Agni with his bright and steady flames bending towards the right communicated to her the welfare of Hanūmān.[3]

Agni's wife is Svāhā.[4] He is, however, said at one place to have begotten Kumāra by depositing his energy in Gaṅgā at the request of the gods.[5] The sage Suprabha[6] and the Vānara Nīla[7] are also said to be his sons. He is also said to have produced the Śveta mountain by entering Śiva's energy in conjunction with Vāyu.[8]

(ii) Mythical Saints

In the list of divinities collectively invoked or described as flocking in the sky to witness a fight, competition or any such other momentous event happening on the earth the Rāmāyaṇa generally includes a class of saints who are indiscriminately called *Ṛishis*, *Maharshis*, *Paramarshis*, *Viprarshis*, *Brahmarshis*, *Devarshis*, *Munis*, *Siddhas*, *Sādhyas* and *Cāraṇas*.[9] This class of saints is a miscellaneous one being comprised on the one hand of individual sages like Durvāsā and Nārada, and on the other of groups like that of :

(i) Siddhas, Sādhyas and Cāraṇas who possess no distinct individuality except what can be gathered from their nomen clature;

(ii) Bālakhilyas, which is a group of sages possessing a certain distinct individuality in the sense that they are always described as anchorites (*vaikhānasas*)

1. *havyakavyāśī*, R. VI 98/1.
2. R. VI 53/18-26; R. VI 58/5-11; R. VI 82/22 ff.
3. R. V 49/31 ff.
4. *Agneḥ Svāhā yathā patnī*, R. V 19/24.
5. R. I 34/11-23.
6. R. VII 98/4.
7. R. I 17/13 N. S.
8. R. I 33/21.
9. For references vide : R. I 10/68; R. IV 62/44; R. VI 100/42; R. VII 24/4; R. II 28/26; R. III 28/26; R. III 30/14; R. II 28/20; R. VI 37/57.

and as drinkers of the rays of the sun (*marīcipāḥ*);[1] and

(iii) The personifications of stars and constellations, prominent among them being the *Saptarshis*[2]—the seven *Ṛishis* (Marīci, Aṅgirā, Atri, Pulastya, Pulaha, Kratu and Vasishṭha) who are personifications of the seven stars of the constellation Ursa Major. Of these some are referred to in the Rāmāyaṇa as stars and also as individual characters actively participating in the progress of the drama.[3]

A close perusal of the account of individual sages and of those belonging to the various groups noted above reveals that Vālmīki's conception of a *ṛishi* is, "an inspired person (human or divine) possessing a glorious pious record which enables him to be invested with certain divine traits such as supernal vision, the power to bless and curse, the power to fly in the air, free access to the spheres of the gods and the like". With the exception of Śukra who is sometimes described as the preceptor of the *Asuras* and the Rākshasas and in that capacity aiding them against the *Devas*,[4] the *ṛishis* always sympathise with the forces of good and try to foster their cause. It is difficult as well as unnecessary to speak of all the sages mentioned in the Rāmāyaṇa as their number is very large. We, however, describe here Nārada and Bṛihaspati, as each of them has a distinct individuality.

Nārada who is called a *ṛishi*, *maharshi*, *viprarshi*, *viprendra* and *devarshi*[5] is an interesting example illustrating the indifference with which the poet employs these terms. He is also called *brahman* (holy) and *kālatrayajña*[6] (knower of the three times—past, present and future), and his main accomplishments are that he is *mahāyogabalānvitaḥ* (possessed of the great power of *yoga*) and *nṛityagāndharva-kovidaḥ*[7] (proficient in dance

1. R. III 39/18, 32.
2. R. IV 36/57.
3. For example Pulastya—R. VII 1/33 ff; R. VII 21/1 ff.
4. R. VII 31/6 ff.
5. R. VII 24/5; R. VII 23/13; R. VII 24/4; R. VII 23/22 and R. VII 23/1 respectively.
6. R. VII 23/13 and R. I 1/9 respectively.
7. R. VI 27/14 and R. VII 24/4 respectively.

and music). His meetings with Vālmīki in the opening canto of the Bāla-Kāṇḍa[1] and with Rāvaṇa in the Uttara-Kāṇḍa[2] clearly bring out his two principal characters, viz. (i) of being almost a moving encyclopaedia on account of roving from place to place and (ii) of fostering disputes. The Rāmāyaṇa beautifully sums up his entire character in one expression viz. *deva-gandharva-vihāra-samara-priya.*[3]

Bṛihaspati is a complex character. He has attained the position of a star in the sky.[4] He is a god[5] as well as the priest of the gods.[6] He is *vācaspati* (Lord of Speech) noted for his eloquence and wisdom.[7] In his capacity as the preceptor of the gods he restores to life the dead and injured gods by divine medicinal plants treated with *mantras*,[8] and commands great respect.

(iii) **Divine Races** :

Associated with the Devas and sharing most of their traits are hosts of benevolent beings like the Yakshas, the Gandharvas, the Kinnaras, the Apsarasas, the Guhyakas, the Bhūtas, the Vidyādharas, the Nāgas (Pannagas and Uragas)[9] and the Patagas (or Pataṅgas). Out of these no detail is given in the Rāmāyaṇa about the Patagas except that they generally appear in conjunction with the Uragas in the lists

1. In this meeting Vālmīki enquired of Nārada whether he knew of a person with almost super human qualities such as benevolence, continence etc. Nārada, in reply, named the Dāśarathi Rāma.—R. I 1/1 ff.

2. In this meeting Nārada suggested to Rāvaṇa that he should employ his prowess in subduing Yama and then he himself rushed to Yama to inform him about Rāvaṇa's designs.—R. VII cantos 23-24.

3. R. VII 23/13.

4. *Bṛihaspatibudhārkenduśukrāṅgarākarāhavaḥ*, R. II 44/10.

5. *Devo Vācaspatiryathā*, R. V 28/28.

6. *Śakrasyeva Bṛihaspatiḥ*, R. VII 21/7.

7. *Satyavādī madhuravāg devo Vācaspatiryathā*, R. V 28/28.

8. R. VI 27/3.

9. The Nāgas, Pannagas and Uragas are synonymous terms, But sometimes distinctions are tried to be drawn among them. Thus R. III 14/28 N. S. describes Nāgas as sons of Surasā while Pannagas are said to be the children of Kadru. Nāgojī-Bhaṭṭa records the opinion of Tīrtha and Kataka who respectively hold : *Nāgā bahuphaṇāḥ sarpāḥ, tadanye Pannagāḥ* and *nirvishāḥ Nāgāḥ, tadanye Pannagāḥ*.

of other divinities [1] The Nāgas who are described as 'like gods'[2] are believed to be the children of Surasā (the Nāga-mātā).[3] There are frequent references to their splendid town, Bhogavatī in the *Pātāla* which is believed to be strongly guarded by the Nāgas.[4] In this town resides Vāsuki, the lord of serpents.[5] Takshaka, Śaṅkha and Jaṭī are some of the other chiefs of the Nāgas.[6] Rāvaṇa is known to have attacked the town Bhogavatī, vanquished the Nāgas and even raped Sundarī, the wife of Takshaka.[7] However, the all time enemy of the Nāgas is Suparṇa (Garuḍa) whose very presence becomes intolerable to them.[8]

The Vidyādharas, as their very name suggests, are repositories of great wisdom (*mahāvidyāḥ*).[9] Though essentially spirits of air, the Vidyādharas, being fond of sports go to the mountain peaks (which are their usual haunts) for merry-making.[10] On Citrakūṭa, Rāma showed to Sītā lovely sport-fields of the Vidyādhara ladies.[11] Since the Vidyādharas are described as timid by nature an unusual sight or sound easily frightens them.[12]

Though bracketed in a passage with the Rākshasas as night-rangers[13] the Yakshas are always grouped with beings of benevolent disposition. Perhaps it is only to emphasise their good character that the Uttara-Kāṇḍa narrates the mythical story which alludes to their association with 'worship.'[14] The Yakshas are the attendants of Kubera and live with him on

1. R. III 53/2; R. IV 32/38; R. IV 36/42, 70.
2. *devakalpaiḥ*, R. IV 60/16.
3. *Surasāṃ Nāgamātaram*, R. IV 62/12.
4. R. III 36/13; R. IV 33/50; R. V 1/23; R. V 2/5; R. VII 26/3-4.
5. R. IV 33/51; R. VII 26/4.
6. R. V 78/8.
7. R. III 36/13; R. VII 26/3-4.
8. R. VI 28/4-7. (Also see p. 221 infra).
9. *Darśayanto mahāvidyāste tu Vidyādhararshabhāḥ*, R. IV 61/33.

According to E. W. Hopkins this great wisdom is "The Yoga trick of diminishing their size".—Epic Mythology, p. 175.

10. R.IV 61/28-33.
11. R. II 107/11.
12. R. II 110/1, 5; R. IV 61/28.
13. R. I 31/18.
14. R. VII 4/13 N. S. (Contd. next page)

Kailāsa in the North[1] though they can be seen on other mountains also such as Himavān and Mahendra,[2] and even in air in company with other righteous beings like the Devas, the Gandharvas etc.[3] The Uttara-Kāṇḍa represents them as militant beings, employing for them epithets like *raṇa-viśārada* and *yuddha-śālī*[4] but in the Bāla-Kāṇḍa they are called *alpa-vīryāḥ*.[5] With females of other divine races (such as Gandharvī, Kinnarī etc.) a Yakshiṇī is also recognised as a beautiful woman,[6] and her eyes are believed to be particularly handsome.[7]

The Guhyakas are a group allied with the Yakshas. They are also benign beings living on Kailāsa and other mountains[8] as attendants of Kubera.[9]

References to the Bhūtas are often vague in the Rāmāyaṇa. Thus in passages like *sādhu sādhviti bhūtāni pra-śaśaṃsus-tadā harim* and *bhūtāṇyākāśa-cāriṇi tamūcuḥ Plavageśvaram*[10] the term *bhūta* is liable to be understood as standing for beings in general rather than for a separate group. However, in various other passages where they are mentioned along with Suras, Asuras, Ṛishis, Mahoragas, Yakshas, Gandharvas etc. they must be recognised as a distinct class of beings.[11] In the Sundara-Kāṇḍa thousands of Bhūtas, speedy like mind and possessing faces bedecked with ear-rings are said to carry the Pushpaka.[12] This may indicate that like the Yakshas and the Guhyakas the Bhūtas are also to be included among the attendants of Kubera, though sometimes they are also associated with Rudra (Śiva) who is called *Bhūtapati*.[13]

Dr. E. W. Hopkins assigns a different meaning to the word *yakshāmaḥ*. He writes in his Epic Mythology, p. 41, "......Some of these creatures cried *rakshāmaḥ*, "let us guard", while others cried *yakshāmaḥ*, "let us gobble", so guards and goblins they became." We beg to submit that this is not the spirit of the text.

1. R. V 78/4.
2. R. IV 36/19; R. IV 60/16.
3. R. I 40/13; R. IV 61/90.
4. See—*Yakshān raṇaviśāradān* (R. VII 13/4) and *Yakshāṇām yuddha-śālinām* (R. VII 14/2).
5. *Alpavīryāḥ yadā Yakshāḥ*, R. I 23/2.
6. R. V 27/9.
7. *Svakshī Yakshī*, R. VII 4/37.
8. *Guhyakaiḥ sevitaśśivaiḥ*, R. II 107/22.
9. R. IV 36/33.
10. R. IV 62/38 and 65 respectively.
11. R. VI 37/134; R. VI 46/155.
12. R. V 5/40.
13. R. II 118/24; R. III 19/34; R. VI 37/3.

Like the Vidyādharas the Kinnaras also bear close relationship to the mountainous regions. Their presence is described on Citrakūṭa, Mahendra, Suvela, Droṇa, the Himavān and the hills in Janasthāna.[1] The Mahendra is described as being frequented by hosts of Kinnaras[2] and on Citrakūṭa both Rāma and Bharata observed Kinnaras possessing divine forms and sporting in company with their female partners.[3] Like the Vidyādharas, the Kinnaras are also very timid,[4] but it is only a Kinnarī who serves as an ideal type of figure for the sullen picture of a lady in separation from her lover[5] or of any lady in melancholy state.[6] Most probably the Aśva-mukhīs described in the Kishkindhā-Kāṇḍa as having their dwelling places on the Maināka[7] belong to the class of the Kinnaras.

The Apsarasas, literally explained in the Rāmāyaṇa as women sprung from the essence of waters at the time of the churning of the ocean,[8] are divine courtezans. It is said that in the beginning when they appeared from the sea-water, neither the Devas nor the Dānavas accepted them, so they became *sādhāraṇīs*, i.e. belonging to all.[9] Befitting their role the Apsarasas possess an extremely comely frame of body, the charms of which are heightened by magnificient dress, ornaments and other accomplishments like graceful gait and musical voice.[10]

1. R. II 106/13; R. IV 33/32; R. V 54/6; R. VI 3/21; R. IV 36/19 and R. III 73/7 respectively.
2. *Bahukinnarasevitaḥ*, R. IV 33/32.
3. R. II 106/13; R. II 107/10.
4. R. II 110/5.
5. Cf. R. V 31/1.
6. *Patiteva Kinnarī*, R. II 12/24.
7. R. IV 36/56.
8. R. I 41/21-22.
9. *Apratigrahaṇāttāśca sarvāḥ sādhāraṇīkṛitāḥ*, R. I 41/25.
10. Thus Rambhā is described in the Uttara-Kāṇḍa as an ideal of feminine beauty (*Ityeshā hyupamā strīṇāṃ svarge(a)pi varavarṇinām*) She is depicted as dressed in an apparel looking like a sable cloud and bearing (on her face) a dainty *viśeshaka* ornamentation which was rendered attractive by flowers of all seasons. Her face was like the moon; her complexion golden; her thighs tapering like the trunk of an elephant; her arms delicate like lotuses; her waist like the cenre of *vajra*; her hips expansive like the sandy bank (of a river); her feet possessing the lustre of bloomed lotuses and having beautiful fingers. In her voice she was a lute; in her gait she was a female swan; and her teeth were like *kunda* flowers. (R. VII 32/11-14.)

Further, the Apsarasas in general, are known to be experts in the arts of dance and music, and particularly in the art of amorous sports.[1]

Their numbers are fabulous. Sixty *koṭis* (crores) of them are said to have come out of the sea waters.[2] 'Thirty thousand' and 'several thousands' of celestial damsels are said to have been deputed by Indra and Kubera respectively in response to the call of the sage Bharadvāja.[3] However, the prominent Apsarasas are Ghṛitācī, Menakā, Rambhā, Miśra-keśī, Alambushā, Tilottamā, Hemā, Muñjakeśī, Varūthinī, Puṇḍarīkā, Vāmanā and Urvaśī.[4] Quite often when the Devas (specially Indra) become apprehensive of the intentions of a sage they employ these Apsarasas to seduce him and it is only with reluctance that they accept such an assignment.[5] Nevertheless, their charms have proved availing against the ascetics and their notable victims are Viśvāmitra and Madakarṇi. Viśvāmitra fell a prey to the charms of Menakā and Rambhā[6] (—sometimes the name of Ghṛitācī is also mentioned in connection with Viśvāmitra)[7] and Madakarṇi became so fond of the five Apsarasas who had come to seduce him at the bidding of the Devas that he built a beautiful house in a lake and lived there ever enjoying their company.[8] Sometimes, the Apsarasas are also referred to as attending upon the sages in their *āśramas*[9] or upon a gallant or a meritorious person arriving in the heaven from the earth.[10]

The Rāmāyaṇa is assiduously silent about the early history of the Gandharvas. No doubt, Kubera is sometimes called the

1. Vide : *Nṛityagītaviśāradāḥ* (R. IV 42/18) and *Krīḍārativihārābhiḥ* (R. III 39/19).
2. R. I 41/22.
3. R. II 104/46-47.
4. For references see R. II 104/17, 49 and R. III 53/17.
5. Rambhā could be persuaded by Indra to proceed against Viśvāmitra only on the assurance that he will himself be present there along with Kandarpa (to assist her). R. I 60/5-6.
6. R. I 59/5 ff., R. I 60/8-11.
7. R. IV 28/6-7.
8. R. III 12/15-17.
9. *Pūjitañcopanṛittañca nityam apsarasāṅgaṇaiḥ*—the *āśrama* in the Daṇḍakāraṇya. R. III 4/3.
10. R. VII 28/2-3, 10-11; R. VII 79/40.

king of the Gandharvas also,[1] but the leaders of the Gandharvas are Śailūsha, Grāmaṇī, Bhikshu, Suvalgu, Nārada, Tumburu, Gopa, Parvata and Sūryamaṇḍala.[2] Of these the first two and the last five are named in different contexts as kings of the Gandharvas.[3] The name of Śailūsha is rather more frequent in the Uttara-Kāṇḍa. His daughter Saramā, it is said, was married to the Rākshasa Vibhīshaṇa[4] and it was against the descendants of Śailūsha, established on the either side of the river Sindhu that a military expedition was launched jointly by the kings of Ayodhyā and Kekaya under the leadership of Bharata.[5] Inspite of all this the Gandharvas appear to be the closest companions of the Devas—they are associated with them not only in the witnessing of a combat or a marvel, in greeting or cheering a hero, in attending a festival but also in sacrifices where the gods assemble to receive their share of the oblations.[6]

The resort of the Gandharvas appears to be on the mountains where not infrequently they are represented as guardians of plant life. Thus Sugrīva told the Vānara-party bound for the South, that on the Ṛishabha mountain there was a forest of sandal wood which was guarded by Rohita Gandharvas.[7] Similarly, he asked the party going to the West to avoid a clash with the Gandharvas on the Pāriyātra mountain by not touching the fruits and the roots there.[8] In the Yuddha--Kāṇḍa Hanūmān when attempting to pluck certain medicinal plants from the Droṇa mountain had to face a strong resistance from the Gandharvas.[9] There are references to the *lokas, nagaras* or *bhavanas* of the Gandharvas but there is a suggestion in one passage that those were of a deceptive character being different from what they appeared.[10]

1. *Yaksha-Rākshasa-Gandharva-Kinnareśvṇa*, R. IV 36/4.
2. For references see R. II 104/48; R. IV 33/56.
3. R. II 104/48; R. VII 11/24.
4. R. VII 11/24.
5. R. VII 102/11-20.
6. R. I 40/25; R. I 69/28; R. III 35/42.

Note : *Tato Devāḥ sa-Gandharvāḥ Siddhāśca Ṛishibhiḥ saha,*
Bhāga pratigrahārthaṃ vai pūrvameva samāgatāḥ. (R. I 10/51).

7. R. IV 33/54-56.
8. *rakshanti phalamūlañca*, R. IV 35/30-31.
9. R. VI 81/101-102.
10. *Naiva vyaktaṃ svaram manye darśanaṃ kiñcideva tu,*
Gandharvanagara prakhyā māyaishā rakshasā kṛitā. R. III 50/15.

Various fights of the Gandharvas are alluded to in the Rāmāyaṇa but a Gandharva, serving as an ideal of beauty, seems to be an easy-going person given to pleasures. Sampāti referred to the Gandharvas as exceedingly lewd[1] and on the Mahendra mountain, prior to Hanūmān's flight, the Gandharva couples were seen engaged in drinking and dalliance.[2] Tumbura was cursed by Kubera for his excessive attachment to Rambhā.[3] The Gandharvas appear to be primarily devoted to the pursuit of fine arts like dance and music. *Kaiśikācārya*, which is explained by Nāgojī-Bhaṭṭa as a teacher of *gāna-vidyā* and *nṛitya-vidyā* is a term employed as an epithet for the Gandharvas,[4] and music is popularly known after them as *gāndharva*.[5] Tumburu and Nārada are specially noted for their proficiency in music.[6] In Bharadvāja's hermitage, for the entertainment of Bharata and his army, the Gandharvas sang and played on their musical instruments while the Apsarasas danced.[7]

(iv) Evil Spirits

Parallel to the Devas the Rāmāyaṇa refers to a class of beings who, no doubt, possess almost all the traits of the Devas but are distinguished as a group hostile to the Devas on account of their opposition to goodness.[8] The Daityas, the Dānavas, the Asuras, the Rākshasas, the Yātudhānas and the Piśācas

1. *Tīkshṇakāmāstu Gandharvāḥ*, R. IV 59/9 N. S.

Attention may incidentally be drawn here to the *Gāndharva* marriage which is the most loose form of marriage requiring only mutual agreement of the parties. Perhaps this also explains the numerous marriages of the Gandharvas with the Rākshasas. (R. VII 4/1-2, 27 and R. VII 11/24).

2. *Nānā Gandharvamithunaiḥ pānasaṃsargakarkaśaiḥ*. R. IV 67/45 N. S.

3. R. III 5/41-44. This account of Tumburu agrees very closely with the *yaksha* of the Meghadūta and might have been the source of inspiration for Kālidāsa.

4. R. IV 62/40 (*Kaiśikaṅgānanṛityavidyā, tadācāryaiḥ Tumburuprabhṛitibhir Gandharvaiḥ*—Tilaka-Ṭīkā).

5. Cf. Nārada's epithet, *nṛityagāndharvakovidaḥ* in R. VII 24/4.

6. R. V 97/42; R. VII 24/4.

7. R. II 104/26.

8. An interesting illustration of this distinction between these two groups is presented in course of the Lāṅkā war where the *Devas* were cheering up Rāma while the *Asuras* were cheering up Rāvaṇa, R. VI 84/8.

Compare also E. W. Hopkin's remark about the *Asuras*—"Opposition to light and goodness, love of and use of *māyā*, illusion or deception (tricks),

constitute this hostile group possessing an innate evil inclination. For convenience of treatment we may divide them into two groups : formed of the first three (viz. Daitya, Dānava and Asura) and the last three (viz. Rākshasa, Yātudhāna and Piśāca) respectively. Though there might have been once some distinction among the Asuras, Daityas and Dānavas, this had practically disappeared by the time of the Rāmāyaṇa which interchanges them freely.[1] Similarly interchangeable are the members of the second group; though the Rākshasa class can be shown to have two subdivisions, namely Rākshasas by birth and Rākshasas on account of having adopted Rākshasa culture and ways of life.[2]

In the group of the Daityas, the Dānavas and the Asuras the Daityas (also called Daiteyas) who derive their name from their mother Diti, the wife of Kaśyapa[3] should be looked upon as the principal ones. They are also called Asuras (*a—surāḥ*) because they disowned Surā, the daughter of Varuṇa who had appeared from the ocean as a result of the joint effort of the Devas and the Daityas.[4] The entire earth is said to have belonged in the beginning to the Daityas.[5] But later, being dis-lodged of their position by the Devas assisted by Vishṇu they had to hide themselves in the nether regions which subsequently became their permanent abode.[6] Hosts of Asuras are believed to be living in the bottom of the sea.[7] On his way to Varuṇa's home, through the waters of the sea, Rāvaṇa is said to have come across a host of the Daityas

a roaring voice, ability to assume any shape, or to disappear, are their general characteristics; in which they differ from Rākṣasas not at all and except for the first element not from the gods."

—Epic Mythology, p. 48.

1. Dundubhi and his son Māyāvī are described as *Asuras* in R. IV 8/25 and R. IV 7/27 respectively. But elsewhere the former is referred to as *Daityāpasada* (R. IV 8/32) and the latter as *Dānava* (R. IV 7/56). Similarly Maya is a *Ditijaḥ* (born of Diti =*Daitya*) at one place (R. VII 11/6), a *Dānavarshabha* and *Dānavendra* at another (R. IV 42/11, R. V 78/7) and an *Asura* at the third (R. IV 27/22).

2. For details vide chap. XIV infra.

3. *Ditiśca janayīmāsa Daityāṃścaiva yaśasvinaḥ.* R. III 19/17

4. R. I 41/25-28.

5. *Yeshāmiyaṃ vasumatī purāsīt sa-mahārṇavā.* R. III 19/17.

6. R. VII 7/21.

7. The sea is called *asura kshayam*, R. V 73/3 (Note also R. IV 61/56).

known as Nivāta-Kavacas who lived in their town Maṇimati and with whom, on the advice of the Pitāmaha, he entered into an alliance.[1] Aśma-nagara was another town belonging to the Daityas in the same region.[2] In the ocean, again, a town Prāg-jyotisha is mentioned where the Dānava Naraka resided.[3] In a few cases the mountain caves are said to be the home of the Asuras and the Dānavas. On being pursued by Bālī Māyāvī, the son of Dundubhi ran for his life to the mountain cave, his home, where he lived with his other kindred.[4] Maya also, a Dānava, lived in a cave in the Vindhyas which served for him as a strong-hold.[5]

The Asuras are noted for their *māyā* (illusion).[6] The chief Asuras and Dānavendras (e. g. Namuci and Kālanemī) are called *māyavīs.*[7] Śambara is known as a *bahu māyaḥ* and so is Maya a *māyāvī.*[8] One passage refers to a machine of the Dānavas.[9] Maya is renowned as an architect of the Dānavas just as Viśvakarmā is of the Devas.[10] He is said to have built several beautiful houses in Laṅkā.[11] The splendid garden inside the cave on the Vindhya mountain in which there were lovely golden trees and artificial lakes with golden fish was also his construction.[12] These references indicate that this group (of Asuras and Dānavas) was noted for craftsmanship, and had reached a high stage of material culture.

The second group of the evil beings consists of the Rākshasas, the Yātudhānas and the Piśācas. Of these the Yātudhānas are completely identical with the Rākshasas.[13] A story

1. R. VII 26/4-12.
2. R. VII 26/15.
3. R. IV 35/39.
4. R. IV 7/31 ff. (Note 61—*nihataśca mayā yuddhe sānugaḥ sahabāndhavaḥ.*
5. R. IV 42/13-14.
6. *Āsurī māyā,* R. III 60/13.
7. R. VII 5/32-33.
8. R. II 11/13 and R. IV 42/11 respectively.
9. *Tasya nirdaśato dantāṃśchuśruve dantanisvanaḥ.* *Yantrasyāveshṭyamānasya mahato Dānavairiva.* R. VI 71/18.
10. *Dānavamukhyānāṃ Viśvakarmā babhūva saḥ,* R. IV 42/12.
11. R. V 5/12.
12. R. IV 41/20-24.
13. The term *Yātudhāna* is very freely and frequently employed for the Rākshasas in the Araṇya-Kāṇḍa, R. III 29/27; R III 30/5, 8; R. III 38/6.

in the Uttara-Kāṇḍa attributes their origin to Yadu, the son of Yayāti by Devayānī, but there also the term Rākshasa stands in apposition to them.[1] The Piśācas generally appear in conjunction with the Patagas and the Uragas[2] but the Rāmāyaṇa provides no help towards the unfolding of this relationship. At various places the Piśācas are mentioned with the Rākshasas and identified with them. To wit, it is said that in Laṅkā Rāvaṇa asked the Piśācīs to wait upon Sītā and to look upon her with the same regard as was due to himself or his queen. But immediately after his words the poet refers to these 'Piśācīs' as 'Rākshasīs'.[3] Dancing and rejoicing in drinking of blood and eating of raw meat are no distinctive traits of the Piśācas in the Rāmāyaṇa, for these are equally shared by the Rākshasas as well. All these classes had by Vālmīki's time become associated with some mythical elements.[4] But as they were essentially human, we propose to deal with them in a separate chapter.

(v) Divine Rivers, Mountains, Trees, Birds etc.

This last group is comprised of deified rivers, *tīrthas* (holy places), mountains, birds etc. They were held to be divine in the sense that they were believed to be the forces of good possessing power to bless and confer boons and hence deserving worship. The members of this group are also invested with several human traits, for example, mountains and cows can speak like human beings. But leaving the case of a few like Gaṅgā, Samudra and Himavān, their anthropomorphism is of a very rudimentary character.

Waters of the rivers are themselves holy and render holy the person or place that touches them. Thus by *abhisheka* (bath) and *ācamana* (sipping) people secure outer and inner purity

1. *Rākshasān yātudhānāṃstvaṃ janayishyasi dāruṇān*, R. VII 60/8.
2. *Piśācapatagoragāḥ*, R. III 53/2; R. IV 36/42, 70.
3. *Rākshasīśca tathoktvā sa Rākshasendraḥ pratāpavān*, R. III 60/17.
4. *Pātitaḥ sa tu Kaikeyyā sthānādishṭād yatheshṭataḥ,*
   Pradishṭo Rakshasām bhāgaḥ parvaṇīvāhitāgninā. R. II 46/5.

Also : The Rākshasas follow an army to the battle-field in order to enjoy a feast of human flesh and blood—

Māṃsāśanāni sattvāni Rakshāṃsi sumahānti ca,
Anugacchanti Bharataṃ pipāsanto hyasṛgbahu. R. VII 102/23.

and by offering *tarpaṇa* bring happiness to the departed ones. Rivers are invoked to grant wishes. Sītā implored Bhāgīrathī to help Rāma in the successful completion of his father's orders and vowed for her an elaborate *pūjā* on Rāma's regaining his kingdom.[1] The spot where more than one rivers met was considered extremely holy. Bharata paid his respects to the Prayāga, the meeting place of the Gaṅgā and the Yamunā[2] and so did Rāma and Lakshmaṇa to the confluence of Sarayu and Jāhnavī.[3]

Rivers as a rule are called the daughters of the mountains and the wives of the ocean. Thus Gaṅgā is frequently spoken of as the daughter of Himālaya[4] and the queen of Samudra.[5] Sugrīva in his account of the South referred to the river Kāverī as proceeding to meet her lover Samudra with whom she had fixed up an appointment.[6] Sometimes the diverse moods of the rivers are alluded to. It is said that at the sight of the wicked Rāvaṇa Godāvarī was suddenly smitten with fear and that her flow slowed down.[7] Similarly Gaṅgā, sympathising with the bewailing Rāma, approached him to communicate to him the whereabouts of Sītā, but then, she withdrew for fear of the Rākshasa (Rāvaṇa).[8] Gaṅgā's pride is also alluded to when she wanted to disappear in the nether regions carrying with her flow Śaṅkara who was preparing to hold her on his head.[9]

The personification of the ocean who serves as an ideal symbol of serenity[10] and as an ideal dwelling place for the Nāgas, the Asuras, the Daityas and also the Rākshasas is a little more developed one. The ocean is called Sāgara after the name of Sagara[11] whose sixty thousand sons enlarged him in their attempt to search the missing sacrificial horse. The Sāgara

1. R. II 56/15-20.
2. R. II 102/20.
3. R. I 22/8-9.
4. *Himavataḥ sutā* and *Śailendra duhitā*, R. I 32/21, 25 respectively.
5. *Samudramahishi*, R. II 51/3.
6. R. IV 33/24.
7. R. III 46/8 N. S.
8. R. III 69/30-32.
9. R. I 43/5-6 N. S.
10. *Gāmbhīrye sāgaropamaḥ*, R. II 3/33.
11. R. I 40/37.

owes on that account a debt of gratitude to the descendants of Sagara and ever tries to repay it. Thus he persuaded Maināka, his protege against the *Gotrabhid* (Indra), to emerge out of the waters and offer a resting place to Hanūmān who was an agent of Rāma, a scion of the Ikshvāku family.[1] Sāgara is also said to be a friend of Daśaratha with whom he is believed to have fought a battle against the Asuras.[2] At the conclusion of this war he presented to Daśaratha a bright head-ornament (*Cūḍāmaṇi*) as a souvenir.[3] Dundubhi challenged him for a duel but he cleverly avoided it by directing him to Himavān.[4] He also felt extremely agitated on seeing Rāvaṇa carrying away Sītā.[5]

Rāma implored Samudra for granting passage to him and the Vānara army, but the latter showed no inclination towards fulfilling that request because just as the elements (earth, air, sky, water and light) maintain their (respective) natures so also it was the nature of Samudra to be unfathomable.[6] However, he offered to assist Rāma by holding his waters (motionless), so that Nala could build a bridge across the waters. The Rāmāyaṇa describes the figure of Sāgara in this context. He appeared before Rāma accompanied by Pannagas of flaming faces, and huge Nāgas of brown, yellow and dark colours—each possessing seven hoods, seven faces and flaming tongues. On the head he was wearing a wonderful garland of divine flowers, and others made of heated gold. He was also bedecked with a cluster of ornaments studded with gems originating in himself. On all sides he was surrounded by prominent rivers, (his wives), the chief among them being Gaṅgā and Sindhu.[7]

Many forms of the ocean are spoken of in the Rāmāyaṇa. There are popularly speaking four seas,[8] though seven are also alluded to.[9] The ocean is usually the abode of Varuṇa[10]

1. R. IV 61/93.
2. R. V 96/43 ff.
3. R. V 96/59.
4. R. IV 8/3-9.
5. R. III 60/10.
6. R. V 96/23.
7. R. V 96/14-19.
8. *Nadīpatibhyaścaturbhyaḥ*, R. VI 109/68.
9. *Saptānāṃ tu samudrāṇām*, R. III 81/4.
10. *Varuṇālayam*, R. IV 8/4.

though the *kshīroda* is the home of Vishṇu who rests there on his serpent cot.[1] The waters of the sea are considered holy and are specially propitious in a king's coronation.[2]

A mountain is the home of the various divinities and their rendezvous. The Meru and the Kailāsa are each termed as the 'abodes of the gods';[3] the Droṇa is the habitat of the Kinnaras;[4] on the Citrakūṭa, Rāma saw Kinnaras, Vidyādharas and Guhyakas having a pastime;[5] and on the Mahendra, when Hanūmān was preparing for his flight across the ocean, there were sporting the Siddhas, Cāraṇas, Kinnaras and Vidyādharas.[6] There are some purely mythical mountains like the Udaya and the Asta (the starting point and the point of culmination respectively for the sun's journey), the Pāriyātra[7] and the Mandara—this last is believed to have been employed as the churning rod by the gods.

Mountains are symbols of firmness[8] and hugeness. It is said that in the beginning they had wings and could fly like birds. The sight of the floating mountains inspired great awe in the heart of the people and so Indra chopped off their wings by his thunder-bolt. Only Maināka escaped because he concealed himself in the waters of the sea.[9] Among the mountains Himavān is the most important one from the point of his personification. He is lord of mountains.[10] His wife is Manoramā, the daughter of the mount Sumeru, and by her he has two

1. *Kshīrodaśayanīyan te Śeshasyopari*, R. VI 27/26.
2. R. II 16/4; R. IV 19/31; R. VI 109/67-72.
3. *Kailāsam bibudhālayam*, R. IV 56/54 and *Devānāmālayam Merum* R. VI 41/39.
4. *Droṇe bahu-Kinnarasevite*, R. VI 3/21.
5. R. II 107/10-11, 22.
6. R. IV 61/18, 28.
7. The Pāriyātra is one of the seven *Kulaparvatas* which are sometimes designated as the ancient 'doors of heaven'. E. W. Hopkins writes about them in his Epic Mythology (p. 8) : "The seven are the Orissa chain, the southern part of the Western Ghats, and the northern part (these three being called Mahendra, Malaya and Sahya), the range called Śuktimat (in the east), the Gondwana range called *Ṛkshavat*, the (Eastern) Vindhya, and the Northern and Western Vindhya called *Pāriyātra*; among which Mahendra (from which Hanūmat leaps) is best known to the epic poets as a sacred place."
8. *Sthairye ca Himavāniva*, R. I 1/20; R. II 125/23.
9. *Dvitīyaḥ parvato yathā*, R. IV 60/10; R. IV 61/35.
9. R. IV 61/131-135.
10. *Śailendro Himavān nāma*, R. I 32/19.

daughters, Gaṅgā and Umā. The elder one (Gaṅgā) was given (in marriage) to the gods on their request and the younger one was married to Rudra after she had propitiated him by her penance.[1] Himavān is thus the glorious father-in-law of Śaṅkara.[2] Himavān's son is Maināka who still possesses the power to extend upward, downward or sideward and who lies deep in the waters of the sea, blocking the passage of the Asuras residing in the *Pātāla*.[3] There are fragmentary references to the rivalry between Himavān and Vindhya. The Vindhya is said to have become angry with the sun who walked the deasil around the Himavān but not himself. He, therefore, started growing to obstruct the passage of the sun. The rivalry was, however, set at rest by Agastya who asked the Vindhya to let him pass over and not grow till he did not return—and the Vindhya still awaits the return of the sage.[4] These mountains sometimes speak like human beings.[5] Himavān was even challenged for a duel by Dundubhi.[6]

The mountains are considered holy. The sight of the Citrakūṭa, for instance, is believed to inspire pious thoughts in one's mind and to ensure one's welfare.[7] Bharata before leaving the Citrakūṭa circumambulated it[8] (and thus expressed his sense of regard for the hill). A gold mountain in the South[9] and the Ṛishyamūka[10] are described as inaccessible to the unholy and the sinful. About the latter it is also stated that on awakening a person got the wealth he had seen in his dream there.[11]

In addition to the rivers and mountains there are a number of other places which are considered holy in the Rāmāyaṇa. It is the association of some holy act or personality which renders them holy. Thus the spots where Vishṇu recovered Earth from

1. R. I 32/20-26.
2. R. I 36/4.
3. R. IV 61/96-98.
4. R. I 36/4; R. III 15/15; R. VII 20/41.
5. R. IV 61/114 ff.
6. R. IV 6/29-34.
7. R. II 58/31-32.
8. R. II 126/3.
9. R. IV 33/39.
10. R. III 79/27.
11. R. III 79/29.

Bali Vairocana and gave it over to Indra, where Kāma was rendered bodiless by the fire of Śiva's wrath, where Bhagīratha practised penance, and where Vindhya and Himavān looked at each other with rivalry[1] are all considered holy. So was the hermitage of Agastya an extremely sacred place where a liar, a cunning or a crafty person, a wicked or a wanton could not live.[2]

Like gods and men who are children of the Prajāpati Kaśyapa all birds and animals also are believed to have their origin from the same Prajāpati, if not directly from his wives then from his daughters and grand daughters.[3] Of these the cow, on whom depended their oblations to the gods and the

1. R. I 27/2 ff.; R. I 21/6; R. I 39/13 and R. I 36/4-5 respectively.

2. R. III 15/20.

3. It is said that the Prajāpati Kaśyapa married eight of the sixty daughters of the Prajāpati Daksha. We note in the following table the children that were born to them :

(a) Aditi—Thirty-three sons, viz. 12 Ādityas, 8 Vasūs, 11 Rudras and 2 Aśvins.

(b) Diti—Daityas (their number is not given).

(c) Danu—One son, Aśva-grīva.

(d) Kālakā—Two sons, viz. Naraka and Kālaka.

(e) Tāmrā (D) Krauñcī—son—Ulūkas.
(D) Bhāsī—son—Bhāsas.
(D) Śyenī—sons—Śyena and Gṛidhra.
...Haṃsas
(D) Dhṛitarāshṭrī—sons ...Kalahaṃsas
...Cakravākas
...Aruṇa
(D) Śukī—daughter—Natā—(D) Vinatā, sons
...Garuḍa

(f) Krodhavaśā (D) Mṛigī—son—Mṛigas
...Ṛikshas
(D) Mṛigamandā—sons ...Sṛimaras
...Camaras
(D) Harī—son ...Haris (lions)
...Vānaras (apes)
(D) Bhadramadā—daughter—Irāvatī—son—
Airāvata
(D) Mātaṅgī—son—Mātaṅga
...Golāṅgūlas
(D) Śārdūlī—sons
...Vyāghras

(Contd. next page.)

manes, in fact their very means of subsistence,[1] was held to be the most sacred by the ancient Indians. To touch a cow with the foot was considered sinful;[2] on the other hand her gift to the *brāhmaṇas* was considered extremely meritorious and formed an important part of social and religious performances.[3]

The Rāmāyaṇa refers to the divine cow Surabhi who is described in the Araṇya-Kāṇḍa as the child of Kaśyapa from his wife Krodhavaśā, and the mother of two daughters, Rohiṇī and Gandharvī whose off-springs are the kine and the horses respectively. Popularly she is the mother of the cows[4] (the bovine class) and feels very much distressed on seeing her sons (oxen) being pressed hard under the burden of the plough and being beaten by the farmer when completely worn out by toil and hunger.[5] Her tears are feared even by the Devarāja (Indra) as portending evil for the gods.[6] The Uttara-Kāṇḍa associates her with Varuṇa in whose abode she ever issues forth the sweet flow of milk which forms the *Kshīroda*.[7] She is so venerable that even the wicked Rāvaṇa did not proceed further without paying her his respects.[8] As Kāmadhenu she is identified with Śabalā, the wonder-cow of Vasishṭha.[9]

The Rāmāyaṇa also alludes to the four elephants, the mythical guardians of the quarters. Thus the sons of Sagara digging the earth in search of their missing horse saw Virūpāksha supporting the earth in the East, Mahāpadma in the South,

(D) Śvetā—son—Diśāgaja
(D) Surabhi—daughter ...Rohiṇī—daughter...Gau
...Gandharvī—son...Vāji
(D) Surasā—sons—Nāgas
(D) Kadrukā—sons—Pannagas
(g) Manu—sons—Brāhmaṇas, Kshatriyas, Vaiśyas and Śūdras.
(h) Analā—sons—Vṛikshas.

R. III 14/7-33 N. S.

1. *Atra kavyañca havyañca prāṇayātrā tathaiva me.* R. I 48/39.
2. *Padena hanyāt gāṃ suptāṃ yasyāryo(a)numate gataḥ*, R. II 83/4.
3. On the occasion of the *Aśvamedha* Daśaratha gave gifts of cows to the Brāhmaṇas (R. I 10/39-40). Cows were also given at the time of marriage, R. I 68/28.
4. *Gavām mātā*, R. II 80/17.
5. R. II 80/23-24.
6. R. II 80/21.
7. R. VII 26/17.
8. R. VII 26/20.
9. R. I 49/1.

Saumanasa in the West and Bhadra in the North.[1] In addition to these there are also mentioned Sārvabhauma, the elephant of Kubera[2] and Airāvata (or Airāvaṇa) of Indra.[3] This latter is believed to be a white elephant born of Irāvatī, the grand-daughter of Kaśyapa. To Indra also belongs the horse Uccaiḥ-śravā who sprang from the ocean at the time of the churning[4] of the ocean.

Among birds only Garuḍa (variously known as *garutmat*, the winged, *suparṇa*, of lovely wings, *tārkshya*, the son of Tārksha-Kaśyapa, *pakshi-rāja* and *patagottama*, the lord of birds) is noteworthy.[5] He is son of Vinatā the great-grand-daughter of the Prajāpati Kaśyapa. Aruṇa the charioteer of Sūrya is his brother and Sumati his sister.[6] Sumati was married to king Sagara and on that account Garuḍa is called *mātula* (maternal uncle) of the sixty thousand sons of Sagara.[7] Garuḍa bears an everlasting hostility towards the serpents—*pannagāśana*, *bhujagāri* and other synonyms are his popular epithets—who are possessed with panic the moment they smell of him and try to slip away from his sight in whichever direction possible.[8] His principal feat is the carrying off of ambrosia from the home of Mahendra disregarding the blazing flames that were set around it as hurdles.[9] He is also glorified for having saved the Bālakhilyas from getting crushed under the heavy branch of the Sucandra-nyagrodha as it gave way under his own weight rendered heavier by the elephant and the huge tortoise whom he was carrying as food on his onward journey to the Mahendra-bhavana for ambrosia. He is said to have carried a long distance the entire branch along with his load (of the elephant and the tortoise) and dropped it over a habitation of the Nishādas.[10]

1. R. I 37/12-21. The names in R. I 6/24 N. S are Airāvata, Añjana, Vāmana and Mahāpadma.
2. *Aupavāhyam Kuberasya Sārvabhauma iti śrutaḥ*, R. IV 36/61.
3. *Mattairāvaṇavāhanam*, R. III 28/24.
4. R. I 41/28.
5. R. III 35/15; R. II 45/26; R. VII 23/4; R. I 38/16 respectively.
6. R. I 35/14.
7. R. I 38/16.
8. R. VI 28/7.
9. R. III 39/37.
10. R. III 39/30-34.

Garuḍa is renowned for his great speed. He ranges in the sky like a meteor throwing the clouds topsyturvy. The gush of wind produced from his wings causes a tremor in the mountains, a strong flutter in the waters of the sea and overturns a large number of trees.[1] Vishṇu has a great liking for him on account of his might and speed and employs him as his conveyance. Garuḍa not only serves Vishṇu as his conveyance but also assists him in actual fighting. He flung away the Rākshasa Mālyavān fighting against Vishṇu[2] and released Rāma and Lakshnaṇa in the Laṅkā war from the effects of Indrajit's *sarpa-bandha.*[3]

The mythical trees alluded to in the Rāmāyaṇa are few. There are solitary references to the Śālmalī, the deceptive tree in the *Yama-nagara* having iron thorns covered under golden flowers and leaves of lapises,[4] and the Sucandra Nyagrodha on the sea-coast having branches extended to a *yojana* on each side.[5] The most well known is the Kalpa-vṛiksha which is, however, only casually mentioned in a passage of the Kishkindhā-Kāṇḍa.[6] To this list may be added the Śyāma Vaṭa at Prayāga which was specially mentioned by the sage Bharadvāja to Rāma and party. The sage specifically told Sītā to worship this tree and pray to it for obtaining her heart's desire.[7]

1. R. VI 28/5.
2. R. VII 7/16-18.
3. R. VI 28/9-11.
4. R. III 59/24.
5. R. III 39/29.
6. R. IV 27/5.
7. R. II 59/5-6.

CHAPTER X

SOME PHILOSOPHICAL IDEAS

Being primarily a *kāvya*, the Rāmāyaṇa neither presents nor aims at presenting any philosophical system. No doubt, there are a few stray passages giving cosmogenic accounts according to which the universe is said to have been created by God out of his own *māyā śakti*[1] or to have sprung from pre-existent matter[2]. But on such meagre information it is not possible to build Rāmāyaṇa metaphysics. There is a solitary reference to the *Lokāyatikas* in the Ayodhyā-Kāṇḍa[3] and the materialistic approach is also voiced by Lakshmaṇa[4] in the Yuddha-Kāṇḍa. This only shows that as in the times of Yāska[5] so in the Rāmāyaṇic period there was an under current of heresy which perhaps insisted on upholding direct perception as the only source of knowledge and also displayed lack of faith in accepted canons.[6]

There are some references to the ephemeral character of life, especially when one philosophises about death.[7] But, as we shall shortly show, there is nothing to prove that the people of the period had a pessimistic view of life or an escapist tendency. Even the concept of *moksha*—which is the summum bonum of life according to most Indian philosophic systems, heterodox as well as orthodox—is absent.

We have already seen that Yama, as lord of the dead was an important god in the Rāmāyaṇic pantheon.[8] The Rāmā-

1. *Saṃkshipya hi purā lokān māyayā svayameva hi,*
   Tvameva māyayā sārdham apaḥ pūrvam ajījanaḥ...R. VII 106/4 ff.
2. *Pūrvaṃ salilamevāsīt pṛithivī yatra nirmitā,*
   Tataḥ samabhavad Brahmā svayambhūrvaradaḥ prabhuḥ...R. II 123/3 ff.
3. *Kaccinna lokāyatikān brāhmaṇānupasevase,*
   Anarthakuśalā hyete mūḍhāḥ paṇḍitamāninaḥ....R. II 114/30.
4. R. VI 61/15-37.
5. *Anarthakā hi mantrāḥ*, Nirukta, I 15/2.
6. Cf. *Pratyakshaṃ yattadātishṭha paroksham pṛishṭhataḥ kuru.*, R. II 122/16.

Also : *Bhūtānāṃ sthāvarāṇāñca jaṅgamānāñca darśanam,*
Yathāsti na tathā dharmastena nāstīti me matiḥ. R. VI 61/16.

7. R. II 88/21-22; R. II 119/6-13; R. II 121/3, 6; R. IV 15/57, 59.
8. Vide pp. 198-199 supra.

yaṇa also frequently refers to the *Pitṛis* as a class of divine beings living in a separate region known as the *Pitṛiloka*, and their close association with Yama is clearly alluded to.[1] The word *Preta* also occurs and refers to beings who are associated on the one hand with Piśācas and Rākshasas[2] and on the other with Yama, who is often known as *Pretarāja*.[3] But it is to be noted that this state of the soul (viz. as *Preta* or *Pitṛi*) was not an ever-lasting one, for the Aryans believed in the doctrine of metempsychosis. According to this doctrine the soul (with its *liṅgadeha* or astral body which always accompanies it) having reaped the corresponding fruits of its meritorious or sinful deeds returns to this world to be born in some form or the other. This leads us to the consideration of the *Karma* doctrine which is correlated to the theory of transmigration of soul.

The *Karma* doctrine offers on the one hand the most plausible explanation for the various disparities that exist between man and man and on the other inspires tremendous faith in human action. According to this doctrine human happiness or misery is a result of *karma*[4] (action) and there is neither loss of *karma*[5] nor reversal of effort.[6] Daśaratha speaking to Kauśalyā says that whatever actions, good or bad, a man performed, he surely reaped its fruit in course of time.[7] This idea is made more clear in the following words of Mandodarī : "The performer of meritorious deeds reaps good results whereas an evil doer earns evil."[8] It was on this very principle again that Rāma turned down the proposal of Bharata for staying in the forest for fourteen years in his place. Rāma declared before the assembly at Citrakūṭa that neither he nor Bharata could annul any pledge or purchase effected by their father during his life time.[9] What he meant was that whatever happiness or

1. R. VI 98/12.
2. *Piśācapretarakshobhirjushṭānyucchritabhojanaiḥ*...R. II 36/22.
3. *Pretarājānam*, R. VII 24/5.
4. *Buddhim rūpaṃ kulam putrān śauryam gāmbhiryamera ca,*
   Prāpnuvanti narā loke nirjitam pūrvakarmabhiḥ. R. VII 14/21.
5. *Avaśyaṃ kriyamāṇasya karmaṇo dṛiśyate phalam*, R. IV 40/8.
6. *Na ca dharmo(a)pi saṃhāryo hyadharmaphala saṃyutaḥ,*
   Sa eva phalamabhyeti dharmo nādharma nāśanaḥ., R. V 47/29.
7. *Yadācarati kalyāṇi naraḥ karma śubhāśubham,*
   So(a)vaśyam phalamāpnoti tasya kālakramāgatam., R. II 69/5.
8. *Śubhakṛichubhamāpnoti pāpakṛitpāpam aśnute.*, R. VI 111/26 N. S.
   Cf. also : *Yādṛiśaṃ kurute karma tādṛiśam phalam aśnute.*, R. VII 14/20.
9. II 124/27.

misery had been ordained for one could not be mitigated by the offer of some one else to experience the same.

Generally on seeing an evil doer having good time or a righteous person suffering hardships, people become sceptic about the doctrine of *Karma*. What is forgotten in such cases is the fact that the former state (i.e. an evil doer having good time) becomes possible due to the working of some merit acquired in the previous birth and the latter (i.e. a righteous person suffering hardship) is caused by a certain evil of the previous birth obstructing the good fruit of meritorious actions performed in the present life. During her forced stay in Laṅkā Sītā wondered as to what sort of a grievous sin she had committed in her previous life that she had to experience such hardships.[1] Rāma also was confident of having repeatedly committed sins in the previous birth as a result of which he had to pass from one misery to another in the present life.[2] Kauśalyā was sure that in her previous birth she must have cut the paps of kine and thus prevented their calves hungering after their mother's milk from drinking it so that now for that sin she was forcibly deprived of Rāma by Kaikeyī.[3]

Normally *karmas* require a certain interval of time to yield their corresponding results[4]—one birth or several births. However, depending upon the character of a certain *karma* and also the circumstance in which it is done there can be quick or immediate results; in cases of intense merit or sin (*utkaṭa puṇya* or *pāpa*) the results are accelerated so as to be reaped by the doer in his life time, almost immediately. The working of this principle can be particularly seen in case of boons and curses which number very large in the Rāmāyaṇa. The cases of kings Daśaratha and Daṇḍa may be cited as examples. The former performed the *Putrīyā ishṭi* and got in return from the *Prājāpatya Nara* the holy *pāyasa* on eating which his wives conceived and were delivered of four illustrious sons;[5] the latter (Daṇḍa)

1. R. V 20/18.
2. R. III 63/4 N. S.
3. R. II 46/18-19.
4. *Na tu sadyo(a)vinītasya dṛiśyate karmaṇaḥ phalam*
Kālo(a)pyaṅgī bhavatyatra sasyānāmiva paktaye., R. III 49/27 N. S.

Also : *Adṛishṭaguṇadoshāṇāmāhitanāñca karmaṇām,*
Antareṇa kriyā yeshāṃ phalakāle pravartate., R. III 72/18.

5. R. I cantos 11 and 14 (Note ; *Rājannarcayatā devān sadyaḥ prāptam phalaṃ tvayā*, R. I 11/18).

was cursed by the sage Śukra to perish along with his kingdom in consequence of the offence of committing rape upon his (the sage's) daughter.[1]

The *Karma* theory presupposes a dispenser—and that dispenser is 'Fate'. 'Fate' is a very old conception. In primitive times its application was spread over a very wide range. It comprised within its scope all happenings in which the cause and effect relationship was not discernible to the human eye. Thus' drought and flood, hail-storm and lightning, famine and epidemics were all attributed to 'Fate'. Gradually as human knowledge advanced with the progress of time the province of 'Fate became narrower and narrower but basically the conception remained the same, namely, 'a divine agency in whose working human intellect can point out no cause and effect relationship and whose presence is felt by man only through its working which is invariably sudden and hence unpredictable.'

In the Rāmāyaṇa Rāma is the best expositor of this conception of 'Fate'. He resorted to it in order to pacify Lakshmaṇa who was getting furious on seeing the plans of coronation being frustrated by Kaikeyī. Rāma also explained the sudden change of Kaikeyī's heart and the consequent misery upon himself as being decreed by 'Fate'. He said, " Fate was that which was above comprehension and it was beyond the power of creatures to avert its consequences ......No one could contend with Fate which was hidden from man's view until its decree was executed......Setting aside all human calculations that which appears suddenly and imperceptibly was indeed the working of Fate."[2]

The above words of Rāma bring out three salient points in the conception of 'Fate' :

(i) 'Fate' is beyond the power of human control.
(ii) Its working is always sudden and inconceivable.
(iii) It is cognisable only through its own working.

1. R. VII 83/6 ff.
2. *Yadacintyantu taddaivam bhūteshvapi na hanyate,*
Kaśca daivena Saumitre yoddhumutsahate pumān,
Yasya nu grahaṇaṃ kiñcit karmaṇo(a)nyanna dṛiśyate.
Asaṅkalpitameveha yadakasmātpravartate, ...
Nivartyārabdhamārambhairnanu daivasya karma tat. R. II 22/20-24 N S.
N.B. The reading is different in the N.W. (vide R. II 22/15-17).

The most important of these is obviously the first because it distinguishes the working of 'Fate' from all other actions which are characterised by an apparent cause and effect relationship and also because it makes 'Fate' the most dreaded phenomenon.

It may be observed here that this conception of 'Fate' when linked with the doctrine of *Karma*, underwent a significant modification. Formerly all happiness and misery, profit and loss, birth and deliverance were caused by 'Fate' but the *Karma* doctrine sought to explain them with reference to man's own actions, performed in this birth or the previous births. When the two conceptions were fused together 'Fate' lost the character of being a determining factor; it was now reduced only to the position of a dispenser. Since the *karmas* of the previous births were beyond the range of human knowledge all happiness and misery retained the label of 'Fate' though now the responsibility of causing them rested with the man himself, i. e. on his actions. 'Fate', however, retained its awe due to its imperceptibility and suddenness.[1]

A careful reader will not fail to notice that in this modified conception of 'Fate' mutually opposite elements got linked together. On the one hand there was suddenness, because the working of 'Fate' was beyond the range of human knowledge and on the other there was definiteness, because for each good or bad action there was bound to be a corresponding good or bad result. The believers in 'Fate', therefore, fall under two categories :

(i) Those who are impressed by the vagaries of 'Fate' seem to have developed an attitude of resignation and appear to be lacking in self-confidence. These are votaries of a pessimistic view of life and are prone to condemn all initiative. Thus Rāma declared to Bharata at the Citrakūṭa meet : "No creature is endowed with the power of exercising any control over the course of events, —man has no independent status (in nature); Destiny tosses him from place to place. All collections are ultimately to waste away; all rise is to culminate in fall; all associations have their end in separation; and the goal of life

1. *Atarkyamapyaniśceyaṃ daivaṃ kastu vilaṅghayet.*, R. VI 81/20.

is death."[1] Followers of this view paint man as a helpless babe before the all powerful 'Fate' and very loudly proclaim the futility of all human effort. "A man does not succeed in overcoming Destiny", is the opinion of a chamberlain of Bālī.[2] Likewise, according to Sthūlajaṅgha Destiny was the supreme power and human effort was of no avail.[3]

(ii) Those who believe in the prominence of *karmas* in shaping their present lot neither become arrogant by prosperity nor restive by adversities. Both in weal and woe they maintain their mental repose and ever strive to ameliorate their future state by performing good deeds. Their approach towards life is that of optimism and they represent the healthier aspect of 'Fate'. They derive inspiration from virtue and are the sincerest promoters of values in life. Thus Sītā cheerfully condoned all the suffering she had experienced in Laṅkā and pleaded in defence of the Rākshasa guards (whom Hanūmān presently desired to kill) saying that she had to experience all that suffering on account of her adverse fortune caused by vicious deeds of the previous birth.[4] Getting ready to suffer the curse pronounced by an enraged *brāhmaṇa* king Nṛiga consoled his son in the same strain and said, "Destiny who has brought upon you this misery is all powerful in this world. My child, do not be dejected, for a man receives (in this life) all happiness and misery as his reward of deeds done in the previous birth."[5]

Incidentally, it might be noted here that Vālmīki has employed seven words to convey the idea of 'Fate'. ' They are *daiva, kāla, vidhi, bhāgya, kṛitānta, niyati* and *bhavitavyatā*.[6] Of these *daiva* which means 'chance' or 'divine will' is Vālmīki's most favourite expression. His fondness for this word is perhaps explained by the sense of vagary of the divine will which is present most in this expression. Equally vague is the word *kāla* which correctly stands for 'time' and is perhaps

1. R. II 119/2-3.
2. *Na hi daivamanutkramya mānusheṇeha sidhyati*, R. IV 15/60.
3. *Daivameva parammanye paurushantu nirarthakam*, R. VI 81/162.
4. R. VI 94/36.
5. R. VII 55/39-40.
6. R. VI 25/37, R. V 10/54, R. V 34/4, R. II 65/34, R. VII 100/28, R. IV 25/4 N. S. and R. II 70/48 respectively.

employed only metaphorically in the sense of 'Fate'. Perhaps the word *kāla* is employed to convey the sense of 'Fate' because the actions of the previous existence appear as workings of 'Fate' in the present life, only after they have become ripe with the passage of time. Vālmīki has himself explained the term *vidhi* as denoting that agency which makes a man act according to the (pre-ordained) divine arrangement.[1] In fact, the sense of forced obedience to pre-ordained regulations is more or less present in every Sanskrit synonym of 'Fate'. The words *bhāgya* and *kṛitānta* come nearest in explaining the Hindu conception of 'Fate'. *Bhāgya* literally means the allotted share (resulting from the merit or demerit of former birth) and *kṛitānta* is the result (*anta* i. e. end) of actions done (*kṛita*) in past existence. These terms clearly point at a definite relationship existing between the working of 'Fate' (in present life) and actions (of the previous one). The word *kṛitānta* is Vālmīki's favourite next to *daiva* . The words *niyati* and *bhavitavyatā* do not further elucidate the concept of 'Fate'.

As we have already seen 'Fate' is an agency responsible for bringing to people the rewards of their previous evil as well as good deeds, still the characters of the epic have recalled 'Fate' mostly when something unpleasant has happened. In the Rāmāyaṇa Triśaṅku, Yajñadatta, Daśaratha, Kauśalyā, Bharata, Lakshmaṇa, Sītā, Vasishṭha, Tārā, Bālī, Hanūmān, Sampāti, Vibhīshaṇa, Sthūlajaṅgha, Rāvaṇa and Nṛiga[2]—all recognise the force of 'Fate'. Rāma is particularly a staunch devotee and, as pointed out earlier, the best exponent of 'Fate'. The reader of the Rāmāyaṇa is sometimes struck with wonder at the readiness with which Rāma resorts to this idea in times of distress. It seems, as if, strongly controlling all his desires he has completely surrendered himself into the hands of the divine will. His words to Tārā are worth noting in this connection. He says, *Niyati* is the prime cause in this world, and the source of the accomplishment of actions. And *Niyati* it is that leads men to actions. No one is the lord of another person, and no one leads him to actions. People are subject to

1. *Vidhiḥ kila naraṃ loke vidhānenānuvartate.* R. IV 56/4 N. S. (The reading in the N. W. (IV 48/4) appears to be defective).

2. For references vide : R. I 54/25; R. II 70/48; R. II 67/5; R. II 65/34; R. II 82/2; R. VII 52/4; R. VI 24/20; R. II 84/22; R. IV 15/44; R. IV 16/88; R. V 10/54; R. IV 48/5; R. VI 22/27; R. VI 81/162; R. V 81/23; R. VII 55/39-40 respectively.

their actions of previous existence and Time aids them."[1] The attendant pessimism is also observable in the following words : "All collections are ultimately to waste away; all rise is to culminate in fall; all associations have their end in separation and life ends in death."[2] It must be added to his credit that inspite of such seeming disinterest and indifference he always tried to answer the call of duty, and perhaps this justifies his claim for being called the *Maryādā-purushottama*.

In the Rāmāyaṇa practically all characters seem to be definite about their conception of 'Fate'. Whenever a calamity overtakes them they perceive therein the hand of 'Fate' and quietly submit themselves to the ordeal. There is only one character, Lakshmaṇa, who seems to raise a voice of revolt against 'Fate'. In his opinion 'Fate' was the cry of the powerless and the weak. Those who were mighty and whose prowess was held in esteem by the people paid no regard to Destiny. Lakshmaṇa was always confident of averting the consequence of Destiny by dint of his manliness.[3]

It is obvious that the above two extremes represented by the words of Rāma and Lakshmaṇa proceed from faith in human action and the lack of it. So far as Vālmīki is concerned he strikes the middle course. According to him, success is always attained with the union of both *daiva* and *purushakāra*.[4] He favours the idea of 'Fate' in distress to avoid frustration[5] and strongly recommends manliness and effort under all circumstances.[6] Fortitude and energy are sterling qualities in man and one possessing them never perishes even in the face of great hardships. "Perseverance", says Vālmīki, "is the source of good fortune; perseverance brings about supreme happiness......, perseverance, for certain, brings people to all profitable objects. Whatever one does with vigour bears fruit."[7]

1. R. IV 25/4-5 N. S..

N. B. The text in the N. W. appears to be broken at this point, therefore, we have adopted these verses from the N. S. The critical edition from Baroda also retains them.

2. R. II 119/3.
3. R. II 23/19-22.
4. *Daivapaurushasaṃyogāt siddhirnityamavāpyate*, R. VI 38/12.
5. Cf. R. III 72/6, 13.
6. Cf. R. IV 5/4, 6.
7. R. V 7/10-11.

This view is in agreement with Vālmīki's general outlook on life which is, 'an unceasing effort for the attainment of bliss'. He recognises that human life is not a bed of roses and that there are briers strewn in the path of one struggling for prosperity. But it is his firm conviction that one who does not give up the struggle ultimately achieves his object, may be after a period of long suffering even of a hundred years.[1]

1. *Eti jīvantamānando naraṃ varshaśatādapi*, R. V 28/8.

CHAPTER XI

FOOD AND DRINKS

Food is the basic requirement of life. Primitive man subsisted upon raw meat and wild fruits and roots and in this respect was little distinguished from the birds and beasts of the forest. At a very early period, however, he started taming wild animals and raising crops and thus laid foundations of civilisation and culture.

The ancient Indian attached great importance to food. He recognised that it was food which enabled a man to use all his faculties[1] and that purity of thought depended upon purity of food.[2] He also developed the culinary art and the evidence of ancient Sanskrit literature testifies to the popularity in that period of various preparations of meat and cereals rendered extremely delicious on account of being dressed by a number of spices and condiments.

In the Rāmāyaṇa the general term for food was *bhakshya*[3] or *bhojana*.[4] Vālmīki speaks of four varieties of food, viz. *bhakshya* (hard food such as requires mastication), *bhojya* (soft food as may be eaten without mastication), *coshya* (preparations which are sucked) and *lehya* (food stuffs which are licked).[5] Of these the first two, viz., *bhakshya* and *bhojya* were prepared of meat and cereals and under the last two came fruits and honey and their various preparations. The mention of *sūpa* (and *sūpakāras*) shows that sauce was an important component of the meal of the people of those times.[6]

Among cereals the Rāmāyaṇa mentions rice (variously known as *taṇḍula, śāli* and *kalama*), wheat (*godhūma*), barley (*yava*), beans (*māsha*), gram (*caṇaka*), *mudga, kulattha, śyāmāka*

1. ......*athānnasyāyai drashṭā bhavati śrotā bhavati mantā bhavati boddhā bhavati kartā bhavati vijñātā bhavatyannam upāssveti.*, Chānd. Up., VII 9/1
2. ......*āhāraśuddhau sattva-śuddhiḥ*......, Chānd. Up., VII 26/2
3. R. I 9/70, 71; R. I. 48/27.
4. R. I 48/22.
5. *Bhakshyaṃ bhojyañca coshyañca lehyañca vividhaṃ bahu*, R. II 104/20.
6. R. II 104/69; R. VII 68/22.

and *nīvāra.*[1] Of these the last two appear to be inferior grains and were especially eaten by the ascetics living in the forest. Rice seems to have been the staple food grain of the Aryans in that period and was used by them in various forms.[2] Thus boiled rice was known as *odana* or *bhakta,*[3] parched rice as *lājā,*[4] milk rice as *pāyasa*[5] and a mixed preparation of rice, beans and sesamum (*tila*) as *krisara.*[6] Unbroken (unhusked) grains of rice (*akshata*) were used in various religious performances.[7]

Sugarcane[8] and its products *guḍa* (molasses) and *śarkarā* (sugar)[9] were extremely popular. Sugar and especially molasses were used in preparing various kinds of sweets and sweet drinks.[10] The word *mishṭānna,*[11] sweets, occurs in the Rāmāyaṇa in a number of passages. Besides, *apūpa, pūpa* and *modaka*[12] and *rāga-shāṇḍava*[13] are specificially mentioned as food

1. *śālitaṇḍulabhojanām*, R. I 5/16; *prabhūtaṃ kalamakshetram*, R. IV 9/39; *yavagodhūmavanti*, R. III 21/15; *ayutaṃ tilamudgānāṃ gacchantvagre...... caṇakānāṃ kulatthānāṃ māshāṇāṃ...*, R. VII 93/25, *pacathastatra nīvārataṇḍulān*, R. III 79/22. *āhārāścaiva kartavyā......śyāmāka nīvāra......*R. II 31/18.

2. Dr. S. N. Vyas interprets *anna* in R. II 104/20 (=II 91/20 N.S.) as synonymous with rice preparation (Rāmāyaṇa Kālīna Saṃskṛiti, p. 74). Such a meaning is, however, supported neither by dictionary, nor by commentary.

3. R. I 48/27 and R. V 33/5.

4. R. I 48/26.

5. R. II 83/16

6. R. II 83/16 (Note Tilaka-Ṭīkā –*kṛisaraṃ tilamudgataṇḍulātmakam*).

7. R. IV 19/26.

8. *ikshūṃśca*, R. I 48/26.

9. R. I 48/29 and R. II 104/72 respectively.

10. R. I 48/28-29.

11. R. I 48/28; R. II 83/24.

12. R. I 48/28; R. II 104/69 and R. VI 108/14 respectively.

The last reference (*mālyamodakahastaiśca nāgarair Bharato vṛitaḥ*) incidentally shows that *modaka* was also required in certain religious ceremonies, presumably to offer *naivedya* to the deity.

Dr. Omprakash explains that *modakas* were generally prepared with rice or wheat flour fried in clarified butter mixed with sugar, some aromatic spices and thin slices of the kernel of cocoanut.

(Food and Drinks in Ancient India, p. 112, f. n. 5).

13. *rāgashāṇḍavasaṃyuktān*, R. V 6/16.

The preparation *rāga-shāṇḍava* is explained by the Tilaka-Ṭīkā as *keśarādibhiḥ kṛitavarṇāḥ shaḍrasopetāḥ pūpā rāgakhāṇḍavāḥ*. Sometimes, the word is treated as a compound and its components *rāga* and *shāṇḍava* are explained as two separate drinks. Thus, according to Dr. Omprakash,

(*Contd. next page*)

preparations. The mention of *saktukāras* in the Ayodhyā-Kāṇḍa indicates that the practice of eating the flour of barley, first fried and then ground, also obtained in the society.[1]

Cow fares very prominently in the Rāmāyaṇa as the principal article of gift for the *brāhmaṇas*. Its milk (*gorasa*) was considered extremely nourishing and formed an important item of food. Besides, milk and its products served as sauce with other food preparations.[2] The processes of curdling and churning were pretty well-known and the people also knew to extract butter out of curd. Curd (*dadhi*) and butter-milk (*takra*)[3] were extremely relished by the people in that period.

Eating of meat was very common in the society. Particularly the Rākshasas were very fond of it and indulged in indiscriminate eating of non-vegetarian dishes.[4] They did not

"A preparation of juices from fruits such as pomegranates and raisins was called *rāga*, if it was liquid in form, and *ṣāṇḍava*, if the juices were reduced to a thick consistency." (Food and Drinks in Ancient India, p. 120) It may be added that *khāṇḍava* as a food preparation occurs independently also in the Rāmāyaṇa. (R. I 48/28)—Note Tilaka-Ṭīkā : *khāṇḍavaḥ bhakshya viśeshaḥ*.

It may further be added that in various contexts Vālmīki employs the word *uccāvaca* which expression vaguely conveys the idea of variety. Dr. Omprakash has, however, remarked that "Some good quality sweets were called *khāṇḍava* and *uccāvaca-bhakshya*." (Food and Drinks in Ancient India, p. 112). The text, as already indicated, does not offer any clue on the strength of which the idea of sweets may be ascertained.

1. R. II 94/24.
2. *Vyañjanārthañca Saumitre gosahasramupākuru*, R. II 35/23.
3. R. I 48/28 and R. II 104/71.

It is interesting to note that a faulty reading in the Southern recension has misled Dr. S. N. Vyas and Dr. Omprakash, both of whom treat *takra* and *kapittha* as identical. *Kapittha*, in fact, is a tree on which monkeys dwell (—vide Monier Williams, p. 250 column 3). Its fruit, it seems, smells like *takra*.

Compare the readings :

Yauvanasthasya gaurasya kapitthasya sugandhinaḥ. R. II91/72 N. S.

Gorasasya ca takrasya kapittha samagandhinaḥ. R. II 104/71 N. W.

N. B. It is amusing to point out that in the very next verse the reading in the N. W. is defective. It reads :

Hradāḥ pūrṇānnaśālāśca dadhnaḥ śvetasya cāpare. R. II 104/72 N.W. The first half of this line gives no happy sense. The sense is clear in the N. S. which reads, *Hradāḥ pūrṇā rasālasya*.........R. II 91/73 N.S. (*Rasāla* is a liquid preparation of curd.)

4. R. V 6/12-15; R. VI 38/32-33, 78-79, 95. The female guards of Sītā have been described as *sarvabhakshāḥ* in R. V 12/16.

hesitate to eat raw meat[1] and even cannibalism obtained among them.[2] In one passage the Kirātas have also been described as raw meat eaters.[3] The Aryans had, however, developed the notion of clean and unclean meat.[4] Thus, while eating of monkey's flesh was censured among them,[5] that of deer and ram was[6] held extremely meritorious. Oblations to gods and manes were usually prepared of them.[7] Moreover, the flesh of hare,, iguana, hedge-hog, porcupine and tortoise was specially recommended for the *brāhmaṇas* and the *kshatriyas*.[8] Besides, eating of fish and of various aquatic creatures and birds[9] was fairly popular. Fish was generally killed with a hook[10] though Vālmīki also alludes to the peculiar practice of killing fish by arrows.[11] A cow, as a rule, formed part of the *madhuparka*[12] offered to a distinguished guest.

The *kshatriyas* resorted to hunting for excercise and diversion as also for obtaining food. Rāma and party mostly subsisted in the forest upon the meat of various kinds of animals (generally deer) that they killed in hunting.[13] No taboos with regard to eating of meat by *brāhmaṇas* either had yet developed. On the other hand, non-vegetarian dishes were very common, almost a ncessity in the *śrāddha* feasts where the *brāhmaṇas* were invariably the principal invitees.[14] Similarly in *Aśvamedhas*

1. The Rākshasas are generally described as *piśitāśanās*, R. III 11/13.
2. *Rakshāṃsi purushādāni*, R. III 1/13. Kumbhakarṇa is said to have made a meal of twenty-one men, R. VI 38/79.
3. R. IV 32/21.
4. *medhyān kṛishṇamṛigān*, R. II 109/35.
5. R. IV 13/18.
6. R. II 60/23; R. III 14/12 ff.
7. R. II 60/26.
8. R. IV 13/18.
9. R. III 79/7-8.
10. R. III 57/6.
11. R. III 79/9.
12. Vide p. 153 supra.
13. R. III 8/21.

Shri Balachand Shastri has taken great pains to show that Rāma abstained from eating of meat throughout the period of his exile. He has suggested ingenuous explanations of passages in which meat-eating by Rāma is stated or implied.

(Vide his article, "Śrī Rāmāyaṇa men māṃsāhāra", Kalyāṇa 5, Rāmāyaṇāṅka, p. 139)

14. Mention may incidentally be made here of the queer mode of killing *brāhmaṇas* employed by the two Rākshasa brothers Vātāpi and Ilvala.

(*Contd. next page*)

fabulous numbers of animals were slaughtered[1] and their meat was consumed by the *kshatriyas* as well as the *brāhmaṇas*. Among various classes of workmen accompanying Bharata to Citrakūṭa the poet also mentions *māṃsopajīvinaḥ* which indicates that there were regular meat shops in Ayodhyā.[2] It may, however, be added that already the scale had started tilting in favour of vegetarianism because it was being felt that meat eating went against a life of piety, and that at least an ascetic, who repaired to the forest primarily to lead a righteous life should abstain from eating meat.[3]

Popularity of meat, naturally tended towards the introduction of various methods of preserving and preparing it. Thus meat was seasoned and preserved for future use.[4] Meat was roasted on iron pikes[5] and sometimes cooked with other food. Soup preparation from meat was also a favourite non-vegetarian dish of those times. To add to its flavour meat was dressed with various spices and condiments.[6] In fact, seasoning of food in general by clarified butter (*ājya*), oil (*taila*) and spices was fairly common.[7] Clarified butter and oils of sesamum and mustard seeds were used for frying.[8] It may be noted that Vālmīki has employed the word *rasa* in the sense of flavour of food also and in the Bāla-Kāṇḍa edibles of six tastes, namely, *madhura* (sweet), *amla* (sour), *lavaṇa* (salt), *kaṭuka* (pungent), *tikta* (bitter) and *kashāya* (astringent) are mention-

Ilvala would invite *brāhmaṇas* to the *śrāddha* feast in which food prepared from the flesh of Vātāpi (who was transformed into a ram for the purpose) was served. After the invitees had eaten that food Ilvala would accost Vātāpi to come out and the latter would do so by rending open the bellies of the *brāhmaṇas*., R. III 14/12-16.

1. R. I 10/21-23.
2. R. II 94/20.
3. Cf. *Nanu śāntātmabhirvāpi sarvabhūtadayāparaiḥ,*
   Bhavitavyam phalāhāraiḥ nityamāśramavāsibhiḥ. R. V 81/16.
4. *ārdram māṃsañca śushkañca*, R. II 96/8. Also R. II 109/39.
5. *śūlyāṃśca*, R. V 6/15.
6. R. V 6/14, 19-20.
7. The word *nishṭnāna* occurring in R. II 91/67 N. S. has been explained by Dr. S. N. Vyas in the sense of seasoning of food. (Rāmāyaṇa Kālīna Saṃskṛiti, p. 75). The N. W., however, reads *mishtānna* in its place. (R. II 104/69).
8. R. VII 93/24; R. IV 19/26.

ed.[1] Sweetness was imparted to the preparations by mixing molasses and sugar and also perhaps juices of certain fruits. For the sake of other flavours various other things like curd, vinegar and spices[2] were used. Among spices ordinary salt (*lavaṇa*), a special kind of salt known as *sauvarcala*, pepper (*marica*) aloes (*agaru*) and nutmeg (*jāti* and *śālūka*)[3] were known.

Fruits and vegetables also formed important items of food of the people of those times.[4] Specially the diet of the hermit consisted primarily of fruits, esculent roots and tubers that could be easily procured from the forest.[5] The fruits (or fruit trees) mentioned in the Rāmāyaṇa are mango (variously known as *āmra*, *rasāla* and *cūta*), plantain (*kadalī*), pomegranate (*dāḍima*), jujube (*badarī*), wood-apple (*bilva*), rose apple (*jambu*), careya arborea (*pilu*), cocoanut (*nārikela*), walnut (*akshota*), dates (*kharjūra*), jack-fruit, (*panasa*), emblic myrobalan (*āmalaka* or *āmalakī*), palmyra (*tāla*), disopyros embryopteris (*tinduka*—a variety of orange) mimusops kauli (*kshīri*), ghironji sapida (*priyāla*), marking nut (*bhallātaka*), feronia elephantum (*kapittha*), citrus (*bījapūraka*) and gmelina arborea (*kāśmari*).[6] In addition to these the lotus stalks were also used as food.[7] Some of these fruits, it may be noted, were used for making condiments and drinks.

Among beverages the first and foremost is naturally water. The Aryans had recognised its manifold utility at a very early period which fact is reflected down to this day in the conception of *tīrtha* and the daily *tarpaṇa* to *Savitṛi* and the *Pitṛis*. For the latter it constitutes their principal food. In the Rāmāyaṇa Rāma also is said to have taken only water as his food (*bhojya*)

1. R. I 48/23.
2. R. V 6/14, 20.
3. R. VII 93/25; R. V 6/14; R. III 39/24; R. III 39/23 and R. III 79/6 respectively.

N. B. R. V 11/23 indicates that the practice of mixing certain perfumed powders to make the preparations sweet-smelling also obtained in that period.

4. R. V 6/16; R. VII 84/3.
5. Cf. R. II 69/31; R. IV 61/122.
6. R. II 59/7 (Also R. II 104/30 and 52); R. II 20/22; R. II 59/7; R. II 60/9; R. II 104/30; R. IV 35/23; R. III 39/13; R. II 107/7 R. III 20/17; R. II 60/9; R. II 104/30; R. II 104/52; R. I 22/14; R. II 16/6; R. II 31/18; R. II 60/9; R. II 104/30; R. II 107/8.
7. *mṛiṇālaiḥ prāṇadhāraṇam*, R. II 56/37.

on a few occasions.[1] Drinking water was usually had from natural sources such as rivers, springs and water-falls, failing which from such artificial sources as lakes, wells and tanks. Clear, cool, sweet and health-giving water having the fragrance of lotus was considered extremely good for drinking.[2] Besides water, people of Vālmīki's times were in the habit of drinking butter-milk, fruit-juices, sugar-cane-juice and honey.[3] In *madhu-parka* (which was offered to a guest), as its name suggests, honey must have formed the principal item. The Vānaras were particularly fond of honey. The royal garden in Kishkindhā (unlike its counterparts in Ayodhyā and Laṅkā which were known as *Aśoka-vanas*) was not only just named *Madhu-vana* but was actually an extensive grove of honey. It seems that every Vānara longed to find admittance into it and also for an opportunity to partake of honey produced and preserved in it.[4]

In addition to the above, intoxicating drinks were also very widely popular among the people—both men and women[5] of those times. Vālmīki mentions *śauṇḍikas* and *pānabhūmis* (taverns) in Ayodhyā[6] and names a section of Rāvaṇa's palace as *pāna-bhūmi*.[7] In Ayodhyā 'drinking' was so popular that the aroma of wines could be felt in the atmosphere of the town and drunkards could be seen staggering on the roads.[8] It may be noted further that not only the Rākshasas and the Aryans unreservedly indulged in drinking spirituous liquors but even the Vānaras who were purely vegetarians in their food habits fully shared this weakness with their contemporaries. Thus the highways of Kishkindhā also were filled with the fragrance of *madhu* and *maireya*.[9]

1. *Adbhireva hi Saumitre vasāmo(a)dya niśāmimām*, R. II 48/8 and *jalamevādade Rāmaḥ*, R. II 51/26.
2. R. III 79/10-11.
3. R. II 104/71; R. II 104/69; R. II 104/15 and R. V 59/1 ff.
N. B. Animals were also given sugarcane juice to drink. R. II 104/57.
4. R. V cantos 58-59.
5. R. V 5/57-58; R. VII 44/14.
6. R. II 94/14; R. II 127/12.
7. R. V 6/11.
Dr. S. N. Vyas is not correct in describing this *pāna-bhūmi* in Laṅkā as a tavern. He has confusedly associated the description of the Rākshasas in R. V 5/11-12 N. S. with that of the *pāna-bhūmi* in R. V canto 11 N. S. (Vide Rāmāyaṇa Kālīna Saṃskṛiti, pp. 92-93).
8. R. II 127/19-20.
9. R. IV 26/8

The employment of the word *krita-surā* as distinguished from *surā* in the Sundara-Kāṇḍa[1] indicates a two fold division of liquors, viz. natural (*surā*, like *Kādambarī*) and artificial (*krita-surā*) i. e. fermented.[2] The same Kāṇḍa further speaks of four varieties of spirituous liquors (*āsavas*) viz. *pushpāsava, phalāsava, mādhvīka* and *śarkarāsava* being distilled from flowers, fruits, honey and the juice of sugar-cane respectively.[3] The other terms employed for wine in the Rāmāyaṇa are *madirā, āsava, sīdhu, maireya* and *vāruṇī*.[4] Of these *maireya* was an extremely popular variety. *Vāruṇī* was perhaps a very strong drink,[5] while *pītamaṇḍā* was one which had lost its spirituous element.[6]

As may naturally be expected soldiers were very fond of wines. They considered *pāna* as a stimulant[7] and freely indulged in it. For drunkards, *surā* was a panacea against all sorrows[8] and they preferred it to everything else.[9]

1. R. V 11/22 N. S.
2. *Surā vrikshebhyaḥ kadambādibhyaḥ svataḥ prādurbhūtāḥ, kritasurā śauṇḍikairutpāditāḥ.*, Tilaka-Ṭīkā on R. V 11/22 N. S.
3. R. V 6/23.
4. R. II 114/33; R. V 4/47; R. V 6/24; R. IV 26/8 and R. VI 10/9 respectively. According to Dr. Omprakash the *sīdhu* was distilled from the juice of sugar cane and *dhātakī* flowers and the *vāruṇī* was prepared from the juice of palm fruits and dates. (Food and Drinks in Ancient India pp. 118-119).

The war elephants were regularly given *madirā* to drink and this was considered so important that the king was expected to supervise it personally. R. II 114/33.

5. *Mām mohayati dushṭātmā pītamātreva Vāruṇī*, R. VI 10/9.
6. *Hritasāramidaṁ rāshṭram pītamaṇḍāṁ surāṃ yathā*, R. II 39/12.

It may be added that Dr. S. N. Vyas recognises one more kind of spirituous drink, viz., *sauvīraka* (R. III 47/45 N.S.) He explains it as a cheap variety of spirituous liquor inported from Sauvīra. (Rāmāyaṇa Kālīna Saṃskriti, p. 89).

The commentators, it may be pointed out, unanimously explain *sauvīraka* as gruel (*sauvīrakamāranālaṁ kāñjikam*) and in our opinion the spirit of the passage also supports that meaning.

7. *pānam balasamīraṇam*, R. VI 60/91 N. S.
8. *Surāmānīyatāṃ kshipraṃ sarvaśokavināśinīm*, R. V 19/49.
9. R. II 104/54, 60.

It may be noted that this wide popularity of 'drinking' in the Rāmāyaṇic society is looked with strong repugnance by some of the modern scholars. Thus Dr. S.N. Vyas in his 'Rāmāyaṇa Kālīna Saṃskriti (p. 93) opines that majority of passages testifying to the popularity of 'drinking' in the epic are later interpolations. (*Contd. next page.*)

In view of the various preparations of cereals and meat noticed above one would be justified in supposing that the culinary art was fairly developed in that period. The processes of boiling, cooking, roasting, seasoning and dressing of food were known and were very popular. The Rāmāyaṇa refers to cooks (*sūdāḥ*) who were experts in the art of cooking.[1] In the royal palaces there were special officers known as *paurogavas* to supervise the cooking in the kitchens[2]. Cooking was generally the business of women[3] though men (including princes) also were perhaps adept in this art.[4] Kings and the rich employed professional cooks in their kitchens, who in those days also seem

To show that 'drinking' was not received with approbation in that society but was, on the other hand, severely condemned, the following passages are cited from the Rāmāyaṇa.

(i) *Vikarishyati rathyāsu surāpam brāhmaṇaṃ yathā*, R. II 12/78 N. S.

(ii) *Madye prasakto bhavatu yasyāryo(a)numate gataḥ*, R. II 75/41 N. S.

(iii) *Āsīt paramasammūḍhaḥ prāśya vipraḥ surāmiva*, R. II 84/4.

(iv) *Aninandātmanātmānaṃ surām pītveva vedavit*, R. II 37/26.

(v) It is included among the ten vices against which a king was to guard himself. (R. II 100/68 N. S.)

(vi) *Na hi dharmārthasiddhyartham pānameva praśasyate,*
Pānādarthaśca kāmaśca dharmaśca parihīyate., R. IV 33/46 N. S.

Of these, it is interesting to find, that the passages from the Ayodhyā-Kāṇḍa (viz. i-v) have been rejected in the critical edition from Baroda as spurious. The last verse (viz. vi) cited from the Kishkindhā-Kāṇḍa is missing in the Lahore edition and even a casual consideration of the context in which it appears in the N. S. will show that it is a misfit there.

Nevertheless, it is not our object to assert that 'drinking' was commended by the Rāmāyaṇic society or that the poet looked at it with favour. In our opinion, as is evidenced from earlier literature, the *kshatriyas* were generally in the habit of drinking wines and presumably it was forbidden for the *brāhmaṇas* and ascetics.

Cf. also the following remarks of Vaidya, C. V.,

"........These and other facts go to prove beyond the shadow of a doubt that the Indo-Aryans especially the Kshatriyas were given to the habit of drinking in the epic period. By the end of that period, however, the generality of the Indians were teetotallers especially the Brahmins though the Kshatriyas with their usual conservatism continued the use of liquor. (Epic India, pp. 115-116).

1. R. V 17/13; R. V 6/20; *bhakshya-saṃskāra kuśalān*, R. VII 68/22.
2. R. V 6/50.
3. Sītā did the cooking in the forest, R. II 109/36-39.
4. After Sītā's abduction by Rāvaṇa Lakshmaṇa, it seems, was doing the cooking for Rāma and himself. (Note : R. III 79/8-9)

to have been men[1]. The Rāmāyaṇa also mentions a number of kitchen utensils such as *sthālī, kumbha, kalaśī, kalaśa, ghaṭa, pātrī, śarāva, karaka* and *galvarka*[2]. Of these the last three were particularly used for drinking wine.

It seems that the people took three meals a day—breakfast in the morning,[3] lunch in the afternoon[4] and dinner in the evening.[5] Men perhaps did not take their meals with women. On the other hand, the practice seems to have been that women took their meals after their husbands and other male members in the family had done so.[6] Moreover, one was expected not to partake of sapid food by himself alone; he was to share it with his friends and dependents.[7] In fact, as we have elsewhere shown, it was the righteous duty of every householder to make partners in his food the gods, manes, various living creatures (*bhūtas*) and guests.[8] It may be noted here that there was not the least of hesitation in offering a most modest meal to gods (or guests), for the principle was that what food a person ate himself the same he offered to his gods.[9] The reference to Guha offering edibles to Rāma and Bharata[10] shows that there were no taboos in receiving food from a *nishāda*. However, one was not expected to eat food offered by a *cāṇḍāla*.[11]

The Rāmāyṇa also testifies to the practice of big feasts being generally given at the time of sacrifices.[12] On such occasions well-dressed persons served food to the guests.[13] They were required to be polite and regardful, for any disregard

1. R. V 6/20; R. V 17/13; R. VII 68/25.
2. R. II 104/70-71; R. II 127/12; R. IV 61/29; R. III 1/24; R. III 67/6; R. III 47/15.
3. R. V 17/13. (It is also suggested in R. II 71/7).
4. R. VII 44/15.
5. Rāvaṇa had most probably taken his dinner late in the evening. (R. V canto 6.)
6. R. II 60/31.
7. *Ekākī mishṭamaśnātu*, R. II 83/24.
8. Vide pp. 152-153 and 158 supra.
9. *Yadannaḥ purusho rājaṃstadannāstasya devatāḥ*, R. II 116/36.
10. R. II 51/13-14 and R. II 96/8 respectively.
11. R. I 55/15.
12. R. I 10/7-12.
13. R. I 10/13.

shown on such occasions towards the invitees was sure to ruin the host (*dātā*).[1] It may also be noted in passing that though the plant *nāga-vallī* was known[2] betel chewing after meals is conspicuous in the Rāmāyṇa by its absence.

1. R. I 9/89-90.
2. R. III 82/43.

CHAPTER XII

DRESS AND ORNAMENTS

Nature has made 'dress' an imperative necessity for mankind by depriving it of the furs or tough skin with which she has provided the birds and beasts of the world. Primitive man covered himself with leaves, bark or skin to protect his limbs against the roughness of weather. But erelong in the history of mankind dress came to be recognised as an important mark of civilised living. The inventive faculty of man took into consideration the requirements of different climates and created countless varieties of dress materials and styles. The study of this subject in any ancient society, it may be pointed out, suffers from limitations as one can scarcely form an accurate idea of a people's dress in the absence of adequate information which is generally missing in the work of an ancient poet, in whose times cap-a-pie descriptions (of characters) had not yet become a norm. Thus, it is interesting to note that the Rāmāyaṇa even when it mentions 'tailors'[1] and 'needle'[2] seldom refers to a stitched garment as forming part of a man or woman's attire.[3]

The evidence in the Rāmāyaṇa indicates that the dress of the people in that period consisted of two oblong pieces of cloth (which we might name as *adhovastra* and *uttarīya*[4]), which were worn differently by men and women. In case of men, perhaps, the *adhovastra* was worn round the loins from the waist below, and the *uttarīya* might have been hung around

1. *prāvārikāḥ*, R. II 94/16; *vastrakarmakṛitaḥ* ?, R. II 94/22.
2. *akshi sūcyā vimṛiśasi*, R. III 52/35.
3. It is, no doubt, true that silence of a poet with regard to a particular point or article is not conclusive in itself still the reader of the Rāmāyaṇa, can not fail to notice that in female dress no 'petti coat' as an under-garment or a bodice to cover the breasts has been mentioned by the poet anywhere in the epic. Likewise, in the dress of a male, a jersey or a vestment (*aṅgarakhā*) does not find mention. *Kañcuka* is the only stitched garment mentioned in the epic.
4. The term *adhovastra*, it should be made clear, does not appear in

(*contd. next page*)

the neck and kept flowing down from over both the shoulders.[1] In times of necessity it might have also served them as a napkin.[2]

Like men, women also donned two pieces of clothes. That neither of them was a stitched one is clear from a reference to Añjanā in which we are told that her dress was gently waved by Wind, with the result that her fair face, together with her well developed breasts and round thighs, were exposed to view.[3] The *uttarīya* of women was most probably a little longer than that of men, for it was employed by them as a mantle to cover the face, the shoulders and the breasts.[4] It was completely

the Rāmāyaṇa; and in case of the males the *uttarīya* has not been specifically mentioned. In fact, the second garment worn by males is very rarely mentioned. We infer its existence from the mention of an *uttarīya* in religious books and also from the fact that the dress of males and females is generally referred to in the dual number (Vide R. II 40/7, 9; R. II 103/2; R. VI 28/16).

N. B. A *brahmacārī* (*ekavastra dharaḥ*........., R. III 41/12) and one banished by the king (*vāsasaikena vānaraḥ*...... *nirvāsayāṃāsa*......, R. IV 7/66) wore only one garment, the *adhovastra*. The *brahmacārī* most probably used the antelope's skin as his *uttarīya*.

A few *Rākshasas* (and those leading a solitary life in the interior of the forest) perhaps used only skins to cover their limbs (Cf. R. III 5/9). A passage in the Sundara-Kāṇḍa indicates that sorcerers wore cow's hide as their upper garment. (R. V 2/29).

1. Dr. S. N. Vyas opines that "There was some difference in the dress of various castes, especially the *Brāhmaṇas*, so that it was possible to make out the caste of an individual on the basis of his habiliment." (India in the Rāmāyaṇa age, p. 212). His observations are based on the following passage of the Araṇya-Kāṇḍa: *Dhārayan brāhmaṇaṃ rūpam Ilvalaḥ saṃskṛitam vadan*, R. III 11/56 N. S. It may be pointed out that *dhārayan brahmaṇaṃ rūpam* has been specifically mentioned here because *Ilvala* was a Rākshasa. If he were to appear in his original Rākshasa form no one would confide in him and fall a victim to his mischief. But to catch the ascetics unawares he used to disguise himself as a *brāhmaṇa*—Aryan. This does not indicate that the *brāhmaṇa's* dress or of any other *varṇa* was of a particular sort. (Vide also p. 16 supra).

2. Cf. Rāma wiped his tears from the face with the end of his cloth: *mukham aśrupariklinnaṃ vastrāntena parāmṛishṭavān*, R. IV 5/7.

3. IV 57/11-12.

4. We have noticed elsewhere (p. 114 supra) that in the Rāmāyaṇic period the purdah (veil) obtained among women of the elites. Naturally,

loose, for Sītā, being carried by Rāvaṇa, unnoticed by him, easily removed her *uttarīya* and dropped it amidst the Vānaras on the Ṛishyamūka hill.[1] During her captivity in Laṅkā she wore only the lower garment with one end of which she covered her upper body also in times of necessity.[2] This suggests that in the Rāmāyaṇic period also the *adhovastra* was donned by women very much in the style of the modern *sārī*.

Other items of dress mentioned in the Rāmāyṇa are :

(i) *Ushṇīsha*[3]—a covering for the head—turban,

(ii) *Kañcuka*[4]—a cloak; and

(iii) *Upānahau*[5]—a pair of sandals—wooden or made of leather.

The first two, viz., *ushṇīsha* and *kañcuka* perhaps formed part of the uniform of servants. There is a reference to *prāvaraṇa* in the Araṇya-Kāṇḍa but the context in which it appears does not help one in determining whether it is a reference to a 'cloak-like garment' or just to a covering of cloth.[6]

Thus the dress of people in the Rāmāyaṇic period appears to have been simple in a way. But the wearers chose the finest of materials and looked to the fineness and richness of their texture. Expressions like *mahārha vastra* (or *mahārha vasana, mahārha-ambara, mahārhavāsas*), *pravara vastra, uttama vastra, divya vastra, varāmbara, rucirāmbara, paramāmbara, agryāmbara* and

the *uttarīya* must have served as the veil to cover the head and the face on such occasions. Thus the *uttarīya* of women of that age seems to correspond to modern cunni or dupaṭṭā (scarf).

1. R. 60/2-3.

2. To avoid the sight of Rāvaṇa Sītā tried to cover her breasts with the end of her yellow garment :

Saṃhatau ca sujātau ca stanau stavaka sannibhau,
Pracchādayantīm savrīḍam pītasyāntena vāsasaḥ. R. V 14/22.

3. *Kañcukoshṇīshiṇaḥ*, R. VI 95/42. (In R. VI 53/20 and R. VI 82/23 Indrajit and Rāvaṇa respectively, performing *yajña* before going to the battle field, are also described as *raktoshṇīshadhara*.)

4. Ibid.

5. *pādukopānahaścaiva*, R. II 104/75. (Also *vārāhe cāpyupānahau*, R. IV 19/26.)

6. *Saṃpravṛittā niśā Sīte nakshatrasamalaṅkṛitā,*
Jyotsnā prāvaraṇaścandro dṛiśyate dyotite(a)mbare. R. III 3/31.

N. B. In addition to the articles of dress noted above the poet also mentions carpets (*kutha*, R. II 76/20), bed covers (*paristoma*, R. IV 17/18), blankets (*kambala*, R. IV 41/32), rugs (*āstaraṇa*, R. V 5/48) silken cushions (*saṃstara*, R. II 107/23) and quilts.

sūkshma or *tanutara vāsas* are very common in the Rāmāyaṇa.[1] The dress of ladies in Rāvaṇa's palace displayed a rich variety;[2] and the cloth of their dress was so fine that a regular stir was produced in it by their breath as they slept.[3] Likewise, Rāvaṇa's apparel was made of exceedingly refined cloth which was light and white like the foam of churned nectar.[4] The dress of the rich especially was usually embellished with gold and silver embroidery.[5] Bharata was distressed to observe the golden fibres of Sītā's *uttarīya* sticking into the blades of grass on which she had slept in the forest.[6] Likewise, the night-wear of Rāvaṇa was made of golden fibres (*mahā-rajatavāsasam*).[7]

Dyeing of cloth was very popular . The hermit's dress and perhaps also of servants was usually dyed in yellowish red colour (*kashāya*).[8] An *abhisārikā* proceeding on a tryst attired herself in blue.[9] The garment of Añjanā was yellow and having a red border.[10] Rāvaṇa (and the Rākshasas in general) seem to have favoured red dresses[11] and Sītā perhaps had a special fancy for the yellow garments.[12] Some passages indicate that white garments were considered pure and auspicious[13] while the black and the red colours for the Aryans

1. R. IV 41/32 (R. II 109/18, R. II 81/7, R. II 87/15), R. IV 18/12, R. V 13/19, R. III 36/26, R. V 3/22, R. V 3/12, R. V 2/33, R. V 5/89, R. II 40/7, R. II 100/117 respectively.
2. R. V 5/57.
3. R. V 5/76.
4. R. V 13/19.
5. Dr. S. N. Vyas suggests that bordered and embroidered clothes were known as *saṃvīta-vastra*. (Rāmāyaṇa-Kālīna Saṃskṛiti, p. 50). That his assertion is not correct can be easily seen from R. III 46/3 N. S. where Rāvaṇa is described as *slakshṇa-kāshāya saṃvītaḥ*. Rāvaṇa was appearing before Sītā disguised as a *parivrājaka* and it is utterly unbelievable that the poet wants to suggest that he was wearing embroidered garments. (Also note the use of the word *saṃvīta* (=clad or covered in) in R. II 8/7; R. II 20/17).
6. R. II 100/17.
7. R. V 5/100.
8. R. VII 99/9; R. II 17/3.
9. R. VII 32/11. Cf. *Nīlī-abhisārikā*, Shastri, S. N., The Laws and Practice of Sanskrit Drama, p. 220.
10. R. IV 57/11.
11. R. III 54/9; R. V 40/2; R. VI 82/22.
12. A passage of the Uttara-Kāṇḍa refers to the *pītāmbara* of Janārdana (R. VII 5/27).
13. R. II 20/7; R. V 21/12; R. VII 46/14.

(*Contd. next page.*)

and the yellow for the Rākshasas signified inauspiciousness.[1]

As already indicated above, various materials were used for making dresses. The dress of a hermit was usually made of grass, leaves, bark of trees and skin (especially of an antelope).[2] The towns-men, however, used hemp (*śaṇa*) cotton (*kārpāsika*)[3], silken (*kauśeya*)[4], linen (*kshauma*) and woollen clothes.[5] The dress of the rich was generally made of silk and linen. Linen clothes were perhaps considered auspicious and holy. Rāma was dressed in linen while performing *pūjā* on the eve of his coronation.[6] For receiving the brides the queens of Daśaratha had dressed themselves in linen.[7] Yellow silk, it seems, was the favourite of Sītā, for whether in Ayodhyā, Pañcavaṭī or Laṅkā, she is always described as clad in *pītakauśeya.*[8] Rāvaṇa while attending the court was dressed in superior linen[9] and even the coffin-sheet of Daśaratha was made of the same cloth.[10]

Among other things clothes also formed popular articles of gift. With the messengers sent to Kekaya to fetch Bharata

N. B. New (unwashed) clothes (*ahatavāsas*) were considered pure and were especially used on ceremonial occasions. R. II 16/6.

1. Black—R. II 75/14; R. V 74/13; R. VI 52/26; Red—R. II 75/10. Yellow—R. V 21/20, 24.
2. R. II 31/20; R. II 41/6; R. II 45/19; R. IV 41/34.

Cf. "There is, however, no doubt that clothes made of grass were actually used in India in ancient times. Herodotus assists us at this place and records; "These Indians wear a garment made of rushes which when they have cut the reed from the river and beaten it, they afterwards plait like a mat and wear it like a coat."—Vaidya, C. V., Epic India, p. 131.

3. R. V 56/130.

N. B. The Rāmāyaṇa being primarily an account of kings and noblemen rarely refers to cotton clothes which must have been the wear of the common man.

4. In one passage of the Kishkindhā-Kāṇḍa the poet refers to a town of cocoons (*pattanaṃ kośakārāṇām*, R. IV 32/17. Note Ṭilaka-Ṭīkā—*kauśeyatantūtpādaka jantūtpattisthānabhūtam.....*).
5. There is no direct mention of woollen garments in the Rāmāyaṇa (N. W.) but their existence may be inferred from the various references to *kambalas* (and also to *ajā*, *avi* and *mesha*).

The N. S. mentions *āvikam* and *aurṇam* in R. VI 75/9.

6. R. II 8/7.
7. R. I 72/10.
8. R. II 40/9; R. III 3/35; R. III 51/11; R. V 10/23.
9. R. V 45/4.
10. R. II 87/32.

and Śatrughna Vasishṭha sent costly garments as gifts[1] which were reciprocated by the Kekayarāja by carpets, blankets, superior dresses (*mahārhāṇi vāsāṃsi*) and various skins.[2] King Janaka, on the occasion of Sītā's marriage, gave excellent blankets, skins and silken garments (*dukūlāni*) as dowry (*kanyā-dhana*)[3]. Rāma and Sītā while leaving for the forest distributed clothes among the *brāhmaṇas* and dependents.[4] Clothes were also distributed among the *brāhmaṇas* on the occasion of a *pūjā*, a *śrāddha* or a *yajña*.[5] Kings and princes bestowed costly garments upon their servants as rewards or as mark of their pleasure.[6]

Fondness of Indians for ornaments has become proverbial.[7] In the Rāmāyaṇa-period too, "both males and females delighted in wearing ornaments and richness of India in precious stones and metals and in pearls enabled them, perhaps engendered in them the desire to wear ornaments in profusion."[8] The poet has employed about a dozen synonyms of gold in the Rāmāyaṇa[9], and a mention of gold, silver and various jewels is very common in the descriptions of the town Laṅkā and its people.[10] Among precious stones the

1. R. II 76/4.
2. R. II 76/20.
3. R. I 70/3.
4. R. II 33/37; R. II 35/5, 7, 18.
5. R. II 56/20; R. II 90/2; R. IV 19/28; R. VII 94/14.

N. B. A passage in the Uttara-Kāṇḍa (*...paṭṭaiḥ kauśeya sammiśraiḥ... śuśubhe tatra Liṅgañca*......R. VII 19/42) refers to Śiva-liṅga decked by silken garments. Dr. V. S. Agraval points out that the practice of offering garments to idols was common in ancient India and that such garments were known as *kośa*. Bāṇabhaṭṭa in his Harshacaritam specifically refers to a *mukha-kośa* offered to Śiva. It is plausible that the passage of the Uttara-Kāṇḍa noted above is referring to this very practice.

(For derails vide Agraval, V. S., Prācīna Bhāratīya Lokadharma, pp. 26-27).

6. R. VI 43/29; R. VI 106/54.
7. In the Rāmāyaṇic period warriors adorned their weapons, animals and chariots also with gold, silver and other precious gems.
8. Vaidya, C. V., Epic India, p. 133.
9. *Kañcana* (R. V 5/13); *kārtasvara* (R. V 5/25); *cāmīkara* (R. V 5/45); *jāmbūnada* (R. V 5/30); *tapanīya* (R. V 5/28); *mahārajata* (R. V 5/100); *rukma* (R. V 6/13); *suvrṇa* (R. V 5/45); *hāṭaka* (R. IV 2/20), *hiraṇya* (R. IV 2/20) and *hema* (R. V 5/9).
10. Vide early cantos of Sundara-Kāṇḍa.

Rāmāyaṇa mentions *pravāla* (ruby), *vaiḍūrya* (cat's eye), *indra-nīla* and *mahā-nīla* (sapphires), *vajra* (diamond), *vidruma* (coral) and *sphaṭika* (crystal)[1]. Besides, *muktā* (pearl) and *danta* (ivory) are also mentioned.[2] The skilled artisans of that period made beautiful articles of decoration with this material to enhance the beauty of person and place[3].

The ornaments used by the people in that period may broadly be classified as follows :

(a) **Ornaments for the head and face :**

Mukuṭa[4] and *kirīṭa*[5] were ornamental head-dresses for the males. In the Rāmāyaṇa Rāvaṇa's golden *mukuṭa* is described as thickly set in pearls.[6] Women, perhaps, did not wear *mukuṭa*.[7] The ornament worn by them on the head was known as *cūḍāmaṇi*. The prominent *cūḍāmaṇi* mentioned in the epic is of Sītā and it appears to have been of the shape of a ring and was studded with jewels and pearls.[8] In addition to the *cūḍāmaṇi* women also wore *tilaka* which though described as an ornament for the face[9] was perhaps, like the modern *ṭīkā*, worn on the head and used to be a little suspended on the fore-head.

The general term for the ornaments of the ear was *avataṃsa*.[10] The only ornament of this class mentioned in the Rāmāyaṇa is *kuṇḍala*. It was extremely popular and was worn by men and women alike.[11] As its name suggests, the *kuṇḍala* was of the shape of a coil. Ladies in Ravaṇa's palace wore

1. For references vide R. V 1/49; R. V 50/18; R. III 48/1; R. V 5/29; R. III 61/8; R. V 50/18 and R. III 61/8 respectively.
2. R. III 47/5 and R. III 61/8 respectively.
3. Note for example the descriptions of the palace and the royal garden in Laṅkā, R. V 5/25 ff. and R. V 9/26 ff. respectively.
4. R. I 6/11; R. V 45/2.
5. R. III 30/28.
6. R. V 45/2.
7. R. V 5/118 associates *mukuṭa* with the ladies of Rāvaṇa. But a comparison of this (and the following verses) with R. V 10/25 N. S. will show that it is the description of Rāvaṇa and not of the ladies.
8. R. V 35/61-62; R. V 65/4-5.
9. *mukhe ca tilakam*, R. II 12/12.
10. R. II 109/32; R. V 1/24.
11. (i) *sukuṇḍaladharāḥ.........striyaḥ*, R. V 5/71.
    (ii) *kuṇḍalābhyāṃ vibhūshitaḥ* (Rāvaṇaḥ), R. V 17/32.

golden *kuṇḍalas* inlaid with lapises and diamonds.[1] Their *kuṇḍalas* also appear to have been furnished with tiny bells which produced a jingle at the slightest movement.[2]

Vālmīki does not mention any ornament for the nose. Perhaps piercing of the nose and wearing an ornament into it had not yet started.

(b) Ornaments for the neck :

Ornaments for the neck (*graiveya*)[3] are perhaps of the longest standing and down to the present day even men of sobre taste have expressed a liking for the *mālā*. In the Rāmāyaṇa such ornaments have been mentioned under different names such as *hāra*, *srak*, *mālā* (or *mālya*), *hemasūtra* and *nishka*.[4] Of these the *nishka* was a necklace made of golden beads or coins.[5] The *srak* is described in the Yuddha-Kāṇḍa as a golden string interspersed with jewels.[6] The *mālā* of Bālī, given to him by Indra, is described as a golden chain interspersed with ivory.[7] *Hāras* of pearls, lapises and only gold are mentioned in the Sundara-Kāṇḍa.[8] Necklaces were usually long and fell on (the chest) or in between the breasts.

(c) Ornaments for the hand :

Ornaments for the hands are often collectively mentioned as *hastābharaṇa*,[9] and *aṅgulīya* (rings, usually with names inscribed thereon) for the finger,[10] *valaya*[11] and *pārihārya*[12] (brace-

1. R. V 5/125.
2. R. V 5/78.

N. B. The N. S. mentions two more ornaments of the ear—*karṇa-veshṭa* and *śva-daṃshṭra* (R. V 15/42 N. S.). According to C. Shivaramamurti, the former is a square made of gold with a full-blown lotus carved on it, the stalk of which is twice curled over the ear-lobe and then hung freely. *Śva-daṃshṭra* is an ear-ornament shaped like a flower, or a dog's teeth—Amarāvatī Sculptures in the Madras Government Museum, p. 108.

3. *grīvā graiveya bhūshitā*, R. III 67/27.
4. For references vide R. I 6/11; R. III 1/78; R. III 58/30; R. IV 8/30; R. V 3/22; R. V 5/73.
5. R. V 43/12; R. VI 44/22; R. VI 55/5.
6. R. VI 65/25.
7. R. IV 16/50.
8. R. V 5/72-73.
9. *nāhastābharaṇopetaḥ*, R. I 6/12.
10. *Rāmanāmāṅkitañ cedaṃ divyam paśyāṅgulīyakam*, R. V 31/17.
11. R. V 5/141.
12. R. V 5/82.

lets) for the wrist, and *keyūra*[1] and *aṅgada*[2] (bracelets) for the upper part of the arm are separately mentioned. Both men and women had a liking for these ornaments.

(d) **Girdle** :

The use of the girdle worn round the waist, slightly suspended on the hips at the back, was common.[3] Besides serving as an ornament it helped in supporting the lower garment. This latter sense is very well expressed by the various names of the girdle employed in the Rāmāyaṇa such as *mekhalā-dāma*, *śroṇī-sūtra* and *raśanā-guṇa*.[4] *Kāñcī* was also a variety of the girdle.[5] At more than one place Rāvaṇa has been described as wearing a golden *śroṇī-sūtra*[6] which indicates that the use of the girdle was common among men also.

(e) **Ornaments for the feet** :

Only one ornament has been mentioned for the feet and that is *nūpura*. It was worn on the ankles. Perhaps it was fitted rather loosely, for it is generally mentioned as 'slipping from the foot.'[7] It was worn only by women.

In addition to the precious stones and metals men and women alike used flowers for decking themselves.[8] The practice of wearing garlands of flowers around the neck and of adorning the locks, the ears and the arms by means of flowers was very common. In the forest Rāma and Lakshmaṇa roamed wearing *vanamālās* in their necks[9] and *āpīḍas* (wreaths) on their crowns.[10] In Citrakūṭa Rāma decked the hair of Sītā with bunches of *kesaras*.[11] In Pañcavaṭī when Rāvaṇa lifted Sītā, a shower of sweet smelling

1. R. V 3/9.
2. R. V 5/108.
3. *Jaghanaṃ tava vispashṭaṃ raśanāguṇa-śobhitam*, R. II 12/7.
4. R. II 81/7; R. V 17/31 and R. II 12/7 respectively.
5. R. V 2/27.
6. R. V 17/31; R. VI 44/23.
7. R. III 58/27; R. V 5/141.
8. Vide : *Utpalaiḥ puṇḍarīkaiśca kumudaiścāpi pādapaiḥ,*
   Vāpyaḥ samupaśobhante sāmānyāḥ pramadā iva., R. IV 23/14.
9. R. II 109/32.
10. R. II 109/32.
11. R. II 109/21.

flowers fell from her head upon the abductor.[1] Samudra as he appeared before Rāma wore over his crown a lovely wreath of divine flowers;[2] and Rambhā, decorated her person with divine flowers to meet her lover.[3] According to a passage of the Ayodhyā-Kāṇḍa the people of South were especially fond of wearing a chaplet of flowers.[4]

It is interesting to note that the people of the Rāmāyaṇic period were also very particular about their personal decoration for which the term was *prati-karma*[5] or *alaṅkāra-vidhi.*[6] In royal palaces there were ladies and old men proficient in the arts of bathing (*snāpakāḥ*),[7] anointing (*anulepakāḥ*)[8] and personal decoration (*prati karmaṇi nishṭhitāḥ*).[9] Cleaning of teeth with sticks[10] and of limbs with various powders and medicinal herbs[11] was very common and almost everyone besmeared the body with different kinds of scents (*gandha*), cosmetics (*aṅgarāga*) and unguents (*anulepana*[12])—among them the sandal paste was the most common. Both Rāma and Rāvaṇa are said to have applied to their limbs—specially arms—soft, fragrant and refreshing red sandal paste.[13] Añjanā

1. R. III 58/15, 23.
2. R. V 96/16.
3. R. VII 32/10.
4. *Kurvanti kusumāpīḍā śirāṃsi surabhīṇyapi,*
   Meghaprakāśaiḥ phalakairdākshiṇātyā suyodhinaḥ, R. II 106/14 f.n. 13.

"This verse", writes K. S. Ramaswami Sastri, "seems to refer to the partiality of the Tamils for wearing flowers. Two great Tamil scholars of today—Mahavidwan R. Raghava Iyengar and Rao Sahib M. Raghava Iyengar—are of opinion that the verse refers to the ancient Tamil custom of Tamil kings wearing special flowers symbolising the particular military errand undertaken by them."—Studies in Rāmāyaṇa, Part I, p. 20.

5. *Drashṭum iccāmi Vaidehīm......pratikarma-samāyuktām*, R. VI 95/
6. *Alaṅkāravidhau yuktāḥ......varastriyaḥ......*, R. VI 102/3. 8.
7. R. II 35/21.
8. Ibid.
9. *Striyaśca kula-vṛiddhāśca pratikarmaṇi nishṭhitāḥ*, R. VI 95/23.
10. R. II 104/74.
11. R. II 104/74; R. IV 19/7.
12. For references see R. I 6/11; R. V 2/33; R. VI 8/18; R. IV 41/32; R. II 94/29; R. V 17/39; R. VI 102/2-3.

N. B. A melancholy person—e. g. a lady in separation from her husband—was naturally averse to such decoration., R. II 127/15.

13. R. V 17/7; R. V 16/16; R. II 5/112.

was seen by Vāyu, with her body smeared with red sandal paste after her bath.[1] Sītā was presented by Anasūyā with an extremely superior type of paste and unguent, the application of which was to render eternal loveliness to her limbs.[2] The royal garden in Laṅkā with its trees and plants violently shaken by Hanūmān's feet and tail looked like a harlot whose fragrant ointment had been wiped off (*mṛidita-varṇakā*) in course of the manhandling by her paramour.[3]

Women applied sandal, red *alaktaka* and *lākshā* juice to their feet[4] and superior sandal paste on their breasts.[5] On the face they—sometimes men also—wore a variegated decoration of dots of sandal and other pastes prepared from flowers which was known as *bhakti* or *viśeshaka*.[6] Rāvaṇa wore such *bhakti* as he sat in his court[7] and Rambhā looked very attractive in the pleasing decoration of various colours on her face.[8] A passage in the Sundara-Kāṇḍa indicates that the art of fumigation was also known to the people.[9]

Dressing of the hair formed an important item in toilet. Long hair suspended right up to the hips were perhaps considered as a special mark of feminine beauty.[10] Women parted their hair[11] with the comb and plaited them so as to form a *veṇī* which was held towards the end with the help of a ribbon (*veṇyudgrathana*).[12] Flowers were also set in various styles into the hair for decoration. A lady in separation from her husband, however, did not comb her hair but carelessly tied them into a single braid (*eka-veṇī*).[13]

The fact that young boys wore locks on the sides (*kāka-paksha*) and that the *brāhmaṇas* preserved a tuft of hair on

1. R. IV 58/30.
2. R. III 1/78-79.
3. R. V 9/23.
4. R. II 12/12, 13; R II 64/16.
5. R. II 81,7.
6. Such decorative designs were painted on arches and buildings also and these too were known as *bhakti*—Vide R. V 1/19; R. V 4/50.
7. *Anuliptaṃ vicitrābhirvividhābhiśca bhaktibhiḥ*, R. V 45/5.
8. ......*kṛitair viśeshakair hṛidyaiḥ*......, R. VII 32/11.
9. *Candanāguru karpūrairdivyadhūpaiḥ pradhūpitam*, R. V 4/50.
10. *Veṇyā jaghanasthitayā*, R. V 10/27.
11. Note the word *sīmanta* in R. V 98/21.
12. R. V 22/16.
13. R. V 15/8.

the crown shows that the hair of males were trimmed in various styles. The Rāmāyaṇa actually refers to hair dressers (*śmaśru vardhakāḥ*) whose hands were quick and light,[1] and also mentions the razor (*kshura*).[2] In view of all this we can not agree with Dr. S. N. Vyas who is of the opinion that men of the Rāmāyaṇic period wore moustaches and beards and that their hair was not cropped.[3] His interpretation of the expression *viśodhita-jaṭaḥ* in this context as one who "merely had his matted locks shampooed and restored to their usual youthfulness" (without trimming) is not correct.[4] Perhaps he has been misled by the use of the word *viśodhita* which in addition to its popular meaning 'cleaned' or 'cleansed' also means 'trimmed,' when used in connection with hair. Moreover, the reference to barbers in that context will be completely redundant if the shaving of the beard and trimming of hair was not implied. It is, however, true that the ascetics did not dress their hair; they wore matted hair.

The Rāmāyaṇa also mentions a few articles of toilet such as looking-glasses (*darpaṇa*), combs (*kaṅkata*), brushes (*kūrca*), powders for bathing (*vāsa-cūrṇa*), sandal pastes (*candana kalka*) and collyriam phials (*añjanīḥ*).[5]

1. *Tataḥ Śatrughnavacanānnipuṇāḥ śmaśruvardhakāḥ,*
Sukhahastāśca śīghrāśca Rāghavam paryupāsate., R. VI 109/16.
(also *śmaśru yojakāḥ* in R. II 35/21).
2. *Jihvayā lihyasi kshuram*, R. III 52/35.
3. India in the Rāmāyaṇa Age, p. 220.
4. Ibid.
5. R. II 104/74-76.

CHAPTER XIII

SOME OTHER ASPECTS OF SOCIAL AND ECONOMIC LIFE

We have dealt above with most of the aspects of social life in the Rāmāyaṇic period. But a few facts about social etiquette, sports and recreations and economic life still remain to be stated. We may present them one by one in the present chapter :

Social etiquette[1] :

Etiquette is very intimately associated with civilised living. With the passage of time every society evolves its own form of behaviour, conformity to which meets general appreciation while a departure from the same is looked down upon. Some of the rules belonging to such a code of formal behaviour may be found to be common to practically every society, for their birth is mostly spontaneous. Thus expression of one's joy on meeting a dear one by embracing him or shaking hands with him may be found to be very widely current. But rules regarding reception of a guest or about the regard to be shown to a teacher or an elder may not be the same in every society, for these are primarily expressions not of nature but of nurture which varies from time to time and people to people. Since such a code in a society is generally unwritten it is mostly to be gathered from the actual behaviour of its members andit serves as a fairly dependable evidence for forming a high or low impression about a people.

Early Sanskrit literature shows that from the very beginning the Aryans were particular about the rules of etiquette. By the time of Vālmīki the unwritten code in this behalf had become fairly elaborate and at the same time extremely popular so that

1. The terms denoting etiquette in The Rāmāyaṇa seem to be *ācāra*, *samudācāra* and *upacāra* :

(i) *jagāma samudācāram prayujyācārakovidaḥ*, R. V 76/11.

(ii) *...sopacāraṃ tato Rāmamūcuḥ...*, R. V 92/8.

N. B. The term *ācāra* preceded by the word *loka* is employed in the sense of custom in the Rāmāyaṇa. (Vide p. 175 supra).

the characters in the epic are found paying due regard to these rules in their mutual behaviour. 'Regard for the senior, sincere cordiality to the equal and affection for the junior' was the guiding spirit of all good behaviour in Vālmīki's age. In the society the order of seniority among the four *varṇas* was fixed and a person belonging to a lower *varṇa* was strictly expected to treat with regard the members of the higher *varṇa* or *varṇas*. The *brāhmaṇas* who were the repositories of learning and penance were considered worthy of highest respect and so every member of the other three *varṇas* displayed a most deferential deportment in relation to the *brāhmaṇas*.[1] In the family age and status determined the seniority of a member who on that account commanded great regard from his juniors. The position of the parents in the family was supreme and they were venerated by their children as veritable deities.[2] A preceptor who was responsible for the spiritual birth of the child was accorded a higher place than even the parents.[3]

Various modes of expressing his sense of regard to the senior by the junior were current in that society. Thus on the arrival of a senior the first thing that the junior was to do was to immediately give up his seat and occupy it again only after being permitted by the senior who had been seated and duly honoured.[4] Folding of one's hands, lifting the joined hands to the forehead, bending a little forward with folded hands, touching the feet of the senior and laying oneself prostrate before him, and circumambulating the senior were other popular modes of showing regard to him.[5] These latter modes were generally adopted by the junior when he approached a senior and on such an occasion in accompaniment to his actions he also uttered the words of salutation prefixing to them his (or her) own name.[6]

1. Cf. R. I 6/20-21.
2. R. II 19/19.
(Also note pp. 37-38 and 93 supra).
3. Vide p. 119 supra.
4. R. I 2/26-28.
5. For references see (*prāñjaliḥ*) R. II 5/18; (*śirasyañjalimādhāya*) R. VII 21/6; (*prāñjaliḥ praṇato bhūtvā*) R. I 2/26; (*jagrāhāvanataḥ pādau śirasā patito bhuvi*) R. II 78/2; (*pradakshiṇamupāvṛitya*) R. I 61/28.
6. (*i*) *Nāma saṃśrāvayan Rāmo vavande caraṇau pituḥ*, R. II 5/18.
(ii) *Abhyavādayata kshipram bruvantī Maithilī hyaham.*, R. III 1/50.

The seniors on their part expressed their affection for the junior by pronouncing words of blessing, by smelling him on the head and by embracing him.[1] Embracing and shaking of hands were also the popular modes of greeting among the equals.[2] It may be added that on occasions of large gatherings one was first to show one's respects to the seniors in age and status and then meet one's equals and juniors.[3] This is clear from the actual behaviour of the epic characters and also from the use of the words *yathārha*, *yathākrama* and *ānupūrvī* employed by the poet on such occasions.[4]

To wish one another and make mutual inquiries of welfare are marks of good manners and both the practices were fairly popular in the society of Vālmīki.[5] To cite an example, the sage Bharadvāja, on meeting Bharata, made inquiries about the welfare of his kingdom, the treasury and the capital.[6] In return the *Purohita* Vasishṭha and Bharata asked the sage about his welfare in relation to the body, the *agnihotra*, the pupils and the birds and beasts of the hermitage.[7] It may be pointed out in this connection that no doubt, inquiries were generally directed keeping in view the status and occupation of the addressee, however, there is no indication that, as in later times,[8] a rigid mode was adopted in this behalf for each

1. *Sa mītrā samabhipretya parishvajyābhinanditaḥ,*
Prāpnuhyāyuśca kīrtiñca dharmañca svakulocitam..., R. II 20/11-14.
Also : *tañca sā mūrdhnyupāghrāya parishvajya ca Kaikayī*, R. II 78/3.

N. B. Smelling a junior on the head or embracing him was also indicative of the senior's joy or gratification at some significant achievement by the former. (R. V 68/12; R. VII 74/12).

2. *samparishvajya*, R. II 51/12 and *samprahrishṭamanā pāṇim pīḍayāmāsa pāṇinā*, R. IV 4/12.

3. On returning from Laṅkā Hanūmān paid his respects first to *guruvṛiddha* Jāmbavanta and prince Aṅgada, and then met the rest of the Vānaras., R. V 55/26 ff.

4. R. I 9/74; R. II 103/9.

5. Sometimes such enquiries were made through messengers. Note R. V 28/4 ff; R. V 37/24.

6. *...papraccha kuśalaṃ cāsya rājye kośe pure tathā*, R. II 103/10.

7. *Vasishṭha-Bharatau cainam papracchaturanāmayam,*
Śarīre cāgnihotre ca śishyeshu ca mṛigapakshishu., R. II 103/11.

8. Cf. *Brāhmaṇaṃ kuśalam pṛicchet khsatrabandhumanāmayam,*
Vaiśyaṃ kshemaṃ samāgamya śūdramārogyameva ca., Manusmṛiti, II 27

separate *varṇa* . In the examples, cited above, the sage Bharadvāja asked *kuśala* of the *kshatriya* prince Bharata and the latter asked *anāmaya* of the former, even though he was a *brāhmaṇa*.

A person proceeding on a journey formally took leave of every relation, friend or acquaintance present on the spot.[1] He spoke words of comfort to his wife and children and also smelt the latter on the head[2]. The friends and relations on their part wished him a bon-voyage and prayed for his welfare.[3] They also accompanied him upto the nearest margin of water—the bank of a pond or river.[4]

To express indebtedness for a favour received from another is both a sign of good manners as well as an expression of magnanimity. Ingratitude was severely condemned by Vālmīki's society[5] which recognised the principle that the favour must be returned.[6] There are various illustrations in the epic of characters who have expressed their gratitude to their benefactor. The words of Rāma spoken to Hanūmān after his coronation at Ayodhyā are the most striking in this respect. He said that he would sacrifice his life for the sake of the *Kapi* in consideration of each one of the acts of favour done to him and yet he would not be completely absolved of the debt. However, he wished that this debt should ever remain on him, for its retribution would require that the Vānara should be visited by calamities.[7]

Vālmīki's society was extremely civilised not only in external behaviour but also in the employment of speech. In mutual conversation the people employed sweet and polite speech and addressed one another in a variety of ways. *Bhagavān, bhavān* and *ārya* were the general terms of respect employed for a senior.[8] Among persons of almost equal age and status the popular terms of address were *tāta* and *tvam*[9] and they also

1. ......*āmantrya cāmantrya ca vānaram*......R. IV 58/72.
2. R. IV 15/50-51.
3. R. IV 58/66; R. IV 59/1
4. R. IV 61/50, 55.
5. *Kṛitaghnaḥ sarvabhūtānāṃ sa vadhyaḥ Plavageśvara*, R. IV 27/12.
6. *Kṛite ca pratikartavyameshā tāta satāṃ gatiḥ*, R. IV 61/119.
7. R. VII 40/23-24 N. S. (The verses appear in a distorted form in the N. W. VII 42/22).
8. R. III 1/5; R. IV 61/125; R. II 124/18.
9. R. II 5/28; R. II 120/2, 3.

called one another by name.[1] *Tāta*, *vatsa* and *saumya*[2] were also the most popular terms of endearment employed by the senior for the junior. A lady was generally addressed as *bhavati*, *ārye* and *devi*.[3] It is worth noting that a young lady (whether married or unmarried) was freely addressed even by strangers in terms referring to the charms of her person. Thus Rāvaṇa appearing in the guise of a *parivrājaka* addressed Sītā as *cārusmite*, *cārudanti*, *cāruvistṛitalocane* and *varārohe*.[4] Similar terms were employed for her by Hanūmān also in the Aśoka-Vanikā.[5] A husband, usually referred to his wife as *priye*, *kalyāṇi*, *bhāmini*, *śubhe*, *vilāsini*, *anindite*, *yaśasvini*, *abale*, *dayite*, *manasvini*, *bhadre* and *devi*[6], while he was generally addressed by her as *āryaputra* or *priya*.[7] It may be noted that there was no restriction for the wives on addressing their husbands by their names.[8] Names derived from the names of the parents, the family and the country (or province) were also extremely popular.[9]

A word may also be added here about princely etiquette. A king was by virtue of his position an object of highest regard for his subjects who looked upon him as a veritable divinity. He was generally addressed as *deva*, *rājan* and *āryaputra*.[10] In the *Sabhā* the members paid him their respects by folding their hands unto him or by touching his feet.[11] They also greeted him by such words as *vardhasva* and *vijayasva*.[12] The servants received his command by a little bending of their heads[13] and circumambulated him while taking his leave.[14] It seems

1. R. I 47/7.
2. R. IV 61/118; R. I 20/11; R. III 65/4.
3. R. II 26/11; R. II 83/2; R. II 21/30.
4. R. III 51/15-28.
5. R. V 27/2-10.
6. R. II 13/8, 9, 11, 29; R. II 67/5; R. VI 104/44, 47; R. II 29/23; R. II 31/2, 17, 27; R. II 107/10.
7. R. II 30/2.
8. R. II 33/3.
9. (*Kauśalyāmātaḥ*) R. I 21/2; (*Rāghava*) R. II 32/14; (*Maithili*) R. II 29/20; (*Vaidehi*) R. II 31/16.
10. R. II 17/13; R. VI 2/33; R. VI 8/38.
11. R. V 91/3, 28.
12. (*jayāśishā vardhayitvā*) R. VI 5/17 and (*vijayasvāryaputra*) R. VI 8/38.
13. R. V 42/18.
14. R. V 44/14.

even in those days it was customary for strangers coming to have an audience with the king to bring presents for him.[1] Presents were also exchanged by the kings in their mutual relationship. Vasishṭha sent various presents (on behalf of Daśaratha) to the Kekayarāja through the messengers sent to fetch Bhrata and so did Aśvapati send presents for Daśaratha with Bharata.[2]

Sports and Recreations :

Sports and recreations do away with the monotony of life. Hunting, chariot race and gambling were popular in India as early as the Vedic period. There were also places where people could meet for recreational purposes.[3] As life became more peaceful and prosperous the spirit to enjoy manifested itself in a greater variety of ways.

The Rāmāyaṇa refers to the people of Ayodhyā as *hṛishṭa-pushṭa*[4] and the town as resonant with the sweet music of various instruments and as jubilant with *utsavas* and *samājas*.[5] There are also frequent references to parks and gardens as the haunts of lovers and resorts of sportive people.[6] Occasionally we read of young people celebrating picnics either in

1. Even the ascetics came with 'fruits, roots and holy water.' R. VII 64/6.

2. R. II 74/9; R. II 76/20-24.

3. Cf. "A noted fair was the *Samana* where maidens flocked to make merry and find a husband. They even spent their nights there." Upadhyaya, Bhagvat Saran, Women in Ṛgveda, p. 216.

4. R. I 6/6.

5. R. I 5/15; R. II 61/13; R. II 73/14.

The word *samāja*, it may incidentally be noted, has been distinguished by Pāṇini (III 3/69) from its near parallel *samaja*. The former is explained by him as 'congregation of men' while the latter as 'aggregation of animals'. The word *samāja* appears in Pāli literature also as *samajjā* and is to be met with in the edicts of Aśoka and the Hathigumpha inscription. In R.E.I., it is associated with *yajña*, a religious function, and in the Hathigumpha inscription with *usava* (=*utsava*), a festive occasion or festivity. The inseparable association of *samājas* with *utsavas* is equally borne out by the Jātakas where it has been employed with reference to contests, dances, song and instrumental music.

(For further details see Barua, Beni Madhab, Inscriptions of Aśoka—Part II—note on Samāja, pp. 224 ff. Vide also Agraval, V. S., Prācīna Bhāratīya Lokadharma, pp. 20-21, 37).

6. R. II 73/17; R. II 77/21.

gardens or on the hills.[1] How fond the Rāmāyaṇic people were of sports can further be gauged from the fact that *vaihārika śilpa* (fine arts) was recognised in that age as a fit subject for proficiency even by a prince.[2]

A lively spirit marks the entire behaviour of the Rāmāyaṇic people. But a direct mention to a particular sport is very rare. *Dyūta* is mentioned more than once.[3] But all that we can gather from the epic about *dyūta* is that it was played with the dice (*aksha*) and with a stake (*paṇa*). Vālmīki has made a very interesting reference to the melancholy of a gambler (*dhūrta*) who had lost the stake.[4] There is clear evidence also to show that gambling though popular, was regarded as a vice.[5] The use of the word *ashṭāpada* is believed to indicate familiarity with chess.[6] Of vigorous sports, which might have been popular specially with the *kshatriyas*, we read of wrestling (*mallakrīḍā*)[7] and fowling and hunting (*mṛigayā*).[8] Hunting, fowling and fishing appear to have been fairly popular even though addiction to them was censured. The fish was either hooked[9] or killed with arrows.[10] In hunting beaters[11] and hounds[12] were also employed. An elephant was captured with the help of other trained elephants after being made to fall in an artificial pit.[13] We read also of deer being first captivated by music and then caught by the hunter.[14]

1. R. II 107/10-11; R. IV 61/29-32.
2. R. II 3/17.
3. R. II 94/27; R. V 5/53; R. V 9/20.
4. R. V 5/53.
5. *Aksha* is enumerated among the *kāmajadoshas*.
6. R. I 5/13.
Vide Dikshitar, V. R. R., War in Ancient India, pp. 135-136.
7. R. II 35/24.
8. R. II 94/27 refers to bird catchers (*vaitaṃsikas*).
N. B. R. I 5/21 N. S. shows that duels with wild animals like lions, tigers and boars was also popular in that period. The verse is however missing in the N. W.
9. R. III 57/6.
10. R. III 79/8-9.
11. R. II 112/2.
12. R. III 61/4.
13. R. V 43/20; R. V 90/45.
14. R. II 11/35.

As stated above fine arts were popular among the people. There are copious references to architecture, painting, dance, music and poetry. Of these the popularity of architecture is evidenced from graphic descriptions of splendid constructions[1] and that of music from specific references to music—both vocal and instrumental—which are the most numerous. The two famous capitals of that period, viz. Ayodhyā and Laṅkā have been described as reverberating with the sound of music which was perpetually played there.[2] Music was further, a necessary accompaniment of all functions, social as well as religious. Vālmīki displays familiarity with several technical terms of music such as *tāna* (the musical tone), *sapta-svara* (the seven notes of the musical scale), the base, the middle and the high tones produced from the three *sthānas*, *tāla* (the musical measure), *laya* (cadence) and *mūrcchā* (the musical modulation).[3] There is also a long list of musical instruments which were played upon by the people.[4] Poetry was recognised as

1. Note different architcetural constructions suggested in : *Harmya-prāsāda-bhavana-vimānebhyaḥ*......R. II 30/10.

It may incidentally be noted that the epic employs various architectural terms such as *aṭṭalaka* (a watch tower, R. V 1/18) *bhūmi* (storey, R. V 1/53), *citra-śālā-gṛiha* (a picture gallery R. V 4/41), *gavāksha* (round window, R. VI 102/47), *gopura* (gate or especially town-gate, R. V 2/4, R. VII 52/83), *jāla* (lattice, R. V 5/28), *kakshā* or *kakshyā* (court or inner apartment of a palace, R. II 61/18, R. IV 26/24, R. V 4/20, R. VII 49/12), *kāma-gṛiha* (pleasure resort, R.V 4/42), *kuṭṭima* (levelled floor, R. VI 38/27), *kuḍyā* (wall, R. VI 102/46), *krīḍā-gṛiha* (sport pavilion, R. V 4/41), *maṇi-gṛiha* (R. V 4/41), *nandyāvarta* (a house not having an opening on the western side, R. V 2/23 foot note 1), *niryūka* (a kind of pinnacle, R. V 2/10), *niśā-gṛiha* (R. V 4/42), *nishkuṭa* (a pleasure-grove near a house, R. V 8/3), *pratolī* (principal road through a village R. V 1/18), *prākāra* (city-wall, R. V. 2/6), *rathyā* (a lane, R. VI 54/6), *toraṇa* (an arched portal, R. V 1/56), *sañjavana* (quadrangle, R. V 3/10 N. S.), *sṛiṅgāṭaka* (a cross-way, R. V 49/20), *sopāna* (stair case, R. V 2/27), *saudha* (a fine building, R. V 4/52), *vapra* (rampart, R. V 1/24) *vardhamāna-gṛiha* (a house not having an opening on the southern side, R. V2/23), *valabhī* (a turret or upper room, R. VI 15/18) and *vedikā* (platform, R. V 2/9).

2. R. I 5/15 and R. V 2/4, 8, 11, 22, 26.

3. For references see R. I 4/58, R I 4/42, (R. VII 96/3), R. V 2/26; R. VII 96/26; R. VII 75/2; R. VII 95/14.

4. *bheri* (R. VI 38/46), *ḍiṇḍima* (R. V 5/134), *dundubhi* (R. I 9/32), *kumbha* (R. VI 38/51), *muraja* (R. II 42/41). *mridaṅga* (R. I 5/15), *paṇava*

(*Contd. next page.*)

an art meant for providing aesthetic joy.[1] It was recited with feeling and usually to the accompaniment of a musical instrument.[2] Drama, actors and dancers have been mentioned in different contexts and theatrical performances appear to have been common in towns.[3] Occasionally, it seems, *goshṭhīs* were also held[4] in which people perhaps amused themselves by reciting light poetry. The most popular members of such *goshṭhīs* seem to have been the professional story-tellers[5] who entertained their audience by their wit and humour. The royalty and perhaps also the rich were fond of keeping pet birds and animals. The Kekayarāja had a special breed of dogs brought up in his palace.[6] Likewise, the palaces at Ayodhyā and Laṅkā have been shown as crowded by birds and deer.[7] Unable to find Sītā in the palace of Rāvaṇa Hanūmān suspected that she might be bewailing in some lonely corner like a tame *sārikā* in a cage[8]; and Mālyavān pointed out to Rāvaṇa that ever since Sītā was brought to Laṅkā the *sārikās* were making inauspicious shrieks in the houses.[9]

In the end it may also be pointed out that merriment had become a part of practically every social and religious function. Thus big feasts were held in course of the sacrificial sessions like the *Aśvamedha*[10] and large scale festivities were organised on occasions like the royal coronations.[11] Periodical *saṃskāras* like the *Āgrāyaṇa* also afforded regular opportunities for rejoicings. Special mention must be made in this connection of the festival *Indra-dhvaja* to which there are numerous allusions in the epic. The *Indra-dhvaja* appears to have been a public festival celebrated on the full moon day of *Āśvina*[12] when the

(R. V 5/133), *paṭaha* (R.V 5/128), *śaṅkha* (R. I 9/32), *tantrī* (R. VII 95/14), *vallaki* (R. V 12/23), *veṇu* (R. V 5/15) and *vīṇā* (R. V 5/129). The *koṇa* (quill of a lute) is mentioned in R. VI 38/46.

1. Cf. *ślokeshvatirasāyaṇam*, R. I 2/46.
2. Cf. *gāyetām madhuraṅgītaṃ tantrīlayasamanvitam*, R. VII 95/16.
3. R. I 8/14; R. II 73/14; R. II 75/4; R. II 94/27.
4. R. V 96/101.
5. R. II 75/3-4; R. VII 45/1-3.
6. *antargṛihacarān pushṭān*, R. II 76/24.
7. R. II 16/53, 55; R. V 9/39.
8. *kvacillālapyate nūnampañjarastheva sārikā*, R. V 8/20.
9. R VI 11/36.
10. Vide pp. 169-170 supra.
11. R. II 8/10 ff.
12. R. IV 16/37 N. S.

crops were ripe and ready for being reaped. A week earlier than the actual festival a lofty pole decorated with flags and festoons was raised in honour of Indra, the guardian of rain and also of agriculture. On the final day the ropes or the other contrivances supporting the pole were removed so that it fell down with a great thud.[1] Vālmīki, it seems, had a peculiar fancy for this fall of the *Indra-dhvaja*, for it repeatedly strikes him as an *upamāna* for a person suddenly falling on the ground.[2]

Economic Life :

India is a rich country abounding in natural resources; and the ancient Indians, though highly spiritual in their outlook were never indifferent to economic progress. They recognised the importance of material wealth in life by including *artha* among the *purushārthas*, the objectives of an individual's life. Moreover, in their *varṇa* scheme a large section of the community (viz. *vaiśyas*) had primarily to devote itself to the promotion of national wealth.

The term *vārtā* which stands for national economy and comprises agriculture, cattle-breeding and trade[3] occurs in the Rāmāyaṇa;[4] and there is ample evidence to show that all these three branches were in a flourishing state in that period. Agriculture was, naturally, the primary industry of the country and formed the pivot of economy. The state looked well after the husband-men,[5] for taxes realised on agricultural produce were the main source of state revenue.[6]

Cultivation was mostly done by the husband-men (*kṛishakas*) in agricultural villages known as *grāmas* though agricultural fields (*kshetra*) could easily be seen at the outskirts of the towns as well.[7] The chief crops in that period also appear to have been two—one reaped in autumn and the other in spring. Among the agricultural produce of that

1. R. II 80/40; R. II 88/9; R. III 31/27.
2. For details about this festival vide Agraval, V.S., Prācīna Bhāratīya Lokadharma, Chap. IV.
3. Cf. *kṛishi pāśupālye vaṇijyā ca vārtā*, Arthaśāstra I 4.
4. R. I 3/6.
5. R. II 114/21.
6. We have discussed the State's position with regard to the economic life of the people in another chapter—Vide chapter XX infra.
7. Cf. *grāmān sukṛishṭasīmnaśca*, R. II 50/5.

period references are found to rice (known as *śāli* or *taṇḍula*), barley (*yava*), wheat (*godhūma*), pulses (like *mudga*, *caṇaka* and *māsha*), sugar cane (*ikshu*), cotton (*karpāsa*), oil seeds (like *tila* and *sarshapa*) and various kinds of spices.[1] Crops generally depended upon rain-water[2]; and it was believed that the king could ensure timely rainfall by his righteous conduct.[3] As a safeguard against famine in the event of drought, the king had also to provide irrigation by constructing wells, tanks, dams and canals.[4] The land which was provided with an efficient system of irrigation was known as *adevamātṛikā* i. e. not depending upon rainfall. The king had also to guard against the usual damage done to crops by pests such as locusts, rats and damaging insects.[5] The king had the prerogative to collect *bali* on the agricultural produce, but the prerogative arose from his sovereignty and not necessarily from his ownership of land.[6]

Gardening is a concomitant of agriculture and seems to have been very popular in the Rāmāyaṇic period. Fruits and vegetables formed important part of the daily food of the people[7] and flowers were profusely required for religious purposes and decoration.[8] The art of distilling wine from fruits and flowers was known; and the people were fond of such drinks. The poet generally refers to various types of gardens in his descriptions of the towns.[9] Particularly the pictures of the *Madhu vana* at Kishkindhā and the *Aśoka vana* at Laṅkā are very inpressive. The trees in these royal gardens have

1. See chapter XI pp. 232ff. supra.
2. Cf. R. IV 23/8.
3. Cf. *taṣya vyatikramabhavā bhavishyati......anāvṛishṭiḥ*, R. I 8/12.
Note Tilaka-Ṭīkā, *rājocitadharmavilopanāt*.
Also R. II 70/8; R. VI 110/8.
4. Note R. II 114/21.
5. R. II 114/22-23.
N. B. The word *hiṃsā* occurring in the verse has been explained by Govindarāja as referring to six-fold *ītis* : *ativṛishṭiranāvṛishtirmūshikāḥ śalabhāḥ khagāḥ, atyāsannāśca rājānaḥ shaḍetā ītayaḥ smṛitāḥ*.
6. Vide also Chap. XVII infra.
7. Vide p. 237 supra.
8. Vide pp. 251-252 supra.
9. Vide *ākrīḍa, udyāna, ārāma, upavana, nishkuṭa* and *vana* in R. I 5/10; R. II 73/13, 17; R. II 77/17; R. V 4/41-42; R. VI 72/36.

been described by the poet as yielding fruits and flowers in every season.[1]

Animal husbandry was another important occupation of the *vaiśyas*.[2] In fact, all the three higher *varṇas* were engaged in their own way in the preservation and rearing of cattle. The cow for the *brāhmaṇa* and the horse for the *kshatriya* were indispensable. Cattle in general constituted the principal wealth of the people. The importance of live-stock and animal husbandry can be understood further from the fact that like agricultural villages there also existed in that period separate pastoral villages (*ghoshas*).[3] Horses, elephants, mules and camels were in great demand for the army and therefore great emphasis was laid on the improvement of their breed and their training. It is also likely that animals of good breed, particularly horses, were imported from neighbouring countries.[4] Kings like Aśvapati were also fond of dogs and displayed great interest in bringing up their special breeds.[5] But the position occupied by the cow was unique. The nutritive value of milk and milk products like curd and butter had been recognised very early in India and that was principally responsible for the deep-rooted sentiment cherished by the Hindus for the cow. In the Rāmāyaṇa, the cow, along with the *brāhmaṇa* is the symbol of Aryan culture.[6]

Direct information with regard to industry and trade is very meagre in the epic. Mostly our knowledge regarding these aspects of the economic life of the Rāmāyaṇic people is inferential, being mainly deduced from the references to the material wealth of the people. We have noted in an earlier chapter that the dress of the people was made of different varieties of cotton, silk and wool, and that both men and women were extremely fond of ornaments made in different designs from gold, silver and various other valuable metals and stones.[7] This can be taken as an ample proof of the deve-

1. R. V 10/6, 15.
2. R. II 114/24.
3. R. I 13/11; R. II 94/26.
4. R. V 4/36.
5. R. II 76/24.
6. Cf. *go-brāhmaṇahitārthāya*, R. I 23/13.
7. Vide pp. 245-251 supra.

loped state of the textile industry and of the high craftsmanship of the goldsmith.[1] References to *dhātu* (metal) obtained from the mountains[2] and the complex military equipment which included large numbers of metallic weapons and some elementary machinery testify on the one hand to the knowledge of the refining of metals and on the other to the manufacturing skill of the people. The progress of the leather industry is easily shown from the liberal use of skins and hides for sacred as well as secular purposes.[3] Frequent references to multi-storeyed buildings of varying designs and particularly the description of the palace and the royal garden in Laṅkā evidence the high proficiency achieved by the people in that period in the field of architecture.[4] The poet presents a very luxurious and artistic lay out of Rāvaṇa's palace in which there are references to imposing seats and carpets, costly utensils, various types of musical instruments and artificial birds and animals—all possessing exquisite fineness being fashioned by the workmen with superb diligence out of the costliest material.[5] That all this is not a creation of the poet's fancy but a reality is further indicated by the long list of artisans and craftsmen which appears in the Ayodhyā-Kāṇḍa.[6]

Corporate activity in economic life had become the marked feature of that period. The epic frequently refers to *śreṇis* and *nigamas* which were corporations of artisans and merchants respectively.[7] Corporate activity had become so

1. Vide also *maṇikārāḥ, dantakārāḥ, svarṇakārāḥ, kanakaśodhakāḥ, tantuvāyāḥ, hairaṇyakāḥ, kārpāsikāḥ* and *vastrakarmakṛitaḥ* mentioned in R. II 94/12-22.

2. R. IV 10/17; R. IV 20/8; R. IV 33/17; R. IV 60/15; R. IV 61/25.

Note : Besides gold and silver there are references to various metals: *āyas* (R. V 70/13 and R. VI 51/19); *kālāyasa* (R. V 49/42); *kārshṇāyasa* (R. II 73/14); *śīśa* (R. III 52/38); *kāca* (R. II 94/25); *kāṃsya* (R. II 94/17); *tāmra* (R. II 94/23) and *loha* (R. III 52/38).

3. For various articles made of leather see chapter XXII infra.

4. Vide references to architectural terms noted on p. 262f.n. 1. supra.

5. Cf. *Na tatra kiñcinna kṛitam prayatnāt, na tatra kiñcinna mahārharatnam, Na tatra kiñcinna mahāviśesham, na te viśeshā niyatāḥ sureshvapi.* R. V 5/36.

6. R. II 94/11-27.

7. For details about the corporate bodies vide chapter XXI infra.

patent a fact that even soldiers[1] and priests[2] carried on their functions on the principle of partnership.

We frequently find references to merchants, merchandise and markets.[3] There are allusions to travelling companies of merchants[4] and also to large boats laden with vendibles[5] which might indicate even the presence of foreign trade. There are unambiguous notices of horses of foreign breed.[6] Progress in trade is also evidenced from the references to 'price' and 'money'.[7] Usually the cow served as the standard of value or as a medium of exchange but coins of gold and perhaps also of silver appear to have been in use in that period.[8] Money was required not only for sale or purchase of articles but also for payment of work.[9] Salaried labourers were known as

1. *Kshatriya* guilds are mentioned both in the Mahābhārata and the Arthaśāstra—Vide Majumdar, R. C , Corporate Life in Ancient India, p. 25.

2. Manu lays down that of the sixteen priests, the first group of four would receive about the half, and the second, third and fourth groups respectively half, one third and one fourth of that. Kullūka explains that if, for example, the sacrificial fee consists of 100 cows, each of the first group would receive 12 and each of the succeeding groups respectively 6, 4 and 3. (Manusmṛiti—VIII 210).

The Rāmāyaṇa does not specifically mention this formula but displays familiarity with a certain principle of division of the *dakshiṇā*.

Vide : *Ṛitvijaste tataḥ sarve ādaduḥ sahitāḥ vasu.*
Rishyaśṛiṅgāya mahate Vasishṭhāya ca dhīmate,
Tataste nyāyataḥ kṛitvā pravibhāgaṃ dvijottamāḥ, R. I 10/40-41.

3. R. I 5/5, 8; R II 8/12; R. II 17/44; R. II 18/7; R II 73/19; R. III 41/22

4. R. II 73/19; R. III 67/31; R. IV 12/22.

5. R. V 12/3.

6. R. V 4/36.

7. *dātumarhasi mūlyena sutamekaṃ dvijottama*, R. I 57/16.
na vikreshyāmyaham putraṃ......R I 57/17
vikreyam madhyamam manye, rājaputra nayasva mām, gavām śatasahasreṇa R. I 57/22-23.

8. R. I 57/22-23. Fee to the priests was paid in terms of cows—
Cf. *Nishkṛitiṃ tvaṃ naraśreshṭha hyasmabhyam dātumarhasi,*
Gavām śatasahasrāṇi daśa tebhyo dadau nṛpaḥ.
Daśakoṭīḥ suvarṇasya rajatasya caturguṇam.— R. I 10/39-40.
Besides, *nishka*, it seems, was a gold coin.
Cf. *Saṃvāhakāḥ saliladāḥ puratovācakāśca ye,*
Teshāṃ nishkasahasraṃ tvaṃ vṛittyarthamupakalpaya R. II 35/22.

9. *Santi me kuśalāḥ vaidyāḥ suvibhaktāśca vṛittibhiḥ* R. II 13/10.
Also R. II 35/20-26; R. II 83/9 and
Kaccidbalasya bhaktañca vetanañca yathocitam,
Samprāptakālaṃ dātavyaṃ dadāsi na viśaṅkase R. II 114/44.

karmāntika while *vishṭi* was the term for forced labour who were perhaps only provided subsistence.[1]

Incidentally we may also note in the end that the epic employs certain terms which indicate the presence of certain methods of measurements and counting. Thus *hasta* or *kishku*[2] (standing approximately for one cubit or 18 inches) was the smallest linear measure. Other higher measures were *vyāma*, *dhanu*, *nalva*, *krośa* and *yojana*[3] which have been explained by Monier Williams as 2 *hastas*, 4 *hastas*, 400 *hastas* (or a furlong) and 16,000 *hastas* (or 4 *krośas*) respectively. Among the measures of capacity only one, viz. *droṇa* has been mentioned.[4] In counting, numbers one to ten and the decimal method were known[5] and the terms for counting higher numbers were *śata*, *sahasra*, *ayuta*, *śata-sahasra*, *niyuta*, *koṭi* or *arbuda*, *śaṅku*, *vṛinda*, *mahā-vṛinda*, *padma* and *mahā-padma*.[6]

---

1. Vide Govindarāja on R. II 82/20 N. S.—*vishṭayo bhṛitimantareṇa janapadebhyaḥ samānītāḥ karmakarāḥ; karmāntikāḥ karmānte bhṛtigrahītāraḥ.*
2. *Catushkishkūtsarū divyau daśahastau pramāṇataḥ,* R. VI 52/25.
3. For references see :
   (i) *shaḍvyāmaśatavistīrṇam*, R. VII 12/4.
   (ii) *apāsarpaddhanūṃshyashṭau*, R. VI 18/44.
   (iii) *tasya sūto rathandivyaṃ navanalvam pramāṇataḥ*, R. VI 44/27.
   (iv) *athāśramāt krośamātre*, R. III 68/13.
   (v) *śatānyahaṃ yojanānām*.........R. V 1/4.
4. *droṇamātrapramāṇāni*, R. V 72/10.
5. Note : R. VI 4/51-54.
6. For references see R. V 70/30-34 and R. VI 4/51-55.

Chapter XIV

THE NON-ARYAN PEOPLE OF THE SOUTH

For a long time even after the Aryan settlement in North India in the Vedic period, southern India remained almost isolated from the *Āryāvarta* and aboriginal tribes continued to hold their sway on that part of the country. Most probably Agastya was the first Aryan to cross the Vindhyas and penetrate into the South. Subsequent to this came a series of attacks and counter-attacks by the Aryans and the aboriginal people of the South—each trying to establish its supremacy over the other. Vālmīki has left in the Rāmāyaṇa a very graphic and at the same time most authentic account of this struggle, and even though the peoples of the South have been disfigured by mythological colouring the principal ones among them can still be recognised as human beings and one can easily gather from the epic ample information with regard to their social, political and religious life. Most important from this point are the Rākshasas and the Vānaras.[1]

Among the Rākshasas of the Rāmāyaṇa, one can observe two categories, namely, (i) Rākshasas by birth and (ii) Rākshasas by culture.[2] Rākshasahood, with which is identified savagery and ghastliness, descends upon the members of

1. It is very likely that the *Yakshas*, *Gandharvas*, *Nāgas*, *Siddhās* and the *Cāraṇas* too, originally represented human races. But in the Rāmāyaṇa they have almost assumed a completely mythical character and accordingly we have given their accounts in the earlier chapter on mythology.

We have also left out from our treatment the Gṛidhras. No doubt, Jaṭāyu and Sampāti appear as characters in the epic, but from all the references to them we can know nothing significant except perhaps that they were a nomadic people friendly to the Aryans. *Gṛidhra* might have been their totem.

2. Dr. S. N. Vyas recognises three distinct lines of the Rākshasas, headed respectively by Virādha, Kabandha and Rāvaṇa. (Rāmāyaṇa-Kālīna Samāja, p. 25). It is to be noted, however, that Virādha and Kabandha were not originally Rākshasas. The former was a Gandharva and the latter a divine being (vide R. III 5/4 ff. and R. III 78/1 ff. respectively). Therefore the classification that we have suggested above explains the facts better.

the second category as a punishment for some serious offence.[1] Thus Virādha, Kabandha and a Chāyāgrāhiṇī of the lake on the Gandhamādana had to embrace Rākshasahood because they roused by their mis-behaviour the anger of some august person or other and thereby invited his curse. Combining in themselves the material knowledge of the two groups—the higher one from which they have fallen and the lower one that they have adopted—they acquire certain peculiarities such as greater power, greater savagery and even greater hideousness.[2] These Rākshasas are without exception represented as night-rangers and man-eaters. Their disposition is characterised by treachery, trickery and savagery. Outcast from society, they live their own isolated life, without being the members of any social group. The way their character has been represented turns them almost into mythical beings.

The Rākshasas belonging to the other group (viz. of Rākshasas by birth) are essentially human beings,[3] inspite of the cloak of monstrosity and barbaric splendour imposed upon them by an Aryan poet whose account is vitiated by a bias, natural to a poet describing the culture and achievements of a hostile people.[4] The origin of these people is to be traced to Śālakaṭaṅkaṭā who is in all probability a personification of the night.[5] One important respect in which these Rākshasas

1. Cf. R. III 78/24.

2. Cf. R. III 76/16-20.

3. Compare the following remarks of E. W. Hopkins in this regard. "In the Rāmāyaṇa, the royal Rākshasas are nobler......" and, "The Mahābhārata makes the Rākshasas less human than does the Rāmāyaṇa." Epic Mythology, pp. 46 and 39 respectively.

4. The attitude of the poet towards the Rākshasas can very well be understood from such passages as the following :

(i) *Dīpānāñca prakāśena śriyā cātulayā tatnā,*
Arcibhirbhūshaṇānāñca tām pradīptāmamanyata, R. V 5/54.

(ii) *Sammuktarasanāḥ kāścit...kiśorya iva vāhitāḥ*, R. V 5/70.

(iii) *Āsīdvanamivoddhūtaṃ strīvaṇaṃ Rāvaṇasya tat*, R. V 5/88.

(iv) *Pānabhūnirvinā vahnim pradīptevopalakshyate*, R. V 6/19.

5. Note that Śālakaṭaṅkaṭā is *sandhyā-putrī* (night) (R. VII 3/20) and the Rākshasas are *rajanīcaras*. The Uttara-Kāṇḍa also contains a mythical account of the origin of the Rākshasas. It is said that at the time of creation the Prajāpati created certain beings and asked them to carefully guard the cosmic waters (*ambhāṃsyetāni yatnena rakshadhvamiti*— R. VII 3/11.) Some of them, however, thought that they were asked to 'guard' (*rakshāmo menire kecit*, Ibid 12) while others thought that they should 'injure' or 'hurt' (*kshaṇumeti tathāpare*, Ibid) At this the Prajāpati declared that the

are to be distinguished from the Aryans (and all other peoples of the Rāmāyaṇa) is the 'matrilineal character' of their family life.[1] It was only due to this peculiar character of the Rākshasas that notwithstanding the fact that their father was Pulastya, a *brahmarshi*, Rāvaṇa and his brothers were recognised as Rākshasas because they were born of Kaikasī who was a Rākshasī.

To the Aryans the Rākshasas were aliens both ethnically and culturally. As opposed to the fair Aryans the Rākshasas were dark-complexioned[2] and even the general constitution of their body was different from that of the Aryans. On an average the Rākshasas—both men and women—are represented as possessing prodigious strength and huge forms. The Rāmāyaṇa generally describes them as *mahādaṃshṭra* (possessing long teeth or big jaws), *mahāsya* (large mouthed), *mahākāya*

former would be the Rākshasas and the latter, the Yakshas. Elsewhere in the same Kāṇḍa a distinction seems to have been drawn between the descendents of Śālakaṭaṅkatā and of Pulastva.

(Vide : *Ye vai te rākshasī Rāma ete Śālakaṭaṅkaṭāḥ,*
Ye vai tvayā nihatāste vai Paulastyā nāma Rākshasāḥ. R. VII 7/23.).

In this connection it is to be noted that the mythical line of the Rākshasas said to have originated from the Prajāpati is ultimately connected with Śilakaṭaṅkaṭā; and the Paulastyas also being the offsprings of Kaikasī are no distinct group but a continuation of the Śālakaṭaṅkaṭā line. In our opinion, the separate name for the Rākshasas as 'Paulastyas' and the mythical account of their origin from the Prajāpati are due to later additions by one who failed to appreciate the matrilineal character of the Rākshasas. We feel that the only correct origin of the Rākshasas is from Śālakaṭaṅkaṭā.

1. This fact about the Rākshasas has nowhere been specifically stated in the Rāmāyaṇa. However, there is strong indirect evidence to prove this fact :

(i) The very recognition of Rāvaṇa and his brothers as Rākshasas is based upon this principle.

(ii) In the Rambhā episode (R. VII Canto 32) Rāvaṇa refused to acknowledge Rambhā as his daughter-in-law when she disclosed that she was going to meet by appointment Nalakūbara, the son of Kubera, who was Rāvaṇa's step-brother. Rambhā's stand would have been upheld by a member of the patriarchal family but Rāvaṇa who belonged to the matriarchal group did not respect that relation.

(iii) Among the kinship terms employed by the poet with reference to the Rākshasas, there occur *mātāmaha* (R. VII 31/25; R. VII 10/10) *duhituḥ-duhitā* or *mātṛishvaseyā* (R. VII 30/37; R. VII 31/26) but their counter parts *pitāmaha* and *pitṛishvaseyā* are conspicuous by their absence.

2. Cf. (Rakshasām) *nīlajīmūtavarṇānāmañjanācalavarcasām*, R. III 27/9 (Also R. III 52/27; R. III 76/18.)

(possessing huge body) and *bhīmadarśana* (of frightful aspect).[1] The poet is sometimes even tempted to exaggerate this distinction and to represent the Rākshasas as possessing limbs of various animals. A huge congregation of such deformities is described in the Sundara-Kāṇḍa as guarding Sītā in the Aśoka-Vanikā.[2] It may further be added in this connection that Vālmīki generally expresses this ethnical distinction between the Aryans and the Rākshasas by stating that the former were *mānusha* whereas the latter were not.[3]

What distinguishes the Rākshasas more radically from the Aryans is their hostile disposition towards everything that is valued by the Aryans. Thus the Rākshasas are enemies of sacrifice and the ascetic. *Ṛishi kaṇṭaka, brāhmaṇakaṇṭaka, lokakaṇṭaka, munighna, yajñaghna, brahmahā* and *kratu-kriyāṇām praśamaṅkarāḥ*[4] are the most popular epithets of the Rākshasas. Moreover, the unbridled indulgence of the Rākshasas in wine[5] and women[6] and their lust for wealth inspires the strongest repugnance of the poet for the Rākshasas which he declares by pronouncing that *adharma* was the course of the Rākshasas.[7]

The accounts of the early history of the Rākshasas in the epic are meagre and at the same time not very trustworthy. If the Uttara-Kāṇḍa is to be relied upon, the original home of the Rākshasas would appear to be the southern sea coast[8] from where they moved in hoary past to the Laṅkā-fort and settled there as an independent political power.[9] From references to be found in the other Kāṇḍas also it become almost

1. R. III 76/19, R. III 27/10, R. III 1/17 and R. II 1/19 respectively.
2. R. V 12/4-17.
3. Note *Mānushī manusham kāntam Rāmamicchasi śobhane* and *Na mānushī rākshasasya bhāryā bhavitumarhati*, R. V 19/6 and 9 respectively. (For other references vide R. III 46/5; R. III 61/22; R. V 86/7; R. VI 42/4).
4. R. I 11/2; R. III 35/22; R. I 10/74; R. III 39/9; R. I 18/19 and R. VII 4/41 respectively.
5. Cf. *Surāmānīyatām kshipram sarvaśokavināśinīm*, R. V 19/49. Also R. VI 42/45.
6. *Svadharmo Rakshasām bhīru sarvathaiva sanātanaḥ,*
Gamanam paradārāṇām haraṇam sampramathya ca. R. V 15/5.
7. *adharmo Rakshasām pakshaḥ*, R. VI 11/15.
8. R. VII 7/21; R. VII 10/1.
9. R. VII 4/21.

certain that having earlier suffered a few vicissitudes in their political life they had emerged in contemporary history as a mighty power. With a strong and capable leader in Rāvaṇa they had not only reclaimed their old possessions but by entering into alliance with their strong and powerful neighbours, the Vānaras,[1] they had made their position extremely secure. Moreover, by establishing a military post in the Daṇḍakas they were slowly even trying to penetrate further into the North.[2] It is significant to remember that mighty Aryan kings of that period found themselves utterly helpless in counteracting their onslaughts.[3]

No doubt, the political constitution of the Rākshasas as described in the epic follows the same pattern as of the Aryans inasmuch as we hear even in their case of a king, the council of ministers and the Popular Sabhā. However, the fact that their state was constituted of a single town (viz. Laṅkā) lends a singular character to their political organisation. It is significant to note that in the descriptions of the Rākshasas there is not a single reference to feudal lords or subordinate kings. On the other hand, the frequent use of the term *Gaṇa* with reference to them[4] and the reference to the *kula-vṛiddhas* in their *Sabhā*[5] might indicate that they followed some sort of an oligarchical organisation. It is worth noting in this connection that the entire Rākshasa army in Laṅkā belonged to the king (or the state)[6] and unlike the Vānaras it was not constituted of different units belonging to individual chiefs.

The Rākshasas of the Rāmāyaṇic period were not only a mighty political power, but even in respect of their material wealth they were the most advanced people of their times. The abundance of gold, silver and other jewels such as sapphire, coral, pearl, diamond and ruby in the descriptions of the town

1. R. VII 22/39.
2. R. III 51/25; R. VII 30/35-36.
3. Note the words of Daśaratha in R. I 18/14-18 :
Tena sārdhaṃ na śaktāḥ smaḥ saṃyuge tasya vā balaiḥ.
4. R. V 36/42; R. V 44/56; R. V 46/10; R. V 53/19; R. VI 11/6; R. VI 16/76; R. VII 20/57; R. VII 40/42.
5. *athopavishṭān kulaśīlavṛiddhān......* R. V 44/63.
Also see the account of the 'Sabhā at Laṅkā' in chap. XIX infra.
6. See the note on *Balādhyaksha* under 'Units of the Army' in chap. XXII infra.

Laṅkā gives, in a way, the popular imagination every right to hold that the town was all made up of gold. Power and wealth naturally tended towards the promotion of various types of arts among them. The general description of their town, particularly of the royal palace, is a sure evidence of the high architectural skill of the Rākshasas. One can gather a similar impression about dance, music and painting among them from the graphic picture of the *śālā* of Rāvaṇa's harem.[1] The variety of drinks and other viands,[2] the references to art galleries (*citraśālā*), sport pavilions (*krīḍā-gṛiha*), bowers (*latā-gṛiha*) and pleasure groves (*nishkuṭa*),[3] and the description of their royal garden of exquisite charm[4] are convincing proofs of the fact that the Rākshasas were not just barbarians but that they were a highly civilised race who had by their efforts secured for themselves the choicest pleasures of life known to those times. Hanūmān was so much bewildered at the sight of the opulence in Rāvaṇa's palace that for a moment he thought that he was wandering in some celestial region—the *svarga* or the town of the gods.[5] Further, he considered the ladies in the chamber of Rāvaṇa to be heavenly beings who had come there to enjoy the fruit of the remainder of their merits of the previous births.[6]

The poet very aptly characterises the Rākshasas at one place as men "predominated by the intellect."[7] One observes that as a corollary of this predominance of the intellect the Rākshasas pursued naked sensualism. Thus Mahāpārśva declared in the assembly of the Rākshasas that the very fruition of *dharma* was in *kāma* which was the foundation of the *trivarga.*[8] He also defined *kāma* as the gratification of the senses (by securing for them their objects, viz. the sound for the ear, tangibility for the skin, form or colour for the eye, savour for the

1. R. V 5/43 ff.
2. R. V 6/11-26.
3. R. V 4/41-42; R. V 7/13.
4. R. V 9/7 ff.
5. R. V 5/52.
6. R. V 5/66.
7. R. V 5/15 N. S.

N. B. The parallel verse in the N.W. is R. V 3/12; but the reading in the first quarter is defecive. The poet is inaulging here in *antvānuprāsa* and therefore the reading should be *buddhipradhānān.*

8. *dharmaṃ kāmaphalaṃ viddhi.........etanmūlaṃ trivargasya,* R.V 87/4-6.

tongue and odour for the nose).[1] Similar was the view of Mahodara who considered *kāma* as the spring of all human activity. No doubt, some people think that final beatitude can be achieved through *dharma* and *artha*. But according to Mahodara *dharma* and *artha* were themselves rooted in *kāma* and whatever action a man undertook for his welfare in this life or the life hereafter it could achieve its end only if it was founded on *kāma*.[2] That it was not merely one man's prattle but was the central principle of the Rākshasa culture is shown by the several remarks of the poet for the Rākshasas in the epic. As an example we may recall the one made by him about the *śālā* of Rāvaṇa's harem, which is said to have satiated the five senses of its master by providing for them their five objects.[3] It may be added that this sensuality in their outlook turned them into *loka-kaṇṭakas* (a curse to their fellowmen) and also became the root cause of their downfall.

The account of the religion of the Rākshasas is very intriguing, for we observe two distinct currents, viz. Vedic and non-Vedic simultaneously flowing in their society. Thus several passages of the Rāmāyaṇa refer to the Rākshasas in Laṅkā as engaged in *svādhyāya*,[4] *japa* (the muttering of the sacred *mantras*)[5] and the performance of the *agnihotra*.[6] One passage calls Rāvaṇa a *vidyā-veda-vrata-snāta*[7] and another alludes to the presence of the *brahma Rākshasas* who were well versed in the Vedas along with their six auxiliaries.[8] Besides, one also notes among them the prevalence of such Vedic practices as *svastyayana*,[9] *udaka-kriyā*[10] and the *vivāha*[11] and the *antyeshṭi*[12] *saṃskāras*.

1. *Indriyārthopabhogo hi kāmaḥ satyaparākrama,*
   Śabdagandharasasparśā rūpāṇi vividhāni ca. R. V 87/4-5.
2. R VI 43/7-9.
3. R. V 5/51.
4. ......*svādhyāyaniratāṃstatra*......R. V 2/29.
5. R. V 4/13 N. S.
6. R. V 3/13; R. V 11/36.
7. R. VI 71/59.
8. R. V 13/2.
9. R. VI 74/8.
10. R. III 35/5.
11. R. VII 11/19.
12. R. VI 92/57.
   It may be noted that according to R. III 5/48 burial was the most praiseworthy mode of disposing of the dead body among the Rākshasas. For details about this vide p. 160 f. n. 6 supra.

As distinguished from the above there are references to several practices of witch-craft and sorcery among the Rākshasas. Thus the Sundara-Kāṇḍa specifically mentions the *yātudhānas*[1] and alludes to the Rākshasas carrying handfuls of *darbha* for their weapons and having the sacrificial fireplace for their arms.[2] In connection with the Rākshasas the poet also generally mentions the name Nikumbhilā. According to the Uttara-Kāṇḍa Nikumbhilā was a wood on the southern border of Laṅkā.[3] But from other references it appears that Nikumbhilā was perhaps also the name of a goddess—the tutelary deity of the Rākshasas. It is likely that the Rākshasas made human offerings (*nara-bali*) to this goddess and that 'dance' and 'drink' formed part of the services to the deity.[4] Some passages of the Uttara-Kāṇḍa clearly refer to *Śiva-liṅga-pūjana* by Rāvaṇa.[5] Further, the ascetic practices characterised by severe physical tortures[6] and sacrifices administered by Uśanā[7] and performed with the help of *Rākshasa* (and sometimes *Raudra*) *mantras*[8] also appear to have been popular among the Rākshasas.

It is to be noted that the entire religion among the Rākshasas as peeped through the Rāmāyaṇa is only an instrument for acquiring wealth and power; that spirit of religion which realises itself in the cultivation of such virtues as veracity, tranquillity, continence and the like is completely missing in all such references.

Incidentally, we may note here that the profusion of references to Vedic practices in case of the Rākshasas has led several scholars to hold that the Rāmāyaṇa represents "the spread of Aryan civilization to the south especially to Ceylon (Laṅkā)."[9] Attention is particularly drawn by them to the verses in the Yuddha-Kāṇḍa where Rāma is believed to have

1. E. g. *Yātudhāna śatairguptam*, R. V 4/29.
2. R. V 2/29.
3. R. VII 31/2.
4. *Surāmānīyatāṃ kshipraṃ sarvaśokavināśinīm,*
   Mānusham māṃsamādāya nṛtyāmo (a)tha Nikumbhilām. R. V 19/49.
5. R. VII 19/39-45.
6. R. VII 4/8-9 and R. VII 9/2-7. Vide also pp. 127-129. supra.
7. R. VII 31/6-14.
8. *Hutvāgniṃ rākshasaiḥ mantraiḥ*, R. VI 20/13. Also *juhotyagniṃ raudramantraiḥ*, R. VI 82/13.
9. Weber quoted by Krishnamachariar, M. in his History of Classical Sanskrit Literature, p. 14.

pressed Vibhīshaṇa to perform the last rites of Rāvaṇa probably according to Vedic rites, with a view to effectively induce the entire Rākshasa community to adopt Vedic religion. Dr. Vyas holds that Rāma wanted to introduce Aryan traditions among the Rākshasas.[1] We are, however, not able to uphold such a view, for we do not find the slightest internal evidence in the epic testifying to such an inclination on the part of Rāma. Moreover, Rāma's stay in Laṅkā after the war was too short to be able to exercise any lasting influence upon the culture and religion of the Rākshasas. So far as Rāvaṇa's cremation is concerned it is to be noted that in the whole account there is not the slightest indication that Vibhīshaṇa was not willing to perform the last rites of Rāvaṇa according to the Vedic rites. Vibhīshaṇa's unwillingness was based on the ground that Rāvaṇa was unrighteous, libidinous, wicked and sinful and hence did not deserve such an honour from him. Rāma, however, impressed upon Vibhīshaṇa that all hostilities ended with victory and that they were not to be prolonged even after the death of the enemy.[2]

In the above connection one should not fail to remember that there are copious references to Vedic practices among the Rākshasas even before the death and cremation of Rāvaṇa. Good evidence of the early close contact between the Rākshasas and the Aryans is to be found in the tradition which traces the origin of the former from the renowned sage Pulastya. Rāvaṇa and his brothers who were born and bred in the hermitage of the sage Viśravā must have derived from there good many Vedic practices. Their inherent sinful disposition, however, did not permit them to assimilate the real spirit of Vedic culture and religion.

Next let us take up the Vānaras. In our treatment of the Rākshasas above we have indicated that in a literary work it is often difficult to glean a true picture of a people alien or hostile to the religion and culture of the poet. Usually a poet's vision in such cases suffers from a partiality towards his own

1. But Rāma evidently intended to introduce Aryan customs into the Rākṣasa community by giving Vedic (pitṛmedha) rites to Rāvaṇa. So, at Rāma's insistence Rāvaṇa's body was cremated according to the Aryan style and, thus, the Rākṣasas were sought to be Aryanized in culture.

Vyas, S. N., India in the Rāmāyaṇa Age, p. 34.

2. R. VI 92/39-55.

beliefs and customs and he is apt to colour his pictures of the alien people by mixing elements of his own culture. This tendency works all the more prominently when a poet furnishes accounts of a people who have already surrendered to the dominating influence of the superior culture of the poet with which they have recently come into contact. That Vālmīki was no exception to such a tendency is all the more powerfully illustrated by his picture of the Vānaras. These people as we shall shortly see were so primitive as to prompt the poet to describe them as monkeys. But that they were actually human beings can be shown from the fact that he imposes upon them practically all the salient features of Aryan culture and religion. Thus he describes the cremation (*aurdhva dehikam* or *pretakārya*) of Bālī almost on the same lines as of Daśaratha making reference to the *śibikā*, the *citā*, circumambulation of the *citā* by the son of the deceased and other relatives, the *udaka-kriyā* and the period of impurity (*aśauca*) after the actual cremation.[1] Later on he describes Sugrīva's coronation in a characteristic Aryan style.[2] In this account there is a reference to *homa* in course of which *mantravid dvijas* are said to have offered *haviḥ* purified by *mantras* into the well-kindled fire of the altar. Among the articles required for this ceremony the poet mentions *akshata, lājā, priyaṅgu, madhu, sarshapa, dadhi*[3] and holy water from the rivers and the seas in addition to herbs, flowers, sprouts of various kinds and manifold fragrant substances. There is also a reference to liberal gifts being distributed among the *dvijarshabhas* on this occasion. Moreover, Tārā, desirous of her husband's success in the combat performed the *svastyayana* for him duly reciting the *mantras*.[4] Hanūmān prayed to Sūrya, Mahendra and other gods, obviously to crave their blessings for success in his undertaking.[5] Bālī is believed to have performed the *sandhyā* everyday before sunrise and also muttered the *naigama* verses.[6] A few references would also

1. For references vide R. IV 18/verses 10, 18, 29, 30 and R. IV 19/1.

2. Note the account in R. IV 19/22ff.

3. It is worth remembering that with reference to the Vānaras the poet neither refers to agriculture nor to cattle rearing.

4. *Tataḥ svastyayanaṅkṛitvā mantravadvijayaishiṇī*, R. IV 12/10.

5. R. IV 60/18.
6. R. VII 22/17.

indicate that in their mutual behaviour the Vānaras were extremely suave and courteous.[1]

It is, however, necessary to remember that in the Rāmāyaṇa there is also another side of the Vānara-picture which reveals itself in marked contrast to the one just now shown above. For referring to these people the poet freely employs the various synonyms of *vānara* (monkey) such as *plavaṅgama*, *kapi*, *śākhā-mṛigendra* and *vanaukasa*[2] and he unhesitatingly likens these people in their features and disposition to the monkeys. He describes them as brown in complexion,[3] having long hair all over the body[4] and usually does not forget to mention their tail.[5] Their constitution is invariably described as robust; but unlike the Rākshasas they employ in fighting their natural weapons, viz. the arms, the feet, the nails, the teeth and the very weight of their body.[6] *Nakha-daṃshṭrāyudha*[7] is thus their usual epithet in this respect. The cry of the Vānaras is expressed by the poet as *kilakilā*[8] and when they are beside with joy, they are described as beating their arms, kissing their tail and jumping and shouting.[9] Inconstancy (*capalatā*) and fickle-mindedness (*calacittatā*, *asthira-cittatā* or *laghucittatā*)are stated to be the outstanding characteristics of their nature.[10] These are alluded to not only by the poet and his non-Vānara characters but even by the Vānaras themselves.[11]

It may be deemed profitable to recount here a few more facts about the Vānaras of the Rāmāyaṇic period :

(i) The food of the Vānaras is repeatedly declared to be fruits and roots.[12] In addition to this they were fond of *madhu* (honey) and *maireya* (an intoxicating

1. For example : *kapiṃ senāpatiṃ vākyamabhivādya prasādya ca uvāca vānaraṃ tatra*............R. IV 35/3.
2. R. VI 2/11; R. V 44/35; R. IV 1/12; R. VI 2/40.
3. See the epithet *piṅgāksha* for the Vānaras. R. IV 61/64;
4. Vide : *dudhuve ca sa romāṇi*, R. IV 61/39.
5. Vide : *anurūpañca vṛittañca lāṅgūlaṃ lomabhiścitam*, R. IV 61/40.
6. R. V 41/12-13.
7. R. I 15/13; R. V 36/48; R. VI 3/37.
8. R. V 55/29; R. V 96/86.
9. R. V 5/146.
10. R. IV 1/12; R. IV 46/10; R. VI 33/8; R. VI 108/21.
11. R. IV 1/12; R. IV 46/10.
12. R. IV 13/13; R. IV 33/41; R. IV 39/5; R. VI 100/11-12.

drink which at least in their case must have been made principally of juices of flowers or fruits).[1] Nowhere does the poet refer to agriculture, cooked food or cattle-rearing with reference to the Vānaras.

(ii) The hordes of Vānaras, Ṛikshas and Golāṅgūlas arriving in Kishkindhā in pursuance of the orders from the central authority bring "divine herbs, fruits and roots" as presents to their royal master, Sugrīva.[2]

(iii) No doubt, there are references to the dress of the Vānaras —men and women[3]—but at the same time there are a few passages which might indicate that the Vānaras remained nude.[4] This is, however, certain that their dress was not only simple but elementary—consisting of one upper and one lower garment. There is not a single reference in the epic to a stitched garment of the Vānaras.

(iv) In spite of all the glitter of a capital town and the royal palace, Kishkindhā and the residential quarters of Bālī and Sugrīva remain a mountain cave (*giri guhā*).[5]

(v) The sex relations of the Vānaras are extremely loose—verging almost on promiscuity.[6]

Obviously the epic furnishes two opposite pictures of the Vānaras and to determine their exact position in between these two extremes is indeed a difficult task. Some would give greater credence to the first category of references and believe that by the time of Rāma the Vānaras had completely adopted the Aryan culture.[7] We, however, find it difficult to subscribe to such a view, for the gulf between the primitive stage in which the Vānaras actually appear to be and the highly cultured stage represented by the Aryans of Vālmīki's times is very wide. To

1. R. IV 26/8; R. V 59/10, 17-23.
2. R. IV 30/36.
3. R. IV 57/10-11.
4. Note : *sphigdeśenātitāmreṇa rarāja sa mahākapiḥ*, R. IV 61/68.
5. *nishpapāta guhāmukhāt*, R. IV 7/26.
6. Vide pp. 46-48 supra.
7. Cf. Vāli's cremation also makes it abundantly clear that the Vānaras had become completely Aryanized and that their outlook and spirit was Aryan.

Vyas, S. N., India in the Rāmāyaṇa Age, p. 50.

say that the Vānaras suddenly switched over from the former stage to the latter is a gross violation of the principles of evolution. In our opinion the Vānaras were a primitive people perhaps still emerging from a nomadic state. Not only in comparison to the Aryans, but also in comparison to the Rākshasas, the Vānaras were backward both materially and culturally. The only fields where they might appear to excel their contemporaries are 'medicine' and 'bridge-building' in which Sushena and Nala respectively are believed to be past masters. The ascription of some Aryan practices to the royal family of the Vānaras of Kishkindhā might either be due to its contact with the neighbouring Aryans, or to Vālmīki's unfamiliarity with the actual Vānara customs regarding coronation, disposal of the dead etc.

Before closing this account of the Vānaras it must be pointed out that Vālmīki has no clear idea of the origin and past history of the Vānaras. He generally calls the Vānaras the sons of the *Devas* and the *Gandharvas*;[1] and sometimes he gives independent stories to explain the birth of individual Vānara heroes, from different gods.[2] The Bāla-Kāṇḍa commences the history of the Vānaras with the incarnation of Vishṇu on earth as son of Daśaratha. It is said that at the instance of Brahmā the Vānaras were brought into existence by the *Devas* specifically to serve as allies of Rāma in his struggle against the Rākshasas.[3] The individual Vānaras, however, refer to their glorious past, when they used to be invited by the *Devas* presumably to assist them in their fight against the *Asuras*.[4] In that hoary past they are believed to have possessed so much speed and strength that one of them (Jāmbavān) is said to have circumambulated the earth a number of times and even participated in the churning of the ocean and in extracting out of it the herbs and *amṛita*.[5]

Frequently the poet refers to three classes of these people designating them as Vānaras, Ṛikshas and Golāṅgūlas.[6] Some-

1. *Devagandharvaputrāśca*, R. IV 31/34 (Also R. V 91/75).
2. Birth of Hanūmān from Vāyu—R. IV 57/7 ff.
Birth of Bālī and Sugrīva from Indra and Sūrya respectively, R.VI 4/29-43.
3. R. I 15/1 ff.
4. Note R. V 56/123.
5. R. IV 56/44, 52-54.
6. R. IV 31/32-33.

times he even tries to draw distinction among them by pointing out certain differences in their complexion and features[1]; but more often he alludes to them collectively by the common term 'Vānara'. In a few passages a traditional enmity between the Hastins and the Vānaras is also alluded to[2] but the material on such points is so meagre that it is well nigh impossible to unfold these facts of Vānara history.[3] Can it be that the Hastins were a totemistic tribe at feud with the Vānaras ?

---

1. Cf. *Tāmrāḥ nīlāḥ sitāḥ śvetā haritā ghorakarmaṇaḥ*, R. VI 3/2.
2. Cf. *Yo Gaṅgāmanuparyeti trāsayan gajayūthapān,*
Hastināṃ Vānarāṇāñca pūrvavairamanusmaran. R. VI 3/26.

Hanūmān's father, Kesarī, is also believed to have killed a 'Gaja', R. V 30/24.

3. In the absence of dependable internal evidence scholars have made fanciful surmises with regard to the identity of these people and their designation, Vānara. Thus Shri Manmatha Nath Ray identifies these Vānaras with the *vrātyas* of the first migration, who had taken to the fresh fields and pastures new of the Deccan on the advent of the Aryans of the second migration......" ("An estimate of the civilisation of the Vānaras as depicted in the Rāmāyaṇa"—Prince of Wales, Saraswati Bhawan Studies, Vol. V, 1926). This view would make us believe that after a long period of civilisation these people had receded to a primitive state by the time of the Rāmāyaṇa.

According to C. V. Vaidya the Vānaras were the aborigines of the South who were "called by that name from their monkeyish appearance...... They were also like monkeys active, ferocious and given up to pleasure...... (Riddle of the Rāmāyaṇa, p. 153).

Dr. Bulche also identifies the Vānaras with the aborigines of the Vindhyas and opines that the name Vānara was given to them either because 'monkey' was their insignia or their totem. (Rāma Kathā, p. 117)

N. B. In the present chapter we have deliberately refrained from repeating such information about the Rākshasas and the Vānaras as has been already given in other chapters. Our object here mainly has been to present the distinctive character of the culture and civilisation of these people by drawing attention to those salient points where they are distinguished from their contemporary Aryans.

CHAPTER XV

STATE

Society and state are institutions very closely inter-related. While the gregarious instinct in man impels him to lead a corporate life, his reasoning faculty urges him to evolve a sound political organisation. The circumstances, however, under which the primitive man first secured essentials of state life remained enshrouded in the mists of obscurity, and ancient Indian political thinkers while dealing with the subject took recourse to legends and mythology and regarded the state as a divine institution which was created by God to ensure security and justice for mankind against the law of the jungle which had somehow set in among them at the end of the golden age.[1] The account of the origin of the state in the Rāmāyaṇa, or rather of the monarch with whom the ancient Indians very often identified the state, follows the same pattern. In the account in the Uttara-Kāṇḍa a golden age is visualised in which the people on the earth had no king, though Śatakratu was the ruler of the celestials. Men, therefore, are said to have approached Brahmā with a prayer to confer upon them, on the analogy of the gods, a king who would be foremost among them and by worshipping whom they would be freed from all sins. The story goes on to relate that in response to the prayer of the people Brahmā sent for Indra and the other *Lokapālas*. He, then, created a sound (*kshupa*) from which originated a being under the name of *Kshupa*. In his person Brahmā placed in equal proportions the energies of all the *Lokapālas* and then declared him king of men.[2]

It need hardly be pointed out that this is not the true origin of the state in India or elsewhere. Actually the Indian state probably evolved from the institution of the patriarchal joint-family. "The Ṛgvedic evidence", states Dr. A. S. Altekar,

1. Mahābhārata, XII 58,. Digghanikāya, Vol. III pp. 84-96 and Ādipurāṇa, III 30 ff.—Jinasena, quoted by Altekar, A.S.. State and Govt. in Ancient India, pp. 23 and 25.

2. R. VII 79/16-20.

"shows that the Aryan society in that early period was divided into families, *janmans*, *viśas* and *janas*. *Janmans* seem to have corresponded to a village consisting of people claiming a common descent, and a number of such villages joined together by a bond of kinship seem to have constituted a *viś*; its chief was known as a *viśpati*......several *viśas* made a *jana* or tribe, which had its own *janapati* or the king."[1] In a subsequent period, however, as life became more and more stable, the tribal character of the political organisation changed and the territorial conception of the state became settled. By the time of the Rāmāyaṇa, it may be remarked, all over India, among the Aryans, the state displays a territorial character. This is amply clear from the fact that the idea of a state is conveyed through such terms as *rāshṭra*, *rājya*, *janapada* and *vishaya* which in the Rāmāyaṇa principally refer to the region rather than its inhabitants.[2]

The only type of state[3] found in the Rāmāyaṇa is monarchical. The evidence of the epic shows that India of those times was covered with a network of states invariably governed by a king. As regards their territorial character they usually comprised a capital town (*pura*), a few other towns (*nagaras*) and a number of agricultural and pastoral villages (*grāmas* and *ghoshas*). A vast state ruled by one emperor and extending from sea to sea, is unknown to the Rāmāyaṇa. The *Aśvamedhas* were, no doubt, common enough but they were performed in the Rāmāyaṇic period primarily with a religious or cultural motive. There is nothing to indicate that they led to the subordination of the adjoining states.

1. State and Govt. in Ancient India—pp. 30-31.

2. It may also be noted that the term *viśāmpati* as a title of the king is of frequent occurrence in the Rāmāyaṇa. (R. I 9/10; R. II 4/15; R. III 81/11). It is perhaps a relic of an earlier age when state was of the tribal character.

3. No doubt, the political constitution of the Rākshasas evinces a few traits of oligarchical organisation but in the absence of definite information regarding important points, viz. who were entitled to vote, what were the qualifications for membership of the assembly, how voting took place, what was the period for which members of the assembly were elected, whether the president was elected for life or a shorter period or was elected at all and what were the powers of the assembly, we are not in a position to confidently assert that oligarchies did exist in that period.

The royal court of Ayodhyā is, no doubt, often described in the Rāmāyaṇa as being attended to by subordinate kings,[1] and the Bāla-Kāṇḍa specifically mentions *sāmantas* coming to Ayodhyā to pay their tribute to Daśaratha.[2] Moreover, Rāma asserts in the Kishkindhā-Kāṇḍa that the entire earth with its mountains and forests belonged to the Ikshvākus.[3] However, any impression that the above references are likely to create regarding the universal authority of the Ayodhyan princes[4] quickly evaporates when one remembers that the southern boundary of their kingdom could be reached by only one day's journey on the chariot from Ayodhyā,[5] and that the independent Kekaya and the Videha kingdoms existed to its North-West and East respectively. The military expeditions sent by Rāma against Lavaṇa and the Gandharvas in the Uttara-Kāṇḍa under the leadership of Śatrughna and Bharata respectively also relate the same story. Rāma's statement in the Kishkindhā-Kāṇḍa too, even if it be taken at its face value, does not amount to much, for Kosala was not the only Ikshvāku state of India. And that Bālī was not prepared to assign it even that value is proved by his statement accusing Rāma of unlawfully interfering in the affairs of a country and people who fell outside his jurisdiction.[6]

Imperialistic ideas, however, are in the air as indicated by the existence of words like *samrāṭ*, *sarvarāja*[7], *cakravartī*,[8] and *adhirāja*[9]—all of these applied to Daśaratha and his sons.

1. R. I 5/14 N.S.; R. II 3/52-55; R. II 92/7.
2. *sāmantarājasaṅghaiśca balikarmabhirāvṛitām*, R. I 5/14 N.S.
3. R. IV 16/63.
4. Dikshitar, V.R.R., "Rāmāyaṇa ke kucha rājanītika siddhānta aur śāsana saṃsthāyen"—Kalyāṇa, Rāmāyaṇāṅka, V, p. 348.
5. Rāma and party started from Ayodhyā late in the morning and after a night's rest on the bank of the Tamasā river they crossed the Kosalas and reached Śṛiṅgaverapura the next day. (R. II 50/27) It may also be noted here that Guha was only a personal friend of Rāma and not necessarily a vassal of the Ikshvākus, for had he been one such he should have been present in Ayodhyā at that time in connection with Rāma's consecration as *yuvarāja*.
6. R. IV 13/11.
7. *Pṛithivyāṃ sarvarājo(a)smi, samrāḍasmi mahīkshitām*, R. II 13/21.
8. *Rājā Daśaratho nāma........cakravartikule jātaḥ*, R. V. 25/2.
9. *yo bhokshatyadhirājavat*, R. II 57/13.

But from what we know of the extent of Daśaratha's territory, the use of these terms appears to have been rather of a loose character. That feudatories also existed in that period is indicated not only by the references to certain *sāmantas* who offered tribute to Daśaratha but also by reference to rulers whose policy, army, treasury etc. were subordinate to other rulers and who for that very reason were comparable to ordinary people (*prākṛitāḥ janāḥ*).[1]

The use of the word *prakṛiti* is very common in the Rāmāyaṇa but it has been employed either in the sense of the subjects[2] or for the ministers and state officials.[3] Nowhere does it convey the sense of the constituents of the state viz. *svāmī* (king), *amātya* (ministers), *jana* (people), *durga* (fortress), *kośa* (treasure), *daṇḍa* (army) and *mitra* (allies).[4] However, it will be wrong to suppose from this, that the notion that the state as a political unit was constituted of different elements was absent in that period. There are various passages in the Rāmāyaṇa in which these different limbs of the body-politic are mentioned. Thus in a passage of the Kishkindhā-Kāṇḍa, with the exception of the *amātyas* all the elements referred to above are collectively mentioned;[5] and that the *amātyas*, too, were an indispensable limb of the state is indisputably proved by various other references in the epic. Just to serve as an

1. *Yeshāṃ cāraśca kośaścha nayaśca jayatāṃ vara,*
   Asvādhinā narendrā ye prākṛitaiste naraiḥ samāḥ., R. III 37/8.
2. R. II 6/14; R. II 29/16; R. II 47/4; R. II 93/6.
3. R. II 86/14; R. II 93/6; R. II 113/30; R. II 115/9.
4. *Svāmyamātyajanapadadurgakośadaṇḍcmitrāṇi prakṛitayaḥ.*
   Arthaśāstra, VI 1.

Also : *Svāmyamātyā jano durgaṃ kośo daṇḍastathaiva ca,*
Mitrāṇyetāḥ prakṛitayo rājyaṃ saptāṅgamucyate.
Yājñavalkya Smṛiti, I 353.

N.B. "The Śukranītisāra (I 61-62) compares the seven *aṅgas* of *rājya* to the organs of the body viz., the king is the head, the ministers are the eyes, ally the ear, treasury the mouth, the army the mind, the capital and *rāṣṭra* are hands and feet." Kane, P. V., *History of Dharma-śāstra*, Vol. III, p. 18.

5. *Yasya daṇḍaśca kośaśca mitrāṇyātmā puraṃ janaḥ,*
   Pūrṇāny tāni sarvāṇi sa rājyaphalamaśnute.. R. IV 22/11.

It may incidentally be noted that in this list Vālmīki includes *jana* and omits *janapada*. In this respect his enumeration agrees with that of Yājñavalkya Smṛiti.

example may be cited the passage from the Araṇya-Kāṇḍa which states that a king who acted without consulting his ministers was sure to lose erelong his position.[1]

It may also be pointed out in this connection that the enquiry with regard to a king's welfare is generally directed in the Rāmāyaṇa with reference to one or more of these elements of the state. Thus Vasishṭha asked king Viśvāmitra whether it was all well with his exchequer and allies,[2] and likewise, sage Bharadvāja asked prince Bharata about the welfare of his capital, kingdom and *treasure.*[3] Such references besides recognising the importance of these elements also indirectly indicate their relative importance. In a monarchical state the position of a king was unequivocally super-eminent.[4] The Rāmāyaṇa expressly states that success in an enterprise depended upon the king.[5] The next in importance came the ministers, the treasure, the army and the allies, among which it is difficult to determine as to whom Vālmīki attached relatively a higher or lower position.

A brief discussion about the relationship between the state and the citizens may not be out of place here. We have seen above that the state as an institution was recognised by Vālmīki as posterior to society and that it existed for the benefit and well-being of the people. Moreover, the theory of taxation according to which the people are required to render to the state a portion of their produce (or otherwise income) in consideration of the protection granted by it also points at the fact that the state exists primarily for the benefit of the people.[6] A king is repeatedly referred to in the Rāmāyaṇa as 'the protector of the people' and 'the securer of their happiness and well-

1. R. III 45/17.
2. R. I 48/9.
3. R. II 103/10.
4. Cf. "The authorities are agreed that the ruler is the most important or the first of the seven. Kauṭilya puts the matter very forcibly and realistically when he states that the briefest exposition of the elements of *rājya* is to say that the king is the State." Kane, P. V., History of Dharmaśāstra, Vol. III, p. 18.
5. R. III 44/10.
6. Cf. "Some works describe the king as a servant of the people whose wages or remuneration for the protection he affords is the taxes he raises." Kane, P. V., History of Dharma-śāstra, Vol. III, p. 27.

being'. According to the conception of Vālmīki a king was to regard his subjects with affection and justice even as a father regards his children.[1] In theory and partly in practice also Vālmīki recognised that sovereignty primarily vested among the people who had the right not only to formally sanction a king's succession to the throne but also to stop it if it went against their interests. Thus Daśaratha had to seek the approval from his subjects of his proposal of appointing Rāma as the *yuvarāja*,[2] and Sagara banished his eldest son Asamañja, for his practices were objected to by the subjects.[3] Vālmīki, however, does not throw sufficient light on the constitutional measures that could be resorted to by the people against a self-willed ruler except that from a few passages of the Ayodhyā-Kāṇḍa it can be reasonably inferred that migration to the neighbouring state was perhaps one such.[4]

That for Vālmīki, the state was a beneficient institution, is a fact proved not only by his view regarding the origin of the state but also by the account that he gives of the plight to which the people could be reduced if there was no king. Thus in the absence of a king, he apprehends that a strong sense of insecurity would prevail among the people with the result that all religious, cultural and economic activity in the state would be paralysed. A son would not abide by the commands of his father; a wife would not follow her husband; and a pupil would not listen to the wholesome advice of his preceptor. No one would respect anybody's proprietary rights; so all initiative in earning wealth would be lost. The farmer would not sow seeds in his field; nor would the merchants move about with their merchandise. In such a state the *brāhmaṇas* being harassed by the *dasyus* would not feel inclined to undertake the performance of sacrifices, and likewise, the ascetic striving to realise

1. Cf. R. III 7/15-16; R. VI 95/55; R. VII 95/15
2. Vide p. 311 and Chap. XIX infra.
3. R. II 39/19 ff.
4. R. II 36/18-24; R. II 49/27.

N.B. Dr. P. V. Kane is of the opinion that there were very real checks and limitations that effectively prevented a king from exercising his unlimited powers. He adds, that these checks, though real cannot be called constitutional in the sense in which that word is used in modern times. For details vide History of Dharma-śāstra, Vol. III, pp. 96-98.

the Self within himself would not freely move about. People would not build public places or assemble to divert themselves with the performances of actors and dancers. Lovely maidens would not sportively move on the streets nor lovers haunt the trysts.[1] In short, in the absence of a king it is the law of the jungle which would prevail everywhere and the poor and the weak would be oppressed by the rich and the powerful.[2]

The above account, incidentally also reveals that the agency of a king was deemed extremely necessary for the discharge of the functions of the state which extended broadly to all the departments of men's life. The primary functions of the state were naturally security against foreign aggression, protection of person and property and maintenance of law and order. It may also be pointed out that unlike the tendency of the modern states to bring within the sphere of their direct control as large a field of man's activities as possible, the ancient state confined itself mainly to its above noted constituent functions. Vālmīki seems to have clearly felt that the smooth functioning of the religious, economic, literary and other social institutions could be possible only when the state duly discharged its functions.

To a certain extent the state appears to have been theocratic in that period. Slaying a *brāhmaṇa* was a grievous sin likely to degrade even a god or a king.[3] *Brāhmaṇas* were perhaps free from state taxation and at least in theory the state existed for the welfare of the *brāhmaṇas*[4] (and the cow). In actual practice also the *brāhmaṇa purohita* was an indispensable state officer and he held a position of eminence among the ministers of a king. Great kings like Daśaratha and Janaka are described in the Rāmāyaṇa, as completely under the guidance of their respective *purohitas*—Vasishṭha and Śatānanda—who were also in all probability the Prime-Ministers in their respective states. This will indicate that Vālmīki's conception of a state was theocratic to a great extent. This much, however,

1. R. II 73/9-23.
2. R. II 73/24-25. Also : R. VII 63/22.
3. Vide R. II 45/11; R. VII 76/12; R. VII 86/3ff.
4. Cf. *gobrāhmaṇa hitārthāya*, R. I 23/13.

is true beyond doubt, that Vālmīki did not recognise an absolute authority of the king to rule over the subjects. In his conception it was *dharma* which reigned supreme.[1] The king was only an agent of the state to enforce with strictness and impartiality the *dharma* which was neither of his making nor necessarily of his choice. The *dharma* was mostly enshrined in religious works and time-honoured traditions and customs of the society. While introducing a ruler (or a rule) Vālmīki generally employs the qualifying phrase "ruling according to *dharma* and *nyāya*."[2] That this force of *dharma* in the society was not imaginary but real is shown from the fact that Rāma's going to the forest could not be stopped by Daśaratha or his ministers (nor by the representatives of the people themselves) even though it was so dearly cherished by everyone, only because this would have involved a gross violation of the fundamental principle, *dharma*. In the Uttara-Kāṇḍa also Rāma had to chastise the *śūdra*, who violating his (*varṇa-*) *dharma* was practising penance as a hermit in the forest.[3]

1. *dharmo hi paramā gatiḥ*, R. VII 2/9.
2. Cf. *rājāpi dharmeṇa tadā rañjayan sunayaiḥ prajāḥ*, R. I 14/1.
3. R. VII 78/21.

Chapter XVI

INTER-STATE RELATIONSHIP

Early India had a large number of states. As everyone of them was eager either to increase its power and influence or to maintain at least its distinct individuality, inter-state relations naturally happened to be a matter of vital interest to them. Ancient political thinkers refer in this connection to the *maṇḍala* theory, which with the *vijigīshu* (the ambitious conqueror) at the centre seeks to explain his relationship with the other states around him.[1] The Rāmāyaṇa, no doubt, does not elaborate the theme, but herein is distinctly present the nucleus of this theory. Thus the terms *vijigīshu*,[2] *mitra*[3], *amitra*,[4] *madhyastha*[5] and *udāsīna*[6] occur in the Rāmāyaṇa and clearly indicate that in a political gamut the other states could be related to a particular one as its ally, enemy, or neutral. Whether the terms *madhyastha* and *udāsīna* bore also the technical sense that they have in Kauṭilya's Arthaśāstra is not clear.

The allies (*mitra*) occupied such an important position that, as we have seen in the previous chapter, they came to be regarded as one of the limbs of the state. Political alliances were a necessity for the proper maintenance of balance of power and naturally, a ruler was ever anxious to strengthen the bond of friendship with his allies.

We do not find any specific mention of permanent resident embassies for fostering friendly relations between the allies. But we read occasionally of *dūtas* who were sent to the

1. Arthaśāstra, VI 2. Also : Altekar, A. S., State and Govt. in Ancient India, pp. 289-290.

Cf. "All our works place before kings this ideal of conquest, domination or self-aggrandizement at the expense of one's weak neighbours." Kane, P. V., History of Dharma-śāstra, Vol. III p. 218.

2. R. III 21/7; R. IV 23/20; R. V 32/20.
3. R. I 48/9; R. II 5/31; R. IV 22/10; R. IV 27/8; R. V 32/22.
4. R. I 7/6; R. II 5/31; R. VI 11/10.
5. R. II 5/31.
6. R. I 7/6.

courts of the neighbouring rulers for carrying out specific missions.[1] Further, the Rāmāyaṇa alludes to the presence of allies at Ayodhyā on ceremonial occasions like the coronation of a prince[2] and in a state of emergency like war.[3] A passage in the Araṇya-Kāṇḍa indicates that in case of semi-independent states (*asvādhīnāḥ*) the Sovereign exercised control over their espionage, treasury and policies (perhaps foreign ?).[4] In such cases it is reasonable to presume that a representative of the imperial power stayed at the court of the feudatory rulers.

As compared to the *mitra* the position of the *amitra* was in a way of even greater consequence, for the entire political theory meant for the guidance of the *vijigīshu* was conceived primarily in relation to him. If the enemy was noble and virtuous the *vijigīshu* was to employ *sāma* i.e. conciliatory measures. If he was greedy then he was to have recourse to *dāna* i.e. giving of gifts etc. If he was alarmed or distrustful then *bheda* i.e. sowing of dissensions and if he was arrogant and sinful then *daṇḍa* i.e. open assault were regarded as the right policies to pursue.[5] The epic does not furnish actual instances in which *sāma* and *dāna* were employed as political measures by any ruler for achieving his object. But there are striking instances of *bheda* and *daṇḍa*.

Espionage, as we shall show in a subsequent chapter, was an important institution in the Rāmāyaṇic period and it was not unusual for a king to seduce through his spies the senior officers of the enemy. When Mālyavān, a senior minister of Rāvaṇa tried to dissuade him from pursuing the policy of war against Rāma, his master (Rāvaṇa) suspected him of having been instigated by the enemy.[6] Rāvaṇa expressed similar doubts about his charioteer's loyalty when he suddenly withdrew from the battle-field in the Laṅkā war.[7] A very impressive use of *bheda* was made by Hanūmān to foil the attempt of Aṅgada who in a bid to establish himself as an independent

1. R. I 9/86-87; R. I 64/1 ff; R. II 74/10. Also see Chapter XXII infra.
2. R. II 3/52-53.
3. R. VII 40/43-44.
4. R. III 37/8.
5. R. V 82/8-9.
6. R. VI 12/6-7.
7. R. VI 86/7.

power in the Ṛikshabila in the Vindhyas was trying to alienate the Vānara chiefs of his party from their master, Sugrīva.[1] The last measure, *daṇḍa*, was recommended only in extreme cases when other measures had proved completely unavailing.[2] Mandodarī pointed out to Rāvaṇa that the first three expedients (viz. *sāma*, *dāna* and *bheda*) were auspicious for kings but *yuddha* (or *daṇḍa*) was inauspicious and hence it was to be avoided by them.[3]

The epic also displays familiarity with *shāḍguṇya* or six-fold policy[4] which embodied the guiding principles for a king in determining his relationship with the foreign states.[5] The six policies enumerated under *shāḍguṇya* are *sandhi*, *vigraha*, *āsana*, *yāna*, *saṃśraya* and *dvaidhī-bhāva*. Of these the first (viz. *sandhi* or peace) was resorted to when one found oneself in a position weaker or equal to that of one's enemy.[6] In such circumstances peace was to be effected by surrendering to the enemy the object of his desire.[7] Tārā, for instance, suggested to Bālī that he should make peace with Sugrīva by declaring him *yuvarāja*, as he was then in a stronger position with an ally in Rāma[8] on his side. In course of the Laṅkā war, after the fall of Prahasta, the Commander-in-chief of the Rākshasa forces, a similar move was suggested to Rāvaṇa by Mandodarī.[9] The Uttara-Kāṇḍa alludes to a treaty between Rāvaṇa and Bālī according to which the resources of one could be freely utilised by the other.[10] *Yāna* and *vigraha*, the next two policies, stood for the 'military march' and the 'actual war' respectively. These were useful only in case of one who was stronger than

1. Kishkindhā-Kāṇḍa, cantos 45 and 46. (Note R. IV 46/7).
2. R. V 90/9.
3. R. VI 35/39-40.
4. *Shāḍguṇyasya padaṃ vettā nītikartā ca Rāghavaḥ*, R. VII 61/22.
5. Cf. *Shāḍguṇyasya prakṛitimaṇḍalaṃ yoniḥ.*, Arthaśāstra, VII 1.
6. R. VI 11/11.
7. R. VI 41/22.
8. R. IV 10/8-20.
9. R. VI 35/33-39.
10. R. VII 22/38.

Note : This seems to correspond to the *karma sandhi* of the Arthaśāstra. (Vide Dikshitar, V.R.R., War in Ancient India, p. 317).

his adversary.[1] In the epic, these are amply illustrated by the behaviour of Rāma who, followed by the Vānara army, marched against Rāvaṇa, his enemy, and destroyed him along with his followers.

Āsana in the sense of 'staying in siege' has been mentioned in the Kishkindhā-Kāṇḍa and it is said that this policy could be fruitfully employed by a stronger party at feud with a weaker one and not vice-versa.[2] The fifth policy was *saṃśraya* or 'seeking the protection of a more powerful king against one's enemy'. This is illustrated in the behaviour of Sugrīva who sought the assistance of Rāma for regaining the Vānara kingdom from the hands of his stronger enemy, Bālī. About the last policy, *dvaidhī-bhāva* there is no information in the epic.

It may be added that while determining a certain course of policy to be pursued by himself a king had to take into consideration the fact that the results in an undertaking depended upon two factors—providential and human. Since the former was unforeseen and beyond human control he could give the utmost consideration only to the latter.[3] Thus in every case, before determining the course of action, he had carefully to appreciate his own position as well as that of the enemy and also the exigencies of time and place.[4] He had also to visualise the position which was likely to develop as a consequence of his policies[5] and always act with a view to strengthening his own position and weakening that of the enemy.[6]

---

1. R. VI 11/11.
2. R. IV 54/12 N.S. (Note R. VI 11/10).

Also cf., "The Third method of *āsana* is loosely interpreted by some scholars as 'neutrality'; but it may mean 'holding a post against an enemy''. Dikshitar, V.R.R., War in Ancient India, p. 320.

3. R. V 32/23; R. V 81/20-24.
4. R. V 81/3.
5. R. V 81/4.
6. R. V 81/5.

N.B. The ideas expressed in the verses referred to above under the foot notes three to six bear a very close resemblance to those of Artha-śāstra, VI 2.

CHAPTER XVII

KINGSHIP

In primitive times when society was in its tribal stage and when its peace and security were often in danger on account of frequent internal quarrels among its members and attacks from outside by invading hordes, the rule of a strong man must have been considered conducive to the best interests of all concerned. The parables in the Vedic literature clearly show that kingship in India arose out of a military necessity.[1] The Rāmāyaṇa, as already indicated in an earlier chapter, makes no mention of any form of government except the monarchy; and one of the accomplishments that Vālmīki regards as necessary for an ideal king was that he should be a military leader; he should, if enraged, be a terror even to the gods on the battle-field.[2]

We need not consider here the question of the caste of the Vedic king. But by the time we reach the Rāmāyaṇic period, the *varṇa-vyavasthā* had become so deeply rooted in India that *kshatriyas* alone were considered fit to become rulers.[3] In all states belonging to the Aryans, the rulers were invariably *kshatriyas*. Among the non-Aryans, however, we hear of the *Rākshasa-rāja* Rāvaṇa (and later Vibhīshaṇa) in Laṅkā, of the *Vānara-rāja* Bālī (and later Sugrīva) in Kishkindhā and of the *Nishāda-rāja* Guha in Śṛiṅgaverapura. Besides, there are references to *Mleccha* kings,[4] and *janapadas* (States ?) belonging exclusively to *Śūdras* and *Ābhīras*.[5]

We find also that kingship had become hereditary and the rule of primogeniture had also come to be fully recognised. The pedigress of Daśaratha and Janaka,[6] and the statements of

1. Vide Aitareya Brāhmaṇa (I, 14) and Taittirīya Brāhmaṇa (II 2.7.2) quoted by Altekar, A. S., State and Govt. in Ancient India, p. 70.
2. R. I 1/4.
3. R. I 10/37-38.
4. R. II 3/55; R. II 5/11.
5. R. IV 35/6.
6. R. I cantos 66 (verses 17-32) and 67 (verses 2-13).

Daśaratha, Mantharā, Kaikeyī, Bharata Vasishṭha and Sugrīva[1]—all point to this very fact. The statement of Kaikeyī, namely, Bharata also will surely receive the hereditary kingdom from Rāma after the lapse of a hundred years[2] does not indicate that the kingdom was to rotate among brothers, for no such practice is anywhere alluded to directly or indirectly by Vālmīki. One cannot even argue that such a practice might have obtained in the land of Kaikeyī's father, for Mantharā (who was a *jñātidāsī* and should have, therefore, been perfectly familiar with the customs of that land) clearly brought out the fallacy of Kaikeyī's wishful thinking by pointing out that all sons of a king were not installed (as rulers) over the kingdom, for that would surely lead to mighty chaos.[3]

Rulers of the period had begun also to assert their divinity. There are a number of passages in the Rāmāyaṇa which expressly state that a king was a divinity. We may refer here to the statements of Rāma and Rāvaṇa which are of a representative character. Rāma told Bālī that a king was a divinity ranging on earth under the semblance of man and was, therefore, neither to be injured nor insulted.[4] According to Rāvaṇa a king represented five gods, viz, Agni, Soma, Indra, Varuṇa and Yama and therefore, one was to render him ungrudging and complete obedience.[5] These passages make it amply clear that the notion of king's divinity appears in the Rāmāyaṇa for two purposes. Firstly, it is resorted to by the kings themselves to elicit absolute obedience from their subjects and secondly it refers to the functional semblance between the king and the various guardians of the *Lokas*. Nowhere in the Rāmāyaṇa the person of a king is held divine;[6] nor does the epic anywhere appear to subscribe to the view that the king's authority was absolute.

A few references in the Rāmāyaṇa might lead a cursory reader to believe that the ruler had proprietary rights in the

1. R. II 4/9ff; R. II 10/17-20; R. II 10/8; R. II 123/32; R. II 116/2; R. IV 7/22 respectively.
2. R. II 10/12.
3. R. II 10/18, 20.
4. R. IV 14/21.
5. R. III 43/12.
6. Cf. *rājānam mānusham prāhuḥ...*, R. II 116/4.

kingdom; that it was his personal property which he could dispose of as he pleased. Thus, at Citrakūṭa, in the presence of the entire gathering there, Rāma revealed to Bharata that their father Daśaratha, at the time of his marriage with Kaikeyī (Bharata's mother), pledged the kingdom in favour of the son (to be) born of Kaikeyī.[1] In the early cantos of the Ayodhyā-Kāṇḍa it actually appears as if Daśaratha first offered the kingdom to Rāma but afterwards when Kaikeyī demanded her two boons from him he gave away the entire kingdom to Bharata.[2] In the Uttara-Kāṇḍa Rāma appears to be apportioning the kingdom among his sons and the sons of his brothers.[3]

Such a deduction, however, about the king's right would be found erroneous when the evidence noted above is carefully examined and when the total evidence available in the epic on this point is taken into account. As regards the promise of Daśaratha made to his father-in-law (Aśvapati), we should remember that Daśaratha was without a male issue at that time and might have, by then, lost all hopes of getting one by the previous wives. He could, therefore, have reasonably hoped that if a son were born to Kaikeyī he would also be the eldest and there would be nothing irregular in fulfilling the promise. Later, when due to some divine agency sons were born to his principal three wives and the son of Kauśalyā (and not of Kaikeyī) happened to be the eldest, Daśaratha faced a great dilemma. He realised that Rāma had a clear constitutional right to succeed; even though his promise to the Kekaya ruler went against it. When the princes came of age the king, therefore, arduously tried to secure conditions which would be favourable to Rāma's succession. Daśaratha, conveniently sent away Bharata from Ayodhyā and in his absence tried to put through a plan of Rāma's coronation as *yuvarāja*,[4] making it public only at the fag end. He hoped to confront the other party with almost a *fait accompli*.

As to Daśaratha's offering the kingdom first to Rāma and then to Bharata, there is nothing in the Rāmāyaṇa that

1. R. II 107/3 N.S.
2. Cf. (Kauśalyā) R. II 65/7.
3. R. VII/Cantos 103 (verses 9-10), 104 (verses 3-14), 109 (verses 17-19) and 110 (verses 8-9).
4. Note Daśaratha's words in R. II 6/18-19, 23-24.

would conclusively lead to such a deduction. We never find Daśaratha expressly saying 'yes' to the boons of Kaikeyī or himself asking Rāma to go away from Ayodhyā. Actually he found himself placed in a terrible *dharma-saṅkaṭa* (conflict of two duties, opposed to each other, but simultaneously presenting themselves before a person). He desperately wished not to break his promise to Kaikeyī and at the same time to see Rāma installed in his rightful position. And so his suggestion to Rāma was that the latter should imprison him and forcibly take over the crown.[1] To ignore in this whole affair the constitutional position of Rāma, who alone, under the rule of primogeniture, was competent to create a vacancy for Bharata is to deprive the epic of the entire moral significance for which it has primarily stood for all these ages.[2]

With regard to the last point, viz., Rāma dividing the kingdom among the members of the following generation, we should note that what was received by the sons of Lakshmaṇa, Bharata and Śatrughna were portions not of the hereditary kingdom but subsequent accretions. We may not be wrong even in holding that technically these portions never formed part of the hereditary kingdom of the Kosala kings, for even before they were conquered, Rāma had in anticipation coronated his brothers as rulers of the lands against whom they were sent to lead the expeditions.[3] That a provision (or a convention) to the effect of creating a new kingdom, so to say, from the freshly acquired territory under a younger brother by his ruling elder brother existed in that period is evidenced also by the illustration of Kuśadhvaja, who was coronated king of Sāṅkāśyā by his elder brother Janaka after Sudhanvā, the original ruler (of Sāṅkāśyā) had been defeated and slain in a battle.[4]

1. ....*tasmānnigṛihya mām mūḍhaṃ rājā bhavitumarhasi*, R. II 58/24.
2. Cf. Law, Narendra Nath, Aspects of Ancient Indian Polity, pp. 58-59.
3. R. VII 66/7-12; R. VII 102/16-19; R. VII 104/3, 10-11.
4. R. I 67/15-18.

N.B. It may be pointed out that ordinarily the practice obtaining in that period was that the territories of a vanquished king were not annexed by the victor. However, in certain exceptional circumstances—say, for example, when the opponent got killed in the battle (presumably without a direct successor—e.g. Sudhanvā) or when he and his dynasty

Contd. next page

The real position of the king in this respect becomes distinctly clear when one considers it vis-a-vis the position of the people, the subjects or citizens of the state. No doubt, the society of Vālmīki recognised the principle that the kingdom should remain in a royal family, passing on from generation to generation among its members according to the rule of primogeniture. It was, however, not prepared to accept as a corollary of this that it created absolute proprietary right of the king in the state. The state primarily belonged to its people, the king being there not for his personal benefit, but for the prosperity and welfare of the people. This position of the people in the period of the epic is powerfully revealed by the fact that succession in royal families was not just a matter of course; it necessarily required the approval of the officers of the state and the representatives of the people.[1] Moreover, the succession of the eldest son of the ruler was not binding upon the people in each and every case. For this rule to become operative it was necessary that :

(i) the eldest son should be born to the ruler of a regularly wedded and befitting (and also perhaps *kshatriyā*) wife;[2] and that :

(ii) he should himself be virtuous.[3]

were noted for their notoriety (e.g. Lavaṇa)—the victor put an end to the old rule. In such cases it devolved upon the victor to ensure sound administration in the conquered country. (Cf. *yo hi vaṃśaṃ samutpāṭya pārthivasya parikshaye, na vidhatte puraṃ tatra Narakam so (a) vagāhate*.. R. VII 65/42.

Specially in cases where the conquered territories lay at an appreciable distance from the victor's own seat of government and thus rendered his effective control on the new land rather impracticable he must have felt it more desirable to install there as ruler a near relation of his. It was exactly the position so far as the cases under reference above are concerned.

1. Vide the account of the *Sabhā* at Ayodhyā in Chapter XIX infra.
2. R. II 5/25.
3. Note the following :

(i) *guṇavatsvitareshu vā*, R. II 10/19.

(ii) *anujāto hi me sarvair guṇair jyeshṭho mamātmajaḥ...*, R. II 4/9.

(iii) *na caiva rājyaṃ viguṇāya deyam*, R. IV 23/38.

Note also the apprehensions of Bharata expressed by him in R. II 78/45-47 on being informed by Kaikeyī that Rāma had departed to the forest on being so ordered by Daśaratha.

Particularly if the second requisite was not fulfilled by his eldest prince the king was himself expected to put aside his claim and banish him from the kingdom, for otherwise, the subjects were expected to rise against the ruler and force him to exile the prince.[1]

We may in connection with the relationship subsisting between the king and the subjects consider also the checks on the ruler's authority. A king was required to be a supporter and upholder of law.[2] Moreover, an ideal conduct unimpeachable in every respect was demanded of him, for not only the people were prone to follow the 'first citizen'[3] but also because the society believed that evils and mishaps among the people were caused by the wrongs of the ruler.[4] The drought in the Aṅgadeśa was attributed to some default of Romapāda, its ruler[5] and, likewise, the premature death of his son was attributed by the *brāhmaṇa* to the misrule of Rāma.[6] The kings strongly dreaded public infamy, specially the censure of the sages and the good[7] and this served in that period as a fairly effective measure to keep the kings on the righteous track. We may, however, confess here that inspite of the fact that constitutionally Vālmīki recognised the position of the people in a way higher than that of the king, he does not refer to any constitutional measures[8] (except perhaps mass migration to a new territory) that could be resorted to by the people against a king having despotic tendencies. No doubt, there existed a Popular *Sabhā* as an important political organisation, however, as will be shown in a subsequent chapter we are not in a position to determine the extent of its control upon the king.

1. Vide the case of Asamañja in R. II 39/21-25.
2. R. I 7/17; R. I 19/8; R. VII 62/12-13; R. VII 84/12.
3. Cf. *yādṛig bhavati rājā tu tādṛiśi bhavati prajā,* R. VII 45/19. (Also R. V 81/11).
4. R. VII 76/17-18
5. R. I 8/12.
6. R. VII 76/10.
7. R. II 14/8; R. VII 47/12

Noteworthy is Rāma's reply to Lakshmaṇa in R. II 57/26-27.

8. Worthy of note is the helplessness of Vasishṭha against the despotic Viśvāmitra who was forcibly driving away his cow, Śabalā. (Note R. I 49/10-11).

Further, in the Rāmayāṇic period, it is not a king's rights but his duties that are specially stressed. The king's office was never sinecure in India. It was burdened with heavy responsibilities and the king's duties were onerous and numerous. We shall take notice here only of the principal obligations which it was absolutely necessary for the king to discharge.

The word *rājan* though literally derived from the root *rāj* (to shine) is in Hindu polity generally associated with the root *rañj* (to please).[1] Thus, according to Hindu political thinkers *prajānurañjana* (pleasing his subjects) is considered to be the primary duty of a king.[2] This ideal, according to Vālmīki, was to be realised by a king through the employment of wholesome policies conducive to public welfare and by adherence to *dharma* (Law). In fact, from his ideal king, Vālmīki demanded a complete dedication to the cause of the subjects so much so that he was to remain prepared to gladly sacrifice, at the call of the people, his dearest and nearest, nay his very life.[3]

As a primary condition of *prajānurañjana* the king had to ensure perfect security of life and property of his citizens against external as well as internal dangers.[4] For preventing any external danger likely to arise in the form of invasion by an enemy he was required not only to grow in strength but also

1. Jayaswal, K. P., Hindu Polity, p. 189.

2. Cf. R. I 14/1; R. VII 62/6.

N.B. Vālmīki's ideal king is famed as Rāma because by his noble qualities he pleased his subjects. (R. I 1/22-23).

3. Cf. "The epic exhibits as an ideal that a king should even give up his dear wife if asked to do so by his subjects : a popular and somewhat crude way of expressing the king's position, but all the same enshrining the radical demand of Hindu constitution from its king to sink his individuality into his office.", Jayaswal, K. P., Hindu Polity, p. 353.

To the above may be added the following from the Rāmāyaṇa—R. I 23/15, 17; R. V 44/12; R. VII 47/15.

4. R. I 19/9.

It may also be pointed out that protection of the subjects was not merely a pious obligation on the part of the king. In a sense it was legally binding upon him, for the taxes that he realised from his subjects were expressly on the understanding that he would in return protect them (and tend them) as his own children. (R. III 7/14).

to see that by his judicious and timely alliances a proper 'balance of power' was maintained.[1] Within the state he had to protect his subjects against the rage of the Rākshasas,[2] the menace of the *Dasyus*[3] and the threat of diseases and famines.[4] Moreover, he was also required not to harass his people himself[5] or through his officers[6] by such acts as the unlawful seizure of their wealth. It may further be added that the king's duty to protect was not limited only to the townsmen and the countrymen but also extended to the hermits living in the forest.[7] In fact, his responsibility towards these latter was still greater, for the belief was that a king who righteously protected his subjects became entitled to a sixth part of the great religious merit that was reaped by an ascetic subsisting on fruits and roots.[8]

It was a king's duty also to provide internal security in a state. In ancient India, as we have already indicated in an earlier chapter,[9] legislation did not fall within the purview of the king's authority. However, its enforcement primarily depended upon the king. The weak and the poor could coexist in the society with the strong and the rich only when law and order were maintained by the king.[10] He was the guardian of *dharma* (Law) and for its efficient and effective administration, the authority to punish the wrong-doer was

1. R. VI 11/10.
2. Daśaratha was required by Viśvāmitra to send Rāma to protect the latter's sacrifice against Mārīca and Subāhu. (R. I 17/4 ff.); Rāma promised to rid the Daṇḍakāraṇya of the menace of the Rākshasas (R. III 11/4ff); and Rāma deputed Śatrughna to kill Lavaṇa and thus protect the sages living on the bank of Yamunā. (R. VII 65/3 ff.).
3. R. II 4/22; R. V 100/33.
4. Cf. R. I 1/90; R. VI 105/3; R. VI 110/6-8; R. VII 61/8-9.
5. R. II 114/16; R. V 100/34.
6. R. II 114/16.
7. R. III 4/19.
8. R. III 7/17.

Cf. *Yaduttishṭhati varṇebhyo, nṛipāṇāṃ kshayi tat phalam,*
Tapaḥ shaḍbhāgamakshayyaṃ dadatyāraṇyakā hi naḥ.

Abhijñāna Śākuntalam, II 13.

9. Vide p. 291 supra.
10 R. II 73/24-25, 27.

vested in him.[1] An able king so utilised his authority that for fear of it, people of their own accord abided by the righteous course.[2] The *dharma* relating to the *varṇas* need a special mention here, for according to Vālmīki a king was particularly to ensure their rigid observance by the members in the society.[3] It is well known that Vālmīki's ideal king, Rāma, went to the extent of slaying the *śūdra*, Śambūka, who in contravention of these principles was practising penance in the forest.[4]

Protection, in fact, was only a means to an end—the end being welfare. That 'national welfare' formed an important duty of a king, according to Vālmīki, is evidenced from the fact that he generally terms a king as *rāshṭra-vardhana*[5], *śarma-dātā*[6] and *vṛiddhi-kāmo hi rāshṭrasya.*[7] Moreover, he visualises that under the rule of such a king the kingdom was prosperous with wealth and corn and that the people were hale and hearty.[8] The main stay of national welfare in that ancient society were agriculture, cattle-rearing and trade and these, according to Vālmīki, a king was keenly to supervise.[9]

We have noted above that as head of the government the king was ultimately responsible also for any and every 'right' or 'wrong' happening in his country.[10] It was necessary for him, therefore, to personally supervise the state affairs. Moreover, he was to frame his policies with due reflection and never to be procrastinating in their execution.[11] Presiding over the

1. R. III 4/18.
Cf. *Daṇḍaḥ śāsti prajāḥ sarvā, daṇḍa evābhirakshati,*
Daṇḍaḥ supteshu jāgarti, daṇḍaṃ dharmaṃ vidurbudhāḥ.
Manusmṛiti, VII 18.
2. R. VII 61/12.
3. R. I 1/94.
4. R. VII 77/27.
5. R. II 3/54.
6. R. III 4/17.
7. R. II 3/32.
8. R. VI 110/2 ff.
Moreover, a country is generally described by Vālmīki as *sphīta*, R. I 5/1; R. IV 35/6.
9. R. II 114/24.
10. R. III 55/11.
11. R. II 114/12-14.

Sabhā, the court of justice, formed a part of his daily routine.[1]

But for all this responsible work, careful training was felt necessary. In order to prepare the prince to eminently shoulder in his future life as king the heavy responsibilities of public administration very great attention was paid to his education and training. Vālmīki has left ample material in this behalf and particularly from the account of the education and accomplishments of Rāma and his brothers, one can easily form a general idea about the training of a prince in that period.[2] It may be stated at the very beginning that the entire training and education of a prince was directed towards three ends viz., (i) inculcating in him a sense of high respect towards *dharma,* the animating force of the entire social and political life of those times, (ii) invigorating him with a strong urge for public welfare, and (iii) fashioning him into an efficient and strong administrator.

No doubt, study of the Veda along with its auxiliaries and of other sacred scriptures formed part of the princely curriculum in the times of Vālmīki.[3] However, as is naturally to be expected, greater emphasis was laid on military training and training in the art of administration. *Dhanurveda,* as the term for military science, had become popular in those days and a prince was expected to master it.[4] He was taught the use (both offensive and defensive) of various arms, missiles and super-missiles.[5] By regular practice he was to become adept in riding over the horses and the elephants and also in breaking and training them.[6] Since chariot-warriors formed the core of military strength of those times a prince was given special training in driving and fighting from chariot.[7] Special significance was being attached to the elephants and so *hasti-śikshā* also seems to have formed an important part of a prince's military training.[8] Mastery had also to be acquired by a prince in

1. Note p. 308 infra.
2. R. II 3/9 ff.
3. R. II 2/8; R. II 3/12.
4. R. I 50/17-18; R. II 2/28; R. II 3/18-19; R. II 4/20; R. V 29/14.
5. R. I 25/2 ff.; R. I 26/2 ff.
6. R. II 3/18.
7. R. II 2/28.
8. Ibid.

swimming, galloping and hitting at the target.[1] Daśaratha and Rāma are said to have acquired the unique skill to shoot at invisible objects locating them merely by the sound.[2] A prince was also trained in leading the army, attacking the foe and fighting on the battle-field.[3] In short, he was prepared to become active and energetic and not negligent and dilatory.[4]

Arthaśāstra[5] had come to be recognised as the science of politics and formed complementary to *Dhanurveda* in the training of a prince. Under this, special emphasis must have been laid in making a prince adept in the employment of the four political expedients viz. *sāma* (negotiation), *dāna* (bribery), *daṇḍa* (open assault) and *bheda* (sowing dissensions) and the six measures viz. *sandhi* (peace), *vigraha* (war), *yāna* (marching), *āsana* (sitting encamped), *dvaidhī-bhāva* (dividing his forces) and *saṃśraya* (seeking the protection of a more powerful king).[6] Special lessons with regard to the collecting of dues from the people and the manner of expending them must also have been given.[7]

1. R. II 2/28-29.
2. R. II 4/20; R. II 70/15.
3. R. II 3/19.
4. R. II 1/26; R. II 3/14.
5. R. II 2/28.

N.B. "The words *arthaśāstra* and *daṇḍanīti* are applied to the science of government from two different points of view. *Artha* is defined in the Kāmasūtra (I. 20) as 'education, lands, gold, cattle, corn, domestic utensils and friends and the augmenting of what is acquired.........'Therefore when wealth and prosperity of all kinds is the spring and motive of giving a name the science treating of these is called *arthaśāstra* and when the government of the people and the punishment of offenders are the main ideas the same is called *daṇḍanīti*", Kane, P. V., History of Dharmaśāstra, Vol. III p. 7.

6. A specific mention of the 'four expedients' and the 'six measures' is not to be met with in the account of the prince's education given in the early cantos of the Ayodhyā-Kāṇḍa. However, the former (viz., the expedients) are mentioned collectively as well as severally at several places; and among the 'six measures' *sandhi*, *yāna* and *vigraha* are alluded to in different passages.

(For reference see R. V 32/20; R. V 38/2-4; R. V 80/9-10 (For 'expedients') and R. IV 11/3; R. VI 11/10 (for 'measures'). Six 'measures' are collectively mentioned in R. VII 61/22).

7. R. II 3/16; R. II 114/55-56.

It may be added that the importance of practical training was fully recognised. Generally, it seems, towards the end of his course the prince was associated with certain departments of public administration.[1] Rāma, we learn, was from time to time asked by his father to conduct a few military operations (presumably against the rebellious *Dasyus*).[2] He was also required to attend public business (*paura-kārya*) which he discharged to the satisfaction, among others, of the *Naigamas*.[3]

Moral discipline was of utmost importance for the prince in those days, specially in view of the fact that constitutional checks against the authority of the king were practically non-existent. Thus by making him conversant with ancient religious and didactic stories[4] and by associating him with virtuous persons of mature age and experience[5] he was trained to become truthful, righteous, virtuous, compassionate, grateful, sacrificing, self-restrained, conquering anger, not malevolent, ungrudging, unenvious and free from blemish.[6] At one place tranquillity, benevolence, compassion, righteousness, veracity, piety and prowess are expressly enumerated as qualities of a (good) king.[7] Moreover, Vālmīki also refers to certain *doshas* (vices) against which a prince was to guard himself. Thus fourteen *doshas*, viz. atheism, untruthfulness, anger, inattention, procrastination, disregard of (or non-appearance before) the wise, indolence, gratification of the senses, consultation with a single person concerning the needs of the kingdom, taking counsel with those that are cognisant of evils alone, omission to take in hand a task that has been decided upon, divulgence of counsel, non-application of salutary words or practices and marching against all the foes at one and the same time were enumerated by Rāma to Bharata, and he was asked to abstain from them.[8] Besides,

1. Cf.........*Vārtāmadhyakshebhyaḥ, daṇḍanītiṃ vaktṛiprayoktṛibhyaḥ*—Arthaśāstra, I 5.
2. R. II 3/2; R. II 4/22.
3. R. II 3/4 (variant 7).
4. R. II 2/15-16.
5. R. II 3/27.
6. R. II 3/9-21.
7. R. IV 16/58.
8. R. II 114/66-68.

reference is also made to vices arising from anger (*krodhaja*) and passion (*kāmaja*).[1]

The education of a prince, however, was not to be altogether dry. Fine arts like painting and music also formed a part of his curriculum.[2]

There lie scattered in the Rāmāyaṇa some passages by piecing which together we can form some idea of the king's daily time table. It may be remarked, however, that the information contained in the Rāmāyaṇa on this point does not create an impression that the daily routine of the king was as rigid and strenuous as detailed in the works on polity—say, for example, the Arthaśāstra.[3]

A king was awakened from sleep very early in the morning by sweet music and eulogies of professional bards and panegyrists.[4] Immediately on waking he finished his bath and toilette and repaired to the royal *vedi-gṛiha*. There he offered oblations to the sacred fire and worshipped the *Devas*, the *Pitṛis* and the worthy *brāhmaṇas*.[5]

After perhaps finishing his breakfast he came out into the *bāhya kakshyā* where the *purohita*, the ministers and other officers and Heads of *Nigamas* waited for him. Accompanied by them he went to the *Sabhā* for the transaction of public business.[6] Sometimes, it seems, he also listened to discourses on *dharma* by wise men and sages.[7]

The afternoon was a free time with the king and he usually spent it in the royal garden in company with the

1. R. II 5/28.
Commenting on this verse Govindarāja writes :
Mṛigayāksho divāsvāpaḥ parivādaḥ striyo madaḥ,
Tauryatrikam vṛithādhvā ca kāmajo daśako gaṇaḥ.
(*Ityetāni kāmajāni*).
Paiśunyaṃ sāhasaṃ droha īrshyāsūyārthadūshaṇam,
Vākdaṇḍayośca pārushyaṃ krodhajo(a) pi gaṇo(a)shṭakaḥ.
(*Ityuktāni krodhajāni ca vyasanāni*).
Cf. Manusmṛiti, VII 47-48.
2. R. II 2/4, 29: R. II 3/17.
3. I chap. 19.
4. R. II 15/14-15; R. VII 40/2ff.
5. R. VII 40/11-12.
6. R. VII 40/12-18.
7. R. VII 40/21.

inmates of the harem—dining and drinking with them[1]. Part of the afternoon was also spent in the *madhya kakshyā* in listening to jesters and story tellers and also in receiving reports from the spies.[2]

The Rāmāyaṇa does not say much directly about the king's programme in the evening and the night. A solitary passage in the Ayodhyā-Kāṇḍa directs the king not to be under the sway of sleep but to wake up early and reflect over the means of acquiring wealth.[3] The scene in the Sundara-Kāṇḍa, however, shows that till late in the night Rāvaṇa enjoyed dance, music and amorous sports.[4]

To carry out their duties effectively, the kings must have felt also the need of being backed by religious sanctions. The Brāhmaṇas speak of three ceremonies for consecrating a king.[5] The normal ceremony of coronation was the *Rājasūya*. The *Vājapeya* and the *Sarva medha* sacrifices were also related with a king's coronation. "The *Vājapeya*", as Dr. K. P. Jayaswal remarks, "probably did not partake of political nature in its origin, it being primarily designed to celebrate something like an olympic victory. It was, later on, adopted for royal and religious consecrations.[6] The *Sarvamedha*, as is suggested by its name, was 'a sacrifice for universal rule' and was performed only by emperors.[7]

The Rāmāyaṇa speaks of the *Rājasūya* and *Vājapeya* sacrifices, but it appears that in Vālmīki's age even the *Rājasūya* had lost its political character. From a statement of Sītā in the Ayodhyā-Kāṇḍa the relation of the *Rājasūya* with a king's coronation is suggested[8]; but another statement of Rāma in the same Kāṇḍa disproves this. Rāma has referred to Daśaratha, his father, as 'the performer of several *Rājasūyas* and *Aśvamedhas*.[9]

1. R. VII 44/1 ff.
2. R. VII 44/29; R. VII 45/1-20.
3. R. II 114/12.
4. R. V 5/97 ff.
5. For details about the coronation cermony in the Brāhmaṇa period vide Jayaswal, K. P., Hindu Polity, Chapters XIV-XV.
6. Hindu Polity, p. 199.
7. Ibid.
8. R. II 17/19-20.
9. R. II 114/4.

Obviously, the *Rājasūya*, had it retained its political significance, could have been performed by Daśaratha only once in his life time, namely, at the time of his own coronation as king. This conclusion is further corroborated by Rāma's proposal in the Uttara-Kāṇḍa to perorm a *Rājasūya* after his coronation.[1] The *Vājapeya* is also mentioned in the Ayodhyā-Kāṇḍa and the Yuddha-Kāṇḍa. In the Ayodhyā-Kāṇḍa the *brāhmaṇas* are said to have performed the *Vājapeyas* for their religious merit;[2] while in the Yuddha-Kāṇḍa,[3] these were performed by Rāma not with any political end in view but for their religious merit alone.

The Rāmāyaṇa mentions a coronation ceremony on several occasions. The first reference is in the Ayodhyā-Kāṇḍa where preparations for Rāma's consecration as *yuvarāja* are seen going on.[4] Next, we hear in the Kishkindhā-Kāṇḍa of Sugrīva being crowned king of the *Vānara rājya*.[5] The third is the coronation of Vibhīshaṇa. This is described in two stages, as it were; first, before the commencement of the Laṅkā war[6] (in anticipation, so to say)[7] and next, after the Laṅkā war when the throne of Laṅkā actually fell vacant.[8] The most important is the coronation of Rāma, which took place at Ayodhyā, after he returned from exile.[9]

Of these, the *yauvarājyābhisheka* slightly differed from the regular *rājyābhisheka*, for it was performed for a prince when his father was still ruling as king. Moreover, its object was only to formally declare the prince as heir-apparent. The first coronation in the Ayodhyā-Kāṇḍa, though incomplete, was of this very character. This account in the Rāmāyaṇa brings to light three things—first, it points at the requisite qualifications in a prince before he could be selected as a *yuvarāja*;

1. R. VII 85/4.
2. R. II 47/23.
3. R. VI 110/12.
4. R. II cantos 3-8, 16 and 29.
5. R. IV 19/22 ff.
6. R. V 94/1-3.
7. Of a similar nature was the coronation of Śatrughna when he proceeded against Lavaṇa., R. VII 66/7-13.
8. R. VI 93/16-16.
9. R. VI 109/33 ff.

next, it gives details of procedure in the selection; and finally it sheds some light upon the ritual itself.

The first qualification for selection as the *yuvarāja* was that the prince should be the first-born son of the consecrated senior wife of a king (most probably belonging to the *kshatriya varṇa*) having an equal status with the king.[1] Next, he should have endeared himself to the subjects by his virtues, particularly by his benign disposition towards them and by displaying a sincere desire for the welfare of the state.[2]

The procedure of selection as described by Vālmīki in this Kāṇḍa is remarkably precise with respect to its details. It is said that perusing over the accomplishments of prince Rāma, Daśaratha, the king in office, first, adjudged the prince's fitness for being appointed *yuvarāja*.[3] He then placed his proposal before the cabinet and sought its approval.[4] Next, he called a meeting of the Popular *Sabhā* or *Parishad* and explaining to the members his deservedness for retirement proposed that his eldest son (Rāma), who was worthy in every respect, be coronated *yuvarāja*.[5] The house having supported its approval of the king's resolution by recapitulating the various amiable qualities in the prince,[6] the resolution was adopted. In that very sitting of the *Sabhā* the king, presumably the ex-officio Chairman, within the hearing of the members, issued instructions for the implementation of the decision of the *Sabhā*;[7] probably as was customary, he formally introduced the prince-elect to the house and conveyed to him the decision of the house.[8]

The above account clearly shows that the appointment of a prince as the heir-apparent was not merely a matter of course, nor did it depend entirely on the sweet-will of the reigning king. It is amply clear that the people exercised effective control in the selection of their would-be ruler.

Next, we come to the ritualistic details connected with the

1. R. II 5/25.
2. R. II 3/4, 32; R. II 5/26.
3. R. II 3/29-30.
4. R. II 3/35.
5. R. II 4/1-12.
6. Ibid 15-31.
7. R. II 5/3.
8. R. II 5/8.

yauvarājyābhisheka. It seems that in the evening, previous to the actual coronation, it was customary for the mother (of the prince-elect) to arrange for certain propitiatory rites.[1] The same evening, the chief *purohita*, who was fully conversant with the Vedic *mantras*, administered a fast to the prince and his wife and made them perform, for their own welfare, certain other rites.[2] Later, the prince bathed himself, and in company with his wife repaired to the shrine of *Nārāyaṇa*[3] (which was situated within the precincts of the palace). There, raising the vessel of clarified butter unto his head (by way of paying reverence) he duly offered oblations into the fire for the great *Devatā* and partook of the remaining quantity of the *haviḥ*.[4] With his mind and speech controlled, he, then, meditated on the god *Nārāyaṇa*, and lying down on a bed of *kuśa* grass in company with his wife, he solemnly passed there the whole night.[5]

The ceremony in the Ayodhyā-Kāṇḍa is broken at this stage; the coronation having been abandoned on account of Rāma repairing to the forest in consequence of Kaikeyī's demand. However, Vālmīki furnishes a long list of articles required for the coronation and also indirectly refers to a few rites. The articles collected for the ceremony were a well ornamented excellent seat (*bhadra-pīṭha*) of *audumbara*; water brought from the sacred confluence of the holy rivers Gaṅgā and Yamunā and from other holy streams, lakes, wells, ponds and rivers; water brought from all the oceans; all kinds of seeds, scents and various gems; chariots, holy grass and flowers; unused clothes and golden vases; sprouts of fig tree and lotuses; well-decorated golden jars, the lovely yellow pigment (*gorocanā*), fried paddy, curd, clarified butter and honey; holy earth and water brought from various *tīrthas*; a pair of beautiful chowries with gem-laid handles; a brilliantly ornamented beautiful parasol; a rutting elephant; a chariot and a white horse; eight propitious maidens completely adorned with ornaments; daintily bedecked youthful and

1. R. II 6/35-36.
2. R. II 7/11.
3. R. II 8/1.
4. R. II 8/2-3.
5. R. II 8/3-4.

lovely dancing girls, white flowers and flutes; a sword and a bow; a white bull wearing golden strings; a lion-seat with a covering of tiger skin; fire fully ablaze; and bards and panegyrists with musical instruments.[1] 'Sprinkling' was the principal rite of coronation. In Vālmīki's age sprinkling over the prince's head with holy waters mixed with curd and honey was done by *brāhmaṇas* versed in the Vedas.[2]

After the *abhisheka* the *yuvarāja* was perhaps taken round the city in a splendid procession, which was formed, among others, by the senior state officers and principal citizens of the town.[3] He was seated over a splendid seat (*bhadrāsana*) in a chariot and an umbrella looking like the full moon and having hundred ribs was held over his head[4], and he was fanned with a pair of chowries.[5] He was eulogised with auspicious songs by the panegyrists, encomiasts and family bards.[6] In the procession, an excellent white horse, bearing auspicious marks, preceded the prince-elect;[7] and elephants and bulls who had been delivered three times, and who possessed auspicious marks, followed him.[8]

The main coronation is, however, the last, which took place at Ayodhyā after Rāma returned from the forest at the expiry of the term of his exile. This time Vālmīki mentions no preliminaries. The ceremony starts right with the *abhisheka*. The man in charge of the ceremony is, of course, Vasishṭha, the chief *purohita*.[9] He got Rāma, accompanied with his wife, seated on a gem-laid throne and then the 'sprinkling' commenced.[10] It is noteworthy that after the sprinkling was (first) done by the *brāhmaṇas* (Vasishṭha and others), the *ṛitviks* and the maidens to suggest a general approval of the prince as their ruler by the people, the ministers,

1. R. II 16/2-14.
2. R. II 29/15.
3. R. II 29/16.
4. R. II 29/12.
5. R. II 29/13.
6. R. II 29/14.
7. R. II 29/18.
8. R. II 29/17.
9. R. VI 109/73.
10. R. VI 109/75-76.

army officers and chiefs of guilds also poured water over Rāma[1] (and Sītā). After the 'sprinkling' the family crown was placed over the head of Rāma by Vasishṭha and the other *ṛitviks*.[2] This indicated vesting of kingship in him and his recognition as king. Immediately after this a 'Durbar' was held in which, again it is noteworthy, presents were given to *brāhmaṇas* and allies.[3]

Among the Vānaras and the Rākshasas also, it seems, kingship was hereditary and the succession of the eldest son to the throne of his father was the recognised rule. A *yuvarāja* is mentioned in case of both, the Vānaras and the Rākshasas,[4] but nowhere, any details with regard to the conditions or procedure of selection or of the ceremony connected with such an installation are given. In fact, the conditions under which the Vānara princes of the Rāmāyaṇa were coronated kings were rather abnormal, for Bālī was coronated king of the Vānaras when perhaps his father had suddenly died, and Sugrīva became king by contriving the death of Bālī through Rāma. Naturally, there are no references to the people or ministers and other state officials considering the question of succession of a prince in a *Sabhā*. However, there are faint indications that normally their will was respected, It is said that after the death of the Vānara king, Ṛiksharajas, Bālī was installed as 'Lord of the Vānaras' by the Vānara ministers, for he was the eldest prince.[5] The ministers and townsmen are again reported to have installed Sugrīva as king when Bālī was missing (and reported dead).[6]

The ceremony of regular coronation among the Vānaras also was practically of the same character as we find earlier in the Ayodhyā-Kāṇḍa. There is, no doubt, no reference to the prince-elect observing a fast, but before the 'sprinkling' the *mantravit brāhmaṇas* offer oblations into the fire here also.[7] A slight change is noticeable in the main ceremony, the

1. R. VI 109/79 (variant in f n. 10).
2. R. VI 128/64-67 N.S.
3. R. VI 109/87-99.
4. R. IV 19/41; R. V 90/32.
5. R. IV 7/22.
6. R. IV 7/50-51.
7. R. IV 19/29.

'sprinkling'. Here, the 'sprinkling' is done by the Vānara chiefs, Gaja, Gavāksha, Gavaya, Śarabha and others.[1] May be, these are the counterparts of the subordinate rulers, state-officers and representatives of the people who had assembled at Ayodhyā. Among the articles of *abhisheka* there are minor changes. Here, to the holy waters of *abhisheka* are added auspicious herbs,[2] and the number of handsome maidens is doubled.[3]

No details are supplied by Vālmīki about the coronation among the Rākshasas. However, it is clear that sprinkling formed the essential ceremony even among them.[4]

---

1. R. IV 19/25-37.
2. R. IV 19/24, 32.
3. R. IV 19/27.
4. R. VI 93/11-12.

Chapter XVIII

KING'S COUNSELLORS AND EXECUTIVE OFFICERS

Neither the ministers nor their joint body finds a mention in the Ṛigveda. In the immediately succeeding period of the Yajurveda and the Brāhmaṇas, however, one comes across the *ratnins* whose functions and status have been the subject of much controversy.[1] In the post-Vedic period we read of ministers who form an indispensable limb of the body politic, next in importance only to the king. The epics as well as ancient Indian Law-books emphasise the need of the minister's counsel and co-operation.

The importance of ministers for the king is very well brought out by Vālmīki when he calls them the king's *sahāya*[2] and *suhṛid.*[3] nay, his very *svajana.*[4] Moreover, the Rāmāyaṇa apprehends total ruin of a state in which a self-willed monarch acts without consulting his ministers;[5] the position of such a king remains ever unstable.[6] Vālmīki considers a minister to be the king's best help and it is he who advises the king about his welfare.[7] "The state policy", says Vālmīki, "has to follow the counsel (of councillors)"[8] and that, "It is in the counsel of councillors that a king's victory is rooted."[9]

For ministers Vālmīki employs the words *amātyas, sacivas* and *mantrins.*[10] As these terms denote the same persons

1. Ghoshal, U.N., Studies In Indian History And Culture, pp. 411-413.
2. R. V 89/15; R. V 100/9.
3. R. VI 71/39, 43.
4. R. II 79/4 N.S. (Note, *svajano mantryādiḥ*—Tilaka-Ṭīkā.
5. R. III 40/6.
6. R. III 45/17.
7. R. V 100/8.
8. R. V 81/24-25.
9. R. V 77/6.
10. The terms *amātya* and *saciva* are as old as the Vedic period. The word *amātya* occurs in the Ṛigveda (VII. 15.3) and the term *saciva* appears in the Aitareya Brāhmaṇa (XII.9). For details vide Kane, P. V. History of Dharmaśāstra, Vol. III p. 104.

(*e.g.* Sumantra[1] and Hanūmān)[2] it would appear *prima facie* that they have a similar or identical connotation. But from the descriptions of Daśaratha's ministry it is clear that a distinction was recognised by Vālmīki between the counsellors (known as *mantrins*) and the executive officers (known as *amātyas* or *sacivas*).[3] The two groups taken together formed the king's ministry. Moreover, since the *amātyas* or *sacivas* were also *ex-officio* members of the ministry they are also sometimes styled as *mantrins*.[4]

Describing the ministry of Daśaratha Vālmīki speaks of two groups—one consisting of Vṛishṭi (Dhṛishṭi), Jayanta, Vijaya, Siddhārtha, Arthasādhaka, Aśoka, Dharmapāla and Sumantra who are styled *amātyas*[5] and the other of Vasishṭha, Vāmadeva[6] and others who are cited as *mantrins*.[7] The former of these groups (collectively known as *Saciva-maṇḍala*)[8] was permanently in charge of the state affairs; it also had the right of counselling the king.[9] Thus the members of this group acted in a dual capacity; they were counsellors or *mantrins* as well as excutive heads of their departments or *amātyas*. The members of the second group, on the other hand, were merely counsellors or *mantrins*.

1. Sumantra is *amātya* in R. I 7/2-3, *mantrī* in R. I 8/4 and *saciva* in R. II 115/13.

2. Hanūmān is *amātya* in R. V 25/15, *saciva* in R. IV 2/24 and *mantrī* in R. VII 41/16.

Note also : The six ministers of Rāvaṇa accompanying him in his *digvijaya* are cited *sacivas, amātyas* and *mantrins* in R. VII 24/21, 22, 23 respectively.

3. Sometimes *saciva* is explained by the Tilaka-Ṭīkā as *upa-mantrī* (R. VI 7/2), but such a distinction is not borne out by internal evidence.

4. Those who are *sacivas* in R. VI 29/2 are called *mantrins* in R. VI 29/6.

5. R. I 7/2-3.

6. These two were also the *ṛitviks*. (R. I 7/1).

7. R. I 7/1. Other names of this group are given in R. II 73/2. They are : Jābāli, Kāśyapa, Mārkaṇḍeya, Gautama and Maudgalya. In R. VII 77/4 these names are again repeated as forming the group of counsellors of Rāma with the only exception that there the names of Nārada and Kātyāyana are added to the list.

8. R. II 115/13.

Manu also recommends seven or eight *sacivas* (Manusmṛiti, VII 54). It is difficult to determine whether the figure eight of the *Saciva-maṇḍala* in the Rāmāyaṇa is incidental or it refers to the number of the *sacivas* in general in that period.

9. R. II 3/35.

They had no executive duty to perform, nor did they perhaps permanently reside in the capital. Whenever any emergency arose or very urgent matters of state had to be transacted, they could be summoned by the king most probably through the agency of the *purohita* (Vasishṭha) who, besides being one of them was also the most influential member of that group, and as it were, their permanent spokesman at the centre. Daśaratha summoned this group (namely *mantrins*) to counsel him when in consultation with his *sacivas* he was planning to consecrate Rāma as *yuvarāja*.[1] When Daśaratha died they as a body went to the *Sabhā*[2] and along with the *amātyas* requested Vasishṭha to put one of the members of the Royal family on the throne as the kingdom was bound to suffer from evils of anarchy if no king was appointed.[3] They are mentioned also as approving the proposal of Vasishṭha, namely, that prince Bharata be called from his maternal uncle's house.[4] Later, when Bharata declined to accept the throne offered to him they accepted (along with other members of the *Sabhā*) Bharata's counter proposal to approach Rāma and request him to return to the capital.[5] In Rāma's own reign we find them summoned on three occasions—firstly when on the untimely death of his son a *brāhmaṇa* laid on the king and his *mantrins* serious charges of maladministration,[6] secondly when Rāma was thinking of performing the *Aśvamedha*,[7] and lastly when he had to decide the important question of restoring to Sītā her lost status.[8] Thus to a certain extent they performed the same function as the *Parishā* of Aśokan inscriptions[9] and the *Mantri-parishad* of

1. R. II 3/38.
2. R. II 73/1.
3. R. II 73/3ff.
4. R. II 74/4.
5. R. II 92/28.
6. R. VII 77/3-5.
7. R. VII 93/2-3.
8. R. VII 98/2-5.
9. Cf. "Going by Buddhaghosha's definition of *Parişā*. Aśoka's *Parişā* or Kauṭilya's *Mantri-parishad* may be treated as a representative body of all officials of the state under a monarchical constitution. Its members, whether known by the name of *Mahāmātras*, *Amātyas* or *Sacivas*, were the *rājākṛits*, Pāli *rāja-kattāro*, or King-makers backed by the collective popular will which was always behind them. The Rāmāyaṇa (II 29/1 N.S.) in describing the ministers who put their resolution before Bharata, calls them King-makers (*sametya rājakarttāro Bharataṃ vākyam abruvan*)."
Barua, Beni Madhab, Inscriptions of Aśoka, part II, p. 292.

Kauṭilya which had to be summoned on occasions of an *ātyayika-kāryā*.[1] As wise *brahmarshis*, the repositories of penance and Vedic learning this class of *mantrins* has sometimes been referred to also as *guravaḥ* or *rājaguravaḥ*,[2] *dvijāḥ* and *brāhmaṇāḥ*. Thus the king's *Mantrimaṇḍala* was a joint body constituted of the *sacivas* or *amātyas* and also the *brāhmaṇa* counsellors.

As to the distribution of duties among the *amātyas*, there is no clear indication of it in the Rāmāyaṇa. If the names of Daśaratha's ministers be indicative of their functions, which is not unlikely, we may perhaps infer something from their names. Griffith has suggested that the ministers Dhṛishṭi, Jayanta and Vijaya meaning 'Boldness', 'Victorious son of Indra', and 'Conquest' respectively, were associated with the portfolio of War; Siddhārtha and Arthasādhaka meaning 'the successful man' and 'one efficient in the acquisition of riches or wealth' respectively, with Finance; Aśoka meaning 'without sorrow' and Mantrapāla meaning 'one who protects *mantra* or the sacred texts' with Law and Justice; and Sumantra with miscellaneous affairs. This last officer was the Royal Bard, the Royal Charioteer, the Royal Equerry and the Private Secretary to Daśaratha.[3] But even if this general reasoning be accepted, it is difficult to associate Aśoka with

1. *Ātyayike kārye mantriṇo mantriparishadam cāhūya brūyāt*, Arthaśāstra, I.15.

2. R. I 8/4; R. II 73/1; R. II 73/3 and R. II 74/1.

Note : The Bombay recension of the Rāmāyaṇa reads *rājakartāraḥ* (R. II 67/2 N. S.) for *rajaguravaḥ* of the North Western recension (R. II 73/1). This term again appears in the Bombay recension in II 79/1 N.S. (but the Lahore edition completely drops this verse). The commentators explain it as *rājño (a) śesha kāryakartāraḥ* (Tilaka-Ṭīkā), *rājocitakarmanirvāhakāḥ* (Rāmāyaṇa-Śiromaṇi-Ṭīkā) and *rājābhisheka kāryakartāraḥ* (Govindarāja)

The term also occurs in the Atharvaveda (III 5/7) and the Dīgha Nikāya (II 233). Dr. Jayaswal explains it as 'high functionaries or ministers' (Hindu Polity, p. 195). This view has been criticised by Dr. A. S. Altekar in his work, The State and Government in Ancient India (p. 76). His objection is that "the *raja-kartāraḥ* referred to in the Rāmāyaṇa are not King-electors but the *Brāhmaṇas*, who were entrusted with the duty of offering the coronation ablutions to the king." Dr. Altekar, it is evident, fails to appreciate the constitutional position of these *brāhmaṇas*. We have shown above that they were the 'Counsellors' of the king and formed an important section of the king's *Mantri-maṇḍala*.

Dr. U. N. Ghoshal also takes up the question of the *rāja-kartāraḥ* (Studies In Indian History And Culture, pp. 411-412), but he does not refer to the Rāmāyaṇa.

3. Griffith quoted by Dharma, P. C., Rāmāyaṇa Polity, p. 52.

law and justice merely on the ground that a minister can cause sorrow to the people by interfering with their person and property. Similarly Mantrapāla may not mean 'one who protects the sacred text', for in political contexts the word *mantra* stands more often for 'Diplomacy' and thus Mantrapāla may have been minister in charge of 'foreign affairs.' Arthasādhaka may similarly have been connected with finance, Dharmapāla with justice, and Sumantra perhaps with the king's Ministerial Council. But all this can at the most be regarded as a plausible surmise. In fact, the suggestion for the different portfolios in the ministry should come from what Vālmīki considered to be the aims of the state. If we keep this in view and then analyse the description of the evils to which according to the Rāmāyaṇa a state could be subject in the absence of a ruler and also consider certain other references we can easily infer that the main tasks with which a ministry could be concerned were maintenance of law and order, defence of the state, justice, financial administration, foreign affairs and ensuring the unobstructed performance of one's duties—religious as well as secular. On the basis of these functions we can think of the existence of the following departments :

(a) The Department of Ecclesiastical Affairs :

In the Rāmāyaṇic period religious affairs were much more important than they are now and the *purohita* who was perhaps in charge of them was one of the most important functionaries of the state. He was the royal *upādhyāya* and the chief counsellor; in certain spheres he was in no way inferior to the king himself.

At Ayodhyā Vasishṭha was the *purohita*.[2] He was a *brahmarshi* fully conversant with *mantras* (sacred verses)[3] and has been described as the family deity of the Ikshvākus.[4]

1. Cf. R. II 114/11, 13.
2. *piturishṭaḥ purohitaḥ*, R. II 88/20.

N.B. Technically a *purohita* is to be distinguished from a *ṛitvik* but in the Rāmāyaṇa the *purohita* Vasishṭha is also referred to as *ṛitvik* (R. I7/1) and *upādhyāya* (R. II 114/5).

3. *mantravin mantra pāragaḥ*, R. II 7/4.
4. R. I 66/14.

Daśaratha consulted him in all matters, specially in religious ones where the *purohita* was almost the final authority.[1] He administered a fast to Rāma in connection with his *Yauvarājyābhisheka*[2], related the genealogy of Daśaratha on the occasion of the marriage of the princes[3] and conducted the king's (Daśaratha's) funeral.[4] He could read omens and suggest means to ward off presaged evils.[5] But not only that, during Daśaratha's reign and also after that he was probably the most influential figure in the political sphere. He was practically the chief minister, though the designation *mahāmātya* belonged to Siddhārtha.[6] He had complete hold over the king and the ministry. The king has been described as *Vasishṭha-vaśavartin*[7] and the ministry even in the lifetime of Daśaratha always abided by his verdict and looked up to him for guidance in all matters.[8]

Vasishṭha presided over the *Sabhā* in the absence of the king and carried on the administration during the period of interregnum.[9] When requested by the *dvijas* and the *amātyas* to "install a descendant of Ikshvāku as king of the realm" Vasishṭha proposed that Bharata be called from his maternal uncle's house and asked to accept the throne conferred upon him by (the late) king Daśaratha. The proposal being accepted he sent words to Bharata to come immediately, for an *ātyayika* business was waiting for him.[10] Vasishṭha was also the

1. R. I 66/14
2. R. II 7/2 ff.
3. R. I 66/17 ff.
4. R. II 87/1 ff.
5. R. I 70/11-14.
6. R. II 39/18. May be that Siddhārtha was the chief of the *Sacivamaṇḍala*.

It may incidentally be noted that the Bombay recension reads *mahāmātra* for *mahāmātya* in the verse quoted above. This term has been interpreted by Dr. P. C. Dharma (Rāmāyaṇa Polity, p. 50) as "Prime Minister"—which, however, is not in consistence with her own statement in which she calls Vasishṭha the *de facto* Prime Minister.

The word *mahāmātra* literally means "one of great measure" and it was a common designation of all the ministers. This fact is proved by R. II 89/15 where Dharmapāla is cited as *mahāmātra*.

(For a similar use of the term *mahāmātra* in Aśoka's times vide Barua, Beni Madhab, Inscriptions of Aśoka, Part II, pp. 287-289. Vide also Arthaśāstra, I 10).

7. R. I 17/2.
8. R. II 73/30.
9. R. II cantos 73, 74 and 92.
10. R. II 74/4-7.

spokesman of the members of the *Sabhā* at the time of offering the throne to Bharata and later in approving the proposal of Bharata to go to Citrakūṭa to persuade Rāma to return to the capital.[1] He sat by the king when the latter presided over the law courts. His advice was sought by Rāma along with that of other *dvijas* and *amātyas* when the *brāhmaṇa* whose son had met with untimely death was laying charges of maladministration at the door of Rāma and his Counsellors.[2]

Vasishṭha, no doubt, was a powerful personality. But that it was no individual position which he enjoyed can be inferred from the position of Śatānanda in Janaka's kingdom in the Rāmāyaṇa[3] and also from Kauṭilya's statement even for a later period that the king should follow a *purohita* as a student, his teacher; a son, his father and a servant, his master.[4]

(b) The Department of Defence :

Another important department was that of 'Defence'. It was probably under the charge of the *senāpati*, an officer known to us also from sources earlier than the Rāmāyaṇa.[5] He was the Commander-in-chief of the Royal forces and was expected to be proficient in the science and art of war.[6] Prahasta who was the *senāpati* at Laṅkā was his master's spokesman[7] and probably the convener of his war councils.[8] He was also Rāvaṇa's war minister. Under the *senāpati* were various military officers like the *vāhinīpati*, the *balādhyaksha*, the *yūthapas*, the *nāyakas*, etc.[9]

(c) The Department of Finance :

The important department of 'Finance' may have been under a minister called the *kośādhyaksha*.[10] Of Daśaratha's

1. R. II 92/3, 23
2. R. VII 77/3.
3. Note : *Śatānanda-mate sthitaḥ*, R. I 64/13.
4. Arthaśāstra, I 9.
5. For details see Dikshitar, V.R.R., War in Ancient India, p. 222.
6. R. II 114/43.
7. R. V 46/2-3; R. V 90/61
8. R. VI 8/39.
9. Vide Chapter XXII infra.
10. R. II 41/14.

amātyas Artha-sādhaka might have had something to do with finances. When a state went in financial difficulties, it was only a minister proficient in financiery science who could heip the king by his counsel. Rāma advised Bharata to prefer such a *paṇḍita* to thousand fools.[1] Under the Finance minister might have been other officers like the *dhanādhyakshas* whose main function seems to have been the collection of wealth.[2]

(d) The Department of Justice :

Justice may have been under the charge of a *dharma-mantrī*, perhaps the same as the *amātya* Dharmapāla of Daśaratha's ministry. In ancient India, as already noted, the state was not competent to enunciate new laws; it was only to enforce the *dharma* as gathered from the sacred texts and the practices of the *āpta-jana*. Often, this must have presented conflicts and doubts, to remove which there must have been a consultative body in the state consisting of the *brāhmaṇas*, well versed in the Dharma-śāstras and other sacred lore. This body must have helped the king in determining what was to be accepted as *dharma* being in consonance with the principles of equity and the spirit of piety and what was to be discarded as *adharma* being against the same. Vālmīki actually refers to *dharma-vācakas* (or *dharma-pāṭhakas*) and *vyavahārajñas* (i.e. conversant with secular law) accompanying a king when he presided over a law court.[3]

(e) The Department of Foreign-Affairs

An important function of this department perhaps was to collect intelligence through spies about the plans of the allies, neutrals and foes[4] and to advise the king on the four-fold policy of *sāma* (conciliation), *dāma* or *dāna* (appeasement or gifts), *daṇḍa* (war) and *bheda* (causing dissensions in the

1. R. II 114/17.
2. R. I 65/2; R. II 41/14-17.
3. R. VII 61/4 (f. n. 6 *dharmapāṭhakaiḥ*)

Their position may be compared to that of the *brāhmaṇas* and *mantrins* who according to Maṇu (VIII, 1) accompanied the king to the Law-court.

4. R. I 7/6.

enemy's camp). It had also to keep an eye upon the various state officers (*tīrthas*)—a measure necessary in the interest of the security of the state.[1] A regular corps of spies, envoys and ambassadors was maintained by this department. Rāvaṇa had spies of the status of *amātyas*[2] and among the Vānaras Hanūmān, a senior minister of Sugrīva and Aṅgada, the *yuvarāja* acted as envoys for their master.[3]

Before closing this section the position of the *yuvarāja* may be considered. He figures in the list of the *tīrthas*[4] and in the Rāmāyaṇa he appears invariably to be associated with the ministry. *Yuvarāja* in the Rāmāyaṇa does not necessarily seem to be a title of the eldest son of the reigning sovereign, a successor-designate to the throne. The Rāmāyaṇa describes Rāma being appointed a *yuvarāja* at Ayodhyā in the times of Daśaratha.[5] But Rāma, when he became king, appointed Bharata as *yuvarāja*, Lakshmaṇa having declined to accept the offer.[6] At Kishkindhā, Tārā suggested as a diplomatic move the appointment of Sugrīva as *yuvarāja*,[7] even though Bālī had a grown up and able son, Aṅgada. At Laṅkā Vibhīshaṇa was actually the *yuvarāja*,[8] even though Rāvaṇa had at the time mature and able sons like Meghanāda, competent to join him in his expeditions and in the deliberations of the Council.

It is not clear whether the *yuvarāja* had any definite portfolio. This, however, seems certain that he was associated more or less with the reigning sovereign in the task of administration and in attending to the important affairs of the state. Rāma, a non official *yuvarāja*, as we may call him, even before the decision of his appointment to that office, led small operations against turbulent elements in the kingdom.[9] At the instance of his father he attended to all the *paura-kāryas* to the

1. R. II 114/48.
2. R. VI 1/1.
3. R. V 47/2 and R. VI 16/53 respectively.
4. See the 'table' at the end of this chapter.
5. R. II 4/10 ff.
6. R. VI 109/114-116.
7. R. IV 10/20.
8. R. V 90/32.
9. R. II 4/22.

satisfaction of all concerned.[1] Aṅgada was appointed leader of the party sent to search the southern direction and discover Sītā.[2] Vibhīshaṇa was left in charge of the entire administration at Laṅkā when Rāvaṇa went out on *Trailokyavijaya*.[3]

The exact details of the working of a ministry are not clear from the Rāmāyaṇa. But as pointed out above, in matters concerning the state a king was not expected to act being led by his own impulses and passions. It is likely, therefore, that in every matter he consulted the most important of his ministers, generally one, two or three.[4] After preliminary deliberations with them he was to place the matter before the ministry as a whole, giving them the fullest liberty to express their views. Ordinarily the ministers agreed with the king, but when a matter came up for discussion in a council meeting and the ministers were required to express their opinions, they were expected neither to be influenced by the wish of the king nor to be over-awed by his authority.[5] Moreover, they were expected not to misguide the king being actuated by their own desires, interests or passions.[6] They were to be guided by the scriptures and speak salutary words for the good of the king. Vālmīki declares, "Where the gain and the loss (attendant upon it) (or the points for and against) as also the uncertainties (or doubts) arising therein are examined, that is to be termed 'deliberation'; the rest is just an adventure."[7] Very important matters, affecting the welfare of the state had to be placed also before a General Assembly called the *Sabhā* or the *Parishad*.[8]

There must have been occasions when the interests of the

1. R. II 3/2 ff.
2. R. IV 56/74.
3. R. VII 31/38.
4. There appears to be a tendency to form a small body inside the *Saciva-maṇḍala* consisting of three or four persons with whom the king constantly conferred. (*Kaccinmantrayase naikaḥ kaccinna bahubhiḥ saha*, R. II 114/13. Compare : *'Na' iti Kauṭilyaḥ Anavasthā hyeshā. Mantribhistribhiścaturbhirvā saha mantrayeta.*, Arthaśāstra, I 15.)

Moreover, consultation with a single person concerning the needs of a kingdom, and taking counsel of those who were cognisant of evils alone—these two are enumerated in the list of faults among kings. (R II 100/66 N.S. Cf. the reading in R. II 114/67 which appears to be defective).

5. R. IV 25/19.
6. R. I 7/8 N.S.
7. R. V 89/17.
8. Vide Chapter XIX.

state demanded that the ministers should differ from the king. In a council meeting, therefore, differences of opinion occurred now and then. Vālmīki has recognised three categories of deliberations : "That deliberation was the best where ministers engaged in deliberations arrived at a unanimous decision in accordance with the *śāstras*. A middling one was that where an agreement was reached after good deal of discussion and (preliminary) dissension. The worst was that where each defined the thing differently and as a result , oblivious of the main subject of discussion, the councillors failed to arrive at any agreement.[1] From the expression, "working in harmony" employed for the ministers of Daśaratha it is obvious that this was the objective of every ministry.[2] If a minister talked too much unnecessarily, or wilfully obstructed the business of a council, he could be asked to leave it.[3]

The appointment of the ministers was done by the king. Loyalty to the state was the primary qualification for selection as minister, hence the persons selected came from local, rich and noble families that had been in the service of the king for some generations in the past.[4] At Laṅkā and, perhaps, also at Kishkindhā a very large number of the ministers was selected from the royal family itself. Vālmīki invariably describes the ministers joining their masters in military expedition[5] and refers to them as 'heroic' (*śūrāḥ*),[6] 'possessed of prowess' (*dṛiḍhavikramāḥ*) and 'masters of military technique' (*śastrajñāḥ*).[7] This shows that mostly the ministers entrusted with executive functions were recruited from the *kshatriya* class and that they combined civil and military duties. Ability was another important consideration in the selection of a minister.[8] Worthy

1. R. V 77/13-15.
2. *parasparenāviruddhāḥ*, R. I 7/11.
3. That this was a principle recognised not only in theory but also in practice is clear from the case of Vibhīshaṇa who was forcibly turned out of the *Sabhā* by Rāvaṇa. (R. V 90/62-63).
4. R. II 114/35.
5. The ministers of Viśvāmitra (R. I 50/10) and Rāvaṇa (R. VII 13/1) joined their masters when they went out on military expeditions. The ministers of Arjuna of Māhishmatī also resisted Rāvaṇa and his followers when the latter came to attack their master, R. VII 20/31.
6. R. II 114/10.
7. R. I 7/7 N.S.
8. R. I. 7/13.

of mention among the accomplishments of a minister are his learning,[1] proficiency in the art of war and peace,[2] discriminating understanding in matters of religion and law,[3] skill in replenishing the treasury and the levy of troops[4] and cleverness in reading the motives of others[5] and vigilance in guarding the state secrets.[6] Ministers were expected to be wise (*matimantaḥ*), pure (*śucayaḥ*), resourceful, endowed with enthusiasm (*vikrama*) and dignity (*prabhāva*), steady (*dhṛitimantaḥ*), unavaricious (*alubdhāḥ*) self-controlled (*vijitendriyāḥ*), free from partiality (*sama-darśinaḥ*) and men of integrity (*anuraktāḥ*).[7]

Ministers of that early period were very closely associated with the king.[8] They had to assist him not only in the task of

1. (*edavedāṅgapār gau*) R. I 7/1 ; (*prāgatajñānavijñānāḥ*) R. I 7/9.
2. (*sandhivigraha tattvajñāḥ*) R. I 7/18 N.S.
3. (*dharmācāravivekajñāḥ*) R. I 7/7.
4. (*kośasaṅgrahaṇe yuktāsthathā balaparigrahe*) R. I 7/7.
5. (*iṅgitajñāḥ*) R. II 100/15 N. S.
6. (*mantra saṃvaraṇe ś ktāḥ*) R. I 7/19 N.S.
7. For references see R. I 7/2-7; R. II 114/17; R. VII 38/6.

Note : Sometimes Vālmiki refers to *ashṭāṅga-buddhi* as a qualification of a minister (R. IV 46/3). The term is explained by the Tilaka-Ṭīkā as :
Śuśrūshā śravaṇaṃ caiva grahaṇaṃ dhāraṇaṃ tathā,
Ūhāpohārth vijñānaṃ tattvajñānaṃ ca dhīguṇāḥ.
Cf. Arthaśāstra, VI 1.

8. Ministers accompanied the king :
   (i) When he received a sage—
      (a) Lomapāda received Ṛishya-Śṛiṅga with his *amātyas* (R. I 12/26).
      (b) Lomapāda received Vibhāṇḍaka with his *mantrins* (R. I 13/17).
   (ii) When he was out—
      (a) Daśaratha went with his *amātyas* to bring Ṛishya-Śṛiṅga (R. I 9/15).
      (b) Haihayarāja was accompanied with his *amātyas* when sporting in the waters of the Revā. (R. VII 20/24).
   (iii) When he received a dignitary—
      (a) Guha came forward to receive Rāma with his *amātyas* (R. II 51/10).
   (iv) When he was attending the *paura-kārya*—
      (a) Rāma was accompanied with his *mantrins*. (R. VII 61/4).
   (v) In an expedition—
      (a) *Amātyas* and *mantrins* of Viśvāmitra joined him. (R. I 48/32-33).
      (b) *Sacivas* of Rāvaṇa joined him (R. VII 13/1).
   (vi) When he was making a new settlement —
      (a) Prahasta asked Rāvaṇa to settle down in Laṅkā with his *amātyas* (R. VII 10/33).
   (vii) When he received an envoy—
      (a) Hanūmān was received by Rāvaṇa in company with his *mantrins* (R. V 45/11).
   (viii) When a prince was to be crowned (R. II 16/31).

Contd. on next page.

administration but also in the transaction of his personal affairs. From coronation to cremation and from the seat of justice (*dharmāsana*) to the field of battle, they were the king's constant companions. The king consulted them when framing policies whether relating to the replenishing of the treasury or declaring of war. Administration of law and justice was, as shown above, one of their important duties. They had to protect the weak from the strong, the poor from the rich, and ensure impartial justice and sympathy for all citizens.[1] They had to see that peace reigned in the kingdom in such a way that the ruler could declare, "There is no thief in my kingdom; none is impure or wicked or loose charactered."[2]

Replenishing the treasury was the minister's responsibility. But, in their zeal to collect money they were neither "to set free a thief who had been caught, interrogated and found with the stolen property" nor "fine a respectable, pure-minded and innocent person accused of theft by some one".[3] They were also not to extort money from the *brāhmaṇas*.[4]

To defend the state the ministers resorted to military measures as well as diplomacy. They maintained the army in a state of efficiency[5] and kept a vigilant watch over the activities of the neighbouring states by deputing spies to the department of every *tīrtha*.[6] Sometimes they acted also as envoys and ambassadors.[7] They determined the king's course of action and guided him in his choice of the four expedients, viz., *sāma*, *dāna* (or *dāma*), *bheda* and *daṇḍa*. Specially before declaring war they considered the pros and cons of their policy, weighed the relative strength of the enemy and their own, and kept

(ix) When a prince was to be married (R. I 65/4).

(x) When a king was to be cremated —

(a) The *mantrins* and *amātyas* of Daśaratha joined his funeral (R. II 85/32 and R. II 88/25).

(b) The *sacivas* of Bālī joined his funeral (R. IV 18/24).

(c) The senior *amātyas* joined Rāvaṇa's funeral. (R. VI 92/58).

1. R. I 7/8; R. II 114/59.
2. R. I 7/14-15.
3. R. II 114/57-58.
4. R. I 7/10.
5. R. I 7/7.
6. R. II 114/48.
7. Vide the role of Hanūmān in the Sundara-Kāṇḍa.

in view also the future consequences.[1] Every care too was taken to see that their counsel remained absolutely confidential.[2]

A minister naturally tried to please his master. But a good minister never submitted blindly to the will of the king nor acted in a manner which, though agreeable and pleasing, went against the king's interests. It was the duty of the ministers to restrain a king going astray and do what was right as well as good for the king.[3] The ministers who did not prevent a king from following an evil course deserved death according to Vālmīki.[4]

Ministers had no joint or collective responsibility. They were appointed by the king and were responsible to him. The king consulted them in all matters. They were to render him help by examining the soundness of whatever moves and measures he contemplated.[5] Ordinarily a king was expected to listen to the opinions of his ministers and accept their counsels made in accordance with the *Śāstras* though, constitutionally he was not bound to accept them.

The measure of confidence and respect a minister enjoyed depended to a very large extent upon his king. A law-abiding and righteous king like Daśaratha behaved very submissively to his senior ministers. He reproached himself and condemned his own action as very arbitrary when he acted without consulting his ministers.[6] Hanūmān under Sugrīva could make bold to accuse his master of neglect of duty towards his benefactor Rāma.[7] But, the position was reverse under a self-willed monarch like Rāvaṇa. He demanded naked submission and tolerated no criticism.[8] He was not prepared to listen to anything, however true and wholesome it might be, if it was jarring to his ears and failed to satisfy his vanity.[9] A

1. R. III 40/23-24.
2. R. I 7/19 N.S.
3. R. III 44/6-7.
N.B. The N.S. reads *vadhyāḥ* in place of *buddhāḥ* and that seems to be the correct reading. Cf. R. III 41/6 N.S.
4. Ibid.
5. R. V. 100/9.
6. R. II 63/21-22.
7. R. IV 25/10-23.
8. R. III 43/8-11.
9. R. V 90/32; R. VI 5/5.

minister persisting in the honest discharge of his duty against Rāvaṇa's will was openly insulted and even threatened with death by him.[1]

Administration of the kingdom was carried on by the king with the help of high officials known as *tīrthas*. Conventionally, their number was fixed as eighteen and the list included, besides the departmental heads of varying ranks, officers of the royal household as well. Vālmīki refers to them along with their number (eighteen)[2] but does not supply their designations. In the table at the end of this chapter we give the lists of the *tīrthas* as given in the Arthaśāstra and in the three principal commentaries of the Rāmāyaṇa along with the English equivalents suggested by scholars.

It is to be observed that the lists of the commentators agree with one another except that while the *sabhya* is *vyavahāra-nirṇetā* in the lists of Tilaka and Rāmāyaṇa-śiromaṇi commentaries, he is the 'Council secretary' according to Govindarāja.[3] The description of the *sabhya* given by Govindarāja appears to be correct and we should interpret the *vyavahāra-nirṇetā* of the other two commentaries also in the sense of one who decided the ceremonial procedure of the court. If, however, we shall give the word the sense of a 'Judge' the functions of the *sabhya* will get confused with those of the other two officers, viz., the *prāḍvivāka* and the *dharmāsanādhikṛit*.

In their understanding of the list given in the Arthaśastra there is disagreement at several points between Doctors Shamasastry[4] and Jayaswal.[5] Dr. Shamasastry counts twenty *tīrthas* by splitting the words *mantriparishadadhyaksha* and *durgāntapālāṭavika* of the text as "Assembly of Councillors (*mantriparishad*), Head of Departments (*adhyakshaḥ*), Officers in charge of fortifications (*durgapāla*), boundaries (*antapāla*) and wild tracts (*āṭavika*)." Dr. Jayaswal's interpretation would

1. R. III 43/22-23.
2. R. II 114/48.
3. *Sabhyaḥ pratidinaṃ sabhālaṅkaraṇarājamantriprabhṛitisamucitāsanavidhāna sabhyāna yanāsabhyanirodhana yathocita niveśana sabhā niḥśabdīkaraṇa sabhā rakshaṇādividhāyijananirvāhakaḥ.*, Govindarāja on R. II. 114/48
4. Kauṭilya's Arthaśāstra (Translated by R. Shamasastry, p. 23.)
5. Hindu Polity, pp. 302-303.

have, instead, only three officers namely 'the President of the Council', 'the Minister in charge of Home defences' and 'the Minister in charge of Frontiers'. The words *senāpati* and *nāyaka* in the Arthaśāstra list have been rendered by Dr. Shamasastry as 'the Commander of the army' and 'the City constable' respectively. Dr. Jayaswal understands by them 'the Minister for the army' and 'the Generalissimo' respectively. In the Arthaśāstra, the *nāyaka* was required to join the *vardhakī* and the *mauhūrtika* in measuring (i.e. selecting) the site for the military camp;[1] to be in the forefront, when the camp moved;[2] and to arrange the army in battle array with the *senāpati*.[3] This clearly shows that he was a senior military officer. He was, however, very much junior in rank to the *senāpati*, because Kauṭilya fixed 12000 *paṇas* as his annual pay, while the *senāpati* drew 48000 *paṇas* annually.[4] To regard the *senāpati* as 'War minister' too, does not seem to be correct, because the *senāpati* in the Arthaśāstra was required actually to be on the battle-field, fighting and arranging the army.[5] Dr. Shamasastry's rendering of *sannidhātṛi* as 'Chamberlain' does not appear to be right. In arriving at this meaning he has been guided, it seems, by the word *sannidhi* (=nearness, proximity; and hence *sannidhātā*= one who ever attends upon the king).[6] The third conjugational *ubhayapadī* root *dhā* from which this word is derived means 'to put', 'to place', and the words like *nidhi* and *nidhāna* meaning a store, a treasury, are derived from this very root. From the functions also of the *sannidhātṛi* in the Arthaśāstra, it is clear that he was in charge of the Royal stores[7] and there-

1. *Vāstukapraśastavāstuni nāyaka-vardhakimauhūrtikāḥ skandhāvāraṃ vṛittaṃ dīrghaṃ caturaśraṃ vā, bhūmivaśena vā caturdvāraṃ shaṭpathaṃ navasaṃsthānam māpayeyuḥ*, Arthaśāstra, X 1.

2. *purastān-nāyakaḥ*, Arthaśāstra, X 2.

3. ......*senāṃ senāpati-nāyakau vyūheyātām*, —Arthaśāstra, X 5.

4. Arthaśāstra, V 3.

5. Arthaśāstra, X 3 and 5.

6. Kauṭilya's Arthaśāstra (Translated by R. Shamasastry), p. 63.

7. *Sannidhātā kośagṛiham paṇyagṛihaṃ koshṭhāgāraṃ kupyagṛiham āyudhāgāraṃ bandhanāgāraṃ ca kārayet*......
Bāhyamābhyantaraṃ cāyaṃ vidyādvarshaśatādapi,
Yathā pṛishṭo na sajjeta vyayaśeshaṃ ca darśayet, Arthaśāstra, II 5.
Also : *Sannidhātā kṛitāvasthamanyaiḥ kośapraveśyam pratigṛihṇāti*, Arthaśāstra, VIII 4.

fore, it is correct to call him the 'Minister of Treasury', as does Dr. Jayaswal. The Arthaśāstra mentions an officer *samāhartṛi* with extensive powers and numerous functions.[1] He was not only to collect the Royal revenue but also had the authority to spend government money for promotion of trade, agriculture and industry and such other projects as promised an increase in the king's income.[2] He enjoyed judicial powers and ran an intelligence department on a large scale.[3] Kauṭilya says that the *nāgaraka*, the city Superintendent, was a miniature of the *samāhartṛi*, discharging the same functions at the capital city which the latter did in the *janapada*.[4] Thus the *samāhartṛi* might have been the 'Provincial Governor'. The renderings of *samāhartṛi* as 'The Collector General' and 'the Minister of Revenue' by Doctors Shamasastry and Jayaswal respectively, are not happy, because they do not cover all his functions. The *pradeshṭṛi* was the first officer under the *samāhartṛi*. He was required to inspect the work of the village and district officers (*gopa* and *sthānika* respectively) and also to collect *bali*.[5] He also discharged some judicial functions, mainly on the criminal side.[6] Dr. Shamasastry has named him 'Commissioner' while Dr. Jayaswal has left him untranslated saying, 'his functions are not clearly known'.

The rendering of the term *praśāstṛi* is also not correct. Dr. Shamasastry translates this term as 'Magistrate' at one place, as 'Commander' at another and as 'Instructor' on the third.[7] Dr. Jayaswal seems to equate him with the 'Superintendent of Jails' of Govindarāja. Kauṭilya clearly associates

1. *Samāhartā durgaṃ rāshtraṃ khaniṃ setuṃ vanaṃ vrajaṃ vaṇikpathaṃ cāvekshetа*, Arthaśāstra, II 6.

2. *Evaṃ kuryāt samudayaṃ vṛiddhiṃ cāyasya darśayet,*
Hrāsaṃ vyayasya ca prājñas sādhayecca viparyayam. Ibid.

Also : *Samāhartā pūrvamarthanātmanaḥ kṛitvā paścādrājārthaṃ karoti, praṇāśayati vā parasvādāne ca svapratyayaścaratīti.* Ibid.

3. Ibid IV 4.

4. *Samāhartā janapadaṃ cintayedevam utthitaḥ.* Ibid. II 35.

Also : *Samāhartṛivannāgarako nagaraṃ cintayet,* Ibid. II 36.

5. *Gopa-sthānika sthāneshu pradeshṭāraḥ kāryakaraṇaṃ balipragrahaṃ ca kuryuḥ,* Arthaśāstra, II 35.

6. *Pradeshṭārastrayastrayo vāmātyāḥ kaṇṭakaśodhanaṃ kuryuḥ,* Ibid, IV 1.

7. Kauṭilya's Arthaśāstra (Translated by R. Shamasastry), pp. 23, 307 and 438 respectively.

him with the commissariat[1] and this seems to be his old function, because in the Rāmāyaṇa also, he is referred to in connection with the march of Bharata to Citrakūṭa.[2]

A comparison of the Arthaśāstra list with those of the three commentaries shows that the numbers one to six, the fourteenth (*karmāntika*), the seventeenth (*durgāntapāla*) and the eighteenth (*āṭavika*) are the same in both the enumerations.[3] Numbers nine (*sannidhātṛi*), twelve (*paura*), thirteen (*vyāvahārika*) and fifteen (*mantriparishadadhyaksha*) seem to have their parallels in the *dhanādhyaksha*, *nagarādhyaksha*, *dharmādhyaksha* and *sabhya* respectively of the commentaries. Number sixteen (*daṇḍapāla*) appears with the same designation in the list of the commentaries but there is wide divergence between the functions of the two. The rest of the functionaries in the Arthaśāstra list do not agree with those of the other lists.

Besides the above mentioned collective reference to the *tīrthas* in the *Kaccit sarga* of the Ayodhyā-Kāṇḍa, the Rāmāyaṇa mentions a number of officers,[4] some of whom correspond to the designations in the *tīrtha* list. Thus connected with the king's harem there are two titles—*antaḥpurādhyaksha*[5] and *stryadhyaksha*.[6] It is very much likely that it is one officer with two designations[7] agreeing with the *antarvaṃśika* or *antaḥpurādhikṛit* of the *tīrtha* lists. He was an old man wearing yellow robes, holding a staff in his hand as a mark of his office and having free access to the inner apartments of the king.[8] Connected with the royal household at Ayodhyā there are two more officers in the Rāmāyaṇa—one is the royal *vaidya*[9] and the other a tutor for the princes, who besides

1. *Purastādadhvanassamyak praśāstā grahaṇāni ca,*
Yāyādvardhakivishṭibhyām udakāni ca kārayet, Arthaśāstra, X 1.

2. R. II 104/42.

3. The order of these functionaries is, however, different in the different lists. For that see chart at the end of this chapter.

4. This is in addition to the Executive Heads (*amātyas* or *sacivas*) and the Counsellors (*mantrins*) who have already been treated earlier in this chapter.

5. R. VI 95/14.

6. R. II 17/3; R. VI 95/17.

7. The same *antaḥpurādhyakshas* of R. VI 95/14 are called *stry[illegible]hyakshas* in R. VI 95/17.

8. R. II 17/3. Cf. the *Kañcukin* of the Sanskrit plays.

9. R. II 13/10.

training them in the military science, taught them the Artha-śāstra.[1] The *kośādhyaksha*, the Chancellor of the Royal Exchequer, who has been described as *vyāpṛitaṃ vitta sañcaye*[2] and the *antapāla*[3] are the same as the *arthasañcayakṛit* or the *dhanādhyaksha* and the *ṛāshṭrāntapāla* respectively of the *tīrtha* lists of the Rāmāyaṇa commentaries. The *kośādhyakshas* were ordered by Daśaratha to follow Rāma in the forest with the treasury and to give rich robes and choice ornaments to Sītā which would suffice for her for fourteen years in the forests. The *antapālas* were summoned by Sugrīva to present themselves with their following at the capital within a week's time. The title *āraksha* also seems to apply to the *antapāla*.[4] In addition to the above, there are some military officers who will be treated in a subsequent chapter.

1. The *ācārya* Sudhanvā (R. II 114/9).
2. R. II 39/14 N.S.
3. R. IV 22/24.
4. (*Ārakshо me hatastāta*) R. III 31/40 N.S.

Note : *Ārakshо (a) ntapālaḥ*, Govindarāja.

Chapter XIX

SABHĀ

A state in the Vedic period was a small one, usually consisting of the capital and some villages. Though the institution of kingship had come into existence in this period, the popular element had not ceased to exercise its control in the task of administration. We hear frequently of the *Sabhā* and the *Samiti* in the *Saṃhitās* definitely having political rights of discussing and deciding matters of interest and concern for the village and town population. The importance of the *Samiti* can be understood from the fact that it could re-instate an exiled king and the latter earnestly prayed that "his *Samiti* for ever be in agreement with him."[1]

In the Rāmāyaṇa we do not find any reference to the *Samiti*,[2] but the word *Sabhā* is of frequent occurrence and has been employed in various senses. Vālmīki's *Sabhā* is a place of meeting for the king and his ministers;[3] it is a social club where perhaps people play and gossip;[4] it is the king's court where justice is meted out to the appellant;[5] and lastly it is an 'Assembly' which discusses important matters concerning the state.[6] In this last sense, the words *Saṃsad*[7] and *Parishad*[8]—sometimes also spelt as *Parshad*—have been used by Vālmīki as

1. *Dhruvāya te samitiḥ kalpatāmiha.*, Atharva Veda, VI 88/3.
2. The word *samiti* as part of the epithets for kings is, however, common. Thus in various passages Rāma, Bāli, Rāvaṇa and Indrajit are called *samitiñjaya* and *samitinandana* (R. IV 15/12; R. VI 79/11; R. VI 105/8; R. VII 36/8). But the word *samiti* in these passages means army' or 'war' and not an 'Assembly'. The word *samiti* also appears in R. VI 11/31 N.S. But there too, it does not convey a technical sense (vide Tilaka-Ṭīkā, *samitau samāgame*) ; the 'Assembly' is denoted there by the word *sabhā*.
3. *Sametya rājaguravaḥ sabhāmīyurdvijātayaḥ*, R. II 73/1.
4. *Nārājake janapade kārayanti narāḥ sabhāḥ*, R. II 73/13.
5. *Sabhā yathā Mahendrasya Varuṇasya Yamasya ca*, R. VII 61/5.
6. *Tena vibh·āj..tā tatra sā sabhāpi vyarājata*, R. II 5/22 (Also R. V 90/28)
7. *Mantraṃ jñātvā mayā proktaṃ vākyaṃ Rākshasasaṃsadi*, R. V 90/57.
8. *Tataḥ parishadaḥ sarvā āmantrya vasudhādhipaḥ*, R. II 4/1.

N.B. The word *parishad* (or *parshad*) is also employed in a general sense of 'the assembly of people' in R. VII 97/5.

synonyms of *Sabhā*. First, we shall take up the *Sabhā* in the sense of the 'Assembly', for it looks like the successor of both the Vedic *Sabhā* and the *Samiti*, though with powers very much attenuated.

The Sabhā at Ayodhyā

In the third canto of the Ayodhyā-Kāṇḍa, we find Daśaratha discussing with his ministers the question of appointing his eldest son, the virtuous Rāma, as his heir apparent.[1] On their agreeing to his proposal the king hastened to summon a meeting of the *Sabhā*[2] which he addressed in the following significant words : "Bearing the heavy burden of duty in the interests of the people I have now become old and fatigued. Therefore, with the permission of the honourable members, I wish for rest after installing, in the interests of the subjects, my worthy and eldest son, Rāma, as heir apparent."[3] The (representatives of the) subjects welcomed the proposal of the king and expressed gratification at the admirable qualities of Rāma which had endeared him to the subjects in general and to the people of the *Ābhyantara* and the *Bāhya* sections of the *Paura* and the *Jānapada* (bodies)[4] in particular. At this the king thanked the 'Assembly' and in their presence issued orders for the execution of their decision.[5] He also summoned Rāma before the 'Assembly' and after

1. R. II 3/35 ff.
2. R. II 3/52-53.
3. R. II 4/3-12.
4. R. II 4/13 ff. (Note 28-29).

Note : The account at this stage in the N.S. is slightly different from what we have noted above. There it is said that after the speech of Daśaratha the *brāhmaṇas* and the *balamukhyas* along with the *Paura-Jānapadas* conferred among themselves and then unanimously approved of the king's proposal. The king (in order to satisfy himself whether their decision was taken independently or due to a prejudice for himself) asked them to explain the grounds on which the decision had been taken by them. In reply they enumerated the various qualities of prince Rāma and stated that he was highly spoken of by the people of the *Ābhyantara* and the *Bāhya* sections of the *Paura* and the *Jānapada* bodies. (R. II 2/19-51 N.S.)

N.B. This account of Daśaratha asking the members to explain as to why they wished to appoint Rāma as *yuvarāja* when he himself was righteously governing the state appears in the N.W. also. But there it is slightly transposed; there it appears in course of the account of the ministerial council meeting and not of the General Assembly meeting. (R. II 3/41-51).

5. R. II 5/2-5 (Note the words : *teshāmevopaśṛiṇvatām* in 3).

communicating to him their decision he briefed him on the duties of an heir-apparent.[1]

An emergent meeting of this 'Assembly' appears to have been held again in canto ninety-two of the Ayodhyā-Kāṇḍa.[2] This meeting too was preceded by a meeting of the ministerial council; in fact, it was occasioned by the latter, for Bharata had declined to accept the kingdom offered to him by the ministers and had instead proposed to bring Rāma back from the forest.[3] In the absence of the king, this meeting of the 'Assembly' was summoned by Vasishṭha[4], the *de facto* Prime Minister. When all were assembled Vasishṭha again formally offered the kingdom to Bharata saying, "This kingdom, free from troubles, has been given over to you by your father and elder brother. Enjoy this kingdom consecrating yourself as king and assisted by the ministers."[5] Bharata criticised Vasishṭha for making an unrighteous proposal to him and re-iterated his resolve to offer the crown to Rāma whom he regarded as its only rightful claimant.[6] Bharata's stand was

1. R. II 5/8 ff.

2. Note : Due to the inadvertence of the early editors the account of this second 'Assembly' meeting has become split up into two parts. Canto 86 of the Ayodhyā-Kāṇḍa should immediately precede canto 92 with which it is directly connected; in the present setting it is congruous neither with what precedes i in the text nor with what follows it.

A comparison of this portion of the Ayodhyā Kāṇḍa with its counterpart in the N.S. also corroborates the fact that canto 86 in the N.W. has been dislocated from its original position. After describing the meeting between Bharata and Kauśalyā in canto 75 the N.S. takes up consecutively in canto‹ 76 to 78 the account of Daśaratha's cremation and other rites connected therewith. Canto 79 states that on the fourteenth day after Daśaratha's cremation the ministers headed by Vasishṭha requested Bharata to accept the kingdom; but the latter declined the offer. The following canto gives the account of the preparation of the *rāja-mārga* from Ayodhyā to the bank of the Ganges. Canto 81 refers to the preparation for the 'Assembly' meeting and canto 82 to the meeting itself.

All this account appears in cantos 84-92 in the N.W. and with the exception of canto 86 the rest of the material in the N.W. closely agrees with that in the N.S. The material of canto 86 of the N.W. appears in canto 81 of the N.S., i.e., after the meeting of the ministers with Bharata but before the meeting of the 'Assembly'. And this appears to be its correct location. Therefore, in the N.W. also canto 86 of the Ayodhyā-Kāṇḍa should appear after canto 91 but before canto 92.

N.B. For a similar dislocation in the cantos describing the *Sabhā* of the Rākshasas vide f. n. 1 on p. 344 infra.

3. R. II 90/4 ff.

4. R. II 86/8-11.

5. R. II 92/6.

6. R. II 92/9-20.

unanimously greeted by the 'Assembly' and their approval was formally announced by Vasishṭha.[1] Bharata felt very happy at this and assured the honourable members that he would try all measures to bring Rāma back from the forest (and to persuade him to accept the kingdom).[2] In the presence of all the members he directed Sumantra, the Royal *sūta*, to issue orders for the journey (to Rāma's hermitage).[3]

The above accounts make it clear that the Popular *Sabhā* was an important institution in the administration of Ayodhyā. These accounts also provide some valuable information concerning the constitution, function, status and working of the *Sabhā*.

The *Sabhā* consisted of 'Officials' and 'Non-officials'. The first group was constituted of the *mantrins* (i.e. the *brāhmaṇa* counsellors) and the *amātyas* or *sacivas* of the king.[4] The second group, namely, of Non-officials, on the other hand, consisted of the representatives of the people—The *Paura-Jānapadas* and the *Naigamas*—and tributary kings (i.e. the representatives of the nobility).

We have already dealt in the preceding chapter with the *mantrins* and the *amātyas* who constituted the group of official members of the *Sabhā*. As to the *Paura-Janapadas* who represented the people, it may be noted, that the term is a derivative compound from the words *pura* and *janapada* and ordinarily it means the inhabitants of the *pura* (capital town) and the *janapada* (the rest of the country). But as constituents of the *Sabhā* the *Paura-Jānapadas* appear to have been given a secondary sense which, though derived from the primary one just referred to, is in some way different and technical. In the Rāmāyaṇa, it is amply clear that there was a *Paura-Jānapada* body with its Inner (*Ābhyantara*) and Outer (*Bāhya*) circles and that its representatives had a right to sit in the

1. R. II 92/22-28.
2. R. II 93/2.
3. R. II 93/3-4.
4. According to the N.S. the *balamukhyas* seem to be the third constituent of the official section of the *Sabhā*. [*Brāhmaṇā balamukhyāśca Paura-Jānapadaiḥ saha, sametya te mantrayituṃ samatāgatabuddhayaḥ*, R. II 2/19-20 N.S.] These *balamukhyas* were senior officers of the army receiving due honour from the king. (Cf. R. II 114/42).

Popular *Sabhā* of Ayodhyā.[1] The existence of corporate organisations of traders and merchants in ancient India bearing the designation *Nigama* or (*Naigama*) is unambiguously proved from literary and epigraphical sources other than the Rāmāyaṇa also. Their heads were generally known as *Nigama-vṛiddhas* or *Nigama-mukhyas*. That in the Rāmāyaṇic period they enjoyed certain judicial powers is testified to by various references in the epic. They are also invariably associated with every coronation mentioned in the epic. In the second Assembly meeting summoned by Vasishṭha they are mentioned among the invitees along with *mantrins* and *anya-pradhāna-jana*.[2] This shows that the representatives of the *Nigamas* (or *Naigamas*) also formed a part of the Non-official group of the Popular *Sabhā* at Ayodhyā.[3] Lastly, the kings of various quarters attending the meeting of the *Sabhā*, summoned earlier by Daśaratha[4] and later by Vasishṭha[5], have to be regarded as the feudatories of the Ayodhyan kings. That feudatories constituted an important element of the *Sabhā* can be seen almost from the beginning of the ancient period of Indian history. Thus all the prominent interests in the state being represented in the 'Assembly' by their different representatives, it is obvious that the voice of the Popular *Sabhā* was regarded as the voice of the people as a whole, even though it is difficult to assess the amount of its responsibility to the people.

No doubt, the power of initiative in governmental work rested, as now, with the government, the king (or in his absence the Convener ?) summoned the meeting of the Popular *Sabhā* to ascertain the popular view with regard to measures vitally concerning the welfare of the state. Such measures were discussed beforehand by the king and his *sacivas*. Then, these were brought before the Popular *Sabhā*

1. For detailed discussion about the *Paura-Jānapadas* vide section (a) (The *Paura* and the *Jānapada*) in chapter XXI infra.

2. *Sumantraṃ Jaiminiṃ caiva Vāmadevaṃ Jayaṃ tathā,*
Mantriṇo Naigamāṃścānyān pradhānāṃśca tathā janā!, R. II 86/11.

3. For detailed discussion about the *Naigamas* vide section (b) (The *Nigama* or *Naigama*) in chapter XXI infra.

4. *Prācyodīcya pratīcyāśca dākshiṇātyāśca bhūmipāḥ,*
Mlecchāścānye subahavaḥ pārvatīyāśca saṅgatāḥ., R. II 3/55.

5. *Udīcyāśca pratīcyāśca dākshiṇātyāśca keralāḥ,*
Karṇadhārāśca sāmudrā ratnānyupaharanti te., R. II 92/7.

for discussion with a view to take this larger body into confidence. But the *Sabhā* did not merely approve or disapprove the government proposals; it also gave reasons for doing so. Whether the *Sabhā* was competent to make an alternative concrete proposal is uncertain.[1] The evidence in the Ayodhyā-Kāṇḍa indicates that generally it was assumed that the 'Popular Assembly' would agree to the well-considered proposal of the government. Daśaratha, for instance, had even before putting the matter before the *Sabhā* for its acceptance, sent out messengers inviting people to the ceremony of installing Rāma as *yuvarāja*. What he would have done if the *Sabhā* dissented from his view can be anybody's guess.

Sabhā at Laṅkā

The word *Sabhā* has also been employed by Vālmīki in connection with the meetings held at Laṅkā. Of these, the one in the Sundara-Kāṇḍa[2] stands distinctly separate from the rest in the sense that it was a large gathering summoned to make the momentous decision of making War or Peace with Rāma. Vālmīki furnishes a very graphic account of the entire proceedings which is of great significance for our study.

After the havoc wrought by Hanūmān in Laṅkā, Rāvaṇa summoned a meeting of his *Sabhā* and when all were assembled he said, "Hanūmān came and entered this town. This is the time for holding counsel. You deliberate upon what is beneficial......Rāma is coming followed by a huge Vānara host. So in this conflict with the Vānaras, you consider what is salutary for me and the town."[3] The Rākshasas flattered Rāvaṇa by recounting his feats and concluded by saying, "All these were killed by you in the battle single handed and hence you should rise (against Rāma and the Vānaras also)."[4]

1. The N.S. contains the following two verses :
Yadidam me(a) nurūpārtham mayā sādhu sumantritam,
Bhavanto me(a) numanyantāṃ kathaṃ vā karavāṇyaham.
Yadyapyeshō mama prītirhitamanyad vicintyatām,
Anyā madhyasthacintā tu vimardābhyadhikodayā. (R. II 2/15-16 N.S.)
These verses expressly state that the 'Assembly' had the power to uphold or reject the government's proposal and to sugggest an alternative measure.

2. R. V Cantos 77-90.

3. R. V 77/3-19.

4. R. V 78/1-17 (Note 15).

Prahasta, the Commander-in-chief, was slightly abashed at the devastation of Laṅkā by Hanūmān and confessed that it happened because they were negligent and over confident. But he assured the king that the story would not be allowed to repeat itself.[1] Some of the members wanted permission to march immediately against the enemy and destroy him.[2] When all were thus assuring Rāvaṇa of victory and were pleading for war against Rāma, Vibhīshaṇa, the *yuvarāja*, argued that an appeal to prowess (*vikrama*) should be made with regard to a business only when the end sought could not be attained through the other three means (viz., conciliation, gift and creating dissension). Moreover, prowess brought the desired result only when carefully directed against those (enemies) who were negligent, or in the hands of other enemies, or under divine affliction.[3] According to Vibhīshaṇa, Rāma belonged to none of these categories. On the other hand, he was strong and law-abiding. Hence, Vibhīshaṇa saw no gain in picking up a quarrel with Rāma. He was of the opinion that Maithilī should be returned to Rāma, for, otherwise, he apprehended total ruin for Laṅkā and the Rākshasas.[4]

Vibhīshaṇa's words gave a new turn to the deliberations.[5] Now there were two views before the *Sabhā* and therefore, Rāvaṇa tried to meet Vibhīshaṇa's arguments. He accused Rāma of unrighteousness, for to live in a forest with a lady luxuriously bedecked with ornaments was unprecedented and against all canons. Moreover, Rāma's perversion to all practices of *dharma* was evident from the fact that he carried arms in the forest and had destroyed a number of

1. R. V 79/3-5.

2. Note the statements of Durmukha, Vajradaṃshṭra, Yakshahanu and Kumbha in canto 79 of the Sundara-Kāṇḍa.

3. R. V 80/9-10.

It may incidentally be noted that Vibhīshaṇa's present pleadings present an interesting contrast to what he said earlier in R. V 48/13-16.

4. R. V 80/11-32.

5. *Vibhīshaṇa vacaḥ śrutvā dharmārthasahitaṃ tadā,*
Mantribhiḥ saha medhāvī mantrayāmāsa Rāvaṇaḥ, R. V 81/1.

Rākshasas.[1] Recognising the efficacy of deliberations Rāvaṇa requested the members to reconsider the matter coolly and arrive at a unanimous decision which, he assured, he would abide by.[2] At this, Prahasta, replying to Vibhīshaṇa, pointed out that Rāma, though weak, had adopted a threatening attitude against the Rākshasas by sending Hanūmān who was devoid of all qualifications of a *dūta*. In fitness of things, therefore, they had to take up the challenge.[3] Mahodara supported the view of Prahasta and added that they were in a more advantageous position than the enemy, for the hurdle of the sea was insurmountable and, besides, they occupied a fortified position. Moreover, he added, that the *niśā-yuddha* was positively going to bring them victory. He suggested, therefore, that the fort may be equipped with men, ammunition and provisions and that the way the army had to be deployed should be decided there and then.[4] Virūpāksha also favoured war and added in support that the Vānaras were by their very nature fickle and it was impossible for the unsteady to gain victory.[5]

Vibhīshaṇa tried to defend Rāma's action (viz., killing of Rākshasas) on the plea that he was strong and confident of his powers.[6] At this Indrajit felt that perhaps Vibhīshaṇa was frightened. Therefore to instil courage in him, he loudly boasted of the family traditions and particularly of his personal achievements.[7] This resulted in a brief row between Vibhīshaṇa and Indrajit and their respective supporters.[8] Vibhīshaṇa accused Rāvaṇa of rash and violent policies and persisted in his demand to return Sītā to Rāma.[9] At this point, Rāvaṇa intervened again in the debate, requesting a decision in favour of War and asking Vibhīshaṇa to join

1. R. V 81/18-19.
2. R. V 81/24-30.
3. R. V 82/10-20 (Note 12).
4. R. V 83/11-23.
5. R. V 84/5 ff.
6. R. V 85/11-12.
7. R. V 86/2-7
8. R. V 86/9-14 and R. V 87/1-20.
9. R. V 87/24-51.

Rāma if he so wished.[1] Vibhīshaṇa, however, persisted in criticising Rāvaṇa and the 'Assembly' and even announced his decision to join Rāma.[2] As a result, Vibhīshaṇa was banished from Laṅkā, but not by Rāvaṇa alone, for Prahasta communicated the decision to him in the words, "It is not possible for you to stay (here). You may go, wherever you please, for the king Rāvaṇa and the mighty Rakshasas are angry with you."[3]

The first point to be noted about the *Sabhā* described above is the large number of its members. This meeting was attended by *mantrins*, *amātyas*, friends and relations of the king[4] of whom twenty-nine individual names (besides Rāvaṇa) have been mentioned by Vālmīki. Of these Prahasta, Durmukha, Vajradaṃshṭra, Yakshahanu, Kumbha, Vibhīshaṇa, Indrajit, Mahodara, Virūpāksha, Mahāpārśva and Hara took active part in the discussion during the session. It is interesting also, to note that the personal *amātyas* (in this context, personal secretaries) of Vibhīshaṇa were not only present in this 'Assembly', but had also the liberty to speak in defence of their master.[5] It may further be noted that they left the 'Assembly' with Vibhīshaṇa though not expressly asked to do so by Rāvaṇa or Prahasta.

The Laṅkā state, as we have observed in an earlier chapter, was slightly different in her constitution from the Aryan states of the Rāmāyaṇa.[6] Naturally, her political institutions differed in character from the political institutions of the Aryan states. At Ayodhyā, the *Sabhā* was a relic of the more powerful *Samitis* and *Sabhās* of the Vedic period. But at Laṅkā, it was even then a powerful 'General Assembly' representative not only of various interests and classes of the society but, perhaps, also of families. When Rāvaṇa summoned the meeting of the *Sabhā*, his runners began to range Laṅkā; and going to every house, they fearlessly collected the Rākshasas from places

1. R. V 88/6-26 (Note 15 and 26).
2. R. V 89/2-21 (Note 16 and 19).
3. *Na śakyaṃ bhavatā sthātuṃ gaccha yā te gatirmatā, Kruddhaste Rāvaṇo rājā Rākshasāśca mahābalāḥ.*, R. V 90/63.
4. R. V 77/8.
5. R. V 87/18.
6. Vide p. 274 supra

of sport, bedrooms and gardens.[1] Then some Rākshasas set out for the meeting mounting cars, and some mounting proud coursers, and some others on foot.[2] On coming to the Assembly Hall, they touched the feet of the sovereign and being honoured by him in turn they occupied their seats—some sat on raised seats, some on cushions of *kuśa* and some on the floor.[3] Next came the *mantrins*, the *amātyas*, the army chiefs and the *yuvarāja* Vibhīshaṇa.[4] These were made to sit in order of merit by Prahasta and Śuka.[5]

As regards the procedure of the meetings, it should be observed as a contrast to the meeting of the *Sabhā* at Ayodhyā that Rāvaṇa had no previous consultation with his *sacivas* or *amātyas* on the matter to be placed before the *Sabhā*. He straight away called a meeting and explained to the members the occasion and the object of the meeting. He referred to three types of men and likewise three types of counsels : "The *purushottama* is he", Rāvaṇa remarked, "who confers with his *mantrins* or *amātyas* who are competent to make decisions and

1. *Rākshasāstadvacaḥ śrutvā Laṅkāyām paricakramuḥ,*
Anugeham avasthāya vihāraśayaneshu ca.
Udyāneshu ca Rakshāṃsi codayanto hyabhītavat., R. VI 11/19 N.S.

Note : There is a very elaborate account of the *Sabhā* of the Rākshasas in the Sundara-Kāṇḍa of the Lahore edition (N.W.). This account in the N.S. (Yuddha-Kāṇḍa) is incomplete, being broken at two places—in cantos 9 and 16. The cantos 6 to 17 in the N.S. have somehow lost their original order. Moreover, some portion which should have appeared after canto 16 (and before canto 17) seems to be missing. A comparison with the Lahore edition makes it amply clear that the account of the *Sabhā* preserved in two pieces in the N.S. (first in cantos 6-9 and next in 12-16) is, in fact, the account of one *Sabhā*-meeting held in Laṅkā. The canto 10 in the N.S. which gives the account of an informal advice given to Rāvaṇa by Vibhīshaṇa on his personal initiative, should actually appear before canto 6, i.e. before the account of the *Sabhā* actually begins. (It is so in the Lahore edition—V canto 76.) Canto 11 and the early verses of canto 12 in the N.S. which furnish valuable information regarding the procedure for calling a meeting of the *Sabhā* should also be placed at the beginning of Canto 6.

N.B. We have followed the Lahore edition in giving the account of the meeting of the *Sabhā* and the N.S. for the procedure and other details of the *Sabhā*.

2. R. VI 11/20 N.S.
3. R. VI 11/23 N.S.
4. R. VI 11/25-27 N.S
5. R. VI 11/28 N.S.

N.B. The varying status of the members of the *Sabhā* at Laṅkā is amply illustrated by the varying modes of their conveyances and also by the difference of their seats in the Assembly Hall. This incidentally also reflects the widely representative character of the *Sabhā* of the Rākshasas.

are interested in his well-being, and with his friends and relations. Duly reflecting upon a subject he proceeds to action, providing against providence. The *madhyama-nara* deliberates unaided but decides upon a righteous course and also proceeds unaided. The *adhama-nara*, however, reflects not upon the merits or demerits of the case but depends upon providence and is procrastinating.[1] Likewise, the *uttama-mantra* was that wherein the councillors, engaged in deliberations in accordance with the *śāstras*, arrived at a unanimous understanding. In the *madhyama-mantra* councillors, previously holding different opinions, agreed (unanimously) to a particular decision purely in consideration of the end to be achieved.[2] The *adhama-mantra* was that, where in the midst of differences and dissensions, the matter (under consideration) was completely lost sight of and there was not a whit of agreement."[3] The purpose of Rāvaṇa in referring to these principles was to bring home to his councillors the importance of a unanimous decision which was to be arrived at after due deliberations.[4]

It is to be appreciated that the discussion which ensued was free and frank. Every member freely expressed himself and whatever he said was duly supported by reasoning.[5] Only Vibhīshaṇa tried to carry his point without proper argument. Rāvaṇa pointed at this, saying, "Skipping over all doctrines of the *śāstras*, one who is wanting to win one's point merely by one's obstinacy—obviously, this is the mark of a fool."[6] But even he was not prevented from speaking until the king became convinced of his partisanship with the enemy.[7]

1. R. V 77/8-11.

2. The difference between the *uttama-mantra* and the *madhyamamantra* lies in the *śāstra-dṛishṭi*. The deliberation and the decision in the former have necessarily to be in accordance with the *śāstras*, but not so in the latter. Here, the ends justified the means.

3. R. V 77/13-15.

4. Cf. *Tasmāt sumantritaṃ kṛitvā bhavanto mantrisattamāḥ,*
Kāryaṃ ca pratipadyeta bhavet kṛityatamam mama., R. V 77/16.

5. Attention may be drawn to the fact that the Rākshasas were, as Hanūmān had remarked earlier, *bala-darpitā janāḥ* (R. V 38/3). Leaving therefore, the interception of Vibhīshaṇa whose motives were undoubtedly questionable, the tone of the entire meeting was in keeping with the character of the Rākshasas.

6. R. V 88/12.

7. R. V 90/30 ff. (Note 37).

Then, he was made to leave the hall through Prahasta, the Commander-in-chief and also perhaps the Convener of the Council. Worthy of remark is the fact that the first time when Vibhīshaṇa placed his point before the *Sabhā*, neither Rāvaṇa, nor any other member of the Council got angry with him. On the other hand Rāvaṇa, Prahasta, Mahodara and Virūpāksha tried to counteract Vibhīshaṇa's point and justify their own stand. Rāvaṇa, as a matter of fact, re-iterated his faith in the efficacy of 'Counsel' (*mantra*) and once again asked the Rākshasas to examine fully the point and arrive at a unanimous understanding.

As observed above this *Sabhā*-meeting is the only one of its nature held at Laṅkā. It is not possible to say anything about the status and rights of the *Sabhā*. All that we can infer on the basis of what has been said above is that at Laṅkā there was some sort of a 'General (National) Assembly', which was widely representative in character. Matters of vital concern for the state, such as the declaration of war, were discussed here. Members had full liberty to express themselves, though one could not press one's point without proper reasoning. The king was the 'President' of the 'Assembly'. We cannot say what would have been his position or of the 'Assembly' if the two did not see eye to eye with one another.

Sabhā as Ministerial Councils

In a restricted sense the word *Sabhā*, as already pointed out earlier, stood for ministerial councils also. There is reference in all to four such meetings of the ministerial council at Ayodhyā—one in the Bāla-Kāṇḍa and the rest in the Ayodhyā-Kāṇḍa. In the first of such meetings Daśaratha received the messengers of Janaka and decided to proceed to Mithilā to celebrate the marriage of prince Rāma with the daughter of Janaka[1]. The second meeting was a preliminary to the 'General Assembly' meeting and was called by Daśaratha to consult his ministers on the question of appointing Rāma as *yuvarāja*.[2] The rest of the two meetings, held after the death

1. R. I 64/2 ff. (Note verse 14 with f.n. 9)
2. R. II 3/35-51.

of Daśaratha, were of a special character in the sense that these were convened in the absence of the President, the king. In the first of these, held immediately after the death of Daśaratha, the *brāhmaṇa* councillors along with the *amātyas*, requested the royal *purohita* (and Prime Minister), Vasishṭha, to install a scion of the Ikshvāku family on the vacant throne, for otherwise they apprehended a state of anarchy all over the kingdom.[1] Vasishṭha suggested that Bharata be brought back from his maternal uncle's house (and be requested to accept the crown). The council having approved this suggestion, messengers were immediately sent to Girivraja.[2] The last meeting, held on the fourteenth day after the cremation of Daśaratha, was a follow-up of the preceding one, in the sense that in pursuance of the decision of the earlier meeting the ministers requested Bharata to accept the kingdom. Bharata, however, declined the offer on the ground that the installation of a younger brother on the throne while a virtuous elder one was living was against the tradition of the Ikshvāku family. He, therefore, announced his decision to go to the forest and persuade Rāma to become king. The council warmly welcomed the proposal of Bharata.[3]

At Laṅkā, the poet refers to six meetings of the ministerial council. In two of these[4] Rāvaṇa, in company with his *mantrins* and *sacivas*, received the envoys of Rāma (viz. Hanūmān and Aṅgada). The only interesting information supplied by Vālmīki in the account of one of these meetings is a point of Council etiquette, viz., Rāvaṇa did not address Hanūmān directly but talked to him through Prahasta,[5] perhaps the Secretary of the Council in the present context.

The rest of the four council meetings held at Laṅkā were meetings of the war-councils. Of these the first was held when Rāma's army had crossed the ocean and was preparing to lay siege.[6] Rāvaṇa reprimanded his *sacivas* for neglecting their

1. R. II 73/1 ff.
2. R. II 74/1 ff.
3. R. II 90/4 ff.
4. R. V Cantos 44-49 and R. VI 16/68-85.
5. R. V 46/2-3.
6. R. V canto 100.

duty; having decided upon 'War' (in the 'General Assembly' meeting held earlier) they had slept over the matter not caring even to appoint spies to gather information of the enemy movements.[1] The *sacivas* were ashamed for a moment but soon the same boastful attitude, so characteristic of the Rākshasas, asserted itself, and they started bragging by recounting the earlier achievements.[2] Dhūmrāksha suggested a surprise attack[3] which Mahodara rejected saying that such a tactic would have been proper if the enemy was on the other side of the ocean or was attempting to cross the ocean; but now it was too late. For the present, he advised that they should strengthen the defence of the town and prepare for a straight fight to score a victory.[4] An interesting thing to note about this meeting is the protest of Atikāya against the policy of war being pursued against Rāma. He criticised Rāvaṇa for forcibly seizing Sītā and keeping her a captive in Laṅkā. He also suggested that Sītā may be returned to Rāma after showing her due honour.[5] Unfortunately, since the canto has abruptly closed the account of the meeting is broken here.

The next meeting was held after Śuka and Sāraṇa, and Śārdūla and party—the spies appointed by Rāvaṇa—had brought information about the strength of the enemy and his chiefs of the army. No details of this meeting have been given by Vālmīki. There is just a reference that Rāvaṇa summoned his *mantrins* and after holding a brief meeting with them he entered the inner apartments.[6] The last two meetings appear to be emergent meetings. The first was probably called by Prahasta[7] and was attended by the queen-mother who along with *mantri-mukhya* Avindhya[8] and Mālyavān requested Rāvaṇa to release Sītā (and thus put an end to this hostility with Rāma).[9] The main business of this meeting perhaps was

1. R. V 100/5-11.
2. R. V 100/12-24
3. R. V 100/25-27.
4. R. V 100/28-31.
5. R. V 100/32-39.
6. R. VI 7/2-5.
7. R. VI 8/39-40.
8. R. VI 10/25-28.
9. R. VI 11/8 ff.

to take effective measures of defence of the town, for the enemy, it was reported, was just on the point of making a severe assault. Rāvaṇa appointed Prahasta in defence of the eastern gate; Mahāpārśva and Mahodara of the southern; Indrajit of the western; himself of the northern along with Śuka and Sāraṇa; and stationed Virūpāksha with many Rākshasas in the centre.[1] The next meeting also was an emergent meeting held after the death of Prahasta, the Commander-in-chief.[2] This was held at the instance of the queen who went to the *sabhā* (council hall) with Mālyavān, Yūpāksha and other ministers and made a last effort for putting an end to this hostility between Rāma and the Rākshasas.[3] She in her own name and in the name of the ministers who had come with her expressed disapproval of the confinement of Sītā[4] and suggested that some ministers be sent to return Sītā to Rāma and thus effect peace. She was of the opinion that in this matter the services of Vibhīshaṇa who was already there in Rāma's camp should be availed of.[5] Rāvaṇa turned down the proposal, declaring that he might break but would never bend. He, however, assured her of victory.[6]

Obviously, the above is an account of the war-councils of Rāvaṇa and hence they centre round only one subject—"War". Measures and counter-measures to be adopted against the enemy were decided upon and detailed in these councils. We would not be wrong to suppose that other matters of civil administration also were likewise considered in these ministerial councils. An interesting thing to note about these councils at Laṅkā is the presence of the queen and the queen-mother. They appear to be competent not only to attend the meeting of the *Sabhā* but even to summon a meeting. The presence of the queens in the *Sabhā* is to be noted at Kishkindhā also where in a fragmentary account of the only meeting of the ministers, they were present by the side of Sugrīva.[7] Perhaps this speaks of the status of women among the Rākshasas and

1. R. VI 12/16-21 (Note 16).
2. R. VI cantos 35-36.
3. R. VI 35/10-11.
4. R. VI 35/33.
5. R. VI 35/34-39.
6. R. VI 36/6-15.
7. R. IV 26/30.

N.B. Tārā on this occasion interceded for Sugrīva and cleverly pacified Lakshmaṇa (R. IV 28/1 ff.).

the Vānaras where they were not kept out of politics and political decisions. These *Sabhās* had obviously an advisory character.

To complete the list of war-councils we may also mention two such meetings held in Rāma's camp. The first was an emergent meeting called by Rāma on Vibhīshaṇa's arrival[1] and the second was held when Rāma followed by the Vānara host, having crossed the ocean, had reached the enemy territory.[2] The members attending the first meeting were, Rāma (President) and Lakshmaṇa, Sugrīva and his *sacivas*—the monkey chiefs, including Aṅgada, the *yuvarāja*. Vibhīshaṇa was added to the list in the second meeting. The object of the first meeting was slightly delicate—one from the enemy camp was offering to join the Vānara camp. Rāma asked the members to express themselves on the point, one by one, supporting their opinions with reasoning.[3] Sugrīva had already suspected the motives of Vibhīshaṇa and suggested his imprisonment.[4] Aṅgada was not clear in his mind; he was of the opinion that Vibhīshaṇa should be discarded if his company was risky and be received if he could be useful.[5] Śarabha, therefore, first wanted to ascertain the motives of Vibhīshaṇa through spies.[6] Jāmbavān outright opposed Vibhīshaṇa's acceptance, for he argued: one who was not loyal to one's own kith and kin could not be true to others.[7] Mainda recommended that Vibhīshaṇa be first interrogated and then from his tone and expressions his motives might be ascertained.[8] Last to speak was Hanūmān. He first of all rejected the previous suggestions showing that they were not practicable and concluded saying, "Considering well thy preparations for war and Rāvaṇa's vain conduct, and hearing of Bālī's destruction and Sugrīva's installation on the throne,

1. R. V 91/111-113 and cantos 92-93.
2. R. VI 13/1 ff.
3. R. V 92/5.
4. R. V 91/106-109.
5. R. V 92/11-15.
6. R. V 92/16-17.
7. R. V 92/18-19.
8. R. V 92/20-22.

he has, impelled by his good sense, come here, desirous of gaining the ground." "Moreover", Hanūmān pointed out, "the services of Vibhīshaṇa would prove of immense value in gaining our end, for no better information about the secrets of the enemy—of his fortification, strength of the army and other things—could be had than what a deserter like Vibhīshaṇa was capable of giving".[1] Rāma took the hint and upheld Hanūmān's proposal under the plea of granting *abhaya* to the refugee.[2] In the second meeting, plans of assault, military positions and some other details such as the pass-word were decided.

The accounts of these meetings in Ayodhyā and Laṅkā also provide us information on a few other matters connected with the *Sabhā* and the same we may note here.

The king was the *ex-officio* President of the *Sabhā* and in this capacity, he was perhaps known as *Netā*.[3] He had, it seems, a convener under him. The meeting of the *Sabhā* was summoned by the President though in the absence of the President or in a state of emergency (*ātyayika kṛitya*) the convener also could call a meeting of the *Sabhā*.[4] Runners (*dūtas*) were sent to invite and collect the members.[5]

The President was the first to arrive at the *Sabhā* (the council hall) and to occupy his seat.[6] The council hall was either attached to the palace (as was the case at Ayodhyā and perhaps also at Kishkindhā)[7] or it was a detached building situated at some distance from the royal palace (as at Laṅkā).[8]

1. R. V 92/27-44.
2. R. V 92/47-50; and R. V 93/17.
3. (*yatra netā ca guṇavān*) R. V 89/15.
Dr. Shyam Lal Pandeya in his Janatantravāda : Rāmāyaṇa aur Mahābhārata Kālīna, p. 111, calls the President of the *Sabhā* as *madhyastha*. He cites in support the following line from the Rāmāyaṇa :

Anyā madhyasthacintā tu vimardābhyadhikodayā (R. II 2/16 N.S.).

This is obviously a misunderstanding of the text. *Madhyastha-cintā* in the verse means 'dispassionate consideration' (—see Tilaka-Ṭīkā).

4. Vasishṭha called a meeting of the *Sabhā* after the death of king Daśaratha (R. II 92/1ff.). In a state of emergency Prahasta convened the meeting of the *Sabhā* (R. VI 8/39-40).
5. R. VI 11/17 N.S.
6. R. II 3/54; R. VI 11/23 N.S.
7. R. II 5/12; R. IV 26/24 ff.
8. Rāvaṇa had to drive in his car from his palace to attend the meeting of the *Sabhā* (R. VI 11/4 N.S.).

In the latter case the king proceeded to attend the meeting of the *Sabhā* in a luxurious car yoked with trained steeds. Officers fully equipped with arms went before him while some guarded his flanks and the rear. As he crossed on there arose the loud blare of trumpets and the uproarious sound of conches. People standing on either side of the highways joined their hands, bowed down their heads and uttered the words of blessings.[1]

The council hall (*sabhā*) was an imposing structure. The one at Laṅkā was paved with silver and gold; had its interior decorated with crystal; and was gracefully covered with silk embroidered with gold. It was guarded by six hundred *Piśācas*.[2] At Ayodhyā also the *sabhā* was built entirely of gold and appeared very charming and dazzling being set in gems.[3] Moreover, it was provided with galleries for the visitors[4] and was open in the front and on the sides.[5]

After the king was seated on his lofty and well decorated seat, there entered the other members.[6] They came gaudily dressed in silk and gold and entered with folded hands and bowed to the king.[7] They sat facing the king in order of their merit (*yathārha*), each according to his rank (*yathāmukhya* or *ānupūrvyā*).[8] In the *Sabhā* of Rāvaṇa there were two officers, Prahasta and Śuka, to look to the seating arrangements. They provided some with raised seats, and some with cushions, while some were made to sit on the floor.[9] The order of seats is also indirectly suggested by Vālmīki in connection with the reception accorded to Bharata and party by Bharadvāja. There, first sat the prince (i.e. the king), next to him the *purohita* and the *mantrins*, then the *senāpati* and lastly the *praśāstā*.[10]

1. R. VI 11/3-13 N.S.
2. R. VI 11/14-15 N.S.
3. R. II 86/9.
4. N.B. Even before the meeting of the *Sabhā* concluded, the friends of Rāma carried the happy news to Kauśalyā. (R. II 5/33).
5. Daśaratha could see Rāma coming on his chariot towards the *Sabhā* (the Council Hall)., R. II 5/12.
6. R. VI 11/16-17, 22 N.S.
7. R. VI 11/23, 29 N.S.
8. R. VI 11/24, 25, 28 N.S.
9. Ibid.
10. R. II 104/41-42.

When the members, known as *sabhāsadaḥ*[1] (or *sabhyas*) were seated, the convener who sat facing the king requested him to begin the proceedings.[2] The king then addressed the members in such terms of respect as *āryamiśrāḥ* or *bhavantaḥ*[3]. He explained to them the occasion of the meeting and placed before them the matter for their consideration. It was open to the king to express his own mind in the beginning or to reserve his opinion till others had expressed themselves.[4] Members were asked to speak one by one and to back their opinions with sound logic[5]. They were expected not to shout (but to speak in a mild regulated tone), nor to make a false statement[6], nor to speak for mere argumentation or being impelled by their skill in oratory, nor by the vanity of being gifted with a superior intellect, nor for self aggrandisement.[7] While deliberating upon a point the members were neither to be divided by difference of opinion, never coming at accord, nor to be in league with one another.[8] In short they were expected to be mindful of the *kārya-gaurava* and speak only in that light.[9] A member holding a different view from the rest and not prepared to agree with the views of the rest had the right to walk out—whether in protest, can not be determined.[10] On the other hand a member whose presence was considered undesirable for any reason by the council was made to leave the hall.[11] When all had expressed themselves the king announced the decision and invariably orders were issued to the executive officers (*amātyas* or *sacivas*) sitting in the council for the implementation of the decision.[12] The meeting was then adjourned.

1. R. II 92/21; R. VI 11/30 N.S.
2. R. VI 12/4-5 N.S.
3. R. II 3/45; R. II 93/2; R. VI 12/9 N.S.
4. Daśaratha expressed his feelings just in the beginning (R. 4/2 ff.) while Rāvaṇa first invited the opinion of his councillors. (R. V 77/19).
5. R. V 92/5.
6. R. VI 11/30 N.S.
7. R. V 92/25.
8. R. V 83/9.
9. R. V 92/25.
10. Vide Mālyavān in R. VI 12/14-15.
11. R. V 90/63.
12. E. g. R. II 5/3 ff.

Chapter XX

REVENUE AND JUDICIAL ADMINISTRATION

I

Ancient Indian political thinkers fully realised the importance of 'Finances' for the progress and security of the state. They recognised *kośa* as an important element of the body-politic[1] and according to one view in the Rāmāyaṇa *artha* was the most important in the *trivarga* (for a king), inasmuch as, *dharma* and *kāma* depended upon *artha* for their realisation.[2] Moreover, income and expenditure formed an indispensable part of a prince's education[3] and a king was advised to ponder in the last watch of the night every-day over the means of acquiring wealth.[4] In case of the ministers also 'replenishing the treasury' was an important qualification[5] and a wise king valued one able minister, who would help him to wade through a financial crisis much more than a motley crowd of fools.[6] In short, 'Finance' was one of the essential constituents of a kingdom; a kingdom devoid of *dhana* and *dhānya* was as worthless as *surā* bereft of its spirituous contents.[7]

The main source of filling the treasury was 'taxes',[8] which were considered as a sort of wages received by the king from his subjects in consideration of the protection granted by him to them. Collection of the taxes and protection of the people were inter-dependent; the one could not be justified without the other. Vālmīki says that the sin of that king was great, who took one sixth of his subjects' income (as taxes), but did not protect them as his own children.[9] The different *varṇas* living in the kingdom also tried, each in

1. Vide pp. 287-288 supra.
2. R. VI 61/40.
   Cf. *Artha eva pradhānaḥ iti Kauṭilyaḥ*, Arthaśāstra, I 7
3. R. II 1/26N.S.
4. R. II 114/12.
5. R. I 7/7.
6. R. II 114/17.
7. R. II 39/12.
8. The term for 'tax' in the Rāmāyaṇa is *bali.*, R. II 83/7.
9. Ibid.

its own way, to repay the protection and other benefits secured for them by the king. The *brāhamaṇas* contributed a part of their religious merit;[1] the *kshatriyas* served in the army; the *vaiśyas* surrendered a portion of their income; and the *śūdras* paid the royal dues in the form of manual labour (*vishṭi*).[2] Obviously the most substantial contribution to the state revenue was the one made by the *vaiśyas*, who, as we have seen in an earlier chapter, were engaged in the profit-making occupations of those times, viz., trade, agriculture and cattle-rearing.

Besides taxes, there were two more sources of state revenue, namely, fines realised from convicts[3] and gifts and tributes[4] received by the king on ceremonial occasions from his vassals, allies and subjects. These latter were known as *bali* (or *upahāra*)—*bali* in this case retaining the sense it had in an earlier period of our history, namely, of voluntary offering.[5]

The share of the king (realised by him as taxes) is stated everywhere in the Rāmāyaṇa to be one-sixth of the income of the subjects.[6] It is difficult to say whether this rule was rigidly and uniformly adhered to by the kings in that age or was just an ideal. It may not be unreasonable to presume that this rate (viz., one-sixth) was primarily applicable to agricultural produce, and that particularly in case of income from trade a higher rate was charged. It may further be added that in times of pecuniary hardships, for example, in a state

1. R. III 7/17.
Cf. *Tapaḥ shaḍbhāgamakshayyaṃ dadatyāraṇyakā hi naḥ.*
Abhijñāna Śākuntalam, II 13.

2. R. VI 127/6 N.S.

3. Sometimes a king could be tempted to fine an innocent person or let loose a thief for the sake of money. Such practices have, however, been condemned by Vālmīki., R. II 114/57-58.

4. R. II 92/7; R. IV 30/36.

5. Cf. "The term *bali*, originally used to denote voluntary offerings made to gods for securing their favour came to be applied later to the presents and taxes offered to the kings, more or less voluntarily."
Altekar, A.S., State and Govt. in Ancient India, p. 256.
It may be added, however, that by the time of the Rāmāyaṇa and even much earlier, the subjects had started making regular payments of taxes to the ruler.

6. *balishaḍbhāgam*, R. II 83/7; R. III 7/14.

of emergency caused by a war, a king must have been constrained to discover new methods of increasing his income. Unfortunately, the Rāmāyaṇa provides no information on these points.

The revenue was mostly collected in kind. Moreover, the articles received by the king as gifts consisted not only of gold, silver and other precious gems, but also horses, elephants, chariots, sheep and goats, various kinds of clothes and such other material.[1] Naturally, the Finance department required the services of several officers to fully discharge its responsibilities. We have already indicated that in the ministry there was an *artha-mantrī* who had under him officers like the *kośādhyakshas* and *dhanādhyakshas*.[2] Besides, the list of *tīrthas* mentions *samāhartṛi* (the collector-general) and *karmāntika* (superintendent of manufactories) also[3] who may have been associated with the 'Finance department'.

There is very meagre information in the Rāmāyaṇa regarding state expenditure. We do not know whether there was any system of 'budgeting' in Vālmīki's times. However, the principle that 'income should always exceed expenditure' was fully recognised.[4] A verse in the Ayodhyā-Kāṇḍa states in a very general way that a king should spend his wealth in the interest of the *Devas*, the *Pitṛis*, the *brāhmaṇas*, the guests, the warriors and the friends.[5] But the major portion of the state revenue was probably spent on the running of the administration (i.e. in making payments to the ministers and other state officers), the maintenance of the army (i.e. in disbursement of salary and ration to the army personnel and securing equipment for them)[6] and the royal household. We have noted earlier that the ministrant functions of the state were very few in that period. But in his own interest the king probably under-

1. R. VII 41/8-9.
2. Vide pp. 323 and 334 supra.
3. Vide the 'table' at the end of chapter XVIII supra.
4. *Āyaste vipulaḥ kaccit kaccitsvalpataraḥ vyayaḥ*, R. II 114/55.
5. R. II 114/56.
6. Rāma specifically instructed Bharata to be particular about the distribution of pay and rations to the soldiers, R. II 114/44.

took works conducive to the promotion of trade and agriculture. The Kosaladeśa, we are told, was provided with efficient system of irrigation so that the husbandmen had not to depend upon rain-water, and that it was *sphīta* (prosperous), presumably on that account.[1] The national highways also seem to have been maintained in good condition so that transport of men and goods was safe and easy.[2]

II

However cultured and advanced a society may be still on account of the various human limitations and weaknesses several types of disputes are bound to arise from time to time among its members. In order to prevent the law of the jungle from operating in such cases it is extremely desirable that there should be a central authority to protect the rights of the weak and the poor and to ensure justice for everyone in the society. In ancient India such an authority was vested in the king who was the one fountain of equity and justice for all alike. It may be recalled that the king was not the creator or maker of Law.[3] The Law, in fact, was enshrined in the Vedas and other scriptures, the ancient traditions and customs, and the practices of the good. The king was responsible only for its enforcement.

For the effective enforcement of Law there was invested in the king the authority to punish. Thus, like Yama, the divine chastiser, he was the supreme *daṇḍa-dhara* on earth.[4] This *daṇḍa* (i. e. the authority to punish) is extolled in the Rāmāyaṇa as the virtual protector of mankind[5] and it is emphasised that the king should not employ it arbitrarily or

1. R. II 100/45-46 N.S.
2. The Rāmāyaṇa describes a number of journeys :
 (i) Of Rāma from Ayodhyā to Śṛiṅgaverapura.
 (ii) Of Bharata from Kekaya to Ayodhyā.
 (iii) Of Daśaratha from Ayodhyā to Mithilā.
 (iv) Of Śatrughna and party from Ayodhyā to Mathurā.
3. It is, however, true that as a leading member of the society the king was expected to display exemplary behaviour and thus establish new standards which might subsequently become 'ideals' for others to follow. It is perhaps in this spirit that Rāma is described by Hanūmān in the Sundara-Kāṇḍa as *maryādānāñca lokasya kartā sthāpayitā vibhuḥ*, R. V 29/11.
4. *Yastu Yāmyo bhaved bhāgastena śāsati sa prajāḥ.*, R. VII 79/22. (Also R. III 4/17)
5. R. III 4/18.
Cf. *Daṇḍaḥ śāsti prajāḥ sarvā daṇḍa evābhirakshati,*
Daṇḍaḥ supteshu jāgarti daṇḍaṃ dharmaṃ vidurbudhāḥ.
Manusmṛiti, VII 18.

recklessly,[1] for the sufferings of those who were wrongfully punished (by the king) were sure to ruin the king along with his family and belongings.[2] As the guiding principles for a king in the exercise of *daṇḍa* and the administration of justice we may note the following :

(i) The wrong-doer must be punished—In the interest of peace and security in the state it was felt absolutely necessary that a wrong-doer must be punished.[3] Such a punishment was deemed to be conducive to the ultimate welfare of the wrong-doer also, for the belief of those times was that after undergoing punishment, awarded by the king, men were rendered pure, and that they became entitled to entry into heaven.[4] Moreover, by awarding due punishment to the offenders the king himself acquired merit and attained heaven.[5]

(ii) Impartiality—No justice is conceivable unless the king and his officers are guided by a staunch sense of impartiality. It was, therefore, necessary that in the administration of justice considerations of family relationship, of wealth or personal bias should not weigh upon the mind of the king and his officers. It is said about the ministers of Daśaratha that in the discharge of their duties they would punish their own sons, if found guilty, and that they would not cherish any evil even against an enemy if he was innocent.[6]

(iii) Thorough investigation—The king was not to hold *prima facie* a person guilty merely because a charge was levelled against him. In the interest of justice, it was necessary, that each individual case be fully investigated by the experts; and that the punishment be awarded only when the accused was found guilty.[7]

(iv) Lastly, the punishment was to be proportionate

1. *Daṇḍena ca prajā rakshan na ca daṇḍamakāraṇam*, R. VII 81/8.
2. R. II 114/60.
3. *daṇḍaścāpyapakārishu*, R. IV 16/58; R. V 82/9.
4. R. IV 14/19.
5. R. VII 81/9.
6. R. I 7/8.
7. R. II 114/57-58.

to the offence. This also implied that for the fault of one many could not be made to suffer.[1] In the forest, Lakshmaṇa reminded Rāma of this principle on several occasions and thus helped the latter to restrain his anger.

For the administration of justice, the king was required to appear everyday in the *Sabhā* (the court) and there, being seated on the seat of justice (known as the *dharmāsana*)[2] he was to grant audience to the *kāryārthīs* i.e. petitioners coming to the *Sabhā* with a cause (*kārya* or legal business).[3] As already indicated earlier, attending the *Sabhā* in the morning formed an important part of the daily routine of a king[4] and the evidence in the Uttara-Kāṇḍa reveals that a king failing in the discharge of this duty incurred sin and at the same time invited displeasure of his subjects.[5]

The *Sabhā* (meaning the court of law in the present context) was presided over by the king himself. It also included various other members known as *sabhyas*. It was their duty to assist the king in the administration of justice.[6] They may be termed the 'jury' of that ancient period. Thus the *Sabhā* of Rāma described in the Uttara-Kāṇḍa consisted of the Royal priest, Vasishṭha, learned *brāhmaṇas* competent to interpret sacred and secular law, *mantrīs* fully conversant with law, *kshatriya* counsellors who were experts in politics, and *Naigamas* (i.e. representatives of corporations of merchants).[7] No doubt, the decision in every case was taken by the king himself. But according to the nature of the case he must have consulted jointly or severally, the above-noted members who represented the different *varṇas* and interests of the society. About the king's *Sabhā* we may presume that it also served as the final Court of Appeal in the state.

The term for a legal dispute was *vyavahāra*.[8] On the

1. R. III 71/12.
2. *dharmāsanagato rājā*, R. VII 61/3.
3. *kāryārthinastu Saumitre vyāpārayitumarhasi*, R. VII 61/6.
4. Vide p. 308 supra.
5. R. VII 55/18.
6. R. VII 63/32.
7. R. VII 40/17-18; R. VII 61/4-5.
8. A legal dispute is termed *vyavahāra* in the Smṛitis (Manusmṛiti, VIII 1). In the Rāmāyaṇa also this term is found employed in a few cases. Thus one of the qualifications of a minister was that he should be a *vyavahārajña* (R. VII 61/4). In R. I 12/21 (*vyavahāreshu te dharmaḥ kartavyo hṛidi nityaśaḥ*) it is clearly employed in this technical sense.

basis of the evidence available in the Rāmāyaṇa it is difficult to state whether a distinction between the civil and the criminal cases was distinctly realised in that period or not. However, it is clear that the Rāmāyaṇic society recognised certain crimes[1] in which it was felt to be the duty of the king to punish the culprits. Thus treason[2], incest[3], polluting one's preceptor's bed[4], abduction of others' wives[5], murder (especially of a *brāhmaṇa*)[6], killing of a cow[7], unlawful seizure of another's property[8] and theft[9] were some of the serious crimes. As a general rule punishments for offences were severe. Not only heavy fines[10], physical torture[11] and solitary confinement were common;[12] but even for such offences as theft capital punishment was awarded.[13] In certain cases the culprit was taken round the city with beating of the drum so that his case served as an eye-opener to the people.[14] The spirit behind these punishments was that they should serve as powerful deterrents for the people against committing offences. We are expressly told about Rāma's rule in the Uttara-Kāṇḍa that for fear of the *rāja-daṇḍa* everyone abided by the bounds

1. Sometimes the same act is declared as an *aparādha* as well as a *pāpa*. It may be pointed out in this connection that viewed from the point of view of religion or righteousness a particular act was to be considered a *pāpa* (sin); the punishment for which was some sort of torture in *Naraka* (hell). From the point of view of law the same act was an offence or a crime and for this the person had to suffer punishment at the hands of the king.

2. R. II 83/8; (*rājahā*) R. IV 13/15.

3. R. IV 18/22-23 N.S.

4. *yatpāpaṃ gurutalpage*, R. II 83/6.

5. *kaccinna paradārān sa mama bhrātābhyapadyata*, R. II 78/47.

6. (*brahmahā*) R. IV 13/15.

7. (*goghnaḥ*) R. IV 13/15.

8. R. II 78/45-46; R. V 100/34.

9. R. II 114/58; R. V 22/7.

10. R. II 114/57-58.

11. R. V 26/10 N.S.

12. *saṃyatā bandhaneshu*, R. IV 7/7.

13. R.V 22/7. (Executions, it seems, were carried out in the mornings.)

Incidentally, it may also be pointed out that capital punishment for theft was perhaps the rule in Kālidāsa's times also. Vide Abhijñāna Śākuntalam, Act VI, *Praveśaka*.

14. R. V 49/5, 17.

of righteousness[1] so that Rāma's *Sabhā* had not much work to do.

About the procedure of trial there is a faint indication in a verse of Ayodhyā-Kāṇḍa. According to it, it seems, an accused was first taken into custody (*gṛihītaḥ*) by the royal officers. Next, an investigation was carried on with regard to the charge (*pṛishṭaḥ*), in course of which the accused was interrogated and the available evidence on the point was recorded.[2] Last of all the decision was announced and executed—if the accused was found guilty (*sakāraṇaḥ*) he was awarded punishment, and in case the guilt could not be proved against him, he was acquitted.[3] As already indicated the king's responsibility was very great in this regard, for gross demerit was to result for him in case the wrong-doer succeeded in evading punishment or the innocent unlawfully suffered.[4]

1. R. VII 61/12.
2. 'Witnesses' were also known in that period. It was expected of them that they will base their evidence on truth, and not on personal considerations., R. II 83/13.
3. R. II 114/58.
4. R. II 114/57-58.

CHAPTER XXI

LOCAL ADMINISTRATION

A country in Vālmīki's times was variously known as *deśa*[1], *janapada*,[2] *rāshṭra*,[3] *vishaya*[4], and *rājya*[5]. It usually comprised of two parts, viz., the metropolis and the rest of the country. Vālmīki generally alludes to such a division by employing the term *pura* for the capital and *rāshṭra*, *janapada* or *vishaya* for the rest[6]. Since the capital was the seat of government and also the military headquarters it was invariably fortified and also known as *rājadhānī*[7] and *durga*.[8] The rest of the country was generally further divided into different units of varying character and extent. Thus small villages (hamlets) were known as *saṃvāsas*[9], pastoral villages as *ghoshas*[10], agricultural villages as *grāmas*[11], commercial ports as *pattanas*[12] and towns as *nagaras*.[13]

Substantial information with regard to local administration in the different units of the country just alluded to above is very meagre in the Rāmāyaṇa—in fact, it is non-

1. *Pāñcāladeśān*, R. II 74/11.
2. *Kosalo nāma muditaḥ sphīto janapado mahān*, R. I 5/1.
3. *hṛitasāramidaṃ rāshṭram*, R. II 39/12.
4. *amitravishayam prāptāḥ*, R. VI 13/2.
5. *Rājya*, it may be noted, was a political unit.
6. (i) *nāsīt pure vā rāshṭre vā......*, R. I 7/14.
   (ii) *......pure janapade cāpi nirvṛitiśca bhavishyati*, R. VII 72/6.
   (iii) *......vishaye vā pure vāpi......*, R. IV 13/11.
7. *rājadhānīm piturmama*, R. II 52/20.
8. R. V 68/5.

All the principal capital towns described in the Rāmāyaṇa (viz. Ayodhyā, Mithilā, Kishkindhā and Laṅkā) were forts.

9. *grāmasaṃvāsavāsinām*, R. II 50/6.

(Vide Tilaka-Ṭīkā—*grāmāḥ mahāntaḥ saṃvāsāḥ svalpagrāmāḥ*.

10. R. II 94/26.
11. Ibid.
12. R. IV 38/21.
13. The conception of a country, of course, included hills and forests also, but these we have not mentioned above, for these are not significant from the point of local administration.

existent. We are casually given to understand that the capital of the Kosaladeśa, viz. Ayodhyā was connected by road with the Aṅga-deśa[1], Mithilā[2], Girivraja[3], Śṛiṅgaverapura[4] and Mathurā[5], and that these roads were maintained in fairly good condition so as to make possible a chariot-ride. In the description of the town Ayodhyā we are also told that the *rāja-mārga* was daily swept and sprinkled with water.[6] A few passages also seem to suggest some arrangement for lighting on the streets[7] and water supply in the town.[8] On a few occasions we are further told that at the behest of the ruler the town—invariably the reference is to the metropolis—was gorgeously decorated to celebrate a royal wedding[9] or a royal coronation[10], or to accord a royal reception to a dignitary.[11] Lastly, references to public parks and public buildings[12] in the towns and the descriptions of the towns themselves[13], strongly suggest that notions regarding town-planning existed in that period. All these facts lead one to believe that some sort of municipal administration did exist in that period. However, as already indicated above, there is nothing in the Rāmāyaṇa to shed clear light on the character or extent of such administration. The term *paura-kārya* is sometimes understood as referring to municipal administration.[14] But as we know, this term has a comprehensive connotation, being applicable to every sort of 'public business', and in the Rāmāyaṇa it very often stands for 'legal business'[15].

1. Vide Daśaratha's journey from Ayodhyā to the Aṅgadeśa, R.I 9/15-17.
2. Vide Daśaratha's journey from Ayodhyā to Mithilā, R. I 65/6-7.
3. Vide the journey of the *dūtas* from Ayodhyā to the Kekayadeśa, R. II 74/11-16; R. II 77/1 ff.
4. Vide the account of Rāma's journey, R. II cantos 47-50.
5. Note Śatrughna's expedition against Lavaṇa, R. VII cantos 68-71
6. R. I 5/4, R. II 7/18.
7. R. II 8/18.
8. *varānnapānasalilām*, R. I 5/16.
9. R. I 72/6-7.
10. R. II 8/9-19.
11. R. I 9/30-32.
12. R. I 5/10, R. II 73/13.
13. Note the description of Ayodhyā in R. I 5/2 ff.
14. Dharma, P.C., Rāmāyaṇa Polity, p. 67.
15. R. VII 55/4 ff.

In the passage of the Ayodhyā-Kāṇḍa where Rāma is said to have attended to *paura-kārya* at the behest of his father, Daśaratha[1], there is nothing to show conclusively that it refers to municipal administration and not legal administration. It may also be pointed out in this connection that in various contexts there occur in the Rāmāyaṇa certain terms such as the *Paura* and the *Jānapada*, the *Śreṇi*, the *Nigama* (or *Naigama*), the *Gaṇa* etc. We know on the testimony of literary and epigraphical evidence that in ancient India there were corporate organisations bearing these titles and that in their own way they also participated in the task of local administration. It may be deemed desirable, therefore, to examine here these terms and to make an attempt towards ascertaining their connotation.

(a) The Paura and the Jānapada

In the Vedic times, the *Samiti* was a very popular institution occupying an important place in the political life of those times. Towards the close of the Vedic period, however, as the tribal basis yielded its place to the territorial one—to the formation of states—and as a consequence, when large monarchies or empires came into being the functioning of the *Samitis* became well-nigh impossible. Dr. Jayaswal is, however, of the opinion that even in the subsequent period the *Samitis* did not completely disappear from the political life of the country; in fact, they were incarnated in the form of another institution, viz., the *Paura-Jānapada.*[2]

The word *paura-jānapada* is a compound formed of two components, namely, the *paura* and the *jānapada*, which are derivatives from *pura* (meaning the capital) and *janapada*

1. R. II 3/2-4 (Note the reading of verse 4 as given in f.n. 7).

It is to be noted that the *Naigamas* felt very happy with Rāma's discharge of *paura-kārya*. It will be shown in the following pages that the *Naigamas* exercised certain judicial powers and that in matters concerning the *Nigama* (or *Naigama*) they had a right to be consulted by the king (or his nominee). This also corroborates the view that the *paura-kārya* was legal business and not municipal business.

2. Jayaswal, KP., Hindu Polity, p. 239.

(meaning the whole area of a kingdom minus the capital) respectively. Of these the former (viz. *paura*) may stand for 'an inhabitant of a *pura*' or 'a member of the *Paura* institution', and likewise the latter (viz. *jānapada*) may denote 'an inhabitant of a *janapada*' or 'a member of the *Jānapada* institution'. The mediaeval commentators being completely ignorant of such institutions always render the terms *Paura* and *Jānapada* (or the collective term *Paura-Jānapada*) as the people inhabiting the (capital) town (*pura*) and the (rest of the) country (*janapada*). No doubt, the use of the term (*Paura-Jānapada*) in the plural does not preclude in any way the possibility of its denoting the technical sense (viz. the members of the *Paura* and *Jānapada* institutions). Still, its significance is fully established from those passages where it occurs in the singular, not in the sense of one man but in the collective sense. Dr. K.P. Jayaswal cites in this connection a passage from the Ayodhyā-Kāṇḍa of the Rāmāyaṇa in which the *Paura-Jānapadas* i.e. members of the *Paura* and the *Jānapada* institutions have been mentioned along with the *Naigamas* as waiting respectfully at the royal gate for Rāma's consecration as crown prince.[1] From another passage of the same Kāṇḍa of the Rāmāyaṇa Dr. Jayaswal further opines that the *Paura* and the *Jānapada* institutions consisted each of two sections, the Inner (*Ābhyantara*) and the Outer (*Bāhya*).[2] The Outer (*Bāhya*) *Paura* was perhaps constituted of the representatives of the various corporations in the capital, while the *Jānapada-Bāhya* was not one collective body but a collection of scattered units, viz., the corporations of the *grāmas*, *ghoshas*, *nagaras* and *pattanas*. The Inner *Paura* and *Jānapada* was perhaps a joint body constituted of the various Presidents (*mahattaras*) of the *Bāhya-Jānapadas* and the selected members (the Elders or *vṛiddhas*) of the *Bāhya-Paura*. This joint character of the Inner Council which was the executive council and which had a permanent seat in the metropolis perhaps explains the tendency of the poets to employ the term *Paura-Jānapada* collectively and in the singular.

1. Hindu Polity, p. 240.
2. Ibid., p. 247.

According to Dr. Jayaswal,[1] the references to the *Jānapadas* and the *Deśa-saṅghas* in the Dharma-Sūtras and the Artha-śāstra, the copious references to the *Paura-Jānapadas* in the works of classical Sanskrit writers, the reference to the *Jānapadas* in Khāravela's inscription and above all the discovery of the *Jānapada* seals at Nālandā are conclusive testimonies to the existence of the *Paura-Jānapada* institution in ancient India.

Dr. Jayaswal further identifies the description of the municipal government noticed by Megasthenes at Pāṭaliputra with the *Paura* organisation and derives a detailed account of the municipal functions discharged by it. He dwells more upon the political functions of the *Paura-Jānapada* which may succintly be noted below :

1. They had a say in the matter of the nomination of the Crown Prince.
2. They could depose an unlawful ruler.
3. They could compel a king to remove a minister or senior state officer on the charge of mal-administration.
4. They were approached and begged by the king for a new tax.
5. They could demand and get industrial, commercial and financial privileges for the country.

The above theory of Dr. Jayaswal has been very vehemently criticised by reputed authorities like Doctors N.N. Law[2] and A.S. Altekar.[3] For various reasons it is not possible for us to re-open the question here in its entirety. Nevertheless, we deem it necessary to examine the position in so far as it pertains to the evidence contained in the Rāmāyaṇa.

At the very outset it must be conceded without the least of hesitation that there are a number ef passages in the Rāmāyaṇa in which the word *paura-jānapada* may be

1. For Dr. Jayaswal's *Paura-Jānapada* Theory vide Hindu Polity, part II, chapters XXVII and XXVIII.

2. Vide Law, N.N., (his article) 'The *Jānapada* and the *Paura*' in the Historical Quarterly Vol. II, Nos. 2 and 3 of July and September, 1926 respectively.

3. State and Govt. in Ancient India, pp. 136-146.

clearly taken to denote the people of the town and the realm.[1] The doubt is, however, raised by the most of the passages of the Ayodhyā-Kāṇḍa which seem to indicate a technical character of the term *Paura-Jānapada*. Such references may be noted below for benefit of perusal :

1. The *Paura-Jānapadas* are seen to be present in the 'General Assembly' of the Kosala-deśa which was summoned by Daśaratha to consider the question of Rāma's selection as *yuvarāja*. What is noteworthy in this connection is that the *Jānapadas* are described here as having their (permanent) quarters in the metropolis.[2]
2. Among the qualifications of Rāma considered worthy for his selection as *yuvarāja*, one note-worthy was that the *Ābhyantara* and the *Bāhya Paura-Jānapada* people in the capital and the country spoke highly of the prince.[3]
3. When the resolution was unanimously adopted the *Paura-Jānapadas* (referred to here only by the term *Paurāḥ*) repaired to their homes and feeling extremely delighted offered worship to the gods.[4]
4. On the coronation day the *Paura-Jānapadas* are seen respectfully waiting at the royal gate along with the members of another corporate body, viz. the *Naigamas*.[5]
5. In course of his enquiries about the welfare of Bharata and his kingdom, Rāma refers to the *Paura-Jānapadas* saying, "Do the *brāhmaṇas* versed in all religious lore, together with the *Paura-Jānapadas* wish for thy happiness, O highly wise one."[6]
6. The *Paura-Jānapadas* are seen to be present at the Citrakūṭa meet also Bharata actually requested them to press upon Rāma the desirability of his returning to Ayodhyā.[7] They, however, expressed their inability to do anything in the matter, for they found that Rāma's stand was firmly

1. R. II 118/11; R. VII 40/22; R. VII 45/5.
2. ...*purālayairjānapadaiśca mānavaiḥ*, R. II 3/65.
3. R. II 4/29.
4. *Te cāpi paurāḥ nṛipatervacastacchrutvā tato lābhamanantamāpuḥ,*
Narendramāmantrya gṛihāṇi gatvā devān samānarcuratīvahṛis hṭāḥ., R. II 5/36.
5. *Paura-jānapadaśreṇī naigamaścāgato janaḥ*, R. II 16/27.
6. *Kaccitte brāhmaṇāḥ sarve dharmakāmārthakovidāḥ,*
Na śocanti mahāprājñāḥ paurajānapadaiḥ saha., R. II 114/65.
7. *Āsīnastveva Bharataḥ paurajānapadañjanam,*
Uvāca sarvān samprekshya kimāryaṃ nānuyācatha, R. II 124/18.
(N.B. N.S. reads *nānuśāsatha* for *nānuyācatha.*, R. II 111/19 N.S.).

rooted in righteousness.[1] Rāma invited the attention of Bharata to the words of the *Paura-Jānapadas* and referred to them as 'having morality for their vision.'[2] Rāma again looked to them for support while rejecting the offer of Bharata to live in the forest for fourteen years in place of his elder brother.[3]

The opponents of Dr. Jayaswal maintain that all these references to the *Paura-Jānapadas* in the Rāmāyaṇa stand for 'the townsmen and the countrymen' and not for the members of any corporate bodies like the *Paura* and the *Jānapada.* We may note below their principal objections and also incidentally examine their validity.

With regard to the references to the *Paura-Jānapadas* in the *Sabhā* of Daśaratha, Dr. N.N. Law seems to have the following three objections:[4]

1. The gathering included not merely the *Pauras* and the *Jānapadas* but also the rulers of various kingdoms and the subjects of various territories. The gathering was thus extremely motley and the *Pauras* and the *Jānapadas* are by no means given a very prominent place in the *śloka* in the Rāmāyaṇa in which the presence of the different classes of people is mentioned.
2. The *Paura-Jānapadas* meet in the 'Assembly' in response to an invitation sent by king Daśaratha and not in answer to a notice formally issued by a convener associated with either or both of the supposed *Paura* and *Jānapada* bodies.
3. The decision about making Rāma his heir-apparent was already taken by Daśaratha in consultation with his ministers. The object of calling the people at large to his court was to make an announcement of his decision before them and to ascertain whether it met with their assent.

1. *Te tamūcurmahātmānam paurajānapadā janāḥ....*
Ato na śaknumo hyenaṃ vivartayitum ojasā, R. II 124/19-20.
2. ......*etannibodha vacanaṃ sarveshāṃ dharma cakshushām.*, R. II 124/21. (N.S. reads *suhṛidām* for *sarveshām,* R. II 111/22 N.S.)
N.B. Perhaps the *suhṛidas* mentioned in R. II 59/18 N.S. are these very *Paura-Jānapadas.*)
3. *Uvāca Rāmaḥ samprekshya paurajānapadañ janam,* R. II 124/26.
4. The *Jānapada* and the *Paura* (H.Q. Vol. II, 1926) p. 638.

It may be pointed out in this connection that Dr. Law seems to refuse to grant any constitutional position to the *Sabhā* referred to in the opening cantos of the Ayodhyā-Kāṇḍa. We have shown earlier[1] that there did exist a popular *Sabhā* in Ayodhyā with a representative character and competent to discuss vital matters concerning the state (like the appointment of a successor to the ruler). We had also shown that it was a matter of procedural detail that the king, the *ex-officio* President of the *Sabhā*, before bringing any resolution before it, discussed the same with his cabinet. We may add that such a practice continues to obtain even in modern times in countries having a parliamentary rule. Further, the presence of other sections (like the kings or subjects of other territories)[2] in the *Sabhā* only indicates its widely representative character. We fail to understand what bearing this point can have upon the existence or otherwise of the *Paura* and the *Jānapada* institutions in that period. Even with a relatively subsidiary or an inferior status the *Paura-Jānapadas* can equally be the common townsmen and countrymen or the members of the *Paura-Jānapada* body. Equally fallacious is the objection, namely, the members of the *Paura-Jānapada* were summoned by the king and not the convener of such body (or bodies). For, this point, if rigidly pursued, will reflect upon the political rights of the *Paura Jānapada* members, indicating that on the occasion of a meeting of the *Sabhā* they were directly invited by the President. We may incidentally add that to seek such details in a *kāvya* will generally prove misleading. We definitely know, for example, that there was a corporate organisation of merchants with the designation *Nigama* (or *Naigama*). Nowhere in the Rāmāyaṇa

1. Vide the chapter on *Sabhā*, pp. 336-340 supra.

2. It may be pointed out that Dr. Law's rendering of *pṛithagjānapadānapi* as subjects of other territories is misleading. The verse reads:

Nānānagaravāstavyān pṛithagjānapadānapi,
Samānināya medinyām pradhānān pṛithivīpatiḥ., R. II 1/46 N.S.

The correct meaning of this expression is "his Governors in various towns" (Vide Tilaka-Ṭīkā—*nānānagaravāsinas tatrādhikṛitān bhinna bhinna janapadasvāminaśca.*)

a notice is served to its members by any conevner of such organisation to present themselves at the coronation ceremonies of a prince, and yet, we find the *Naigamas* almost invariably present in every coronation described in the Rāmāyaṇa.[1]

Arguing almost on the same lines as Dr. N.N. Law, Dr. A.S. Altekar also states that even if it be assumed that the term *Paura-Jānapada* in the Rāmāyaṇa denoted a constitutional body of citizens it is clear that it wielded no effective powers; it could neither veto Daśaratha's plan to banish Rāma nor induce the latter to return home as desired by them.[2] Dr. Altekar fails to appreciate the fact that in the period of the Rāmāyaṇa *dharma* was a very powerful force restraining the caprices of the ruler and the ruled alike. Leaving aside for a moment the powers and wishes of the *Paura Jānapadas* we may remember that king Daśaratha whose powers cannot be the least doubted in this respect and whose wishes are also no secret, found himself utterly helpless in stopping Rāma from going to the forest, only because, now, it had become a question of adherence to *dharma*, which was everyone's paramount concern in that period.[3]

Dr. Altekar also points out that the term *Paura-Jānapada* is generally used in the plural, sometimes in the singular, but never in the dual. He wonders, why the *Paura* and the *Jānapada* if they really constituted two houses of Parliament should never have been referred to in the dual.[4] We have noted earlier that according to Dr. Jayaswal there were two sections, *Bāhya* and *Ābhyantara*, of the *Paura* and the *Jānapada* bodies, and also that the *Bāhya* sections of the *Jānapada* were many (—there being perhaps independent corporate bodies in the *grāmas*, *ghoshas*, *nagaras* and *pattanas*). The Inner sections of the *Paura* and the *Jānapada*, having their permanent seat in the capital invariably worked jointly; and being a collective body they are, therefore, either referred to in the plural or in the singular. We may add here that neither Dr. Law nor Dr. Altekar has taken pains to explain the use in the

1. Vide p. 375 infra.
2. State and Govt. in Ancient India, p. 138.
3. Note the words of the *Paura-Jānapadas* in R. II 124/20.
4. State and Govt. in Ancient India, p. 137.

singular of the term *Paura-Jānapadam* which according to Dr. Jayaswal is a conclusive evidence to show that it refers to the members—not one person—of a Corporate Body. Nor do the above scholars try to offer any satisfactory explanation for the expression *purālayaiḥ-jānapadaiḥ*. (Why are the *Jānapadas* (the countrymen) said to have had permanent quarters in the metropolis?)

The last contention of Dr. Jayaswal's opponents is that the terms *vṛiddhas*, *mukhyas*, *śreshṭhas* and *mahattaras* convey no technical sense; and that they do not refer to the Presidents or Aldermen of the corporate bodies. According to them, these terms should be understood to denote their primary sense of an elder, chief, and pre-eminent.[1] It may be pointed out that this objection is no longer tenable. The cumulative evidence of the Pāli canonical works, the Dharma-śāstras and various inscriptions has fully established that such terms more often than not stood for the Heads of various corporate bodies.[2]

It may be added in this connection that following Dr. Jayaswal, Dr. P.C. Dharma opines that the terms *grāam* and *ghosha* occurring in the Rāmāyaṇa might refer to the territorial units villages, or the political units, the village organisations. She further states that the Outer section of the *Jānapada* which was the collective name for the local corporations of the villages and the corporations of the provincial towns looked after the local interests, mainly municipal and economical. The local municipal administration of the metropolis, according to her, was managed by the *Paura* with its municipal councillors or *śreṇi-mukhyas* and its presidents.[3] All this, we may state, is at best a suggestion, for there is no internal evidence in the Rāmāyaṇa to support it. For our part, it is, no doubt, true that the references in the Rāmāyaṇa seem to indicate that in the times of Vālmīki there was a twin *Paura-Jānapada* body with Outer and Inner sections having political rights to participate in the delibera-

1. Dr. Law, N.N., The *Jānapada* and the *Paura* (H.Q. Vol. II, 1926), pp. 396 ff. and Dr. Altekar, A.S., State and Govt. in Ancient India, p. 141.
2. Vide Majumdar, R. C., Corporate Life in Ancient India, Chap. I.
3. Rāmāyaṇa Polity, p.. 66-67 (Also see p. 373 infra).

tions of the 'General Assembly' at the centre. But, beyond this there is no dependable evidence in the epic which can help us to determine the constitution, character or functions of this body.

(b) The Śreṇi:

Next, we may take up the term *śreṇi* which occurs very frequently in the Ayodhyā-Kāṇḍa. The commentators of the Rāmāyaṇa appear generally to take it in the literal sense of a 'row' and explain it as an 'assemblage of the town-people or subjects' (*prajā-samūhāḥ* or *nagara-vāsi-samūhaḥ*).[1] Twice, however, the Tilaka-Ṭīkā seems to assign a technical sense to this term when it explains *Śreṇi* as *nānā-jātīya-saṅgha*, i.e. 'association of men of various castes.'[2]

It may be pointed out in this connection that the term *Śreṇi* is very commonly to be met with in the Jātakas, the Mahābhārata, the Arthaśāstra, the Dharma-sūtras and the Smṛitis. It has been shown by scholars that the term *Śreṇi* appearing in this literature signifies a corporation of people belonging to the same or different castes, but following the same trade and industry. The Dharma-sūtras, further clearly state that these corporations were competent to frame rules for their own guidance which were recognised as valid in the eyes of law. Looking to this character of the *Śreṇis* both Indian and European scholars have felt inclined to render the term as 'guilds.' The literature cited above provides ample information with regard to the structure and functions of these 'guilds' in ancient India.[3]

1. Vide Rāmāyaṇa-Śiromaṇi-Ṭīkā on R. II 124/23 and R VI 108/14 respectively.

2. Vide Tilaka-Ṭīkā on R. II 105/11 N.S. and R. VI 127/4 N.S.

It may be added that the explanation in the Tilaka-Ṭīkā looks like a part of the definition of *Pūga* given by Kāśikā on Pāṇini (viz. *Nānājātīyā aniyatavṛittayo(a) rthakāmapradhānāḥ saṅghāḥ pūgāḥ*—Kāśikā on Pāṇini V 3.112). The distinguishing feature of a *Śreṇi* is "the pursuit of the same trade or industry by all its members", which, however, has not been touched upon by any commentator of the Rāmāyaṇa.

3. For details about the *Śreṇis* in ancient India vide Majumdar, R.C., Corporate Life in Ancient India, Chapter I, and Dr. Mookerji, R.K., Local Government in Ancient India.

So far as the evidence in the Rāmāyaṇa is concerned it becomes clear that there used to be *mukhyas* (chiefs) of the *Śreṇis*, who on the occasion of a royal function, such as the coronation of a prince, were invited by the ruler to participate in the ceremonies.[1] The Ayodhyā-Kāṇḍa of the Rāmāyaṇa gives a long list of artisans and merchants who accompanied Bharata to Citrakūṭa as he went to persuade Rāma to return to Ayodhyā.[2] At the end of this list are mentioned *Śreṇi-mahattaras*.[3] Later, at Citrakūṭa also the words of Bharata[4] clearly allude to the presence of the *Śreṇis* among the assemblage. These references most unambiguously testify to the presence of 'guilds' in Ayodhyā and also indicate that they were recognised by the rulers. It is interesting to add that the list under reference includes *astropajīvinaḥ*,[5] which is perhaps a reference to the guild of militant people corresponding to the *kshatriya-śreṇi* of Kauṭilya.[6]

It may also be noticed here that Dr. P.C. Dharma, laying her sole credence on the solitary interpretation of *Sreṇi-mukhya* as *vīthī-pradhāna* by Govinda-rāja, concludes that the town Ayodhyā was divided for municipal administration into wards (—*vīthī*=*śreṇi*) and that each ward was supervised by a Ward-Councillor or City Father.[7] Such an interpretation of the term *Śreṇi*, as far as we are aware, is neither supported by the Dharma-sūtras or Smṛitis nor by any epigraphical evidence. Moreover, it goes against the accepted connotaion of the term as just shown above, which we may add, perfectly suits the context in the Rāmāyaṇa.

(c) The Nigama or Naigama.

Allied in character with the *Śreṇi* there was another

1. R. II 29/16.
2. R. II 94/12 ff.
3. R. II 94/26.
4. *śṛiṇvantu me parishado mantriṇaḥ śreṇayastathā*, R. II 124/23.
5. R. II 94/12. (Gorresio's edition of the Rāmāyaṇa refers to *Sayodha Śreṇi*.) Cf. Majumdar, R.C., Corporate Life in Ancient India, p. 25.
6. Arthaśāstra, XI 1.
7. Rāmāyaṇa Polity, p. 68.

It may be added that Govindarāja himself interprets *śreṇayaḥ* in R. II 79/4 N.S. as *naigamāḥ*.

organisation in ancient India, viz. the *Nigama* or *Naigama.*[1] In fact, the *Nigama* (or *Naigama*) seems to have been an offshoot of the *Śreṇi*. Already in the period of the Jātakas a differnce is discernible in the organisation of the artisans on the one hand and the traders and merchants on the other. Soon perhaps the latter formed themselves into an independent body with the designation *Nigama* (or *Naigama*). In case of the *Śreṇis* (the organisation of the artisans) heredity of profession and localisation of industry were more or less indispensable factors. Such might not have been the case with traders and merchants. Perhaps this fact formed the main factor responsible for their branching off from the parent organisation.[2] Dr. K.P. Jayaswal is right, therefore, in explaining *Naigama* as the association or guild of the City Merchants.[3] Since the *Nigama*, it may be pointed out, consisted of the wealthy and more cultured people in the society it had a wider field of activity and wielded greater powers.[4]

As compared to the *Śreṇis* the references to the *Naigamas* are more frequent in the Rāmāyaṇa. In the explanation of this word Govindarāja quotes from the lexicons of Amara and Vaijayantī[5] and generally he interprets it as *paurāḥ*. The other two commentaries, viz. Tilaka and Rāmāyaṇa-Śiromaṇi also sometimes render it as *paurāḥ*, but more often as *vaṇijaḥ*. This last interpretation is only partly correct, for, as noted earlier the term *Naigama* stands not for the merchants in general, but for their corporate organisation. The

1. In the Rāmāyaṇa both the words *Nigama* and *Naigama* are to be met with. Technically the terms *Nigama* as well as the *Naigama* stand for a 'Corporate body' and so the word *Naigama* may mean a Corporate body of merchants or a member of such a body.

2. Majumdar, R.C., Corporate Life in Ancient India, p. 5.

3. Hindu Polity, p. 252.

It may further be added that according to Dr. Jayaswal the word *Nigama* (which literally means the place or house wherein people resort) stood for the meeting place or the bourse in the capital where merchants and tradesmen in the capital met. (Ibid. p. 254).

4. For details vide Jayaswal, K. P., Hindu Polity, pp. 252-254. and Mookerji, R.K., Local Government in Ancient India.

5. *Nigamo niścaye vede pure pathi vaṇikpathe.* (Vaijayantī).

Vaṇikpathaḥ puraṃ vedo nigamaḥ. (Amara)—quoted by Govindarāja on R. II 15/2 N.S. and R. II 59/19 N.S. respectively.

commentators of the Rāmāyaṇa, being perhaps oblivious of the technical character of the *Naigamas* interpret the word in the Uttara-Kāṇḍa (where the presence of the *Naigamas* is mentioned a number of times in the *Sabhā*, Law-court, of Rāma) as 'Vedic scholars'.[1] In fact, as observed earlier about the *Śreṇis*, the *Naigamas* also enjoyed certain judicial powers and their representatives had a right to be consulted by the king in matters relating to them.

That the organisation of the *Naigamas* in the period of the epic was perhaps of the same character as of the *Śreṇis* is evidenced from the fact that like the *Śreṇi-mukhyas* the Rāmāyaṇa also refers to *Nigama-mukhyas*.[2] In one passage there is a mention of the *Nigama-vṛiddhas*[3] who attended the court of Rāma along with the *kula-vṛiddhas*. This perhaps indicates that experienced people fully conversant with the rules and conventions of the *Nigama* were deputed to represent the organisation in the king's court.

The Rāmāyaṇa further shows that the *Naigamas* enjoyed a very high status in the society and commanded great respect from the rulers. After the departure of Rāma and party to the forest, Daśaratha reproached himself for having rashly acted without consulting his well-wishers, the *amātyas* and the *Naigamas*.[4] Rāma invited, among others, the *Naigamas* for consultation when the *brāhmaṇa* whose son had prematurely died was accusing him of maladministration.[5] Like the *Śreṇi-mukhyas*, the *Naigamas* also participated in the coronation ceremonies. In the Ayodhyā-Kāṇḍa they are seen among the distinguished assemblage waiting at the royal gate on the day of Rāma's coronation.[6] In fact, they are also invariably associated with every coronation mentioned in the Rāmāyaṇa.[7] We

1. Rāmāyaṇa-Śiromaṇi Ṭīkā on R. VII 40/18 and R. VII 61/3.
2. *mukhyā ye nigamasya ca*, R. II 15/2 N.S.
3. *tathā nigamavṛiddhāśca*, R. VII 40/18.
4. R. II 59/18-19 N.S.
5. *purodhasam upādhyāyaṃ bhrātarau naigamāṃstathā*, R. VII 77/2.
6. R. II 16/15, 27.
7. R. VII 66/8; R. VII 109/1-2. (This must, however, be made clear that the *Naigamas* (and also *Śreṇis*) are not to be found among the Vānaras and the Rākshasas.)

might even observe that in this respect they were enjoying a privilege in preference to the *Śreṇis*, for they are seen participating in the actual ablutions.[1]

It may be noticed in passing that Dr. P.C. Dharma associates the *Naigamas* also with the municipal administration.[2] She, however, neither makes clear the specific municipal functions which the *Naigamas* might have discharged in the times of the Rāmāyaṇa nor does she cite any passage from the epic which will indicate this aspect of the *Naigama* organisation.

(d) The Gaṇa

An intricate term is *Gaṇa*. It is variously interpreted by modern scholars. Thus according to Dr. D.R. Bhandarkar it means "a combination of individuals formed for a definite object" or "a corporate body of individuals formed for a definite purpose."[3] Dr. K.P. Jayaswal usually understands 'republics' by this term[4] and Prof. R.C. Majumdar assigns three meanings to it, viz. (i) Corporation of traders, (ii) Corporation of villages and (iii) a Federation of different groups or communities.[5] Sometimes the term *Gaṇa* stands also for a certain unit of the army.[6]

A more frequent use of the term *Gaṇa* in the Rāmāyaṇa is with reference to the Vānaras and the Rākshasas. The Vānara kings Bālī and Sugrīva and the ruler of Laṅkā, Rāvaṇa, are very often introduced as *Gaṇeśvaras*.[7] The popu-

1. R. VI 109/79 (f.n. 10).
2. Rāmāyaṇa Polity, p. 70.
3. Dr. Bhandarkar, D.R., quoted by Ghoshal, U.N. in his Studies In Indian History And Culture, p. 360.
4. Hindu Polity, pp. 24 ff.
5. Corporate Life in Ancient India, pp. 2, 58 and 94 respectively.
6. In the N.S. the Ayodhyā-Kāṇḍa refers to *Gaṇavallabhas*. Vasishṭha is said to have invited them to the meeting of the *Sabhā* summoned by him to formally offer the crown to Bharata., (R. II 81/12 N.S.).
Gaṇavallabhāḥ senā-nāyakāḥ (Tilaka-Ṭīkā).
Gaṇavallabhāḥ senādhiśāḥ (Rāmāyaṇa Śiromaṇi-Ṭīkā).
Gaṇavallabhāḥ gaṇādhyakshān (Bhūshaṇa-Ṭīkā).
7. (i) R. IV 17/3 N.S.; R. IV 32/10 N.S. ; R V 62/10; R. V 93/1 (for Vānara rulers).
(ii) R. V 39/22; R. V 46/10; R. VI 16/76; R. VII 20/57 (for Rāvaṇa).

larity of this term for the Vānara and the Rākshasa rulers and the rigid absence of such a reference for any Aryan ruler, prompts one to believe that the poet is perhaps alluding to the special character of the political constitution of the Vānaras and the Rākshasas. Kātyāyana defines the term *Gaṇa* as 'a collective organisation of *kulas*'[1]. In the Jātakas also, the term *Gaṇa* stands for a federation of diferent *kulas* and they frequently refer to the Licchavī-*gaṇa*[2]. A sitriking character of the *Gaṇa* constitution was that here the authority to rule was vested in certain families of the tribe. From each family, the senior-most male member was consecrated and he was known as *kula-vṛiddha*[3]. It is significant to note that in the assembly at Laṅkā, Vālmīki alludes to the presence of the Rākshasa-*vṛiddhas*[4]. Moreover, we have pointed out earlier that perhaps there was family representation in the 'Assembly' of the Rākshasas[5]. In the case of the Vānaras, the poet does not furnish any detail about the constitution of their *Sabhā* or the political character of their state. The only striking thing that we learn about them is with regard to their army. We are told that the Vānara army that followed Rāma and Sugrīva in the expedition over Laṅkā was constituted of different units belonging to individual chiefs.[6] All this evidence might indicate that the political organisation of the Vānaras and the Rākshasas probably corresponded in some measure to the *Gaṇa* type of the Licchavī state[7].

1. *Kulānāṃ hi samūhastu gaṇaḥ samparikīrtitaḥ*, Kātyāyana quoted by Majumdar, R.C., Corporate Life in Ancient India, p. 94.

2. Vide Majumdar, R.C., Corporate Life in Ancient India, pp. 92-94. It may be recalled that the period of the Jātakas and Kātyāyana comes nearest to the period of the Rāmāyaṇa. Their evidence is evidently most useful and reliable in interpreting the conditions reflected in the Rāmāyaṇa.

3. Agraval, Vasudeva Sharan, Pāṇini-Kālīna Bhārata Varsha, p. 436.

4. ......*iti Rākshasa-vṛiddhānāṃ teshāṃ sañjajñire kathāḥ*, R. V 44/58. Note also the verse 56 of this canto in which it is said that Hanūmān was presented by Indrajit before......*sagaṇāyarājñe*.

5. Vide pp. 343-344 supra.

6. R. VI cantos 2-4.

7. Incidentally it may be pointed out that even the Ṛigveda displays its familiarity with the *Gaṇa* type of political organisation. (Vide X 34/12).

(e) The Vāra

In the end, we may also refer to the *Vāra* which occurs in a solitary passage of the Ayodhyā-Kāṇḍa in connection with the levellers etc. who were sent by Bharata to prepare the passage for the army.[1] One of the commentators explains the term as the corporate organisation of artisans[2].In a later period of the Pratihāras there are copious references to local bodies styled as *Vāra* and to their chiefs, the *Vāra-pramukhas*, who discharged certain municipal and judicial functions[3]. A similar institution in the form of sub-committees of the larger 'Village-Assembly' existed in the times of the Colas also having the designation *Variyam*[4]. With the meagre and rather late evidence at our disposal it is not possible to state whether the *Vāra* of the Rāmāyana had any feature in common with these later *Vāras* and *Variyams*.

1. R. II 80/5 N.S.

2. ......*svavāraṃ svasvajātīyasaṅghaṃ samāsthāya*, Rāmāyaṇa-Śiromaṇi-Ṭīkā) on II 80/5 N. S.

3. Vide Dr. Dasharath Sharma's article, Pratihāra Sāmrājya Men Pañcāyatī Rājya (pp. 6-10), published in Viśvambharā, Hindī Viśvabhāratī Anusandhāna Parishad, Bikaner. Vide also Siyadoni Inscriptions, Ed. by Kielhorn, E.I. Vol. I pp. 173 ff.

4. Sastri, Nila Kanṭa, K.A., Studies in Chola History And Administration, pp. 131 ff.

Chapter XXII.

THE ART OF WAR AND MILITARY ORGANISATION

The Rāmāyaṇa is primarily an account of the struggle between the Rākshasas and the Aryans. During this period, the former having established themselves in Laṅkā under the leadership of Rāvaṇa were gradually trying to expand Northwards. They managed to by pass the Vānaras and the Haihayas by entering into alliance with them[1] and were soon moving even further, with their out posts in Janasthāna.[2] In the interest of their survival, the Aryans had to come into clash with the Rākshasas and put an end to their advance. Thus the instincts of self-expansion and self-preservation which are the breeding grounds of war are at the back of the story of the Rāmāyaṇa and naturally, therefore, like the Mahābhārata the Rāmāyaṇa is also a war poem. It provides us with ample information regarding the military organisation, the techniques of warfare and several other questions relating to war; and these we will discuss in the present chapter.

Causes of War:

In the history of all ancient nations there has been an age wherein men lived for action and for the honour which comes from it. "Such men", as C.M. Bowra remarks, "are moved by an important element in the human soul, the self-assertive principle, which is to be distinguished equally from the appetites and from the reason and realises itself in brave doings."[3] Display of heroism and the spirit of adventure have often led kings and knights to wars in ancient India, sometimes of great magnitude. In the Rāmāyaṇa, the

1. R. VII 22/37; R. VII 21/18.
2. R. III 39/44, 46.
3. Heroic Poetry, p. 1.

adventures of Dundubhi[1] and the exploits of Rāvaṇa[2] are illustrative of this very spirit. The ideal of *digvijaya* also has the same spirit at its root. However Dr. P. C. Chakravarti may like us to believe that the aspirant for paramount sovereignty was actuated by a longing to establish a common political organisation for the whole country corresponding to cultural unity which existed from very early times in the whole of India,[3] yet it is probably more of a fact that a great hero launched over such a project mainly to assert his authority and was inspired, as pointed out by Dr. V.R.R. Dikshitar, by "the mastery motive."[4]

Passion and emotion combined with the spirit of adventure led to the capture and abduction of maidens belonging to the neighbouring kingdoms and countries, and they often served as a cause of war. In the Rāmāyaṇa the great Laṅkā war was the result of the abduction of Sītā by Rāvaṇa;[5] Janaka was attacked by a host of princes for the sake of a maiden[6]; and Bālī's downfall was caused by his illicit connection with the wife of his younger brother.[7] Sometimes wars were fought to revenge wrongs. Paraśurāma, for instance, is known to have waged a war against the *kshatriyas*, for the Haihaya king was responsible for the death of Jamadagni, his father.[8] A righteous king had also to undertake to fight for granting protection and ensuring good rule for those oppressed by a tyrant. Śatrughna was sent by Rāma to fight against Lavaṇa in pursuance of a petition made by the oppressed sages of the territory near Mathurā.[9] A similar reason for entering war was to help the allies as did Sugrīva to help Rāma, and Madhu to help Rāvaṇa.[10] Lastly, in a

1. R. IV 8/2-35.
2. R. VII cantos 13 to 37.
3. The Art of War in Ancient India, p. 182.
4. War in Ancient India, p. 31.
5. R. III 58/10; R. VI 96/2.
6. R. I 62/18-19.
7. R. IV 16/70.
8. R. I 71/25-27.
9. R. VII 65/2 ff.
10. R. IV 29/10; R. VII 31/49 ff.

country spread over by a net-work of small independent and semi-independent states, the ambition of a great king naturally must have been to extend his sway upto the natural frontiers.[1] Rāma sent Bharata against the Gandharvas and after defeating them annexed their territories.[2]

Vālmīki also takes up the question of the causes of war and says, "The land, the gold, the silver and the cattle are the (four) sources of war."[3]

Ethics of War:

We have no information about any accepted code of fighting in the Vedic period. A critical study of the Vedic literature, however, makes it clear that the *Asuras* were fairly advanced in the art of war and that they sometimes resorted to unscrupulous and unclean methods to gain victory over their enemies.[4] In the Rāmāyaṇa the Rākshasas have been declared *kūṭa-yodhis*[5] and *māyāvis*[6] in their fights. Daśaratha pleaded before Viśvāmitra the inability of Rāma to fight against the deceitful Rākshasas, for the Rākshasas

1. Cf. The Aitareya Brāhmaṇa, VIII 4/1, which states that monarchy at its highest should have an empire extending right up to the natural boundaries.

2. R. VII cantos 102 and 103.

3. *Bhūmirhiraṇyaṃ kupyaṃ ca paśavo vigrahāspadam*, R. IV 16/62.

4. Dikshitar, V.R.R., War in Ancient India, p. 60.

5. *Prakṛityā Rākshasāḥ sarve māyayā kūṭayodhinaḥ.*, R. VI 28/27.

Incidentally we may note that the *kūṭa-yuddha*, as shown by Dr. V.R.R. Dikshitar, was in vogue in India from the time of the Vedas. The Atharva Veda gives us a number of battle charms with the use of plants like *aśvattha*, to overcome an enemy. It also contains certain rites of sorcery against hostile warriors, and the use of incantations. The main feature of this mode of warfare was the use of *mantras* and of charms and spells.

Commenting on this mode of warfare in the period of the Rāmāyaṇa, Dr. Dikshitar further writes, "The *āsura* form of war is mentioned in the Rāmāyaṇa. A feature of this was the employment of the diplomatic instrument *māyā*. Guile is chiefly used to overcome the enemy......A ruthless war was *āsura-yuddha*. But it was rarely indulged in, and we may conjecture that it is a relic of the ancient warfare fought by the primitive tribes who had neither a code of chivalry nor a code of ethics."

War in Ancient India, pp. 89-90.

6. *Iyaṃ tena nṛiśaṃsena māyā māyāvinā kṛitā*, R. VI 9/13.

were *kuṭa-yūddāḥ*.[1] Among the Rākshasas themselves Rāvaṇa[2] and his sons[3] (specially Megha-nāda) were dexterous fighters in this mode of warfare. Meghanāda is said to have acquired the *Tāmasī-māyā* from Śiva having propitiated the Lord by various sacrifices.[4] In the Laṅkā war he beheaded an illusory Sītā on the battle-field to deceive the enemy[5] and is said to have become invisible while fighting.[6] He employed his *māyā* against the *Devas* also and caused darkness to spread all over.[7] Vidyujjihva was, among the Rākshasas, another expert in the employment of *māyā*. He prepared an illusory head and bow of Rāma to convince Sītā that her husband had been killed on the battle-field by the Rākshasas.[8] The protagonists of this mode of warfare declared that in fighting recourse should be had to anything that would cause pain to their enemies.[9]

It may, however, be remembered that the *kūṭa-yuddda* though deprecated as unrighteous became an accepted mode of warfare under Hindu military science and regular training was imparted to a warrior of this mode as well. The idea was that against an unrighteous enemy employing 'deceit', one may not find oneself handicapped. In wars, to pay the enemy in the same coin was the accepted principle.[10] In the Rāmāyaṇa, molestation of Mandodarī by Sugrīva and party to disturb Rāvaṇa in his sorcery[11] and setting fire to the

1. *kūṭayuddhāḥ hi Rākshasāḥ*, R. I 18/6.

2. Rāvaṇa has been described as employing his *Māyā* in the Uttara-Kāṇḍa. When fighting against the *Yakshas*, he assumed a thousand shapes to contrive the destruction of his adversaries. He successively assumed the shapes of a tiger, a boar, a cloud, a hill, the ocean and a pond and thus wore full many forms and was not visible in his native shape., R. VII 14/27-28.

Earlier in the Araṇya-Kāṇḍa he appeared before Sītā, disguised as a *parivrājaka*., R. III 51/2.

3. R. VI 48/11.

4. R. VII 31/9, 10.

5. R. VI 59/30.

6. *Adṛiśyaḥ sarvabhūtānāṃ kūṭayodhī niśācaraḥ*, R. VI 21/17.

7. R. VII 35/24.

8. R. VI 7/7.

9. *Pīḍākaramamitrāṇāṃ yatsyātkartavyameva tat*, R. VI 59/29.

10. *Na hi dushyati loke(a) smin pāpe pāpaṃ samācaran*, R. VI 82/49.

11. R. VI 82/47.

town of Laṅkā with fire-brands at night by the party of Rāma[1] were acts of this very nature.

As against *kūṭa-yuddha* there was *dharma-yuddha*, the righteous war, also known as *prakāśa-yuddha*. *Dharma-yuddha* was a war carried on on the principles of *dharma*, meaning in the present context the *kshātra dharma* or the laws of kings and warriors.[2] Here, *śaurya* (valour) devoid of *nīti* (ethical principles) was not valued; on the other hand, it was recognised that the waging of war without regard to moral and ethical principles degraded men to the level of carnivorous animals.[3]

The first principle of righteous war, worthy of mention, is that non-combatants were not to be attacked.[4] In contrast with the theory and practice of modern wars, in ancient India, the civil population with its normal life-routine remained unaffected by wars. Viśvāmitra was termed of 'execrable ways' by Vasishṭha for destroying his hermitage,[5] and Yajñadatta being hit by Daśaratha's arrow wondered, as to how could the slaying of one like him, who subsisted on what the forest yielded, and never injured others, could be sanctioned by the scriptures.[6] Equally popolar and respected was the principle of granting immunity from all fear to one who was seeking refuge.[7] Vibhīshaṇa was received by Rāma because the practice of the good was not to slay even a wicked-minded enemy, if he, with folded palms and a poor heart craved for shelter.[8] Moreover, if an enemy, proud or terrified, sought shelter in an affright, he was to be saved by a great man even at the risk of his own life.[9]

Quite a large number of principles of warfare are the

1. R. VI 54/6.
2. R. VII 7/3. Note the use of the word *kshātra-dharma* (Also in R. VI 37/67).
3. Cf. *śauryaṃ śvāpadaceshṭitam*, Raghu-vaṃśa, XVII 47.
4. *ayudhyamānān......na tvaṃ hantumihārhasi*, R. VI 20/35.
5. R. I 50/28-29.
6. R. II 69/26.
7. Rāma was moved to be merciful even to the offending crow (Jayanta) when he begged for life bending low at his feet, for 'a fugitive had to be protected', R. II 109/52.
8. R. V 93/8.
9. R. V 93/9.

demands of chivalry. An enemy, for instance, was to be attacked and his belongings seized, only after openly challenging him to a duel. Sītā condemned Rāvaṇa as a coward, for he did not win her in war duly announcing himself as a combatant to her husband.[1] The code of chivalry also demanded that an enemy who was not engaged in fight with one, but was engaged in conflict with another person was not to be attacked without a warning. Bālī strongly expostulated Rāma for attacking him, while he was engaged in fighting with Sugrīva. He wondered, what merit Rāma had reaped by destroying one who was not engaged in fight with him.[2] In fact, Bālī had all the time felt confident that he would not be attacked by Rāma, for he felt assured that, "Rāma observed the *dharma*."[3] In course of the Laṅkā war also Hanūmān refrained from avenging himself upon Rāvaṇa on finding that the latter had then engaged himself in fight with Nīla.[4] Not only that, but a great hero was even expected to allow the enemy an opportunity to recover and be refreshed and not to kill him if he was wearied and exhausted.[5] Likewise, an enemy was not to be attacked when he was drunk and was sporting with females. The *mantrīs* of Arjuna requested Rāvaṇa to challenge their king some other time, for at that moment he was sporting with his harem in the Revā waters.[6] Lastly, it was the righteous duty of every one to come out for fighting when challenged by an enemy. One could be excused only if one confessed defeat by openly saying, "I am vanquished", and here too he was expected to direct the challenger to some other knight who might be capable of accepting the challenge. On Himavān expressing his inability to accept Dundubhi's challenge the latter demanded of the former to name one who could engage with him in a duel.[7]

1. R. III 59/9.
2. *parāṅmukha vadhaṃ kṛitvā ko nu prāptastvayā guṇaḥ*, R. IV 12/29.
3. R. IV 13/9.
4. R. VI 37/66-67.
5. R. VI 37/131.
6. R. VII 20/27.
7. R. IV 8/14.

Seizure of women or some other distinguished article of the enemy as mark of victory appears to have been a common practice of those times. In course of his *digvijaya,* Rāvaṇa captured many maidens of his foes[1] and seized the Pushpaka from Kubera as a mark of victory.[2] To capture alive the adversary was also a sign of victory. Meghanāda asked his father to retire from battle because he had taken the leader of the *Devas* (viz. Indra) a prisoner.[3] Such a position (that he should be taken a prisoner by the enemy) was the most despicable one for a hero, for the highest glory for a warrior lay in dying while fighting on the field of battle. It was believed that by arms he won fame and wealth on earth and the *Mahendra lokas* were ensured for him after death.[4] Not to turn back from the field of battle was strictly expected of a warrior and a hero took pride in joining to his name the epithet "unretreating in battles".[5] At the same time the ambition of a warrior was to meet death in straight fight. To be killed treacherously was also a cause of lament for the hero. Tārā felt much tormented to think that Bālī, her husband, was treacherously killed by Rāma.[6]

Before closing this section we may record a few laws governing the behaviour of kings in course of wars. To attack a state (or king) without rhyme or reason was considered an abominable cruelty and so Bālī strongly condemned Rāma for killing him when "he had done him no wrong either in his kingdom or in his city."[7] Likewise, a certain sense of equity was desired to be observed in avenging oneself upon a wrong-doer. Lakshmaṇa, trying to pacify Rāma who being enraged on Sītā's abduction by Rāvaṇa was preparing to rid the universe of all Rākshasas, pleaded that "all

1. R. V 9/69 N.S.; R. VII 30/2.
2. *Pushpakaṃ tasya jagrāha vimānaṃ jayalakshaṇam,* R. VII 14/32.
3. R. VII 35/37.
4. R. IV 16/113; R. VII 28/13-14.
5. *saṃyugeshvanivartināṃ,* R IV 15/20; R. IV 29/13; R. V 11/5; R. V 18/12.
6. R. IV 16/29.
7. R. IV 13/11.

should not be made to suffer for the wrongs of one."[1] Then, the *rāja-dharma* required of every king to send an 'ultimatum' to an enemy through a regular *dūta* before making an assault. It was in pursuance of this very principle that Rāma, after crossing the ocean, sent Aṅgada with a last offer to Rāvaṇa to return Sītā and surrender.[2] Lastly, it was a moral obligation of the victorious king to see that the subjects of the vanquished state, were not rendered *anātha* after the death of their ruler. He (the victorious ruler) was either to appoint a scion of the previous king as ruler to that conquered state or install one from his own family as king there. In any case, he was to ensure good rule in that state, for otherwise, he was sure to be transported to hell after death.[3]

The army and its divisions :

Protection of the person and property of his subjects was the primary duty of a king and to discharge it successfully he needed an absolute authority, the *daṇḍa*. In ancient India, army was the only instrument of this *daṇḍa*. The importance of the army can well be understood from the fact that along with the king and the ministers the army also constituted one of the limbs of the body-politic.[4]

The original fighting man must have been a foot soldier. With the addition of a car-warrior, a two fold division of the army had already come into existence during the Vedic period. By the time of the epics, however, the horse and the elephant were also incorporated in the fighting corps. The term *caturaṅga bala* and allusions to the chariots, the elephants, the horses and the foot soldiers as constituting the army are profusely available in the epic.[5] A relation of this

1. *Na caikasya kṛite lokānutsādayitumarhasi*, R. III 71/12.
2. R. VI 16/52 ff. (Note *rājadharmam anusmaran* in 52).
3. R. VII 65/42.
4. Vide pp. 287-288 supra.
5. In the Rāmāyaṇa the Aryan princes and the Rākshasas are described as having strong and large units of Infantry, Cavalry, Elephantry and the Chariot-corps. Thus ten-thousand elephants, sixty-thousand cars with bowmen, a hundred-thousand horses mounted by riders and a large number of surveyors, civil engineers, miners, architects, carpenters etc. are said to have followed Bharata to Citrakūṭa. (R. II 94/3 ff.) The Vānara army, however, was constituted only of Infantry.

For the word *caturaṅga* and its constituents vide R. I 18/10;-R. I 49/11-12.

fourfold division of the army with the game of chess is often pointed out. References to the game of chess are common in the literature but the term *caturaṅga* is met with only in the epics and hence V.R.R. Dikshitar is of the opinion that "the principles of chess supplied ideas to the progressive development of the modes and constituents of the army".[1]

In ancient India when the function and powers of the state were limited, a king could not afford for all times to maintain large armies. "The Hindu monarchical state," B.K. Majumdar points out, "did not possess standing armies before the 6th century B.C."[2] In times of war with neighbouring countries and tribes, therefore, he had to depend upon different sources for raising his army. Based presumably on the area or source of recruitment, a sixfold division of the army was thus recognised.[3] The army, according to this conception, was supposed to consist of six limbs, viz., hereditary troops (*maula-bala*), mercenaries (*bhṛitya-bala*), guild levies (*śreṇi-bala*), units supplied by feudatory chiefs or allies (*suhṛid-bala*), troops captured from the enemy (*dvishad-bala*) and forest tribes (*āṭavī bala*). An indirect reference to these different sources is available in the Rāmāyaṇa. Advising Rāma not to receive Vibhīshaṇa as a friend, Sugrīva says : "Avoiding forces from the enemy, a king should collect the hereditary troops, the mercenaries, forces supplied by the allies and the forest tribes".[4] It is interesting to point out that though the term *Śreṇi* occurs in the Rāmāyaṇa at various places,[5] Vālmīki has omitted in his enumeration above, the guild levies. Whether this omission has been caused because in the times of Vālmīki the trading communities had not developed a defensive power of their own or because like some later writers[6] Vālmīki also considered the *śreṇi-bala* as a source of weakness for the state, is difficult to pronounce.

1. War in Ancient India, p. 156.
2. The Military System in Ancient India, p. 22.
3. Chakravarti P.C., The Art of War in Ancient India, pp. 2-3.
4. R. VI 17/24 N.S.
5. Vide pp. 372-373 supra.
6. Cf. Arthaśāstra, Books VIII and XI.

Some political thinkers have called the army *shadaṅga* by adding to the well-known four limbs the force of counsel (*mantra*) and the power of treasury (*kośa*).[1] Sometimes by adding the commissariat (*vishṭi*), navy or admiralty (*nāvaḥ*) spies (*carāḥ*), and advisers (*deśikāḥ*) to the *caturaṅga* an eight-fold division of the army is also mentioned.[2] It may be observed in this connection that importance of *mantra*[3] and *kośa*[4] as indispensable factors in wars was duly recognised by Vālmīki. The position of spies is clear from the fact that they were called the 'eyes of the king'[5] and also from the part they played in the Laṅkā war. That commissariat was also indispensable for the army is clear from the description of the march of Bharata to Citrakūṭa.[6] Though fighting ships are clearly mentioned in the Ayodhyā-Kāṇḍa[7] it is definite that admiralty did not form a regular part of the army. The 'advisers' perhaps are not different from the members of the war council (and they have already been discussed in an earlier chapter).[8] Thus, different constituents of a full-fledged army were known to Vālmīki though theoretically he has recognised only a four fold division.

The primary unit of the army was infantry. As in all other countries, in India also the foot soldier was the original fighting man.[9] With the introduction of the car warrior in the army the position of a foot soldier, in the Vedic

1. Kāmandaka, 19/24
2. *Vishṭirnāvaścarāścaiva deśikā iti cāshṭamam, Aṅgānyetāni Kauravya prakāśāni balasya tu.*, Mahābhārata, XII 59/41-42.
3. R. II 114/11; R. V 77/6.
4. R. VI 40/23.
5. R. III 37/9.
6. Accompanying Bharata's army there were surveyors, civil engineers, miners, day-labourers, architects, carpenters, levellers etc., R. II 91/1 ff.
7. R. II 95/10.
8. Vide pp. 346-350 supra.
9. This can be proved from the evidence of the Rāmāyaṇa also. Rāma, though an expert archer, fought practically throughout the Laṅkā war as a foot soldier, excepting the short period when for purposes of fighting aganst Rāvaṇa he was supplied with a chariot by Indra. Moreover, every car-warrior transformed himself into a foot soldier when his chariot was smashed by the adversary.

period itself was very much reduced in importance.[1] By the time of the epics, there are clear evidences that the foot soldier was reduced to the status of a mere follower of the car warrior[2] and was considered "useful only in order to secure a decorous setting for the display of knightly prowess."[3]

In his description of wars, Vālmīki attaches no importance to the infantry. In the Rāmāyaṇa, the infantry has no individuality of its own. It is just a unit to be counted among the different units of the army, and sometimes even this mention is not made.[4] Vālmīki quite often refers to them in the Rāmayaṇa as *śesham*[5] or *avaśishṭam balam*[6], a mass of nothingness whose fate is only to be shot down in hundreds by the adversary when their leader is killed[7] and whose function is more often than not to report to the king, their master, the death of their commander.[8] The importance of the infantry consisted only in its numerical strength because sometimes it could decide the day merely by the weight of its numbers. Otherwise it had ceased to be a regular arm of independent status; an arm which could have its own organisation and tactical methods of offence and defence. Vālmīki's description of the followers is: "Incapable of standing after the death of the leader—commander—like water in a broken jar."[9] With such insignificant position of the infantry it is not unreasonale to surmise that the camp followers were also included under this class and that no clear line of demarcation could be drawn between the two.

1. Atharva Veda, VII 62/1.
2. R. I 28/10.
3. Chakravarti, P.C., The Art of War in Ancient India, p. 15.
4. R. V 42/4.
5. *jaghāna śesham tejasvī* R. III 31/35.
6. *Balaṃ tadavaśishṭaṃ tu nāśayāmāsa vānaraḥ*, R. V 42/39.
7. Compare in this connection the remark of E.W. Hopkins : "He (the knight) never makes a pre-meditated attack upon the foot soldiers alone, but when their chief is killed, of whom they are, like the horses, an appendage, they ought to disperse; and if they do not, they are shot as nuisances, not as antagonists." (J.A.O.S. XIII, p. 205).
8. R. V 39/59; R. VI 30/39-40; R. VI 35/2; R. VI 52/114.
9. R. VI 34/49.

Information regarding the arms and equipment of the infantry is very scanty in the Rāmāyaṇa. It is only at one place that the foot soldiers are clearly mentioned to have carried the *gadā* and the *parigha*.[1] The principal arm of the infantry was, however, the bow.[2] Generally, a foot soldier carried along with him the bow and the quiver and a sword,[3] and it seems that the use of the shield was also known to him during the Rāmāyaṇic period.[4] It is interesting to note that the entire Vānara host consisted of foot soldiers and yet they carried no arms. Their natural arms were the nails and the teeth,[5] and the foot and the fist[6] which were sometimes supplemented by big rocks and huge trees.[7] The Rākshasas were also adept in the use of such articles though usually they employed various types of arms. The followers of Dūshaṇa were armed with the *Sāla*, *Tāla* and the rocks[8] and Rāvaṇa cudgelled Jaṭāyu with his fists and feet.[9]

Usually a fighter covered his body with an armour.[10] Defensive coverings for the head,[11] the arm,[12] the fingers, the breast and the back[13] were known in the times of Vālmīki. Their use was to exclusive to the car warrior or the foot soldier but perhaps depended upon the rank and status of the warrior. It is interesting to learn that among defensive measures the warriors also applied (oils or powders of) medicinal herbs over their body.[14]

1. R. VI 73/2
2. R. I 1/44.
3. *Sa tu bāṇadhanushpāṇirbaddhāsirvitateshudhiḥ*, R. III 72/2.
4. R. III 30/20.
5. (*mahatī camūḥ*) *ṛikshavānarasampūrṇā nakhadaṃshṭrā prahāriṇī*, R. V 72/1.
6. R. V 41/12.
7. *Śailaśṛiṅgāṇi śataśaḥ pravṛiddhāṃśca mahīruhān*, R. VI 16/18.
8. *Atha te rākshasāḥ......sālatāla śilāyudhāḥ*, R. III 31/2.
9. *Mushṭibhyāṃ caraṇābhyāñca Jaṭāyusham apothayat*, R. III 57/18.
10. *Abhedye ca tanutrāṇe gṛihāṇa laghunī śubhe*, R. II 34/25.
11. R. VI 52/113.
12. R. I 20/29.
13. Ibid.
14. R. VI 52/102.
15. R. VI 49/4. (*Contd. on next page*)

Distance was a great handicap for the infantry. In distant marches, expereince taught the ancient people that the foot soldier, burdened with the heavy load of his arms and armour was already out of breath when he reached the field of battle and thus could not exert his energies to the fullest advantage. This led to the introduction of chariots in ancient warfare. The car warrior being elevated over his adversary, being partly protected from his weapons by the chariot screen, having the facility of carrying a much larger number of weapons along with him and appearing fresh on the field of action was distinctly in a privileged position over the foot soldier.

In India, beginning with the Vedic period right upto the period represented by the Arthaśāstra when emphasis was weighing more on the side of the elephants, the car warriors have been considered the main stay of the army. They enjoy a paramount position in the epics and Dr. P. C. Chakravarti has rightly felt inclined to designate this period as "the veritable chariot age of Indian history."[1]

The principal warriors of the Rāmāyaṇa, with the exception, of course, of the Vānaras, were great car warriors. Daśaratha, Rāma, Rāvaṇa, Indrajit, Aksha and Kumbhakarṇa were all renowned *mahārathis* and *atirathis*.[2] An interesting fact about the car warriors of the Rāmāyaṇa is that they belong exclusively to the noble class. The paraphernalia of the chariot was extremely lavish and perhaps the ordinary soldier could not afford to possess it. This elevated status lent airs to the car warrior and he could assumingly declare on the battle-field, "Stationed in this car, holding the bow and arrows in my hands, I will not fight any one that is ignoble.

About the herbs mentioned in the verse the Tilaka-Ṭīkā says : *āyudhaprahāranivārakaushadhiviśeshaḥ.*

1. The Art of War in Ancient India, p. 23.

2. Vālmīki does not define the terms *rathī*, *mahārathī* and *atiratha*. We quote below their definitions as noted by Dikshitar, V.R.R. in War in Ancient India, p. 13, foot notes 15-16.

Ātmānañca sārathim aśvān sva sainyaṃ rakshituṃ kshamaḥ
Prahartā parasaiyānāṃ yuddhaśāstra viśāradaḥ.
Yuddha śāstreshu nipuṇaḥ sa rathitvena sammataḥ.
Eko daśa-sahasrāṇi yodhayed yaśca dhanvinām,
Pūrvokta lakshaṇairyuktaḥ pārthivasyāpi rakshakaḥ,
Mahārathīti kathito yuddhaśāstraviśāradaiḥ.
Amitān yodhayet yaśca pūrvoktaguṇasaṃyutaḥ
Vijñeyo (a) tirathī nāmnā śastrāstranipuṇassadā.

He that has strength, and that also understands his business,—let him today speedily give me battle."[1] The hopes of the epic army were, naturally, pivoted on the car warrior. He was accorded an impressive send off by the king[2] and he marched to the field of battle flanked and followed by complete units of the army.[3] Kumbhakarṇa was, for instance, followed by high-souled mighty warriors and with elephants of four tusks, steeds and chariots sending out rattle resembling the rumbling of clouds.[4] The importance of the car warrior was also due to the fact that he alone was capable of employing a missile weapon. Rāma, Rāvaṇa and Indrajit employed a number of missiles.

While engaged in operation against the adversaries, the only support of the warrior lay in his alertness. He was required to safeguard himself against his own weaknesses and to be vigilant in taking advantage of the opponent's weakness. His bow and eye alone were his sole protectors. While Lakshmaṇa was preparing to march against Indrajit, Rāma advised him to keep an eye on the enemy's short-comings and safeguard himself against his own failings; that being always alert he should protect himself as much with his eye as with his bow.[5]

A war chariot was called *sāṅgrāmika ratha*[6] and was distinguished from other varieties of chariots.[7] Since the construction of an epic chariot did not materially differ from that of the Vedic car we may note the account of the car given in the Vedic Index.

In the Vedic period the chariot was usually a small sized two wheeled vehicle. It was drawn by two horses, occasionaly by three or even four. The body of the car appears to have been exceedingly light, consisting of a

1. R. VI 52/49.
2. R. VI 33/22-25; R. VI 44/19-25; R. VI 56/6.
3. R. VI 72/6.
4. R. VI 44/32.
5. R. VI 37/44.
6. R. III 71/9; R. VI 18/68.
7. As distinguished from the *sāṅgrāmika ratha* there was the *brahmaratha* used for conveynce by the *brāhmaṇas.*, R. I 29/16; R. II 7/4.

wooden frame work, fixed on an axle tree (*aksha*), fastened by cow-hide thongs. The frame work consisted of a floor (*garta*) to stand on and a guard of some sort round it. It was also provided with a seat (*vandhura*) where the warrior could sit when he wanted. The pole (*isha* or *praugā*) of the car was probably attached to the middle of the axle; and at the end of the pole was the yoke (*yuga*). Normally there was, it seems, one pole, on either side of which the horses were harnessed, a yoke being laid across their necks; the pole was passed through the hole in the yoke (called *kha* or *tardman*), the yoke and the pole being then tied together. The horses were tied by the neck where the yoke was placed, and also at the shoulder, presumably by traces fastened to a bar of wood at right angles to the pole or fastened to the ends of the pole, if that is to be regarded as it probably should be, as of triangular shape, wide at the foot and coming, to a point at the tip. The traces seem to be denoted by *raśmi* and *raśanā*. These words also denote the reins, which were fastened to the bit (perhaps *śiprā*) in the horse's mouth. The driver controlled the horses by the reins, and urged them on with a whip (*kaśā*). The girths of horses were called *kakshya*. The wheels, like the body of the chariot, were of wood. It is probable that originally solid wheels were used, but gradually these wheels were replaced by those with spokes (*ara*). Besides the spokes, a wheel consisted of a rim (*pavi*), a felly (*pradhi*), and a nave (*nabhya*). The rim and the felly together constituted the tire (*nemi*).[1]

Scattered in the Rāmāyaṇa are available references to the following parts of the chariot:

1. *Aksha*[2] The axle of the car.
2. *Anukarsha*[3] A piece of additional wood fastened beneath the car for the purpose of quickly repairing damages done in battle.

1. Vedic Index, Vol. II p. 202, quoted by Chakravarti, P.C., The Art of War in Ancient India, pp. 27-28.
2. R. III 33/28.
3. R. VI 49/11.

3. *Apaskara*[1] Explained by Monier Williams as any part of a carriage, a wheel.[2]

4. *Upastha*[3] A secure place.[4] It was meant for the driver, for Rāma is said to have caused to fall down from the *rathopastha* the driver of Triśirā.[5] "The *Upastha* was the general bottom of the car", says E.W. Hopkins.[6]

5. *Kūbara*[7] The pole of a carriage or the wooden frame to which the yoke is fixed. An ivory *kūbara*[8] and a *kūbara* studded with lapises[9] are mentioned by Vālmīki.

6. *Cakra*[10] The wheel of the car. A war car of eight wheels is also mentioned in the Rāmāyaṇa.[11]

7. *Triveṇu*[12] The Tilaka-Ṭīkā explains it as a pole in the front of the car to support the yoke.[13]

8. *Nīḍa*[14] "It was the little shelf in front where the charioteer stood", says E. W. Hopkins.[15]

9. *Nemi*[16] The rim of the wheel.

10. *Bandhurā*[17] A seat for the warrior.[18] The Tilaka-Ṭīkā explains it at one place as a plank of a chariot.[19]

1. R. VI 33/27.
2. A Sanskrit-English Dictionary, p. 53.
3. R. III 32/19.
4. Monier Williams, A Sanskrit-English Dictionary, p. 211
5. R. III 32/19.
6. J.A.O.S. XIII, p.238
7. R. VI 49/11.
8. R. VI 18/24.
9. R. III 27/14.
10. R. II 110/32 .
11. R. VI 44/28.
12. R. III 33/28 .
13. *Triveṇurnāma rathamukhastho yugādhāra daṇḍaḥ*, Tilaka-Ṭīkā on R. III 33/28.
14. R. V 41/15.
15. J.A.O.S. XIII, p. 238.
16. R. VI 20/21
17. R. V 43/5.
18. Date, G.T., The Art of War in Ancient India, p. 18.
19. *bandhurā rathaphalakā*—Tilaka-Ṭīkā on R. V 43/5

11. *Yuga*[1] The yoke of the car.

12. *Varūtha*[2] The fence rim or guard to prevent the warrior from falling down while engaged in action.

In a passage of the Yuddha-Kāṇḍa Vālmīki has given *nava nalva* as the measure of Kumbhakarṇa's chariot.[3] Obviously this is an exaggeration yet, the fact remains, that with the march of time, as the art of war became more and more complex and the number of arms and missiles multiplied, the size of the war car was also extended. Strength and spaciousness were the main qualities of a war chariot. The chariot of a knight "was crowded with quivers, arrows, spears, swords and javelins."[4] Rāvaṇa's chariot carried "32 quivers, a number of huge bows, terrific maces and a pair of swords."[5] Weapons were arranged in the chariot in an orderly manner so that the knight may be able to quickly lay his hands upon the thing required. Presumably there was a proper place for each kind of weapons. "The swords", it is said about Rāvaṇa's car, "were placed in the sides";[6] and in Aksha's car "the *śakti* and *tomara* were arranged in their respective order."[7]

As already stated, the knight's war car was lavishly decorated. It was richly laid in gold and precious stones;[8] had gold bells emitting out sweet jingle;[9] and carried a rich umbrella of one hundred gold ribs and a gold-pole.[10] Raised to its top, the chariot also had a pennon which was perhaps the ensign of the knight.[11]

1. R. VI 18/70.
2. R. VI 33/27.
3. R. VI 44/27

N.B. *Nalva,* according to Monier Williams is a measure of distance being equal to 400 cubits., A Sanskrit-English Dictionary, p. 530.

4. R. VI 49/11.
5. R. VI 52/24-25.
6. *Dvau ca khaḍgau rath?gatau pārśvasthau pārśvaśobhinau,* R. VI 52/25.
7. *yathākramāveśitaśakti tomarau,* R. V 43/5.
8. *prataptajāmbūnadajālasaṃvṛitam,* R. III 27/14; R. V 43/3; R. VI 83/5.
9. *kiṅkaṇikavibhūshitam,* R. III 27/16.
10. *chatraṃ śataśalākañca...bhagnadaṇḍam,* R. III 68/17.
11. R. II 95/3; R. V 43/4.

Ordinarily four horses were yoked to the war chariot[1] but sometimes chariots driven by eight[2] (and in a passage even one thousand)[3] horses are also mentioned in the Rāmāyaṇa. White chowries and various gold ornaments were used to decorate the horses.[4] The horses of the car were controlled by the driver by means of the reins and the whip,[5] and they were also supplied with protective coverings.[6]

Speed was the main demand of a chariot warrior and naturally this formed the main quality of the horses.[7] Besides, they were required to be capable of standing heavy loads.[8] The chariot had its own strategy in the time of action which depended upon the skilful movement of the horses and hence regular training for the purpose must have been given to them. The Rākshasas also yoked *kharas* (mules) to their chariots;[9] and in the Yuddha-Kāṇḍa, Rāma is seen employing Hanūmān as his vehicle.[10]

Incidentally, mention may be made here of chariots obtained by 'long-continued asceticism' or 'as a result of offerings properly made into fire'. Prince Aksha is described to have "sallied out ascending a car, obtained with long-continued asceticism, embellished with a net of glowing gold, furnished with pennons, having a standard studded with gems, nicely yoked with eight excellent steeds having the fleetness of thought, incapable of being overpowered either by celestials or *Asuras*, competent to course over uneven ground, of the lustre of lightning, sky ranging, completely garnished, equipped with quivers, with swords fastened to the banners in eight directions, with darts and lances arranged in proper

1. R. III 31/11; R. III 32/18.
2. R. V 42/29; R. V 43/4.
3. R. VI 52/16.
4. R. III 27/20; R. VI 83/6.
5. R. III 64/50 N.S. ; R. VI 56/19.
6. R. III 56/12.
7. *manojavāshṭāśvavaraiḥ suyojitam*, R. V 43/4.
8. ......*ashṭahayān mahājavān*......*bhārasahān*, R. V 43/31.
9. *ratham kharaśreshṭhasahasrayuktam*, R. VI 53/7.

N.B. In a passage of the Sundara-Kāṇḍa (44/17) even four tigers of sharp and white teeth are said to have been yoked to his chariot by Indrajit.

10. R VI 37/117.

places, splendid with every object in full measure, bearing golden threads, wearing the brilliancy of the sun and moon, and possessing the effulgence of the sun."[1] The chariot used by Indrajit for fighting was usually offered to him by Agni, who was pleased by the offer of choice oblations. To this chariot were yoked four very strong and inviolable horses. It was furnished with all decorations and arms and it had the singular characteristic of moving invisibly.[2] Such chariots might either be attributed to the *māyā* of the Rākshasas or might reflect the ambition of a chariot fighter.

The success of the car warrior and his fame depended to a very large measure upon the skill of the charioteer.[3] Naturally therefore, the knight took particular care to keep his charioteer satisfied and devoted to himself by offering him gifts and rewards.[4] Attempts on the part of the enemy for bribing the charioteer so that he may render the efforts of his knight futile, were not unknown among the war tactics of the Rāmāyaṇic age.[5] Such a charioteer, if detected by the knight was liable to be capitally punished.[6] A charioteer, though himself not fighting was required to be fully conversant with the art of war and had to be a man of steel—strong enough not to be unnerved even in a deadly conflict.[7] His position was an extremely perilous one, specially in view of the fact that the adversary made him his first target in the melee.[8]

The duties of a charioteer were many and onerous. He was required to present the chariot to the knight, completely in order so that the latter may ascend it and march to the field of action.[9] It was customary for him to greet the knight on such occasions by sounding 'victory' unto him.[10] On the

1. R. V 47/4-6 N.S., Dutt, M.N., The Rāmāyaṇa, Eng. Tr. pp. 1026-1027.
2. R. VI 20/9-10.
3. R. VI 86/5.
4. Cf. *smaryante yadi vā guṇāḥ*, R. VI 86/9.
5. *pareṇopakṛitaṃ vyaktam*, R. VI 86/7.
6. *tena vadhyo (a) si me mataḥ*, Ibid.
7. Cf. *na bhīto (a) smi*, R. VI 86/11.
8. R. VII 6/28.
9. R. VI 44/27-29.
10. *jayāśishā vardhayitvā*, R. VI 44/29.

battle-field, the charioteer was not to act according to his own understanding but had always to regard the knight and his will.[1] To protect the knight and his interest was the one prime concern of the charioteer.[2] For proper discharge of his duties the charioteer was required to be conversant with season and place, with omens and the expression of emotions, with depression of spirits, as also with the relative strength of the combatants.[3] He was to have a knowledge of level and uneven grounds and also the time of conflict.[4] Moreover, a charioteer mounted on a car was to know "when to draw near the enemy, when to turn away from him; when to stay and when to turn round from before the foe."[5] In course of the duel between Rāma and Rāvaṇa the driver of Rāvaṇa's chariot, on perceiving that 'through the stupefication of his inner self his master could not discharge any weapon or draw his bow or put forth his prowess, that the enemy (Rāma) did not persist in smiting him, and that the shafts and various arms discharged by his master were not befitting the occasion' took the car away from the field of battle.[6] When reprimanded by Rāvaṇa he justified his action by pointing out that he had known that Rāvaṇa had been fatigued in consequence of his mighty exertions in the fight; that his car was battered and the steeds of his car were worn out by carrying it and were helpless and perspired.[7]

As already suggested above, there were definite movements of the chariots employed for purposes both of offence and defence. By the skilful movement of his car, Mātali by leaving Rāvaṇa's mighty car on the right enveloped Rāvaṇa with a column of dust raised by the wheels.[8] A vivid description of the clever movements of the war cars is provided by Vālmīki in course of the account of the final encounter between Rāma

1. Cf. *kimartham māmavajñāya macchandamanavekshya ca*, R. VI 86/4.
2. R. VI 86/13.
3. R. VI 86/18.
4. R. VI 86/20 .
5. R. VI 86/21.
6. R. VI 85/34-36.
7. R. VI 86/16-17.
8. R. VI 87/11.

and Rāvaṇa. He says, "And their charioteers drove the cars on, displaying their skill by moving in circles, in rows and diverse other ways.....And displaying many a movement in the conflict they stood again facing each other, the forepart of one car touching that of the other and the heads of the steeds touching each other; and the pennons staioned on one touching those of the other."[1]

In duels between knights, the charioteer was generally killed. On such occasion, the knight, whose charioteer was slain, usually jumped out of his car with a weapon in his hand.[2] But in some cases the handling of the car was also done by him. Indrajit, for instance, himself drove his car when his driver was killed in the encounter with Lakshmaṇa.[3] Incidentally, the above fact shows that 'charioteering' also formed part of a knight's military training.[4]

Though adept in the use of all sorts of weapons[5] the car-warrior was principally a bow man. The bow with him was both an offensive and a defensive weapon. With half-moon shaped arrows, Jambumālī pierced Hanūmān's face; his head with one (arrow) having its front made like a hook and his arms with ten *nārācas*. And the invincible[6] Rāma counter-acted the missiles of Rāvaṇa by a shower of his own arrows.[7] In the handling of his bow, the knight was a past master. Describing the prowess of Rāma to Rāvaṇa, Śūrpaṇakhā remarked that she did not notice Rāma taking out his dread shafts, or discharging them; nor even drawing his mighty bow; she only saw the host being slaughtered by a shower of his shafts.[8] A similar remark is made by Vālmīki about Lakshmaṇa and Indrajit: "On account of their light-handedness, neither discharge of arrows, nor the drawing of the bow, nor the selection of

1. R. VI 89/3, 6-7.
2. R. III 31/13-15; R. 43/33; R. VI 30/28; R. VI 46/9; R. VI 89/42.
3. R. VI 89/42-43 N.S.
4. R. II 2/3.
5 For the list of weapons and missiles vide 'appendix' at the end of this chapter.
6. R. V 40/7
7. R. VI 89/20.
8. R. III 38/7-8.

the shafts, nor the clenching fast of their fists, nor the hitting of aims could be perceived as they fought on."[1] In case of an expert archer, none of the arrows missed the aim, none of them failed to pierce another and none of them went fruitless.[2]

The other equipment of the car warrior can be gathered from the hero in suit described by Vālmīki. About Lakshmaṇa, ready to march against Indrajit, he says, "And donning on his mail, and putting on his armour and his sword, and furnished with arrows, and a bow in his left hand......"[3]

The next limb of the army was constituted of the elephants. The elephant was known to the Vedic Aryans. The occurrence of thr term *hastipa* in the Yajurveda[4] is a strong proof of the fact that the animal was tamed and domesticated. But there is no clear evidence in any of the Saṃhitās to show that the elephant was employed in war. However, in the Rāmāyaṇa there are copious references showing that the elephants formed a regular arm of the army in the times of Vālmīki. At Ayodhyā there was an independent Elephant-unit and ten thousand elephants with full military accoutrements are said to have followed Bharata in his march to Citrakūṭa.[5] Moreover, from Rāma's statement in the Kaccit Sarga, viz., "And do you not feel satisfied with the (recruitment of) elephants with lofty tusks",[6] one can even conclude that gradually the elephants were gaining in importance. This is further corroborated by the fact that Rāma considered it to be a duty of the king that he should personally see that every day in the morning and in the evening the elephants were provided food and drink.[7] To capture elephants the kings occasionally undertook an expedition to the forests.[8]

1. R. VI 68/32-33.
2. R. VI 88/24.
3. R. VI 63/25-26.
4. Vājasaneyī Saṃhitā XXX 11; Taittirīya Saṃhitā III 4, 9, 1.
5. *Daśanāgasahasrāṇi kalpitāni yathāvidhi*, R. II 94/3.
(*Kalpitāni* in the verse is translated by M.N. Dutt as 'duly consecrated' (p. 416). But the Tilaka-Ṭīkā explains it as *kṛitasannāhāni*.
6. *kaccidunnatadantānāṃ kuñjarāṇāṃ na tṛipyase*, R. II 114/27.
7. R. II 114/33.
8. Compare Guha's words—*grahīshyate hastinaḥ kim* ?, R. II 95/4.

It is interesting to observe that Vālmīki alludes to the practice of enticing a wild elephant in a pit artificially covered with grass, through the agency of another elephant trained for the purpose[1].

Elephants were regularly trained for purposes of war. In Laṅkā, Hanūmān had seen well trained elephants capable of crushing hostile elephants, destroyers of hostile hosts and invincible in battles by foes.[2] Battering down of walls, gates and towers of a fortress formed the principal functions of the war elephants in later times[3] but in the Rāmāyaṇa they are conspicuous by their absence in the siege of Laṅkā. Whether they were trained for the purpose in that period is difficult to determine, for the absence of elephants on the side of Rāma is accountable otherwise also, namely to the fact that the army of the Vānaras was constituted only of the infantry.

Riding and training up of elephants formed a part of the military accomplishments of a prince.[4] In the Laṅkā war Triśirā,[5] Akampana[6] and Mahodara[7] have been described by Vālmīki as riding over elephants on the battle-field. The words *mahāmātra*[8] and *totra*[9] occur in the Rāmāyaṇa but it is difficult to state whether the knight fighting from an elephant was himself its driver or was accompanied by the *mahāmātra.* The elephants were also provided with defensive armours[10] and the warrior on an elephant is described to be fighting with a *tomara* and a *śūla.*[11]

The last limb of the army was cavalry. The position of the cavalry in the Rāmāyaṇa seems to be as subsidiary as that of the infantry. Though recognised as one of the regular arms of the army, the cavalry plays no significant role in the

1. R. V 43/20; R. V 90/44-46.
2. R. V 4/37-38.
3. Arthaśāstra, X Chap. 4.
4. R. II 2/28; R. II 3/18.
5. R. VI 18/45.
6. R. VI 37/8.
7. R. VI 50/2.
8. *mahāsattvairmahāmātraiḥ*, R. V 4/21. (The Tilaka-Ṭīkā explains the word *mahāmātra* as *hastipaka*).
9. *totrairiva mahādvipam,* R. III 33/10.
10. R. VII 31/32.
11. R. VI 18/45; R. VI 37/13.

wars described in the Rāmāyaṇa. The only function of the warrior on horse-back was perhaps to follow the car-warrior.[1] The Rākshasa Narāntaka is described in the Yuddha-Kāṇḍa as fighting on horse-back with *prāsa* (a javelin) in hand.[2] The sword must have been used by the cavalry soldier in melee. Though bow and arrow formed the principal weapon of the epic times, the horse-bowman is conspicuous by its absence in the whole of the Rāmāyaṇa.

We have seen above that the horses for the chariot were given regular training but whether similar provision existed for the cavalry-horse as well, is difficult to state. Their speed is certainly referred to at one place and it is indicated that the horses of Āraṭṭa, Vāhlīka and Kamboja were of good breed.[3] The horses were profusely ornamented[4] and were provided with a defensive covering for the chest.[5]

There is no evidence in the Rāmāyaṇa to show that the 'Navy' formed a regular limb of the army. Guha is the only king in the Rāmāyaṇa to possess war boats. He brought forward 500 boats manned with hundred fighters each to intercept Bharata whom he suspected to be advancing against Rāma in a hostile spirit.[6]

Espionage :

In India, which consisted of a congeries of small independent and semi-independent states where one was always eager to swallow the weaker neighbour, the *cara* and the *dūta* were indispensable instruments of security for a king which he achieved by keeping a vigilant watch both within and without through them. Traces of such diplomatic agents are found in Indian literature as early as the Vedas. We find mentioned in the Ṛigveda, besides the *spaśaḥ* (spies) of Varuṇa, the *dūta* and the *cara*;[7] and in the Taittirīya-

1. R. V 42/19.
2. R. VI 49/64.
3. R. V 4/34-36.
4. R. V 4/40.
5. *kāñcanoraśchadān haivā*, R. III 56/12.
6. R. II 95/9-10.
7. For details see Dikshitar, V.R.R., War in Ancient India, p. 339.

Saṃhitā the term *prahita* has been used as distinct from the term *dūta*.[1]

Vālmīki calls the *dūtas* 'the eyes of a king'[2] and declares that the wise king who gathers (a knowledge of) his enemy through spies, can, putting forth a modicum of effort in conflict, neutralise his exertions.[3] He seems to recognise a distinction between a *dūta* (envoy) and a *cara* (or *cāra* or *cāraka* or *praṇidhi*—spy)—the former being an open representative of his master while the latter, a secret one.[4]

The Rāmāyaṇa mentions three kinds of servants. One who being entrusted with an arduous task, after having accomplished it, out of love for the master, does another which is supplementary to the main, is termed a *purushottama*. One who, being deputed to any task, does not, though capable, perform any other work which may be dear to the the king (his master) is called a *madhyama nara*. And he is termed a *purushādhama* who, entrusted with any work of the king, does not, albeit competent, heedfully accomplish it.[5] V.R.R. Dikshitar finds this classification to be a parallel to the three classes of ambassadors, namely *nisṛishṭārtha*, *parimitārtha and śāsanahara* mentioned by Kauṭilya.[6] But, apart from the agreement on numbers there is nothing in common between the two lists. The basis of the gradation in the Rāmāyaṇa is radically different from that of the Arthaśāstra. In the Rāmāyaṇa-classification, "conscientious discharge of the duty" forms the basis of division whereas in the Arthaśāstra it is "the extent of the delegation of the authority by the king (master) to the ambassador" which determines his character.[7] That a conscientious envoy came very near *nisṛishṭārtha-dūta* of Kauṭilya can, however, be shown from a passage in the Sundara-Kāṇḍa wherein is

1. Taittirīya-Saṃhitā, IV 5, 7.
2. R. III 37/9.
3. R. VI 5/21.
4. This distinction is clear from the treatment meted out to them by the enemy. For details vide pp. 408-409 infra.
5. R. VI 1/7-9.
6. War in Ancient India, pp. 340-341.
7. Arthaśāstra, I Chap. 16.

stated, "He alone is deemed fit to act who when asked to achieve an object, having fulfilled his principal purpose, accomplishes many more without marring the prime one".[1]

In the Rāmāyaṇa Hanūmān[2], Aṅgada[3] and Prahasta[4] were employed as *dūtas* by their masters. Of these the par played by Hanūmān very faithfully illustrates the role of an envoy. In the Kishkindhā-Kāṇḍa he anounced himself to Rāma as a *dūta* of Sugrīva and negotiated alliance between Rāma and his own master.[5] A more important part was played by him in the Sundara-Kāṇḍa. Though his specific mission was to find the whereabouts of Sītā,[6] he behaved in Laṅkā as if he were entrusted with absolute authority. After meeting Sītā he reasoned out to himself that since the diplomatic expedients, *sāma*, *dāna* and *bheda* could be of no avail with the Rākshasas, Rāma of necessity shall have to resort to *daṇḍa* (war).[7] In his master's interest he felt it extremely desirable, therefore, that he should study the technique of war of the Rākshasas[8] and the situation and defence of their fort.[9] He, therefore, acted in such a manner that Rāvaṇa had to bring out his forces in an encounter with him.[10] Incidentally, he tried to demoralise the enemy and spread panic among his subjects by announcing that thousands of monkey-chiefs equal to him or even excelling him in strength were stationed under the command of Sugrīva on the other side of the ocean (to crush the Rākshasas).[11] Then again, when offered an apportunity to meet Rāvaṇa (the king) in council, he seized it and to the astonishment of

1. R. V 38/5.
2. R. IV 1/19-24; R. V 46/15.
3. R. VI 16/52-60.
4. R. VII 10/22-23.
5. R. IV canto 2
6. R. IV 34/6.
Note also the words of Jāmbavān :
Vicetuṃ vayam ājñaptā dakshiṇāṃ diśamuttamām, nānetuṃ kapirājena, R. V 58/2.
7. R. V 38/3-4.
8. R. V 38/7.
9. R. V 49/21.
10. R. V 38/8.
11. R. V 39/53-57.

Indrajit allowed himself to be carried a captive before Rāvaṇa.[1]

In the council of Rāvaṇa, Hanūmān announced himself as an envoy of Rāma.[2] He tried to impress upon Rāvaṇa the unrighteous character of Sītā's seizure by him and the ruin awaiting him on that account.[3] He told Rāvaṇa that if by virtue of his *tapas* (penance) he deemed himself incapable of being destroyed by the *Devas* and *Asuras*, he was to remember that Rāma, along with Sugrīva was neither a celestial nor a *Pannaga*, nor an *Asura*, nor a *Gandharva*, nor a *Yaksha* and nor a *Kinnara*. Rāma, he reminded Rāvaṇa, was a man and Sugrīva, the lord of Vānaras; how then would he be able to save his life from them?[4]

Describing Hanūmān's role in Laṅkā V.R.R. Dikshitar adds, ".....Thereupon Hanūmān crosses the ocean to Laṅkā and on the way defeats a few of the formidable Rākshasas apparently appointed by Rāvaṇa to guard the outskirts of his capital. Defeating them all and securing permission from every one of them, Hanūmān reaches the fortress of Laṅkā. Here again, he has an encounter with the guardian deity of the city. The latter is defeated by his prowess and she willingly grants him permission to enter the citadel. Thus we may take it that Hanūmān entered the capital of Rāvaṇa with the permission of those who had the power to grant it."[5] On his way to Laṅkā, we may point out, Hanūmān was confronted by Surasā, the *Nāga-mātā* and Siṃhikā, a Rākshasī. Of these the former (Surasā) was impelled by the *Devas* to appear as an obstacle before Hanūmān, for they desired to ascertain Hanūmān's strength and valour and to see whether he employed some artifice or came to grief.[6] Obviously Surasā was no agent of Rāvaṇa. Siṃhikā's mention by the poet in this connection is also to serve as a test for Hanūmān's insight and imagination. A *dūta* is required of necessity to be shrewd

1. R. V 44/46.
2. *Dūto (a) ham iha samprāpto Rāghavasyātitejasaḥ*, R. V 46/15.
3. R. V 47/15 ff.
4. R. V 47/28.
5. War in Ancient India, p. 246.
6. R. IV 62/12-15.

enough to distinguish between a friend and a foe. Hanūmān fulfilled this requirement by reacting differently to Surasā and Siṃhikā. He entered the wide and gaping mouth of both. He came out from Surasā's mouth by quickly contracting himself[1] while he rent asunder the vitals of Siṃhikā with his sharp nails.[2] His encounter with the guardian deity, Laṅkā, is also not to imply that he entered the town Laṅkā being duly permitted by competent authorities. This becomes distinctly clear if we remember that at this stage Hanūmān was not a *dūta* but a *cara*; and then, he entered Laṅkā by jumping over the rampart and not through the gate.[3]

V.R.R. Dikshitar has further remarked, "When he became weary of the search he thought of assuming the guise of a beggar, an insane person or an ascetic."[4] This is also reading a little too much between the lines. It is to be noted that it was in a state of great despair that the above words came out of Hanūmān's lips.[5] He was fighting shy of reporting to his party and king the failure of his mission and was apprehensive of great disaster befalling Rāma, Sugrīva and the Vānara host if it were to be reported that Sītā was not seen in Laṅkā.[6] By saying that he would turn a beggar or an ascetic he plainly meant that he would pass the rest of his life elsewhere—away from the Vānaras.

The responsibility of a *dūta* was great. An indiscreet move taken by an unreflecting *dūta* regardless of the exigencies of time and place could set at nought actions even on the verge of fruition.[7] Not only that, even good policies chalked out by the king in consultation with his ministers failed to bring the desired end as a result of the agencies of a conceited envoy.[8] Hence, high qualifications were demanded

1. R. IV 62/32-34.
2. R. IV 62/60-61
3. *advāreṇ a mahāvīryaḥ prākāramavapupluve*, R. V 4/2 N.S.
4. War in Ancient India, p. 346.
5. R. V 8/24-56.
6. R. V 8/24.
7. R. V 24/37.
8. R. V 24/38.

of a *dūta*. He was to be a native (*jānapadaḥ*), learned (*vidvān*), upright (*dakshiṇaḥ*), imaginative or resourceful (*pratibhānvān*), representing the truth (*yathoktavādī*) and possessed of wisdom (*paṇḍitaḥ*).[1] He was to be well versed in the lores (*śāstravid*), clever in the employment of speech (*vākya-kuśalaḥ*), well disposed (*suhṛid*), wise (*sapratibhaḥ*), of unimpeachable honesty (*śuciḥ*) and born in a high family (*kule mahati cotpannaḥ*).[2] While delivering his message he was not to get provoked, but was to employ conciliatory tone.[3] For achieving success he was to be endowed with "endurance (*dhṛitiḥ*), audacity (*dhārshṭya*), vigour (*balam*) and skill (*dākshyam*)."[4] Moreover, the office of a *dūta* (and also of a *cara*) was a very high one. Hanūmān, Aṅgada, Prahasta, Śuka, Sāraṇa and Śārdūla were all officers of high ranks. Leaving Aṅgada who was a *yuvarāja* they have been called *sacivas*[5] or *amātyas* by Vālmīki.[6]

The *cara* (or *cāra* or *cāraka* or *praṇidhi*) was a secret emissary and was indispensable in times of war. In war a king employed a regular Secret Service department,[7] whose principal functions were to assess the strength of the enemy,[8] to study his fortification,[9] and to discover his military plans and movements.[10] It was also to detect the secret agents of the enemy moving in disguise in the camp with similar motives.[11] Spies were also employed to ascertain the loyalty of the fugitive officers or relations of the enemy seeking friendship (or service) with the king.[12] Sometimes spies were also instructed to secretly contrive to murder the enemy or his officers.[13]

1. R. II 100/35 N.S.
2. R. V 82/16.
3. Cf. *vacanānmama vitteśaṃ sāmapūrvamidaṃ vacaḥ*, R. VII 10/22.
4. R. IV 62/63.
5. R. IV 2/28; R. IV 19/12.
6. R. VI 1/1.
7. *Vibhīshaṇaṃ cāravidhau niyojya*, R. VI 13/33
8. R. VI 1/4.
9. R. VI 13/7.
10. ......*pravṛittistairupānītā śvo(a)bhisāraḥ purasya ca*, R. VI 9/17; R. VI 82/6.
11. R. VI 1/17; R. VI 5/24.
12. R. V 92/17.
13. R. III 60/27.

After the abduction of Sītā, Rāvaṇa lost no time in appointing eight spies to bring to him information about the movements of Rāma.[1] Soon after laying siege of Laṅkā, Rāma appointed Vibhīshaṇa in charge of the 'Intelligence department'[2] and the latter by employing his personal *sacivas* as spies gathered information about the plans of Rāvaṇa.[3] He hauled up Śuka and Sāraṇa[4] and Śārdūla and party[5] as they were spying in his camp. Practically minute to minute information of the movements of Rāvaṇa was kept by Vibhīshaṇa with the help of his spies.[6]

In order to collect information about the strength and plans of the enemy the spies roamed about in his land variously disguised. The spies of Rāvaṇa surveyed Rāma's camp, disguised as Vānaras; the *sacivas* of Vibhīshaṇa entered Laṅkā as *śakunis* and Hanūmān approached Rāma on the Ṛishyamūka mountain in the guise of a mendicant.[7] Sometimes, officers (or relations of the enemy) pretending to have been offended and expelled from the kingdom by their master entered into the service of the enemy and tried to espy. This can be inferred from the statement of Aṅgada, viz., "Let it be remembered that he (Vibhīshaṇa) has come from the enemy. The Vānara army should in no case confide in him, (for) concealing their (real) motives, people of deceitful dispositions, spy (in the enemy camp) and taking advantage of his weakness smite him."[8]

The treatment accorded by the enemy to the *dūta* and the *cara* differed in as much as the official status of the two differed—(the former was an open representative of his master while the latter was a secret agent). Since a *dūta* was supposed to be delivering the message *adverbum* in pursuance of orders from his master he was not held responsible for

1. R. III 60/26.
2. R. VI 13/33.
3. R. VI 13/7.
4. R. VI 1/17.
5. R. VI 5/24.
6. R. VI 82/6, 9-15.
7. R. VI 1/11; R. VI 13/7; R. IV 2/2 respectively.
8. R. V 92/13.

any stiffness in its word or spirit.[1] For the biggest offence the highest punishment prescribed for him was 'flogging and deforming.'[2] Intercepting Rāvaṇa who had ordered 'death' for Hanūmān, Vibhīshaṇa said, "The killing of this Vānara (a *dūta*) is in every respect unbecoming; it is against the canons of the 'Royal code' and is deemed censurable according to social ethics. No doubt, he is an enemy, and has immeasurably wronged you, yet, the good do not recommend the killing of a *dūta*. Several other punishments for (an offending) *dūta* have been prescribed. Disfigurement of the body, stripes and tattooing are befitting punishments for him."[3] Accordingly, Rāvaṇa ordered that with fire set to his tail, Hanūmān be taken around the principal roads of the town.[4]

The rules for the treatment of the spy were rather unsparing. If detected, he was relentlessly beaten and roughly handled. Śārdūla, when detected, was dragged and pulled by the powerful Vānaras, furiously assailed with thighs, clenched fists, teeth and palms, and he was further dragged in the midst of the army by the enraged Vānaras.[5] Usually a spy was ultimately put to death. Śuka and Sāraṇa, when detected and presented before Rāma, lost all hopes of life.[6] Rāma also called them "deserving to be put to death."[7]

Fortification and siegecraft :

Forts of stone[8] and sometimes of sun-dried bricks[9] stood

1. R. V 48/10; R. VI 94/35.

It may, however, be noted that this rule was not respected by unrighteous kings. Rāvaṇa (R. VII 12/39) and Lavaṇa (R. VII 70/17-18) killed the envoys from Kubera and Māndhātā respectively even before they had finished their speech.

2. R. V 56/127-128.
3. R. V 48/6.
4. R. V 49/5.

Note that Śārdūla was also carried around the camp by the Vānaras., R. VI 6/8.

5. R. VI 6/6-8.
6. *nirāśau jīvitam prati*, R. VI 1/18.
7. *vadhārhau vām pramuñcāmi*, R. VI 1/20.
8. Ṛigveda, IV 30/20.
9. Ṛigveda, II 35/6.

on the Indian soil right in the time of the Vedas and perhaps even earlier. The evidence contained in the Ṛigveda leads one to believe that the pre-Aryan inhabitants of India were excellent fort-builders. The iron castles of the *Asuras* are frequently mentioned in the Ṛigveda.[1] Archaeological finds dating from as early a date as the 6th or the 7th century B.C. also show that stone fortification had perhaps a continuous history in India.[2]

The metropolis in ancient India was invariably surrounded by fortifications, either natural or artificial.[3] The esteem in which the fort was held in India can well be gauged from the fact that it has been recognised as one of the constituents of a state.[4] Moreover, in Indian military science which lays more emphasis on defence rather than on offence it is natural that fort should enjoy a position higher than the treasury, the allies and the army itself.[5] That fort was considered an unfailing form of defence by Vālmīki also can be inferred from a passage in the Uttara-Kāṇḍa which states, "And occupying the citadel of Laṅkā, you will become invincible to foes and capable of destroying them."[6] The name 'A-yodhyā' for Kosala's capital also corroborates this view.[7]

From the detailed and vivid description of Ayodhyā and Laṅkā that Vālmīki has left in the Rāmāyaṇa, his readers can easily form a complete idea of fortification in his times.

Based on the nature of defence, Vālmīki seems to recognise four types of forts. One situated on an island in the midst of a river (or rivers) seems to have been a *nādeya* fort. One built in a valley in the midst of an encircling

1. Ṛigveda, II 20/8.
2. Chakravarti, P.C., The Art of War in Ancient India, p. 130.
3. The Sanskrit name *pura* for the capital town also means a 'stronghold or a castle'. Monier-Williams explains it as a place containing large buildings surrounded by a ditch and extending not less than one *Kos* in length., A Sanskrit-English Dictionary, p. 635.
4. Vide pp. 287-288 supra.
5. Arthaśāstra, VI Chap. 1.
6. R. VII 4/24.
7. *satyanāmnīṃ dṛiḍhadvārām*, R. II 114/50.

range of hills was perhaps a *pārvata* fort. One having the protection of dug out artificial moat is perhaps, implied by a *khānitra* fort and one defended by sea-waters on all sides is perhaps his *ambu-durga*.[1] In making citadels the strategical strength of the site was kept in view and advantage taken of the natural features of the ground. The capital towns Madhumattā[2] and Kuśāvatī[3] were, for instance, built on mountain slopes, both having the Vindhya ranges as their natural defence. Some forts, like that of Ayodhyā raised on plain grounds and having no natural advantage were defended by artificial means,[4] while, some others, like Laṅkā, possessed all the strategic advantages supplied by man and nature.[5]

Capital towns were systematically planned in the times of Vālmīki. Dwelling houses for the subjects, quarters for the ministers and state-officials and palaces for the princes and the king had their definite positions. Public places, highways and crossways were judiciously distributed.[6] For purposes of defence the town was provided with impassable deep ditches full of dreadful aquatic creatures. Encircling the town was a strong rampart above which were erected parapets and pinnacles. Heavy rocks and logs of wood were heaped in the turrets and on the top of the rampart, to be hurled against the enemy forcibly trying to enter the fort. In the rampart there existed a number of huge and strong gates fitted with massive bolts. On the arches of the gates and above them were guards equipped with all sorts of arms, specially the bow. The gates were also furnished with *śataghnīs* and other contrivances which perhaps flung stones and similar other things at the advancing enemy with such speed and force that it caused instantaneous death to hun-

1. *Nādeyam pārvateyañca khānitrañcāmbu vartate*, R. V 70/26.

Note : Five types of forts seem to have been indirectly referred to in R. II 100/68 N.S.—Vide Tilaka-Ṭīkā, *Pañcavargastu—audakam-pārvataṃ vārkshamairiṇaṃ dhānvanaṃ tathā, iti durgam pañcavidham pañcavarga udāhṛitaḥ.*

2. R. VII 81/16-18.
3. R. VII 110/4.
4. R. I 5/6-9.
5. R. V 70/24 ff.
6. R. I 5/3-18; R. V cantos 1, 2.

dreds of them. On the gates, there were also stationed units of the army fully equipped and commanded by a tried and trusted officer. On and along the wall there were erected high watch-towers. They were meant to keep vigilance on the advance of the enemy troops and also served as places for locating both movable and immovable defensive weapons. Large supplies of food and drink were kept stored in the fort and it was always garrisoned with a well-equipped army. Machines and other army-equipment together with numerous forces and drought animals were kept in readiness there.[1]

In times of war special care was taken to guard the gates and the rampart. Twenty-four hour 'guard' was mounted on the strategic positions all over the fort. Rutting elephants were made ready for war; chariots and horses were yoked; and from all quarters mailed and equipped foot-soldiers were seen flocking. On the principal highways, units of army were seen marching on all sides. State-arsenals were filled with supplies of arms and cuirasses; and on all sides and in the centre, large armies under the command of the king, the prince, the Commander-in-chief and other officers of equal rank were stationed for carrying out military operations.[2]

Vālmīki has left a very lively picture of the fort of Laṅkā guarded and protected by the Rākshasas. In the Yuddha-Kāṇḍa, while describing the fortification of Laṅkā to Rāma, Hanūmān says, "Filled with rutting elephants Laṅkā ever rejoices. It is great, thronged with cars and inhabited by Rākshasas. Its gates are firmly established and furnished with massive bolts. And it has four wide and giant gates. (At those gates), there are powerful and large arms, stones and engines whereby an approaching hostile host, is opposed. At the entrances huge rocks are heaped and the bands of heroic Rākshasas have arrayed their hundreds of dreadful iron *śataghnīs*. It has a mighty impassable golden wall having its side emblazoned in the centre with costly stones, corals, lapises and pearls. Round about there is a moat exceedingly

1. R. I 5/3-18; R. V cantos 1, 2.
2. R. V 100/31; R. VI 12/16-21.

dreadful, with cool water, fathomless, containing ferocious aquatic creatures, and inhabited by fishes. At the gates there are four iron draw-bridges, furnished with powerful machines and men. On the approach of hostile forces, their attack is repulsed by these machines, and they are thrown into the ditch. One among these bridges is immovable, strong and fast established; adorned with golden pillars and daises. And dreadful and resembling a celestial citadel, Laṅkā cannot be ascended by means of any support. It has fortresses composed of streams, those of hills, artificial one (lit. dug out with a shovel) and of (sea) waters. And, O Rāghava, it is situated on the other shore of the sea having its limit far away. And way there is none even for vessels,—and its all sides are destitute of division. And that citadel is built on the mountain's brow; and resembling the metropolis of the immortals, the exceedingly invincible Laṅkā is filled with horses and elephants. And a moat and *śataghnīs* and various engines adorn the city of Laṅkā, belonging to the wicked Rāvaṇa. An *ayuta* of Rākshasas, dart-handed, hard to subdue, and all fighting at the front, protect the Eastern gate. A *padma* of experienced Rākshasas, holding swords, lances and bows, are stationed at the Northern gate. An *arbuda* of Rākshasas, car-warriors and horsemen, persons honoured and sprung from noble lines, holding swords and javelins, great heroes and fighting with all missiles protect the Western gate. A *niyuta* of Rākshasas are stationed at the Southern gate. Hundreds and thousands of foot-soldiers and car-warriors, irrepressible and mighty warriors protect the garrison."[1]

The account of the forts in the Rāmāyaṇa will remain incomplete without a reference to what Vālmīki calls *bilas*. The word *blia* literally meaning a hole or a cave seems to have been employed by Vālmīki in a technical sense, viz., a 'mountain fort'. Two significant references to the *bilas* are found in the Kishkindhā-Kāṇḍa. Māyāvī, an *Asura*, being chased by Bālī, the Vānara lord, entered a *bila*, a capacious

1. R. VI 3/10-28 N.S., Dutt M. N., The Rāmāyaṇa, Eng. Tr. pp. 1109-1110).

and impregnable aperture in the earth covered with grass on the surface. Bālī, immediately followed him leaving Sugrīva at the mouth of the *bila*. Significant it is to remember that already in the *bila* the *Asuras*, perhaps relations and followers of Māyāvī, were present, and after a very long time (a complete *saṃvatsara* since Bālī had entered) Sugrīva heard the roars of the *Asuras*. Taking Bālī to have been slain by the enemy, Sugrīva blocked the opening by placing a huge rock there and returned to Kishkindhā.[1]

A more detailed description of the *biladurga* is to be met with in the same book a little further. While searching the Vindhya ranges the Vānara party sent to the South by Sugrīva espied there an un-enclosed cavity and entered it. The Vānaras moved and moved in darkness crossing over an hundred *yojanas* till they saw light. Then they saw golden trees, tanks with large fishes of gold, and lotuses, golden vehicles and elegant dwellings all round veiled with nets of pearls, having golden balconies, with their grounds paved with gold and silver and furnished with lapis-lazulis.[2] From Svayamprabhā, a female ascetic living there, they learnt that that fort, Ṛiksha-vila, was constructed by Maya the 'Viśva-Karmā' of the principal *Dānavas*.[3] That this place was really a fort is clear from a statement of Aṅgada who proposed to permanently settle there with the Vānara-chiefs belonging to his party (and establish an independent Vānara state), for the place was incapable of being approached and abounded in viands, meats, drinks and waters.[4] We will not be wrong to state that this *bila* was also provided with an artificial defence in the nature of an elementary labyrinth, for before their chanced meeting with Svayamprabhā, the Vānaras had roamed about there in darkness for a considerable period[5] and later they were delivered from it by Svaymprabhā, only on the condition that they will cover their eyes.[6]

1. R. IV 7/34-39 and 58-65.
2. R. IV 41/17-33.
3. R. IV 42/11-12.
4. R. IV 45/22-25.
5. R. IV 41/16-19.
6. R. IV 44/13.

The above meaning of the word *bila*, is further corroborate by the use of the word *guhā* made in this context by Vālmīki. This word also literally means a cave but Vālmīki frequently refers by it to the palace of Bālī (and Sugrīva)[1] and at one place it expressly stands for Kishkindhā[2] which was definitely a fort (though elementary in its structure in comparison to Ayodhyā or Laṅkā).

In a country where forts were so common siegecraft must have formed a regular part of military science. All the same, subdual of an enemy fortified in his citadel, must have been a difficult task for a king, specially in an age in which even gunpowder was not known. The most usual tactic employed by an attacking foe in such a case was to cut down supplies of provisions and arms of the besieged by stationing posts at all the overt and covert passages of the fort. When gradually provisions ran short in the fort, the enemy was obliged to throw open the gates of the fort. The disappointed suitors of Sītā besieged Mithilā for one year with the result that Janaka was reduced to a sad state;[3] likewise in the Laṅkā war when Nīla effectively cut down the intercourse of Laṅkā with the outside world, Rāvaṇa complained to Kumbhakarṇa that all his treasures had been exhausted.[4] Sometimes 'use of fire' was also made to destroy the fortification of the enemy and to compel him to come out of his citadel. Hanūmān set fire to Laṅkā with the specific motive of destroying its fortification, hoping that by doing so he will render the task easy for Rāma.[5] Even in course of the Laṅkā war, the Vānara host set fire to the Laṅkā fort by means of fire-brands.[6]

Occasionally the besieging army attempted to force its way through the gates. Ordinarily elephants were employed on such occasions for battering the gates of the fort but as there were no elephants in Rāma's army, this task was attempted by the Vānaras themselves. They tried to break

1. R. IV 11/3; R. IV 20/1.
2. *Kishkindhāṃ yaḥ samadhyāste guhāṃ vānarasaṅkulām*, R. VI 4/48.
3. R. I 62/19-20.
4. R. VI 39/34-36; R. VI 40/23.
5. R. V 50/4.
6. R. VI 54/3 ff.

down the gates, arches and bastions and filled the deep ditches of limpid waters with dust, grass, wood and stones. When attempting to scale the walls of the fort they were attacked with javelins and *bhindipālas* by the Rākshasas stationed on the turrets. The Vānaras in their turn pulled them down and killed them with the blows of their clenched fists.[1]

Incidentally, it may be remarked here that in the Laṅkā war the Rākshasas, though having all the natural advantages on their side, lost to Rāma perhaps only due to the inefficiency of their leader, Rāvaṇa. Rāvaṇa under-estimated the strength of his enemy and positively over-estimated his own strength[2] with the result that he committed serious tactical blunders. He allowed the enemy to cross the ocean safely[3] and take an advantageous position on the Suvela mountain.[4] Thus ultimately he found himself at a disadvantage in meeting the enemy. Moreover, whether it was due to the strategical position of Rāma's army or due to lack of imagination on the part of Rāvaṇa, the Rākshasa-chiefs besieged in the fort came out one by one and naturally did not prove successful against the whole army of Rāma. The scales might have been tilted the other way had Rāvaṇa come out with all his army and chiefs to meet Rāma in an open fight.[5]

Some aspects of military organisation

(a) *Recruitment of troops* :

In early Vedic times when political society had not yet fully emerged from the tribal state, the king did not

1. R. VI 17/10-29.
2. Note the account of Rāvaṇa's War-Council in R. V cantos 77-90.
3. R. V 100/7-8, 30
4. R. VI 7/1.
5. According to Dr. E.W. Hopkins (J.A.O.S. XIII p. 175) the epic descriptions of the city defences are later interpolations and do not belong to the original epics. The material on the point is, however, so profuse in the Rāmāyaṇa and the descriptions of fortification and siege so unambiguous that such a contention with regard to the Rāmāyana cannot be accepted even with reservations. From what has been stated in the section above it can safely be asserted that 'fortification and siegecraft' formed a regular part of military science in the times of Vālmīki.

possess large standing army. But soon the expansionist policy of the ambitious *kshatriya* princes necessitated the maintenance of full-fledged standing armies by the state. By the time of the epics we find exorbitant numbers being mentioned in this connection. Thus Bharata going to meet Rāma at Citrakūṭa was followed, it is said, by ten thousand elephants, sixty thousand chariots and hundred thousand mounted horses.[1] About the Vānaras and Rākshasas, Vālmīki speaks in terms of *ayuta, niyuta, arbuda* and *padma*.[2] Though large armies were maintained by the kings, the practice of raising local levies on the occasion of a grave emergency did not completely die out. In times of war the state-army was supplemented by troops of (feudal) chiefs who came to join the king as his allies. On hearing of the abduction of Sītā by Rāvaṇa Bharata had collected at Ayodhyā a number of kings to offer assistance to Rāma in his conflict with the Rākshasas.[3]

The sources of recruitment of troops as indicated earlier[4] were mainly five viz., hereditary fighters, mercenary fighters, soldiers supplied by feudatory chiefs or allies, soldiers captured from the enemy and lastly those recruited from forest-tribes.[5] The *kulaputras* mentioned quite often by Vālmīki were perhaps the *kshatriya* nobles owing hereditary allegiance to the king.[6] Such allegiance was presumably due to blood or caste relationship. These people enjoyed complete confidence of the king and naturally formed the main stay of his army. Next in importance were the mercenaries.[7] Even in the times of Vālmīki there were people who being completely given over to fighting had earned a name for themselves in wars. They perhaps roamed about in the country in search of employment and could be retained by any king who offered them sumptuous pay and provision. That one

1. R. II 94/3-5.
2. R. IV 30/21-27; R. VI 4/54-56.
3. R. VII 40/43. Compare also Sītā's enquiry in R. V 32/38.
4. Vide p. 387 supra.
5. R. VI 17/24 N.S.
6. R. II 114/46.
7. R. I 18/4.

such unit formed a part of Bharata's army is evidenced from his mention of *dākshiṇātyāḥ-suyodhinaḥ*.[1]

There is no evidence in the Rāmāyaṇa to show that only the *kshatriyas* were employed in the army. That the art of fighting was open at least to the *brāhmaṇas* also is clear from the fact that Paraśurāma wielded his weapons against the *kshatriyas* in open fight[2] and that Vasishṭha resisted the armed attack of Viśvāmitra.[3] In the Rāmāyaṇic period also the *brāhmaṇas* were as much repositories of military science as of other *śāstras*. Sudhanvā, Rāma's teacher in this line, was master par excellence in archery and the use of other missiles.[4] Since the commissariat was not distinctly separate from infantry it can be reasonably surmised that the other classes (*varṇas*) also had access to the army. In cases of dire necessity, such as protracted siege of the fort by the enemy, conscription by the state was also perhaps possible; the military officer of Rāvaṇa is said to have moved from house to house to ask the Rākshasas to join the army.[5]

(b) *Units of the army* :

In view of the fact that large armies were maintained by the kings in Rāmāyaṇic period, it is reasonable to presume that in the interest of administrative efficiency the army was divided into various units. The Arthaśāstra and later politico-military manuals contain definite directions regarding the divisions of the army.[6] The terms *Gulma*, *Vāhinī*, *Pṛitanā*,

1. R. II 106/14 (Also *astropajivinaḥ* and *yodhinaḥ* in R. II 94/12 and 17 respectively.)
2. R. I 70/24.
3. R. I 50/29.
4. *ishvastre paramācāryam*, R. II 114/9.
5. R. VI 74/23.
6. The sister epic (Mahābhārata) divides the army into 9 divisions. The smallest unit is a *Patti* described as consisting of 1 chariot, 1 elephant, 3 horses and 5 foot-soldiers. The next seven units in the ascending order were *Senāmukha*, *Gulma*, *Gaṇa*, *Vāhinī*, *Pṛitanā*, *Camū*, and *Anīkinī*. Each of these was three times as big in its composition as the unit preceding it. Thus the *Anīkinī* was to have 2187 chariots, 2187 elephants, 6561 horses and 10935 foot-soldiers. The last unit was the *Akshauhiṇī* which was ten times in strength than the *Anīkinī*.

Chakravarti, P. C., The Art of War in Ancient India, p. 83.

Camū, *Anīkinī* and *Akshauhiṇī*,[1] are no doubt, found in the Rāmāyaṇa but their use is very ambiguous. From the available evidence it is very difficult to state whether these terms had any definite technical sense attached to them.

Practically the same is true of the 'ranks' of the army officers. The highest military officer (of course, lower in rank than the king, who in the Rāmāyaṇa was invariably in over all command of the army) was the Commander-in-chief, variously known as *senāpati*, *vāhinīpati*, *camūpati* or *camūmukhya* and (*kapi*) *sainyapāla*.[2] He was required to be confident, endowed with intelligence and fortitude, sprung in respectable race and devoted and able.[3] A passage in the Uttara-Kāṇḍa indicates that the ceremony of *abhisheka* took place in case of the *senāpati* also.[4] The office of a *balādhyaksha* was perhaps peculiar to the Rākshasas. As opposed to the Vānaras among whom every chief brought his own following to the theatre of war,[5] the practice obtaining with the Rākshasas was that the chief was supplied with the following by the state.[6] The *balādhyaksha*, was perhaps the officer in charge of the entire army of the state and responsible for providing proper following to the chief marching to the field of battle. *Dhvajinīpati*, *senāgrayodhinaḥ*, *balīmukhāḥ* (or *balamukhyas*) and *nāyakas*[7] were also perhaps some military ranks. The *yūthapas*, *yūthapa-yūthapas* and *mahā-yūthapa-yūthapas*[8] were ranks exclusively belonging to the Vānaras.

(c) *Discipline* :

Discipline is the very core of army-organisation. But

1. R. VI 16/32; R. II 106/1; R. VI 33/38; R. VI 18/4; R. III 29/27 and R. I 18/3 respectively.

2. R. III 27/7; R. III 28/18; R. VI 34/32; R. VI 34/50 and R. VI 50/26 respectively.

It may be noted that at Ayodhyā there seems to have been some distinction between the *Vāhinīpati* and the *Senāpati* who have been separately mentioned by Rāma in R. II 114/29 and 43 respectively.

3. R. II 114/43.
4. R. VII 66/11.
5. R. VI 2/12-42 (Note *svenānikena* and *svabalāni* in 21, 23, 27, 33)
6. R. VI 29/19; R. VI 33/17; R. VI 56/9; R. VI 74/22-23.
7. R. V 42/42; R. V 42/2; R. VI 45/37; R. VI 72/2 and R. V 81/12 respectively.
8. R. VI 2/29 and R. VI 3/15 and 11 respectively.

obviously in an age in which individual display of knightly prowess was the mark for a warrior and when disorder and confusion was the character of fights the notions of discipline could not be the same as today. However, complete wantonness had no scope in the army even in those days. While camping on the sea-shore, strict orders were issued by Rāma that "no Vānara shall move in any circumstance from his lines at will."[1] Similarly during the assault over Laṅkā at night, Sugrīva announced that being physically fit, whoever will turn his back on facing the enemy will be forcibly seized and killed.[2] Likewise, Rāma issued instructions to the Vānaras "not to assume human forms during the fight, for in that case the distinction between the friend and the foe would be lost."[3]

G.T. Date's remark—"The Epic horde is not under very strict military discipline. Friends and foes can mix together at the end of each day's fight and social connexions are not altogether cut off by reason of the hostilities in the field"[4]—is not applicable to the Rāmāyaṇa; may be because, firstly the Laṅkā war (unlike the great war fought at Kurukshetra) was not a war between princes of the same family but between two hostile races and secondly, it was not a case of an open fight in the open field but the laying of a siege of the Laṅkā fort by Rāma. Besides, the activities of Vibhīshaṇa had created such a bad blood between him and the rest of his kinsmen that what to speak of maintaining the social connexions, even the sight of one was intolerable to the other.

(d) *Pay and rewards* :

In times of war (as well as of peace) regular pay and provisions were paid to the army by the king. The king appointed a special officer to ensure regular payment of dues to the army. Irregularity in giving provisions and other dues to the army invariably caused discontent among troops and was a source of great danger to the state. In the Kaccit-sarga

1. R. V 72/24.
2. R. VI 54/47.
3. R. VI 13/30.
4. The Art of War in Ancient India, p. 68.

Rāma enquired of Bharata whether he granted provisions and pay to his soldiers at the proper time and did not delay them. He warned Bharata that if the proper time for granting pay and provisions was passed the servants got wroth with their master and vexed him; and that great was the evil that sprang therefrom.[1] The chief military officers, for example the Commander-in-chief and Knights were kept contented and gratified by additional offer of various gifts and presents. This was necessary to ensure their loyalty and earn a claim on their lives in times of war. Prahasta, while marching against the enemy, pledged not to spare his life, sons, wife or wealth in effecting what was dear to his master, Rāvaṇa, who had variously fondled him by the giving of gifts, showing of regard and speaking of sweet words.[2] Vālmīki also refers to the practice of giving special gifts and rewards to the heroes effecting the death of the hostile ruler. To beguile Sītā by convincing her of the death of Rāma Mahodara suggested to Rāvaṇa that when he returned from the battle-field declaring that he had killed Rāma and Lakshmaṇa and clasped his feet, he (Rāvaṇa) should give him a warm embrace and distribute among his servants wealth, articles of luxury and other enjoyments.[3] Gifts were also given to the soldiers of the army on the occasion of the latter being discharged after a victory in a war. The king made his soldiers sharers in the spoils of war, presumably on the principle that the results of a common enterprise were to be enjoyed commonly. Rāma directed Vibhīshaṇa to honour the huge congregation of Vānaras and Ṛikshas who had displayed valour for him and to reward them by gems and other choice gifts.[4]

Army on the march:

(a) *Time for marching* :

Winter (*hemanta*) has been declared by Vālmīki as the proper time for starting on a military expedition. This season

1. R. II 114/44-45.
2. R. VI 33/14.
3. R. VI 43/28-29.
4. R. VI 103/6-8.

being neither very hot nor very cold is convenient for men and animals to march even long distances. Again, this being the period of harvest and of plentiful water-supply it becomes peculiarly well-suited for military expeditions. Vālmīki declares, "(In this period) the kings bent on conquest and desiring new acquisitions, range about the provinces overflowing with food and milk."[1] Equally good was the spring season in which Rāma marched towards Laṅkā.[2] Astronomical considerations also weighed in deciding the time for march. Rāma issued orders to arrange for the march instantly, for the sun had attained his meridian at that proper moment and was capable of conferring victory. The *Uttarā-Phālgunī* was in the ascendant on that day and the next day the moon was to be in conjunction with *Hasta*.[3] The strategical maxim of military science, viz., 'strike the enemy when he is at a disadvantage' was also not lost sight of. Rāma advised Śatrughna to slay Lavaṇa when rains had set in at the end of summer,[4] for as the Tilaka Ṭīkā points out, "feeling confident that military expeditions were not undertaken in the rains, and anticipating fear from no quarter, Lavaṇa would be moving about without his *śūla*; and that would be the hour of his death."[5]

(*b*) *Order of march*:

Three marches of the army have been described in some details by Vālmīki in the Rāmāyaṇa. Of these, that of Bharata to Citrakūṭa though not intended for waging war against any one, is still useful in providing information about the order of march, and the last two, namely, that of Rāma against Rāvaṇa and of Śatrughna against Lavaṇa, are plainly military expeditions.

The Director of Labour (known as *praśāstā* in the Rāmāyaṇa)[6] who was to prepare path and also to ensure

1. R. III 21/7.
2. R. V 71/3.
3. R. VI 4/3-5.
4. R. VII 67/11.
5. *Varshākāle varshāsu ke(a)pi yuddhārthaṃ na yatanta iti nirbhayo niśśūla eva carati, ataḥ sa evāsya vadhakāla iti bhāvaḥ.*, Tilaka-Ṭīkā on R. VII 67/11.
6. *Tataḥ senāpatiḥ paścāt praśāstā ca nishedatuḥ*, R. II 104/42.
For the meaning of *praśāstā* vide pp. 332-333 supra.

safety and security for those coming behind was perhaps despatched with his retinue of artificers and workmen, a little in advance of the main army. Vālmīki supplies a long list of pioneers which includes levellers, wood-cutters, road-makers, diggers, engineers, surveyors and supervisors who preceded Bharata and his retinue.[1] Rāma also commanded Nīla, the Commander-in-chief, to move in advance with his party to survey the path and to see that food and drink on the path were not poisoned by the enemy.[2]

The army while yet on its way to the theatre of war moved in definite battle-formations, particularly when danger was apprehended. Rāma posted Gaja, Śarabha and Gavāksha in the van, Ṛishabha on the right side and Gandha-hastī and Gandha-mādana on the left side. In the centre moved Rāma himself with Lakshmaṇa moving only at a distance of an arrow's-throw behind him.

Jāmbavān, Susheṇa and Durdharsha were directed to guard the flanks.[3] Shortly after, Panasa, Nala and Kumuda are described as moving in the van clearing the path; Sugrīva, Rāma and Lakshmaṇa are in the centre; Hari guards the right flank and Kesarī, Panasa, Gaja and Ṛiksha move on the (left) side; and Aṅgada and Jāmbavān protect the rear.[4] Nīla, the Commander-in-chief, assisted by Dadhimukha, Prajaṅgha, Jambha and Kapi had the over-all responsibility of protecting the flanks and the whole army.[5] The marching army had to take special care to safeguard itself against the possible attacks of the enemy lying in ambush, particularly so when it was crossing a strategic position. When the Vānara-army was crossing the sea Vibhīshaṇa with *gadā* in his hand stationed himself on the other side of the bridge to meet any possible obstacle from the enemy.[6] It is also worth remembering in this connection

1. R. II 91/1 ff.
2. R. V 71 /8-12.
3. R. V 71/13-18.
4. R. V 71/33-37.
5. R. V 71/38-39.
6. R. V 98/35.

Compare in this connection Mahodara's statement in which rejecting Dhūmrāksha's proposal of making a surprise attack on Rāma encamping on the Suvela mountain he said, "Such a move would have been proper when Rāma was on the other side of the sea or when the bridge was being constructed.", R. V 100/30.

that the army on the march avoided towns and habitations on its way.[1] This was presumably done with a double purpose, viz., (i) to avoid causing unnecessary damage to the life and property of the innocent people and (ii) to safeguard itself against the possibilities of surprise attacks.

The operation against Lavaṇa was a clandestine move and naturally the movement of the army was done in a surreptitious manner. Rāma advised Śatrughna, the leader of the operations, to despatch his whole army in pretty advance and himself to lag behind and later move all alone.[2] He was asked deliberately to delay till the proper time for the attack (which in the case under reference was the setting of the rains—an unusual time for military operations) had arrived.[3] The army itself was to conceal its true character, for it was to include shops with various articles, and songsters and dancers; and the sages were to move in its van.[4] In short, the whole thing was to proceed in a manner that Lavaṇa did not even smell of the impending danger and was ultimately caught unawares.[5]

The Camp

The word employed in the Rāmāyaṇa for a military camp is *skandhāvāra*[6] and fairly considerable information has been supplied by Vālmīki on the point. The first thing to be considered in encampment was the selection of the site. A spot where food and drink were available easily and in abundance and which was fairly secure was selected by the king or the Commander for encamping and the tents were pitched on an auspicious hour. Bharata encamped under an auspicious star and at a favourable hour at the bank of the Gaṅgā on a spot having a rich supply of tasteful fruits.[7] Likewise, Rāma selected a spot on the seashore "abounding in fruits, roots

1. *varjayannagarābhyāśāṃstathā janapadānapi*, R. VI 4/39 N.S.
2. R. VII 67/7.
3. R. VII 67/11.
4. R. VII 67/3, 12.
5. *yathā tvāṃ na prajānīyād......tathā vraja*, R. VII 67/8.
6. *Dadarśa vānarāṇāṃ tu skandhāvāraniveśanam*, R. VI 23/21.
7. *Nakshatre supraśaste ca muhūrte caiva tadvidaḥ*, R. II 91/18.

and water."[1] Bharata's camp was surrounded by an entrenchment and was furnished with ditches and watch-towers (posts?).[2] In Rāma's camp, presumably the sea and the mountain Suvela served as natural defences.

In the centre of the camp there used to be a special tent for the king and around it were tents for his high officers. In the camp prepared by Viśvakarmā at the instance of the sage Bharadvāja, there was in the centre a majestic tent for Bharata and around it were perhaps quarters for his *mantrīs*, the *senāpati* and the *praśāstā*.[3] The army was divided into divisions and was perhaps entrusted to the care of different commanders. When the camp was on the enemy's land and danger was imminent, the army encamped in military formations (*vyūha*). Rāma distributed his army in the *Purusha*-formation. Taking their own forces with them, Aṅgada and Nīla were to be stationed in the centre (*urasi*) of the army, Ṛishabha at the right (*dakshiṇa-pārśva*), Gandhahastī and Gandha-mādana at the left (*savya-pārśva*), Rāma himself along with Lakshmaṇa in the fore-front (*mūrdhni*), Jāmbavān, Sushеṇa and Vegadarśī in the interior (*anta*); and Sugrīva, the lord of the Vānaras was to protect the rear (*jaghana*).[4] Movement in the camp was extremely restricted.[5] Guards were appointed on all sides,[6] presumably to raise an alarm in case of surprise attacks by the enemy and to detect spies of the enemy operating in disguise. The sign to distinguish between friend and foe in Rāma's army was *vānara*.[7]

The Vānara army fought during the day and usually returned to the camp after sunset. Sugrīva, accompanied with Vibhīshaṇa was perhaps in charge of the proper upkeep and maintenance of the camp. He provided medical aid to the wounded, collected intelligence about the enemy and

1. R. VI 16/2.
2. R. II 91/19.
3. R. II 104/41-42.
4. R. VI 24/13-18 N.S.
5. R. V 72/24.
6. R. V 74/12; R. V 97/18.
7. *Cf. Vānaro hyeva naścinhaṃ svajane(a)smin bhavishyati*, R. VI 13/30.

perhaps made arrangements for the conduct of the next day's fight.[1]

The marching army did not consist only of the warriors. The drought animals, the pioneers, the commissariat and the camp-followers also formed part of it. Rāma directed Śatrughna to carry along with him a regular bazaar with shops selling various merchandise and to include dancers and songsters in his troop.[2] Since dancers and songsters also accompanied the army, the soldiers must have been provided with good entertainment in the period of their rest. They had also enough to drink.

At the end attention may be drawn to the fact that after their halt at Śṛiṅgaverapura when the army of Bharata resumed its march the soldiers set fire to their dwellings. The Tilaka-Ṭīkā commenting upon it states : "This is a military practice."[3]

Army in the field :

(a) *Battle-orders* :

On the field of battle the army was arranged in various battle-orders. On the eve of the Laṅkā war, Rāma is said to have arrayed his army in the *Garuḍa* formation.[4] Khara also finding his men scattered, re-arranged them so as to make them compact for a concerted attack.[5] Arranging and re-arranging of the army before and after assault can be inferred from such statements as, "meanwhile let me re-organise the forces"[6], "there came Vibhīshaṇa after laying the forces in their positions",[7] and "I have detailed our troops in quarters and appointed their leaders as per rules."[8]

During the operations there was also arrangement for providing relief on a front likely to give way either because

1. R. VI 25/41; R. VI 75/7.
2. R. VII 67/3.
3. *āvāsamādīpayatām*, R. II 101/21. Note Tilaka-Ṭīkā—*ayaṃ senādharmaḥ*.
4. R. VI 6/11.
5. R. III 29/25-26.
6. *yāvat sarvāṇyanikāni punaḥ saṃsthāpayāmyaham*, R. VI 22/36.
7. *tataḥ sarvāṇyanikāni sthāpayitvā samantataḥ, ājagāma...vibhīshaṇaḥ*, R. VI 25/41.
8. R. VI 63/6.

of the leader being wounded or exhausted due to protracted fighting or a sudden arrival of reinforcement of the enemy. Vibhīshaṇa took the position of Lakshmaṇa when the latter was tired and injured[1] and Jāmbavān was detailed by Rāma to relieve Hanūmān fighting desperately against Indrajit.[2] Order and discipline were observed by the epic-army only before the assault; after the first plunge into the fight complete disorder and confusion prevailed in the lines.

(b) *Some usages of the battle-field* :

(i) *Music and Harangues* :

Music is like second nature of war and its regular accompaniment. To raise the spirit of the soldiers, to instil in them the sense of pride for their king and country and to inject a spirit of chivalry music was played before and during the march of the army. Drawing the attention of Sītā, Saramā asked her to hearken the solemn notes of the kettle-drums, calling upon soldiers to put on their military accoutrement.[3] The Vānaras also employed war-music. The sounds of *bherīs* and conches, accompanied with joyous tumult were common to them.[4] *Śaṅkha, paṭaha, dundubhi, veṇu, mṛidaṅga, bherī* and *paṇava* are the instruments mentioned by Vālmīki in this connection.[5]

Boasts and harangues were also addressed to the followers by their leaders to infuse courage and confidence in them. To the Vānaras terrified by Indrajit, Hanūmān said, "O Vānaras, why do you look so melancholy, and why are you flying away? Why have you renounced your earnest desire for fight? And where is your heroism gone? Do you remain behind me as I go first in the battle. For heroes, sprung from noble families, it is unbecoming to fly away."[6] Typical illustrations of harangues are furnished by Aṅgada and Khara. To the Vānara host, panicky at the dreadful sight of Kumbhakarṇa, Aṅgada said, "Forgetting

1. R. VI 67/36.
2. R. VI 61/1-3.
3. R. VI 9/21.
4. R. VI 10/32.
5. R. VI 19/13.
6. R. VI 60/2-4.

your lineage and prowess, where do you, exercised with fear, fly, like ordinary monkeys? You amiable ones, desist. Why should you save yourselves... We are born in long and noble lines. It is ignoble that for fear, you are running away from battle. Where now is gone that talk of yours with regard to your nobility which you had held in society. Dead is he (though living) who is despised by all and termed a coward. Therefore, do you follow the way frequented by the worthy, and cast off fear. We will either lie down on the earth, being slain, and thus attain the reign of Brahmā incapable of being attained by dastards or achieve renown by slaying the foe in fight."[1] Lest his army be disheartened at the appearance of evil omens, Khara with a laugh addressed the whole body of Rākshasas , saying, "Even as a strong person from prowess counts not a weak one, I do not dwell upon all these mighty portents, dreadful to behold, that have appeared. Even the stars will I bring down from heaven with my sharp shafts; and even Death will I engaged, bring to mortality. Without slaying Rāghava puffed up with pride, as well as Lakshmaṇa, by means of sharp weapons, I return not (from the conflict).....I have never before met with defeat in conflict. You have witnessed it."[2]

(ii) *Medical relief* :

The importance of 'medical relief' for the army needs no introduction. Provision was made to provide medical aid to the wounded even in the Rāmāyaṇic period. Accompanying the army of Bharata were surgeons and experts in the extraction of extraneous substances, and poison-doctors.[3] After the disastrous assault by Indrajit, Hanūmān and Vibhīshaṇa moved about at night with light in hand, providing relief to the rank and file.[4] After his encounter with Rāvaṇa, Rāma assisted by Lakshmaṇa took out shafts from the bodies of the Vānaras. Vālmīki has mentioned in this connection a few herbs, *sandhāna karaṇi* or *sandhānī* (healing the wounds), *viśalyā* (freeing from pain or a specific plant

1. R. VI 45/25-31.
2. R. III 28/19-24.
3. *śalākāśalyahartāro vishavaidyāśca śobhanāḥ*, R. II 94/22.
4. R. VI 53/61.

for healing arrow-wounds), *mṛita-sañjīvanī* (vivifying) and *suvarṇa-karaṇī*.[1] One interesting fact mentioned about them, however, is that they were administered through the nose.[2]

1. R. VI 53/86.
2. R. VI 53/119.

CHAPTER XXII

APPENDIX

Weapons and Missiles

ardha-nālīka, *R. VI* 21/26
aśani, *R. VI* 79/4
asi, *R. V* 43/18
ishu, *R. II* 70/52
ishudhi, *R. III* 72/2
ṛishṭi, *R. V* 70/31
kaṅka-vāsas, *R. VI* 20/25
karṇi, *R. V* 40/7
kārmuka, *R. V* 43/16
kuṭhāra, *R. VI* 52/111
kunta, *R. VI* 79/4 *N.S.*
kūṭa-mudgara, *R. VI* 7/18
kūṭa-yantra, *R. VI* 79/4
kshurapra, *R. V* 42/36
kshepaṇī, *R. V* 4/21 *N.S.*
khaḍga, *R. V* 43/33
gadā, *R. V* 39/31
gadā (*bahu-kaṇṭakā*), *R.* VI 30/35
cakra, *R. VI* 18/67
candra, *R. VI* 20/12
cāpa, *R. V* 44/20
jyā, *R. III* 29/16
tūṇa, *R. III* 9/18
tūṇīra, *R. III* 2/27
tomara, *R. VI* 7/19
triśūla, *R. VI* 30/5
daṇḍa, *R. VI* 29/23
dhanu, *R. V* 40/3
nālīka, *R. VI* 21/26
nārāca, *R. V* 40/7
nistriṃśa, *R. VI* 53/10
paṭṭiśa, *R. V* 42/36
patatri, *R. V* 43/14
paraśu, *R. I* 70/20
paraśvadha, *R. VI* 29/23
parigha, *R. VI* 29/23
prāśa, *R. VI* 30/19
bāṇa, *R. V* 39/31
bāṇāsana, *R. V* 43/24
bhalla, *R. VI* 37/93
bhiṇḍipāla, *R. VI* 17/28
bhushuṇḍi, *R. VI* 13/10
mārgaṇa, *R. VI* 77/1
mudgara, *R. V* 42/31
musala, *R. VI* 7/19
lāṅgala, *R. VII* 6/51
vajra, *R. V* 48/11 *N.S.*
vatsa-danta, *R. VI* 21/26
viśikha, *R. VI* 75/4
vaitastika, *R. VI* 49/45
śakti, *R. V* 70/31
śataghnī, *R. VI* 44/37
śara, *R. VI* 52/51
śita-daṃshṭra, *R. VI* 21/26
śilīmukha, *R. V* 42/23
śūla, *R. V* 42/35
sāyaka, *R. III* 32/19
hūla, *R. VI* 52/111

Esoteric sciences and Divine missiles

atibalā, *R. I* 20/12-18
amogha-śakti, *R. I* 25/13
ari-kampana, *R. I* 25/18
ari-nikṛintana, *R. I* 25/15
ari-paksha-pratāpana, *R. I* 25/17
ari-vidāraṇa, *R. I* 25/12
āgneyāstra, *R. I* 25/11
ārdrāśani, *R. I* 25/10
indrāśani, *R. I* 25/10
indra-vajra, *R. I* 25/6
unmādana, *R. I* 25/16
aishika, *R. I* 25/7
kaṅkāla, *R. I* 25/13
kampana, *R. I* 25/18
kāla-daṇḍa, *R. VII* 25/31
kāla-pāśa, *R. I* 25/9
kālāstra, *R. I* 25/6
kiṅkiṇī, *R. I* 25/13
kaumodakī, *R. I* 25/9
kauverāstra, *R. I* 25/17
krauñcāstra, *R. I* 25/12
gandharvāstra, *R. I* 25/16
jṛimbhaka, *R. I* 26/4
tejo bhyāharaṇa, *R. I* 25/17
tvāshṭra, *R. I* 25/20
daṇḍāstra, *R. I* 25/4
dānavāstra, *R. I* 25/20
daityāstra, *R. I* 25/20
dharma pāśa, *R. I* 25/9
dharmāstra, *R. I* 25/5
dharshaṇa, *R. I* 25/15
nandaka, *R. I* 25/14
nārāyaṇāstra, *R. I* 25/11
pavanāstra, *R. I* 28/14
pāśa, *R. VI* 52/38
paitāmahāstra, *R. V* 44/36
painākāstra, *R. I* 25/11
paiśācāstra, *R. I* 25/17
pramathana, *R. I* 25/15
pramardana, *R. I* 25/15
prasvāpana, *R. I* 25/15
balā, *R. I* 20/12-18
brahma-śiraḥ, *R. I* 25/7
brahmāstra, *R. I* 25/3
madanāstra, *R. I* 25/16
mānavāstra, *R. I* 25/20
musala, *R. I* 25/13
mūrchana, *R. I* 25/18
mohana, *R. I* 25/16
rākshasa, *R. I* 25/17
lohitāmukhī, *R. I* 25/9
vajra, *R. V* 48/11 *N.S.*
varuṇa-pāśa, *R. I* 25/10
vāyavyāstra, *R. I* 25/11
vijaya-śakti, *R. I* 25/13
vishṇu-cakra, *R. I* 25/8
vaidyādharāstra, *R. I* 25/14
śaṅkarāstra, *R. I* 25/8
śushkāśani, *R. I* 25/11
śaiva-śūla, *R. I* 25/7
śoshaṇa, *R. I* 25/15
somāstra, *R. I* 25/20
(*alias śiśira*)
stambhana, *R. I* 25/15
svāpana, *R. I* 25/18
hayaśiras, *R. I* 25/12

Defensive Equipment

aṅguli-trāṇa, *R. I* 20/9
āpīḍa, *R. VI* 18/2

uraśchada, *R*. *VI* 68/18
kavaca, *R*. *VI* 18/2
godhā, *R*. *I* 20/9
carma, *R*. *VI* 9/24
tanutrāṇa *R*. *VI* 59/43

varma, *R*. *VI* 9/24
śirastrāṇa, *R*. *VI* 52/113
sannāha, *R*. *VI* 19/5
hastāvāpa, *R*. *VI* 89/16

CHAPTER XXIII

CONCLUSION

We have given in the foregoing pages a general survey of the social and political institutions of India as reflected in the Rāmāyaṇa of Vālmīki. We may now attempt on its basis to give a consolidated picture of the society of that period and in the end try to discover a few salient features which served as the foundations on which the entire social structure of those times rested.

The Rāmāyaṇa, as we have seen, introduces us to an early period of ancient Indian history when the country was not yet fully Aryanised; and, in particular, the region beyond the Vindhyas in the South was still inhabited by non-Aryans. Of these Vālmīki speaks in fair detail about the Vānaras and the Rākshasas who lived in Kishkindhā and Laṅkā respectively. Though in respect of their religious practices, the Vānaras appear indistinguishable from the Aryans, the account of their features and dispositions and particularly the state of sex relationship among their men and women leave no doubt that they were primitive people who were, perhaps, still in the process of emerging from conditions of nomadic life. The Vānaras have been represented as friendly to the Aryans; and as immediate neighbours they had, probably, greater contact with the Aryan people and their culture than the distant Rākshasas had.[1]

In contrast with the Vānaras, the Rākshasas were an advanced non-Aryan people. Politically, they were a strong power, portending a great threat to the security and well-being of the Aryans, who looked upon them as their worst enemies, primarily because the Rākshasas' outlook on life was radically opposed to theirs. A highly intellectual people they permitted their actions to be dominated by the sensual in life. The *tapas* (penance) and the *yajña* (sacrifice) were

1. Chapter XIV, pp. 278-283 supra

popular among them also; but these they employed solely to achieve wealth and power.[1]

About the Aryans the Rāmāyaṇa furnishes abundant information. Their social structure was founded on and maintained by the twin institutions of *varṇa* and *āśrama* which sought to ensure harmony between the seemingly opposite aims of the individual and the society which in popular minds were irreconcilable. The society was divided into four classes, viz. *brāhmaṇa*, *kshatriya*, *vaiśya* and *śūdra*. Of these, the first three constituted a homogeneous group in the sense that originally they seem to have been divisions of the Aryans themselves, conceived on the principle of the division of labour. They stood out distinct from the last one, viz. *śūdra*, which was constituted primarily of non-Aryans and was differentiated from the rest, in that it was denied any direct access to the Vedic heritage of the Aryans. The *brāhmaṇas* were men, renowned for their mental, moral and spiritual attainments. Their life, as reflected in the Rāmāyaṇa, was invariably dedicated to the cause of *dharma*. The *kshatriyas* were noted for their physical valour and high sense of chivalry. It was their responsibility to ensure for everyone peace and security against all possible dangers. The *vaiśyas* were men devoted to trade, cattle-rearing and agriculture. They not only provided the daily needs of every individual in the society, but also laboured hard to increase national prosperity. The *śūdras* served the society by rendering personal services to the members of the three higher *varṇas*. No doubt, the position of each preceding *varṇa* was regarded as higher than that of the following one; but no member of the higher *varṇa* entertained, on that account, any hatred or contempt for the members of the *varṇa* (or *varṇas*) lower than his own. In that early stage of society, all the four *varṇas* appear to have lived in perfect amity as several limbs of the 'Body Social' and faithfully discharged their respective functions. We find a gradual emergence of the concept of *sva-dharma* which, on the one hand, teaches a person to cherish his own duty as a member of a particular

1. Chapter XIV, pp. 270-278 supra.

varṇa and, on the other, not to meddle with the duties of the other *varṇas*. Naturally, the society did not approve of the attempt of a member of the lower *varṇa* to adopt a course of conduct prescribed for the higher *varṇas*, however righteous or laudable in itself that conduct might have been.[1]

Just as society was divided into four *varṇas*, the life of an individual was divided into four stages or *āśramas* : the *brahmacarya*, the *gṛihastha*, the *vānaprastha* and the *sannyāsa*. Of these, the first stage was meant to give a *brahmacārī* that education and training which, on the one hand, moulded his character in such a way that he could strive to achieve the highest standard of moral and spiritual excellence, and on the other, equipped him for the still nobler task of making his best contribution to society, as was but expected of him. For acquiring such training and education the *brahmacārī* was generally entrusted to the care of very competent teachers under whose guidance he led a very austere life. The next stage was the *gṛihastha-āśrama* which an individual entered at a time when he was equipped for the struggle in life and was full of youthful vigour and unbounded aspirations. This stage was primarily intended for the realisation of *artha* and *kāma* though it was expected that even at this stage these would be subordinated to *dharma*. The *gṛihastha-āśrama* was, in a way, the most important, for it served as the backbone of society in as much as other three *āśramas* depended for the satisfaction of their material needs upon the *gṛihastha*. The *vānaprastha-āśrama*, the third stage, served as a transition from the attachments of life to a complete detachment. Even at this stage, one continued to be an important member of society in the sense that he was required to discharge the responsibility of educating the coming generation. But, at the same time, he stood outside the society, for he almost confined himself to his hermitage in the forest. The principal object of the *vānaprastha-āśrama* was to slowly develop in a person a spirit of complete renunciation which would enable him to enter the last stage, viz. the *sannyāsa-āśrama*. At this last stage he had no formal

1. Chapter II, pp. 14-26 supra

obligations whatsoever. His only pursuit was self-restraint and contemplation of the highest reality. This scheme, it may be observed, was ideal in its conception and at the same time most practical in its effect.[1]

The family was the primary unit of society. It served to mould the personality of the child in a manner that he learned to sacrifice his personal interest in the larger interests of the family and the community and also helped him preserve his cultural heritage. The family was joint and patriarchal in character. At the head of the family was the father whose authority was final and absolute in all matters relating to the family. The mother was loved and respected, but her status was subsidiary to that of the father. Among the members of the younger generation, the eldest son enjoyed a unique position. Next to the father, he commanded the highest respect in the family and enjoyed a number of rights and privileges. But his responsibilities were no less for, in the absence of the father, the burden of the entire family fell primarily on his shoulders. The several members of the family were joined together in a strong bond of affection which taught them to respect one another's rights and feelings. But polygamy, which was fairly popular—specially among the *kshatriyas*—not infrequently succeeded in disturbing the otherwise serene atmosphere of the family.[2]

Marriage was the basis of the family; and its sexual character was subordinated to the sacramental, the object being the creation of a life-long partnership between the husband and the wife in the discharge of their social and religious duties. The emphasis on this ideal led, on the one hand, to the unpopularity of such forms of marriage as *Gāndharva*, *Rākshasa* and *Paiśāca* and, on the other, to the restriction of the free choice of the young men and women in the selection of their life-partners. In marriage affairs, the authority of the father was absolute and, hence, there was no courtship and no genuine *svayaṃvara*. It is, however, worth noting that child-marriages are nowhere in evidence. The society was very particular about the sex-purity of its members, parti-

1. Chapter II, pp. 26-34 supra.
2. Chapter III, pp. 35-43 supra.

cularly women. Naturally, it could under no circumstance tolerate an intimate sexual contact outside the wedlock. The idea of *śulka* (bride-price) was familiar to the society; but the only form of marriage popular in those days seems to have been the *Brāhma*. There appears to have been no restriction on inter-caste marriages, although there is not a single case of *pratiloma* marriage in the Rāmāyaṇic society.[1]

The Rāmāyaṇa presents to us a galaxy of illustrious women-characters like Sītā and Anasūyā. But, on the whole, this period appears to have witnessed a lowering of the general status of the woman in society. No doubt, daughters were not deserted by their parents; nor were they ill treated or neglected by them. But their birth was not as welcome an event in the family as that of a son. The marriage of daughters to suitable husbands presented a great difficulty to the parents though, unlike as in the present age, dowry was not the main cause, and on that account, they generally cursed their lot. As wives, women were theoretically equal partners in the religious and secular undertakings of their husbands. But, in actual practice, the *bhāryā-bhartā* ideal was so excessively emphasised that it, not unoften, reduced the woman to the position of a simple maid-servant of her husband. Equally popular was the *pātivratya* ideal which required the wife to merge her individuality completely into that of her husband, thereby turning herself into a mere shadow of him incapable even of complaining against unfair or ill treatment at his hands. Widowhood was the most dreaded calamity in the life of a woman, for it rendered her even more helpless. As a widow, she was required to lead a life austere and completely devoid of happiness. No doubt, she was not till then looked upon as an object of inauspiciousness in the family or the society, but her position was subordinated to that of the son on whom she depended for her maintenance. The code of sex-ethics was very rigid for women; and as such virginity before marriage and ardent fidelity to the husband after it were strictly demanded of them. Naturally, we cannot think of polyandry, levirate and widow-remarriage in that society.

1. Chapter IV, pp. 51-65 supra.

The society, however, did grant a few privileges to women, such as maintenance, protection and immunity from capital punishment. But these gains were insignificant in view of the fact that in exchange they lost their freedom and individuality. We have lofty women characters in the epic, but their treatment by the society is not what they deserved.[1]

Education, as already stated, was primarily received by a student in the first stage of his life during which he normally stayed with his teacher. Educational centres were mostly situated in forests, though some existed in the towns as well. The subjects of study comprised a wide range of subjects, including a large number of practical sciences and arts. Much desirable information regarding the curriculum, the methods of teaching and such other points of educational interest are missing in the epic. But the exalted characters of the epic serve as the surest evidence of a successful and efficient educational discipline. The high respect for the teacher in society and the very concept of *saṃskāras* (particularly the *upanayana saṃskāra*) clearly show that great significance was attached to refinement through education.[2]

The ascetic, who at the conclusion of the *gṛihastha-āśrama* voluntarily withdrew himself from the material pleasures of worldly life and settled in the peaceful atmosphere of the hermitage, was the cream of society. His chief pursuit was the *brahmarshi* ideal which meant a perfect control over the human frailties like passion and anger. He was, no doubt, no longer a regular member of society; all the same, the reins of society, in a sense, rested in his hands. He was the teacher of the coming generation and kings and the common men frequently visited his hermitage and sought his advice, not only on religious matters but also on social and political ones. In fact, the principles of morality, the practical application of which can be detected in the conduct of every member of the Rāmāyaṇic society, can be shown to have emanated from these centres of learning or the forest *āśramas*.[3]

1. Chapter V, pp. 66-115 supra.
2. Chapter VI, pp. 116-126 supra.
3. Chapter VII, pp. 127-145 supra.

Dharma was a strong directive force in that society, and governed the entire behaviour of the individual. The *dharmas* (duties) of the individuals as members of a particular *varṇa* or *āśrama* were clearly laid down and they were expected to act strictly upto them. Besides, there was a general code of ethics (*sādhāraṇa dharma*) applicable to every individual, irrespective of class, colour or sex. A high sense of morality motivates the behaviour of most of the epic characters and they are even today regarded as embodiments and models of various moral excellences.

Dharma in the restricted sense stood also for the various religious practices. These appear to have come down from two distinct traditions, viz. Vedic and non-Vedic. Of these, the former comprised the daily rites (like *sandhyā* and *agnihotra*), the periodical ceremonies (like *Vāstu-śamana* and a number of *saṃskāras*) and certain optional rituals which only privileged people in the society performed in the hope of securing some special benefits. The second group of religious practices, viz. belonging to the non-Vedic tradition, was formed of a heterogeneous mass which was of a non-Aryan origin perhaps, but had been later accepted and modified by the Aryans. Under this head come various types of worship of gods, trees, rivers and mountains etc.[1]

The divine family had become very large in that period consisting as it did of gods, mythical saints, divine races (like *Yakshas*, *Gandharvas* and many others), evil spirits (like *Daityas* and *Dānavas*) and divine rivers, mountains and so on. The first group (viz. gods) itself had been much enlarged for, besides the Vedic gods, there were now a large number of deified abstractions and fresh products of animism and naturism. The tendency of anthropomorphism and the association of elaborate myths with each class—quite often with individual figures—had made each one distinct from the rest. Significant changes had also occurred in the status of various gods of the Vedic period; for instance, gods like Soma and Sūrya had become completely obscure, those like Varuṇa and Indra had lost their position of eminence, while Vishṇu,

1. Chapter VIII, pp. 146-174 supra.

Prajāpati and Rudra—the last two transformed as Brahmā and Śiva respectively—had become prominent.[1]

The philosophy of the epic cannot be specifically brought under any of the well-known philosophical systems. There is, however, ample evidence to show that the people in this period had a strong faith in the *karma* theory, according to which all human happiness and suffering that an individual experiences spring basically from his own actions. The 'Divine Will' is, no doubt, recognised. But its position is not paramount, for it is now only accepted as the dispenser of the good or the evil fruits of the virtuous or the vicious actions of the individual man. Significant also is the fact that the concept of *moksha* as a state, from which there is no return to the cycle of birth and death, is completely missing in this period. The outlook of man is full of optimism. He readily submits to the sufferings in life, taking them to be the consequences of his own past actions, but is ever hopeful of ameliorating his lot by putting forth better conduct in the present life.[2]

Contempt for the world or its material pleasures is nowhere in evidence in this period. On the other hand, one finds that in their food and drink, in their fondness for good dress and ornaments, in the variety of their sports and means of recreation and in their economic pursuits, the people of this period display a healthy spirit of the joy of life. Thus, they freely helped themselves to a variety of dishes prepared from fruits, milk and cereals. Non-vegetarian dishes were very popular; especially on the occasion of a *yajña* or a *śrāddha* the serving of meat preparations to the *brāhmaṇas* was held to be a pious necessity. Curd and various types of spices were used to add to the flavour of the preparations. Intoxicating drinks were prepared from honey and the juices of flowers, fruits and sugar cane and were very much in use, especially among the members of the fighting class.[3]

1. Chapter IX, pp. 180-222 supra.
2. Chapter XX, pp. 223-231 supra.
3. Chapter XI, pp. 232-242 supra.

The dress of the people—both men and women—was extremely simple. And naturally, in the case of a people of a tropical country, one cannot expect a large variety. Nevertheless, richest variety is met with in respect of the material of which dresses were made. Clothes made of cotton and silk were very much popular, though woollen garments were also sometimes used. And these were made extremely attractive by various types of embroidery in silk, gold and silver threads. There was lavish use of ornaments presenting a rich variety in respect of their shapes and designs as also the material of which they were made.[1]

To ensure peace and prosperity for society, there was in existence a sound political institution, viz., the State. It was constituted of seven limbs,—the king, the ministry, the people, the fortress, the treasury, the army and the allies. The days of mere clan-states were over, as in this period the states were invariably territorial and monarchical in character. There is no indication of the existence of big empires, constituted of smaller units, rendering allegiance to a central authority. At best, we can speak of a few strong monarchies like Kosala, Videha and Kekaya.

The state was conceived to be a beneficent institution, brought into being primarily for the welfare of its subjects. To be more precise, the state was the guardian of *dharma* which in its turn was regarded as an embodiment of Justice and ideal Good. The greatest praise that a monarch claimed in that period was that he ruled his state in accordance with the dictates of *dharma*, as then understood by him and his people.[2]

The government of a state was headed by a king who, among the Aryans, was invariably a *kshatriya*. His office was hereditary and the crown passed in the royal family from father to son according to the law of primogeniture. But this neither created any proprietary rights for him in the kingdom nor did it make his authority absolute. The sovereignty in theory, and partly in practice also, vested in the people, who

1. Chapter XII, pp. 243-254 supra.
2. Chaprte XV, pp. 284-291 supra.

not only had the right to be consulted by the ruler in matters of succession, but were competent also to force a ruler to keep away from succession a prince whose conduct did not meet with their general approval. Unfortunately, however, they do not seem to have evolved any constitutional measures—except, perhaps, mass migration—which could enable them to effectively exercise their rights against a tyrannical ruler. But, in a critical situation, a ruler very often found himself forced to respect public feelings and to regard the welfare of his subjects as his primary concern. Religious and moral training of a ruler, which formed an important part of his early education, and the dread of public odium normally prevented a ruler from turning into a tyrant. Also, the universal belief of that period, namely, that one could secure heaven after death only by a sincere discharge of one's duties, must have served to keep the rulers on the path of righteousness. And that it was so can be seen from the bulk of evidence in the epic where we find the rulers zealously engaged in the task of *prajānurañjana* by ensuring peace within their dominions and security against external dangers, and by pursuing policies conducive to the general welfare of their people.[1]

The maintenance of law and order in society was the king's primary responsibility; and it was for this that he had been invested with the paramount authority of wielding the *daṇḍa*. But, as a safeguard against the degeneration of this authority into tyranny, the ancient society was prudent enough not to vest the king with legislative powers. Law was enshrined in the religious texts and customary usage, neither of which was of the king's making. He was only to enforce it. Moreover, there were distinct principles to guide the king even in the employment of *daṇḍa*; for instance, the wrong-doer was to be punished; each individual dispute brought to the notice of the king was to be immediately and thoroughly investigated; the punishment was to be proportionate to the offence, and each case was to be looked into with strict impartiality.[2]

1. Chapter XVII, pp. 296-315 supra.
2. Chapter XX, pp. 357-361 supra.

If protection of the subjects was the duty of the king, realisation of taxes from them was his prerogative. So deeply implanted had this idea become in the people's mind that even an ascetic living in his dominion was expected to surrender a part of the religious merit achieved to the king in consideration of the protection that he received from him. Besides taxes, the fines realised from the people convicted for offences and, even more, the gifts received from the tributaries did much to supplement the state-revenues. One-sixth of a person's income was universally recognised to be the share of the king, though on certain items and in special circumstances he must have claimed a higher share. We have no information about any other sources of state-revenue, even if any there were. And this entire state-revenue, when realised, was to be spent by the king, not for his personal glory or benefit, but for the maintenance of the army and on works of public-welfare, like irrigation.[1]

Coming to the next *aṅga* (limb) of the state, the ministry, we find that the king was assisted in the task of administration by a team of ministers, consisting of *mantrīs* and *amātyas* or *sacivas*. Of these, the former group consisted of distinguished *brāhmaṇas* who, perhaps, did not permanently stay in the capital, but were invited by the king or the Prime-minister to participate in serious deliberation in an emergency. The second group (viz. of *amātyas* or *sacivas*) consisted mostly of *kshatriyas* of proven administrative and military ability. They were executive heads of various state departments and assisted the king in the day-to-day administration; and since the authority of the state in this period was principally confined to its constituent functions and its size was also comparatively small, the number of these state departments could not have been very large. From an account of the expectations that the people had from their king it seems that usually there were five portfolios, viz., those of ecclesiastical affairs, defence, finance, justice and foreign affairs.[2]

1. Chapter XX, pp. 354-357 supra.
2. Chapter XVII, pp. 316-334 supra.

Popular control might have been exercised through the *Sabhā*, the popular assembly of the state, which discussed vital state matters. It was constituted of two elements, the official element represented by the *mantrīs* and the *amātyas*, and the non-official element represented by the tributary kings and the *Paura-Jānapadas*. Unfortunately, the epic does not shed sufficient light on the constitutional powers of the *Sabhā*. All that can be said in this regard on the basis of the account of Daśaratha's *Sabhā* is that the *Sabhā* was an important institution which commanded great respect of the government (including the king).[1]

The capital was the heart of the state and formed its next important constituent. Invariably fortified, both by natural and artificial means, it was known as *durga* or *pura* and was distinguished from the rest of the country, termed *rāshṭra*. The latter was further divided into smaller units of towns and villages. There is no specific reference to a department discharging municipal functions in these different units of the state, though there are copious references to corporate bodies like the *Paura-Jānapadas*, the *Śreṇis* and the *Nigamas*, which, it seems very likely, participated in their different capacities in the task of local administration.[2]

In an age in which the peace of the Aryan states was always threatened by the presence of the hostile Rākshasas, living at no great a distance from the Aryan outposts, the 'army' was an indispensable instrument of protecting the life and property of the people; and it was only natural that the Aryan kings meticulously attended to the strength and efficiency of their armies. Conventionally, an army was constituted of four limbs, viz., the infantry, the cavalry, the elephantry and the chariot corps. Of these the cavalry was a subsidiary limb, enumerated in the list, more often than not, to uphold the concept of the *caturaṅgabala*. Equally unimportant was the infantry in purely Aryan military formations, its work being mainly that of the camp-followers and the commissariat. The elephantry seems to have been a new

1. Chapter XIX, pp. 335-353 supra.
2. Chapter XXI, pp. 362-378 supra.

addition to the army. Nevertheless, it had come to be recognised as an important limb of the army; and the kings of this period were ever anxious to strengthen this unit by new acquisitions. The hard core of the army, however, was the chariot corps. The nobility specialised in fighting from their chariots. The epic heroes were invariably chariot-fighters. Though an adept in fighting with almost all sorts of weapons, the chariot-fighter's favourite weapon was the bow in the use of which he appears to have achieved a special excellence. He also carried a large variety of other missiles and super-missiles which he used in special emergencies with great skill and effect. Dr. P.C. Chakravarti rightly brings out the importance of this limb of the army by designating this period as, "the veritable chariot-age of Indian history."[1]

The art of warfare was highly developed in this period. Organisation and discipline could be seen even among the rank and file in the camps, during the march and on the battle-field. In actual fights, the Aryan warriors displayed remarkable courage and valour and a strong repugnance for unscrupulous and unclean methods. But since their chief opponents, the Rākshasas, were predominantly deceitful (*kūṭa-yodhīs* or *māyāvīs*) the Aryans too, had, in self-defence, learned to meet these attacks.[2]

Allies commanded an important position in the organisation of a state, for a proper balance of power could be maintained only through judicious alliances. A ruler had to be very discreet in the employment of political expedients and the framing of his policies. He had to keep a very close watch over the developments in neighbouring states; and for that purpose he employed a regular corps of ambassadors and spies. Through the former (ambassadors) he carried on the necessary negotiations with neighbouring states while through the latter (spies) he not only gathered information about the motives and moves of the other kings but also

1. Chapter XXII, pp. 379-402 supra.
2. Chapter XXII, pp. 381-386 and 419-426 supra.

kept close watch over his own high functionaries.[1]

Thus, the Aryan polity of the Rāmāyaṇic period can claim to be a *saptāṅga rājya*, though it mentions only six *aṅgas* and that too only once.[2] The *amātyas*, the seventh *aṅga*, though not mentioned in this reference, have received a fairly good attention at the hands of the poet and have been regarded as indispensable.

If we now take into consideration all the facts, social as well as political, that we have given above, we find that the social and political life of the Aryan community was grounded in *dharma* which embodied not only the entire set of ethical virtues but also a whole code of rules of conduct applicable to an individual at any specific time and place. This *dharma* again, instead of being merely a static body of rules handed down from the early ancestors, was a dynamic force that ensured to the individual and to the society both inward peace and worldy prosperity. Naturally, the *brāhmaṇa*, who was expected to rise above all class-interests and prejudices, possess a wide and impartial vision and to be responsible for carrying this great ideal of *dharma* to the people, commanded the utmost respect in the society of Vālmīki's Rāmāyaṇa.

On the political side, the state was a beneficent institution. Directly, it interfered to the minimum extent with the life of its citizens; but indirectly, by ensuring security and justice for everyone it sought to create conditions for the promotion of their all-round development. The administrative machinery was so conceived and constituted that it could not, in normal circumstances, degenerate into a military despotism. The king was not the absolute master of the state. He was only a guardian of *dharma*; and, in case his conduct went against its dictates, the people could remove him from his office. Ultimately, sovereignty was vested in the people; their best welfare was, therefore, inevitably the supreme concern of the king. He was to have also the highest regard for their opinion. What a good king was expected to secure for

1. Chapter XVI, pp. 292-295 supra.
2. R. IV 22/11.

his people can be understood from the following description of Rāma's reign :—

Dharmeṇa rakshatastasya hṛishṭapushṭajanākulā,
Babhūva pṛithivī sarvā dhanadhānyasamṛiddhinī.
Akālamṛityubhīrnaiva na ca vyālakṛitaṃ bhayam,
Na ca vyādhibhayaṃ tatra Rāme rājyaṃ praśāsati.
Nirdasyurabhavalloko nānarthaṃ kaścidāviśat,
Na ca sma vṛiddhā bālānāṃ pretakāryāṇi kurvate.
Sarvaṃ pramuditañcāsīt sarve dharmaparāyaṇāḥ,
Dṛishṭvā dharmaparaṃ Rāmaṃ naivāhiṃsan parasparam.
Āsīdvarshasahasrāyustathā putrasahasravān,
Nirāmayo viśokaśca Rāme rājyaṃ praśāsati.
Nityapushpā nityaphalāstaravastatra nirvraṇāḥ,
Pushpavantastathā gulmā Rāme rājyaṃ praśāsati.
Vīryavatyastathaushadhyaḥ sarvā rasasamanvitāḥ,
Kāle varshati parjanyaḥ sukhasparśaścha mārutaḥ.
Svadharmeshu pravṛittāśca varṇāḥ svaireva karmabhiḥ,
Ātmadharmaparā lokā Rāme rājyaṃ praśāsati.

It is this *Rāma-rājya* which has through the ages been the dream and the aspiration of the Indian people.

1 R. VI 110/2-9.

BIBLIOGRAPHY

(a) The Rāmāyaṇa :

Rāmāyaṇa of Vālmīki :

(1) (North-Western recension), Ed. by Bhagavad Datta and Ram Labhaya, 7 Vols., Śrīmad-Dayānanda Mahāvidyālaya Sanskrit Granthamālā, No. 12, Lahore, 1931-1947.

(2) (Dākshiṇātya recension), Ed. by Wasudev Laxman Sastri Pansikar, Nirṇaya-Sāgara, Bombay, 1930.

(3) Published with three commentaries—Tilaka, Rāmāyaṇa-Śiromaṇi and Bhūshaṇa—7 Vols., Gujarati Printing Press, Bombay, 1912-1920.

(4) (Baṅgīya recension), Ed. by Pancanana Tarkaratna 3 vols., Calcutta, 1908.

(5) Bāla-Kāṇḍa and Ayodhyā-Kāṇḍa—Critically edited by G.H. Bhatt and P.L. Vaidya respectively, Oriental Institute, Baroda, 1960, 1962.

(6) Published with exhaustive introduction to each Kāṇḍa by Śrīpāda Damodar Satavalekar, Svādhyāya Maṇḍala, Ānandāśrama, Aundha, Sitara District, 1942.

(7) Translated into English prose by Manmatha Nath

Dutt, 3 Vols., Calcutta, 1892-1893.

(8) Translated into English prose by Hari Prasad Shastri, 3 Vols., London, 1959.

(9) Translated into English verse by T.H. Griffith, Chowkhamba Sanskrit Studies, Vol. XXIX, 1963.

(10) Bāla Kāṇḍa --Rendered into English with exhaustive notes, C. R. Sreenivasa Ayyangar, Madras, 1910.

(b) Sanskrit Texts:

Abhijñāna Śākuntalam (Kālidāsa) — Ed. M. R. Kale, Book Seller's Publishing Company, Bombay, 1957.

Aitareya Āraṇyaka — Ānandāśrama Sanskrit Granthāvalī, No. 38, 1898.

Aitareya Brāhmaṇa (Shaḍguru Śishya) — Vol. I Ed. R. Anant Krishna Shastri, 1942., Vol. II Ed. P.K. Narayana Pillai, 1952, University of Travancore, Sanskrit Series Nos. 149 and 167.

Amarakośa (Amarasiṃha) — Khemraj Shrikrishnadass, Bombay, 1930.

Arthaśāstra (Kauṭilya) — Ed. Shamasastry, Oriental Library Publications, Sanskrit Series No. 37/54, Mysore, 1919.

Arthaśāstra (Translated into English, Shamasastry) — Government Oriental Library Series, Bibliotheca Sanskrit No. 37, Part II, Bangalore, 1915.

Ashṭādhyāyī sūtrapāṭha (Pāṇini) — Ed. Brahmadatta Jijnasu, Shri Ramlal Kapur Trust Granthamālā, No. XXIII, Amritsar, 1957.

Atharva Veda — Ed. Ramachandra, 8 Vols., Moradabad, Saṃvat 1986-1987

Bṛihat Saṃhitā (Varāhamihira)	Sarasvatī Bhavana Granthamālā, Vol. 77, Varanasi, 1968.
Chāndogya Upanishad	Upanishad Bhāshya Khaṇḍa 3, Gita Press, Gorakhpur, Vikrama Saṃvat 2013.
Dharmasūtra of Āpastamba	Ed. George Bühler, Bombay Sanskrit Series, Nos. XLIV and L, 1932.
Dharmasūtra of Vasishṭha	Ed. A. A., Führer, Bombay Sanskrit and Prakrit Series No. XXIII, Poona, 1916.
(The) Dīghanikāya	Ed. Bhikkhu J. Kashyap, Nālandā Devanāgarī PāliSeries, Bihar Government, 1958.
Gṛihyasūtra of Pāraskara	Ed. Rajaram, Ārsha Granthāvalī,Vol.V.No. 3, Lahore, 1909.
Kāmasūtra (Vātsyāyana)	Ed. Goswami DamodarShastri, Haridas Sanskrit Grantha Mālā, No. 29, Benaras, 1929.
Kāśikā on Pāṇini	Kāshī Sanskrit Granthamālā 37, Chowkhamba, Banaras, 1952.
Kaṭhopanishad	Nirṇaya Sāgara Edition, Bombay, 1946.
Kāvyaprakāśa (Mammaṭa)	Ed. Raghunath Damodar Karmarkar, B.O.R.I., Poona, 1950
Mahābhārata (Vyāsa)	Gita Press, Gorakhpur.
Manusmṛiti (Manu)	Nirṇaya Sāgara Edition, Bombay, 1887.
Manusmṛiti (Translated into English, G. Bühler)	Sacred Books of the East Series, Vol. XXV, Oxford, 1886.
Nirukta (Yāska)	Ed. Govinda Sastri and Chotupati Sharma, Khemaraj Shrikrishnadass, Bombay, Saṃvat 1969.
Nītisāra (Kāmandaka)	Ed. T. Ganapati Sastri, Trivandrum Sanskrit Series, No. XIV, 1912.

Prithvīrāja Vijaya Mahākāvya(Jayānaka)	Ed. Gauri Shankar Hirachand Ojha and Chandradhar Sharma Guleri, Ajmer, 1941.
Raghuvaṃśam (Kālidāsa)	Nirṇaya Sāgara Edition, Bombay 1929.
Ṛigveda Saṃhitā	Ed. Paropakāriṇī Sabhā, Ajmer, Saṃvat 1998.
Śatapatha Brāhmaṇa	Vedic Yantrālaya, Ajmer, Saṃvat 1959.
Śrīmad Bhagavad Gītā	Gita Press, Gorakhpur, Saṃvat 1995.
Taittirīya Brāhmaṇa	Ānandāśrama Sanskrit Granthāvalī, 1898.
Taittirīya Saṃhitā	Ānandāśrama Sanskrit Granthāvalī, Vols. I-V, 1940-1946.
Uttararāmacaritam (Bhavabhūti)	Ed. Ashubodha and Nityabodha, Calcutta, 1922.
Vājasaneyi Saṃhitā	Nirṇaya Sāgara Edition, Bombay, 1912.
Vedāntasāra (Sadānanda)	Ed. Swāmī Nikhilananda, Advaita Āśrama, Mayavati, Almora, 1949.
Yājñavalkya Smṛiti (Yājñavalkya)	Nirṇaya Sāgara Edition, Bombay, 1909.
(The) Yoga system of Patañjali	Ed. Charles Rockwell Lanman, Harvard Oriental Series, Vol. XVII.

(c) Modern Works :

Agraval, V.S.	Pāṇini Kālīna Bhāratavarsha, Motilal Banarasi Dass, Banaras, Vikrama. Saṃvat 2012.
Agraval, V.S.	Prācīna Bhāratīya Lokadharma, Jñānodaya Granthamālā : No. 3.
Altekar, A.S.	State and Government in Ancient India, Motilal Banarasi Dass, Banaras, 1955.
Altekar, A.S.	Education in Ancient India, Nand Kishore and Brothers, 1951.

Altekar, A.S. — The Position of Women in Hindu Civilization, Motilal Banarasi Dass, 1956.

Aurobindo — Kālidāsa, Ārya Sāhitya Bhawana, Calcutta, 1929.

Barua, Beni Madhab — Inscriptions of Aśoka, Part II, University of Calcutta, Calcutta, 1943.

Beni Prasad — Theory of Government in Ancient India, The Indian Press, Ltd., Allahabad, 1927.

Beni Prasad — The State in Ancient India, The Indian Press, Ltd., Allahabad, 1928.

Bowra, C.M. — Heroic Poetry, Macmillan And Co, Limited, London, 1952.

Bulche, C. — Rāma Kathā—Utpatti Aura Vikāsa, Hindi Parishad, Viśvavidyālaya, Prayāga, 1950.

Chakravarti, P.C. — The Art Of War in Ancient India, University of Dacca Ramna, Dacca, 1941.

Chanana, Devraj — Slavery In Ancient India, Peoples' Publishing House, 1960.

Das, S.K. — Educational system of the Ancient Hindus, Calcutta, 1930.

Date, G.T. — The Art Of War In Ancient India, University of Bombay, Bombay, 1929.

Deshmukh, P.S. — The Origin And Development of Religion In Vedic Literature, Oxford University Press, Bombay, 1933.

Dharma, P.C. — The Rāmāyaṇa Polity, Madras, 1941.

Dikshitar, V.R.R. — War In Ancient India, Macmillan And Company, Limited, London, 1948.

Dutt, N.K. — Origin And Growth Of Caste In India, The Book Company, Ltd., Calcutta, 1931.

Dutt, R.C. — The Early Hindu Civilisation, Punthi Pustak, Calcutta-4, 1963.

Dvivedi, Hajari Prasad — Prācīna Bhārata Ke Kalātmaka Vinoda, Hindi Grantha Ratnākara Kāryālaya, Bombay, 1952.

Encyclopaedia Of Religion And Ethics, Vols. I, II and IV. — Edited by James Hastings, New York, 1951.

Fleet, J.F. — Inscriptions of the Early Gupta Kings and their Successors, C.I.I. Vol. III, Calcutta, 1888.

Ghoshal, U.N. — Studies In Indian History And Culture, Orient Longmans, 1957.

Gore, N.A. — A Bibliography Of The Rāmāyaṇa, Poona, 1943.

Havelock, Ellis — Psychology of Sex, New York, 1938.

Hopkins, E.W. — Epic Mythology, Strassburg, 1915.

Hopkins, E.W. — Ethics of India, Yale University Press, 1924.

Hopkins, E.W. — History of Religions, Ginn And Company, 1896.

Iyer, T. Paramasiva — Rāmāyaṇa And Laṅkā, Parts I and II, Bangalore City, 1940.

Jacobi, H. — Das Rāmāyaṇa, Translated into English by S.N. Ghoshal, Oriental Institute, Baroda, 1960.

Jayal, Shakambari — The Status Of Women In The Epics, Motilal Banarasidass, 1966.

Jayaswal, K.P. — Hindu Polity, The Bangalore Printing And Publishing Company, Ltd., Bangalore City, 1943.

Kane, P.V. — History of Dharma-śāstra, Vols. I-III, Government Oriental Series, Class B, No. 6, Poona, 1930-1941.

Kapadia, K.M. — Marriage and Family in India, Oxford University Press, 1959.

Karve, Irawati — Kinship Organisation In India, Deccan College Monograph Series, 11, Poona, 1953.

Khan, Benjamin — The Concept of Dharma in Vālmīki Rāmāyaṇa, Munshi Ram Manohar Lal, 1965.

Krishnamchariar, M. — History of Classical Sanskrit Literature, Madras, 1937.

Law, Narendra Nath — Aspects of Ancient Indian Polity, Oriental Longmans, Private Limited, 1960.

Macdonell, A.A. — A History of Sanskrit Literature, London, 1905.

Macdonell, A.A. and Keith, A.B. — Vedic Index, Motilal Banarasidass, 1967.

Majumdar, B.K. — The Military System In Ancient India, The World Press, Ltd., Calcutta, 1955.

Majumdar, R. C. — Corporate Life In Ancient India, Calcutta, 1918.

Makhi, Tryambakaraya — Dharmākūtam (Bāla-Kāṇḍa, Ayodhyā-Kāṇḍa, Araṇya-Kāṇḍa and Sundara-Kāṇḍa), Published by K.S. Subrahmanya Sastri and T. Chandrasekharan, 1916-1951.

Malladi, Venkata Ratnam — Rāma The Greatest Pharaoh of Egypt, Bareilly, 1934.

Marshall, John — Mohenjo-Daro and the Indus Civilization, London, 1931.

Meyer, J.J. — Sexual Life in Ancient India, London, 1930.

Monier-Williams, M. — A Sanskrit-English Dictionary, Oxford University Press, London, 1951.

Monier-Williams, M. — Indian Epic Poetry, William and Norgate, London and Edinburgh, 1863.

Mookerji, R.K. — Ancient Indian Education, Macmillian And Compa.ny, Limited, London, 1951

Mookerji, R.K. — Local Government In Ancient India, Oxford, 1920.

Mudgal, B.S. — Political Economy In Ancient India, M/S Mudgal and Co., Kanpur, 1960.

Navlekar, N.R. — A New Approach to the Rāmāyaṇa, Jabalpur.

Omprakash — Food And Drinks In Ancient India, Munshi Ram Manohar Lal, Delhi-6, 1961.

Pandey, Rajbali — Hindu Saṃskāras, Vikrama Publications, Banaras, 1949.

Pandeya, Shyamlal — Janatantravāda—Rāmāyaṇa Aur Mahābhārata Kālīna, Avadha Publishing House, Lucknow, 1956.

Pinkham, Mildreth Worth — Woman In the Sacred Scriptures of Hinduism, Columbia University Press, New York, 1941.

Prabhu, Pandhari Nath — Hindu Social Organization, Popular Book Depot., Bombay, 1954.

Radhakrishnan, S. — Indian Philosophy, Vol. I, George Allen And Unwin, Limited., London, 1951.

Radhakrishnan, S. — The Hindu View of Life, George Allen And Unwin Limited, London, 1954.

Ramgopal — India of Vedic Kalpasūtras, National Publishing Hòuse, Delhi.

Sankaran, A. — Some Aspects of Literary Criticism in Sanskrit, University of Madras, 1929.

Sarkar, S.C. — Educational Ideas And Institutions In Ancient India, Patna, 1928.

Sastri Nilakanta, K.A. — Studies In Cola History And Administration, Madras University Historical Series No. 7, University of Madras, 1932.

Sastri, Ramaswami, K.S. — Studies In Rāmāyaṇa, Parts I and II, Kīrti Mandira Lecture Series No. IX, Baroda, 1944.

Sastri, Srinivasa, V.S. — Lectures On The Rāmāyaṇa, The Madras Sanskrit Academy, 1961.

Shastri, Shakuntala Rao — Women in the Vedic Age, Bhāratīya Vidyā-Bhavana, Bombay, 1952.

Shastri, S.N. — The Laws And Practice Of Sanskrit Drama, Vol. I, The Chowkhamba Sanskrit Studies, Varanasi, 1961.

Shivram Murti, C. — Amarāvatī Sculptures in the Madras Museum, Madras, 1942.

Siddhanta, N.K. — The Heroic Age of India—A Comparative Study, London, 1929.

Tagore, Rabindranath — A Vision Of India's History, Viśva-Bhāratī, Calcutta, 1951.

Upadhyaya, Bhagawat Saran — Women In Ṛgveda, Nand Kishore and Bros., Benaras, 1941.

Vaidya C.V. — Epic India, Bombay Book Depot, Bombay, 1933.

Vaidya, C.V. — Riddle of the Rāmāyaṇa, Kegan Paul, Trench, Trubner And Company, Limited, 1906.

Vidyalankara, Atrideva — Prācīna Bhārata Ke Prasādhana, Bhāratīya Jñānapīṭha, Kashi, 1958.

Vora, D.P. — Evolution of Morals in the Epics, Popular Book Depot, Bombay, 1959.

Vyas, S.N. Rāmāyaṇa Kālīna Samāja, Sastā Sāhitya Maṇḍala, New Delhi, 1958.

Vyas, S.N. Rāmāyaṇa Kālīna Saṃskṛiti, Sastā Sāhitya Maṇḍala, New Delhi, 1958.

Vyas, S.N. India in the Rāmāyaṇa Age, Atmaram and Sons, Delhi, 1967.

Weber, A. The History of Indian Literature, Chowkhamba Sanskrit Studies, Vol. XIII, Varanasi, 1961.

Winternitz, M. A History Of Indian Literature, Vol. I, University of Calcutta, Calcutta, 1927.

JOURNALS AND MAGAZINES

Journal	Article
Bhāratī, Bulletin of the College of Indology, Kāśī, No. 6, Part I.	Raya Krishnadasa—Vālmīki-kṛita Ādi Rāmāyaṇa.
Epigraphia Indica, Vol. I.	Siyadoni Inscription, Ed. by Kielhorn
Historical Quarterly, Vol. II, Nos. 2 and 3, 1926.	Law, N.N.—The Janapada and the Paura
Indian Historical Quarterly, Vol. I, No. 1	Chakravarti Chintaharana—Tradition about Vānaras and Rākṣasas.
Journal of the American Oriental Society, Vol. XIII	Hopkins, E.W.—The Social and Military Position of the Ruling Caste in Ancient India as Represented by the Sanskrit Epics.
Kalyāṇa (Rāmāyaṇāṅka), Vol. V	Balacanda—Śrī Rāmāyaṇa meṃ Māṃsāhāra.
	Dikshitar, V.R.R.—Rāmāyaṇa Ke Kucha Rājanītika Siddhānta Aur Śāsana Saṃsthāyeṃ.
	Shamasastry, R.—Śrī Rāmācandra Kā Aśvamedha Yajña Aur Usakā Mahattva.
Prince of Wales, Saraswati Bhawan Studies, Vols. IV and V	Ray, Manmatha Nath, (i) Food And Drinks In The Rāmāyaṇic Age. (ii) An Estimate of the Civilisation of the Vānaras as Depicted in the Rāmāyaṇa.
Viśvambharā (Vol. I.), Hindi Viśva-bhāratī Anusandhāna-Parishad, Bikaner.	Sharma, Dashrath—Pratihāra Sāmrājya meṃ Pañcāyatī Rājya.

SUBJECT INDEX

(N.B.—Numbers refer to page numbers)

Note :-For kinship terms and weapons and missiles note tables given on pp. 44-45 and 430-432 respectively.

Contd. next page

Contd. next page